RELATIONSHIPS

Relationships:
A Dialectical Perspective

Robert A. Hinde

St. John's College, Cambridge, CB2 1TP, UK
Behaviour Department, Madingley, Cambridge, CB3 8AA, UK

Psychology Press
An imprint of Erlbaum (UK) Taylor & Francis

Psychology Press Publishers
27 Church Road
Hove
East Sussex, BN2 2FA
UK

British Library Cataloguing in Publication Data
A catalogue record for this book is available from the British Library.

ISBN 0–86377–706–6 (Hbk)
ISBN 0–86377–707–4 (Pbk)

Typeset by Lucy Morton & Robin Gable, London, SE12
Printed and bound in the United Kingdom by Biddles Ltd,
Guildford and King's Lynn

Contents

V

PART E   RELATIONSHIP CHANGE

Acknowledgements

An earlier book, *Towards understanding relationships* (Hinde, 1979, ISBN 0123492505) was written just as the study of personal relationships was becoming established as a recognised sub-discipline in the social sciences. Since then enormous progress has been made, and the present volume focuses on the new developments and attempts to present current perspectives. For permission to re-use passages from the earlier book (primarily in Chapters 2, 4, 5 and 8 of the present one) I am indebted to the present copyright holders, Harcourt Brace and Company Ltd.

I am also very grateful to Joan Stevenson-Hinde, who read a draft manuscript and made detailed and helpful comments. I profited also from discussion of a number of issues with Minucha Lisboa and Jessica Rawson, and from detailed comments on an earlier draft by Ann Elisabeth Auhagen and Ellen Berscheid.

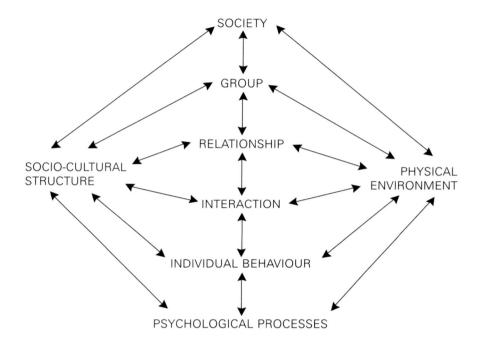

FRONTISPIECE A simplified view of the levels of social complexity. Relationships continually influence, and are influenced by, their component interactions and thus by the individual participants and by diverse psychological processes within those individuals; the groups and society in which they are embedded; the socio-cultural structure of beliefs, values, institutions and so on; and the physical environment. The influences involve behavioural, affective and cognitive processes in the individuals concerned, mediated by the meanings attributed to events and situations. Each level, including that of the individual, is thus to be seen not as an entity but as involving processes of continuous creation, change, or degradation through the dialectical relations within and between levels. (Modified from Hinde, 1975, 1991.)

Preface

People have always been interested in relationships, and novelists, biographers and clinicians have provided a wealth of case histories. In the early decades of this century psychologists provided some important hints as to how an ordered body of knowledge about relationships might grow, but the seeds that they sowed showed little signs of germination for several decades. The material brought together in an earlier book (Hinde, 1979) was embryonic: the systematic study of relationships was just beginning. But in the last 30 years considerable progress has been made. Research workers have probed more deeply into the complexities of personal relationships; theories current then have been elaborated to take better account of real-life relationships; a wider range of relationships and of individuals are being studied. Furthermore, the study of personal relationships now merges with a number of other disciplines—anthropology, child development, cognitive science, communications, psychiatry, social psychology, and sociology, to mention only some. We now have journals specifically devoted to personal relationships, others that also publish important material on the topic, and many edited and authored volumes. As a result the field is moving fast and the study of relationships is now in a very exciting phase—exciting not just as an intellectual enterprise, but because of its potential impact on human happiness. However the data still lack coherence: the field hardly qualifies as a science, using that term to mean an ordered body of knowledge. And the field is growing so fast, it is now hard to keep pace. But perhaps, just for those reasons, an attempt at an overview of at least some of the central issues may be timely.

My aim has been to survey the new material in a way that could indicate a possible route for integrating the knowledge that we are acquiring. Chemistry has its Periodic Table of Elements, Biology its Theory of Evolution by Natural Selection, Physics its Theory of Relativity, Genetics its Double Helix, but the study of relationships has as yet no overarching theory. Although we can be pleased with the progress that the study of personal relationships is making, it is still a very long way from achieving coherence. This is not only because the discipline has not yet reached maturity: the phenomena are of extraordinary complexity, and we cannot (yet?) hope for a simplifying theory that will suddenly bring total insight. The question at the moment is, can we perceive, even if only dimly, the shape that an integrated science of relationships might have? In this book I have tried to survey the data in a manner that indicates a possible route towards finding the integration that we need. I do not suppose that this route will prove to be a final answer, but if we follow it we may stumble across a shorter-cut to our goal.

An initially basic issue is shown in the Frontispiece (for fuller explanation, see Chapter 3). As a background we need to recognise a series of levels of complexity, which include processes within individuals, individuals, interactions, relationships, groups and societies, and also the context of culture and physical environment that permeates them. (This, it will be observed will involve drawing from several social science disciplines.) Each of these levels affects and is affected by the others. This means that each level, including that of the individual, is to be seen not as an entity but as a complex of dialectical processes—dialectical in the sense that tendencies or processes which may appear to be in opposition become integrated into a new reality or truth. Thus no one level can be studied independently of the others—though our own shortcomings make it necessary to focus primarily on one level at a time.

In this book, of course, the focus is on the relationship level, but it will be necessary to keep more than an eye on the others. At the individual level, in so far as the formation of a close relationship is often described as the partial merging of two selves, we need a picture of the nature of the self. A relationship cannot exist without interaction, so this level also is crucial. What the participants do together in their interactions, and what they say to each other (and to third parties) about a relationship, and what they think and feel, influences its future course. Duck, who has done so much to foster the development of the study of personal relationships, has repeatedly emphasised that how the participants communicate with each other, and also what goes on between interactions—reflecting, explaining, reformulating, discussing with third parties—may have a crucial influence on the relationship. And, moving up the levels, every relationship is affected by the other relationships of the participants, and also by cultural factors. The group level and the socio-cultural structure must therefore also come within our orbit.

In attempting to find a route towards integration of our knowledge about relationships, I have not followed the usual sequence of questions (data or theory initiated) through methods to answers, but have started with a section on description. To attempt to be clear about the phenomena is an essential first step: the history of psychology shows how easy it is to enter blind alleys if this is not done. It is thus useful to recognise three analytical stages: the description of relationships, the specification of principles involved in their dynamics, and the recognition of the limitations of applicability of those principles. But understanding requires re-synthesis of the products of our analysis to give comprehension of the whole, and this involves a fourth stage (Tinbergen, 1951). The notion of stages is, of course, only an heuristic device. Because relationships are not entities but dynamic processes, they cannot be described without reference to process, and indeed the characteristics by which a relationship can be described (by participant or by outside observer) may themselves be part of the process. And it would be folly to refer to principles underlying their dynamics without referring immediately to the limitations of those principles. Thinking of research on relationships as involving a series of stages is useful, however, as a way of orienting ourselves in our task and helping us not to confuse description and explanation.

Integrating knowledge about relationships also involves an issue of another kind: we must place new findings alongside what we know already. Over the last two decades studies of personal relationships have progressed from an emphasis on what people do to what people think and feel. The new findings are exciting, and open new perspectives on personal relationships. But if we are to build a body of knowledge about relationships we must not forget the earlier findings: rather we must strive to adapt the old wine-skins to the heady new wine. We must also attempt to see into the future, when further intra-psychic processes, such as defence mechanisms, or the emotional and motivational aspects of relationships, may well become the foci of attention.

Given the continuously interacting processes illustrated in the Frontispiece, full understanding requires yet a further step. Teasing those processes apart, and understanding their interactions, would be facilitated if we could identify relatively stable characteristics of individuals which, in interaction with each other through the successive levels, give rise to the complexity to be seen in those levels. This is merely hinted at in the last chapter.

Discussion in this book is biased in favour of so-called "close" relationships—that is, relationships for whose dynamics such issues as self-disclosure, interpersonal perception, satisfaction, and commitment have considerable importance. It is with such relationships that most of the work has been done—perhaps because they matter most to most people. Indeed, much of the work concerns the heterosexual relationships of young adults in Europe and North America, and even there the conclusions drawn from the data tend to refer to common properties of relationships, and not to their diversity. We need to know much more about the diversity of relationships in the real world. But although we need a wider data base, perhaps for the moment we can search for principles of dynamics in the relationships that have been studied, assessing their applicability to a wider range of phenomena as we become able to do so. An important survey of other types of adult relationships is available elsewhere (Auhagen & von Salisch, 1993, 1996): they are mentioned here only incidentally. Children's relationships involve special problems which arise through their need for caregiving and their developing cognitive competence: coming to terms with these problems will be essential if we are to reach our goal of an integrated body of knowledge about relationships, but children's relationships are mentioned here only to illustrate general principles. Again, a number of recent surveys exist (e.g. Duck, 1993a; Dunn, 1993; Greenberg, Cicchetti, & Cummings, 1990; Rubin, Bukowski, & Parker, in press).

An overview has proved a harder task than I anticipated and, faced by an *embarras de richesse*, selection has been a major problem. Inevitably, the survey is incomplete but, by selecting primarily the more recent and accessible literature, I hope that, while keeping the bibliography within limits, I have made it possible for the reader to find the way back to the earlier literature without too much difficulty. As understanding involves not only examination of the different aspects of complex phenomena, but also examination of how those aspects affect each other, comprehensible presentation has required a good deal of cross-referencing. I have endeavoured, so far as seemed reasonably possible, to make each chapter stand on its own, so I have allowed some repetition. Finally, I hope that it may be understood that "he", "she", "him", and "her" may refer to persons of either sex unless the context indicates otherwise.

The book is divided into six sections. The first three chapters are concerned with the nature of relationships and some of the problems that a science of relationships must confront. Section B provides a framework for describing relationships. It is not, however, purely descriptive, as references to process help put flesh on the bones of description. The reader may therefore find it useful to cross-refer to Section C, where further processes involved in (and theories about) the dynamics of relationships, and their limitations, are reviewed. So far the material has involved analysis. The remaining sections make a start on the necessary process of re-synthesising the products of analysis. Section D presents some material on relationships of special importance to most people—friendship and loving relationships. As relationships are dynamic and constantly changing, it is necessary to pay special attention to the processes involved in their initiation, growth, maintenance, and dissolution: this is the subject-matter of Section E. The last chapter describes, very tentatively, the ways in which integration may eventually be achieved. Although the ordering of the chapters is thus intended to have a certain logic, I have tried to present the material in such a way that they can be read selectively, or in an order suited to the reader.

Before getting down to the meat of the matter, I shall try to illustrate the complexity of the problem by four vignettes, each concerned with successive levels of social complexity.

A Prolegomena

The first three chapters are intended to link those that follow to real life, or at least to real-life situations. Vignettes in Chapter 1 indicate some of the increasingly complex issues involved in individual behaviour, short-term interactions, relationships and groups, and hint at how they can be related to theory. Some of the obstacles to building up an ordered body of knowledge about relationships are discussed in Chapter 2. Understanding a relationship requires some prior understanding of the individual participants and of how they interact, so Chapter 3 presents a brief introduction to some theories of the self-system, and indicates the nature of interactions and relationships. This chapter stresses also the importance of coming to terms with the dialectical relations between successive levels of complexity, as illustrated in the Frontispiece.

1 From Everyday Behaviour towards a Science of Relationships

This is a book about the nature of relationships. Before plunging in, it may be helpful to consider four vignettes which link the analytical approach to situations in real life.

INDIVIDUAL BEHAVIOUR

Suppose that at this moment you are sitting in a chair (behaviour), thinking about what you are reading (cognitive activity), and feeling comfortable (affect). But after a while your mind wanders: you are distracted by thoughts of the wonderful time you had with your friend yesterday (cognition) and you feel a little elated (affect). At the same time you wonder whether you really want to read this book (cognition). You get up and make some coffee (behaviour). Coming back, you nearly trip on the carpet, exclaim loudly with irritation (behaviour, affect), settle back into your chair (behaviour) with relief (affect) and feel content (affect) as you go on reading (cognitive activity).

All the time we are awake we are behaving, and thinking, and feeling, and each of these may influence the others. What we feel is influenced by what we think; and what we think is influenced by what we feel; what we think and feel influences what we do; and what we do influences what we feel and think. Even an apparently simple activity, sitting reading a book, is actually very complicated.

You may ask why you are reading the book anyway. One answer is that you are curious. That, you will say, is a circular answer: we explain your reading by saying you are curious and we believe you are curious because you read. But in general it is far from circular, and almost a truism: it is part of our nature to seek to understand, to be able to predict, to exercise some control over the world we live in and to steer our own way through it. G.A. Kelly (1955) pictured this by saying that we operate as "personal scientists", developing implicit "theories" about our experience in the world so that we can cope with it better. That world is to a very large extent a social world, and it has been convincingly argued that that is why monkeys, apes, and humans have such relatively large cortical areas—we need to cope with a complicated social world (Humphrey, 1976). In practice, the theories that we elaborate about ourselves and about others are only moderately accurate, though we often convince ourselves that they are better than they really are.

To say we act as "personal scientists" is of course a metaphor. It is a way of referring to processes that underlie much of our behaviour, processes that are largely unconscious: the metaphor suggests that they are like the conscious processes of someone investigating an aspect of the world. As a metaphor, it is flexible, and we must be careful to remain aware that it is only a metaphor. Nevertheless it is a useful way of thinking, in part because description in terms of constituent processes at a fine level of analysis might miss properties relevant to a higher level, and in part because, if used with discipline, it gives us interesting insights into our behaviour. Furthermore, it ceases to be circular in so far as it "explains" diverse aspects of our behaviour.

Kelly suggested that, as a consequence of experience, we accumulate a series of constructs by which we construe the world. These constructs are often, but not necessarily, bi-polar—living/inanimate, human/nonhuman, and so on. Each individual construes the world in a different way in accordance with his or her nature and past experience. Because you are reading this book you are probably the sort of person who distinguishes between books and magazines, and between magazines and journals, but to many they would all be just books.

The constructs are interrelated in innumerable but personally idio-syncratic ways, in part by interlocking hierarchies. Thus "chicken" may be subordinated to "bird" and then to "animal" in one person's hierarchy, and to "food" in another's. Although we use labels to discuss constructs, they are not themselves necessarily verbal or dependent on verbal labels. We use these constructs for ordering past experience, making sense of current events, and for predicting the future. Each person's construct system is seen as continually under test by experience, in the light of which the construct system is adjusted, new material is assimilated and the whole accommodated. It is a bit like making a map of unexplored country, adjusting the details as we refine our survey or cover new ground. The superordinated constructs carry more implications for the system as a whole, and are therefore more resistant to invalidation—just as, if we found a particular hill was a bit higher than we thought, we would not give up colouring the high ground brown and the sea blue. Kelly supposed that we use our construct systems to make "theories" with which we organise our experience and with whose aid our behaviour is controlled. In so far as we can understand the present and predict the future, we can control the future—moving into situations where our needs can be satisfied, and avoiding those that are disagreeable or dangerous. However constructs and "theories" are in a dialectical relation to each other—we use our constructs to make theories and adjust our constructs in relation to our theories. One reason that adolescence can be traumatic is that earlier constructs and theories are being challenged.

On this view, we ascribe properties to the self, perhaps partly on the basis of observation of our own behaviour—seeing ourselves give money to charity, we label ourselves as generous, and this affects our future behaviour. The labels we apply to ourselves are based primarily on similarities and differences between ourselves and others: thus the self can be seen only in relation to the social context in which it is embedded. The particular theory each individual has about his/her self enables and restricts social behaviour, and affects both plans and expectations about the future and the accounts of the past fabricated to maintain or change the self-image. And, according to our understanding of ourselves, of the situation we are in, and of those we are with, we select a role—a pattern of activity that follows from that understanding. (Note there is a slight change in metaphor here, the scientist has become an actor, playing the part he sees himself as having been engaged to play.) Although there are a number of roles we could play, we have a "core role structure" (a term which overlaps with "self-concept" or "self-schema"), which provides the means whereby we maintain our identity.

The philosophically minded reader will detect a problem in all this—where is the I who observes the self and plays the role that has been selected? This issue can be pursued in discussions of the nature of consciousness (e.g. Dennett, 1991; Humphrey, 1992): for present purposes we need only remind ourselves that we are speaking metaphorically. We treat the self as someone to think about as if we were thinking about someone else.

Kelly's account is one of a number that stress the social nature of the self (see Chapter 3). We shall meet others in later chapters and find that the metaphors they use overlap with those of Kelly. Bowlby's (1969/1982) Internal Working Model of self and other is one that has received particular prominence lately.

INTERACTIONS

The behaviour of one person is complicated enough. Now imagine an interaction between two.

> Now suppose, while you are reading, someone knocks on the door. You open it to find a little old lady almost entirely covered in a rather ragged grey shawl. You presume that she has come for money, and greet her with a rather hesitant and suspicious "Good morning". She lowers the shawl a little and smiles kindly at you. "I'm your new neighbour", she says, "and I have brought you some flowers from my garden". She produces a bunch of violets from under the shawl. You thank her politely, but now you are a little ill at ease—you want to be on good terms with your neighbour, but not on too good terms: after all, she might become intrusive. Yet again, she seems a kindly person, and perhaps she is lonely: you should be kind to her. However, smiling straight into your eyes, she then turns and walks off through the gate. Did she detect your ambivalence? Did she feel rejected? No, surely not—you took the flowers and thanked her, and you'll do something for her tomorrow to make sure that she realises your gratitude. Yes, you tell yourself that you need not worry.

When the doorbell rings, one usually has no idea who is standing outside. With the first glimpse one forms an impression which is immediately compared with memories of comparable people encountered in the past, or with people one has heard about or read about. The little old women you have met before have usually wanted something, but was there not one once who turned into a fairy godmother—or was it a wolf? So what should one do when such a woman appears on the doorstep? This time you muddled through, feeling apprehension, embarrassment, until she was on her way. You were trying to find a way of behaving that would satisfy both you and her, and you are not sure you succeeded. But after she had gone you could construct a story that explained your behaviour to yourself.

The important issue here, which we shall meet repeatedly in later chapters, is that people are continuously trying to make sense of their own and others' actions. They search for meaning. People need to feel that they have some degree of control over what happens, and to that end need to see the world as predictable—an issue crucial for many aspects of social psychology (Berger, 1993).

There are a number of ways to describe the interaction in this vignette. Duck (1977a, b, 1990, 1994a, b) emphasises that, in their interactions and relationships, people try to create personal meanings for themselves and mutual understanding with their partners. Here it was your uncertainty about whether you had established mutual understanding that led to your feeling uncomfortable.

G.A. Kelly (1955) would say that you were searching for a suitable "role", where "role" is a way of behaving that follows from a particular understanding of another person or of a situation. The role we adopt must be compatible with, and indeed should confirm, the image we have of ourselves—seeing yourself as charitable, you could not have shut the door in her face. But you see yourself as charitable because of past experiences with other people—every individual's personal identity is formed by experience, and especially social experience. And it continues to be formed throughout life—though in some respects resistant to change, it is in dynamic flux. And because you are continually discerning similarities and differences between yourself and others, and between those others, the way in which you construe yourself is closely related to the way in which you construe others, and vice versa.

An approach to the understanding of social behaviour has been worked out in detail by Goffman (1959, 1961, 1963, 1967) and G.J. McCall (1970, 1974). Goffman distinguishes between the expressions an individual *gives* and those he *gives off.* By "gives", Goffman refers to communication in the usual sense. When you opened the door, you said "Good morning" in an entirely proper way. By "gives off", Goffman is referring to the impression an individual creates or tries to create. You might have said "Good-morning" haughtily, benevolently, distrustfully, ingratiatingly... In point of fact, this time you fluffed it—you were not quite sure what impression you wanted to create. But, Goffman would say, the little old lady was watching the expressions you gave off in order to "define the situation"—so that she would know what to expect of you.

In general, it is in the individual's interest to influence this definition of the situation which the others present come to formulate, and he (or she) can do this most readily by expressing himself so as to give them an impression that will lead them to accept his plan. To understand how the individual achieves this, Goffman takes a "dramaturgical perspective", treating the speaker as though he was a performer attempting to create an impression on an audience. In real life an individual may create an impression deliberately; or he may act more or less unconsciously, perhaps falling in with the conventions of the group, or his behaviour may be idiosyncratic and more spontaneous. If the actor dissembles, the listeners may or may not spot what he is up to. If the actor knows that he is likely to be discovered, he may make a false revelation—Goffman emphasises the potentially infinite cycle of concealment, discovery, false revelation, and re-discovery.

Each party to an interaction will be actor and audience in turn, so each will project their definition of the situation, which may or may not be accepted by the other. In the course of interaction, each may shift ground a little—or perhaps adopt a slightly different role. But for the interaction to go smoothly, it is not necessary (or desirable?) that each should candidly express what he feels and honestly agree with the other. Rather each participant conveys a view of the situation that he feels the other will find temporarily acceptable, perhaps concealing some of his feelings behind asserted values to which everyone feels obliged to agree. Each, in other words, must "fit in". But at the same time each individual is allowed to establish tentative rules regarding matters vital to him and allows the other to do the same. Goffman describes such a situation as a "working consensus". As this working consensus is reached progressively, the initial impression made by each party can have a crucial influence on the progress of the interaction. In the same way, the early stages of a relationship may set the tone of later ones: Goffman regards a relationship as arising when an individual plays the same part to the same audience on different occasions.

In this way Goffman analyses a wide range of interactions, ranging from casual encounters to the interactions within intimate relationships, *as if* the individual concerned were playing a part. This involves the individual in projecting a definition of the situation (e.g. "This is my consulting room") and of his self (e.g. "And I am a knowledgeable and competent doctor"). Those parts of the performance that contribute to these definitions are called the "front". The "front" is made up of the physical setting and the personal front, the latter including "appearance", conveying social status, and "manner", concerned with the particular interaction role the performer is playing. There may also be a "back", where the performance is prepared—where, for instance, the doctor instructs his nurse on how to present herself to patients. Disruption of the front may lead to a halt in the sequence of interactions, embarrassment and so on.

Treating social behaviour "as if" it were a performance, liable to be "seen through" by the audience, Goffman provides fascinating insights into what goes on in ordinary social interactions. Of special interest here is his discussion of the extent to which the interactions he describes are in fact performances, and to what extent they are genuine. In the ordinary course of events we treat people as though they were either genuine or dissembling. But status or role in a social situation is not a material thing, to be possessed and displayed; it is a pattern of appropriate conduct, which must be performed to be realised. Goffman thus regards a performer, who is sincerely convinced that the impression of reality that he is staging is the real reality, as being taken in by his own act. Whilst being taken in by one's own act and being cynical about it sound like the extremes of a continuum, Goffman points out that the extremes tend to be more stable than the intermediate regions. In so far as a person is playing a part, that part represents what he would like to be, and in so far as others confirm him in it, he will come to believe that that part is really him.

RELATIONSHIPS

Now let us go a little further, and discuss behaviour between two people who know each other well.

After the little old lady has left you settle back into your chair, comforted by the thought that you had thanked her warmly and by your intention to repay the call tomorrow, and continue reading. But after a few minutes the telephone rings. This time it is your closest friend, someone you've known for years. You are very fond of him—it has often been a relief to discuss problems with him in the sure knowledge that he would not betray your trust. In fact you are a little worried that you might become too fond of him: he sometimes seems a bit assertive, and you don't want anyone else running your life for you. But you greet him warmly, and you chat for a few minutes about what you have both been doing. Then he suggests he should come round and that you go for a walk along the cliffs, a few miles away. There it is again—you'd been planning a quiet day at home with this fascinating book and warm fire and plenty of coffee, and he wants you to get yourself together, put on another coat, change your shoes and go out. You really don't want to stir yourself up, but it is a wonderful fine breezy day, a walk on the cliffs would be wonderful, and after all it's ages since you did anything like that.

So you go. Do you enjoy yourself? Perhaps it really is wonderful on the cliffs: the flowers are just coming out, broken clouds, just enough wind to make little white horses on the sea. And he is very considerate, taking care not to walk too fast—and he brought apples and chocolate with him. Perhaps you were wrong to think him assertive. Next time he rings you won't hesitate.

When you get back you reflect on how, when he rang, there was a comfortable feeling of sinking back into an old routine, you always knew where you were with him. It was not very sensible to have those worries about your autonomy—really he's very considerate. And he is always thinking of wonderful new things to do, so it's never boring to be with him. And so you pick up the book and find you have got to the place where it talks about relationships.

In a close relationship you don't have to search for a new role identity, but just pick up the one that is appropriate for the partner in question. That echoes what you have been thinking and feeling today. In a close relationship, the familiarity makes it unnecessary to think too much about how you should behave—you automatically put on a coat (to use yet another metaphor) suitable for the occasion. With a close friend it's an old coat, one that for nearly all the time you feel comfortable in and, despite its age, keeps you warm. Of course there are times when you wonder if it is the coat you really want to be wearing, whether it really fits *you*. You have quite a number of other coats in your cupboard suitable for other friends and other situations, and which one you choose depends on your memories and feelings about past interactions with the person in question— and perhaps on expectations and hopes for the future. But this is a friend you are fond of, and you do really like the coat you wear with him—you feel it's "like you". Perhaps that is why you are fond of him—because you like the coat you wear with him. One cannot be happy in a relationship unless one likes the sort of person one is in that relationship. We shall see later that this means that you have to keep a number of balances rather delicately poised. You want to be close to him but not (or not yet) so close that you feel as though you've lost control over your life. You want to share your thoughts and feelings with him, but there is a fear that by doing so you make yourself vulnerable and might lose control that way. The familiarity gives you security, but monotony can be boring. You want to do things for him, and you want him to do things for you—but it must be fair, because you'll feel uncomfortable if you feel you are not getting what you deserve, or if you feel you are getting more than you deserve.

THE SOCIAL GROUP

What goes on between two people is often affected by whom they are with. Let us imagine that, instead of going for a walk with your friend, you meet in a group.

> The next day he rings you again and suggests that you and he should join some friends of his for a drink in "The Three Horseshoes". You are really enjoying the book now but, remembering the lovely walk you had yesterday, you agree cheerfully and put on your coat. The friends turn out to be two of his football buddies. They welcome you warmly, buy you a pint, and you are glad you came. You settle down in a corner of the bar. But as the conversation goes to and fro, you begin to feel you are seeing a new side to your friend. With his football buddies he has a certain heartiness which you have not come across before. However you don't want to let him down, and you do your best to fit in. Feeling a little chilly, you take a bright scarf out of your bag and tie it round your neck to fit in over your coat. You try hard but you feel torn—a little guilty because you don't want to let down your friend, and again a little guilty because you are not quite sure that this is a role that really fits you. A few drinks later, you'd really rather leave and be with him alone, but it's your turn to buy a round of drinks and you do not want him to feel that his friends think that you don't know the proper conventions. This time you get your-self some tonic water, but he is on his fourth drink and you begin to wonder if he really is the person you thought you knew—he even makes a remark which you feel is off-colour.

Fortunately his friends soon have to go. You walk back home together, light the fire, and, as the house warms up, you take off your scarf and sit talking. In this relaxed atmosphere you can tell him that you weren't quite certain that you liked his friends. He tells you that they are good chaps really, though perhaps they were showing off a bit for your benefit, and that it's important for him to get on with them because one of them is the boss's son. You know how important it is that he should get on in the firm, and indeed you want him to, so you decide that you needn't say anything about his behaviour in the pub— it was not the real him, he was acting under constraint.

We all feel we are the same person all the time, and yet we adjust our behaviour according to whom we are with. A relationship with one other person is relatively simple compared with interactions with that other person in a group. Somehow you must find a role that suits not only your special friend as he is with you, but also his friends, and yet further the sort of person he likes his friends to perceive you to be. And while when you were with him alone you were to some extent constrained by norms that you both considered appropriate, in a group you felt even more constrained because you felt that your friend might feel that his friends might think less of him if you did not conform to their conventions. You were not sure that you were in sympathy with the way he behaved in the pub, but when you were alone with him he provided you with an account that enabled you to construct your own story and so come to terms with his behaviour.

Relationships are complicated.

2 Obstacles to a Science of Interpersonal Relationships

For most of us, relationships with other people are the most important part of our lives. As individuals we know, though not necessarily at a conscious level, a great deal about how those relationships work. We have been learning about relationships between people since we were born. Indeed some would argue that, by virtue of our evolutionary history, we are predisposed to learn about relationships quickly and to use that knowledge with skill (Humphrey, 1976). Although each of us has only a limited range of experience, we can learn about aspects of relationships that we do not experience ourselves from watching and talking with others, from the distilled wisdom of novelists and bio-graphers, and perhaps less reliably from the folk tales of our culture. Furthermore, the study of interpersonal relations comes within the orbit of a number of scientific disciplines. And yet, in spite of all these sources of information, it cannot yet be said that we have a science, in the sense of an integrated body of knowledge, about interpersonal relationships. But if we are to understand the complex processes by which personality develops, if we are to manage our own relationships successfully, if we are to help and advise others wisely, if we wish to strive to create a society in which positive relationships flourish, we must surely attempt to build up a systematic body of knowledge about relationships. We need a science. We must therefore ask, what is it that has until recently hindered its development?

PREJUDICES FROM OUTSIDE SCIENCE

First there have been and still are prejudices from outside science. Some argue that full understanding of any relationship is possible only for the participants, others that the complexity and diversity of relationships are such that generalisations are unattainable. But full understanding of all aspects of all human relationships is not immediately what we are after—we seek only, or at any rate first, for an understanding adequate to achieve our goals. And from that aim we must not and need not be diverted by complexity.

Yet others fear that full understanding of interpersonal relationships would destroy something of value. "Analysis is total, knowledge is boundless. But I can't stand it," says one of Bergman's characters in a perceptive play on marital relationships (Bergman, 1974, p.192). But if such an argument is to be mounted, it should be directed against all attempts to understand interpersonal behaviour, including those of biographers, novelists, and playwrights, and not just against those of scientists. In any case, the issue is an old one, and need not be pursued. Analytic understanding does not eliminate the whole: Newton did not destroy the beauty of the rainbow. That is not to deny that misplaced cogitation by a participant can induce excessive self-consciousness and reduce the spontaneity of a relationship. If we come to believe that only one type of behaviour is proper in a given relationship, we lose the capacity for mutual adaptation. If we focus on only one aspect, we may magnify it out of all proportion and distort the whole. Thus, as in all such cases, the question should be phrased, "Will the harm, if any, outdo the good?".

Another prejudice involves the supposition that relationships possess subtle properties beyond the reach of the scientist, and must therefore remain the exclusive preserve of novelists, biographers, playwrights, and clinicians (in so far as the latter are not scientists). It may well be that the penetrating insights into individual cases that some writers have achieved would not be attainable in any other way. Perhaps instances of the dialectic between personality and relationship are, at least for the moment, best encapsulated in literary form. But when it comes to systematic knowledge, to abstracting generalisations from their wisdom, even the most sensitive literary criticism, in which the material is assessed not only in its own terms but against the yardstick of life (e.g. Black, 1975), produces conclusions no different from those of the scientists and perhaps less securely based.

Of course there may well be properties of relationships that the scientists' instruments cannot detect—they are in no position to argue about that. But they are obliged to *attempt* to fashion tools suitable for all natural phenomena that they encounter. Hopes, fears, ambitions, tenderness, indifference, empathy, sensitivity and many other seemingly intangible entities form the stuff of which relationships are made, but already progress has been made in coming to terms with them. And if for the moment some subtle properties of relationships are beyond scientists' reach, such properties may nevertheless be correlated with properties that are more accessible. For many practical purposes, it is the extent of such correlations that are important. Some of the properties of an affectionate relationship can be specified with reasonable precision (see p.61), though there are certainly others that are more intangible. If we could use the properties with which we can now cope to discover, for example, the conditions necessary to promote relationships having those properties, it is at least possible that the same conditions would prove to be propitious also for the more intangible ones.

Yet another obstacle to a science of interpersonal relationships arises from the very fact that each of us knows, or thinks he knows, so much about them already. But even our cherished beliefs may be wrong, or may apply only to a limited range of relationships or in a limited range of contexts. Clearly we must use our intuition, but only with the greatest circumspection. This very need for care, for validating every finding and testing the limits of every generalisation, can lead us into complex endeavours which may at times seem to achieve little beyond proving what is already known. The difficulty here is to maintain a proper balance. On the one hand, the temptation to pursue a line of research just because it yields hard data, even though those data are trivial and unlikely to lead anywhere new, must be resisted. On the other hand, it is necessary to formulate each piece of knowledge in a manner that enables it to be incorporated alongside others, and thus contribute to the edifice of knowledge. This must be done even with what we think we know, in part because even if we are correct, the generality of what we know for other contexts and other cultures must be tested.

PROBLEMS FROM WITHIN SCIENCE

General Issues

Selection of Problems and Scientific Respectability. Some prejudices come from within science, for the study of interpersonal relationships does not at first sight provide the sort of material that would allow it to rank highly on the ladder of scientific respectability. Science tends to grow like an *Amoeba,* putting out pseudopodia now here and now there to engulf areas of ignorance, but rejecting indigestible fragments and avoiding areas uncongenial to it. This method of growth leads to the structuring of a value system. Areas of research in which the problems are clear, and where precise techniques are available so that the results can be checked in half a dozen laboratories, become respectable. But it is thought foolhardy and disreputable to enter areas where the course ahead is murky, where the complexity of the material makes it difficult to follow the same path twice, and where the conceptual jungle chokes the unwary. But, if science is not to be trivial, such anticipations of possible difficulties must be reconciled with the importance of problems. The dilemma between the need for rigour and the need for relevance is not new to psychologists, and a growing body of hard-headed scientists have shown that love and hate, and even the trivia of the family breakfast table, are proper grist for their mill.

Use of Metaphors. As mentioned in Chapter 1, in studying relationships, it is as necessary to use metaphors as it is in everyday life, but it is essential to be clear-headed about their use. Thus if we say "The fog lifted from his mind" or "The foundations of an ordered body of knowledge about human relationships have been laid", we are not tempted to look for water droplets coming out of his ears or a book standing on concrete. In the same way metaphors such as "merging two selves" or "having a working model of relationships", while of enormous heuristic value, must be recognised for what they are. This is an obvious enough issue, yet it is often easy to pursue a metaphor beyond the point at which it is useful.

Methodological Problems

Each dyadic relationship involves two individuals, each with a past history and expectations and hopes for the future; it involves cognitive, affective, and behavioural components, each of which influences the others; it exists over time; and it has no clear boundaries, being constantly affected by extra-dyadic influences. It is thus not surprising that the study of relationships is beset by conceptual and methodological difficulties. Many of these will become apparent in later chapters, but some of the principal ones are noted here.

Objective and Subjective Data. A complete description of a relationship would require data on what the participants do, think, and feel. A science of relationships thus requires both objective and subjective data. But data about what individuals do cannot always be obtained by objective means—in part because of the nature of the behaviour, and in part because of the expenditure of time that would be required. It is therefore often necessary to rely on subjects' reports. However, as we shall see, what individuals report about themselves or their relationships may vary with their mood and current situation, it may be obscured or elaborated by defence mechanisms, and constructed as part of an on-going account that the individual makes of his life. Thus it may or may not bear a close relation to what the individual actually did, thought, or felt. That does not necessarily detract from its value as data, as what an individual relationship feels about himself and his relationship will influence its future course.

Descriptive and Explanatory Concepts.   As discussed on p.54, it is desirable to maintain a clear distinction between descriptive and explanatory concepts, yet this is often difficult in the study of relationships because some of the characteristics of relationships are to be explained in terms of processes which are themselves characteristics of the relationship.

Furthermore, many of the concepts used in the study of relationships have woolly edges. This is inevitable, because relationships are part of everyday life, and we are already equipped with means to describe and explain them, yet each of us gives the concepts we use slightly different shades of meaning. To build an ordered body of knowledge about relationships we need reasonably hard concepts, but many of those used in the study of relationships—intimacy, closeness, satisfaction, to cite but three—are defined in different ways by different workers. Sometimes the same word is used to refer to different concepts, and sometimes different words are used for the same concept. This inevitably handicaps communication and reduces the possibility of compatibility between studies—or, worse, causes studies of different phenomena to be treated as though they were the same, or similar phenomena as though they were different. Thus, Fincham and Bradbury (1987a) point out that instruments for assessing self-disclosure and marital satisfaction may overlap, so that any relation between them may be tautologous (see also Glenn, 1987; Newcomb & Bentler, 1981) (further discussion in Chapter 3). Research workers define concepts in ways that they believe foster solutions to their particular problems, but no one of them is in a position to say "My usage is the right usage". The problem is a serious one, yet attempts to dictate correct usage can easily stultify creativity.

Consequences of an Analytic Approach.   Because a scientific approach requires analysis, to be followed by re-synthesis, it is rather easy for a written account of research on relationships to seem both to impoverish and to intellectualise them. The appearance of impoverishment comes from the need to describe aspects or parts of relationships in isolation from the whole. We may discuss the exchange of confidences in a loving relationship, for instance, and it seems that the ecstasy and joy in that relationship are forgotten. The appearance of intellectualisation has at least two sources. First, many relationships just happen—we may think very little about them. This, of course, is not true of most close relationships, which involve a great deal of conscious cognitive activity: indeed one cannot imagine a close relationship between adults in which the participants do not think a lot about it, and what they think may make a great deal of difference to its future course. But all the cognitive and emotional activity in a relationship does not necessarily reach the conscious level, or is not necessarily reflected upon. Second, describing what happens in an interaction takes much longer than the interaction. It may involve reference to events in the past or expected in the future, to events of which the participants were unconscious or only partially conscious at the time, and it may involve the description in words of processes and signals that were near instantaneous and non-verbal.

Analysis has another consequence—one considers separately intimacy, conflict, and so on. By focusing on particular topics, it is easy to give the impression that intimacy is the goal of all relationships, or that conflict is always prominent. One can even neglect the relations between the many characteristics of relationships—though one knows full well that conflict affects intimacy and intimacy affects the incidence of conflict. For such reasons, we must be aware that, even while considering aspects of relationships, it is necessary to see them as wholes. Although the early chapters of this book focus on specific aspects of relationships and specific aspects of their dynamics, later chapters attempt to redress this balance by discussion of issues that involve their integration.

Generalisations or the Understanding of Particular Cases. Another problem involves the finding of a balance between the complexity of the individual case and the need for generalisations. To a large extent, science is a search for generalisations that will explain diverse phenomena, and a science of relationships needs generalisations and needs the statistical techniques that support them—though such techniques are not always used correctly (Karney & Bradbury, 1995a, b). But what matters to this individual may not matter to that, and what matters to either can get lost in the sophistication of the statistics. Furthermore, people behave differently according to whom they are with—in other words, the context in which an individual finds herself is crucial. The context gives meaning to the individual and to the relationship, but what seems like the same context may be seen quite differently by an outsider and by the participants, and even by each of the participants. This is why studies that pool data across individuals, and most studies do and indeed must do so, should be applied to individuals with caution. Studies of groups or populations need to be balanced by the use of case histories, diaries, etc. Above all, we need constantly to refer to the relationships we experience and see around us, so that we can see what is missing from our analyses.

Cross-sectional and Longitudinal Data.   Because what two partners did yesterday affects what they do today, longitudinal studies are essential for many issues. This is especially the case for studies of the predictors or determinants of relationship stability. Yet longitudinal studies are logistically difficult and demand great commitment from the research worker, not to mention security of funding. Often, perhaps too often, it is necessary to make do with a cross-sectional approach.

Use of Experimental Approaches.   If we want to understand the dynamics of relationships in real life, real-life relationships must be studied. However behaviour in real-life situations is influenced by many variables, and evidence of the effectiveness of particular variables can sometimes profitably be obtained by experiment under controlled conditions. There are, of course, dangers in generalising from the laboratory to the outside world.

Choice of Subjects.   To repeat a long-standing lament of workers on social relationships, college students provide a wonderfully available source of data, but how far are such data generalisable? Is the love found in the romantic relationships of students comparable to that of older people or to those in less privileged settings? What is the relation between student love and that of long-married couples? These are important empirical questions (cf. Sears, 1986). Similarly Conway (1995) has emphasised that the idea of womanhood that comes from young women's self-reporting may be misleading as a basis for generalisations. Students may also differ from the general public in other ways relevant to the study of relationships. In these years relationships may form and dissolve more frequently than either earlier or later in life, in part because the environment (home, college, work) is changing. This has undoubtedly coloured the research that has been conducted. Students may also, for instance, be more introspective. Conceivably, they may be more clever.

Cultural Differences.   The problem of cultural differences is ubiquitous. A growing number of studies, some of which will be mentioned later, show how substantial these may be. Yet most of the literature on personal relationships comes from Europe and North America, and is shot through with Western values. One finds, for instance, that self-assertiveness is automatically referred to as a positive trait, selflessness as negative. Not everyone, everywhere, would agree. We must remember that the basic variables in a study may rest on culture-specific values. What holds for California may not be true for Connecticut, let alone for Cambridge, and even less for Calcutta. It would be tedious to specify the location of every study cited in this book, but the reader must be aware that most refer to North America or Europe: not all generalisations are cross-culturally valid, and we often do not know which are and which are not. Values may even differ between sub-cultures within a society, and even between individuals. Especially important for the study of interpersonal relationships is that they may differ between women and men. We must not assume that what brings satisfaction to a woman in a close relationship is the same as what brings satisfaction to a man, and indeed we know that it is not.

This issue is complicated even further by the rapidity of social change. Generalisations about co-habiting couples in the 1960s may not apply to co-habiting couples today, let alone to married ones. And while an individual's answers to a questionnaire or responses in an interview may enable him or her to be labelled as having particular values, ideals, or expectations of one sort or another, what if those values were recently acquired from the peer group and at odds with those to which the individual was earlier socialised? What if they differ from his or her "nature"? And a relationship involves two individuals, whose values may have changed in different directions...

Self-reports.   As noted earlier, for many purposes the most valuable instruments involve questionnaires and self-reports. Such instruments are often most appropriate because how an individual experiences and assesses herself and the relationship is an important determinant of the relationship's future course. However it is important to bear in mind that such instruments are subject to bias, and often tap only overall impressions or focus on salient events, neglecting the moment-to-moment trivialia that, in the long run, cumulatively give a relationship its quality. Diary methods, which make such data more available, have been fruitful but are too little used (Bolger & Kelleher, 1993; Reis, 1995; Reis & Wheeler, 1991). Of even greater potential for the study of relationships is the Double Diary method, in which both partners keep records, whose use has been initiated by Auhagen (1987, 1991).

In any case, self-reports usually concern the respondent's own or the partner's behaviour across a number of situations, and represent evaluative judgements made in the context of a constructed narrative of the relationship. This certainly does not mean that they are unreliable as data, but it does imply that they are unlikely to coincide with the judgements of an observer who has witnessed only a few brief interactions (Noller & Guthrie, 1992).

Thus self-reports, though often used and used appropriately, should not always be taken at face value: they may be influenced by defensive processes or other aspects of the respondent's style or relationship (Harvey, Hendrick, & Tucker, 1988). They can be regarded as partly a true record, partly reflecting the account that the respondent has constructed, and partly as on-the-spot self-justifications.

As an example of how respondents' bias can affect their reports, children were categorised as Securely, Anxiously, or Avoidantly attached to their mothers by the Ainsworth Strange Situation technique, and also rated for Security by both mothers and observers (for further explanation, see Chapter 21). Mothers of children classed in the Secure category rated their children as less Secure than did the observers, while mothers of the other children rated them as more Secure than did the observers. The data suggested that the former mothers had a style that both fostered the Security of their children and enabled them to keep in touch with their feelings and report them in a balanced way; whereas mothers of Avoidant children had a style less conducive to Security in their children which also led to defensive reporting (Stevenson-Hinde & Shouldice, 1995).

In the same vein, Levinger and Breedlove (1966) found that spouses who scored highly on a marital satisfaction index tended to see themselves as more similar than they actually were, while spouses with low scores tended to underestimate their similarity.

A second issue arises when two or more sets of data are obtained from the same individual. For instance, many studies of interpersonal relationships involve comparisons between two or more self-report instruments. Such a procedure, which would not be condoned in other branches of psychology, may be necessary and inevitable if the difficult problems posed by interpersonal relationships are to be solved, but such data must be treated with due caution and with regard for the extent to which biases in the reporter may affect similarly the different instruments.

Theories.   In part because relationships are part of everyone's life, some research on relationships has serendipitous origins. But we need theory to tie together and explain the diversity of human relationships, and to guide the course of research. The study of personal relationships uses, and is giving rise to, numerous generalisations, mini-theories, and theories. Some of these, like interdependence theory (Chapter 19), have proven utility in a wide variety of contexts, but none covers all the phenomena. Although attempts to integrate them are now being made, it is still necessary for the student of relationships to be eclectic, taking data and explanation from where she can, and doing her best to stitch them together. That is the strategy followed in this book. But we must also try to see where they are really saying the same thing but using a different metaphor (Chapter 29).

Conclusion.   The obstacles to building a science of human relationships just listed might make the prospects seem a bit gloomy, but it is a fact that relationships are both complicated and diverse, and we must not expect simple answers. We must not be discouraged by the difficulties, and if you get the bogeys out in front of you, it's easier to deal with them.

SUMMARY

Some obstacles to the building of an ordered body of knowledge about personal relationships are considered. Some of these come from outside science and some from within. Some stem from the complex nature of relationships and the diverse influences on their course, and some from the research techniques necessary to study them.

3 The Self, Interactions, and Relationships

To understand relationships, we must also come to terms with the nature of individuals and of interactions. In this chapter we take up first the nature of the self-system—bearing in mind the caveat in Chapter 1 that our description of the self-system must be in part metaphorical. We shall then comment briefly on the nature of interactions and pursue a little farther what we mean by a relationship.

THE SELF-SYSTEM

We find it convenient, in interpreting people's (including our own) behaviour, to use a concept of "self". We account for the continuity in our own lives by postulating a "self", and we assume that other people have "selves" too. We need not pursue what it means to say that someone *has* a "self", or ask why we do not say that he or she *is* a "self"; nor is it sensible to ask exactly where the "self" is: we can treat the "self" as a convenient abstraction which helps us to tie together the things we observe in the social world.

When we speak about the self in everyday speech, we often intend to emphasise a distinction between the self and others. It is necessary, however, to accept that the nature of the self is essentially social. This has been recognised since the turn of the century. Baldwin (1897) saw thoughts about the self and thoughts about others to be inextricably interrelated. Cooley (1902) and Mead (1934) argued that our views of ourselves, our self-concepts or self-images, can develop only from the ways in which others behave to us, and more recent workers have discussed the processes involved (e.g. Higgins, Loeb, & Moretti, 1995). We can evaluate ourselves only through the ways in which we perceive others to respond to us, and reciprocally, as we shall see, how we see ourselves affects how we see others and how others behave to us. The important issue is the way in which we *perceive* others to perceive us, rather than the way they actually do: we form our self-concepts by interpreting the responses of others to us, incorporating our perceptions of other people's views of us into our views of ourselves. Most important are the views of those with whom we have or have had close relationships, and most especially those in our family of origin. In effect, we tell ourselves stories about our interactions with others, and use those stories to tell ourselves what sorts of people we are (Gergen & Gergen, 1988; Harvey, Weber, & Orbuch, 1990). In harmony with these views, some recent experimental evidence supports the suggestion that it is how we behave in public that affects our self-concepts much more than how we behave when alone (Tice, 1992). The self thus comes to incorporate the psychological processes involved in everyday events; the (relatively) stable views one has of one's appearance, behaviour, traits, competencies, and so on in relation to one's perceptions of those of others and to how one perceives oneself to be perceived by others; and affective experiences associated with self and others—though, as we shall see shortly, that is not all. Comparison with others is of special importance in how one evaluates oneself—one's self-esteem (e.g. Fitness, 1996; Fletcher & Fitness, 1996; Rosenberg, 1988).

Storage of Information

If the self-concept is based on past experiences, we must ask how knowledge of those experiences is stored in long-term memory. A number of schemes have been proposed, and discussion here must be limited. Most have in common the view that information must be stored in networks of modular units within hierarchical systems.

The information stored may concern the self, the situation, other people, and relationships, and comes from diverse sources (Andersen, 1993). Most important is personal experience—as emphasised already, personality is formed largely by experience in interaction with others. But vicarious experience through observation of others, and information from third parties, play a role. Also relevant here are folk tales, myths, books, and the media, whose contents are in dialectical relation to how people actually behave. Soap operas on television, for instance, both mirror relationships in real life and influence the course of real-life relationships. Furthermore the stored information may be affected by reflections on past events or by expectations and hopes for the future. And beyond that, as a mental representation, the self-system must be based within a larger system of knowledge about relationships with others, and how those relationships differ from each other, and contain scripts guiding behaviour in particular situations. We shall return to these issues shortly.

There is evidence both for the view that individuals form summary generalisations on the basis of what they have experienced (schemata, prototypes) and also that they store specific representations of particular individuals or occasions (Reis & Knee, 1996). The cognitive representations are often divided into two sorts. "Procedural knowledge", or "knowing *how*", concerns the skills and rules used in processing information. Thus they may be of the type "If my friend does X, I do Y". "Declarative knowledge" or "knowing *that*", is concerned with characteristics of people or things, and is used explicitly and consciously to provide explanations, plan action, and so on (Baldwin, 1992). Although we tend to think of all knowledge structures as accessible to consciousness, it is important to recognise that much cognitive processing may be irrational, based on associations, laden with emotion, and operating without conscious awareness (Fitness, 1996; Forgas, 1996; Reis & Knee, 1996).

The stored information influences how the individual interprets new information, plans for the future, and behaves from moment to moment. Although discussion has laid emphasis on cognition, this is often inseparable from affect. Thus a person who behaves in a shy manner will see himself as shy and, seeing himself as shy, will continue to feel shy and to behave shyly; and behaving shyly will be seen by others to be shy, so that they are likely to behave to him as though he were shy, confirming him in his belief.

Concepts of the Self and Other

Although the self-system was earlier seen as a cognitive representation of the self based on past experience, it is now apparent that it must involve much more than that. It must involve not only perceptions of the individual as he is, but also of what he might become, could become, or is afraid of becoming (Markus & Nurius, 1986). And, as we have seen, it must include affective and motivational aspects, and thus goals, incentives, and so on.

Cognitive representations of others must be nearly as complicated. Although the ways in which one thinks about the self and others are closely related, there are also some general differences. One is the well-known tendency of individuals to ascribe their own actions, and the consequences of their own actions, to situational factors, and other people's to their personal characteristics (see Chapter 18). Other differences in the ways in which people think about themselves and others can be understood on the premise that one has fuller information about oneself than one can ever have about others. For instance, people tend to think of themselves in terms of what they do, but of others in terms of what they are or seem to be; and of themselves in terms of both non-social and social action, but of others preponderantly in terms of social action (McGuire & McGuire, 1988).

Age Changes and Differences in the Self-concept

The self-concept is not to be seen as a static structure: in the first place it changes to some extent with age and with situation. Thus McGuire and McGuire (1988) found that the proportion of self-descriptions that involve references to others, around a quarter in children and adolescents, decreases with age, with girls using more social references than boys. Self-descriptions are more likely to refer to the same-sex parent but the opposite-sex sibling. Furthermore as children become more sophisticated their self-descriptions become less concrete and more abstract, shifting from perceptions of the self in terms of what one *does* to what one *is*, and from static states to dynamic states of becoming. When the self is described with verbs of action, these tend to shift from overt actions to covert actions with age. There are also trends from physically acting on the world of things to social action; from affective to cognitive covert reaction verbs; and from thinking of oneself in terms of what one is, to thinking also in terms of what one is not.

Gender Differences

The gender differences found in this study are of special interest, and suggest that relationships with others are more important to girls than to boys. In an important chapter Acitelli and Young (1996) refer to a study by Douvan and Adelson (1966) who found that adolescent boys were more likely to respond to interviewers' questions by referring to issues of achievement, autonomy, and occupational plans, while identity development in girls depended on issues of friendship, dating, and popularity (see also Lang-Takac & Osterweil, 1992; Magnusson & Olah, 1981). In adulthood, men's self-concepts are more related to autonomy, women's to connectedness. Thus Acitelli and Young (1996) cite data indicating that while men are more concerned with forming and maintaining relationships regardless of what goes on within them, women care more about monitoring and evaluating the interactions. The masculinity scale in the Bem Sex Role Inventory, on which men usually score highly (at any rate in the West), emphasises assertiveness, independence, and ambition, while the feminine scale is concerned with affection, sensitivity, and understanding.

There is a spectrum of views about the genesis of gender differences. Some lay emphasis on biological determinants. Others suggest that differences in early relationships are responsible (e.g. Dinnerstein, 1976). For instance, Chodorow (1978) has suggested that feminine selfhood is formed within a relationship with the mother-figure, so that representations of relationships play a large part in the self: this leads to an emphasis on empathy, responsiveness to others, and a focus on relationship processes. By contrast, it is supposed that masculine selfhood rests on separation from the primary caregiver, and emphasises autonomy and achievement. An intermediate view accepts biological differences, especially in propensities to learn gender-relevant attitudes, etc. These determine the *direction* of the differences, which are pan-cultural at least to an extent that cannot be accounted for by chance. However the *extent* and *patterning* of the differences are seen as the consequence of socialisation processes which normally act to enhance the initial propensities, and are heavily dependent on cultural norms (Hinde, 1987, 1991).

Situational Effects

McGuire and McGuire's (1988) study also showed that the situation can affect the self-concept. Thus children and adolescents describing themselves tended to emphasise passivity in relation to the family context, activity in relation to that of the school. This was reflected in a greater use of state (as opposed to action) verbs at home.

Whom one is with may affect what one feels about oneself. Brown et al. (1992) showed subjects photographs of attractive and relatively unattractive targets, and then asked them to rate their own attractiveness. The subjects showed a contrast effect, rating themselves as more attractive after they had been presented with an unattractive target. However, if the subjects were made to feel similar to the targets in attitudes and values, their self-ratings were higher after viewing an attractive target, thereby "basking in reflected glory" (cf. Tesser, 1988).

These studies suggest that situational differences in the self-concept depend in part on comparisons with others. McGuire and McGuire (1988, p.102) comment "a woman psychologist in the company of a dozen women who work at other occupations thinks of herself as a psychologist; when with a dozen male psychologists, she thinks of herself as a woman."

These situational differences in the self-concept are in harmony with the view that the self-concept must be seen not as a unitary cognitive structure, but as networks and hierarchies of increasingly context-specific self-concepts. It will be apparent that this is not incompatible with G.A. Kelly's metaphor of "selecting a role" to suit the situation one is in, or Goffman's metaphor of interactants "defining the situation" (Chapter 1). The self-concept is also to be seen in diachronic perspective, forming part of a socially constructed, coherent narrative in which we attempt to understand the course of our lives in a coherent way. We see ourselves as a series of photographs, or better, snatches of videotape, in a family album, linked together by a narrative that we have concocted. This narrative is not only continuously updated, but also changed to maintain coherence with the self-concept itself at any one time, with social conventions, and so on (Gergen & Gergen, 1988; Kihlstrom et al., 1988; Murray & Holmes, 1996; see later). And in this narrative an individual may play more than one part—the self that one is may depend on whom one is with.

Stability of the Self-concept

Although we see ourselves as influenced by the situation we are in, there are also powerful forces that maintain our self-concept. Some of these stem from social conventions or preconceptions. If I behave as a conceited old bore, others will be inhibited by social norms from telling me what they think of me, so I am without a valuable source of evidence on which I might change my self-opinion and behaviour: politeness reigns. Furthermore, if I have behaved as a bore in the past, others will expect me to continue in that way, and behave towards me in a way that ensures that I do.

But more important are internal processes. Our self-concepts are resistant to change partly because they are over-learned and partly because we tend to fit our perceptions of our experiences to our self-concepts rather than modifying our self-concepts to fit them. Thus we construct accounts of our lives in which the central figure does not change. We see ourselves as the same person as we move from context to context through life, believing that we can see how past experiences have influenced us but left us fundamentally the same person. Self-affirmation processes act to maintain a perception of the self as having a certain coherence, stability, competence, and so on (Steele, 1988).

Backman (1985, 1988; see also Secord & Backman, 1974) has suggested that individuals attempt to achieve a psychological state termed "congruency" involving mutual support between an aspect of the self-concept (e.g. a particular characteristic), their interpretation of their behaviour relevant to that aspect, and their perceptions of the relevant behaviours, feelings, and perceptions of some other person(s). Thus a person who views himself as intelligent, sees himself as behaving intelligently, and perceives that others view him as intelligent, would experience congruency. Incongruency is seen as threatening, perhaps because it indicates an inability to deal with one's environment and achieve one's goals. Secord and Backman proposed that people adjust their factual or perceived social worlds in order to achieve congruency in a number of ways:

(a) By *cognitive restructuring* (e.g. misperceiving one's own or others' behaviour or characteristics, or the situation; attending selectively to confirmatory evidence, or selectively encoding and interpreting it; discrediting new information that seems to contradict one's current self-view);

(b) By *selective evaluation* (altering the importance of characteristics so as to increase the importance of congruent systems and decrease that of incongruent ones);

(c) By *selective interaction* (being attracted to others who provided congruency, and vice versa: people prefer to make friends with others who see them as they see themselves);

(d) By *response evocation* (self-presentation in clothing or demeanour that calls for a congruent response, or casting the other into a role that calls for congruent behaviour: for instance, people who see themselves as dominant or likeable behave so that they will be seen that way); and

(e) By *selective comparison* (e.g. associating with someone of less intelligence, thereby confirming one's own).

Of course such attempts are mostly subconscious, and in long-term relationships they are unnecessary because the partner is already likely to confirm the self-concept.

These processes might seem on the whole to tend to produce stability, to conserve the self-concept. However, quite apart from the fact that people change, move through the social structure, grow up, encounter life events, and so on, the formation of any new relationship will involve negotiations about the identities of the partners, and this may lead to a new socially constructed reality. In any interaction, both parties strive to validate their expectancies and to verify their self-views. If their agendas conflict, the conflict must be resolved through processes of identity negotiation. Disagreements in a relationship may involve incompatibility between how a person views herself and how she perceives her partner to view her, and this may lead to cognitive restructuring, and thus to a change in the self-concept. Selective evaluation can lead to changes in one's evaluation of oneself in a manner that increases congruency.

Again, presenting a "new" self to another may induce the other to behave in a way that confirms the new view, and thus to a change in the self-image. Snyder (1984) reviewed experimental studies showing that expectancies of one individual (perceiver) could channel social interaction so as to cause the behaviour of other individuals (targets) to confirm her expectancy (see p.227). Thus targets believed to be hostile become hostile, those believed to be extraverted become social, and so on. But the targets also have ideas about themselves and about social reality, and this also affects the outcome. Thus social reality is co-constructed by perceivers and targets together, each individual playing both roles (Swann, 1987).

Backman (1988) thus argues that the efforts that individuals make to control their objective and subjective social worlds are liable to lead to a compromise "that reflects the efforts of both partners as each attempts to achieve both long-term and short-term goals, including, of course, various forms of congruency." Thus Backman (p.256) sees personality as a product "of all those processes, factors and vicissitudes that have affected the development of the relationships they have with others." Although personality is not infinitely labile and, as we have seen, there are powerful intra-individual forces tending to maintain self-consistency, change in the self-concept can occur (see also Cooper & Fazio, 1984; Festinger, 1957; Scheier & Carver, 1988; Steele, 1988).

The Self-concept and Relationships

Of special importance in the current context is the extent to which the self-concept, and the narratives woven around it, are organised in terms of relationships. Evidence of the extent to which they are so organised is pro-vided, for instance, by the finding that errors in naming individuals often involve the substitution, for the name intended, of the name of someone in a similar relationship to the speaker. Thus a father may call one daugh-ter by the name of another. This implies that knowledge about others is stored at least potentially in terms of the relationship we have with them (Fiske et al., 1991; Fletcher & Fitness, 1996). In a rather different approach to a similar problem, Aron et al. (1991, 1992; Aron & Aron, 1996) argue that a close relationship involves including the other in the self—a meta-phor for describing how the self becomes modified as a consequence of interaction with the other. They cite evidence that, for instance, attributional processes are more similar in individuals who have a close relationship with each other than in strangers; that quality of recall for a close friend's actions are intermediate between recall of one's own and those of a stranger; and that a close relationship may involve sharing the other's characteristics (identification). They describe further experimental evidence in support of their view, thus: (i) There was less self/other differ-ence in allocations of money to a friend than to a stranger. (ii) Subjects recalled fewer nouns previously imaged either with mother or with the self than those imaged with a stranger, suggesting that information relating to the mother was processed more like information relating to the self than that relating to a stranger. (iii) Subjects took longer latencies to make me/not-me distinctions for traits that were different between the subject and spouse than for traits similar for both, suggesting some self/spouse con-fusion (see also Aron & Aron, 1986, 1996; Fiske, 1991, cited pp.62–63).

Planalp (1985) referred to relational schemata as coherent frameworks of relational knowledge used to derive the relational implications of messages. They are modified by on-going experiences in relationships. Planalp and others have argued that these schemata could take the form of the general dimensions of a relationship, or of general expectations about appropriate behaviour in particular situations, or expectations for concrete behaviours, and showed experimentally that relational knowledge guided memory for conversations. Thus in professor–student relationships, perception of the rights and obligations intrinsic to the relationship was crucial.

Baldwin (1992, 1995), in using the concept of "relational schemas", suggested that they contain schemata for self and other, and a script for the expected interaction pattern. Such schemata may involve general beliefs about relationships or about relationships of particular types as well as schemata concerning particular relationships involving accounts of specific interactions, attitudes and attributions (Fletcher & Fitness, 1993, 1996; Fletcher & Kininmonth, 1992; Planalp, 1985).

The extent to which information about the self is organised around relationships differs culturally: Westerners tend to see themselves more as a bundle of internal traits and abilities, while many non-Westerners have a stronger sense of relationships and tend to see the self-in-relation-to-other (Markus & Kitayama, 1991). And in so far as the self is seen in relation to others, the categories of relationships that are used may differ between cultures.

Theories of the Self-system

At this point it will be apparent that we need some way of conceptualising the self-system, and also that that will be no easy task. As one approach, Bowlby's (1982) postulation of an "Internal Working Model" (IWM) of the self, others, and relationships has had an important influence on the field. Bowlby supposed that the young child forms a mental representation or model of the world containing as prominent components models of the self and of each of his or her "attachment figures", and representations of the relationships between them. This IWM is internalised and gradually adjusted to form a guide for social behaviour. It is affect-laden and has motivational implications.

Bowlby's theorising stems from a somewhat different tradition from the work considered so far. For a psychoanalyst of his generation, Bowlby was remarkable for his eclecticism. In elaborating his theory of attachment (Chapter 21), concerned primarily with the manner in which one individual forms a secure base for another, he drew on psychoanalytic theory, systems theory, ethology, and Piagetian theory among others. In using a concept of mental models, Bowlby (1969) was primarily influenced not only by psychoanalytical theory but also by Miller, Galanter, and Pribram (1960), themselves influenced by cybernetics. Bowlby (1973, p.204) later argued that his concept of an internal "working model" is "no more than a way of describing, in terms compatible with systems theory, ideas traditionally described as 'introjection of an object' (good or bad) and 'self-image'." Bowlby's view was that the young child might form more than one model of the self and of each of his "attachment figures", the earlier ones being less sophisticated and unavailable to consciousness. Such multiple models of the same individual might, in some circumstances, be contradictory or inconsistent. As Bretherton (1995) points out, the representation is to be seen not as a dispassionate mapping of reality, but as involving the appraisal and reappraisal of personal and shared meaning systems, involving beliefs about both self and others in a benign or malignant world, and hopes for the future. In its creation, defence processes may distort reality.

Bowlby believed that the capacity to form such models owes its evolutionary origin to their advantages in facilitating insightful behaviour and expectations about future events. They normally permit the development of healthy attachment relationships, being fairly susceptible to updating and fine tuning as relationships progress, though Bowlby indicated that unconscious early-formed models were resistant to modification, and Bretherton, Ridgeway, and Cassidy (1990) suggest that defence processes may inhibit modification. Modification may involve the action of a variety of defence or coping mechanisms which may be generally positive in nature (e.g. anticipation, humour, self-assertion), inhibitions serving to keep potential threats out of awareness (e.g. intellectualisation, repression), distortions that help to maintain self-esteem (e.g. idealisation, devaluation), or disavowals that keep unpleasant ideas out of awareness (e.g. denial, projection), (DSM-1VTM, 1994). For instance, events that threaten the security of an attachment relationship may be blocked from conscious perception or recall.

Since the models embrace expectancies of how self and other would behave in interaction, they are to be seen as effectively models of the child's relationships. The notion of a mental model implies something that can be manipulated cognitively and can thus generate expectations about "What would happen if...". Emotional outcomes can be altered by changing wishes or by the unconscious suppression of wishes. However the word "model" must not be taken too literally, nor to imply the lack of a diachronic element—the models may have the form of stories.

Bowlby's concepts are now being extended and hardened by developmental psychologists and psychiatrists, and links with the work of social psychologists are becoming possible. Stern (1995) writes of "schemata-of-being-with" which are based on the interactive experience of being with a particular person in a specific way, and "representations-of-being-with" which consist of networks of such schemata tied together by a common theme or feature. On his view, a mother's schemata of her baby will include the baby in relation to her, as well as to the father, sibling, grandparents, etc.—each a somewhat different baby who may act differently in the different contexts, and with an historical perspective involving perceived change over time. The mother will also have schemata of her husband—as husband, father, man and so on, in relation to various others, and with a temporal dimension—and of herself.

Bowlby's approach has been related to Schank's (1982) influential modification of script theory, which involves multiple interconnected hierarchies of schemata that determine how new events are decoded and processed and how information is parsed and ordered (Bretherton et al., 1990; see also Honeycutt,1993; Honeycutt, Cantrill, & Allen, 1992; Honeycutt, Cantrill, & Greene, 1989; Honeycutt, Woods, & Fontenot, 1993). Schank distinguished:

(a) *Scripts*—Schemata reflecting specific instances of sequences of behavioural events. The concept is thus similar to Kelly's "personal construct", but more elaborate, involving sequences of actions. For example, an individual might have a script for what to talk about on a first date.

(b) *Scenes*—A general description of a setting and the activities in pursuit of a goal relevant to that setting. Scenes involve scripts based on experiences (personal or vicarious) within such a scene. Thus a scene might include the greeting ritual on meeting a partner on a date.

(c) *Memory Organisation Packets* (MOP)—A memory structure involving a variety of scenes that are related but not contextually bound. This might include scenes of a variety of dating experiences (with their constituent scripts).

(d) *Meta-memory Organisation Packets*—Collections of memory structures. Thus a meta-MOP for developing relationships might contain memory structures for dating, disclosing, etc.

These memory structures, based on actual and vicarious experiences and arranged hierarchically, are held to enable information to be processed and catalogued rapidly, guide action, provide understanding of current events and expectations for the future, and permit planning. (Indeed Berger, 1993, argues that knowledge of events is stored largely in terms of goals and plans.) In so far as the structures relating to a particular issue are related to social conventions, they may be similar between individuals, but they may also be idiosyncratic. While citing evidence that individuals agree on the sequence of actions involved in getting a date, Honeycutt (1993) emphasises that in other situations, such as the de-escalation of a close relationship, the sequence of actions deemed to be appropriate may be less tied to conventions and more a product of individual experience (see also Holmberg & Veroff, 1996). Again, Cole and Bradac (1996) have shown that undergraduates at an American University had clear ideas about the nature of the satisfactions provided by a best friendship, and about the causal relations between the sources of satisfaction. The data are in harmony with the view that we have generalised models of different sorts of relationships superordinated to those of specific relationships.

As another example of a model of the self-system, Greene and Geddes (1988) also emphasise its multiplicity. In their view self-relevant information is held in modular units each of which represents attributes and features relevant to action. These are each composed of more elemental units linked by associated relations. The modular units are supposed to develop as the constituent elements co-vary. The modular units are selectively retrieved from memory and used to guide behaviour and cognition. Only a small set of the self-relevant propositions are activated at a time, so that the self-concept is seen as consisting of the currently activated part of self-relevant information. Thus an individual may have a number of self-concepts which may be in some degree inconsistent, and the self-concept may change with the situation.

It will be apparent that a number of terms—concepts, representations, schemata, scripts, models, modules—used in this field have meanings which, though no doubt subtly different for their authors, overlap and refer to knowledge structures of differing degrees of complexity. However it does not seem impossible that the various approaches can be integrated, for a number of features are compatible with all of them. Thus the knowledge structures are derived primarily from experience, and involve both comparison and evaluation. They involve schemata concerned with the self, with others, and with relationships. Knowledge structures concerned with relationships influence those concerned with the self, and vice versa: the precise relation between the two is unclear. There are also knowledge structures concerned with events, special and routine occasions, and so on. The schemata may be general, having reference to a class of individuals, relationships, or occasions, or may be specific to a particular one. They include emotion scripts, which again may be either general and socially shared, or idiosyncratic, concerned with the course of specific emotions in their own relationships. Affect is thus involved in both the organisation and representation of knowledge about the self, others, and relationships, and in the processing of new information. The schemata

influence behaviour, and are modifiable by behaviour and by new information. They may also show resistance to modification, sometimes leading to psychopathology. The availability of models, schemata, or scripts
at any moment depends on diverse factors including the amount and
intensity of the experience on which they were based, on the degree of
matching with features of the current situation, and current goals and
mood state. The processing of information may be controlled, conscious,
and effortful, or automatic, unconscious, and fast. The knowledge
structures are usually thought of as arranged in hierarchically organised
networks, and also as existing in an historical form which is structured
as a fairly coherent narrative (see Harvey, Agostinelli, & Weber, 1989;
Harvey, Weber, & Orbuch, 1990; Fletcher & Fitness, 1996; Fletcher &
Thomas, 1996).

The parts of this narrative must have some degree of consistency—
though it may also be changed in some degree from moment to moment
to suit circumstances, or in interaction with others. The narrative involves
stored memories which have already undergone assimilation and accommodation into the self-system, and which serve to guide action and create
expectancies about the future. A scheme of how they might guide action
is provided by Fletcher and Fitness (1993): this involves three overlapping
knowledge structures of increasing specificity—general social schemata;
beliefs about close relationships; and accounts, attributions, and attitudes
specific to a particular relationship. When activated, these feed into a cognitive processing component, which in turn leads to a change in cognition,
affect, or behaviour. The self is thus not to be seen as a static entity, but
is in a continuous process of dynamic change.

Perhaps in the long term these models can be integrated into a theory
of mind which in turn will contribute to the still more intractable problem
of consciousness (Dennett, 1991; Humphrey, 1992). That, however, is for
the future. At the moment it is easier to pick out common features of the
approaches than to devise tests to discriminate between them, and it is
their common features that will be used in the discussion of personal
relationships.

Two final words of caution are in order. First, this chapter cannot do
full justice to current work on knowledge structures and the nature of the
self-system—much important exciting work is in progress (e.g. Fletcher &
Fitness, 1996). Second, what we are discussing are only models. Our picture
of the self as an hierarchical structure enables us to explain diverse aspects
of human activity, but we must remember that it is an *"as if"* model, and
not necessarily to be taken literally. Indeed one of the dangers of such
models is that their flexibility enables them to explain almost anything (see
e.g. Shaver et al., 1996a)—data that could disprove them are not easy to
find.

INTERACTIONS

By an "interaction"—or "encounter" in Goffman's (1961, 1963) terminology—we mean such incidents as individual A shows behaviour X to
individual B and B responds with Y. Of course most interactions are much
longer than this, but the question of how long a series of social actions
could be and still qualify as a single interaction need not detain us. Clearly
there is no absolute answer, and any discussion must be based on what is
useful empirically. A useful guide is often the extent to which successive
actions have related goals, foci, references or "meanings". But both exchanged "Good-mornings" and a long discussion could be treated as one
interaction.

All interactions involve at least two participants, and their nature
depends on both of them. For instance, mothers are liable to behave
differently to twins, displaying more "warmth" to one than to the other.
This "warmth" is a characteristic of the relationship of the mother with
that twin, and not necessarily of the mother as an individual. If we say
"She is a warm mother" we must remember that we mean "with that child"
and not necessarily in general. Again, the rank orders of the frequencies
with which 4-year-olds showed particular types of interaction with their
mothers at home (e.g. controls, behaves aggressively) showed at most weak
correlations with the frequencies of similar types of behaviour with peers
at school (Hinde, Tamplin, & Barrett, 1995). That how an individual behaves depends on whom he is with is of critical importance for the study
of relationships: a relationship has properties not predictable from the
characteristics of either participant alone.

Every interaction is, of course, much more complicated than a simple
behavioural description would imply. For one thing, an interaction is not
just a chain response, with B's response supplying the stimulus for A's next
reply. What A does now may continue to affect B much later in the interaction, and behaviour at any one moment may be affected by goals and by
expectations of events still in the distant future.

Furthermore, each participant must assess the other and try to adjust
his/her behaviour so that he/she can induce the other to allow him/her to
behave in a way that seems appropriate. This requires each to monitor the
other's behaviour, and this involves both emotional responses and cognitive interpretations. How A behaves to B will depend on how A interprets
B's behaviour, or how A "reads B's mind". A may see B's cough as a reflex
response to a crumb in the throat, or as a deliberate attempt to interrupt
him. And whichever was "really" the case, B's further behaviour will be
affected by how he perceives A to have perceived his cough. Thus the
attributions the participants make affect their future behaviour. The same
considerations apply to A's own behaviour. At any moment A could

interpret his own behaviour as goal-directed ("I am reading a book"), as impelled ("I stumbled" or "I fell asleep"), or as more or less efficiently goal-directed ("I was trying to read but was too sleepy"). In other words, A not only monitors his own behaviour, but he can monitor his own monitoring (Harré & Secord, 1972). There may be internal dialogues within each participant involving never-ending conflicting evaluations and decisions between alternative courses of action (cf. Billig, 1987), as well as conflict or mutual adjustment of behavioural propensities between individuals. The interaction may involve intensive discussion about the relationship or chit-chat which, though seemingly inconsequential, may in the long run ameliorate or intensify conflict, facilitate or hinder adjustment.

In Chapter 1 Goffman's approach to this complexity was outlined. His "dramaturgical perspective", which involved regarding each participant as an actor trying to create an impression on an audience, is a useful analogy, and if it seems cynical we must remember that the attempt "to create an impression on an audience" may be unconscious, made not by a unitary entity called "I" but by a self with all the complexity noted in the previous section.

RELATIONSHIPS

Definitional Issues—Behavioural Aspects

What do we mean by a "dyadic" or "interpersonal relationship"? We apply the term to husband-and-wife, father-and-daughter, teacher-and-pupil, employer-and-workman, and in many other contexts. Although the way the word "relationship" is used in everyday speech is clear enough, the diversity and complexity of the phenomena involved make any attempt to define precisely what does and does not constitute a relationship inevitably somewhat arbitrary.

At the behaviour level, a relationship implies first a series of interactions between two people, involving interchanges over an extended period of time. The interchanges usually involve a verbal element, and often consist entirely of talk, though it is possible for individuals who never talk with each other to have a relationship.

The interchanges have some degree of mutuality, in the sense that the behaviour of each takes some account of the behaviour of the other. However this mutuality does not necessarily imply "cooperation" in its everyday sense: relationships exist between enemies as well as between friends (Chapter 23), between those who are forced into each other's company as well as between those who seek it.

In addition, "relationship" in everyday language carries the further implication that there is some degree of continuity between the successive interactions. Each interaction is affected by interactions in the past, may affect interactions in the future, and may be affected by expectations of future events. Furthermore a relationship may be enhanced (or eroded) by the way in which the participants think about it between interactions, or discuss it with outsiders. For that reason a "relationship" between two people may continue over long periods when they do not meet or communicate with each other: the accumulated effects of past interactions will ensure that, when they next meet, they do not see each other as strangers. In such a case, and when we say, for instance, that "a separation experience can in some circumstances alter the course of the parent–child relationship", "relationship" refers not to an actual sequence of interactions, but to a potential for patterns of interactions which may be of a certain general type but whose precise form will depend on events in the future. At another level, to be discussed more fully later, when A says that he has a relationship with B he is referring to a narrative in his own mind—a narrative about the past which he expects to be continued.

In general the distinction between an interaction, which involves a strictly limited span of time, and a relationship, which involves past, present, and often future, is clear enough. To discuss how long we must talk to a stranger in the street before we can properly say we have a relationship with him would not be very constructive. But nevertheless it is important to emphasise that a series of interactions totally independent of each other would not constitute a relationship. An essential character of a relationship is that each interaction is influenced by other interactions in that relationship. You might talk to the same telephone operator every day for a week, but if you did not know it was the same person, if each conversation was uninfluenced by what you had learned about the operator as an individual on previous occasions, you could not have a relationship with him or her. A relationship exists only when the probable course of future interactions between the participants differs from that between strangers. Furthermore, although an interaction could be defined as having one meaning or "focus", a relationship is likely to have many, each superordinated to those of numerous types of interactions.

Communication in Relationships

Our representations or models of relationships are made explicit through talk. This includes talk to the self, to the partner, and to outsiders. And talking may change the representations. Thus communication plays a critical role in the dynamics of relationships. As interactions occur, the participants evaluate and represent "events" that they deem to be important. The representations may change with time in accordance with needs and circumstances. The participants convey the representations to each other and to third parties by talk. They also have internal dialogues (involving hopes, regrets, anxieties, strategies, reminiscences and so on), which may also be communicated to others (Duck & Pond, 1989). Although communication is of course an essential part of every relationship, it must not be forgotten that communication between individuals, and also dialogues within individuals, may be non-verbal.

Relationships as Accounts or Narratives

As we have seen, the nature of the effect of one interaction on subsequent ones will depend not only on what actually happened but also on what each partner thinks about what he experienced during that interaction in relation to what he expected or would have liked to have happened, and his expectancy and wishes for the future. While the participants are apart, each may review the course of past interactions, or imagine future ones, or discuss them with a third party in ways that will affect the future course of the relationship. To understand relationships fully, therefore, it is necessary to come to terms not only with their behavioural but also with their affective/cognitive aspects, and to do so whilst recognising that behaviour, affect, and cognition are inextricably interwoven. Furthermore, they are interwoven over time, so that a relationship is to be seen not as a thing but as a *process* over time. And the nature of that process will seem different to each participant and to an outside observer.

A's behaviour in a relationship, and the emotions he or she experiences, are influenced by past experiences. If asked, A can describe many of those past experiences. Not of course that the descriptions will necessarily be accurate, for they will be both selective and distorted, but A will believe them to be related to what actually happened. Furthermore A's behaviour and emotions will also be influenced by anticipations about the future. It is thus reasonable to suppose that A's perceptions of the people and situations he or she encounters, the way A behaves to them and their behaviour in return, A's thoughts about his or her feelings about the behaviour and feelings of others, are coded by A and stored in symbolic form (cf. Asch, 1959; Hebb, 1949). As discussed earlier in this chapter this must result in dynamically organised and interrelated schemata of cognitive representations of individuals, events, etc. and of the motivations, intentions, and affects characterising relations between them (Bartlett, 1932; Neisser, 1976). In other words, it consists of an account of the relationship and has a narrative form. Precisely what is encoded, and the symbols that are used, is of course culturally influenced. They also differ between individuals. New experiences are assimilated to these schemata, which accommodate accordingly. The narrative may be discussed with the partner: sharing narratives provides an opportunity for mutual understanding by bringing the two narratives into line. Or the narrative may be used to discuss an interaction with a third party, or to facilitate re-living it after it is over, or to imagine interactions that may never happen. The narrative is likely to be a little different according to the other with whom it is shared. Real or imagined covert dialogues with others may lead to a change in the narrative (Murray & Holmes, 1996).

Thus relationships can be seen as narratives, and the self as including, and largely constituted by, the narratives of experienced relationships.

Generalising about Relationships

Most relationships involve interactions of diverse types, and those inter-actions affect each other. Any marital therapist would agree not only that what goes on in bed affects what goes on at the breakfast table, but also that the atmosphere at the breakfast table affects that in bed. Indeed, rather than saying that a relationship involves interactions it would be more accurate to say that the relationship is created by the participants out of a series of interactions.

This means that we cannot make generalisations about relationships as easily as we can make generalisations about interactions (Hinde & Stevenson-Hinde, 1987). This point is illustrated at the behavioural level in Fig. 3.1. If we want to make a generalisation about how mothers nurse babies, we can observe a number of mother–baby dyads in the nursing situation, make the measurements or ratings appropriate to our problem, and then make a generalisation from those data. But if we wish to make a generalisation about mother–baby *relationships*, we must observe each mother–baby dyad in a number of types of interaction, make a generalisa-tion about the aspects of interest in each mother–baby relationship, and only then make a generalisation across the dyads about relationships. And we must remember that the generalisation we are talking about here is usually based on an outsider's perception of the relationship.

Social Behaviour versus Social Relationships

Because some of the most important characteristics of interpersonal relationships lie in the affective/cognitive components, because people's behaviour varies according to whom they are with, and because relation-ships have emergent properties, studies of social behaviour are not an adequate substitute for studies of social relationships.

Two points relevant to this issue emerged from a recent study of nursery-school children. Most previous studies of 3–5-year-olds assumed a dimen-sion of "social participation", ranging from the child playing on its own (self play), through playing alongside other children (parallel play), to playing interactively with them (group and interactive play). It was

Interactions approach

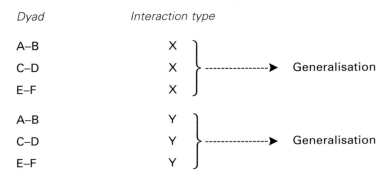

Relationships approach

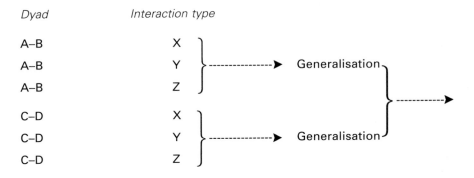

FIG. 3.1 Generalising about interactions and about relationships across dyads from data about behavioural interactions. As relationships have properties that depend on the relative frequency and patterning of interactions, it is not possible to proceed directly from generalisations about interactions to generalisations about relationships. (Modified from Hinde & Stevenson-Hinde, 1987.)

supposed that children mature through stages in which each of these types of play predominates in turn. However analysis of the data showed that how much a child plays on his own, and how much he interacts with other children when playing with them, are separate issues. Some children showed quite a lot of interactive play but also played freely on their own (Roper & Hinde, 1978).

At the same time the extent to which the children formed relationships with each other was assessed in terms of the consistency with which they had the same neighbours. To summarise the data, "good friends" may be defined as children who sat next to each other on at least 35% of the observations. (The data supported the use of this dependent variable as an indicator of friendship; children who were often neighbours were more likely to talk to each other when together than were children who were neighbours less often.) As might be expected, the proportion of children who had at least one good friend tended to be higher amongst those who often showed group or interactive play than amongst those who mostly played in parallel. However the difference was not great, and a number of children with good friends showed much parallel play. These were children who often chose the same neighbours even though they appeared not to interact with them very much. There were also a number of children without good friends who often played interactively. And although, again as expected, children who had good friends tended to score low on the self play dimension, there were some who had good friends and yet were often alone (Hinde, 1978b). These data show for children what we all know to be true for adults, namely that you can be constant but not overtly sociable, and social but yet promiscuous. Social behaviour does not accurately reflect social relationships.

The Social Context

Participants in a dyadic relationship are almost invariably also involved in relationships with other individuals, who in turn may have relationships with each other and with other individuals. Each dyadic relationship is in fact nearly always embedded in a social group, the structure of which provides a further level of complexity. Furthermore this group may interact with other groups within the society, and the relationships, interactions, and behaviour of the individuals will be affected by social norms regulating their conduct with varying degrees of applicability (see Chapter 17).

DIALECTICAL RELATIONS BETWEEN LEVELS

We have referred to a number of levels of behavioural complexity—those within individuals, interactions between those individuals, relationships, groups, and societies (Frontispiece). In addition we have mentioned the norms of behaviour which, together with the values, beliefs, and institutions of the social unit in question, we may refer to as the "socio-cultural structure". (The word structure is important because the norms, values, etc. are not totally independent of each other.) Three points about these levels must be made:

(i)   Each level has properties that are simply not relevant to the level below. For example, the behaviour of an individual may be ambivalent, but ambivalence is simply not relevant to the particular behavioural propensities within the individual that may be in conflict. The behaviour of two individuals in interaction may be coordinated and mesh each with that of the other, or they may be uncoordinated: coordination or meshing is a property simply not relevant to the behaviour of an individual in isolation. And a relationship may involve only one or many diverse types of interaction (see Chapter 5), but this is a property irrelevant to interactions.

(ii)   The explanatory concepts that we use differ with each level of complexity. Thus we might describe (or explain?) the behaviour of a child who fought persistently with sibling and with peers at school in terms of an aspect of his or her personality. But if we were trying to account for a particular conflict with the sibling (i.e. an interaction) we might ascribe it to their both wanting the same toy. And if we were trying to understand why the siblings were always fighting (i.e. relationship level), we might ascribe it to sibling rivalry.

(iii)   Each level affects, and is affected by, others. How an individual behaves in an interaction is affected by his/her behavioural propensities and personality, but behaviour in interactions reciprocally affects his or her psychological characteristics. The course of an interaction affects, and is affected by, the nature of the relationship in which it is embedded. And the nature of a relationship affects, and is affected by, the nature of the group in which it is embedded: for instance A's relationship with B may both affect and be affected by B's relationship with C.

In addition, the socio-cultural structure may both affect and be affected by the various levels of social complexity. For example, as divorce becomes more common it becomes more acceptable, and as it becomes more acceptable it becomes more common. Finally, for the sake of completeness though little discussed in this book, each level may affect and be affected by the physical environment in which it occurs.

It will be apparent that we have built up a picture of considerable complexity, much simplified in the Frontispiece. It must not be forgotten that each interaction depends on both participants, and on complex affective, cognitive, and behavioural processes in each individual. Each relationship may involve interactions of diverse types, and be nested within one or more social groups. Each of these levels may have a socio-cognitive structure that is in some ways unique. And all cause–effect relationships are two-way, involving dialectical relations which must be seen in diachronic perspective. *Thus each of these levels, including that of the individual, must be seen not as involving entities but rather as involving processes of continuous creation, maintenance, or degradation through the dialectical relations between levels.* Although relationship partners may see their relationship as stable or static, thereby retaining a sense of control over their lives, in practice relationships are dynamic, requiring continuing input (though not necessarily interaction) to maintain the semblance of stability (Hinde, 1974, 1991).[1]

An interesting example of the interdependence of the socio-cultural structure, relationships, and individuals is provided by a comparison between Jewish, Protestant, and Catholic families in the Chicago area. Most studies have shown few differences between the family relationships of members of the three religious groups. Although Judaism assigns a major role to the family, there are no hard data to demonstrate clear differences in family-related behaviour. Brodbar-Nemzer (1986), however, argued that the more the family is valued, the more will it play a crucial role in individuals' self-concepts. He therefore suggested that the self-esteem (seen as an evaluative dimension of the self-concept) of Jews whose families are or are not supportive and stable would be more affected by the family atmosphere than that of non-Jews in a similar situation. His data showed that, controlling for education, age, and sex, the self-esteem of c. 120 Jewish respondents was affected more than that of c. 550 Protestants or c. 800 Catholics by the degree of marital support, marital stress, and related variables. (Brodbar-Nemzer acknowledges that the generality of this finding is open to question: the issue here is the relation between cultural values, relationships, and individuals.)

TWO MODELS OF RELATIONSHIPS

It may be helpful to conclude this chapter on the nature of relationships by referring to two frameworks that portray their dynamic nature. The first is due to Kelley et al. (1983). They pictured a dyadic relationship as involving chains of events including affect, thought, and action within each of the participants. These events are interconnected within each person, and events in each person's chain may affect the others. Thus in Fig. 3.2 a young woman P expresses an opinion (P_1) with which O agrees (O_1) and smiles (O_2). P thinks about her remark, sees it has been well received (P_2). O expresses agreement verbally (O_3) and P feels pleased (P_3 and P_4). She smiles (P_5), and so the interaction continues. The interconnections between the two chains may involve many kinds of events (exchange of resources, communicatory signals, actions, and so on); they may be patterned in a variety of ways, of varying strength, frequency, and nature. They may involve facilitation or interference between the two chains, and they may

---

[1]This approach has many points of contact with that of Altman, Vinsel, and Brown (1981).

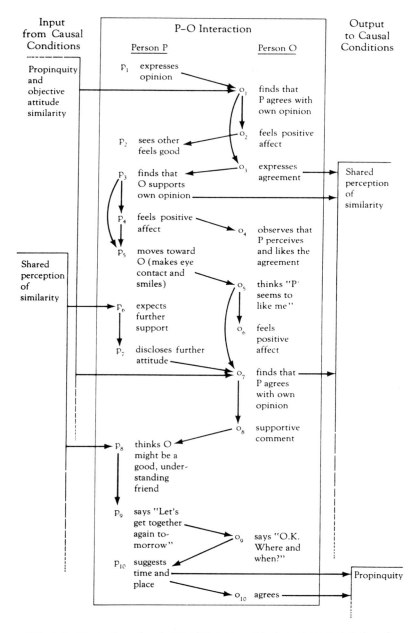

FIG. 3.2 Illustration of an interaction process. The interconnected chains of events for two persons are shown in the centre. Input and output from the causal conditions are shown by horizontal arrows on the left and right respectively. The initial causal conditions (propinquity and objective attitude similarity) are maintained and strengthened and lead to a new causal condition (shared perception of similarity). (From Kelley et al. (Eds.), 1983, *Close relationships*. Copyright © W.H. Freeman & Company. Used with permission.)

be symmetrical or asymmetrical. A close relationship is thus defined by Kelley et al. (1983, p.38) as one involving "strong, frequent and diverse interdependence that lasts over a considerable period of time."

Kelley et al. also refer to "causal conditions", namely relatively stable causal factors that exist over relatively long time periods (long in comparison with the very brief events mentioned earlier) and influence the course of interactions. Such conditions may be in the environment or involve a state of one or both participants. They may affect the chain of interactions as shown in Fig. 3.2, and may themselves be changed as a consequence of interaction.

It will be apparent that this scheme could be adapted to any sort of relationship, and could be seen as aimed at an extremely fine level of description—one that would be unattainable for practical reasons. However that was not the authors' intention: the scheme was intended as a framework within which research workers could identify their special interests and comprehend how their work related to that of others in the field.

The second scheme, due to Bradbury and Fincham (1989), also emphasises the interplay between short-term processes and longer-term conditions, but lays more emphasis on attentional and perceptual processes. It involves distinctions between

(a) Behaviour involved in interaction;
(b) The processing of that behaviour by the other participant. This involves attending to, perceiving, and interpreting it, and experiencing its affective consequences. (Interpretation will, of course, have reference to experience in that and other relationships, and to expectations about the future.);
(c) The proximal context—the current thoughts and feelings that influence the processes described in (b);
(d) The distal context—longer-term, stable variables that also influence both the proximal context and the processing stage. These include personality and relationship characteristics and other relevant variables, including satisfaction with the relationship, relationship beliefs, and emotion knowledge (see also Fletcher & Fitness, 1993; Fitness, 1996).

The relations between these variables are shown in Fig. 3.3 for three transactions. It will be apparent that the proximal context is constantly being updated, and the successive behaviours shown by the participants are guided by the processing stage.

Like the Kelley et al. model, this scheme embraces both the moment-to-moment events in an interaction and the longer-term issues that affect

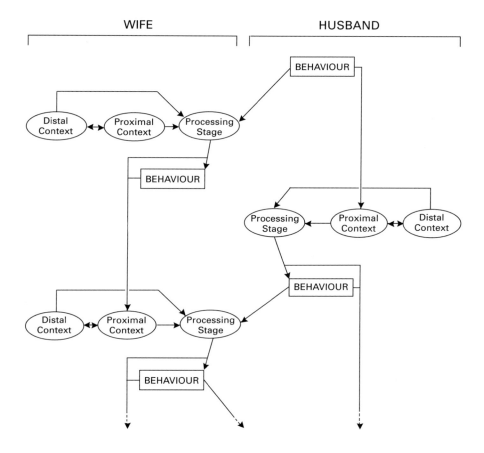

FIG. 3.3   The contextual model of marital interaction (simplified). In the interactions illustrated, the husband's behaviour is processed by the wife in a manner influenced by her proximal and distal contexts, and she then responds. These processes are repeated by the husband, and then by the wife. Each spouse's proximal context is updated frequently on the basis of his/her processing stage and behaviour. (Redrawn from Bradbury & Fincham, in C. Hendrick (Ed.), *Close relationships* (pp.119–43). Copyright © 1989 Sage Publications Inc. Reprinted by permission.)

those events and are influenced by them. Intended specifically for marital interaction, it may lack the generality of the Kelley et al. model, but Bradbury and Fincham claim that it points more clearly to the processes involved in interaction. Of special importance is the emphasis on the relations between behaviour, emotion, cognition, and stored knowledge. Bradbury and Fincham also point out that their scheme has a place for events that occur between interactions (through their influence on proximal and possibly the distal context), and that it distinguishes clearly between the contexts of the two participants.

Neither of these models will be adhered to strictly in what follows, but the general picture of the nature of interactions and relationships that they present is implicit in much of the discussion, and the reader may find that they form a useful background.

SUMMARY

1. The self is seen as involving an hierarchy of knowledge structures, dependent on and modifiable by experience, and referring to self, others, relationships, situations, etc. This is, of course, only a model, useful for guiding research.
2. Interactions involve relatively short-term interchanges.
3. Relationships involve (at the behavioural level) a series of interactions between two individuals who know each other, such that each interaction can be influenced by past interactions and by expectations of interactions in the future. Affective and cognitive components are at least as important as the behavioural ones.
4. Relationships can be seen as narratives.
5. Social behaviour involves a series of levels of social complexity, influencing each other by dialectical relations between levels, such that each level, including the individual, is to be seen as involving processes in time (see Frontispiece).
6. Two models of relationships are described.

B Characteristics of Relationships

An ordered body of knowledge about personal relationships requires a firm basis of description. The chapters in this section are concerned with a variety of categories of dimensions of relationships. A major problem is that of selection: relationships, and especially close relationships, are so complex that it is not always obvious what is primary or important. Chapters 5–15 therefore attempt to group some of the possibilities into categories of dimensions. The earlier chapters are concerned primarily with the constituent interactions, and with more objective aspects of relationships, the later ones with aspects of relationships as wholes (or of participants' views of them), and thus with more subjective aspects.

Although description should ideally be independent of supposed explanation, relationships are in fact dynamic processes, so some reference to process is essential. In any case, bare description would be uninteresting unless reference to process indicated its relevance: the reader may therefore wish occasionally to skip to some of the discussions of process in Section C.

B1 Describing Relationships

Before focusing on the dimensions themselves, it is as well to consider some of the problems inherent in the description of relationships. Unfortunately the description of everyday behaviour is not so simple as it appears at first sight: Chapter 4 considers some of the problems involved.

4 Problems of Description

THE NEED FOR DESCRIPTION

An integrated body of knowledge about relationships must rest on a firm basis of description and classification. Chemistry became a science when Mendeleyev's Periodic Table of elements provided a means for systematising knowledge. Biology became a science when the theory of evolution provided a basis for the work of taxonomists and systematists. This does not mean that either of these classificatory schemes was or is the last word, but only that it provided a base from which to progress. As the examples of chemistry and biology show, such a base is not unmodifiable, for description and classification feed on each other. Increasingly precise description can lead to new systems of classification, and classification can lead to the identification of characteristics that affect the task of description.

A descriptive base has been of equal importance to many anthropologists and some other social scientists. For some experimental and social psychologists the need for description has been less obvious. This was especially the case for those learning theorists who, modelling their approach on that of classical physics, to the detriment of their enterprise neglected the fact that classical physics dealt to a large extent with everyday phenomena, such as falling apples or the appearance of sticks in water, which did not require description. Where classical physics dealt with phenomena that were not immediately apparent, such as the movements of the planets, careful description was essential. Of course interpersonal relationships are also everyday phenomena, but whilst we may manage our relationships with moderate success, we are not always adept at pin-pointing their special characteristics, describing them to others, or gener-alising about them. Only when we can describe and classify relationships in terms of more or less discrete properties can we transform our limited knowledge and research findings into generalisations with specified ranges of applicability.

And the phenomena of relationships differ from those of classical physics. When a stick looks bent in water, it does not make a lot of sense to ask what the stick feels about the water, or whether it minds looking bent to an outside observer. And for as long as we look at it (within reason), it looks much the same. Relationships, as we have seen, are not like that. They exist as processes in time, indeed as intrapersonal processes linked to interpersonal processes linked to interchanges with the extra-relationship world (Frontispiece). And how the participants feel about each other does matter—indeed some would say that that is the relationship. So when we try to describe a relationship, the best we can do is to recognise that we are taking an outsider's view, though that may embrace the out-sider's view of the insider's view of a fluctuating series of interactions between processes (see Duck, 1990, for a discussion of related themes).

DESCRIPTION IS NECESSARILY INCOMPLETE

Although description is logically a necessary basis for a science of relation-ships, it should not aim to be complete, and indeed there are a number of reasons why it can never be so. These arise mostly from the complexity of human relationships. We have seen that each interaction consists of an enormously complicated pattern of actions by both participants: each inter-action is accompanied by emotions and cognitions of many kinds; the nature of the relationship depends in part on the frequency, relative frequency, and patterning of the interactions; and between the interactions each participant may chew over what has happened, perhaps distorting the events, changing their remembered quality, and affecting the future. And, as we have seen, the views of the participants may differ from that of an outside observer.

In addition, relationships are extended in time. At best, description could refer to only a limited span of time, and if the relationship is longer than that, it may be influenced by events that occurred earlier. And the nature of a relationship may change (at any rate superficially) with the context. A heterosexual couple may behave very differently when alone, when with her family and when with his—indeed they may *feel* differently, and each may have thoughts about the other's family which are not shared.

A further problem is that not only may the views of each of the partici-pants, and that of an outside observer, be very different, but the perceptions of each participant of each aspect of the relationship may change with time as they reflect, reminisce, or discuss it with outsiders (Duck, 1990; Duck & Pond, 1989).

Furthermore, relationships are set in networks of other relationships which exist in particular cultures. The several relationships may all affect each other, so where should description stop? This issue is discussed in Chapter 17. It is also important to remember that no relationship is culture-free. "Love" may mean something very different in different cultures (Dion & Dion 1988). "Marital relationship" means something very different in monogamous and polygamous societies, and also within each of these. Many studies in North America describe their subjects as being "in a dating relationship", which would not be a very meaningful description in many other cultures, and even within North America may cover a very wide range of relationships (e.g. Christopher & Cate, 1985). Indeed, it is easy to forget that dating outside the home is a relatively recent phenomenon, still limited to some cultures, and that the relations between the sexes and the course of courtship are still changing rapidly (e.g. Cate & Lloyd, 1992).

In any case, description must be geared to the task in hand. When social scientists first became interested in personal relationships, their obvious complexity was daunting and it was necessary to pick out landmarks that could be used to characterise relationships. The characteristics selected for study were chosen partly on intuitive grounds—they were the characteristics that seemed to matter in real-life relationships. These characteristics, discussed in Chapters 5–15, have proved valuable, and are still valuable, in a number of problem areas—how to deal with conflict, how to predict whether a relationship is in danger of running into difficulties, how best to give social support.

But there must be no pretence that the characteristics with which research has been concerned so far tell us all: the instruments that have been most used take a broad time perspective, asking for instance what the participants have told each other so far; do they feel that they are getting, by-and-large, a square deal; or how committed they feel to adjusting their lives to furthering the relationship in the future. Now we are in a position to use a finer probe. No relationship fits an ideal pattern, the development of a relationship is never smooth, every relationship has its vicissitudes. There are differences in goals, pressures from outside, which lead to the ups and downs with which we are all familiar, but which have so far been little documented. The characteristics of relationships may fluctuate (Altman, Vinsel, & Brown, 1981), perhaps in a cyclic fashion (VanLear, 1991) or episodically (Masheter & Harris, 1986). And the details may be more important than they seem. Although partners may sometimes settle differences by open discussion, it is the talk about trivialia, the mundane matters of living, that may make the problem recede into the background (e.g. Duck & Pond, 1989). The study of relationships is now at a stage when we can begin to pursue these finer details within the picture that we already have. We cannot do this all at once, but must use the knowledge we have already gained to help further advances.

For all these reasons, description has to be, and should be, selective. As understanding increases, we can seek for further detail, adjusting the outline we already have as necessary.

DESCRIPTION AND EXPLANATION

Descriptions should ideally be made in a language that is independent of any theory that will later be used to explain the phenomena observed. In the interests of scientific purity, therefore, we should attempt to describe first, and then turn to theory language for explanation. But for three reasons that course has not been strictly followed in this book. First, it would make for dull reading. Second, as we have seen, relationships require description at more than one analytical level, and description at one level contributes to explanation at another. And third, the selection of characteristics for description is inevitably influenced by current theory, and it is better to make this explicit. It is hoped that the distinction between data language and explanatory concepts will remain clear.

PARTICULAR RELATIONSHIPS OR GENERALISATIONS?

One dilemma facing the student of relationships has already been mentioned. To what extent are we to search for generalisations, valid for particular types of relationship, and to what extent should we, like clinicians, try to discover what makes individual relationships tick? Clearly, a balance must be sought.

The work of many social scientists produces wonderful generalisations, buttressed by multiple regressions, ANOVAs, and path analyses, but we also need to know how far they apply to individuals. Ways out of this dilemma are now being sought from both sides. Simple case studies can lead to a greater understanding of process, at which level generalisations may be more possible. Social scientists are finding that it is often helpful to categorise individuals or relationships along one or more dimensions, and analyse the extremes separately (Hinde & Dennis, 1986; Kagan,1994; Radke-Yarrow, Richters, & Wilson, 1988; Stevenson-Hinde & Glover, 1996). Another route is to go for a generalisation, and then examine the exceptions to that generalisation and find a generalisation about them, and so on (Hinde, Tamplin, & Barrett, 1993a). Yet another route is to use forms of profile analysis (see Cairns, Bergman, & Kagan, in press).

GUIDELINES FOR SELECTION

We have seen that description must be selective, and the art of description lies in the processes of selection. The beauty of the descriptive work of the great nineteenth-century anatomists lay in part in the elegance with which they selected what to describe. In the long term selection is likely to be guided not only by the problems to be solved, but also by the theories thought likely to be useful in solving them. Although this procedure could lead to theories becoming self-verifying, such a danger is minimised if we know what we are doing, and if our data selection is guided not just by a pet theory, but also by its competitors.

In the shorter term, the immediate aim of description is to facilitate the identification of differences. An adequate science of interpersonal relationships must eventually be concerned with differences amongst relationships of very diverse characteristics. Consider the distinction that is often made between, on the one hand, primary or communal relationships characterised by warmth, intimacy, and commitment, and by the apparent unimportance of any tangible exchange or profit motive and, on the other hand, formal, role or "exchange" relationships which have little emotional content and in which the exchange of resources is monitored by the participants (e.g. Mills & Clark, 1982). A related distinction goes back at least to classical Greece, where "Philos-relationships" might refer to kin, affines, or others with whom there was a personal or familial tie (Easterling, 1989). However it will be no surprise that this simple dichotomy, though useful in some contexts, is only a starting point. The relationships with which this book is concerned would all be described as communal, but there are differences between them that have important implications for their dynamics. We all distinguish, for instance, between lovers and friends—though there may be many intermediates. Furthermore, exchanges of resources do in fact play an important, though at first sight perhaps inconspicuous, part even in close relationships both today and in classical Greece (Millett, 1991). We also need to distinguish between relationships within the gross categories—how do best friends differ from friends, for example. Characters useful for the first kind of distinction are not necessarily useful also for the second, or vice versa: it is necessary to have means for describing relationships that will cater for either.

DIMENSIONS AND LEVELS OF ANALYSIS

The task of description would be facilitated if we could specify a limited number of unitary dimensions along which relationships differ, and demonstrate their crucial importance. It would in theory be possible to study a wide range of relationships, measure many of their aspects and then reduce the data by factor analysis or some comparable technique to a limited number of dimensions. A number of such attempts have been made, and in many cases the data were reduced to three principal dimensions, which can be roughly described as love/hate, dominance/subordinance, and involvement/detachment (Becker, 1964; Lorr & McNair, 1963). A number of recent studies have used a circumflex model based on the first two of these dimensions (Wiggins, 1982; see Figure 8.1).

But approaches using factor analysis or a related technique have one obvious problem. However many measures are used initially, some selection is necessarily involved, and the factors extracted from the analysis are inevitably influenced by that initial selection of data. On the view that we do not yet know just what is important and what is not, and therefore do not yet know exactly what to describe or measure, it seems wise to acknowledge the processes of selection. Perhaps it will be as well first to concentrate on what *sorts of* measurements are likely to be useful – that is, to specify *categories* of dimensions.

In trying to specify these categories of dimensions it is reasonable not to discard as preliminary guidelines the qualities we notice in everyday life—for instance whether the participants are affectionate, competitive, understanding, or selfish in their relationships. It seems likely that we have been shaped to make the sorts of judgements we make about relationships in our culture because those particular judgements are based on characteristics likely to be important to us. Though it is not necessary to the present discussion, a biologist might well go further and support the view that we have been selected in evolution to be aware of some characteristics of relationships rather than others. It thus seems proper not to neglect our everyday predispositions in selecting dimensions relevant for the study of relationships.

However here a difficulty emerges. Our judgements about relationships often have a global character: we label them as "affectionate" or "competitive" without specifying the precise criteria by which we make such judgements. Such ratings based on imprecise impressions cannot form the basis of scientific enquiry: we must be able to specify criteria on which the ratings or observations are based. In the early days of studying relationships many of the words used had broad ranges of associations or meanings: in devising an instrument to measure a particular aspect of relationships, much might therefore depend on which particular associations were chosen, and different authors have in fact used the same name for different relationship characteristics. This issue is critical for the development of a science of personal relationships, and it is worthwhile to consider one case in some detail.

The Concepts of "Closeness" and "Intimacy"

Relationships are often described as more or less close, and a participant's perception of the closeness of a relationship may affect its detailed course. "Closeness" implies interdependence between the participants, but research workers have not agreed on how that should be assessed.

Maxwell (1985) produced a "Close Relationships Questionnaire", which included questions concerned with closeness, separation distress, disclosure, naturalness, similarity, following (i.e. seeking each other's company etc.), giving and receiving help, communication, and other variables. This proved to be useful for a variety of types of relationship—female friends, male friends, mothers and children, and married couples—and could be treated as involving a common variable. However there were differences in the items loading on the first factor in factor analysis, and that factor accounted for 71% of the variance with female friends and only 29% with married couples—suggesting the possibility that "closeness" means something different in relationships of different sorts. Maxwell acknowledges another problem found in many instruments of this sort—namely that respondents to a self-report questionnaire tend to ensure that their responses to the various items are mutually consistent.

Another and much used self-report questionnaire for assessing closeness, the Relationship Closeness Inventory (RCI, Berscheid, Snyder, & Omoto, 1989), taps three of the four properties of close relationships postulated earlier by Kelley et al. (1983)—the amount of time two individuals spend together (frequency), the variety of things they do together (diversity), and the degree of perceived influence each has on the other (strength). Berscheid et al. compared the RCI with two other measures—the participant's subjective assessment of the overall closeness of the relationship, and a measure of its hedonic tone. The latter was assessed from the difference between the average reported frequencies of 12 positive and 15 negative emotions. Berscheid et al. found that the frequency distribution of degree of "closeness", gender differences in "closeness", and correlations between "closeness" and the longevity of the relationship, all differed according to which measure was used. Measures of hedonic emotional tone did not distinguish between the family and romantic relationships of a sample of students, but the latter gave much higher scores on the RCI. And only the RCI significantly predicted the durability of the relationships as determined in a follow-up study. However the authors warn against any statement about the "true" or "most valid" method for measuring closeness: not only do the different instruments produce different data, but the validity of any one may vary with the population studied. Consider, for example, heterosexual couples. The vignettes in Chapter 1 have already hinted that close relationships are likely to involve conflicts between autonomy and inter-dependence (see Chapter 10), but the RCI puts heavy emphasis on the latter. But in a long-term traditional marital relationship the wife may come to understand that her husband is not happy accompanying her to the supermarket, and the husband may come to understand that the wife does not like watching football. This mutual understanding is surely indicative of closeness even though it results in their spending less time together.

An earlier conception of closeness in relationships saw it as involving merging or overlapping between the selves (Levinger & Snoek, 1972). This suggested the possibility of assessing closeness by showing subjects diagrams of two circles, overlapping to various degrees, and asking them which most closely represented their relationship (Fig. 4.1: the Inclusion of the Other in the Self scale, IOS, Aron, Aron, & Smollan, 1992). Aron et al. carried out a factor analysis of the three RCI scales, a two-question Subjective Closeness Index, the IOS scale, and the Sternberg Intimacy Scale, the last concerned with both closeness (romantic love and supportiveness) and self-disclosure (Sternberg, 1986; see later). This gave two distinct factors, one loaded by the Subjective Closeness Index and the Sternberg Intimacy Scale, and the other with high loadings for the RCI frequency and diversity subscales. Thus Subjective Closeness and Intimacy as assessed by Sternberg appear to be closely related. They labelled these factors "Feeling Close" and "Behaving Close" respectively. The IOS scale and the RCI strength subscale had at least moderate loadings on both.

The concept of "Intimacy" is in fact often equated with closeness. Many students see them as equivalent terms, while others see intimacy as involving greater intensity or romantic involvement (Parks & Floyd, 1996). Although Hinde (1979) used intimacy as synonymous with self-disclosure (cf. Altman & Taylor, 1973), this has not been general practice, and represents an undue simplification of common usage (see Clark & Reis, 1988). Although self-disclosure was indeed the most frequently mentioned item both when students were asked what they meant by "intimacy" (Monsour, 1992) and what they meant by "closeness" (Parks & Floyd, 1996), it was certainly not the only issue. Other frequently mentioned items were support, shared interests, and explicit expression for closeness; and emotional expressiveness, unconditional support, physical contact, and trust for intimacy. Sexual contact was mentioned in relation to intimacy for cross-sex friendships only, and sharing activities by some men in same-sex and some women in cross-sex friendships. The association of emotional expressiveness with self-disclosure is hardly surprising, since we tend to conceal our emotions from those with whom we do not wish to discuss intimate matters, and trust is often a prerequisite for self-disclosure between individuals who will meet again (Monsour, 1992; see also Helgeson, Shaver, & Dyer, 1987; Waring et al., 1980).

Please circle the picture below which best describes your relationship

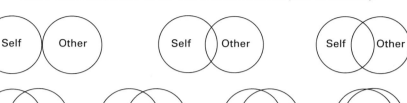

FIG. 4.1   The Inclusion of Other in the Self scale (IOS). (Aron, Aron, & Smollan, 1992. Copyright © 1992 by the American Psychological Association. Reprinted with permission.)

Many measures of "intimacy" do in fact include both "closeness" and self-disclosure along with other issues. For instance McAdams (1988) defined the desire for intimacy as a recurrent preference or readiness for experiences of warm, close, and communicative interaction with others. K.M. White et al.'s (1986) scale for intimacy in married couples involved five components: orientation to the relationship, communication, caring, commitment, and sexuality. Tesch's (1985) Psychosocial Intimacy Questionnaire, like Sternberg's (1986) Intimacy scale, includes items concerned with both closeness and self-disclosure. Perlman and Fehr (1987), reviewing ten definitions, found closeness, interdependence, warmth, and affection to be critical characteristics of "intimacy". In other cases, "intimacy" is more closely tied to self-disclosure (e.g. Altman & Taylor, 1973; Reis & Shaver, 1988; Waring et al., 1980), but it is clear that a relationship with a confidante is not necessarily intimate in any other way, and that sexual intimacy does not necessarily involve any other form of closeness.

Other problems with intimacy arise. A relationship may be seen as "intimate" in some contexts but not others: Perlman and Fehr (1987) suggest that it is profitable to identify sub-types according to the domain (e.g. sexual or recreational) involved. Another issue is that any one relationship may be seen as intimate by one partner but not by the other. Thus intimacy is a property of the relationship, but may be perceived differently by the two partners. Yet it is often assessed by a self-report instrument assessing the perceptions of only one partner (Acitelli & Duck, 1987).

The existence of diverse ways of defining and measuring a dimension, as with intimacy and closeness, poses a major problem for building a science of relationships, as compatibility between studies is hard to obtain. When a construct is measured in diverse ways, the implication must be that we are working with a multidimensional concept, and that it would be better to work at a finer level of analysis. But that poses another problem. We have seen that the approach of Kelley et al. (1983), illustrated in Fig. 3.2, might be taken to imply a very detailed level, but studies carried out at that level would involve an unmanageable mass of detail. Attempts to link detailed studies of interaction with the properties of relationships are much needed and have indeed been started (Cappella, 1984, 1988), but for the moment, and perhaps for practical reasons in the long run, we need to find a middle way. Very fine analysis leads to an unmanageable mass of detail, too little leaves us with ill-defined or multiply defined concepts. The course followed here is to use "closeness" and "intimacy" only in a broad descriptive sense (except when it is necessary to refer to past studies), and to seek for the criteria by which people ordinarily label relationships as "close", "intimate", "affectionate", "controlling", and so on. Often this is roughly the same level as some of the constituent scales used in the instruments mentioned earlier. Of course we cannot pursue all the criteria that contribute towards judgements about relationships, but later chapters will discuss such categories of dimensions as the quality of interactions, power, self-revelation, interpersonal perception, commitment, and satisfaction, with the implication that these are the sorts of issues on which impressions (conscious or unconscious) of intimacy, closeness, and affection are made. This of course does not mean that intimacy is the same as, for instance, satisfaction, for distressed relationships can be intimate and intimate relationships unsatisfactory. But these are dimensions whose meaning is reasonably clear and about which agreement on measuring instruments, suitable at least in specified contexts, can reasonably be hoped for.

But there is no implication that there is a ubiquitously useful level of analysis. The global terms like "intimate" and "close" are not only category terms used by outsiders to describe diverse but usually associated properties of relationships, but are also used by the participants themselves to label and to evaluate their own relationships, and how they label them may affect their future course. Thus we need to work at this global level as well. Indeed such terms may refer also to desiderata, to what individuals want their relationships to be like or not to be like, and thus may be important in a third way, to refer to the motivations of the participants.

In summary, then, in describing relationships within any one sociologically defined category (see p.69) we may be guided initially by the preconceptions of "high-level" categories we derive from our culture; we must identify the empirical criteria on which those properties are identified; we can examine the extent to which, and in what circumstances, those criteria are interrelated; but we must not lose sight of the way individuals describe relationships in the everyday life in which we are interested.

Categories of Dimensions

As an example of this problem, consider the label "affectionate relationship". We might apply this in many circumstances—to peers, parent-and-child, lovers, or married couples, to mention a few. But in each of these cases the individuals concerned will be doing different things together, and their "affection" will be expressed in different ways. What then are the characteristics that lead us to categorise a relationship as "affectionate"? They might include the following:

(a) The partners do a number of different things together.
(b) If they are apart, each partner may try to restore proximity, real or imagined.
(c) Each partner likes to do things that please the other.
(d) Each partner organises his or her behaviour in accordance with the on-going behaviour of the other—in other words, their behaviour meshes.
(e) The presence of the partner reduces anxiety.
(f) The partners are ready to reveal themselves to each other.
(g) The relationship is likely to have a reasonably long duration.

Of course, these are not the only properties on which the label "affectionate" may be based (see e.g. Fehr, 1989, 1994, on love), and not all of these are necessary in any one case. For instance, we might want to add "gentleness" as a quality of the interactions. Furthermore, these characteristics are not peculiar to affectionate relationships: for instance, meshing may also be characteristic of the behaviour of long-standing enemies. The issue here is that while a scale of degree of "affection" might be useful for some purposes, a finer level of analysis is likely to be more useful for understanding the dynamics of relationships. We need items that we can hope to measure on at least an ordinal scale; items that we could use, for instance, to investigate the circumstances in which "affectionate" relationships flourish, in the hope that other less tangible characteristics of affectionate relationships might turn out to be associated with them. It is an empirical matter whether the separate items of this sort are correlated with each other.

Although these lower-level items may lead us to an understanding of the dynamics of relationships, the higher-level labels of everyday speech may still be of value. For one thing, one individual may express affection verbally, another physically, and another in both. For another, as mentioned earlier, the labels that individuals use to describe and evaluate their relationships may affect their future course.

Thus, in Chapters 5–15 we shall discuss some categories of criteria that seem valuable for describing relationships. These concern the properties of the relationships themselves, and not those of the participants. Each category may contain one or many dimensions, and each dimension may be assessed in terms of one or a number of interrelated measures. The categories move from ones concerned with individual interactions to those concerned with the relationship as a whole, and from the more objective aspects of behaviour to the more subjective aspects of thoughts and feelings. There is no absolute certainty that the categories chosen are the right ones: the choice has been based in part on intuition, in part on the possibilities for assessing the dimensions in question, and in part on the availability of data. They may well be extended or refined as we learn more.

CLASSIFYING RELATIONSHIPS

We need not only to describe relationships, but to classify them. We have already noted the distinction between communal and exchange relationships, but that does not take us very far. In everyday life relationships are usually classified initially by what the participants do together—teacher–pupil, doctor–patient, business colleague, husband–wife, and so on. There are, however, certain exceptions. Kin relationships are classified according to the nature of the relatedness (e.g. aunt–nephew), and friends are identified more by the quality of the interactions than by what the participants do together (Chapter 23). Within each of these categories, there is often a need for sub-categories, such as best friend, close friend, friend, and acquaintance, though the distinctions are seldom clear-cut. Some of these will be mentioned in later chapters.

Yet another route is to try to find some fundamental aspects of relationships by which they can be distinguished. For instance, some have focused on six categories of resources exchanged in social relationships (Foa & Foa, 1974; see Chapter 20); or on control, trust and intimacy as ways in which individuals control "distancing" within relationships (Rogers & Millar, 1988); or on the cognitive models which have been said to govern social relationships. The latter are described by Fiske (1992) as the "Communal Sharing" model, in which individual distinctiveness is ignored; the "Equality Matching" model based on reciprocity and fair exchange; the "Authority Ranking" model based on hierarchical status; and the "Market Pricing" model based on calculations of personal cost and benefit. A given relationship may conform to different models at different times. In support of this model Fiske investigated the "natural errors" made, for instance, when one calls a familiar person by the wrong name, misremembers the person with whom one has been interacting, or directs one's behaviour towards the wrong person. The data showed that most of the errors involved individuals with whom the subject interacted in the same mode. (There was also a tendency to confuse people of the same gender. Other factors, such as age, race and name similarity, had smaller effects (see Fiske, Haslam, & Fiske, 1991).[1])

Another approach is to select a limited number of characteristics, either intuitively or on the basis of some form of factor analysis, and use them as the basis of a classificatory scheme. For instance, Ainsworth's scheme for classifying parent–child relationships is discussed in Chapter 21. A number of schemes have been advanced for classifying marital relationships. As an example, Fitzpatrick's (1984) classification of marital types may be considered in a little more detail. The first step was to devise an instrument for assessing dimensions presumed to be of interest for the relationship in question. More than 200 items were reduced in pilot studies to 64, and factor analysis of these gave 8 dimensions (see Table 4.1) for a Relationships Dimension Instrument. A clustering procedure on the responses to the Relationships Dimension Instrument then permitted the development of a typology of individuals. A three-cluster solution provided the clearest explanation of the data, the clusters having individuals who saw themselves as having the following characteristics:

(i) *Traditional*. Considerable self-disclosure between spouses, but reticence with outsiders. Conventional sex roles. Interdependent. Accurate at predicting how each rates him/herself on a variety of personality characteristics. High level of dyadic adjustment. Do not avoid conflict.

(ii) *Independent*. Uninhibited in expressing their feelings to the spouse, but see spouse as less revealing to them. Spontaneous. Liberal sex roles. Believe that relationships should not constrain autonomy. Husbands often masculine sex-typed and wife androgynous. Wife accurate at predicting husband's self-definition, husband less accurate. Dyadic adjustment not particularly high. Exhibit a high degree of interdependence and engage in, rather than avoiding, conflict.

(iii) *Separates*. Less self-disclosure. Relatively inhibited in expressing positive feelings to each other. Ambivalent ideologically: conventional sex roles, but non-conventional about individual freedom. Husbands masculine, wives neither instrumental nor expressive. Poor predictors of each other's self-definitions, with husbands better than wives. Less companionship and sharing. Avoid conflict.

---

[1] Haslam (1995) has compared the approach of Foa and Foa with that of Fiske in a sample of 500 undergraduate relationships in an attempt towards unifying theories of relationship forms, though acknowledging that the response categories of Foa and Foa refer to the resources exchanged, while Fiske's models refer to systems of rules or principles.

TABLE 4.1
Representative Statements from the Relational Dimensions Instrument

---

Ideology of Traditionalism
   A woman should take her husband's last name when she marries.
   Our wedding ceremony was (will be) very important to us.

Ideology of Uncertainty and Change
   In marriage/close relationships there should be no constraints or restrictions on
      individual freedom.
   The ideal relationship is one marked by novelty, humour, and spontaneity.

Sharing
   We tell each other how much we love or care about each other.
   My spouse/mate reassures and comforts me when I am feeling low.

Autonomy
   I have my own private workspace.
   I think it is important for one to have some private space which is all his/her own and
      separate from one's mate.

Undifferentiated Space
   I open my spouse's/mate's personal mail without asking permission.
   I feel free to invite guests home without asking my spouse/mate.

Temporal Regularity
   In our house, we keep a fairly regular daily time schedule.
   We serve the main meal at the same time every day.

Conflict Avoidance
   If I can avoid arguing about some problems, they will disappear.
   It is better to hide one's true feelings in order to avoid hurting your spouse/mate.

Assertiveness
   My spouse/mate *forces* me to do things I do not want to do.
   We are likely to argue in front of friends or in public places.

Source: Fitzpatrick, 1984. By permission of the author.

Of course, the two partners to a marriage may not fall into the same category. Fitzpatrick found that 60% of the couples fell into one of the "pure" marriage types and 40% into one of the six possible mixed types. Amongst the latter, the Separate husband/Traditional wife was the most distinctive. Such marriages, involving a withdrawn husband and a companionate wife, were even more sex-typed in their interpersonal behaviour than the Traditionals.

A discriminate function analysis separated the marriage types on three dimensions of dyadic adjustment—satisfaction, consensus, and cohesion. The data indicated that the Traditionals scored more highly on all three dimensions than the others. The typology predicted a number of other areas of marital functioning (e.g. Fitzpatrick, Vangelisti, & Firman, 1994).

A replication on an Australian sample yielded generally similar data, though with some differences which could be ascribed either to cultural differences due to the different location or to the lapse of time (Noller & Hiscock, 1989). The ideology of traditionalism was less marked in this sample, and the Traditionals seemed to be more appropriately described as "Connecteds". The Connecteds had less need for autonomy than the Independents, and were more involved in their relationships than the Separates.

Gottman (1994) has produced a classification of marriage types on the basis of the styles used in conflict situations. Canary (1995) points out that it bears considerable similarity to Fitzpatrick's scheme. Thus Gottman recognises three functional and two dysfunctional types. Of the three functional types, "Conflict minimisers", like Separates, are rather distant from each other; "Volatile couples", like Independents, thrive on conflict, and are spontaneous and expressive; and "Validating couples", like Traditionals, are emotionally interdependent and show neutral affect in managing conflict. The two dysfunctional types engage in defensiveness, withdrawal, and contempt for each other.

Other methods for classifying relationships will be mentioned later. A review of the conceptual problems in categorising relationships, and a comparison of different approaches in the context of communication in marriage, is given by Dindia and Fitzpatrick (1985).

SUMMARY

1. Description is necessary for an ordered body of knowledge about relationships but, for a variety of reasons, description is necessarily incomplete.
2. Description should ideally be independent of explanation.
3. Description should be such as to facilitate the identification of differences. It must be guided by the problems to be solved and by the theories likely to be useful—and by their competitors.
4. A level of analysis appropriate for description must be found. It is useful to focus on a level intermediate between the terms we use in everyday life to describe the qualities of relationships, and the moment-to-moment aspects of interactions.
5. The concepts of "closeness" and "intimacy" are discussed as exemplifying the extent to which the concepts used in research may overlap.
6. The nature of the categories of dimensions used in the description of relationships in later chapters is discussed.
7. Relationships themselves must be classified.

B2   The Constituent Interactions

Chapters 5–7 are concerned with the nature of the interactions within relationships—with what the individuals do and how they do it. The focus is thus on the objective aspects of interactions, though it is necessary to begin to consider how each participant perceives what the other does.

5 Content and Diversity of Interactions

THE CONTENT OF INTERACTIONS

This chapter is concerned with what the two individual participants in a relationship do together. This is a logical starting point because the initial categorisation of relationships that we make usually refers primarily to what the participants do either together, or in fulfilment of their joint responsibilities. "Teacher–pupil" or "doctor–patient" relationship describes the general nature of the activities of the individuals concerned. Even terms like "mother–child" or "husband–wife" relationship, which may imply the biological characteristics of the participants or institutional aspects of the relationship, still refer primarily to what they do together or cooperatively. We do not necessarily regard a child that has been adopted as having a mother–child relationship with his natural mother, and we speak of couples as "married only in name". That we usually classify relationships in this way does not imply that the divisions are fundamental. Certainly the use of such labels may differ between cultures, and in some societies certain relationships may be invested with a significance which is lacking in others (e.g. mother's brother). But it is often convenient to categorise relationships according to their everyday labels, and these do in fact provide a convenient framework for comparing and contrasting relationships (Auhagen & von Salisch, 1996).

Each such label usually implies a range of types of interaction, not all of which must necessarily occur if the label is to be applied, and which may be accompanied by others not usually implied by it. A mother does not have to nurse her child for us to recognise their relationship as a mother–child relationship, nor is the label ruled out if they often play bezique together. Furthermore the ranges of interactions implied by different labels often overlap extensively. Although in our culture 100 years ago father–child and mother–child relationships showed little overlap, now many types of interaction may be common to both.

Notwithstanding that flexibility, it is only because there are some regularities in the ways in which the various types of interaction are grouped within relationships that it is possible for us to label relationships with such terms as mother–infant or teacher–pupil. These regularities are in part biological; the properties of a relationship involving a child are in part a consequence of the child's immaturity. More important are utilitarian issues and conventions imposed by society. What teacher and pupil, employer and secretary, or academic colleagues do together is dictated in part by the initial purpose of their relationship and in part by conventions specifying what is appropriate for people in such relationships. The specification may be inhibitory—limitations on the individuals between whom sexual intercourse may take place are an example (Argyle & Henderson, 1985; see Chapter 17).

Although most generally recognised categories of relationship are defined in terms of the content of the interactions, there are certain obvious exceptions, such as kin relationships (e.g. aunt–nephew) and friends. The latter are discussed in Chapter 23.

The grouping of types of interaction within relationships raises a question, to which as yet we have no answer, which is especially pertinent to the relationships of a young child. Does it matter how the interactions of a young baby are parcelled up into relationships? We have strong evidence that certain types of interaction have important influences on a child's social development—not just those involved in nurturant care, but also the looking–looking away games that babies play with their mothers (Stern, 1977), the rather more boisterous games that are common with fathers (Lamb, 1976), the joint looking at representational material (Dunn & Wooding, 1977), the games that develop with peers, and so on. What we do not know is whether it matters how these various types of interactions are distributed amongst the several social companions. For example, if the mother were to take over the father's role in addition to her own, and play boisterous games as frequently and with the same quality as he would have played them, would this make any difference at all to the child's personality development? Or, to put the question in another way, are any differences between children who grow up in one-parent and two-parent families due merely to differences in the content and frequency of the interactions in which they are involved? Or is the way in which those interactions are associated with particular individuals also important? Data on this problem are needed.

It is important to recognise that labels such as "husband–wife" or "teacher–pupil" relationship may be used in two ways. On the one hand, they may refer to the properties of one particular relationship or of a category of relationships in the real world. It could be, for instance, that an anthropologist studying a new society had collected data on 100 married couples and wrote a description of "the husband–wife relationship" in that culture based on observations of and discussions with married couples. But such labels are also used in a quite different sense to refer to what participants in such relationships are supposed to do in that society—to their rights and duties. Of course it may be that no couple ever behaves as an ideal married couple is expected to. Either they may strive to, but fail, in which case the institutionalised ideal relationship can be regarded as a goal, and thus as a determining cause, of their behaviour. Or they may just not be interested in behaving that way. Even if they are not interested, the label may affect how third parties treat them, and thus their own relationship. Thus in either case the ideal may be important as a determinant of their behaviour, even though it is likely to be very different from the actual fact (see Chapter 17).

So far we have used the contents of the interactions within a relationship as a means of labelling relationships in ways that are recognised in the society. But within any one such category of relationships, we may differentiate particular ones according to the presence or prominence of certain types of interaction. Thus we are perhaps more likely to describe a mother–infant relationship as a warm one if play is frequent than if it is scarce, though of course other criteria also contribute to our judgement. Indeed we may go further and distinguish amongst mother–infant relationships that contain play according to the kinds of play involved—whether or not physical contact is involved, for example. Thus "Content of interactions" may be applied at a number of levels of analysis according to the sort of discrimination at which we are aiming.

Of special interest in this context are activities that must be performed, but may be the responsibility of either partner. As a consequence of cultural changes in the West, a number of recent studies have been concerned with how husbands and wives divide their time between joint activities and extra-marital activities (e.g. Clark, Mills, & Powell, 1986) and with how they divide responsibility for household tasks and child-care. For instance Stafford, Backman and Dibona (1977) compared married with cohabiting (and thus supposedly less traditional) couples and found that the women in both were responsible for the major part of the housework—though this was somewhat less so in the cohabiting couples.

As might be expected, the determinants of the division of labour are multiple. In one study, the father's psychological state played a role: fathers who were neurotic outpatients took less part in child-care and domestic chores than controls (Collins et al., 1971). But individual characteristics operate with a background of cultural norms, often based on traditional notions, against which the partners construct their own practices. Most important here are the gender-related attitudes of the partners (Atkinson & Huston, 1984). Gervai, Turner, and Hinde (1995), studying families in Cambridge and Budapest, found that parents with more traditional views on male–female relations tended to be more gender-stereotyped in their behaviour and to have more sex-biased expectations of their children. Interestingly, Budapest parents were more gender-biased in their attitudes than Cambridge parents, but less gender-typed in their role-sharing behaviour: the latter difference was in part a matter of necessity, related to greater maternal employment outside the home in Budapest. In another study the father's involvement in child-care was related to the mother's work-hours and to the father's feminism; while his involvement in house-work reflected discrepancies in income, the wife's reflected her occupational prestige and aspects of the marriage (Deutsch, Lussier, & Servis, 1993). The authors suggest that non-traditional attitudes of the men led them to take part in child-care, which is a rewarding occupation, but did not ex-tend to housework, which they used their power to avoid.

Data on what marital partners do and do together have been used to construct a typology of marriages among young American couples (Johnson et al., 1992). The following five variables were included:

(a) Gender asymmetry in participation in the labour force—i.e. whether both spouses were employed, and how long they worked for.
(b) Sex-typing of household work—i.e. whether the husband performed traditionally masculine tasks and the wife traditionally feminine ones.
(c) Differences between spouses in leisure time spent with friends.
(d) Differences in leisure time spent with kin.
(e) Amount of leisure time spent together.

Cluster analysis revealed four major types of marriage:

(a) *Symmetrical.* Both partners participate in the labour force and di-vision of household chores is relatively unsex-typed. Spend less lei-sure time together than the other types (42%).
(b) *Parallel.* Husband the primary breadwinner, housework tradition-ally sex-typed. Spouses spend relatively little time together; differ-entiated with respect to leisure time spent with friends or kin (27%).
(c) *Differentiated companionate.* Gender-differentiated instrumental roles. Husband more involved in the labour market than the wife, but spend more leisure time together than other types (21%).

(d) *Role reversed*. The wife is the primary breadwinner, and traditional gender roles are reversed. Non-traditional sex-typing in household chores. Spend considerable leisure time together (10%).

However the groups did not differ in marital satisfaction, and the authors point out that the generality of this typology, which was based on 100 couples in central Pennsylvania, should be assessed.

That there were no differences in marital satisfaction between the marital types in this study could mean merely that the couples in each group had been able to work out a *modus vivendi* that suited their expectations. We shall see later that the decrease in women's positive feelings towards their husbands in the *post partum* period may be related to violated expectations about the sharing of housework and child-care (Ruble et al., 1988). Such expectations may be very deep-rooted. In professional families with young children where husband and wife had jobs of approximately equal status, Biernat and Wortman (1991) found that husbands took a smaller share in child-care and domestic chores than did the wives. Nevertheless the wives tended to be satisfied with what their husbands did, and dissatisfied with themselves. This dissatisfaction in the wives seemed to stem from internalised gender stereotypes and comparisons with more traditional female relatives. The wives' perceptions that the husbands' careers took precedence contributed to the husbands spending less time in child-care and the wives compensating by spending more. Amongst those who were in business, wives and husbands were happiest about their performances as spouses when the husband's career took precedence and when he earned more money than his wife. The authors remark on the ambivalence about sex roles inherent in a situation where egalitarian beliefs are associated with internalised more traditional norms about gender role behaviour.

Although much of the work on dual career couples focuses on the problems that must be solved, the positive side must not be forgotten. We have seen that a close relationship can be seen as including the other in the self: Gilbert (1993) argues that, whereas traditional marriages tend to involve one giving and the other receiving, the sharing in dual career marriages offers an even greater opportunity for an individual to be more than he or she would be if alone.

THE DIVERSITY OF INTERACTIONS

A related characteristic concerns the diversity of types of interaction that occur. If a relationship involves only one type of interaction, as for instance a relationship with a drinking companion or business colleague, it can be described as single-stranded or uniplex; if many, as multi-stranded or multiplex. The distinction is of course not absolute, and again depends on the level of analysis. Thus the mother–infant relationship could be called uniplex, involving only maternal–filial responses: or multiplex, involving nursing, playing, protecting, and so on. The important issue is the extent of diversity of behaviour involved, not the dichotomy.

Within a multiplex relationship, interactions of one type may be influenced by those of another. Just because a relationship involves two individuals known to each other, the content or quality of one interaction may be affected by that of any other. This is a common enough observation, and has been emphasised especially in the course of discussions of marital therapy. The sexual components of a couple's relationship affect, and are affected by, the other things that they do together. Clearly the effects of one type of interaction on others are likely to be richer, the more diverse the interactions in the relationship.

But diversity is also important in another way. For many, the sharing of experience with one or more others is an important source of satisfaction. The more contexts in which the participants in a relationship interact, the more of their natures can be mutually revealed. In some cases, indeed, actual interaction may not be essential—areas of experience common to both may play an important part in a relationship. Two doctors who work in the same hospital may have much to discuss even though they never meet in the wards, and parent and child may become in some ways closer when the latter marries because a type of experience is shared. Those who have lived for a while in remote places, away from the facilities and constraints of civilisation, feel upon their return an urgent need to converse with others who have had a similar experience, and feel a special bond with them (Hinde, 1978c). And if one partner in a marriage is very involved in a profession, the other may feel great need for a social network where problems can be shared and discussed (Weiss, 1974).

There can be a negative as well as a positive side to sharing a wide variety of activities. Doing many things together may provide a route to greater understanding, but it may also provide more opportunities for conflicts to arise, depending on the activity concerned and the partners' preferences for it (Surra & Longstreth, 1990).

SUMMARY

1. With the exception of friends and kin relationships, relationships are categorised primarily on what the participants do together—the content of their interactions.
2. Labels such as "husband–wife" may refer either to what the participants in such a relationship actually do together, or to what the incumbents of such roles are expected to do.

3. Content of interactions may be used to differentiate types of relationship, or to differentiate relationships within a category.
4. The manner in which child-care and household chores are shared is an important aspect of many relationships.
5. The diversity of types of interactions within a relationship may be important because the greater the diversity, the more interactions of one type may be influenced by others, the more aspects of the personalities of the participants are revealed, and the more experience they share.

6 Qualities of Interactions and Communication

VERBAL AND NON-VERBAL COMMUNICATION

Though the bill may be correct and the change exact, it matters how the cashier in the supermarket handles our purchases: a grumpy interaction may not colour the whole day, but it will certainly affect the probability of our return. And the more important the relationship, the more important the qualities of the interactions: use of the label "loving" for a relationship depends on the qualities as well as on the content of the interactions, and there is clear evidence that being a good parent is not just doing the right things. For example, Ainsworth (1979) and her colleagues found that how a mother held her baby (i.e. tenderly and carefully or briskly and awkwardly) was more closely related to other properties of the mother–infant relationship, and especially to how the infant responded to close bodily contact, than was how much she held it.

In this chapter, therefore, we shall consider various aspects of the "qualities" of interactions. Just how many qualities are likely to be important is quite unknown: perhaps repertory grid techniques (pp.119–122) could be used to provide an answer. But any such answer is likely to be specific to the particular sub-culture: what qualities matter, and when, depends very much on the context. Expectations about the quality of interactions with policemen differ between Londoners and New Yorkers, and the perception of gruffness or courtesy by the experienced traveller depends on where he or she is. Here, however, we shall concentrate on some of the problems of studying the qualities of interactions within a particular cultural context.

What matters, of course, is not the objective quality of what happens, but how that quality is perceived by each participant. And how it is perceived will depend on their expectations for an interaction or relationship of the type in question, expectations which will differ not only between cultures, but also according to how the participants perceive past interactions, their present moods and their hopes for the future. Furthermore the perceived quality of any particular interaction may change with time as the participants turn over what has happened in their minds, perhaps in the light of subsequent experiences with each other or conversations with other parties. Reminiscences, daydreams, memories will change the remembered quality of past interactions, and this in turn may influence the future (Duck, 1990; Duck & Pond, 1989).

Amongst the most important types of interaction, and a major contributor to the quality of relationships, is conversation—whether it be discussion of topics of mutual interest, attempts to solve relationship problems, or just chit-chat. Regretting its neglect in most earlier studies of close relationships, Duck and Pond (1989, p.21) regard talk as the "engine of process" in a relationship, emphasising that "active processes such as talking, acting together, disclosing, making joint decisions, arguing and the like are in fact the key social processes." In an initial encounter between strangers, a single sentence may reveal a great deal about the character of the speaker. In a close relationship conversation is both indexical, in that it conveys the emotional status of the interaction; and instrumental, in that it is the means by which the business of the relationship is carried on (Miller & Boster, 1988). The ability to make skilful use of conversation is an essential part of being socially competent, and provides a basis for mutual understanding and closeness (Planalp & Garvin-Doxas, 1994). The manner and extent to which the participants talk with each other is thus both a central characteristic of their relationship and a major factor in its dynamics: the nature of their relationship affects how people talk, and how they talk affects the nature of their relationship. Although the probable importance of casual talk is now widely recognised, there is much need for more research on just how it contributes to relationship satisfaction and stability.

The view that conversation was neglected in the earlier studies of relationships is certainly correct, but this does not mean that verbal intermediaries, either interpersonal or intrapersonal, are ubiquitous in social interaction. The extent to which information is processed non-verbally has been stressed by psychologists for many decades (e.g. Hebb, 1949; Miller et al., 1960). Furthermore much of talk's impact is mediated by the non-verbal communication that accompanies it. As a tool for studying the dynamics of relationships, non-verbal behaviour has proved powerful in distinguishing distressed from non-distressed couples (Gottman, 1979; Noller, 1987).

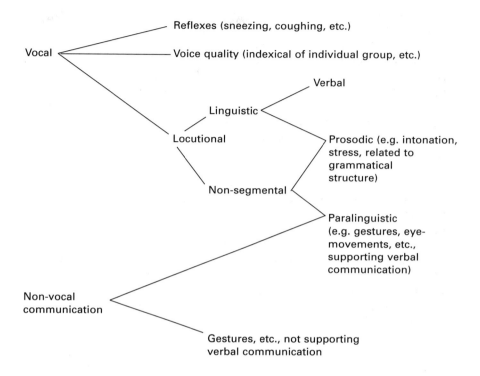

FIG. 6.1   Relations between verbal and non-verbal communication. (Hinde, 1972. Reprinted by permission of Cambridge University Press.)

In the absence of dissembling, the non-verbal concomitants of speech are more or less direct expressions of the speaker's affective state, itself an important determinant of the quality of interactions. An individual's affective state affects the organisation and representation of social information; attributions and the evaluation of self, partner, and relationship; and what is subsequently remembered (Forgas, 1982; Forgas, Levinger, & Moylan, 1994). However, as we shall see, non-verbal and non-vocal communication are not always direct expressions of feelings but may be contrived or feigned, as well as being culturally patterned (Ekman, 1985; Ekman & Friesen, 1969; Ekman & Davidson, 1995).

In studying communication in relationships, and especially in the identification of problems in relationships, it is necessary, at least as a first step, to focus both on the sending and on the reception of messages. We can ask whether the message sent corresponded with the sender's intent, whether it was interpreted correctly by the recipient, and the extent to which the verbal content was in harmony with the prosodic features (vocal tone, emphasis, etc., Fig. 6.1) and with the non-vocal (paralinguistic) elements that accompanied it (cf. Noller, 1984, 1987). Indeed, one may go further and enquire whether the participants not only understood what each other said, but whether they took it fully on board: were they really engaged each with the other, or merely stating positions? Most messages are not fabricated by the sender-as-an-isolated-entity, but are suited to the intended receiver and to the situation. Thus the message itself is a relational entity. And the receiver may or may not interpret it in the light of the perceived properties of the sender and the relationship. It is also important to recognise that any message may have one or more of a number of consequences—the provision of information; regulation of interaction; expression of intimacy or the reverse; the exercising of control; presentation of an image of the self or of the relationship; and the management of affect (Patterson, 1988). These consequences may overlap, and may or may not be intended.

In addition, as always, analysis must be followed by re-synthesis: conversations must be seen not just as strings of messages but also as wholes. Spencer (1994) sees the unfolding conversational sequence as allowing each speaker to accomplish conversational goals, emphasising how, for instance, a conversation may define the level of closeness that each partner desires. Conversations taken as wholes may solve problems, provide enlightenment, communicate biases and feelings, to an extent far beyond what is possible in individual utterances.

Two further points must be made here. Some psychologists like to limit the term communication to intentional acts, while others, and also anthropologists, use it more widely. Verbal and non-verbal communication are discussed here because they provide clues to the participants about each other's feelings and intentions, and to the outsider about the quality of the interaction: the presence or absence of intention to communicate is not a primary issue, partly because the distinction is unlikely to be either ubiquitously possible or useful. Quite apart from the difficulty of detecting intentionality, experimental evidence indicates that intentional communication and mere expression may be inextricably intertwined. Zivin (1982) placed two children in a situation in which they had to compete for a desirable object. If they could see each other's faces, a particular facial expression used in agonistic contexts usually appeared. If an opaque partition was placed between them, its incidence dropped markedly. The decrease can presumably be ascribed to the fact that intentional communication was no longer possible: that it continued at all is evidence for a non-intentional expressive element (see also Hinde, 1972b, 1985). While the intentionality of a message can thus become a fuzzy issue, we shall see later that whether a sender's intent was interpreted correctly by a receiver can be an issue of the greatest significance.

Finally, it is sometimes convenient to divide emotional expression into that which is positive and that which is negative, and studies using such a dichotomy will be cited later. It is important to remember, however, that emotional expression is likely to contain ambivalence: a jealous spouse may be angry with a partner *because* their relationship is a loving one. Furthermore, the meaning of emotional expression, whether good or bad, is a matter of personal interpretation by both parties (Duck & Wood, 1995b; Retzinger, 1995). Thus Retzinger prefers to regard anger, grief, and fear as painful, but not necessarily as negative.

THE PROBLEM OF ASSESSMENT: THE COMMUNICATION OF QUALITY

Almost by definition, the assessment of quality poses a problem. Yet it is meaningful to say that a couple kissed each other tenderly, or argued passionately. Such judgements are overall judgements, often based on multiple criteria. Just as "intimate", "close", or "affectionate" as applied to a relationship involve a number of characteristics of the component interactions, so also may the qualities of interactions depend on diverse criteria. In the long run it may be the judgements themselves, especially those made by the participants, that matter, but it is as well to consider the nature of the characteristics on which they are based. Those important for assessing the qualities of interactions can be categorised as follows.

Intensity

The quality of an interaction may be indicated by the intensity of the behaviour shown by the participants. They may whisper, talk, or shout, speak slowly or fast, spar or clout each other. Usually but not inevitably related to this, their state of physiological arousal may vary. Of course what matters may be not the physical characteristics of the behaviour, but the meaning attached to it in the context in which it occurs. Whispering may indicate collusion or affection according to whether a third party is or is not present; shouting may mean anger or excitement according to the other expressive movements that accompany it.

Content and Presentation of Verbal Material

One indicator, and often the most important indicator, of the qualities of an interaction may be the content of the verbal utterances. Categorisation of verbal material may not be easy, but considerable progress has been made in some contexts. The message may be coded as positive, neutral, or negative (e.g. Gottman, 1979, 1982; Noller, 1987; see earlier). It may be categorised as involving control, neutral speech, friendliness, compliance, and so on (e.g. Hinde et al., 1993a). Or particular features may be examined—for instance the use of first person plural pronouns may indicate a sense of closeness (Brown & Gilman, 1960).

Of course it is not only the content of the verbal message that is important. Every speech act involves a verbal message given in a particular style (Ruesch & Bateson, 1951; Watzlawick, Beavin, & Jackson, 1967). Thus each message contains, in addition to its explicit content, a command or meta-communicational aspect that defines how the message is to be taken. This may carry information about the communicator's definition of herself, or of the role identities (pp.7–11) that she wishes to be included or excluded from the relationship, and thus a definition of the relationship itself. For example the words "I'll do it for you", whilst carrying the explicit message that the speaker will perform a task for the recipient, can also carry a whole range of implications about the nature of the relationship. These may range from "I love you and it gives me pleasure to do things for you" to "It is a great nuisance to me and it is improper for you to put me in a situation in which I have to offer to do it". While the superficial content is the same in each case, the quality is not. These meta-communicational aspects of an utterance are often carried by its prosodic features (e.g. intonation, see Fig 6.1), or by the paralinguistic features (vocal or non-vocal gestures and expressions) that accompany it (Lyons, 1972). They can, however, be carried verbally—"I'll do it for you, if I have to"—just as the content of a communication can be verbal or non-verbal (see also later discussion of politeness).

As the previous example shows, it is by no means necessarily the case that the meaning of the verbal content of an utterance accords with that of the style. Prosodic and paralinguistic features may convey subtle shades of meaning that may do anything from enhancing to totally denying the verbal message. Thus the listener must interpret what the utterance "really" means (Norton, 1988), and in doing so take the whole conversational sequence into account.

In facilitating (or contradicting) interpretation of the verbal message, clues such as tone of voice or direction of gaze may be valuable indicators of the quality of the interaction. Thus in interviews about the marriage relationship, the interviewees' tones of voice provide indicators of their views of the warmth of the relationship (Rutter & Brown, 1966). Brown, Birley, and Wing (1972) have used such information for predicting relapse from schizophrenic illness after a patient has been released from hospital. Using an "index of expressed emotion" based on the number of critical comments made about the patient by a relative, and also on the degree of hostility and emotional over-involvement (assessed in part from tone of voice), they found that 58% of patients from homes with a high index, but only 16% of those from homes with a low index, relapsed within nine months. Vaughn and Leff (1976) replicated these findings and also found the index useful for predicting relapse in depressed patients. Gottman, Markman, and Notarius (1977) have developed a coding system using both verbal content and aspects of non-verbal communication to assess distress in married couples (see later).

Prosodic features have also been used to characterise differences between mother–child relationships involving "normal" and "disturbed" children. Whilst in the former case mothers used a more assertive intonation when expressing approval or disapproval than in neutral situations, mothers of disturbed children tended to do the reverse (Bugental & Love, 1975).

But the interpretation the listener makes will depend also on him/her. One listens, marks, and learns more in some situations than in others, more to some people than others, more to some topics than others—and these depend on characteristics of the hearer. Different people may ascribe different meanings to the same utterance, interpret tone of voice or context in idiosyncratic ways, and have different criteria for what is satisfactory (Krokoff, Gottman, & Roy, 1988; Fitzpatrick, 1988). For instance, we tend to monitor the amount of respect that we receive, and some expect more respect than others: such people may be especially sensitive to this aspect of a message or to the style in which it is given. During pregnancy women become more sensitive to the intent and meaning of both verbal and non-verbal communication (Rubin, 1975), as well as insecure about their appearance and capabilities (Ruble et al., 1990). Men also may feel anxiety and ambivalence during their wives' pregnancies (Gerzi & Berman, 1981).

Daly, Vangelisti, and Daughton (1987) devised an instrument for assessing general conversational sensitivity: individuals scoring highly make more high-level inferences when listening to social exchanges, categorise conversations into smaller chunks, emphasise the characteristics of conversations in their memories of interactions, and refer to the self more in reporting conversations, than less sensitive individuals. Individuals high in conversational sensitivity tend to be high on self-monitoring (see p.117), private self-consciousness (see p.216), perceptiveness, self-esteem, assertiveness, empathy, and social skills. But in addition, individuals may change from moment to moment, interpreting a given message differently according to their mood (Noller & Guthrie, 1992).

Although it is always tempting, and indeed necessary, to try to extract the "real meaning" from an utterance or conversation, it is as well to think carefully about what that means. Is one concerned with the meaning for this partner, or for that? Are we interested in what the speaker intended, or what the listener thought was intended? What were the consequences, and were they intended? And are we sure that anything was intended at all? Some utterances and conversations are essentially mindless, involving habitual routines that may have the unintended consequence of keeping the relationship going but are themselves almost without meaning (Miller & Boster, 1988). What matters, at risk of being repetitious, is how the interactants themselves (consciously or unconsciously) interpret the message—that is, how they incorporate it into the narratives of the inter-action or relationship that each is elaborating.

Communication often involves, either overtly or by implication, an exchange of the participants' views of themselves. In ordinary life the extent to which individuals' views of themselves are supported within their relationships may be of crucial importance both for them and for the future of their relationships. A proffered definition of self or relationship, if not confirmed, may be either rejected, or it may be "disconfirmed". Dis-confirmation implies a negation of the reality of the person who suggested the definition. Such disconfirmation may be produced by misunderstanding (intentional or not), inconsistency, a change of subject, and so on. It may involve either the content of the message or its meta-communicational aspect ("contradiction" or "paradox"), and it may invalidate the claim for recognition or the definition of the relationship made by the originator of the message (Watzlawick et al., 1967).

The way in which a message may be tailored to convey the intent or status of the sender, or to convey an appropriate impression on the receiver, can be illustrated by the issue of politeness. We can ask "What's the time?" or we can say "Can you please tell me the time?" or "Would you please be kind enough to tell me the time?". Which form we use depends on our appraisal of the situation and our relationship with the addressee. Too abrupt a request may threaten the hearer's autonomy, and so we rephrase it to minimise that effect. Brown and Levinson (1987) have suggested that increases in the hearer's power, the distance of the relationship, and the extent to which the act involves an imposition on the addressee, all add to the weightiness of the act, and thus to an increase in the use of politeness. Holtgraves and Yang (1992) confirmed the importance of these variables but found that they did not act additively. Differences in the values placed on the three variables go some way towards explaining cultural differences (see also Goody, 1978; Roloff et al., 1988). However, Holtgraves and Yang attributed the greater apparent politeness of Koreans as compared with US citizens to the greater situation-sensitivity of the Korean language rather than to an intrinsic difference in politeness.

As another example, "double voice discourse" is a style in which the speaker expresses a double alignment. While primarily oriented to the self, the speaker also pays attention to the companion's point of view. She is thus able to pursue her own agenda, and at the same time protect the other's self-esteem (Gilligan, 1982, 1987; Sheldon, 1992).

However, politeness can be a problem. Individuals with negative self-views often persist in behaving in ways that alienate those who would be fond of them. In doing so, they may be affirming their own self-image, but they are not acting in their own social interests. Swann, Stein-Seroussi, and McNulty (1992b) asked why this should be so. Part of the answer seems to be that their partners conceal their aversion behind a façade of kind words. Although the partners' non-verbal behaviour may display their real feelings, individuals with negative self-views overlook these clues. Thus Swann et al. suggest that people with negative self-views live in worlds where they are deprived of the corrective feedback that could help them to help themselves. The same may apply to people with over-positive self-views.

Humour has long been recognised as a way of dealing with stress or contentious feelings. The concept of a "joking relationship" which covers underlying feelings of hostility is well-known to anthropologists. Krokoff (1991), investigating the manner in which married couples use humour to cope with stress at work, proposed two models. In the "coping model" he suggested that higher levels of job distress would be associated with spouses using more humour in the context of negative emotions, while in the "companionship model" he suggested that higher levels of job distress would be associated with less laughter and humour in the context of positive interactions. In a study of married couples videotaped in discussion and responding to a questionnaire, Krokoff showed that the companionship model was more applicable to white-collar than to blue-collar husbands; the coping model to blue-collar husbands and wives. Both were more applicable to blue-collar wives than to white-collar wives.

Not surprisingly, the verbal style used in communication differs according to the closeness of the relationship (Hornstein, 1985), and there is also an effect of gender. Using an instrument that assessed both closeness and distance in the relationship (correlation –0.71), Fischer and Sollie (1986) found that the women participants usually took responsibility for keeping going a conversation with a friend or acquaintance of their own choice, but used more questions with an opposite-sex than with a same-sex interactant, and more subtle verbal behaviours, such as active listening responses, with other women. Closeness to an opposite-sex respondent was associated with the use of body postures, facial expression, and affective responses, while distance in same-sex interactions was related to less eye gaze and less positive body postures. Amongst the men respondents, closeness did not correlate significantly with any of the verbal or non-verbal behaviours, and distance with only two out of sixteen (see also Mulac et al., 1988).

Conversations, however, are not entirely idiosyncratic: conventions and rituals, culturally acquired, keep the interchanges within appropriate bounds. For instance, an individual who discloses too much early on in an acquaintance may be evaluated negatively. Kellermann et al. (1989) have provided data in harmony with the view that there is a knowledge structure (Memory organisation packet, MOP, see p.33) which organises scenes in conversations between strangers in the process of becoming acquainted. The scenes are centred on topics, each consisting of a set of utterances with a single overarching objective. Each scene occurs with a limited number of linguistic variations or "scripts" that colour the actions in each scene. The behavioural sequences are seen as organised by the MOP in order that the speaker's current goals can be achieved. On this view, the relative order of scenes in initial conversations is relatively stable, with variations to meet particular situations. Kellermann (1991) showed that, while a number of different topics may be possible at any given stage in an initial interaction, what is appropriate at one point may not be appropriate later.

Although we have stressed how the prosodic and paralinguistic features of communication may assist interpretation of the meaning or quality of an interaction, it is also the case that the nature of an interaction, and especially the social context, may affect the meaning of a message (Berger, 1993; Montgomery, 1988a; Smith, 1977). The complexity of the issues involved is demonstrated by Goody's (1978) study of questioning in the Gonja (West Africa). Starting with the view that asking a question not only compels a response, but also carries a message about the relationship between the individuals involved, Goody showed how the precise meaning assigned to the act of asking a question can vary. She classified questions according to two dimensions—one running from requests only for infor-mation (e.g. "What time is it?") to rhetorical questions, and the other from control to deference. Questions could be classified in terms of their position on these two dimensions (Fig. 6.2). For example, questions used in greet-ing ("How are you?") might be rhetorical and with a very small control element, whilst questions asked by a superior to an inferior to set him at his ease and promote social contact would be low in requirements for both information and control. Of special interest here is Goody's description of the mutual influences between social status and the meaning assigned to questions. Where status is not clearly defined, the mode of questioning can help determine the role relationship, but if role relationships are established, constraints are thereby imposed on the meaning assigned to questions asked.

Non-vocal Communication and Emotion

As we have seen, prosodic and paralinguistic features may convey the meaning to be ascribed to verbal messages. But non-verbal communica-tion may also be important in the absence of the spoken word. The signals

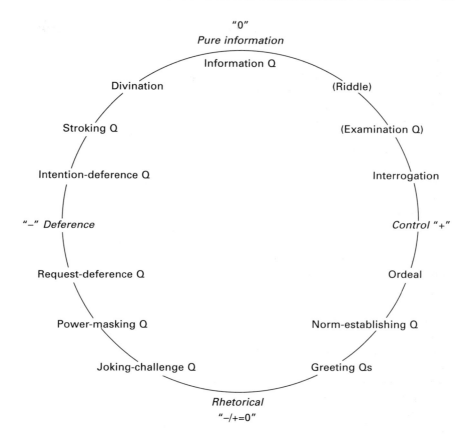

FIG. 6.2 Four modes of questioning in Gonja, showing specific institutionalised types of questioning, and the relative emphasis on information (report) and on command. Question types in brackets are from European society for comparison. (Goody, 1978. Reprinted by permission of Cambridge University Press.)

used fall into two groups—"expressions of the emotions", and other signals used in interpersonal communication.

Although there is considerable disagreement among research workers as to which emotions qualify as primary emotions, Ekman (1992) lists Happiness, Unhappiness, Fear, Anger, Disgust, Contempt, and (probably) Surprise as having distinct facial expressions, with Interest, Awe, and Embarrassment as possible additions. Ekman has focused primarily on emotional expression, and others have cast their nets more widely. The omission of love has been criticised by Shaver, Morgan, and Wu (1996b), and love, hate, anger, and jealousy are regarded as distinct emotions by

Fitness and Fletcher (1993) in terms of their prototypical characteristics and the cognitive appraisals that accompany them.

In any case, the facial expressions of Happiness and Unhappiness each serve for several distinguishable emotions—respectively Amusement, Pride, Contentment, and Sensory Pleasure; and Guilt, Shame, Sadness, and Regret. Each of these is also primary in the sense that they differ in their antecedent conditions, context, physiological mechanisms and consequences, and may also differ in the vocalisations and bodily postures/gestures that accompany them. Furthermore, expressions of the primary emotions may occur in different variants depending on intensity, the presence of other emotions, and so on. Some of the emotions that we distinguish may share one form of expression: thus amusement, relief, pride, sensory pleasure, and exhilaration share a particular form of smiling, its several meanings being distinguishable by the context. On the other hand each emotion may have a variety of related but different expressions. Thus 60 anger expressions have been distinguished, conveying subtleties of intensity, the extent to which the anger is controlled, its spontaneity, and so on (Ekman, 1992; see also Fehr & Baldwin, 1996). Nevertheless anger is to be considered as a state discrete from the other primary emotions.

Whilst these signals are usually interpreted unconsciously in real life, investigation of how the subtleties of meaning are conveyed may require elaborate and time-consuming analysis. Ekman and Friesen (1978) have devised a "Facial Affect Coding System", based on assessment of the degree of contraction of individual muscles, which has proved to be a powerful tool for this sort of research. For further discussion, the reader is referred to Ekman (1993) and Ekman and Davidson (1995).

This leaves open the issue of how many distinct emotions receive lexical labels, a matter which clearly differs between cultures, and even allows the possibility that an emotion can be experienced but have no label in a particular culture (Ekman, 1992; see also Ekman & Friesen, 1969). And, as discussed in other chapters, experiences of more complex emotions, like jealousy (Chapter 10) and romantic love (Chapter 24) may differ between cultures (e.g. Berscheid & Walster, 1974a; Fitness, 1996; Rosenblatt, 1974; Salovey & Rodin, 1989).

Other facial expressions and gestures used in communication, either to enhance verbal communication or independently of it, may have little or no cross-cultural generality. Discussion of recent work in this area is beyond the scope of this book, and the reader is referred to Argyle (1975), Benthall and Polhemus (1975), Ekman (1982, 1993), Ekman and Davidson (1995), Ekman and Friesen (1969, 1975), Hinde (1972), Keeley and Hart (1994), Scherer and Ekman (1982) and Simpson, Gangestad, and Nations, (1996).

But it is important to emphasise that all emotions are in part social constructions. Individuals share socially constructed knowledge structures about the nature and course of emotions in the context of different situations, such as getting married, or bereavement. These knowledge structures may operate either at a general level, applicable to all situations of a given type, or at a specific level. Individuals use this knowledge to understand each other and to manipulate each other, to assist their interpretations of each other's behaviour and to guide their own. There are cultural differences in who can show which emotions to whom, and when (e.g. Ekman & Friesen, 1969), and there are also cultural, situational, and individual differences in the extent to which emotions are suppressed or exaggerated. Experience with an emotion appears to augment its availability, so that frequent experience of anger may make one more likely to be angry in future. The self-system is thus to be thought of as including emotion knowledge structures or scripts (Clark, Pataki, & Carver, 1996; Fehr & Baldwin, 1996; Fitness, 1996; Forgas, 1996).

One special difficulty with the study of non-vocal communication in relation to interpersonal relationships must be emphasised. Perhaps as an inevitable consequence of the use of the scientific method, the signals that have been most studied are the culturally accepted ones. These are, perhaps, of special importance in the early stages of a relationship or in interactions between individuals who are not specially intimate with each other. But at least some of the non-vocal communication in an intimate relationship depends, consciously or unconsciously, on idiosyncratic signals. For obvious reasons, these are more difficult to document (but see Lock, 1976).

Affective state as expressed by non-verbal signals can be contagious, the mood state of one partner assimilating or being influenced by that of the other. This is of special importance in relations with depressed persons. Individuals trying to help a depressed person may become depressed, anxious, or hostile themselves. This is more likely to be the case if the helper tries to give advice, or indulges in chit-chat or joking, than if they acknowledge the depressed person's state and rely on supportive listening (Notarius & Herrick, 1988). The processes involved here have been investigated by Horowitz et al. (1991), who conducted experiments involving a confederate who expressed self-derogations, other-derogations, or non-derogating self-disclosures, and recorded the responses of the subjects. On the basis of their data the authors suggested how the affective state of a depressed individual may influence that of a helper. Initially the depressed person appears submissive and this elicits dominant behaviour (suggestions, advice, etc.) from the would-be helper. The depressed person submits, and the depression persists. Over time the person does not change, and in due course the helper sees the depressed person as having ignored the advice given and as non-compliant. The non-compliance seems hostile, so that the depressed person no longer seems submissive, and is accused of hostile manipulation (see also pp.143–147).

The extent to which emotions are contagious may also depend on the relationship between the individuals concerned. In an experimental study involving students acting as teachers and learners, Hsee, Hatfield, and Carlson (1990) found strong evidence for emotional contagion, though somewhat surprisingly the students in the more powerful roles were more likely to acquire the emotions of the less powerful than vice versa.

But as well as contagion between the participants, emotions may spread from behaviour to feeling within an actor. By acting as if we possessed a particular mood or trait, we may actually come to possess it. This operates both for desirable moods and traits, and for undesirable ones. Our outward behaviour may affect our own self-appraisal and thus our self-concept. For instance people tend to internalise both externally imposed roles and statements they are forced to make that are actually incompatible with their own attitudes. However, if social circumstances require individuals to act in a way that is contrary to their self-concepts, they can employ "distancing behaviour", which enables them to buffer themselves from the ill-effects of their own negative self-discrepant behaviour. This consists of a variety of intentional and unintended behaviours such as wrapping the arms around the chest, sticking out the tongue, rolling the eyes, verbal disclaimers, and so on. They not only protect the actor from the consequences of his or her own behaviour, but also the respondent or an observer (Fleming & Rudman, 1993).

Relations Between the Behaviour of the Two Participants

A fourth category of characteristics conveying the quality of interactions concerns the extent to which the behaviour of each participant meshes with that of the other. Thus an assessment of maternal warmth might well involve measures not only of how much and in what ways a mother cuddles her baby, but also of how quickly she starts to cuddle him after he comes to her—that is, measurement of the behaviour of one participant in relation to that of the other. Caregivers do in fact differ markedly in their sensitivity to a baby's signals (Ainsworth et al., 1978; Sander, 1977).

"Sensitivity" can, of course, be primarily unilateral. But of special interest in the present context are cases in which each participant guides his behaviour in accordance with the on-going behaviour of the other. On a short timescale, a quality of the interactions of both lovers and boxers lies in the extent to which their movements are directed in accordance not only with the movements of the partner or opponent, but also with his (or her) intended movements. Stern (1977), on the basis of a frame-by-frame film analysis, has shown that about half of Muhammad Ali's left jabs were of shorter duration than the generally agreed fastest visual reaction time of 180 milliseconds. Yet the opponent managed to evade most of them. He could not have done this by responding to the preliminary phases of the jab. Somehow he must have successfully decoded Muhammad Ali's behavioural sequences in a manner that enabled him to escape the jabs.

The presence or absence of phenomena that could be described as behavioural meshing may be of critical importance in many human relationships. Sander (1977) sees mother–infant bonding as the interfacing of two adaptable systems where each partner has attuned his or her behaviour to the "behavioural programmes" of the other. Failure of synchrony between the activities of infant and caregiver induced experimentally (Trevarthen, 1979), or because the infant is in the charge of a number of different caregivers, may result in distress and in distortion of the infant's pattern of sleeping and waking (Sander et al., 1970). If normal mothers simulate depressive symptoms in interactions with their infants, the infants respond with negative affective expressions and eventually with disengagement.

At a quite different level, and amongst adults, the way in which the participants in a relationship may adjust the lengths of their verbal utterances so that neither holds the floor to the exclusion of the other, could also be called behavioural meshing. This has been documented, for instance, in husbands and wives (Kendon, 1967), and ground controllers and astronauts (Matarazzo et al., 1964). Thus in an unstructured interview context, reciprocity of speech rate and convergence in latency to respond led to judgements of social competence (Street, 1984), and external judges, listening to audio tapes on which there was or was not convergence on speech rate, content, and pronunciation, rated the persons higher on convergence as more likeable, effective, and cooperative (Giles & Smith, 1979). Cappella (1984, 1988) presents a review of work in this area. Finally, meshing must be essential for a dyad to behave as a unit in presenting a point of view to others (Goffman, 1959).

TENSIONS IN COMMUNICATION: DECEPTION

Because, in everyday life, we expect conversations to proceed smoothly, students of relationships tend to call attention to the ways in which they sometimes go wrong, the misunderstandings that occur, the conflicts that arise. We must not let the pendulum swing too far: most conversations do proceed smoothly. But at the same time every utterance is to some extent the resolution of conflicting desiderata, even if the speaker is not immediately aware of the problems. Spitzberg (1993) has listed some of the tensions that may affect any communicatory act:

   i. Appropriateness vs. effectiveness. Effective interaction may be in danger of violating rules, norms, or expectancies.
  ii. Politeness vs. assertiveness. Politeness, at least in some degree, is viewed as a universal conversational imperative (see above), while assertiveness has been viewed as a key to psychological and social well-being (one might add that the balance between these two, at least at the level of overt expression, differs culturally: the former is more emphasised in Japan, for example, the latter in the USA).
 iii. Communality vs. instrumentality. This is related to the distinction between feminine and masculine gender identities, and clearly poses problems for, for example, a female manager who tries to be a leader yet retain her femininity.
  iv. Social vs. relational competence. What is seen as competent at the societal level may not be so at the relational one.
   v. Adaptation vs. control. Is it more appropriate to adapt to a situation, or attempt to control it?
  vi. Competence vs. incompetence. Individuals may enhance their appearance of competence by manipulating the apparent difficulty of a problem, or appear incompetent in order to make subsequent moderate performance appear competent.
 vii. Short-term vs. long-term objectives. Sometimes the former must be achieved for the sake of the latter, sometimes they must be sacrificed.
viii. Connectedness vs. autonomy. Common tensions in nearly all relationships (see pp.157–158).
  ix. Consistency vs. flexibility. How far should one present a consistent face to the world, and how far should one adapt to one's several relationships? Is it deceitful to be a chameleon?

Tensions of these sorts, and especially those imposed by social conventions or the attributions made about one's behaviour by the partner or by others, are liable to occur in all close relationships. Furthermore it may be far from apparent how to resolve them: actions that appear appropriate at the time may subsequently prove to have been ill-judged, whereas actions that seem destructive may serve to reframe issues or stimulate the development of a relationship (Spitzberg, 1993).

In any case, in most relationships the participants show only parts of themselves. Of course, the closer the relationship, and the more different things they do together, the more is exposed, but there are probably always at least some secret thoughts. Indeed, they may be essential for the maintenance of the relationship (see Chapter 12). Some lies may be collaborative, protecting the relationship: the participants do not attempt to detect them, nor would they profit from doing so (Andersen, 1993). Thus the boundaries between aspects of the self that are irrelevant, those that are not exposed, and outright deception is often hazy.

Given the underlying tensions, and given the possible discrepancies between verbal messages and their non-verbal concomitants, a simple dichotomy between truth and falsehood distorts real life. Nevertheless experimental studies concerned with the detection of deception are of considerable interest. For instance, using an experimental situation DePaulo, Stone, and Lassiter (1985) found that lies told by women were more easily detected by judges than lies told by men; lies told to opposite-sex targets were more easily detected than those told to same-sex targets; ingratiating lies were more easily detected than non-ingratiating ones; and senders addressing an attractive person were seen as less sincere than senders addressing an unattractive target.

McCornack and Parks (1986, 1990) reviewed studies indicating that the ability to detect deception is not related to the ability to determine the speaker's underlying affect, and that individuals perform better at detecting deception than at identifying the underlying affect, scoring less than chance on the latter. In their own study of romantically involved dyads, they found that the ability to detect deception in a partner declines as "intimacy" (measured by Rubin's love scale) increased, but that women were more accurate than men (see also Levine & McCornack, 1992). Ekman (1985) has written extensively on clues to deception.

QUALITIES OF INTERACTIONS AND OF RELATIONSHIPS

Sometimes similar qualities are found in all the interactions of a relationship: a couple may behave sensitively, affectionately, or competitively in all contexts. More usually, the interactions within a relationship have diverse qualities. The distinction may be between interactions of different content, a couple behaving passionately in bed but coldly at the breakfast table. Or it may lie in the context: father and son may interact warmly at home but distantly in public, and siblings may be competitive in the presence of their parents but mutually supportive at school.

Sometimes the behaviour of one partner differs in quality from that of the other. Even when that is the case, it is still necessary to see the qualities as properties of the relationship rather than of the individual participants. If one partner behaves sensitively, the other is the recipient of that behaviour, and there is no necessary reason to suppose that all possible recipients would have elicited equally sensitive behaviour. Even where the initiative appears to lie with one partner rather than the other, the quality of the interaction may depend on both. Whilst many aspects of an individual's behaviour are consistent across contexts, an interaction depends on both participants, and it is usually safer to regard its qualities as properties of the dyad.

COMMUNICATION IN LONG-TERM RELATIONSHIPS

Communication between people who have known each other for some time may be almost uninterpretable by an outsider—there will be agreed conventions, cloaked references to past conversations or events, hints at old disagreements, nudges about future expectations, and so on. Controversial topics may be introduced circumspectly and obliquely, and the long-term future of the relationship is likely to be implicit in everything that is said (Miller & Boster, 1988).

However, as we have seen, routine, mundane, everyday conversation may be important for the maintenance of relationships. Talking, rather than other activities, provides a way for persons to present their inner symbolic life to each other. Conversations, in the view of Duck et al. (1991), are more than mere means to gain compliance, and have symbolic force for creating, sustaining, and manifesting relationships. More than that, they are the means by which the participants in close relationships align the narratives of the relationship that each is concocting, and thus provide a route to intimacy. Using a structured self-report form for respondents to record their recollections of conversations, Duck et al. (1991) were able to investigate various aspects of conversations in non-laboratory situations. For instance, females rated conversations as having greater value, and as being accompanied by more change in the relationship, than males. The value and quality of conversations differed according to the nature of the relationship. Quality was rated as highest in interactions with best friends and lowest with strangers, but quality of conversations with lovers was, surprisingly, rated as less than those with relatives or friends. Conversations were seen as mutually controlled by females, but males tended to see them as under their own control. This is in harmony with findings that mutually controlled conversations are seen as of higher quality than those in which one or other partner has control, and a tendency for females to be seen as higher-quality communication partners than males. The preference for females as interactants, found in a number of other studies, is thus related in part to their role in communication, and not to their mere presence.

QUALITY OF COMMUNICATION AND OF THE RELATIONSHIP

Not surprisingly, the quality of the communication in a relationship is closely related to its overall quality: happily married couples are more likely to understand each other's messages than are unhappy ones (Dindia &

Fitzpatrick, 1985; Navran, 1967; Noller, 1980, 1984). Familiarity with the partner can increase one's confidence that one is understanding messages correctly, even to the point of over-confidence (Sillars & Scott, 1983). The factors that are conducive to good communication, and the causes of poor communication, are thus issues of considerable importance. Studies in this area have usually involved asking couples to discuss issues of conflict between them in the laboratory, or to convey ambiguous messages to each other in a given positive, negative, or neutral style. The participants may be asked to comment on a videotape of the interaction, or to record the intent and perceived intent of the messages passed. Such procedures may permit separate assessment of the accuracy of the coding and decoding of messages (Noller, 1987). Although they may seem artificial, the artificiality may be just such as to bring out the tensions in the relationship, and they have proven validity.

Such studies show that happy couples are better at decoding the intent of messages than unhappy ones, and women are more accurate than men in detecting their partner's feelings (Noller, 1980). For happy couples the intent and perceived impact of messages tend to coincide, but participants in unhappy marriages tend to perceive the impact more negatively than the sender intended (Gottman et al., 1976). Noller (1987) pointed out that this could be either because unhappy couples decode messages more negatively than they were sent, or because the messages sent are more negative than they intended. Furthermore distressed couples tend to reciprocate negative messages, becoming locked into a cycle of negativity, whereas non-distressed couples seem to be able to deal with negativity in the partner (Gottman et al., 1977; Levenson & Gottman, 1983, 1985).

Some studies show that partners are accurate in decoding the negative feelings that their partners report expressing, and respond appropriately, but are inaccurate in perceiving the partners' positive feelings. Gaelick, Bodenhausen, and Wyer (1985) reported that partners attempted to reciprocate the emotions that they perceived their partner to display towards them, but actually did so only in the case of hostility. In this study men tended to interpret their partner's failure to express love as hostility, while women tended to interpret absence of hostility as love.

In such conversations about conflictful issues, what the participants actually say may fail to differentiate happy from unhappy couples, but judges can make a satisfactory discrimination by using aspects of non-verbal communication (Gottman et al., 1977). Verbal behaviour is monitored more closely and is under tighter intentional control than non-verbal, and attitudes can leak through non-verbal behaviour more easily (Fletcher & Thomas, 1996).

Using both a series of ambiguous messages which could be sent and interpreted as positive, neutral, or negative (Kahn, 1970), and analyses of natural conversation, Noller (1987) analysed this issue further. Special interest attached to the degree of agreement or discrepancy between the verbal, vocal (tone of voice, etc.), and visual (gestures, facial expression) channels. Some of the findings she discusses can be summarised as follows:

(a) Poorly adjusted subjects were more negative in their interactions, and their negative messages were more intense, as indicated especially by tone of voice, than well-adjusted subjects. They also sent more messages in which the channels were discrepant.

(b) Well-adjusted couples (as assessed by an independent instrument) were better at decoding each other's non-verbal messages than poorly adjusted ones. The differences were principally due to the husbands.

(c) This was partly due to the fact that the unhappy subjects (especially husbands) tended to rely on the visual channel in decoding, although the vocal one gives greater accuracy.

(d) Unhappy husbands were poor communicators, while unhappy wives wanted more communication from their husbands. Wives were more expressive.

(e) Husbands decoded with a negative bias, while wives tended to have a positive bias.

(f) Although most messages involved neutral words, affect was conveyed by non-verbal signals. Smiles accompanied positive messages more often than negative ones. Tone of voice was especially important in negative messages. "Leakage" of negative affect may occur non-verbally even when the intent is positive.

(g) In "direct messages", verbal, visual, and vocal channels are all either positive, neutral, or negative. Poorly adjusted couples sent more direct negative messages, well-adjusted couples more positive ones.

(h) Well-adjusted couples were more aware of their decoding and better able to predict the accuracy of their spouse in decoding. Low-adjusted couples were over-confident in their ability to decode the messages of their spouses (Noller & Venardos, 1986).

Such studies have, of course, great importance for marriage guidance and counselling. In addition, they provide some of the most useful links between the qualities of interactions and those of relationships (see also on this issue Cappella, 1984, 1988).

Although good communication goes with a good relationship, the direction of the effect is not always clear. Montgomery (1988a, b) considers three possibilities. The first is that there is a constitutive association between the two, such that good communication constitutes a good relationship. The second is that both the quality of communication and that of the relationship are results of an underlying factor, like love, or compatibility. A third possibility is that there is a causal link between the two, good communication having a positive effect on the relationship, and perhaps vice versa. Montgomery suggests that all three approaches may have validity.

SUMMARY

1. The qualities of interactions depend on the participants' or the observers' *perceptions* of what went on, more than on what actually did. Verbal utterances and non-verbal signals, which may or may not be associated with verbal interchanges, are among the most important indicators of quality.
2. The quality of an interaction may be conveyed by (a) the intensity of the behaviour; (b) the content and presentation of verbal material, including its meta-communicational aspects. The sensitivity of the listener, and the interpretation placed on the communication, may be critical. Prosodic and paralinguistic features may influence the interpretation. Politeness also plays a role; (c) non-vocal communication; and (d) the extent to which the behaviour of the two participants meshes each with that of the other.
3. Communication often involves some degree of tension. The boundaries between irrelevancies that are not communicated, issues that are suppressed, and deliberate deception, are hazy.
4. There are reciprocal influences between the qualities of a relationship and those of its component interactions. Emotion may be contagious.
5. The quality of communication in long-term relationships is closely tied to the nature of the relationship. Distressed and non-distressed couples differ in the nature of their communication.

7 Relative Frequency and Patterning of Interactions

So far we have been concerned primarily with the content and quality of individual interactions. But how people feel about their relationships may depend not only on the separate interactions, but on the relations between them—on the relative frequency of different types of interaction; or on the way in which they are patterned in time. However often the partners kissed, a relationship would hardly be called affectionate unless "affection was expressed" also in other ways. Nor would one partner consider the relationship to his/her partner affectionate if the latter expressed affection only in public, and not in private. An employer may judge his employee's efficiency not by how often he does what is required, but by how often the employee does it in relation to how often he is asked—does he take the initiative and act without an order? Several different issues arise here.

CLUSTERS OF CO-VARYING PROPERTIES

As we have seen, our assessment of a relationship as affectionate depends on a number of different criteria. Many other judgements similarly depend on multiple criteria, and we may be the more ready to apply a label, the more criteria are met. However, one point must be emphasised here. Different items indicative of the same quality may be alternatives to each other. They might then be negatively correlated with each other, rather than positively. Thus one mother might greet her child with physical contact, and another with verbal endearments. A positive correlation between items is not a necessary condition for them to be regarded as indicators of the same quality.

RATIO AND DERIVED MEASURES

In assessing the qualities of a relationship from data or interactions, the frequency of a particular type of event may tell us something different, and usually something less relevant for the future of the relationship, than its frequency relative to the frequency with which each of the participants wanted it to occur. Thus how often a couple go out to a meal together may be much less important than how often they go out relative to how often each wants to go out.

Many workers are prejudiced against ratio measures, for two reasons. First, they feel they are too remote from actual behaviour. Whether or not that is the case, if they are more meaningful to the individuals concerned the argument can be discounted. Second, it is argued that ratios can have misleading properties, and may lead to scaling distortions. This is a real worry for some sorts of studies, though animal data indicate that ratio measures can have as much consistency over age as do the absolute measures from which they were derived (Hinde & Herrmann, 1975).

RELATIONS BETWEEN
HETEROLOGOUS INTERACTIONS

Some properties of relationships result from the relative frequencies of interactions of different sorts. To consider first a relatively simple case, suppose that a mother seldom encourages her child to explore and often restricts its exploratory sallies, we might describe the relationship as restrictive. If the opposite were the case, we might say that the mother was encouraging independence. If she both often took the initiative in encouraging exploration and often restricted the child's own initiatives, we should call it a controlling relationship. And if she did neither we might call it permissive, or perhaps sensitive (Table 7.1). Note that it is the relationship that we are labelling, not the interactions and not the mother,

TABLE 7.1
Heterologous Interactions

Mother	Restrictive	Encourages Independence	Controlling	Permissive
Stimulates exploration	–	+	+	–
Restricts initiative	+	–	+	–

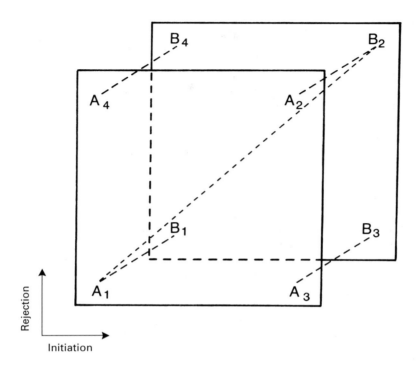

FIG. 7.1   Heterologous interactions: propensities of both partners considered. (Modified from Hinde in Auhagen & von Salisch, 1993.)

who might behave differently with a different child. Although in this case it is suggested that the labels are applied by an outside observer, such labels are important because participants evaluate their relationships in part by similar criteria, and such judgements affect a relationship's future course.

In general, however, the propensities of both partners should be considered. Suppose the two partners differ in the frequency with which they are prone to initiate interactions and to reject their partner's initiations (see Fig. 7.1). The relationship A_1, B_1 might be described as mutual passivity; A_2, B_2 as mutual control or conflict; A_3, B_3 as cooperation; A_4, B_4 as mutual rejection; A_1, B_2 as, perhaps, submission by A or domination by B.

As another example indicating that a given quality of a relationship may depend on interactions of diverse types, Baumrind (e.g. 1971) identified

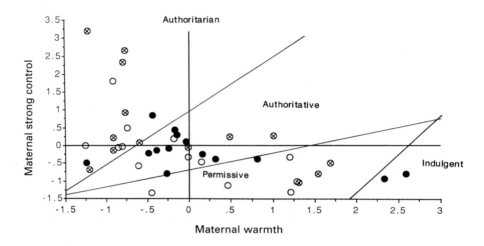

FIG. 7.2 Relations between aggressive behaviour of 4-year-olds in pre-school, and two dimensions of mother–child interaction at home (maternal strong control and maternal warmth). Filled circles, open circles, and crossed circles indicate children in the lowest, middle, and highest third on observed aggression in pre-school. (Modified from Hinde, Tamplin, & Barrett, 1993a, in *Aggressive Behaviour, 19*, 85–105. Copyright © 1993 Wiley-Liss, a subsidiary of Wiley and Sons, Inc., and reprinted by permission.)

three groups of parents. Authoritarian parents attempt to control their children with an absolute sense of values and no allowance for the child's point of view. Authoritative parents expect the child to behave in a mature way, enforce rules and standards gently but firmly, recognise the rights of both children and parents, and encourage warm verbal give-and-take. Permissive parents take a tolerant, accepting attitude and make few demands. A fourth group, extreme in such respects and expressing much warmth, may be termed Indulgent. Baumrind found that children with Authoritative parents had the most favourable outcomes on a number of dimensions, including hostility outside the home. In a more recent study of 4-year-olds, those who were least aggressive in pre-school tended to be those whose mothers provided a balance between warmth and strong control. (The lines in Fig. 7.2 were drawn by eye, but two replications gave closely similar data.) However this does not necessarily mean that maternal warmth and strong control were the critical factors: examination of the exceptions to this generalisation indicated that maternal warmth and strong control were markers of more general properties of the relationship (Hinde et al., 1993a).

It is possible to take this one step further by considering the structure of relationships in terms of the correlations between the frequencies of reactions of different types. So far data are available only for different types of interactions of 4-year-olds with parents and siblings at home and with adult teachers and peers in pre-school. As examples, Figs. 7.3a and b show the correlations between different types of interaction with parents and teachers. Each interaction frequency was expressed as a proportion of the total frequency of interactions with the exception of non-compliance, which was expressed as a proportion of the controls received.

In both cases a group of generally positive interactions is shown to the right, and generally negative ones to the left, though the significant negative correlations between these two groups were indirect, via neutral or only mildly negative interactions.

Figure 7.3a shows that the more often mother and child interacted, the more likely they were to have a high proportion of friendly interactions; the more often mothers were friendly the more often they were solicitous; and the more often they were solicitous the less often did they disconfirm their child and the less often was the child non-compliant. Long sequences of interactions (indicated by a high proportion of answers and a low proportion of initiations) were associated with the positive group, short sequences with the negative group. Table 7.2 summarises some of the differences between the four types of relationship studied. For instance, the more often mother and child interacted, the more likely were the interactions to be positive, but the opposite was true for adult-teachers. Children who often initiated interactions with their mothers, often received initiations from them: this was not true with the teachers. The more often a child was dependent to its mother, the more likely was it to be disconfirmed; but at school, the more dependent the child, the more friendly was the teacher. The teachers answered demanding children, and initiated to undemanding ones. The fact that some behavioural items have different associations in different relationships is in harmony with the view that there is a need for caution in equating behaviourally similar items across contexts (Hinde et al., 1993b).

PATTERNING OF INTERACTIONS

It is intuitively likely that differences in the patterning of interactions between two relationships can be of crucial importance, even though they are given with similar frequencies. For instance, a mother–infant relationship in which the mother picks up the baby only when it is crying is likely to have a different course from one in which the mother avoids picking up the baby at such times, even though the baby is picked up equally often in both cases. One view is that the infant's current activity is reinforced by

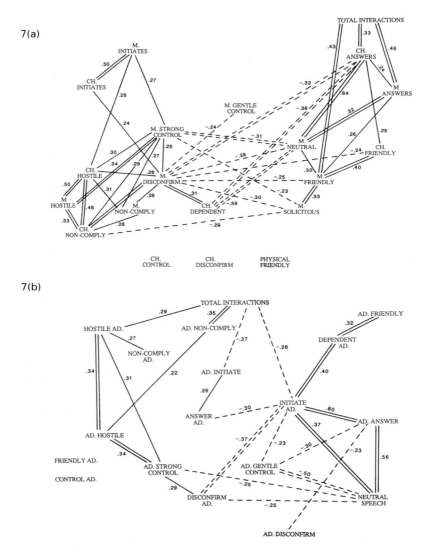

7(a)

7(b)

FIG. 7.3 The behavioural structure of relationships, as indicated by the associations between the frequencies of interactions of different types. (a) Child and Mother at home. (b) Child and Adult (teacher) in school. Each type of interaction is indicated by the subject (e.g. "M Initiates" indicates mother initiates an interaction to the child) or by the object (e.g. "Hostile Ad." indicates child hostile to adult. All frequencies were expressed as proportions of the Total number of interactions except for "Non-comply", which was expressed as a proportion of the number of control statements by the partner. Continuous lines indicate positive Pearson correlations (single line, P < 0.01; double line, P < 0.001): discontinuous lines similarly indicate negative correlations. (Hinde, Tamplin, & Barrett, 1993b. Reprinted by permission of the British Psychological Society.)

104

TABLE 7.2

Summary of the Four Types of Relationships

	Mother	Sibling	Girls with peers	Boys with peers	Adults
(a) Separate groups of positive and negative items?	Yes	Yes for negative items, small group of positive ones	Yes	Yes	Yes, but positive group involved child dependence
(b) Positive group negatively intercorrelated with negative groups?	Only to weakly negative items	Only indirectly	Primarily through neutral speech	Primarily through neutral speech	Primarily through neutral speech
(c) Total interactions associated with positive or negative group?	Positive	Positive and negative	Positive	Positive	Negative
(d) Reciprocal (initiations by associated with initiations to, etc.) or complementary (initiations by associated with answered)?	Reciprocal	Complementary	Reciprocal	Complementary	Complementary
(e) Long sequences associated with positive or negative group?	Positive	Positive, if initiated by elder, negative if initiated by younger	Positive	Negative	Adults initiate to undemanding children, respond to demanding ones
(f) Adult or elder strong control associated negative with?	Yes (non-involvement by sons; tensionful relationships with daughters)	At most weakly	Yes	Yes	Yes
(g) Adult or elder gentle control associated with?	Negatively to M. disconfirms (more positive in boys than girls)	Total interactions	Positively with interactive	As girls, but positively with peers disconfirms	Negatively with the positive (dependent) group
(h) Child dependence associated with?	Neglect but not hostility; more positive responses in boys than girls	—	—	—	Positive

Summary of structural characteristics of relationships between 4-year-olds and mother, sibling, peers and adults (teachers). Those interactions described as "positive" and "negative" are those lying to the right and left respectively in Fig. 7.3. (Modified from Hinde, Tamplin, & Barret, 1993b.)

maternal attention (e.g. Gewirtz & Baer, 1958; Gewirtz & Boyd, 1977). However this may not be the only issue, for data obtained by Ainsworth (1979) indicate that those babies whose mothers pick them up most readily in any one quarter of the first year are likely to be among the ones who cry least in the next quarter. Of course those mothers who respond quickly to their infants' cries may also differ in many other respects from mothers who are less responsive, so the effect on crying may be indirect. Latency is only one characteristic of the mother's response; many other features of her response may affect the baby's subsequent crying behaviour.

Another type of patterning concerns the sequencing of positive, neutral, and negative outcomes provided by one partner for the other. For example, it is often suggested that courtship is more likely to be successful if the potential lover does not show complete devotion from the start but rather changes from a neutral or even negative attitude to one of admiration. Experimental data are in harmony with this view. Aronson and Linder (1965) arranged that students, who believed themselves to be engaged in interviewing a second student who was actually a confederate, should hear intermittent evaluations of themselves from the interviewee. These evaluations were either consistently positive, consistently negative, or changed from initially negative to positive or initially positive to negative. It was found that the subjects were attracted to the interviewee, or agreed with her opinions most (Sigall & Aronson, 1967), when they had received negative evaluations changing to positive, next most when the evaluations had been consistently positive, less when the evaluations had been consistently negative, and least when they had changed from positive to negative. As the total number of positive and negative evaluations received in the two changing conditions were similar, it is clear that the sequence matters.

Such data are of course open to a number of interpretations, and the would-be wooer would be ill-advised to start off with negative interactions deliberately. One possibility is that negative evaluations changing to positive are preferable to consistently positive ones because the positive ones reduce the dissatisfaction induced by the earlier negative ones, and that the reduction in dissatisfaction is rewarding. Another possibility is that evaluations that are consistently positive or negative are regarded as lacking in substance and insufficiently related to the subject's behaviour, whereas evaluations that change are interpreted by the subjects as directed to them personally. The latter explanation would account also for the fact that the positive–negative sequence engendered less attraction or tendency to form similar opinions than the all-negative sequence, even though the latter contained a higher total number of negative evaluations.

SUMMARY

1. Some qualities of relationships may depend not, or not only, on the qualities of the individual interactions, but on their relative frequency and patterning.
2. Some judgements of relationships depend on the content and quality of interactions of diverse types.
3. Others depend on the ratio between the frequency of an interaction and its desired frequency.
4. The ratio between the frequency of one type of interaction and another may also be a key to the quality of a relationship. The relations between different types of interaction differ between relationships of different types.
5. The temporal patterning of the different types of interaction may matter.

B3 Give and Take in Relationships

Here we are again concerned primarily with what the participants in a relationship do together, but it is the behaviour of each participant in relation to that of the other that is the focus of attention. Thus Chapters 8 and 9 discuss the extent to which the partners behave similarly or differently to each other, and why sometimes similarities and sometimes differences seem conducive to the well-being of the relationship. Whichever is appropriate, the participants sometimes find themselves at cross-purposes, and this may lead to conflict and even to one controlling the behaviour of the other: these issues are discussed in Chapters 10 and 11.

8 Similarity versus Difference: Similarity/Reciprocity

In some interactions the two participants each behave similarly, while in others the behaviour of each differs from, but complements, that of the other. Similarity or complementarity[1] in behaviour could be based on similarity or complementarity in personal characteristics. A considerable amount of research has been concerned with assessing the importance, for interpersonal attraction or for the growth or stability of relationships, of similarity on the one hand and complementarity on the other. Not surprisingly, neither is ubiquitously important: the important issue, therefore, is to try to specify which is important where.

RECIPROCITY VERSUS COMPLEMENTARITY

Interactions in which the participants show similar behaviour, either simultaneously or alternately, directed towards each other, will be referred to here as reciprocal: interactions in which the behaviour of each participant differs from, but complements, that of the other as complementary

---

[1] These terms, unfortunately, have been used in other contexts. Reciprocity may refer to a balanced exchange of resources, while complementarity can refer to situations where the behaviour of one individual is simply a function of the behaviour of another. Confusion is enhanced by another use of reciprocity to describe the situation where dominance behaviour induces submission, or vice versa—an interaction that would be described as complementary on the terminology used here. There is no right or wrong here—but there is a need for consistency.

(see also Ross, Cheyne, & Lollis, 1988). Thus when two children engage in rough-and-tumble play they may alternately chase and be chased, push and be pushed, as first one and then the other takes the initiative; the sequence of interactions is reciprocal. But when a mother interacts with her baby, she may show caregiving behaviour and the baby filial behaviour: the behaviour of each partner is complementary to that of the other. Similarly, in male–female sexual behaviour the part taken by each may be complementary to that taken by the other. Dominance–subordinance interactions are by definition complementary.

In part because the individuals in any dyad usually differ in some way, whether in potential for achieving dominance or giving advice or whatever, relationships in which all interactions are reciprocal are probably rare. But some relationships, such as those between peers, colleagues, or drinking companions, approach this condition. By contrast, relationships in which all interactions are complementary are common. For instance, the formal relationships in hierarchically arranged organisations like armies and businesses are of this type. In such relationships, the status difference is likely to be in the same direction in all contexts: in a traditional army it is difficult for an officer not to be in the "boss" position even during off-duty hours. Indeed individuals may feel discomfort if their rank relationships in different contexts are not similar, and will attempt to maintain congruence between them (Homans, 1974). The implication is that it is better to be clear about who has the higher status, for uncertainty promotes anxiety.

However, in the more sophisticated personal relationships there need be no congruence in the direction of complementarity in different aspects of the relationship. One partner may take the lead in some contexts, and the other in others. Indeed the interactions within close relationships may show complex patterns of reciprocity and complementarity, with idiosyncratic patterns of imbalance. It is then not possible to characterise a relationship as a whole as either reciprocal or complementary, but only the constituent interactions.

Further complexity arises from the fact that complementarity may occur with respect to many different properties—dominance/subordinance, maleness/femaleness, nurturance/succorance (Henderson, 1974), achievement/vicariousness, etc. It is important to note that such labels are valuable only in so far as each applies to a property common to a number of interactions. Consider the relatively simple case of dominance/subordinance. If we observe merely that B always does what A wants, and D always does what C wants, it adds nothing, and may mislead, to say that A and C are dominant to B and D respectively. But if, in addition, A often criticises B, A sometimes hits B, and B cringes when A approaches, and if the direction of interactions between C and D follows a similar pattern, dominance/subordinance becomes useful in more than a descriptive sense, and begins to be explana-

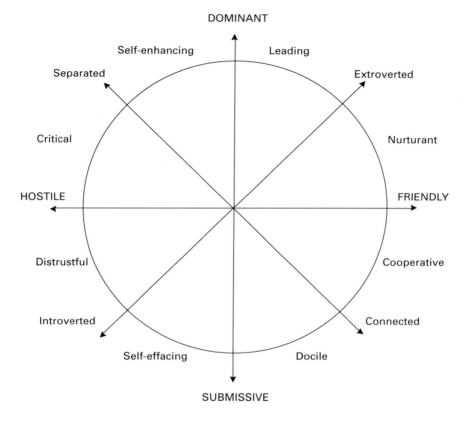

FIG. 8.1   The interpersonal circle. (Modified from Strong et al., 1988.)

tory: several aspects of the relationship can be embraced by one concept (Miller, 1959). This issue is of course a general one. Whilst there is no need for the directions of complementarity with respect to any property to be congruent in different contexts, labels such as dominant/subordinate or nurturant/succorant are the more useful, the more contexts to which they apply.

Although it is primarily at the interaction level that the concepts of reciprocity and complementarity are useful, complementarity may change even in the course of an interaction (Berne, 1967), and different complementary properties may even be present in one interaction—a male's sexual partner could be female, dominant, and nurturant simultaneously.

At the interaction level, reciprocity is to be expected with some types of interaction and complementarity with others. Figure 8.1 is a version of the Interpersonal Circle, originally seen as illustrating a set of theoretical concepts (Leary, 1957) or personality domains, but useful here for describing interpersonal behaviour. There are two orthogonal dimensions, Dominant–Submissive and Friendly–Hostile, and two intermediate ones. Behaviour related to dominance is liable to elicit behaviour opposite to it in the Interpersonal Circle, so that dominating behaviour invites submissive behaviour and submissive behaviour invites dominating behaviour. By contrast behaviour related to the friendly–hostile dimension invites behaviour similar to it: friendly behaviour invites friendly behaviour and hostile invites hostile. Strong et al. (1988) therefore predicted that, in an interaction, certain behaviours would be likely to be linked—leading by one partner and docile behaviour by the other, nurturant and cooperative, self-enhancing and self-effacing, critical and distrustful—while others would be unlikely to occur together—leading by one partner and self-enhancing by the other, nurturant and critical, cooperative and distrustful, docile and self-effacing. They arranged for pairs of undergraduate women to collaborate in creating or agreeing on stories for two pictures. One woman in each pair was a confederate who performed a scripted role which emphasised one of these eight interpersonal behaviours. The effect of each confederate behaviour on each subject behaviour was analysed. The data on the whole confirmed the predictions.

In general, other research has supported the prediction that friendly or affiliative behaviour elicits a reciprocal or similar response, but has been equivocal as to whether dominance/subordinance elicits complementary behaviour. For example, in accordance with the prediction Horowitz et al. (1991) found that individuals high on a measure of self-derogation were judged to be submissive and elicited dominating interactions. However Bluhm, Widiger, and Miele (1990) found that, while affiliative behaviour by one partner did indeed induce affiliative behaviour by the other, behaviour with a dominant/submissive other was determined more by general aspects of dominance/submissiveness in the individual's interpersonal style, and less by the behaviour of the partner. There was, however, some suggestion that behaviour with a submissive other was influenced by the individual's general affiliative style (see also Wright & Ingraham, 1986a).

Common experience suggests that the pattern of reciprocity/complementarity is a critical aspect of the dynamics of a relationship. Some needs can be satisfied only by someone with a similar need, others only by a partner with a complementary one.[2] A child wanting to play searches for another like himself, but a merchant with goods to sell seeks a cus-

---

[2] It would be equally easy to use the language of "role expectations", each partner having a series of "role expectations" with respect to his or her own future behaviour and that of the partner (Kerckhoff & Davis, 1962; Murstein, 1967a; G.J. McCall, 1970). Compatability

tomer who needs to buy, not another merchant. In forming close personal relationships, most people have a complex pattern of needs, which could best be met by someone with some similar and some complementary characteristics. However, much of the earlier research in this area was concerned with establishing that either one or the other was important in interpersonal attraction, with a seeming disregard for whether the interactions occurred within a relationship or not. Nevertheless some interesting principles emerged from the earlier studies and, as we shall see, research is now more sophisticated.

In the remainder of this chapter we shall be concerned with the role of similarity and reciprocity, leaving complementarity to Chapter 9. An important aspect of complementarity, involving control of one partner by the other, will be considered in Chapter 11.

SIMILARITY/RECIPROCITY

Similarity as a Factor in Close Relationships

People tend to make friends with, and to marry, others who are similar to themselves. What counts as similar is, of course, a further issue and depends on both cultural and individual propensities. But a number of studies (mostly conducted in the USA) have shown that married couples or chosen partners tend to come from similar backgrounds; to have similar religions; to have had similar family relationships; to have similar physical characteristics; or to have or to perceive each other to have similar cognitive abilities, attitudes, values, and personality traits (Berscheid & Walster, 1974b; Burgess & Locke, 1960; Byrne, 1971; Epstein & Guttman, 1984; Jensen, 1978; Murstein, 1971c ; Rogler & Procidano, 1989; Rushton, 1989; Vandenberg, 1972). Comparable data are available for adolescent friends (Kandel, 1978) and for student friendships. Individuals who became friends were found to be more similar in personal constructs than those who did not, while friends who stayed together were more similar than those who later separated (Duck, 1973a, b; Duck & Allison, 1978). Again, Hendrick, Hendrick, and Adler (1988) found that dating partners were substantially similar in their beliefs about love (see Chapter 24) and on measures of disclosure, commitment, investment, and satisfaction. Sexually involved couples tend to be more similar in their attitudes to sexuality than randomly paired dyads (Cupach & Metts, 1995).

The effect of similarity extends even to depression (Rosenblatt & Greenberg, 1991) and to temporary mood. Temporarily dysphoric and non-

---

of role expectations might involve either reciprocal or complementary behaviour from the partner. Complementarity would be more important in relationships involving marked "role" differences, such as traditional marriages and work teams involving diverse skills.

dysphoric students were observed conversing in all possible combinations. Those in mixed dyads were less satisfied, perceived each other as colder, and spoke about increasingly negative topics more than those in dyads similar with respect to dysphoria (Locke & Horowitz, 1990).

Comparing couples who had been married for four years with couples who had separated or divorced, Bentler and Newcomb (1979) found more similarity in personality in the still-marrieds. Only one of 28 trait-labels was significantly more similar in the divorced group, and that was clothes-consciousness. Other studies have found homogamy to be a powerful predictor of marital stability or satisfaction (Burleson & Denton, 1992; Cattell & Nesselroade, 1967; Kurdek, 1991b; Tzeng, 1992). Caspi and Herbener (1990) assessed the personality of spouses at two points, 11 years apart. The subjects tended to have spouses similar to themselves, and the more similar they were at the first assessment, the more consistent was personality across time. Caspi and Herbener thus suggest that (a) people tend to choose spouses similar to themselves and (b) spousal similarity promotes personality consistency.

However, it must be remembered that the relations between similarity and attraction or relationship stability are statistical only, and there are many exceptions. Some studies have failed to find a relation. Vera, Berardo, and Berardo (1985) found that marriages heterogamous for age were not less happy, and Weller and Rofe (1988) that women in ethnically mixed marriages in Israel were not less happily married than those in homo-gamous marriages. Hill, Rubin, and Peplau (1976), in a study of college couples, found that those who remained together over a two-year period were no more similar to each other in attitudes than those who broke up, though they were more similar in age, intelligence, and educational aspirations. Again, individuals with a "secure attachment style" (assessed as discussed in Chapter 21) tend to marry someone with a similar style, but there is some tendency for those with an "avoidant style" to marry someone with an "ambivalent" one, and vice versa (Kirkpatrick & Davis, 1994; Senchak & Leonard, 1992). However Latty-Mann and Davis (1996) have argued that the data may be explicable in part by the greater desirability of "secure" partners.

Thelen, Fishbein, and Tatten (1985), instead of using an impersonal personality inventory, arranged for couples to discuss marital situations and assessed their behavioural styles in terms of dominating, energising (i.e. the energy and initiative brought to interpersonal relationships), and communicating. Analyses showed significant positive correlations between spouses on dominating and communicating, but not on energising.

There are, of course, reasons why the relations between similarity in attitudes or personality on the one hand, and interpersonal attraction as assessed in the laboratory or clinic on the other, might not be apparent amongst people attracted to each other in real life. One lies in the nature of the tests. Assessments in an impersonal situation may not be closely related to the behavioural style an individual shows in real life, let alone in relation to a particular partner; and, as we have seen, people may behave differently according to whom they are with, so that assessments of behavioural style made in interactions with one partner may not be an accurate guide to what the individual is like in other contexts. And in any case it may not be similarity *per se* that matters, but the meaning attached to it (Byrne, 1971). Another reason is that the characteristic on which similarity was assessed may not be relevant to the relationship or for the stage in its development. For example, similarity in preference for activities is more important than similarity in attitudes for friendships between young men (Werner & Parmelee, 1979). This is in harmony with the finding that the tendency of young children to choose playmates of the same sex is related to activity preferences: boys who enjoy rough-and-tumble play, and girls who do not, tend to select same-sex friends. As children get older, similarity in age, race, physical attributes, and activity preferences becomes less important for friendship, and similarity in attitudes, tastes, and interests becomes more so (Berndt, 1982; Dunn, 1993; Ladd & Emerson, 1984). Again, the importance of similarity may be more important in the earlier stages of relationship formation: later the necessity for cooperating over joint tasks may involve a greater emphasis on complementarity (Murstein, 1987).

A further complication arises from the fact that the relative importance of similarity in activity or attitudes may depend on other aspects of the personality. Jamieson, Lydon, and Zanna (1987) found that for low self-monitors (individuals who claim their actions depend on their own inner feelings and attitudes) attitude similarity was more important than activity similarity, but for high self-monitors (who claim their actions are determined largely by the environment) the opposite was the case. But both attitudes and activity similarity were of some importance for both.

In any case, similarity (or complementarity) in the partner's characteristics merely sets the stage for the growth or maintenance of a relationship. We need to know why similarity tends to be attractive, and how it contributes to the dynamics of a relationship. But before going any further, it is necessary to describe two techniques.

Methodology: Two Important Techniques

Of the two techniques to be described here, one has been much used in laboratory studies of the effects of attitude similarity on interpersonal attraction, and the other, though used less extensively, throws light on ways in which people assess similarities and on differences in the ways in which people construe the world, and is based on concepts to which we have already referred (Chapter 1).

Attitude Similarity and Interpersonal Attraction.   Much of the earlier experimental work in this area concerns not on-going relationships or even interactions, but the extent to which one individual is attracted to another on the basis of certain limited types of information. Often the issue is the extent to which one individual says he or she would find another attractive, given evidence about the similarity/dissimilarity in attitudes between them. An experimental technique which has been much used involves first asking subjects to complete attitude questionnaires. Later they are asked to rate another person (the "stranger"), from his answers to the questionnaire, on a scale of six seven-point items. This "Interpersonal Judgement scale" contains two items concerning how much the subject believes he would like, and enjoy working with, the stranger. The questionnaires with which the subjects are presented come from "bogus strangers", having been falsified in each case to agree or disagree to a given extent with the subject's own attitudes. The more similar the subject perceives the bogus stranger's attitudes to be to his or her own, the more highly the stranger is rated on the two rating scale items concerned with attraction (e.g. Byrne, 1971).

Although most of the experiments have been carried out with North American college students and have involved the assessment of inter-personal attraction as a result of attitude similarity, Byrne and his colleagues have extended these findings in a number of directions. Comparable data have been obtained for younger and older subjects in a variety of cultures. Other methods of presentation and other measures of attraction, verbal and non-verbal, have been used. The findings appear to be uninfluenced by a number of personality variables in the subjects, though need for affiliation, social avoidance, and distress may play some role. The effects of stimulus characters of the stranger on attraction interact with those of attitude similarity in predictable ways (review in Byrne, 1971). It is important to note that Byrne stressed that it is the meaning attached to similarity that is important for attraction. Not surprisingly agreement on issues held to be important has more influence than agreement on less important issues (Griffitt, 1974).

We may note that it has been claimed that it is not so much a question of similarity in attitudes leading to liking, as dissimilarity leading to repulsion (Rosenbaum, 1986). Evidence against this hypothesis has, how-ever, been obtained experimentally. In a bogus stranger experiment with the number of dissimilar attitudes held constant, attraction increased with the number of similar attitudes (Byrne, Clore, & Smeaton, 1986; Smeaton, Byrne, & Murnen, 1989).

One possible reservation about these studies is that they are largely concerned with the subject's response to a stranger in a highly artificial situation, with no interaction possible. This was in fact part of a deliberate policy, an attempt to find consistent cause–effect relations in a laboratory setting. Furthermore, attitude similarity still leads to attraction if interaction is allowed, though the non-verbal behaviour shown accounts for variance in attraction and similarity beyond that due to the attitude similarity (Cappella & Palmer, 1990).

Other criticisms of a relation between attitude similarity and attraction are reviewed by Monsour (1994). A major issue in relating the experimental data to real-life situations is that in the latter similarity is discovered or negotiated in the course of interacting. To some extent, any initial impression of similarity may be artificial, conversational partners tending to avoid areas of potential disagreement, downplay differences, and act politely by seeking safe topics. The growth of a relationship involves the construction of a common frame of reference: this is discussed further in Chapter 26.

However, it is important that comparable data had earlier been obtained by Newcomb (1956, 1961) in a more natural situation. Newcomb assessed the opinions and values of male college students at various points over a 16-week period. The students were initially strangers, but lived together throughout the experimental period. Those whose pre-experimental opinions and values were similar tended to become friends later on, but not necessarily straight away. Since opinions and values did not change substantially, one issue could be that friendships formed gradually as individuals discovered others similar to themselves.

Personal Construct Analysis.   We are concerned here with a self-report technique which can be used to assess how individuals see themselves, others, and the world. It can thus be applied to assessing how far people encode their experience in similar ways. It has been used in fewer studies than the "bogus stranger" technique just described, but there are promising indications that it reveals issues of considerable importance in close personal relationships, especially in relationships at a moderately advanced stage (see Neimeyer & Neimeyer, 1985). The basic outlines of the theory on which the technique is based have been mentioned already (pp.3–5), but will be summarised again here.

G.A. Kelly's (1955) Personal Construct Theory focuses on people's attempts to make sense of the world they encounter, and to test that sense in terms of its ability to predict the future. We each construe the world in our own way by means of systems of constructs which may concern objects, values, opinions, attributes, etc., and are interrelated in part in interdigitated hierarchies.

Although it is necessary to use verbal labels to discuss constructs, they are not themselves necessarily verbal or dependent on verbal labels. Any discrimination that can be made can provide a construct, but constructs do not refer only to discriminations made in the past. They are valuable for ordering past experience, but also, and more importantly, for making sense of current events and for predicting the future. Each individual's personal construct system is seen as continually under test by experience, and as continually elaborated through experience. It embraces all that has been learned, the individual's goals, intentions, and values. Kelly emphasises that interpersonal interaction depends on some degree of mutual understanding, on the extent to which the individuals construe each other's construct systems correctly (see also Chapter 3).

This approach is put into practice through the repertory grid technique, which attempts to assess the patterning of a person's constructs (Fransella & Bannister, 1977; Ryle & Lunghi, 1970). For example, an individual might be asked to name 20 or 30 people important in his (or her) life. Then three of those people would be selected, and the individual would be asked to specify one way in which two of them differed from the third. He might answer that two were sensitive and the third was not. He would then be asked to extend this distinction to all the other people in the list. Then another triad would be selected, and he would be asked again to say how any two differed from the third. This time two might be honest and one dishonest. This distinction also could be applied to all people on the list. Repetition of the procedure would generate a matrix with people along the top and (bipolar) constructs down the side. The entry in each cell would specify how the construct applied to the individual concerned. Each entry might be in the form of a yes/no answer, but more usually a rating of how far the constructs applied or a rank ordering of the individuals in terms of the construct is used. In practice, 20–30 constructs seem to suffice for most individuals.

Factor analysis of such a matrix can show to what extent the constructs are in fact similar to each other and thus redundant, and to what extent they are genuinely different. Comparison of the columns will show how far the subject perceives the various individuals as similar to each other. If the subject himself is included, then comparison of his column with others will show how far he sees himself as like particular others, and how far different from them.

In this example the items in the grid were individuals, but they could equally well have been events, possible choices of action, dyadic relationships, or whatever suited the case in hand. And while the comparisons are usually made in terms of constructs that the subject himself supplies, some can be supplied by the investigator or therapist. These could be, for instance, "like me", "as I'd like to be", or "like I used to be". The factor

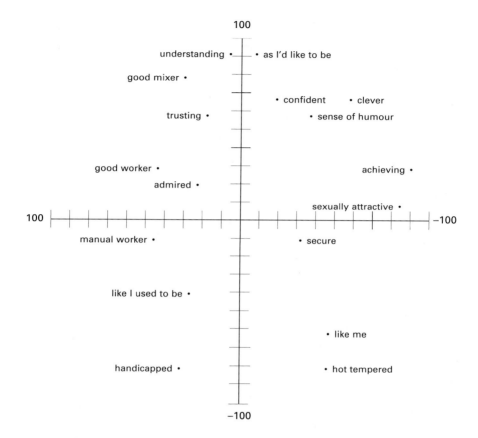

FIG. 8.2 Repertory grid obtained from a man who had lost a leg in an industrial accident. Scores along two axes for supplied and elicited constructs. (Bannister & Fransella, 1971.)

analysis then shows the relation of these supplied constructs to those supplied by the subject. As an example, a grid derived from the matrix made by a patient who had lost a leg in an industrial accident is shown in Fig. 8.2. In this grid, constructs close together are alike in meaning. The axes, derived from the factor analysis, are deliberately unlabelled. It will be seen, in this example, that the patient tended to rank the same people as high on "like me" as he ranked low on "understanding". This implies that he did not see himself as an understanding person. Although the patient's difficulties appeared at first sight to stem from his accident, the grid suggests they may have been more long-standing. Thus the position of "like I used to be" was a long way from "as I would like to be", and the latter was closer to "understanding" and a "good mixer" than to "good worker" (Bannister & Fransella, 1971).

Kelly argued that similarities between the construct systems of two individuals would facilitate social intercourse between them. Two individuals can communicate more fully if each has some grasp of the way in which the other works, of how he sees the world. The more each shares the other's view of reality, the more can be left unsaid, and the more easily does communication extend beyond superficialities. Extending this view, Duck (1973a, b) has argued that similarity in construct systems is likely to facilitate friendship formation in two ways. First, it will facilitate communication and understanding. Second, and perhaps more important, each partner's construct system will provide an external validation for the system developed by the other.

The bogus stranger technique has been concerned primarily with attitude similarity in previously unacquainted individuals, while the repertory grid technique probes more deeply into the personality. Duck has argued that construct similarity may be more important for the later development and maintenance of friendship than it is early on. He therefore compared the value of a personality test (California Personality Inventory) with that of the content similarity of constructs in Reptests for recently acquainted subjects and established friendship groups. The CPI predicted attraction in the former, but not in the latter. The Reptest predicted the established friendships in the second group (Duck, 1977b).

In a later more elaborate experiment 20 male and 20 female students, living in the same campus residence, were followed over an eight-month period. At one month, three months and eight months after first acquaintance they reported their sociometric choices and completed three personality tests. The tests were (a) The California Personality Inventory (CPI), which provides a gross personality profile; (b) The Allport-Vernon Scale of Values (AVSV), which provides rather less easily available information about the subjects' value systems, and (c) a Kelly Repertory Grid in which the subjects' constructs were categorised into four mutually exclusive and exhaustive categories. Although in other studies similarity on the CPI has been found to be correlated with attraction after acquaintances of a few minutes, here none of the tests was correlated with friendship after one month. The AVSV was related to sociometric choice at three months, and the rep grid at eight months. Duck and Craig (1978) argue that this supports the view that different types of personality information will be sought in support of one's own personality at different stages of acquaintance. As we have seen, relationships are dynamic and ever-changing, so that partners must constantly revise their constructions of one another and of the relationship. Thus similarity in construct systems at one time may not be enough in the long term: construct systems must be sufficiently flexible to adapt to relationship change (Duck, 1977b).

Thus we see that psychological similarity between individuals, as assessed by the bogus stranger and repertory grid techniques, can make an important contribution to mutual attraction. This does not mean, of course, that individuals who are similar will necessarily become friends: we have already seen that the nature of the similarity and the stage of the relationship are also important issues. In addition, similarity must be perceived and be meaningful in order to be effective: partners may fail to reveal their similarity to each other, or may lack the opportunity to do so (Duck & Craig, 1978; Duck, 1982b; Huston & Levinger, 1978). Indeed, some liking may be necessary for similarity to be revealed. In addition similarity may be misperceived to be present when it is not (pp.234–236).

Why is Similarity Attractive?

We have seen that like tend to associate with like in real life, that laboratory experiments demonstrate a relation between attitude similarity and interpersonal attraction, and that similarity in construct systems seems to be important for established friends. How are these findings to be accounted for? We may consider a number of possibilities, not with the presumption that one or more is right and the others wrong, but in the expectation that some will be right in some cases and others in others. It will become apparent that most, though not quite all, of the evidence deals with initial attraction and not with long-term relationships. Nevertheless it is of interest in showing the value and limitations of experimental approaches.

Propinquity.   People may tend to encounter others like themselves for reasons that have nothing to do with their personal preferences. They may live near each other, and people who live near each other tend to share social characteristics of wealth, race, class, etc. They may meet at school or college, or at their jobs, and again there is a likelihood that those in the same institution will be or become more similar to each other than they are to outsiders. While propinquity may be the result of economic forces, individuals also actively choose to live near people like themselves (Kerckhoff, 1974).

Propinquity may also facilitate mutual attraction between individuals who are not similar. Room-mates may be attracted to each other even though markedly dissimilar (Newcomb, 1961). A possible explanation for this lies in the influence of mere exposure. Moreland and Zajonc (1982) have shown that repeated exposure enhances the attractiveness of a wide range of stimuli. Hinsz (1989) used this finding to explain the facial resemblance he recorded in engaged and married couples by pointing out that people are most often exposed to their own mirror images and to people genetically similar to themselves.

Another aspect of propinquity is that it is simply easier to have a relationship with someone who lives nearby than with someone at a distance. In exchange theory terms (see Chapter 19), proximity allows people to exchange resources with less cost than is possible for individuals living far apart (Thibaut & Kelley, 1959).

Social Pressures and Social Norms (see also Chapters 17 and 25). Choice of friend or spouse is often constrained by social pressures. Such social pressures are particularly potent over matters of race, religion, and social class. Marriages between spouses of different status tend to show less marital happiness, stability, and value consensus than marriages between spouses of similar status. In reviewing evidence on this issue, Pearlin (1975) emphasised that negative consequences probably follow only when someone who thinks status is important marries someone of lower status. Of course many marriages between persons of different race or status involve conscious rejection of social prohibitions against such liaisons, and the accompanying interpersonal commitment may strengthen the bond.

The sources of these social pressures are themselves complex, and involve the relations between the self-concepts of individuals growing up and identifying with the group or groups in which they are living and with the norms and values of those groups. These may involve both norms of acceptability and restrictions on categories of persons with whom it is not appropriate to associate, as with caste systems.

Inherited Predispositions.   Biologists, finding that strangers tend to elicit aggression whilst members of the same group tend to elicit affiliative responses in a wide range of species, have suggested that this may also be true of man. This could supply a basis for in-group affiliations. While this is a reasonable view, hard evidence is obviously difficult to come by. In any case it is in no way contradictory to the theory of internalised social pressures, for social learning to differentiate between group members and outsiders, or between persons moderately similar and different from the self, could occur under the influence of inherited predispositions (Bateson, 1996; Hinde & Stevenson-Hinde, 1973).

Priority Preferential Pairing.   It has been suggested that partners in close relationships may resemble each other because the more attractive individuals pair off first, thereby as it were removing themselves from the market place, and so on (Kalick & Hamilton, 1986). This has been substantiated only by computer simulation, whose basic assumptions have been criticised by Aron (1988).

Parallels between human relationships and those of non-human primates should be made only with extreme caution, but it is worth noting that a comparable mechanism has been suggested for certain aspects of the patterning of relationships in non-human primates. Within a group the individuals are often arranged in one or more dominance hierarchies. As is well known, monkeys spend a lot of time grooming each other—an activity which may have some cleansing function, but is certainly more important in social communication, and has been regarded as an analogue of "social approval" (Hinde & Stevenson-Hinde, 1976). A number of workers have found that, within any dyad, the subordinate monkey tends to groom the more dominant one more than vice versa, and that individuals tend to direct their grooming more towards others close to them in the dominance hierarchy than to ones much higher or much lower than themselves. Seyfarth (1977; Seyfarth, Cheney, & Hinde,1978) has suggested that this can be accounted for on two assumptions—that high-ranking individuals are more attractive than others, and that access to preferred partners is restricted by competition, the results of which can be predicted from the dominance hierarchy. The high-ranking females, who meet little or no competition, interact with others of high rank; middle-ranking females, who meet competition from those higher in the hierarchy, "compromise" by grooming others of middle rank; and low-ranking females can interact only with each other. Seyfarth (1977) simulated the field data in a computer model which was also able to accommodate other influences on grooming interactions, such as the degree of genetic relatedness between individuals and the special attractiveness of newly parturient females.

Similarity Faute de Mieux.   Another closely related possibility is that like associates with like, not because, if given a free choice, each would prefer someone like himself, but because each assumes that the costs of obtaining someone better would be too great (see Aron, 1988; Homans, 1974; Walster et al., 1966). This view has been assessed especially in studies of the choice of dating partners in North American colleges and universities, the main attribute discussed being physical attractiveness.

Walster et al. (1966) suggested that the choice of a dating partner depends on balancing the possible gains against the costs. Individuals tend to assume that it would be more difficult to date an attractive partner than a less attractive one because attractive partners are more sought after and therefore will have other offers. The perceived probability of acceptance thus decreases with increasing attractiveness of the chosen partner. There are costs in being rejected—embarrassment, the ridicule of one's friends, unhappiness, and so on. These costs will depend on various aspects of one's situation and also on one's own opinion of oneself. The higher the costs, the less risk is the chooser likely to be willing to run. The greater the attractiveness of the chooser, the lower the probability that anybody he or she asks for a date will reject him/her. Thus the more attractive the person looking for a date, the more attractive should be the dating partner that he or she will select. The higher the costs, the less risk is the chooser likely to be willing to run. If the chooser balances the gains of the more desirable partners against the costs of possible rejection, he or she is likely to choose someone more or less like himself or herself.

In a study to assess this thesis, the subjects were students at a dance who thought they would be paired by a computer on the basis of questionnaires they had completed. As predicted, the more attractive the student, the more desirable he expected an appropriate partner would be. In fact the students were paired at random. They were asked, during an intermission, how much they liked their partner and whether they would seek to prolong the acquaintance. However, the data showed little influence of the physical attractiveness of the respondents (rated by independent judges) on their own responses. Perhaps not surprisingly, all subjects, whatever their own attractiveness, were prone to like attractive partners.

Other studies have provided some support for the matching hypothesis for opposite-sex couples (e.g. Murstein, 1971c), but the evidence has been on the whole rather weak (Stroebe et al., 1971). Most data indicate that subjects prefer dates with individuals of high attractiveness and desirability, regardless of their own attractiveness (Berscheid & Walster, 1974b). Even though some of the studies showed that a person's own attractiveness affected his selection of a dating partner, the individuals selected were far above the chooser's own level of attractiveness (Stroebe, 1977). Interestingly, in one study the subject's estimate of his or her own attractiveness was found to provide better evidence for matching than attractiveness as assessed by an independent rater (Stroebe et al., 1971), and in another study to show a closer relationship with the subject's assessment of the probability that he would be accepted by the stimulus person (Huston, 1973).

Some additional support for the matching hypothesis is claimed from a study by Kiesler and Baral (1970). Students whose self-esteem had been lowered by the experimenter behaved more romantically with a female confederate who was only moderately attractive, whereas students whose self-esteem had been raised behaved more romantically with an attractive one. It has also been suggested that individuals will choose the most attractive partner from amongst others whom they have already met, but tend to choose someone more like themselves if they are to be responsible for initiating contact (Berscheid et al., 1971; Walster, Walster, & Berscheid, 1978a); however the evidence is not clear (Stroebe, 1977).

In these studies, almost the only independent variable considered was physical attractiveness. Murstein (1971a, b, c) has argued that, in the early stages of courtship, couples will assess each other on a whole series of dimensions, of which physical attractiveness is but one. On this view individuals are likely to be attracted to others whose *overall* attractiveness is similar to their own, though that attractiveness may involve assessment of status, background, professional potential and so on as well as physical characteristics. Some evidence in support of this view is available (see Murstein, 1971b, c; Walster et al., 1978a).

On the whole, therefore, it seems that, in the early stages of relationship formation, people are motivated to do as well for themselves as they can. We shall see later that, as a relationship develops, the issues may change.

Acquisition of Similarity. Another possibility is that similarity of attitudes or personality are a consequence rather than a cause of mutual association. Blankenship et al. (1984) assessed personality variables in students before acquaintance, and again two years later. On the second occasion the students were asked to make 10 nominations of friends from amongst classes of approximately 50 students. Reciprocally chosen pairs were more similar on an authoritarianism scale at the time of the choices, but had not been more similar before they became acquainted. Religious items in the scale accounted for the increase in similarity, involving increasingly firm non-verifiable beliefs. Similarity in intellectualism characterised those reciprocally chosen pairs that persisted to the fourth year. The authors interpret the data as indicating that choice and increased similarity co-occurred.

Were similarity a consequence of association, one would expect that married couples would tend to resemble each other more, the longer they had been married. Couples followed by Gruber-Baldini, Schaie, and Willis (1995) became more similar in tasks of verbal reasoning and intellectual ability over 14 years and in attitudinal flexibility over 21 years. The effect occurred primarily in husbands in higher-status occupations and wives with fewer changes of profession.

Kreitman et al. (1970/1971) studied 60 married couples in which the husbands were receiving outpatient treatment for neurosis, and 60 control couples. The patients' wives tended to be more disturbed than the control wives. The evidence was against assortative mating; early in marriage the patients' wives had not differed on any measure of disability from the controls, but later they came to do so. It thus seemed likely that interaction during marriage led to the disturbance in the patients' wives. Speculating that this might be associated with more face-to-face interaction in the patients' marriages, and poorer extramarital social relationships in their wives, Nelson et al. (1970) sampled the activities of the couples in both groups. Evidence in favour of both hypotheses was obtained.

However, other studies of neurosis in marriage have not favoured an explanation in terms of the acquisition of neurotic symptoms by the initially non-neurotic partner. Although a number of studies indicate that married couples show greater than chance similarity in neurotic status, this could be due to assortative mating. Murstein (1967b), for example, found that college students tend to become engaged to others similar to themselves in this respect. One possibility is that couples whose members resemble each other in this respect are more likely to marry, whilst couples who do not are more likely to separate: Murstein showed that dating couples who did not progress towards marriage showed a negative correlation on an index of neuroticism, whereas couples who progressed showed a positive correlation.

In any case, evidence that the acquisition of similarity is important is equivocal. Caspi, Herbener, and Ozer (1992), in a study of 165 happy and unhappy couples, found that spousal consistency on the Vernon and Allport scales of values averaged .36 at the time of engagement and .39 twenty years later. Thus similarity did not increase over time. They argue that husbands and wives remain similar because they change in the same direction, and that this is accounted for by the environment they share.

That living together may preserve similarities is also suggested by a study by Newcomb et al. (1967). They found that women who had acquired liberal attitudes at college in the 1930s still had liberal attitudes 25 years later in part because they married liberal husbands who continued to provide support for their liberal views.

In general, one must conclude that the evidence for the acquisition of similarity is not strong. Even if cross-sectional evidence existed, it may be noted, it would have to be interpreted with care: similarity could be enhancing the longevity of marriage rather than being produced by it.

However some longitudinal studies are of special interest. E.L. Kelly (1955) found that husbands and wives did not tend to show more attitude similarity after 18 years of marriage than at the time of engagement. However Uhr (cited Barry, 1970) divided these couples into those happily and unhappily married. The happy couples showed more attitude differences at engagement, but became more alike, whereas the unhappy ones became more unlike. The changes were most marked in the happily married wives, who had changed to become more like their husbands, and in the unhappily married husbands, who had changed away from their wives. It is, of course, important to note the date of Kelly's study: whether a similar differential effect would be found 40 years later is an open issue.

Somewhat comparable evidence comes from a cross-sectional study by Ferreira and Winter (1974). These authors used a questionnaire to assess the extent to which married couples would show "spontaneous agreement" (i.e. agreement before discussion) on a wide range of problems. The couples were divided into normals and abnormals, the latter having had at least one family member (parent or child) with emotional problems or having been involved in psychiatric therapy, delinquency, or a criminal offence. In spite of the crude criteria for separating the groups, a clear difference was found, with the normals showing more spontaneous agreement than the abnormals. However this difference was not present amongst couples that had been married for three years or less; the degree of spontaneous agreement increased with length of marriage amongst the normals, but did not amongst the abnormals. Thus amongst these couples, normals showed more spontaneous agreement the longer they had been married, and the abnormals did not. The authors acknowledge the difficulties in interpreting cross-sectional data of this sort, and again it is possible that similarity enhances the longevity of marriage rather than being produced by it (see also Chapter 13).

Similarity per se is Reinforcing. A number of authors have suggested that interaction between similar persons is rewarding *per se*, and thus likely to be continued. There are a number of reasons why this should be so. At an everyday level, it could be because they share similar values or ways of looking at the world, and this fosters communication and minimises tension (G.A. Kelly, 1955, see pp.4–5) or that similar others are likely to embody one's own ideals (Wetsel & Insko, 1982). Or it could be that norms placing a high value on similarity in others are internalised early in life (Lewis, 1975).

Another explanation that has received much attention is that similarity in attitude is reinforcing because it provides confirmation of the subject's actions or opinions (Byrne, 1971; Clore, 1977; Clore & Byrne, 1974). On this view every individual needs to assess social reality correctly, and the perception of reality can be validated only by others (Festinger, 1957). We thus need "consensual validation" of our world by others. If we find that others share our attitudes we are attracted to them, it is suggested, because we believe that they will confirm our social beliefs. This would perhaps be even more probable if they construed their experiences of the world in the same way as we do (see pp.119–123). To be more precise, it is suggested that similarity, in providing consensual validation, produces positive affect, and is for that reason reinforcing. Byrne did in fact find that it is reinforcing to be agreed with (see also Kelvin, 1970).

Predicting from this that the attractiveness of similarity would increase with the need for consensual validation, Byrne et al. (1966) compared the effects on attraction of similarity over unverifiable beliefs with those of similarity over verifiable facts. As expected, similarity was associated with attraction more in the former case than in the latter. A number of other experiments indicate that the more uncertainty there is about an opinion an individual holds, the greater the attractiveness of individuals who offer support (Wheeler, 1974; see also Blankenship et al., 1984, cited earlier).

Byrne and Clore (1967) likewise predicted that subjects would be more attracted to a bogus stranger who appeared to have attitudes similar to their own if they were themselves temporarily confused. Accordingly they gave subjects various kinds of confusing experience, such as viewing meaningless films, before testing them in the manner described. Moderate disturbance increased the effects of similarity on attractiveness, though high disturbance did not. (See also Byrne & Griffitt, 1966; Swann et al., 1992a, cited p.451).

One finding of special interest was that a subject's attraction to another (assessed as indicated on pp.117–119) may be affected not only by the number of agreements on elements within an attitude scale, but by the way in which those agreements were structured (Tesser, 1971). To exemplify the meaning of structure here, suppose six attitude items are presented (X_1, X_2; Y_1, Y_2; Z_1, Z_2), and the subject (P) sees the two Xs, Ys, and Zs to involve related issues, another individual (O) would show a degree of evaluative similarity if he agreed with P on any four of the six items, but he would show structural similarity if the agreements and disagreements concerned related issues (e.g. agreed over both Xs and both Zs, but not over either Y). Tesser did in fact find attraction was related to both evaluative and structural similarity. This study provides an interesting link with the work on similarity in construct systems, discussed on p.122.

The consensual view can be taken one step further. The formation of a close relationship goes beyond the partners validating each other's views of the world and involves the construction of a new and shared meaning system, a new joint narrative of the relationship. Thus the importance of similarity may lie in the recognition that the sharing of meanings and the active co-construction of a new meaning system are possible (Dixson & Duck, 1993).

Similarity and Self-esteem.   People need not only to confirm their own attitudes and opinions, but also to maintain or enhance their self-esteem. This can be achieved if an individual seeks out relationships that will enable him or her to express characteristics believed to be self-defining, and in which he or she can be protected from negative evaluations, whether this involves interacting with similar or dissimilar others. Some people are better at doing this than others. People with high self-esteem seem to be more certain about their self-defining attitudes, and thus can more confidently assess how they would fit into the available social situations, than those with low self-esteem. Setterlund and Niedenthal (1993) have evidence that this is achieved by comparing the self with each of all possible situations and choosing that in which the match is best. Those low in self-esteem were more likely to have romantic liaisons (Dion & Dion, 1973; see p.438). A sophisticated approach to the problem of when similarity will and will not enhance self-esteem is discussed on pp.140–141 (Tesser, 1988).

Similarity and Being Liked.   An important precursor for making a friend or falling in love is an indication that one would be liked by the other. Thus another explanation for an effect of attitude similarity on liking, not incompatible with the previous ones, is that attitude similarity indicates that liking is likely to be reciprocated (Aronson & Worchel, 1966). On this view, the attractiveness of similar others would be related to the desire to be liked (Walster & Walster, 1963). Subjects who were confident of being liked would be less likely to choose to interact with similar others than subjects who did not expect to be liked. This prediction was confirmed: indeed subjects who had been assured that they would be liked preferred dissimilar others to similar ones, whereas subjects who expected not to be liked preferred similar others. In this same experiment, some subjects were instructed to interact with others who would like them. Such subjects tended to interact with similar others.

These results therefore raise the possibility that the relation between attitudinal similarity and liking in the bogus stranger experiments is not due to similarity enhancing attractiveness directly, but to its affecting beliefs about the probability of being liked. In those experiments almost the only thing the subject knows about the bogus stranger is the extent to which he answers a set of questions similarly to himself. If the answers are similar, this may lead the subject to believe that the stranger would like him, and thus predispose the subject to like the stranger. It is in fact found that if the subject is also given knowledge of whether the (bogus) stranger does or does not like him the effect of attitude similarity versus dissimilarity on attraction is either absent (Aronson & Worchel, 1966) or much smaller than that of like versus dislike (Byrne & Griffitt, 1966; Condon & Crano, 1988). Such experiments suggest that consensual validation is inadequate to explain the attractiveness of similarity. Positive or negative evaluations have an even greater effect on attraction than does similarity or dissimilarity of attitudes on impersonal topics.

Similarity and Role Satisfaction.   In the later stages of courtship, individuals assess each other for compatibility on a wide variety of dimensions. Murstein (1971c) has suggested that the extent to which people will find role satisfaction with partners perceived overall as similar to themselves, or with individuals they see as different, will depend on individual personality characteristics. The argument depends on the view that the partner chosen is likely to be perceived as similar both to the chooser's ideal partner and to his or her ideal self. However individuals differ in the extent to which they are satisfied with themselves. An individual who is satisfied with himself (i.e. where there is a close correlation between his perception of himself and that of his ideal self) is likely to choose someone like himself, but one who is dissatisfied with himself will choose someone close to his ideal self and ideal partner, who will therefore be unlike himself.

Murstein therefore asked each member of 99 university dating couples to complete a modified version of the Edwards Personal Preference Schedule on behalf of his or her self, ideal self, fiancé(e) and ideal partner. The results showed that the subjects with high self-acceptance chose partners perceived as more like themselves than did those with low self-acceptance.

In a related study, Bailey, Finney, and Bailey (1974) predicted that individuals who thought well of themselves would select friends similar in intelligence to themselves, whereas individuals not satisfied with their own intelligence would select a partner complementary to themselves. However the data did not support the attractiveness of similarity in either case. The authors explain their findings as follows. For those with high self-acceptance there was no relation between their actual ability and their perception of their own intelligence. Therefore, it is suggested, they selected a friend less bright than themselves to maintain their own unrealistic view of themselves. The low self-acceptance subjects were more realistic in their self-estimates, but tended to choose friends nearer to their ideal—perhaps in order vicariously to fulfil that ideal—or perhaps so that they could bask in reflected glory (see pp.140–141 and Tesser, 1988).

Similarity per se versus Establishment of Positive Beliefs.   The immediately preceding hypotheses have involved two rather different views. One is that perceived similarity of a stranger produces an affective response more or less directly, the other that perceived similarity produces positive beliefs about the likelihood of being liked or of finding role satisfaction. Byrne, though suggesting a relatively direct effect via "consensual validation", has been careful to emphasise that, while experiments on interpersonal attraction can often be described in simple stimulus–response terms, cognitive intermediaries must be involved. "Human beings ... are actively engaged in remembering, informing, expecting, inducing and deducing even in the limiting confines of an experimental situation" (Byrne, 1971, p.255).

In practice the bogus stranger situation by its very nature minimises any attraction arising from possible beliefs about future interaction. This was highlighted in an experiment designed to test the commonsense prediction that agreement or disagreement on sexual matters should be influenced by the sexual identities of the individuals concerned. With the prediction that similarity vs. dissimilarity of sexually relevant attitudes would have a greater effect on attraction towards someone of the opposite sex than to someone of the same sex, subjects were given sexual and achievement items from the Personal Preference Schedule. Although subjects were more attracted to bogus strangers who gave responses similar to their own, there was no confirmation of the initial prediction. Byrne et al. (1974a) suggest that differential attraction to a member of the opposite sex as a result of agreement on sexual issues would be found only in a situation in which further interaction was anticipated. Consensual validation can be provided by a member of either sex in the absence of further interaction, but similarity would be important in facilitating the subject's goals only if the stranger were of the opposite sex and future interactions were anticipated.

Thus Byrne and Clore argue that similarity can augment attraction by producing consensual validation, but in addition acknowledge the possibility that both similarity and dissimilarity can affect attraction by inducing beliefs about future rewards. Ajzen takes a more extreme view— namely that there is no need to suppose that similarity is attractive *per se*, for it is so only when it leads to the establishment of positive beliefs about the other person (Ajzen, 1974, 1977). This view is based on the supposition that information is actively processed, some items being accepted and others rejected, and that the whole is evaluated according to the past experience of the subject. It is then argued that, if attribute desirability and attribute similarity are separated, similarity may have little effect on attraction—a view which received experimental support (Ajzen, 1977).

There is in fact considerable evidence that similarity is often important in so far as it indicates that the other person is likely to provide benefits (see also Coombs, 1966; Johnson & Johnson, 1972). Furthermore the evidence that the effectiveness of similarity is related to a desire to be liked (see earlier; also some support in Layton & Insko, 1974), or as promising role satisfaction, can be seen as concerning special cases of perceived similarity inducing positive beliefs. Ajzen (1977) cites a number of studies showing how somewhat contradictory data on the effects of similarity can be reconciled on the view that similarity is attractive when it leads to the formation of positive beliefs.

On this view, then, the importance to an individual of the perceived similarity of a real or bogus stranger lies in the beliefs engendered. In the case of attitude similarity, this could be important because it validates the individual's view of the world and enables him to deal with it more competently (Byrne & Clore, 1967). But similarity in attitudes or in other characteristics is important primarily because of concomitant predictions about future benefits—for instance, similarities in interests or outlooks and lack of friction from gross disagreements (see also Lott & Lott, 1974).

Similarities might predict desirable qualities of interaction, greater potential for meshing, or similar viewpoints on how much meshing matters. More importantly, similarity may predict the possibility of elaborating a common meaning system.

Is Similarity Always Attractive?

Although similarity has obvious advantages as a basis for attraction and for relationships, the attractiveness of similarity is not ubiquitous. For example, a later replication of Newcomb's field study of students gave only weak support for a role of attitude similarity, except where attitudes to self were considered (Curry & Emerson, 1970). Izard (1960) gave a personal preference schedule to an entire freshman class. Six months later subjects were asked to name the three individuals they liked most and least in their class. The personality profiles were similar for subjects and their friends, but not for subjects and those they liked least. So far so good, and the study was later replicated. But a later study with college seniors did not show any relationship between similarity and attraction. Izard speculated that similarity in one's friends might become less important with maturity.

Again, Griffitt and Veitch (1974) assessed attitude similarity by a questionnaire method, and friendship choices, amongst men living together in a crowded shelter for 10 days. Although attitude similarity was significantly greater amongst those who became friends than amongst those who did not, the difference was not very great, amounting to agreement on about 4% of the attitude items. Thus even if attitude similarity was a factor in friendship choice, it does not seem to have been a very important one.

Indeed, in some circumstances dissimilarity may be attractive. McCarthy and Duck (1976) suggested that once two individuals had established a relationship on the basis of a degree of similarity, moderate disagreement might be attractive. This prediction was confirmed with a modification of the bogus stranger technique for an early-to-middle phase of friendship development, but not later. Other studies showing that, if an individual knows that she/he will be liked by another, there may be a preference for dissimilarity have been cited by Aron and Aron (1996). They regard such data as evidence for their self-expansion model (p.30), a dissimilar other providing opportunity for expansion of the self by incorporation of the other.

Similarity can also provoke dislike—a finding not easy to accommodate on anything but an information processing approach. For instance, the perceived similarity of another may reduce one's own feeling of being special. Paradoxically, interaction with someone different from oneself can be important just because it provides evidence for the differentiation of the individual and confirms his personal integrity: perhaps such an effect can occur only in a relationship that is already close and positive.

These diverse findings are not irreconcilable. Similarity may be important for providing consensual validation and also, perhaps later, because it engenders positive beliefs. Some similar attitudes may augur well for the future of a relationship, but others may be irrelevant, and in other areas differences may be preferred. And as a relationship progresses, the balance between similarity and difference may change.

Thus in real-life relationships the effects of similarities and differences are closely interwoven. A philosopher may be attracted to other philosophers, but bored by those who think exactly as he does and excited where a limited difference of opinion bodes fruitful and enjoyable debate (see also Campbell & Tesser, 1985).

SUMMARY

1. In reciprocal interactions, the partners show similar behaviour directed towards each other, while in complementary interactions the behaviour of each differs from, but complements, that of the other.
2. Friendly and hostile behaviour by one interactant tend to elicit similar behaviour from the other: dominance and submissive behaviour tend to elicit a complementary response.
3. There is considerable evidence that similarity between the partners in a variety of characteristics is associated with mutual attraction and/or relationship stability.
4. The bogus stranger technique for demonstrating a relation between attitude similarity and attraction, and the repertory grid technique for assessing how individuals construe the world, are described.
5. There are a variety of reasons why similarity might lead to attraction, and why the partners in a relationship might be similar. In general, similarity may be attractive because it provides consensual validation, or because it bodes well for future interaction.
6. A degree of dissimilarity may also be attractive.

9 Similarity versus Difference: Difference/Complementarity

COMPLEMENTARITY IN CLOSE RELATIONSHIPS

While similarity in *attitudes* or *personality* is usually positively related to attraction or relationship stability, it has also been suggested that people are attracted to those with *needs complementary* to their own. The very fact that most people prefer to live with someone of the opposite sex shows that complementarity over some issues is important though, as we shall see, attempts to generalise about patterns of complementarity in other characteristics are fraught with difficulties.

Clinically, the importance of need complementarity has long been apparent, and we shall return to more evidence on that issue later. Winch (1958, 1967) attempted to test the importance of complementarity in marriage. He focused on 12 "needs"—abasement, achievement, approach, autonomy, deference, dominance, hostility, nurturance, recognition, status aspiration, status striving, and succorance, and the personality traits of anxiety, emotionality, and vicariousness. A number of young married couples matched for their general life circumstances were studied, their needs being assessed by interview and questionnaire techniques, and by a Thematic Apperception Test.

Winch looked for complementarity of two sorts. On the one hand, two individuals could have needs similar in kind but yet complement each other because their needs differed in intensity. For instance one might be high on a need for dominance and the other low. The Parsons and Bales (1955) model of marriage fits this type, with the husband primarily instrumental in the extra-familial world and secondarily expressive, and the wife the reverse. On the other hand, needs could be similar in intensity but different in kind. An individual with a high need for abasement might complement one with a high need for dominance.

Winch claimed that couples tended to have needs that complemented each other's in a higher proportion of cases than would be expected with randomly matched couples. Using a variety of data reduction techniques, he suggested that most of the marriages in his study fell into four groups distinguishable along the dimensions of dominance/submissiveness and nurturance/receptivity.

A few later studies have claimed to produce evidence that complementarity is important in the initiation or maintenance of other relationships. For instance schoolboys (but not girls) were found to choose friends who were complementary in a variety of ways as assessed by the Rorschach test and other techniques (Hilkevitch, 1960). Again, Stewart and Rubin (1976) cite evidence showing that power-motivated men tended to seek alliances with weaker subordinates, and to have wives who were dependent and submissive (see also Wagner, 1975).

But Winch's analysis has been sharply criticised on methodological grounds by Tharp (1963a, b), and later studies of the part played by complementarity in friendship and marriage have produced conflicting results. Many indicate that complementarity plays no, or at most a minor, part (e.g. Izard, 1960; Meyer & Pepper, 1977; Murstein, 1961; Seyfried, 1977). Winch (1967), in accepting some of these criticisms, argued that complementary needs must be compatible with group norms. For instance, given societal values, a passive husband/domineering wife relationship is likely to be less satisfactory than the reverse. But in general, while the concept of need complementarity makes intuitive sense, studies attempting to show that complementarity across the board is important have not been successful.

For example, let us consider the issue of masculinity/femininity. Since the dimensions of dominance–submissiveness and nurturance–receptivity are closely related to stereotypic sex-role behaviour, it was proposed that complementarity along the dimension of masculinity versus femininity might be conducive to marital happiness. Individuals high on self-reported masculinity are competent with instrumental behaviours, usually less good at initiating interactions and less ready to discuss negative thoughts and feelings, while those high on femininity readily engage in intimate disclosures and are emotionally supportive in close relationships (Ickes, 1985; Lamke et al., 1994). Early studies, in which masculinity and femininity were seen as opposite poles of a single continuum, seemed to confirm the beneficial influence of complementarity.

However more recent work suggests that masculinity and femininity should be seen as independent dimensions (Bem, 1975, 1981a, b; Spence,

Helmreich, & Stapp, 1975). Spence et al. divided individuals into four gender role categories—Masculine (above the masculinity and below the femininity median), Feminine (above the femininity and below the masculinity median), Androgynous (above both), and Undifferentiated (below both). Using this approach, Kurdek and Schmitt (1986a) found that masculine men tended to pair with feminine or undifferentiated women, and androgynous individuals tended to pair together. However complementary partner choice was not necessarily related to long-term satisfaction. Couples in which one or both partners were androgynous or feminine reported the highest relationship quality, those in which one partner was undifferentiated or masculine the least.

In another study Antill (1983) found that the happiness of married couples (assessed by the Spanier Dyadic Adjustment Scale, which has four scales assessing dyadic consensus, satisfaction, cohesion, and emotional expression) was greatest in couples where both partners were high on femininity: androgyny contributed only because androgynous individuals were high on femininity. Background data in this study permitted some speculation about the dynamics involved. The wife's femininity seemed to be especially important early in marriage, perhaps because such wives fill a traditional role. Husbands' femininity became important later, perhaps when children demanded a nurturant role from both parents. Interestingly, the happiness of each spouse was related more closely to his/her assessment of the partner's femininity than to the partner's own assessment of his/her own femininity (see p.252).

Of course such data do not mean that complementarity never contributes positively to a relationship. We have seen that each partner is likely to have many needs, some demanding reciprocity and others complementarity of different sorts. A husband may take the lead in some contexts, and the wife in others (e.g. Seyfried, 1977). And we have also seen that complementarity may become more important later in some relationships, as cooperation over tasks becomes more necessary (Murstein, 1987). Spouses define their relative positions on dominance, reaching consensus about control in the several areas of married life (Rogers & Farace, 1975). Canary and Sereno (cited Canary & Cupach, 1988) found that both intimacy (in the sense of knowledge of the other) and consensus were related to how the partners perceived their interactions and correlated highly with both satisfaction and a measure of communication patterns associated with relationship growth.

A further issue arises from the fact (already noted) that needs as assessed in a laboratory or clinical setting may be a poor guide to need satisfaction in a real-life relationship. Some needs can be satisfied outside the relationship (Levinger, 1964), and need gratification can be delayed so that a relationship may work because the partners' apparently incompatible needs are satisfied at different times. The reconciliation of diverse needs may be facilitated by the development of norms which regulate the synchronisation of activities, permit turn-taking, reduce differences of opinion, and so on (Thibaut & Kelley, 1959).

In any case, compatibility does not involve only the potential for appropriate reciprocity or complementarity in particular types of behaviour. For one thing, compatibility over who initiates change in activity is also necessary. Two people who both like to be initiators are likely to be at odds. And if we are really to understand a relationship, we must ask not only "Who takes the decisions in this context and in that?" but also "Who decides who should take the decisions?" and even perhaps "Who decides who decides who should take the decisions?" (see pp.147–149).

Yet another possibility was suggested by Winch (1958) and also by Cattell and Nesselroade (1967)—that individuals may be attracted to others who possess characteristics that they lack themselves (see also Aron & Aron, 1996). This need-completion view differs from need complementarity in that emphasis is laid not on interaction between subject and potential friend, but on psychological completion. Although these investigators found little evidence for their hypothesis, there are data showing that individuals often perceive their friends as having traits that they admire but lack themselves (Thompson and Nishimura, 1952; see also Bailey et al., 1974).

A more subtle approach to this issue is due to Tesser (1986, 1988; Campbell & Tesser, 1985; Tesser, Millar, & Moore, 1988). He assumes that people are motivated to maintain positive self-evaluations. (Self-evaluation is seen as a momentary state of self-regard, not to be confused with self-esteem, which is a relatively stable variable defining differences between individuals. Self-evaluation concerns performance rather than the attitudes or aspects of personality considered so far.) Tesser suggests that a positive self-evaluation can be achieved both by basking in the reflected glory of others (reflection) and by evaluating oneself against another (comparison). Three factors affect the occurrence of reflection or comparison—the relevance of an activity to one's own self-definition, the relative standards of performance of self and other on that activity, and the closeness of the relationship. Closeness to the partner predicts the occurrence of both reflection and comparison. If the activity is not self-relevant, one is likely to be attracted to someone who is expert in it, thereby basking in reflected glory. But if it is self-relevant, one may be attracted to someone who does less well than or equally to oneself, but not to someone who is much better unless the other's superiority is acknowledged and accepted by both. Evidence in support of this self-evaluation maintenance model has come from a number of studies: for instance when a person is outperformed by another in a self-relevant activity, he or she will increase the physical distance between self and other, and see the other as less similar to self (e.g. Tesser, Millar, & Moore, 1988).

In a relationship two people are involved, each wanting to maintain his or her self-evaluation. There is no problem if the domains in which each performs well are high in relevance to the self but not to the other. However, as we have seen, similarity often attracts, so this is often not the case. Pilkington, Tesser and Stephens (1991) therefore propose that, in a successful romantic relationship, partners' performances should complement each other so that each can obtain satisfaction from his or her own success and reflected glory from the partner's. Support for this view was obtained in a study in which the importance of 68 performance areas or activities to students involved in romantic relationships were assessed. The students reported on the self-relevance of the activities to themselves and to their partners, and on whether they were better than the partner in each area or vice versa. Where relevance to themselves was high, respondents saw themselves as out-performing their partners on more activities than they saw their partners out-performing them, and vice versa. Thus individuals benefited in comparison with the partner by high performance on activities that were highly self-relevant, and obtained reflection benefits in activities that were not. It also appeared that romantic partners considered their own and their partners' needs in a complementary fashion: where relevance was high for one partner and low for the other, the former was reported as being superior.

In some relationships it may be necessary to distinguish between attraction for instrumental reasons (i.e. to achieve a certain goal) and emotional attraction (where interaction itself is the goal). School children were tested (in a factorial design) on a task of high relevance (intelligence test) or low relevance (literature knowledge). The results indicated that instrumental attraction was higher to a better performing other than to a similarly performing one, especially under conditions of high relevance, whereas emotional attraction was higher to a similarly performing other than to a better performing one, regardless of relevance. Yinon, Bizman, & Yagil (1989) suggest that a better performing other induces ambivalence—there might be benefits in interacting (e.g. doing homework together) and there might be threats to one's self-esteem. They therefore argue that it is necessary to ask not in general whether individuals tend to interact with a better or with a similar other, but what kind of interaction they would like to have with a better as compared with a similar other.

In view of such considerations, it is clear that we should not expect to understand most relationships in terms of simple patterns of reciprocity and complementarity. However, studies designed with due respect for the complexities of real-life relationships could give hope for progress.

For example, Schutz (1960) postulated three types of "compatibility"—originator compatibility, or agreement on who should initiate interactions;

interchange compatibility, or agreement over how much interaction should occur; and "reciprocal" compatibility, or compatibility (reciprocal or complementary in the present terminology) between the types of behaviour the partners like to show. Schutz further suggested that these types of compatibility could be found in three categories of need—need for inclusion (i.e. to interact and associate with others), for control, and for affection. He investigated the relation between the three types of compatibility and the three needs in a group of students. The students answered questionnaires measuring their needs within these three categories, and also answered a sociometric questionnaire indicating which three others they would select as room-mates and which three they would select as travelling companions on a long car journey. The nature of compatibility differed between the two role relationships: room-mates showed all three types of compatibility at more than chance level, but travelling companions only reciprocal and originator compatibility. Furthermore, for room-mates affection was most important, whilst control was most important for travelling companions. Although the legitimacy of Schutz's three categories of need, and thus his detailed conclusions, may be questioned, his general conclusion that different types of role relationships require different types of compatibility is in keeping with common sense (see also Rychlak, 1965). Kerckhoff and Davis (1962) found complementarity on the Schutz scales amongst dating couples to be predictive of permanency in the relationship.

Another study of interest here was designed to assess the effects of personality differences between the individuals concerned (Hendrick & Brown, 1971). Subjects were assessed for introversion–extroversion on the Maudsley Personality Inventory. They were then presented with the answers to the questionnaire of two (bogus) strangers, one answered in a predominantly extroverted and the other in a predominantly introverted way. The subjects were then asked how they thought they would get on with these people in a variety of contexts. The contexts were chosen to cover a number of different role relationships. Extroverts rated the extrovert higher as reliable friend, partygoer, and leader, but had no preference between extrovert and introvert in the role of honest and ethical person. Introverts, however, preferred the extrovert as a fellow partygoer, and as a leader, but the introvert as a reliable friend and as an honest and ethical person. Thus whether or not the subjects preferred a stranger similar to or unlike themselves on this dimension depended on their own personality and on the context in which they expected to interact with him.

With the current emphasis on cognitive processes, such experimental studies have tended to become unfashionable among research workers, but they can be seen as indicating limits within which cognitive and emotional compatibility must be sought. They demonstrate that research that attempts to take note of the complexity of real-life relationships, aimed at finding out what is important to whom and when, can be worthwhile.

Weiss (1974) has adopted a rather different approach. Impressed by the loneliness of individuals who were parents without partners, and by the loneliness of a rather different sort experienced by married couples living in a strange neighbourhood, Weiss used his clinical experience to draw up a list of "provisions" or needs which are normally met in relationships with others. His list was:

1. Attachment, providing a sense of security and place.
2. Social integration and friendship, providing shared concerns.
3. Opportunity for nurturance, as when taking care of a child provides a sense of being needed.
4. Reassurance of worth, provided by relationships that attest to a person's competence.
5. A sense of reliable alliance, usually provided by kin, and involving a sense of dependable assistance if needed.
6. Obtaining of guidance, important to individuals in stressful situations.

Although Weiss (1975, p.25) regarded his list as "a framework for thinking, lightly filled in with observations and conjecture" he suggested that a satisfactory life organisation would make available a set of relationships that would furnish all these provisions. He pointed out that these different provisions may be incompatible to some degree within any one relationship—the assumptions of friendship, for example, may be incompatible with the provision of opportunity for nurturance.

SOME ASPECTS OF SOCIAL SUPPORT

Weiss's work raises the general issue of social support, the subject of an extensive literature. The concept of "Social support" can be used as a unifying concept appropriate for a wide range of relationships, and be seen as an essential component in their initiation, maintenance, and dissolution (Newcomb, 1990). How much such a global concept aids understanding of the dynamics of relationships, and how much it hinders understanding of the individual case, must be seen as open issues. Certainly, in assessing the amount of support a needy person receives it is important to distinguish between individuals to whom the potential recipient merely feels attached and those who actually provide support, and between support given out of duty, and that given when the support-giver feels real empathy for the recipient (Davis & Kraus, 1991). Some earlier studies of the effectiveness of social support failed to find a relation to psychiatric state or sense of well-being because the instruments used to assess the support received did not discriminate between feelings of attachment and real support received. O'Connor and Brown (1984) found a relation of positive self-evaluation and psychiatric state to support received, but not to felt attachment. Very close relationships, those the respondent felt to be very important and could not imagine being without, did not always yield practical help.

Studies of social support illustrate a number of issues of general importance for complementary interactions. For example, success depends on both parties: individuals who are offered help do not necessarily accept it, but may reject or devalue it. One explanation is that receiving help from another may be damaging to the recipient's self-esteem. Fisher, Nadler, and Whitaker-Alagna (1982) have suggested that if the proffered aid is perceived as more threatening than supportive by the intended recipient, the latter may respond defensively, showing negative affect, refusal, or grudging acceptance, and negative evaluations of the helper. Whether defensiveness is shown may depend on the nature of and need for the help offered, the nature of the relationship between helper and recipient, and so on. Thus, in a study of undergraduate siblings defensiveness was only moderate, perhaps because helping is a norm in the sibling relationship. When it occurred, however, it was correlated with perceived conflict in the relationship, dominance relative to the sibling, low self-esteem, self-esteem that was high relative to the sibling, and low feelings of entitlement. The authors suggest that the consequences of receiving aid on feelings of self-worth mediate responses to proffered help.

Another case is provided by the giving of advice in supportive relationships. It is tempting, when trying to help someone in trouble, to offer advice prematurely, because that satisfies one's own need to help. However, the troubled individual may not want to accept the advice: thus bereaved individuals may prefer companionship and sympathy. Or acceptance of an outsider's advice may force an individual to change his/her interpretation of the causes of a difficult situation, perhaps shouldering blame. And the acceptance of advice may involve acknowledging the superior status of the donor. Tripathi, Caplan, and Naida (1986) showed that the freedom to reject advice could facilitate the acceptance of other forms of social support and have beneficial effects on the relationship. This was especially the case in obligatory (e.g. parent–adolescent) relationships, where social support alleviated strain better when the child was free to reject the parental advice. In voluntary (e.g. friendship) relationships, high acceptance of advice implies trust, and high acceptance of advice coupled with high levels of social support is thus efficacious in alleviating strain.

A related issue is that the precise form of support offered may be critical. Cancer patients found expressions of concern, love, and understanding helpful, but attempts to minimise or to maximise the problem, or to be overly protective, unhelpful (Lehman & Hemphill, 1990; see also Dakof &

Taylor, 1990). More generally, the importance of the personal meaning attached to offers of support must be emphasised. Sarason, Pierce, and Sarason (1990) point out that "Would you like to see a movie tonight" might be a request for support, an offer of support, or neutral.

In any case, we have seen that complementary interactions within a relationship must not be considered in isolation from other aspects of the relationship in which they are embedded, as well as the emotions and cognitions of those involved. Albrecht and Halsey (1992) studied the relationships between staff nurses and their managers. Those relationships in which the nurses reported receiving high levels of support and the managers reported giving such support were characterised by strong mutual trust, certainty about each other and the nature of the relation-ship, and discussion about innovations and new ideas. In such cases the complementary roles of the participants must therefore not be considered in isolation, but in the context of other aspects of their relationship, with-out presuppositions as to what is primary.

In general, it has been suggested that the factors affecting the probabil-ity of effective support can be divided into four categories (Dunkel-Schetter & Skokan, 1990; Sarason, Pierce, & Sarason, 1990):

(a) *Stress factors*, both as objectively present and as seen by both potential recipient and potential donors of support. Recipient and donor may not see the situation similarly, so that proffered help may be un-welcome or seen as inappropriate, or desired help may be denied. And the readiness of a potential donor to provide help may be affected by the extent to which he or she is affected by the stressor, either directly or indirectly as a consequence of helping.

(b) *Recipient factors*. Support may be affected by the way the recipient (and donor) perceive themselves, others, and personal relationships. For the recipient, at least three issues are important:

   (i) The recipient's level of distress—though under some circumstances severe distress can elicit negative reactions in a potential donor and reduction in support.
   (ii) Coping activities by the recipient. Individuals who send out appropriate signals or seek appropriate support are more likely to receive it.
   (iii) The characteristics of the recipient: for instance, potential recipients with high self-esteem are more likely to receive support.

Sarason et al., referring to Bowlby's (1980) "working models"—cognitive representations of the self, or others and of relationships, which play a role in expectations of and responses to others (see pp.31–32)—postulate a personal characteristic, termed "the sense of support", which plays an important role in the attributions that people make about others and about the nature of supportive relationships. For instance, they found that a person's expectations about the supportiveness of others' social networks were related to their attributions about the supportiveness of their own network. In keeping with Bowlby's approach, they postulate also a "sense of acceptance", involving beliefs that others love us and accept us for what we are. When others provide us with support, we conclude that we must have some commendable attributes. (Tolsdorf, 1976, uses a somewhat similar concept termed "network orientation".) The sense of acceptance is thus part of a constellation that includes a positive self-image, a favourable view of social relationships, and an expectation that others value us. The sense of support and the sense of acceptance may affect the readiness to give support, readiness to receive support, and the way in which attempts by others to provide support are interpreted. (We may note here that Lefcourt, Martin, and Saleh, 1984, showed that the effects of social support were greater for individuals with a high internal locus of control— that is those who felt in control of their own lives.)

(c) *Donor factors.* A key issue here may be the feeling of empathy for the potential recipient. This is likely to be decreased if blame is attributed to the recipient, but increased if the potential donor feels responsible. A focus of attention on the potential recipient, likely to be increased by appropriate appeals for support, is also important. Of course many other factors may also operate, including the perceived cost to the donor.

(d) *Relationship factors.* The relationship between donor and recipient, and the network of relationships of which they form part, may all influence the support given and received. Intimacy, satisfaction, norms of social responsibility, and reciprocity may all play a role. Social support in the context of a conflictual relationship may increase stress for both parties, creating a feeling of inappropriate indebtedness in the recipient, and guilt and ambivalence in the donor. The recipient may perceive the donor as having evil intentions, or an obligation to restore equity. Spousal support may be more effective when it is invisible, perhaps because the recipient's need for help is not then highlighted (Reis & Knee, 1996). Or the donor may see the recipient as unaccepting of advice and uncompliant. Barrera and Baca (1990) found that both conflict with the donor and orientation towards the social network influence satisfaction with the support.

As discussed in Chapter 19, individuals prefer exchanges in which they neither provide more than they receive, nor receive more than they provide. In the short term, conflict may make the recipient of support feel obliged to restore equity (see p.345) by undervaluing the support given. In the longer term, Antonucci, Fuhrer, and Jackson (1990) suggest that individuals keep account of support received and given with a long time perspective, so that it is possible to give help in the expectation of being a recipient in the future, or to be a persistent recipient (as in old age) but able to maintain self-respect by virtue of memories of being a donor in the past. These authors found cultural differences in the perception of reciprocity amongst elderly recipients of support.

COMPLEXITY IN THE BALANCE BETWEEN RECIPROCITY AND COMPLEMENTARITY

Thus we must expect close relationships, and especially marital relationships, to be built upon complex patterns of needs in the two partners, needs which affect each other and are satisfied in varying ways in reciprocal and complementary interactions inside and outside the relationship. What is important is not reciprocity or complementarity over large areas of the relationship, but compatibility, involving either reciprocity or complementarity, appropriate in nature and direction, in each content area within the relationship (e.g. Murstein, 1967a; review Seyfried, 1977). Furthermore what is important may change as a relationship develops (Chapters 25–28).

Having recognised the possible complexity of patterns of reciprocity and complementarity, it is important also to remember that there are likely to be limits on the complexity that exists in any one case. Just because each interaction within a relationship affects and is affected by others, complementarity along such dimensions as dominance/subordinance or nurturance/succorance has some tendency to be similar in the different types of interaction of a relationship. As we have seen, dominance/subordinance relations are not confined to the barrack square or the office, but obtrude in interactions off-duty or after hours. Similar processes limit the complexity of the pattern of dominance/subordinance even in close personal relationships. And in so far as each participant has traits or is believed to have traits consistent from one behavioural context to another, and the other accommodates him or herself to them, complementarity is likely to have some degree of consistency across contexts.

We may consider a case in which the role of complementarity has been assessed in a clinical sample. Kreitman and his colleagues (Collins et al., 1971) investigated the relative roles of 120 married couples—60 in which the husbands were neurotic patients and 60 controls. They concentrated on certain family functions—child-rearing, choice of dwelling, financial arrangements, maintenance of social relationships, holidays, and entertainments. In studying the roles of husband and wife in these areas they distinguished three levels of activity—executive (what is actually done), executive decision-making (deciding what is to be done), and how responsibility for executive decisions in each area is determined. For example, a husband might actually make the holiday booking, the wife might decide where they should go, and the husband insist that she should make the decision and accept responsibility for it. In this study attention was concentrated on executive decision-making. By an interview technique each area was scored in terms of eight categories: five of these referred to degrees of husband or wife domination (the mid-point here being joint decisions), one was used for where husband and wife were divided and acted in opposition, one for "not applicable", and another for not known cases.

The data prompted a division of marriage into those where one partner generally dominated the other, and those in which neither dominated. The latter were split into those where each partner collaborated cooperatively (cooperative marriages) and those where each partner was more or less equally active, but distinct areas were demarcated for each spouse (segregated marriages). The distribution of the marital types is shown in Table 9.1.

It will be seen that, although the differences were not large, the patient–spouse marriages tended to show more husband-dominated and segregated marriages than the controls, and fewer cooperative marriages. Joint decision-making was less common, the more severe the husband's pathology. The authors raise two interesting possibilities. One is that the role pattern of the wife in the neurotic marriage may not be of her own making, and may therefore be conducive to the increasing neurosis that is sometimes seen in the wives of neurotics. The other is that the wives' role

TABLE 9.1
Distribution of Decision-making Patterns in Patient and Control Couples

	Dominated by		Non-dominated	
	Husband	Wife	Cooperative	Segregated
Patients	14	10	16	20
Controls	6	14	29	11

The couples were divided into those in which executive decision-making was dominated by one or other partner, and those in which it was not. The latter were divided into those in which decisions were taken predominantly cooperatively, and those in which they were divided between spouses according to content area (segregated). Husband and wife dominated marriages were defined differently because the areas chosen for examination tend to reflect the wife's activity more than the husband's. (Modified from Collins et al., 1971, by permission of the Royal College of Psychiatry.)

patterns could serve as a protective device for the wives: perhaps with an irritable and self-absorbed husband it is actually easier for the wife to assume certain roles herself and leave others to the husband, rather than live in continuous strife.

ACCEPTANCE OF THE PATTERN OF COMPLEMENTARITY BY THE PARTNERS

Kreitman's study raises another important point. It is not only the pattern of reciprocity vs. complementarity within a relationship that is important, but the extent to which both partners recognise the pattern for what it is and accept it. Dominance between married couples is often measured by questionnaires given to both participants. Thus in Ryle's (1966) Marital Patterns Test members of couples are each asked questions of the type "I cannot win an argument with her" and "She cannot win an argument with me", being required to answer "True", or "Untrue", or "Uncertain". On its own such a test provides a measure of how each participant sees this aspect of the relationship, and thus how far they agree, but fails to show how far their pictures resemble reality, or of how far they accept their perception of the relationship. We shall return to this issue in Chapters 13 and 14.

In ordinary life, lack of acceptance of the pattern of reciprocity versus complementarity may become evident by disqualificatory replies by one partner to the meta-communicational aspects of the other's communications (see p.82). A related issue arises from Berne's (1967) distinction between three "ego states"—Parent, Adult, and Child. These are seen by Berne as coherent sets of feelings, accompanied by appropriate behaviour, potentially present in all individuals. Normally only one takes charge. The ego state that is dominant can be inferred from the current behaviour and feelings, and the terms are self-explanatory. Thus the Child is innocent, spontaneous, and fun-loving; the Adult mature and orientated towards reality; and the Parent authoritative. The Parent state may be either directly active, when the person responds as his own parent did, or indirectly active, when the response is of the type the person's parent would have wanted. Similarly the Child may behave as he would have done under parental influence—for instance precociously or compliantly; or the Child may involve a spontaneous expression, for instance of rebellion and creativity.

Berne suggests the transactions between two individuals can be analysed according to the ego states involved at the time of the interchange, though these may change from moment to moment. The nature of interactions depends on which ego state of the initiator addressed which ego state of the respondent, and which replied. For instance, if a patient asks for a glass of water, and the nurse brings it, the Child of the initiator has addressed the Parent of the respondent, and the Parent of the respondent has replied. Or if a man says to his friend "It is a nice day", and the friend replies "Yes it is, I was thinking of cutting the lawn", the transaction is Adult to Adult with Adult replying. Berne classifies such transactions, in which the ego state of the respondent addressed by the initiator is the ego state that replies to the initiator, and where that reply goes to the ego state of the initiator that addressed it, as "complementary".[1] In "complementary" transactions each partner is attempting to cooperate with the other, and the interchange is likely to continue. However the respondent may reply with an ego state different from that addressed, and/or reply to an ego state different from that which initiated the interchange. The remark "Where are my cufflinks?" is directed from Adult to Adult, but the reply "You always blame me for everything" is a Child to Parent reply. Such transactions Berne describes as "crossed". With crossed transactions, communication is likely to be broken off. The reply disqualifies the claim, latent in the initial remark, for a relationship of a particular type.

Berne introduces a further complication in describing the manner in which transactions can be conducted at two "levels" simultaneously—an overt social level and a covert psychological one. A salesman addressing a customer at an overt Adult–Adult level may be in reality appealing to the Child in him.

This transactional analysis is concerned in the first instance with the course of interactions, but Berne has applied it also to the course of long-term relationships. For instance he describes a married couple in which the husband was dominant and forbade the wife certain activities in which she was actually afraid to indulge. At the overt social level the husband's Parent was addressing the wife's Child, but at a covert psychological level the transaction was between the wife's Child and the husband's Child, the husband's dominance being a cover for his own insecurity. Berne describes this as a "game" and has developed a taxonomy of "Games people play".

This type of analysis could also be applied to the difficulties that some couples experience after the birth of their first child (see p.73). The wife may need the husband to drop the Adult–Adult role so that she can play Child to his Parent for a while: the husband, on the other hand, seeing the wife's solicitude directed towards the newborn, may play Child and hope for her to play Parent to him.

Berne's model of the three ego states is an "as if" model, which provides a convenient way of describing interactions and the rituals, games and so

---

[1] This terminology is of course different from that used elsewhere in this book. "Complementary" in Berne's sense has therefore been placed in quotation marks.

on built up from them. While his taxonomy of games is not to be taken too seriously, it provides a useful way for conceptualising the multiple levels at which relationships operate.

SUMMARY

1. Earlier claims that complementarity could form a basis for relationships were over-stated.
2. Masculinity/femininity can be seen as a form of complementarity which is a basis for many relationships. However satisfaction seems to be highest in couples in which both members are high in femininity.
3. Complementarity may be important in some aspects of a relationship but not in others. Some needs demand complementarity and others reciprocity.
4. Individuals may be attracted to others who lack characteristics that they lack themselves. Individuals are likely to be attracted to someone who is expert in an activity that is not relevant to them, thereby basking in reflected glory, and to someone who is equally or less expert than themselves in an activity that is self-relevant.
5. Compatibility is a more relevant consideration than complementarity.
6. Some studies on the conditions that facilitate the giving and receipt of social support are discussed.
7. Some complexities in the balance between reciprocity and complementarity are considered.

10 Conflict and Power: Conflict

NATURE AND ASSESSMENT

The Ubiquity of Conflict

Some degree of conflict is virtually inevitable in every relationship. It may be conspicuous, taking the form of rows or fights, but more usually it is so subtly interwoven with positive feelings and pleasurable interactions that it goes unnoticed. Indeed the defence mechanisms of the participants may ensure that they are unconscious of conflictual issues, and the retrospective accounts that people give of their relationships often focus on their positive sides, with past conflicts swept under the carpet. Nevertheless, conflict in close relationships may be important because the basic issue is often the nature of the relationship itself rather than the overt topic of disagreement.

This is not to paint a pessimistic picture of close relationships: in most cases conflicts are dealt with constructively and smoothly, and they may play only a minor role in the relationship as a whole. However McGonagle, Kessler, and Schilling (1992) found that unpleasant disagreements typically occurred once or twice a month in a community sample of close relationships. In another study, Straus and Sweet (1992) found that verbal or symbolic aggression (which included a spectrum from verbal abuse to threats of violence) had occurred within the last year in three-quarters of a representative sample involving 5232 American couples, the median incidence being 3 to 4. Its frequency decreased with age and with the number of children, but was greater in drug users. Burgess (1981) put the

153

frequency of arguments as high as once a day in unhappy marital partners, and weekly in happy ones. This chapter, therefore, is concerned with
why conflicts occur and how people deal with them (see Cahn, 1990, for
a review).

Conflict is used here for a whole spectrum of situations from that in
which the partners in a relationship merely have conflicting short- or long-
term goals, without the conflict actually surfacing, to argument and even
violence. Conflict may be difficult to distinguish from competition: for
instance, sibling rivalry may lead one child to strive to be seen by the
parents as better than its sibling in order to obtain rewards distributed by
the parents.

The majority of studies of conflict are concerned either with children in
families, marital partners, or students in dating relationships. Conflict in
childhood and adolescence is extensively discussed by Shantz and Hartup
(1992): this chapter is based primarily on studies concerned with the other
two groups.

Constructive and Destructive Conflict

Conflict is not necessarily a bad thing. It may be merely a symptom of a
change in the nature of the relationship, the most obvious example being
the relationships between adolescents and their parents. During adolescence
the relative roles of child and parent change, and the rules that govern the
relationship must be renegotiated. Basically, the issue is one of autonomy
and connectedness (see pp.157–158), but the move is towards a different
sort of connectedness and not a severance. During this period, there is
often a decrease in emotional closeness and warmth (Paikoff & Brooks-
Gunn, 1991), an increase in negative affect and an increase in conflict
(Flannery et al., 1993; Montemayor, 1983). The decrease in positive affect
is temporary, and usually increases again postpubertally (Papini, Datan, &
McCluskey-Fawcett, 1988).

But beyond that, conflict may be a central force in developmental
change, for good or ill. As Shantz and Hartup (1992, p.2) state: "No other
single phenomenon plays as broad and significant a role in human development as conflict is thought to. Many different functions—cognition, social
cognition, emotions, and social relations—are thought to be formed and/
or transformed by conflict." And in adult relationships, conflict can be
constructive, providing an impetus and a focus for sorting out problems
(Braiker & Kelley, 1979; Deutsch, 1969; Hicks & Platt, 1970). In a lovers'
quarrel, one partner may become more convinced of the other's commitment, and his/her own trust may be augmented. Conflict can pave the way
for discussion and understanding. Indeed some suggest that conflict is

necessary for real intimacy to be achieved. Gottman (1994, p.159) has gone so far as to write, "The most important advice I can give to men who want their marriages to work is to try not to avoid conflict", though not everyone would agree that this advice is ubiquitously applicable.

In role theory terms, the fit between the role identities (see pp.9–11) of two individuals is unlikely to be perfect: conflict is most likely to be constructive if the incompatible goals or views are relatively trivial, and involve details of the relationship rather than its central core; if both partners are committed to the relationship; if the issue is discussed openly; and if there is a norm of trust.

From another perspective, alienation from a close personal relationship may stem from dissatisfaction with one's own role identity, or with the role support one is given, or with the demands made on one for role support, any of which may well lead to a decrease in intimacy and a disruption of the relationship (M. McCall, 1970). Increasing intimacy requires adjustment of each individual's role identities—the further development of some and the suppression of others. Or, to put it in other terms, the definition of the relationship is bound to need adjustment by both parties. Or yet again, the narratives that both parties are constructing need to be brought into line.

Conflict arising from a real conflict of goals has been contrasted with "autistic" conflict—that is, conflict that has no objective basis in the situation, but stems from the internal states of the participants (Holmes & Miller, 1976). In practice, such a distinction is difficult to maintain. Real conflict may become partially autistic if one or other participant "goes too far" (i.e. disregards the societally imposed standards of behaviour which normally operate to keep conflict in check). Or a dispute involving a genuine conflict of interest may spread to areas of the relationship in which there are no conflicting goals, and the resulting "autistic" elements may then be seen by the participants as real. This is especially likely to occur if the primary issues in the conflict are intangible.

Perhaps the most potent factor in the escalation of conflict is distrust. Distrust may be, and often is, fostered by misperception of the partner, a failure to "read the other's mind" correctly. The perceived failure of one partner to justify the other's trust may lead to a sense of betrayal, with disastrous consequences for the relationship. Threat, distrust, and misperception represent three interrelated factors promoting the initiation and escalation of conflict (Holmes & Miller, 1976). Each partner is likely to attribute blame to the other.

Thus conflict can have positive or negative consequences for a relationship. Even the expression of anger at a partner's perceived neglect can lead either to reconciliation or to further alienation (Bowlby, 1973). Too often, however, there is a vicious circle: anger conceals a sense of shame produced by alienation, and the anger is expressed in a way that negates respect for the partner, leading to shame and anger in the latter and thus to escalation (Retzinger, 1995).

The Assessment of Conflict

Earlier experimental techniques used in laboratory or consulting room to assess conflict involved games often based on the Prisoner's Dilemma paradigm (see pp.339–340) (e.g. Apfelbaum, 1966; Deutsch & Krauss, 1965; Epstein & Santa-Barbara, 1975; Kelley & Stahelski; 1970a, b, c). However the extent to which the results of such tests will generalise to real-life situations is far from clear.

More valuable for research and clinical purposes have been techniques that involve simply getting couples to talk with each other about problems important to them. Given gentle handling, couples will talk naturally even in the presence of cameras and physiological recording devices (e.g. Gottman, 1979; Noller, 1984). Although such techniques appear simple, recording and interpretation of the data requires considerable sophistication. A disadvantage of such methods in some cases is that it overlooks the fact that in real life some couples do not necessarily agree on what they are quarrelling about. In a study of 98 dating couples Klein and Milardo (1993, p.61) found that partners' interpretations of a recent conflict were "so divergent that they seemed to reflect two entirely different realities."

Among other instruments commonly used are the Dyadic Adjustment Scale (Spanier, 1976), which assesses primarily marital satisfaction, cohesion, consensus, and affectional expression; and the Areas of Change Questionnaire (Weiss & Perry, 1979), which assesses desired changes in a marital partner. Many studies use subject reports—for instance daily telephone interviews (e.g. Christensen & Margolin 1988).

SOME SOURCES OF CONFLICT

Conflict may concern the immediate goals of the two partners. It is unlikely that the goals of any two people would always coincide so precisely that their behaviour meshed perfectly. Mismatch may be overt, but resolution is often reached within the heads of the participants as they reflect and consider the relationship in the intervals between interactions. Interests usually continue partially to overlap and partially to conflict, and although a *modus vivendi* is worked out, some conflict may persist. Total abrogation of own goals by one partner in favour of those of the other is unlikely to be a viable option because the latter is likely to feel over-benefitted and guilty (see pp.345–347). There is also a tendency to perceive the submitting partner as partially depersonalised, and becoming a non-person.

Surprisingly little attention has been paid to the immediate focus of conflicts, but Kurdek (1994) found that conflict issues in gay, lesbian, and heterosexual couples clustered into six groups—power (e.g. overly critical), social issues, personal flaws, distrust, intimacy (e.g. sex, affection), and personal distance (i.e. other commitments). While the overall frequency of conflict was negatively related to satisfaction, it was especially arguments over power and intimacy that were associated with low satisfaction, perhaps because these are areas in which the partners have a high degree of control over each other's outcomes. Frequent arguing over power was associated with a decrease in satisfaction a year later, but frequent arguing over intimacy was not. Kurdek emphasises that issues relevant to current functioning are not necessarily related to change.

While most conflicts seem to arise from incompatible short-term goals, many of these involve mutually incompatible long-term issues—for instance affection vs. instrumentality, expressiveness vs. protectiveness, hopes for the future vs. fear of rejection (e.g. Holmes & Rempel, 1989), ideal vs. real, and so on (Montgomery, 1993). Three such issues seem pre-eminent, and must be coped with not only during the growth of a relationship but throughout its course (Baxter, 1988, 1990):

(i) *Autonomy vs. Relatedness (Independence vs. Connectedness)*. Individuals have a need to feel that they have some control over their environment. If they lack that feeling, they may experience a feeling of helplessness, and eventually of depression (Seligman, 1975). If they do feel in control of what they are doing, they are likely to put in more effort and have a greater chance of success. The sense of control is influenced by experiences in early childhood: if parental responsiveness is inconsistent, the child is unable to develop stable expectations of control, but if it is sensitively contingent on the child's behaviour, the child acquires a sense of control over his environment (Bowlby, 1969/82). The amount of control an individual feels himself to exercise in his or her personal relationships may well vary from one relationship to another (Cook, 1993).

But the need for control over the environment implies a need to feel independent of the environment, without external constraints, autonomous. Autonomy involves a feeling of inner endorsement of one's actions, a sense that they emanate from oneself and are one's own. Thus intentional actions are not necessarily autonomous: the behaviour of someone who is desperately seeking approval or avoiding guilt is intentional but not autonomous (Deci & Ryan, 1987). It is also useful to distinguish between two meanings of autonomy—"reactive autonomy", the tendency to prefer to act independently, without being influenced by others, and "reflective autonomy", or the tendency to experience a sense of choice about one's behaviour. The former is associated with disagreeableness, poor social adjustment, and greater dependency, while reflective autonomy is related to openness and good social adjustment, and with more honest interaction and relationships. Thus Deci and Ryan (1987, p.1028) have reviewed some factors related to reflective autonomy, showing that it has been associated with a long list of good things: "more intrinsic motivation, greater interest, more creativity, more cognitive flexibility, better conceptual learning, a more positive emotional tone", etc. than intentional behaviours that are not autonomous in the strict sense. Some later studies, reviewed by Hodgins, Koestner, and Duncan (1996), have similarly shown that reflective autonomy is related to positive and natural interaction.

The autonomy vs. controlled distinction is especially important in any relationship involving a power differential—parent–child, teacher–pupil, manager–subordinate, etc. However even in those conditions the extent to which the individual feels his behaviour to be controlled can be ameliorated: if a person can be made to feel that he or she is acting of her own volition, the beneficial consequences may follow (see also Deci & Ryan, 1985). Hence, for instance, the attachment theorist's emphasis on *sensitive* mothering (Ainsworth et al., 1978).

But in addition to the need for autonomy, we also have a need for connection with others, a need to form relationships. And every close relationship depends upon the partners making some concessions, and thereby forgoing a degree of autonomy. But according to Baxter (1990, p.70), "too much connection paradoxically destroys the relationship because the individual entities become lost. Simultaneously, autonomy can be conceptualized only in terms of separation from others. But too much autonomy paradoxically destroys the individual's identity, because connections with others are necessary to identity formation and maintenance." Friendships, romantic relationships, and marriages may break up on the one hand because one partner feels suffocated by closeness and needs more independence and autonomy, or because one feels the other is insufficiently committed (Baxter, 1986). The potentially insidious nature of this conflict between autonomy and connectedness arises from the fact that it can be based in the best of intentions. Attempting to be too close, thereby denying a partner autonomy, may be just as alienating as coldness and isolation. The over-protective parent, the too-caring spouse, the too-directive teacher can be seen as a constraint (see Cunningham & Antill, 1994).

(ii) *Openness (Self-disclosure) vs. Closedness (Privacy).* Relationships depend on communication and sharing which involve exposing the self. Exposing the self, however, increases vulnerability. Permitting oneself to become vulnerable demands trust in the partner. And beyond that, the maintenance of some areas of privacy may be essential for personal integrity. The shame felt as a consequence of an intrusion on privacy may be experienced as an attack by the intruder and flare into anger (Retzinger, 1995) (see also Chapter 12).

(iii) *Predictability vs. Novelty.* The essence of a relationship is that the participants know each other, and knowing each other involves predictability. But individuals also require a degree of novelty: continuing routine, however pleasurable the activities involved, can take the life out of a relationship. For some people, uncertainty and a degree of unpredictability in the partner can make a relationship more exciting (Berger, 1988), and boredom is given as the reason for terminating many dating relationships (Hill, Rubin, & Peplau, 1976). Sternberg (1986) even maintained that some degree of uncertainty and mystery is essential to love.

Leary et al. (1986) have investigated what makes people boring. Analysis of the ratings of 1297 respondents indicated nine principal issues— passivity, tediousness, distraction, ingratiation, seriousness, negative egocentrism, self-preoccupation, banality, and low affectivity. Egocentric and banal behaviours were judged the most boring. In another study, individuals previously rated as boring used fewer disclosures and statements of objective information, but more questions and acknowledgements, than those previously rated as interesting in unstructured laboratory conversation.

These sources of conflict (and others, as listed by Montgomery, 1993) may or may not be perceived by the participants. Sometimes they are not, or they are perceived only as a vague feeling of tension whose source is not apparent. More often they are perceived by one participant but not the other—the protective parent or loving spouse does not see the constraint that he or she is imposing, the confiding friend does not see the expectation of reciprocation as intrusive. But a study of students involved in romantic relationships indicated that such problems were recognised to be present in a high proportion of cases. The conflict between self-disclosure and privacy was rather more frequent than the others in the early stages of relationships, but the others became equally or more frequent as the relationships progressed. In relationships of 23–192 months some conflict over autonomy vs. connectedness was present in 93% of the relationships, and the other two in 72% and 83% (Baxter, 1990). The author recognises that these figures may be influenced by the focusing of respondents' attention on conflictual issues, and that the data were retrospective.

Although Autonomy vs. Connectedness, Disclosure vs. Privacy, and Predictability vs. Novelty are usually discussed as separate issues, in real-life relationships they may be interrelated. Thus disclosure enhances vulnerability, and an increase in vulnerability may affect the need for connectedness. Predictability may lead to a need for autonomy and even for less disclosure. As so often in the study of relationships, analysis brings clarification but may simultaneously demand resynthesis.

Another perspective on the sources of conflict is that of equity or interdependence theory (see Chapter 19). The participants in a close relationship seek, in the long term, a fair exchange of resources. Although there is always a "strain towards reciprocity", whether fairness is ever achieved is another matter: quite apart from the difficulties of agreement about how rewards and costs should be measured, the partners may not see eye to eye on what sort of justice should prevail (pp.354–355). And beyond that, relationships involve obligations and expectations for the future which can never be specified precisely, so that the balance at any moment cannot be assessed. And because rewards given may create obligations for the future, each partner may strive to build up credit. Thus in addition to the strain towards reciprocity there may also be a "strain towards imbalance". Even in the closest relationships, tendencies towards balance and imbalance exist side by side (Blau, 1964).

PREDISPOSING FACTORS

Situational and Personality Factors

A variety of situational and personality factors have been found to be associated with a high incidence of marital conflict (e.g. McGonagle, Kessler, & Schilling, 1992). Among these may be mentioned:

(i) *Length of marriage*. The frequency of disagreements generally tends to decrease with time. A number of factors are probably involved. There may be progressive adjustment between the couple, and situational changes (increases in earnings, children becoming independent) may remove causes of conflict. It must also be remembered that a high frequency of disagreement may lead to early divorce, so that marriages that have lasted a long time may have had less conflict from the start.

(ii) *First vs. second marriages*. Conflict seems to be generally less common in second marriages. Perhaps outside pressures are reduced for people who have stabilised their careers, or perhaps conflictual issues are more constructively dealt with. Just possibly, people get wiser.

(iii) *Lack of social support* (Lepore, 1992). A correlation between lack of social support and marital conflict does not necessarily mean that the former causes the latter, for couples who quarrel may be less likely to receive support, but some effect is strongly suggested by the evidence.

(iv) *Personality*. A variety of personality characteristics have been associated with marital conflict. These include neuroticism, social extroversion, and low impulse control (McGonagle et al., 1992). Terhune (1970) indicated that conflicts may be exacerbated if one of the participants is high on dispositional aggressiveness, authoritarianism, suspicion, etc, and are likely to be ameliorated if one shows egalitarianism, trust, open-mindedness, etc. Perceptual styles that distort cues are likely to lead to an exacerbation of conflicts (Stagner, 1971). On the other hand people with an internal marital locus of control have been found to engage more actively in problem-solving, and those who confront problems in an active way tend to arrive at better solutions (Miller et al., 1986).

Gender differences also can exacerbate conflict issues. Masculine individuals tend to lay emphasis on *doing*, while femininity involves co-operation, sensitivity to relationships and communication. Masculinity tends to be associated with autonomy, femininity with connectedness (Gilligan, 1982; Thompson & Walker, 1989). Feminine individuals can be frustrated by the advice or judgement which masculine partners are prone to give in a conflict situation, while masculine individuals want practical action and not the mere processing of feelings (Wood, 1993).

Buss (1991) investigated the specific sources of conflict to which various personality factors gave rise. For instance husbands and wives low in Agreeableness tend (not surprisingly) to act in a way that upsets their spouses, and those low on Emotional Stability tend to be possessive, dependent, or jealous. Thus, wives of men who were low on Agreeableness and Emotional stability complained of the husbands' condescension, abuse, infidelity, inconsiderateness, alcohol abuse, emotional constriction, and self-centredness. Husbands of wives low in Agreeableness had a similar series of complaints, and husbands of wives low in Stability complained of possessiveness, dependency and jealousy.

(v) *Unrealistic expectations*. Distressed couples tend to have expectations about marriage that are less realistic than those of non-distressed couples (Eidelson & Epstein, 1982). Such expectations may lead a spouse to attend selectively to relatively minor irritations caused by the partner's behaviour, and thereby exacerbate conflicts (Bradbury & Fincham, 1989).

Turning for a moment to student relationships, Laner (1989) found that while a cooperative style was preferred in romantic relationships by both women and men, subjects nevertheless tended to perceive the partner as behaving competitively, and as a consequence tended to do likewise.

(vi) *Incompatibility* on a wide variety of issues may of course lead to conflict. To cite an experimental example, gender role disparity can cause difficulty in making decisions and lead to conflict. Voelz (1985) assessed students as traditional or modern and paired them into heterosexual couples.

Traditional man/modern woman couples had more difficulty in making decisions on a gender-related task, and felt less satisfaction with any consensus reached, than couples without gender-role disparity.

The complexity of the issue of compatibility between the characteristics of the two partners in a heterosexual relationship has been shown experimentally by Zuroff and de Lorimer (1989). Women students were assigned to groups according to their scores on measures of dependency and self-criticism, and asked to rate three characteristics of their real and of their ideal male friends—intimacy, achievement, and masculinity. The data showed that dependency was positively linked to an ideal of intimacy, as predicted, but the magnitude of the effect increased with concomitant self-criticism. The authors suggest that the latter effect could be explained on the view that women who are self-critical and dependent desire intimacy but feel unworthy and unable to receive it, and that only an exceptionally loving man with a high need for intimacy could give them the love that they need. The ideal partners of highly self-critical, low-dependent women were low in intimacy, as though the women were saying "I want to be alone", perhaps because of their fear of being controlled. Highly self-critical women desired men with high achievement motivation, perhaps because they saw such partners as able to bring them the extrinsic rewards of status and social approval. However this relation was absent at low levels of dependency.

(vii) *Positive feedback*. Conflict can easily lead to conflict. This is clearly seen in studies of marriages involving a depressed partner. One study showed that partners in such marriages reported less problem-solving and more destructive behaviour in conflicts: discussions left them sad and angry and they experienced each other as hostile, competitive, less nurturant, less affiliative, and so on (Kahn, Coyne, & Margolin, 1985). Again, the attributions of distressed spouses tend to accentuate the impact of negative behaviours and minimise that of positive behaviours. Thus a distressed spouse might say "He only bought me a present because he felt guilty about neglecting me" or "She forgot it was my birthday because she doesn't care about me any more" (Fincham & Bradbury, 1987a, b). In the same vein, Beach and O'Leary (1993) found that a subsample of newly married couples who were dysphoric (high on negative and low on positive affectivity) were especially vulnerable to marital stress. Thus it seems that a tendency to depression can lead to conflict. But conversely an increase in marital arguments has been shown to precede clinical depression in married women (Paykel et al., 1969), and spousal criticism is a more powerful predictor of relapse in remitted depressives than overall marital quality (Hooley & Teasdale, 1989).

(viii) *Socio-economic status*, and (ix) *Children*. In their study of a white community sample in Detroit, McGonagle et al. (1992) did not find an association between marital conflict and either SES or the presence of children, though other studies have done so. They suggest that children may provide an occasion for disagreement, but not a long-term cause.

Jealousy, an important cause of conflict, is discussed in the next section.

Jealousy

The Nature of Jealousy.   Jealousy, an emotion or emotion-complex which emerges as early as two years of age (Masciuch & Kienapple, 1993), is one of the most destructive emotions that can arise within a close relationship. It has been defined as a disposition, a state, and a predicament (Radecki-Bush, Bush, & Jennings, 1988). White (1980, 1984) sees it as a complex of thoughts, feelings, and actions which follow threats to self-esteem and threats to a relationship. Although jealousy carries a wide range of meanings in everyday speech, it is usually seen as compounded of fear, anger, sadness, and perhaps hatred (Sharpsteen, 1993).

Jealousy is best distinguished from envy in terms of the precipitating situation (Salovey & Rodin, 1989): envy involves desire for the possessions or attributes of another person, whereas jealousy is associated with a threat to a relationship. The two differ also in the associated emotions: jealousy is accompanied by fear of loss, anxiety, suspiciousness and anger, distrust, uncertainty, and loneliness; envy involves feelings of inferiority, longing, resentment, and ill-will, sometimes accompanied by guilt, denial, and awareness of the inappropriateness of the ill-will (Parrott & Smith, 1993; Salovey & Rodin, 1986). In addition, jealousy tends to be experienced more intensely than envy.

White (1981) suggested that the loss or the anticipation of loss associated with jealousy has two aspects—loss of all the good things that the relationship can bring, and loss of self-esteem. These lead to emotional reactions and coping attempts. The hypothesis of two types of loss was confirmed by Mathes, Adams, and Davies (1985) in a questionnaire study of students. They found further that the loss of the rewards expected from the relationship led to depression, and loss of self-esteem led to anger. A suggestion that loss of self-esteem led to anxiety was not confirmed. Not unexpectedly, loss of a partner due to rejection or a rival is a more negative experience than losing a partner in circumstances that can be ascribed to fate.

Buunk and Bringle (1987) extend the list to four types of immediate loss particularly salient in jealousy:

(i) *Inequality*—an individual feels upset because the partner had an affair when she or he had not.

(ii) *Loss of self-esteem*—especially when the rival is seen as superior, sexual competition being especially salient.

(iii) *Violation of specialness*—threats to the exclusiveness, togetherness, and perceived superiority of the relationship.

(iv) *Loss of partner*, though this is a less important threat if there is a sense of the partner's ultimate commitment to the current relationship.

Although, as we have seen, jealousy is often thought to be related to a lowering of self-esteem, the correlations between the two are often small. Salovey and Rodin (1989) have therefore argued that both jealousy and envy arise only when a person's self-worth is threatened in an area that is particularly important as self-defining for that person. Following Tesser (1986; see pp.140–141), they argue that positive self-evaluation may be achieved by a process of reflection, when the attributes or successes of close others make us feel good about ourselves, but if the issue in question is one that threatens our own self-evaluation the success of another may reduce it. Thus a husband may feel pride in his wife's good looks but feel threatened when she earns more than him. Loss of a spouse or partner to someone whom he or she prefers inevitably infringes self-evaluation (see also later).

Numerous scales have been constructed to assess the amount of jealousy a person experiences, but such scales imply that jealousy is unidimensional. In practice the several emotions involved in jealousy may be combined in different ways which have little in common except that all stem from a situation involving threat to a relationship (Buunk & Bringle, 1987). Pfeiffer and Wong (1989) separated the cognitive, emotional, and behavioural aspects of jealousy. Questioning White's (1984) view that the emotions of jealousy follow cognitive appraisal of the situation, they pointed out that a past partner may arouse jealousy even though one is now in a happy relationship and no current relationship is threatened, and that jealousy may arise from irrational worries and suspicions. Furthermore the coping responses made by a jealous individual can be seen not only as coping with cognitively initiated emotion, but as detective/protective measures to safeguard the relationship. Pfeiffer and Wong thus suggest that the cognitions, emotions, and behaviour involved in jealousy do not follow each other sequentially, but can be simultaneous and interact with each other. They therefore devised a scale which assessed separately the cognitive, emotional, and behavioural aspects of jealousy. Cognitions were assessed by asking subjects how often they had various suspicions about their partners, emotional responses by how they would feel in various jealousy-provoking situations, and the behavioural aspects by how often they engaged in various detective and protective activities. These were used together with Rubin's

(1974) scales for assessing Liking and Loving (see p.432) in a study of subjects ranging widely in age. While the emotional component of jealousy was positively related to love, cognitive jealousy showed a negative relation with love. All three components of jealousy were negatively related to liking, and subjects high on emotional and behavioural jealousy tended to score low on a scale assessing happiness in their lives.

Determinants of Jealousy. The appearance of a jealous reaction depends on characteristics of the person concerned, characteristics of the relationship, and (also by definition) the situation (Bringle & Buunk, 1985). Bersheid (1983) has emphasised the importance of personal and relationship characteristics as mediators of cognitive appraisal during jealousy-provoking events. Thus a number of studies have shown jealousy to be felt especially by individuals with low self-esteem and feelings of inadequacy as a partner, anxiety, neurosis, dissatisfaction, an external locus of control and dogmatism, love for and dependence on the partner, poor communication skills, wish for sexual exclusivity, a measure of social disability, and arousability (e.g. Radecki-Bush et al., 1988). Jealousy is likely to be more severe if the partner's behaviour is attributed to a stable characteristic, such as being easily flattered, because of the indication that the situation might recur from time to time and the characteristic cannot be controlled.

It is sometimes suggested that men are more prone to jealousy in sexual situations than are women. This seems not to be the case, but Buss (1994) cites several experimental studies indicating that women experience jealousy primarily to indications that their mates' resources are being diverted to another woman, whereas men are more concerned with sexual infidelity. In partial harmony with this, Buunk (1995) has argued that there is no evidence that either sex responds more negatively than the other to sexual involvement of the partner with someone else, though male jealousy may be more focused on the sexual aspects of the affair. Buunk's own data, drawn from a sample of married or cohabiting individuals asked to imagine jealousy-provoking situations, indicated only that the nature of the response differed: women showed more self-doubt than did men when the partner committed adultery, especially if their self-esteem was initially low. Women adapted to repeated infidelities by their partners more than did men.

In another study on gender differences, Sharpsteen (1995) found that men students, imagining a situation in which they expected to experience jealousy, would seek greater closeness to the partner when there was considerable threat to the relationship but not to their self-esteem. With women, the likelihood of seeking proximity increased if the imagined threat were either to the relationship or to their self-esteem, but not if it were to both. Sharpsteen suggests that, with men, unflattering comparisons with a rival might be more likely to lead to self-promotion or rival-derogation than seeking greater closeness. Women faced with the dual threat may see the partner as no longer a worthwhile source of support, and/or turn their back on the relationship.

Another perspective on gender differences in responses to jealousy-provoking situations is provided by Nadler and Dotan (1992), who assessed the ways in which married Israeli subjects expected the protagonist in a story (who was of their own sex) to feel and behave in a jealousy-provoking situation. Wives expected the protagonist to feel worse when the rival was described as attractive and the spouse's relationship with the rival fairly serious, and attributed the least negative feelings if the rival was attractive but the relationship casual. Husbands, however, rated the protagonist as most attracted to the wife if the rival was portrayed as attractive and the relationship as casual. If the rival was attractive and the relationship fairly serious, husbands rated the protagonist as unattracted to his wife. Thus in this last situation both husbands and wives reacted strongly, but the wives admitted to strong negative feelings, while the husbands reacted as though dissociating themselves from the partner. Nadler and Dotan interpret the wives' responses as attempts to protect the relationship, the husbands' as concern for their own egos with threatened loss of status in a competitive relationship (see also Sharpsteen, 1995, cited earlier).

Male homosexual respondents to a study by Bringle (1995) reported lower levels of experienced and expressed jealousy than heterosexual ones: although the homosexual men felt equally involved (i.e. committed, satisfied, identifying with the partner) as the heterosexual ones, their relationships were less exclusive and tended to have shorter durations. Bringle suggests that individuals who can tolerate other relationships by their partners may pair with partners who desire to have such relationships, and that amongst homosexuals non-emotional extra-dyadic sexual activity may be dissociated from the emotional intimacy of the primary relationship: the data indicated also other differences between homosexual and heterosexual men. Cohorts were studied in 1980 and 1992, and both homosexual and heterosexual men reported higher levels of jealousy and more exclusive relationships in 1992: this may have been a consequence of the incidence of sexually transmitted diseases.

It should be emphasised that the relations between personal characteristics and jealousy may be two-way. Thus not only are individuals with low self-esteem more likely to feel jealousy, but jealousy (or the situation that precipitates it) can lead to lowered self-esteem. "Dispositional jealousy" as an individual characteristic is less predictive of reported jealousy than aspects of the relationship (see also Bringle et al., 1983; Mathes, Adams, & Davies, 1985; Radecki-Bush et al., 1988).

Jealousy from an Attachment Perspective.   Some of the more recent work relating personal or relationship characteristics to jealousy has used the language of attachment theory. As we shall see in Chapter 21, one variant of this approach proposes that characteristics of early relationships become internalised, the individual acquiring "internal models" of relationships which have some resistance to modification. Individuals may be categorised as "secure" or "insecure": the former are more prone to feel trust, satisfaction, and positive emotions. Insecurity is subdivided as "avoidant" or "anxious/ambivalent", and insecure individuals are more vulnerable to threat and jealousy. The "attachment behaviour system", which normally functions to maintain (real or experienced) proximity to the partner or other attachment figure, is activated by threat of separation. Emotional responses, mediated by appraisals of the situation, are triggered, attempts to maintain or re-establish the relationship ensue and, on this view, it is the perceived failure of these attempts that provokes jealousy.

Now coping with jealousy can take a number of forms. The threatened one may attempt to cling to the partner, manipulate the partner by inducing jealousy reciprocally, act so as to increase the positive feelings of the partner about the relationship, feign indifference, bury him/herself in work or other extra-relationship issues, denigrate the rival, and so on (e.g. White & Mullen, 1989). The coping style adopted will depend on the individual's perceptions of his/her ability to cope with the threat. Radecki-Bush, Farrell, and Bush (1993) suggested that the mental models of self and relationships held by an individual as part of his/her attachment style may affect the appraisal and coping responses shown. Individuals with an insecure style might tend to perceive their relationships as more vulnerable and perceive the threat as greater than those with a secure style. In an experimental study of romantically involved students, Radecki-Bush et al. (1993) assessed their attachment styles (see Chapter 21), and also measured depression, jealousy, the intensity of ten emotions, and the likelihood of using five coping strategies. The subjects were asked to imagine scenes posing differing degrees of threat to their relationship. Although the methodology may be regarded as somewhat artificial, and involves comparisons between a number of self-report items (see p.21), the study provided support for a model in which attachment category, depression, and situational threat predicted the appraisal of threat. Appraisal in turn predicted positive and negative perceptions of the relationship and emotions in response to the jealousy-provoking situation. The authors suggest that attachment style and depression function as schemata which influence appraisal of the rival relationship and thus affective and cognitive responses to the situation. Insecure attachment and depression were related to less secure coping strategies.

In harmony with this, Pistole (1989) assessed students with respect to "their most important 'romantic' love relationship", asking them to say what strategies they used over important issues of conflict, though these did not necessarily involve jealousy. Those with a more secure attachment style were more likely to use an integrating strategy than those with insecure strategies. They were also more likely to compromise than the anxious/ambivalent group. The latter were more likely to oblige the partner's wishes than persons in the avoidant group. Other studies have shown that coping styles involving anxiety, protest, and preoccupation with the relationship are found in the insecure–anxiously attached; the use of outside activities, anger, and the dismissal of distress is associated with insecure–avoidant attachment (Stratton & Pepes cited in Radecki-Bush et al., 1993).

The Third Party.   Most research on jealousy has concentrated on the partner who feels threatened and thus experiences jealousy, but it is also necessary to consider the third party. Since jealousy is generally unpleasant, a third party who forms a relationship with someone who already has a competing relationship would seem to be putting him or herself at risk for intense jealousy. Of course, such risk would be reduced in a very free cultural atmosphere, but even there jealousy may arise. Surprisingly, however, data obtained by Bringle and Boebinger (1990) indicate that the effect is less than might be expected. In a study of students who were or had been third parties to a relationship with either a married person or someone who had a pre-existing dating relationship, and of students who were simply in a traditional dating relationship, they assessed by questionnaire the degree of disturbance the subjects would feel if the partner showed intimate behaviour with the spouse, other dating partner, or an anonymous other. They found that third parties to a married relationship reported less jealousy than those in traditional dating relationships. This could not be accounted for in terms of a lower level of dispositional jealousy, and seemed rather to result from the way in which they managed the relationship. They were less involved than those in traditional relationships— perhaps because they limited their own involvement voluntarily or out of necessity. Third parties to dating relationships had less dispositional jealousy, but greater relative involvement than third parties to a marriage, and felt themselves to be more exploited.

CONFLICT TACTICS
Attitudes to Conflict

In a perceptive review of the literature, Noller et al. (1994) pointed out that there is disagreement about the relative merits of confronting and avoiding conflict. Attempts to resolve a conflict may make things worse, and for certain people and certain situations it may be better to let things be—for instance for those who are generally introspective, or when the relationship has clearly differentiated roles and real affection (Rausch et al., 1974). On the other hand, there is considerable evidence that avoiding conflict may cover up unresolved issues and may lead to feelings of resentment and anger. Avoidance of conflict is often characteristic of distressed marriages: of course it also often happens that one partner (usually the wife) wants to resolve the problem and the other to withdraw (see later).

How people handle conflict may depend on their attitudes to conflict and disagreements in their relationship. For instance, disagreements may be seen as an opportunity for discussion which could lead to greater understanding and intimacy, or as a threat to the relationship which has to be avoided, or as a threat to personal integrity and security (Rands, Levinger, & Mellinger, 1981). Furthermore, the participants in a relationship may or may not believe that conflicts are resolvable. Crohan (1992), in a study of nearly 300 black and white couples in the first and third year of marriage, found little agreement between spouses on beliefs about conflict, nor was agreement strongly associated with marital happiness. However the content of beliefs about conflict was related to marital happiness: spouses who believed that conflicts should be avoided reported less marital happiness both concurrently and two years later than couples who believed that conflict should not be avoided (see also Eidelson & Epstein, 1982; and especially Noller et al., 1994). Similarly, relationships in which both spouses believed that disagreements were solvable reported higher marital happiness than those who did not. Since beliefs in one year were related to happiness two years later, it would seem that beliefs affect happiness, but the reverse is also likely to be true.

Attributional Processes

As mentioned already, the causes of a particular conflict episode may lie in the long-term structure of the relationship, rather than in the ostensible issue under discussion. Indeed, between interactions one partner may ruminate about the relationship and foster a grievance, so that the other may be taken by surprise by the vehemence with which an apparently trivial issue is discussed. However, leaving that aside and taking a conflict at its face value, what happens in a conflict depends in large measure on the participants' views of the causes of the problem—do they agree on what they are quarrelling about, and do they attribute blame to the partner, outside circumstances, or themselves? (see Chapter 18).

If the conflict involves one partner complaining about the behaviour of the other, they tend to make different attributions. While the complained-of member tends to excuse his or her behaviour in terms of extenuating circumstances, outside influences, or his/her current physiological or psychological state, the complaining partner tends to ascribe it to the other's personal characteristics or attitudes. Although the latter course can be destructive and, by bringing in other issues, facilitate spread of conflict, it can also serve as a challenge to the actor to prove the attribution wrong by doing better in the future. Fincham and Bradbury (1987b) proposed that judgements of responsibility mediate the relation between causal attributions and blame, and verified this in a study of marital relationships. An egocentric bias in the attributions made by satisfied couples was found at least for negative events, attributions apparently being based on general sentiments about the partner. For positive events the bias may be towards assigning responsibility to the partner (Fincham & Bradbury, 1989a).

The nature of the attributions made may also be influenced by current mood. Forgas (e.g. 1994) has suggested that the effect of mood depends in part on the complexity of the issues. On his view, constructive cognitive processing involves the transformation rather than mere reproduction of cognitive contents, the use of open information search strategies, and generative elaboration of stimuli. Just because complex and serious conflicts require more elaborate and constructive processing than simple ones, mood is more likely to influence the attributions made. The data supported this view. While happy people were more likely to focus on external, unstable, and specific causes in explaining conflict, sad persons were more prone to attribute real-life conflicts to internal, stable, and global causes, especially if the conflict were serious.

Distressed spouses are liable to make attributions about negative behaviour by the partner as reflecting global characteristics, and the opposite for positive behaviour (Bradbury & Fincham, 1990), and given that attributions play a role in determining marital satisfaction (Fincham & Bradbury, 1987c), the question arises, what other characteristics of individuals are related to the tendency to make such attributions? Fincham and Bradbury (1989b) investigated this issue in a study of married couples. They were asked to make independent attributions about selected problems in their marriages, and to rate the extent to which the cause rested in the spouse, affected the problem area, and was likely to be still present when the problem next arose. An overall index as to how much the subject was prone to make maladaptive attributions was then calculated. Dysfunctional beliefs, perspective-taking, self-disclosure, and attributional complexity, were also assessed. (The last refers to the use of complex attributional schemata in the context of the relationship, assessed by an instrument concerned with the preference for multiple causal explanations, awareness that behaviour is a consequence of interaction with others, and so on.)

The extent to which subjects located sources of difficulty in the spouse, and perceived the cause to be stable and global, was positively related to the extent to which unrealistic beliefs were held, and the extent to which the subject used complex attributional schemata. This finding is in keeping with data showing that attributional complexity is associated with a tendency for spontaneous attribution, and frequency of attribution is inversely related to satisfaction. However the making of attributions was not related to perspective-taking, perhaps because the measure was a global one and the ability to take another's perspective differs between the several relationships of a given individual.

Maladaptive causal attributions were negatively related to own marital satisfaction for both husbands and wives. However at the interpersonal level, the fewer maladaptive attributions made by wives, the greater the husbands' satisfaction. This relation was not significant for husbands. As expected, self-disclosure was significantly related to partners' and to own satisfaction, although care had been taken to ensure that the instruments used to measure them did not overlap. The effect of the wives' attributions on the husbands' satisfaction could be explained by the facts that the wives who made causal attributions were poor self-disclosers, and wives' self-disclosure was strongly related to husbands' satisfaction. The gender differences can be ascribed to women's greater concern over "issues of intimacy and caring that are often fostered by self-disclosure" (Fincham & Bradbury, 1989b, p.83). The authors further suggest that the mediating role of self-disclosure results from self-disclosure allowing maladaptive attributions to be corrected.

Behaviour in Conflict Situations

Our focus here is on the strategies that partners use to resolve conflicts, as these may have an important influence on the future of their relationship. A constructive approach may not only resolve the problem at issue, but is also likely to be seen positively by the partner as an indication of commitment and lead to intimacy (Cahn, 1990). But in a conflict situation the behaviour of the participants may be driven by the emotions engendered. Furthermore an individual may use knowledge of emotions to understand or predict the partner's behaviour, or to manipulate it (Fitness, 1996). A negative approach, such as coercion or manipulation, may merely make things worse. If coercion is successful, it is likely to be used again and a negative approach to conflicts to become established (Patterson, 1982); and manipulation involves dishonesty in the relationship (See Noller et al., 1994, for further discussion of this issue). In general, approaches to a conflict situation that involve taking both partners' points of view from the start are, of course, much more likely to be associated with a good relationship in the long run than those involving making attributions about the partner.

Long-term Issues.   In considering how conflicts are dealt with, we may focus first on the longer-term strategies for dealing with autonomy vs. connectedness, self-disclosure vs. privacy, and predictability vs. novelty. Baxter (1990) has grouped these under four headings:

(a) *Selection.* The parties seek to make one pole dominant and exclude the other. Thus they may attempt to be absolutely open with each other, so that intrusiveness is not seen to occur.

(b) *Separation.* The two poles are both recognised but separated by either alternating between them or separating the topic or activity domains for which they are relevant. Thus the partners may agree to do things together at weekends but go their own ways during the week, or agree never to discuss each other's families or earlier sexual involvements.

(c) *Neutralisation.* Again both poles are recognised, but neither is ever achieved fully. Thus one spouse may agree that the other should play golf, but only nine holes a week. Or they may indulge in small talk involving a degree of openness but retain a degree of privacy, or allude to sensitive topics only indirectly.

(d) *Reframing.* The two poles are no longer regarded as opposites. Thus if the spouses perceive the autonomy that each has to do his/her own thing, or the right each has not to discuss certain issues, as part of their connectedness, then the autonomy vs. connectedness dilemma has been reframed.

In the study of student relationships referred to on p.159, Baxter (1990) found that Separation by cyclic alternation and Selection were most frequently used to deal with autonomy vs. connectedness; Separation by segmentation for self-disclosure vs. privacy and predictability vs. novelty, and Neutralization for self-disclosure vs. privacy. Reframing is a cognitively more complex procedure, and may be used more in longer-term relationships. Some strategies were positively correlated with satisfaction with the relationship, and some negatively. For instance satisfaction was positively correlated with Reframing and negatively with Selection.

Each of these terms—Selection, Separation, Neutralisation and Reframing—refers in effect to a means of categorising the ways in which people deal with specific issues, but they can also imply attempts to ensure a long-term restructuring of the relationship to minimise the occurrence of conflict.

Immediate Issues.   Turning to immediate responses to a conflict situation, several classificatory systems have been proposed. We may consider some examples.

Building on an earlier Australian study, Honeycutt, Woods, and Fontenot (1993) contacted a sample of married and engaged couples and investigated the extent to which they endorsed 35 rules derived from a longer list. Factor analysis yielded four factors:

(a) *Understanding* (e.g. should be able to say sorry; resolve problem so both are happy; support and praise other where due).
(b) *Rationality* (e.g. don't get angry; shouldn't argue; don't raise voice).
(c) *Conciseness* (e.g. should get to point quickly; be specific, don't generalise; be consistent).
(d) *Consideration* (e.g. don't talk too much; don't make others feel guilty; don't push your own view as only view).

Honeycutt et al. used a version of Fitzpatrick's scheme (see pp.63–64) for categorising the marriages. Traditionals reported higher levels of rule endorsement for all the rule dimensions than Independents. (There were few Separates.) The couples saw the rules as important and their endorsement as characterising happy marriages. Demonstrating positive understanding during conflict seemed to be an important issue in maintaining a satisfying relationship.

Canary and Cupach (1988) classified behaviour used in conflict situations into three categories:

(a) *Integrative strategies.* These tend to promote the maintenance and growth of the relationship. The partners negotiate about the issue, pointing out positive aspects, expressing trust in the partner, and airing their views until agreement is reached (e.g. Peterson, 1983).
(b) *Distributive or anti-social strategies.* These are destructive, and include sarcasm, threats, hostile questions, attribution of blame to the partner, and so on. They are likely to lead to escalation of the conflict.
(c) *Avoidance strategies.* These minimise or deny the existence of conflict, divert attention, and are generally non-confrontational but may involve indirect attacks, such as attempts to make the partner jealous.

Canary and Cupach (1988) review literature showing that Integrative strategies are associated with a variety of positive aspects of relationships, Distributive strategies with negative aspects, and Avoidance strategies with mostly negative but in some circumstances positive aspects. They conducted a questionnaire study with students which assessed the consequences of these three types of behaviour in conflict situations. The questionnaire asked the type of conflict strategy used in a recent conflict with a partner

in a relationship, their assessment of their partner's communicative
competence (appropriateness and effectiveness of communication) and their
satisfaction with the communication, and trust, control mutuality (i.e.
agreement about control), intimacy, and satisfaction with the relationship.
The model established by a path analysis of the data is shown in Fig. 10.1.

It will be seen from Fig. 10.1 that Integrative strategies contribute positively to relationship satisfaction via effects on the two communication
variables and relationship variables. Distributive strategies contribute negatively to the relationship variables by both indirect and direct effects. Avoidance strategies appear to have no effects on the communication variables,
perhaps because they would go unnoticed, but one's own Avoidance did
have a negative association with satisfaction with the relationship. Avoidance presumably avoids immediate negative feelings, and may also indicate

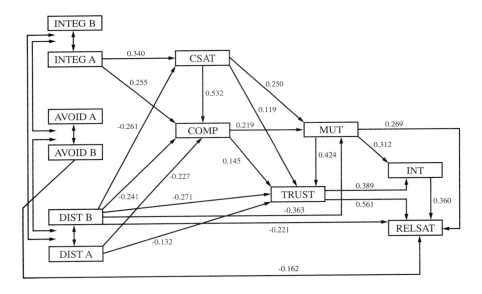

FIG. 10.1 The relations between conflict message strategies (Integrative, Distributive, and
Avoidance) and relationship satisfaction. The figure shows a LISREL model obtained by path
analysis in which one person's perception of the episodic and relationship variables were
combined with the partner's self-reported conflict strategies.

INTEG = Integrative tactics; DIST = Distributive tactics; AVOID = Avoidance; CSAT =
Communication Satisfaction; COMP = Partner's competence; INT = Intimacy; MUT =
Control Mutuality; TRUST = Trust; RELSAT = Relationship satisfaction; A = Person A's
measure; B = Person B's measure. (From Canary & Cupach, 1988, *Journal of Social and
Personal Relationships, 5,* 305–325, copyright © by Sage Publications, Inc. and reprinted by
permission.)

perception that the partner is being competitive or avoidant, whether or not that is actually the case. But dissatisfaction with the relationship may build up.

Kurdek (1995) classified behaviour in conflict situations into three conflict styles—Engagement, Withdrawal, and Compliance. In a study of 155 couples over two years he found that the husbands' satisfaction was more frequently affected by how the wives dealt with conflict than the wives' satisfaction was affected by the husbands' style. The combination of wife engages and husband withdraws brought least satisfaction to both. The data suggested that the conflict resolution style affected satisfaction, and that change in satisfaction affected style, but there was no indication that satisfaction with the relationship affected the style used in resolving conflicts.

In an earlier study, Rusbult, Zembrodt, and Gunn (1982; Rusbult & Zembrodt, 1983) assessed the possible responses of members of student dating couples when the partner behaved destructively. They grouped the possible responses into four categories, each involving a broad set of inter-related reactions.

(a) *Exit*—formally separating, moving out of a joint residence, deciding to "just be friends", thinking or talking about leaving one's partner,

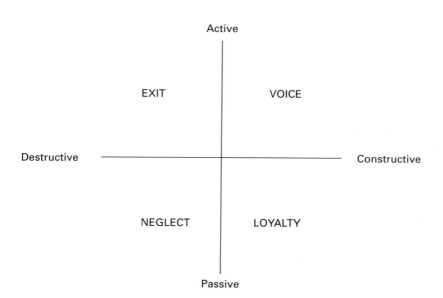

FIG. 10.2 Conflict strategies. (From Rusbult in D. Perlman & S. Duck (Eds.) *Intimate relationships*. Copyright © 1989 by Sage Publications Inc. Adapted with permission.)

threatening to end the relationship, actively destroying the relationship, or getting a divorce.

(b) *Voice*—discussing problems, compromising, seeking help from a
therapist or member of the clergy, suggesting solutions to problems,
asking the partner what is bothering him or her, and trying to
change oneself or the partner.

(c) *Loyalty*—waiting and hoping that things will improve, "giving
things some time", praying for improvement, supporting the partner in the face of criticism, and continuing to have faith in the
relationship and the partner.

(d) *Neglect*—ignoring the partner or spending less time together, refus-
ing to discuss problems, treating the partner badly emotionally or
physically, criticising the partner for things unrelated to the real
problem, "just letting things fall apart", chronically complaining
without offering solutions to problems, perhaps developing extra-
relationship sexual involvements. (Whether extra-relationship involvement is exit or neglect depends on the individual's
intentions—to end the relationship or to stick with it and inadvert-
ently cause it to deteriorate, Rusbult, 1987, p.213.)

These differ along two dimensions Active—(a) and (b)—versus
Passive—(c) and (d)—and Constructive—(b) and (c)—versus Destructive—
(a) and (d)—(Fig. 10.2). Which pattern is followed depends on numerous
properties of the individuals concerned and of the relationship: constructive responses may lead to a reduction in distress.

Destructive actions are, not surprisingly, more common in distressed
than in non-distressed couples, and it seems to be more important *not* to
engage in negative behaviour than it is to engage in positive behaviour
(Montgomery, 1988a, b). Indeed, reactions to Voice or Loyalty are only
weakly related to the functioning of the couple, whereas reactions to Exit
or Neglect have a marked influence on the couple's distress.

However the four categories of response are not necessarily independent.
The tendency to use voice may be reduced by the possibility of exit. It
may also be reduced if exit is not seen as a possible option, since the
plausibility of exit enhances the persuasiveness of voice (Wood, 1993).

An initial tendency to return negative behaviour with negative behaviour
might be predicted from the pervasive tendency to show reciprocity—to
apply the principle of tit for tat. However behaviour is not always directed
towards immediately selfish ends: the recipient of negative behaviour may
value the well-being of the partner or the continuation of the relationship
more highly than her or his immediate *amour propre*. Rusbult et al. (1991)
labelled the tendency to respond to a partner's destructive behaviour by
inhibiting the tendency to reciprocate and instead responding construc-

tively as *accommodation*. They showed that accommodation is more likely if commitment to the relationship is strong, if the partners experience high satisfaction in the relationship, have few alternatives, have invested extensive resources in the relationship, perceive greater normative support for the relationship (i.e. approval of friends), have higher expectations, and perceive the relationship as central to their lives, and if they are more feminine and engage in more perspective-taking. Some of these variables appear to be mediated by commitment. Fig. 10.3 shows a causal model which represents a "plausible account" of the causal links among the variables. It will be noted that perspective-taking and femininity, and to a lesser extent satisfaction, quality of alternatives, and centrality have an effect on accommodation beyond that mediated by commitment. These authors also

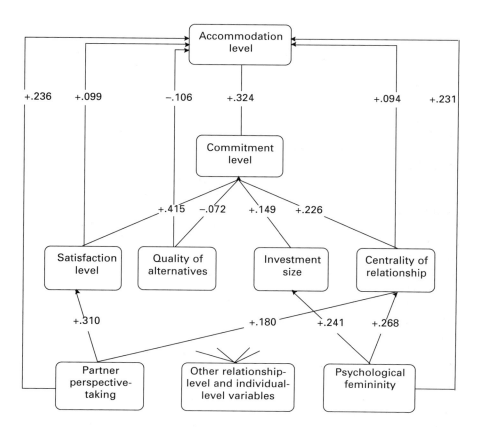

FIG. 10.3 Links between individual-level variables, relationship-level variables, feelings of commitment, and willingness to accommodate. (Rusbult et al., 1991. Copyright by the American Psychological Association, and reprinted with permission.)

showed that the functioning of the couple was more closely related to the male partner's willingness to accommodate than the female's—perhaps because, in conformity with traditional stereotypes, the female is usually mainly responsible for accommodation, so that variations in the male's willingness to accommodate will have the greater effect. Overall, couple functioning was related to the joint level and mutuality of accommodation (see also Chapter 14).

A constructive response to the partner's negative behaviour is likely to be unexpected and to be seen as revealing a desire to forgo self-interest for the good of the relationship (Rusbult, Yovetich, & Verette, 1996). (In the language of interdependence theory it can be interpreted as involving a transformation of the given (self-interested) matrix, see p.343.)

Scharfe and Bartholomew (1995) related Rusbult's Exit/Voice/Loyalty/ Neglect distinction to Bartholomew's (1990, 1993) four categories of attachment styles (see p.393). Studying 64 childless couples in romantic relationships of at least two years' duration, they made two assessments eight months apart. Attachment representations were associated with concurrent and subsequent accommodation to the partners' destructive be- haviours, secure attachment being associated with the use of constructive and inhibition of destructive strategies, and fearful ratings the reverse.

Using a somewhat more elaborate classification of conflict styles, Sternberg and Dobson (1987) found consistency across different personal relationships and conflict situations. The styles considered were: physical force, economic action, wait and see, accept the situation, step down, involve third party, and undermine esteem. In general, conflict-mitigating styles were preferred to those that intensified the conflict.

Prager (1991) classified the communication strategies used by partners as Cognitive (suggest, reason, resolve, etc.), Affective (changing the subject, diverting, deflecting, reconciling, accepting, and appealing) and Coercive. A sequential analysis of the interactions revealed a tendency for partners to respond symmetrically—reasoning tended to elicit reasoning, and hostility/defensiveness was followed by hostility. If one partner focused on an emotional aspect, the other was likely to follow suit, and cognitive strategies led to cognitive replies. Affective and coercive strategies were found to discourage cognitive strategies. Other studies have found that hostile behaviours are more likely to be reciprocated than positive behaviours (see pp.113–114).

While it will be apparent that some of the systems mentioned here have a good deal in common, there is still no general agreement as to precisely how conflict behaviour should be categorised. In any case, useful as classifications of conflict styles may be, it is important to remember that forcing styles into categories may involve an underestimation of complexity. We shall see later how subtle some techniques of persuasion may be, and Rausch et al. (1974) have described how people can learn a diplomacy of psychological pressure.

Gender Differences in Conflict Behaviour.   It is often the case that the partners to a relationship use different approaches to a conflict situation, and a common pattern is for one (often the woman in a heterosexual relationship) to make emotional demands and complaints, while the other (often the man) withdraws or behaves passively. Women use more emotional appeal strategies in conflict situations than do men (Gryl, Stith, & Bird, 1991), while husbands are more inclined not to deal with conflict openly than are wives (Christensen & Heavey, 1990, 1993). Christensen showed that this latter demand/withdraw pattern was associated with marital dissatisfaction, perhaps because withdrawal by the husband may be followed by hostility from the wife, leading to a vicious circle (Noller et al., 1994; Roberts & Krokoff, 1990). It is also possible, of course, that marital satisfaction is primary, or that causation operates both ways.

Several explanations of the gender difference are possible. One is that intimate relationships are more important to women than to men, because women have been socialised to be affiliative and expressive and/or because of a biological difference, whereas men tend to be or have been trained to be independent. Women have higher aspirations for closeness in marriage, itself perhaps due to a difference in their self-concepts (Acitelli & Young, 1996). Thus women are more often threatened by separation, men by loss of autonomy and intrusiveness. Christensen was able to show that the demand/withdraw pattern was in fact more common in couples who had a conflict of interest over issues of autonomy vs. connectedness, with the partner who wanted more closeness taking the demanding role. It has also been suggested that the direction of the gender difference in the demand/withdraw pattern may stem from another sort of inherent personality difference between men and women: men are sometimes said to be more reactive to physiological stress, and this may lie at the basis of their tendency to withdraw (Gottman & Levenson, 1988; see also Fitness & Strongman, 1991 cited in Berscheid, 1994). However, the difference in responsiveness to stress is still controversial, and may depend on the nature of the stressor. Alternatively the difference may arise from the nature of the social structure—specifically the typically greater power enjoyed by men may be associated with little interest in change, and thus a tendency to avoid conflict. Men seem to benefit from marriage more than do women, as some studies suggest that marriage increases a woman's risk of depression but decreases a man's (Jacobson, 1989). Men are therefore likely to have a conservative attitude to marriage, women to press for change.

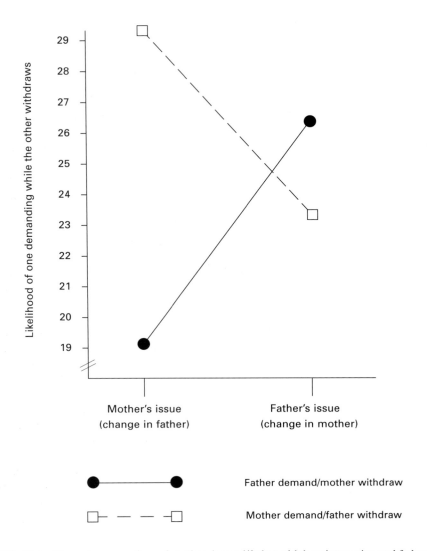

FIG. 10.4 Mean observer ratings of mother-demand/father-withdraw interaction and father-demand/mother-withdraw interaction as a function of whether the issue concerned change in father or mother. (Christensen & Heavey, 1990. Copyright by the American Psychological Association and reprinted with permission.)

Christensen and Heavey (1990) used a questionnaire technique and coded marital interactions to differentiate between individual differences vs. social structure explanations of the gender bias in the demand/withdraw pattern. Both received some support. The wife demand/husband withdraw pattern was more common than the reverse. But there was also an effect of the situation: if discussion was about a wife's wish for a change, the usual wife demand/husband withdraw pattern clearly prevailed. But in the reverse situation there was no significant difference between the tendencies of wife or husband to be the demander (Fig. 10.4). Since analysis showed that the effect of withdrawingness seemed to be greater than that of demandingness, and since other data indicate that women want more changes in marriage than do men, Christensen and Heavey argue that women's role as a demander results from her position in the social structure more than from an inherent gender difference in demandingness. Being more satisfied with the status quo, men tend to be passive in conflict situations, and seek change over fewer issues.

Christensen and Heavey make another interesting point, arising from the view that women want more closeness, men more autonomy. Autonomy can be achieved unilaterally, closeness requires actions by both parties. Any compromise is thus likely to favour the party who wants more autonomy. Thus the woman is likely to want more changes than the man, and this may interact with existing gender differences to produce even greater conflict. The wife is at a power disadvantage, and this may explain women's greater tendency to take the demanding role (Kelley, 1979; Peplau & Gordon, 1985; Wood, 1993). Heavey, Layne, and Christensen (1993) found that the wife demand/husband withdraw pattern was associated with decline in the wife's satisfaction one year later, but the husband demand/ wife withdraw pattern with an increase in the wife's satisfaction.

Other Individual Differences.   It is to be expected that the tactics used in conflict situations will be related to the individual characteristics of the participants. Buss et al. (1987) asked undergraduates to nominate acts used to influence behaviour in close relationships. This produced an instrument giving seven exemplars of each of five categories—Reason, Charm, Regression (e.g. whining), Coercion, and Debasement. Analysis of the replies yielded a sixth category—Silent treatment. These six categories were used in the order listed, with Silent treatment used less than Charm and more than Debasement. Then, using the Eysenck Personality Questionnaire and the Wiggins Interpersonal Adjective Scale, the authors examined the relation between dimensions of personality and the type of influence behaviour used. They found, for example, that individuals high in neuroticism tended to use "silent treatment" and "regression" (e.g. pouting, sulking) in conflict situations. Use of silent treatment was associated also with the adjectives "calculating", "cold", and "quarrelsome", and negatively with "agreeable" and "gregarious".

Steil and Weltman (1992) used a different Adjective Check List in a study of dual career couples, assessing the influence strategies with an instrument that did not include strongly coercive ones. The strategies were characterised along two dimensions—Direct (e.g. stating importance) to Indirect (e.g. hint), and Bilateral (e.g. persuade) to Unilateral (e.g. withdraw). Direct strategies were reported as used most often. Indirect-Unilateral strategies were used most often at home, Indirect-Bilateral at work. Indirect-Unilateral strategies, such as withdrawal, were more likely to be used by the less self-confident subjects, while more nurturant women tended to use Indirect-Bilateral approaches, such as suggesting and smiling. Women said that they used suggesting and smiling more often than did men (see also Falbo & Peplau, 1980).

Two other studies may be mentioned. Stets and Pirog-Good (1990), in their student sample, found that control (both attempted and successful) was negatively related to self-esteem for women, and the successful use of control was negatively related to self-esteem for men. And conflicts were found to be more likely to involve psychological and/or physical abuse if the participants scored highly on a hostility scale (Smith, Sanders, & Alexander, 1990) or had a high need for power as assessed by a Thematic Apperception Test (Mason & Blankenship, 1987).

The use of conflict style to characterise relationships was mentioned also in Chapter 4.

Relationship Differences in Conflict Behaviour. The techniques used in a conflict situation must be seen as a dyadic matter, to be studied in the stream of interaction (Williamson & Fitzpatrick. 1985). Here Fitzpatrick's categorisation of marital types (pp.63–65) has been valuable. For example Independents were found to use more "one-up" behaviours (involving attempts to restrict the behavioural options of the other) than the other types. Traditionals used complementary interaction in neutral discussion but competitive symmetry (each attempting to restrict the other's options) in a conflict situation.

Again using the categorisation of interaction styles into Traditionals, Separates, and Independents, Witteman and Fitzpatrick (1986) addressed the techniques used to gain compliance by 51 married students. The students were asked to carry out two role plays representing areas of potential conflict. Of the three pure types of relationship, Traditionals used arguments whose force came from the expected nature or importance of engaging in an activity. Since such couples tend to share values and to be fairly open with each other, they were able to discuss expected outcomes of actions. They did not use appeals to values or obligations, but did use arguments depending on the individual's conception of the relationship.

Separates tended to focus on the negative consequences of non-compliance, and often used blatant attempts to constrain the behaviour or internal state of the spouse. The Independents appealed to obligations and values of the other, and used both power, with stress on the consequences of compliance or non-compliance, and references to the relationship.

Burggraf and Sillars (1987) also showed that communication about conflict was significantly related to the type of couple, though their data differed somewhat from previous studies. Thus Traditional couples tended to be avoidant and conciliatory, Separates frequently confrontative. No clear sex differences in conversational style emerged. The authors suggest that mutual influence within conversation tends to remove individual speaker differences. VanLear and Zietlow (1990) took this one stage further, showing that the different types of couples find different types of behaviours and interaction patterns satisfying. In a sample of 51 couples, many of them elderly, they found, for example, that a willingness to defer to the partner seemed to be characteristic of satisfied Traditionals, and refusal to defer problematic. While deferral to a dominance attempt was more satisfying for Traditional than for other couple types, a dominating attempt responded to by an expression of identification or equivalence was dissatisfying for Traditionals, but most satisfying for Separates, while Separates found the deferral followed by equivalence particularly unsatisfactory.

Conflict in Distressed Marriages. Distressed and non-distressed couples differ in the way in which they manage conflict (Margolin & Wampold, 1981), and the differences indicate that how conflicts are handled has an important influence on the future of the relationship (Gottman & Krokoff, 1989). In general, studies of interaction patterns in distressed and non-distressed couples discussing a marital problem show that the former display more negative affect and greater reciprocity of negative affect. In some cases there is also more reciprocity of positive affect. Some representative studies are noted in the following paragraphs (see also Chapter 6).

Although Gottman (1979) found that distressed and non-distressed marital couples were equally likely to disagree verbally, the distressed couples were much more likely to express disagreement in their non-verbal behaviour. Furthermore they were more likely to reciprocate negative affect than were non-distressed couples. Other studies show that partners who are dissatisfied with their relationships tend to react to negative messages in extreme ways and to underestimate the frequencies of positive behaviours (Jacobson, Folletti, & McDonald, 1982). While distressed couples tend to be destructive, coercive or rejecting (Schaap, Buunk, & Kerkstra, 1988), happy couples tend to use constructive ways of managing conflict, suggesting compromises or alternatives, and summarising, clarifying, or validating each other's positions (Cousins & Vincent, 1983).

These and other data indicate that low negativity in interaction is a better criterion for distinguishing non-distressed from distressed couples than the incidence of positive interactions. Montgomery (1988a, b) and Rusbult, Johnson, and Morrow (1986a, b) comment that this may be a consequence of the prevailing ideology. People are expected to behave positively, and thus positive behaviour is less salient (see also Acitelli, Douvan, & Veroff, 1993; Reis & Knee, 1996).

Other studies have shown generally similar findings. In a large-scale study of around 1500 individuals in Detroit, McGonagle et al. (1993) showed that increased frequency of disagreement, a negative conflict resolution style, and poor disagreement outcomes were each associated with marital dissolution over a period of about three years. A general negativity factor, derived by factor analysis and involving frequent arguments, tense interactions, low levels of mutual appreciation and of calm problem-solving, failure to compromise, and few satisfactory outcomes, was more powerful in predicting dissolution than either conflict resolution style or poor conflict outcomes. Although McGonagle and colleagues could find no evidence that couples who never engage in conflict are at long-term risk, they point out the importance of distinguishing between the avoidance of issues that might give rise to conflict and withdrawal during the course of a conflict. They found that frequent disagreements and avoidance of disagreements were positively correlated. Couples who both disagreed most frequently and avoided disagreement were most at risk for marital disruption (see also pp.168–169).

On the basis of analyses of audiotaped problem-solving discussions, Krokoff (1987) found that negative affect in the wives was related to their attempts to confront the problem and enforce their own views, and inversely related to attempts to be conciliatory. The husband's negative affect was inversely related to both spouses' attempts to be conciliatory, and to wives viewing the relationship as a resource for helping them with their problems. Gottman and Krokoff (1989) found that withdrawal, defensiveness, and stubbornness were associated with later marital dissatisfaction. This means that the negativity of a husband is less likely to be associated with relationship-maintenance behaviour, which might buffer its impact (see pp.186–187), than is that of wives. This may account for the finding that husbands' negativity predicts declines in wives' satisfaction, while wives' negativity does not have a similar effect on husbands' satisfaction (Huston & Chorost, 1994).

In a study of 20 well-adjusted and 20 maladjusted (not clinical) couples discussing problems in their relationship, Alberts (1988) found that the adjusted couples were more likely to make complaints about behaviour, to show positive affect and to acknowledge agreement than the maladjusted ones. The latter were more likely to complain about personal characteristics, to show negative affect, and to meet complaints with counter-complaints.

Difficulties in discussing marital problems are exacerbated by mis-perceptions. Gaelick et al. (1985) found that participants reciprocated the degree of love or hostility they perceived their partners to show, and believed their own expressions were reciprocated by their partners. How-ever their perceptions were inaccurate in that only hostility, and not love, was actually reciprocated.

As we have seen in Chapter 6, Noller (e.g. 1987) has made extensive studies of non-verbal communication in distressed couples. She found that well-adjusted couples were more accurate at decoding each other's non-verbal messages, more aware of their decoding, and better able to predict the accuracy of their spouses' decoding. Poorly adjusted couples (especially husbands) tended to rely on the visual channel in decoding messages, although the vocal channel gave better accuracy. Their messages were more negative and the negative messages more intense. They also sent more messages in which the verbal, vocal and visual channels carried discrepant messages (Noller et al., 1994). Men tend to display a negative bias in interpreting messages, women a positive one. The evidence indicated reciprocal influences between communication and satisfaction.

Special interest attaches to the use of physiological measures in dis-cussions between spouses. Following up their earlier findings, Levenson and Gottman (1985) found that couples with lower marital satisfaction showed physiological linkage when engaged in a problem-orientated discussion—that is, measures of physiological variables (heart rate, skin conductance) were more closely inter-related. Decreases in marital satisfaction three years later were predictable from the level of physiological arousal at the time of the interaction—even from the basic arousal level taken when the spouses sat silently before the interaction began. However later studies suggested that the physiological data might not be so predictive of marital dissolu-tion as at first seemed likely (Gottman & Levenson, 1992).

Conflict and the Stage of the Relationship

The impact of conflict or negativity on the nature of a relationship appears to change with time. Although conflict has been said to be more overt and explosive in younger couples (O'Brien, cited in Newcomb & Bentler, 1981), there is evidence that it matters less, at any rate at the time. Markman (1981) studied the relation between the ways courting couples perceived their relationship and their subsequent marital satisfaction. Couples dis-cussed solutions to five tasks, rating their perceptions of the positivity/

negativity of their partner's communications. The ratings were unrelated to their reported satisfaction, but the more positively they rated each other's communications at the time, the more satisfied they were with their relationships two and five years later. Although this study involves correlations between two self-ratings, it suggests that some couples might have been unaware of (or denied) early problems which did not produce their effects until later.

Twenty-one couples were studied by interview and questionnaire methods when newlyweds and two and a half years after marriage by Kelly, Huston, and Cate (1985). Retrospective accounts of conflict (e.g. argument) were not related to the couples' feelings about each other in early courtship, but were related to maintenance behaviours designed to improve the relationship. However, with time the relation with maintenance behaviour disappeared. The data thus indicated that early on, but not later, conflict was met by increased attempts to overcome difficulties. Conflict during courtship was, however, strongly related to conflict and to low levels of love and satisfaction in marriage, especially for the wives. (Love in marriage, interestingly, was not significantly related to the reported strength of love during courtship—if anything, the more the couples were in love before marriage, the less they were after.) Although it is dangerous to argue from the absence of a correlation, the absence of a significant correlation between love and conflict before marriage suggests that, at that time, something compensates for conflict or the partners do not pay attention to it. The authors suggested that at that stage the continuation of the relationship depends on the partners misperceiving each other, or on their being more likely to attribute conflict to misunderstandings or circumstances (cf. Markman, 1981, cited earlier; see also p.184). However, premarital conflict did predict satisfaction and dyadic adjustment in marriage, so perhaps when conflicts continue, they are attributed to personal inadequacies in the partner and/or incompatibility, and thus feelings about the relationship change. Partners tend to assess their relationship as a whole, so that the effects of negativity (at least that of the husband) can be ameliorated by positivity; and also that the relations between emotional expression and satisfaction are two-way (Huston & Vangelisti, 1991; Huston & Chorost, 1994; Rusbult et al., 1991).

Noller et al. (1994) were also concerned with what aspects of resolution strategy and behaviour affect satisfaction, and whether the effects are immediate or delayed. These authors studied couples just before, and one and three years after, marriage, and found little change in conflict resolution strategies over this period, again suggesting that destructive communication patterns that cause problems later in marriage may be there from the start. Negativity (threats, verbal and physical abuse) and destructive conflict resolution patterns were related to low satisfaction. Those with low marital satisfaction also tended to avoid or withdraw in potentially conflictful situations—a finding which confirms that withdrawal as a strategy is not conducive to marital satisfaction (see earlier).

Another finding in this study, in harmony with the view that destructive strategies may be present from the start in marriages that eventually break down, was that spouses low in satisfaction increased their positive behaviour and decreased their negative behaviour one year after marriage, but subsequently reverted to their original style. At one year, satisfaction was less for both spouses if positivity was low and disengagement and destruction high. However wife's support and husband's use of reason were negatively related to their own satisfaction, in harmony with the view that spouses low in satisfaction make a special effort at this time. Over the two years the findings were consistent with the view that wives respond to husbands' withdrawal and avoidance by using coercion, and this makes husbands withdraw further.

Although this study involved only 33 couples at all three time points, it is remarkable in that data on both communication and satisfaction were obtained over the presumably critical first two years of marriage. Many subtleties in the changes in interaction patterns over time were revealed, and the authors put special emphasis on the circular nature of some of the effects—conflict style predicted later satisfaction, and low satisfaction predicted later conflict.

Conflict and Closeness

The behaviour used in a conflict situation is likely to differ according to the closeness of the relationship. Prager (1991) investigated the relationship between the conflict management style used by partners (married, or together for at least six months) in a videotaped discussion of the most important disagreement in the relationship, and the "Intimacy Status" of their relationship. "Intimacy" was used to include "closeness" and commitment. The categories, in order of decreasing "Intimacy", were "Intimate", "Merger", "Pseudointimate", "Preintimate", and "Stereotyped". The latter category implied an uncommitted relationship lacking closeness and involvement, and was not found in the study. Contrary to predictions, individuals in the Intimate status category did not show more cognitively orientated or problem-focused conflict behaviour than those in other groups, but showed a balance between the content and emotional aspects of the problem. However women in the Pseudointimate group used more cognitive problem-focused strategies, and women of Merger status used more affective emotion-focused strategies than Pseudointimates. The partners tended to respond to each other in kind, so that coercive and affective acts discouraged problem-focused responses by the partner.

VIOLENCE

Some conflicts escalate into physical violence, and a surprising proportion of murders occur in the context of relationships. In a 1958 study in Philadelphia, half of 588 homicides involved a victim who was either a friend or a relative, and a 1982 FBI report indicates that a least 55% of homicide victims were known to the murderer (Goldstein, 1986).

Of course most violence is much less severe, but in studies in the USA violence seems to be surprisingly common even in relationships that the participants see as close. Shotland (1989) reviews a number of studies indicating that about one-fifth of college women had experienced forceful attempts at sexual intercourse, while Gryl et al. (1991) found that nearly a third of the college men and women in their sample reported violence in their current dating relationship. This ranged from being pushed or shoved to (rarely) the use of a lethal weapon. Surprisingly, however, only 15% of the respondents said the relationship deteriorated as a result.

Although those in violent relationships argued more, felt more angry and resentful, and had more serious disagreements than those in non-violent relationships, and although the negotiation strategies used tended to be evasive, one-sided, and emotional, they did report feelings of love. This is in harmony with a conclusion reached by Bookwala, Frieze, and Grote (1994), who cited studies indicating that a substantial proportion of courtships involve aggression, and that in nearly one third of these cases the aggression is interpreted as love. This must surely reflect values in the sub-culture. Gryl et al. (1991) found that the incidence of violence tended to be greater in those relationships that had lasted longer, and suggest that individuals in love before violence starts are likely to downplay its importance (see also Noller et al., 1994).

A high need for power is associated with physical abuse in men but not in women (Mason & Blankenship, 1987). However Stets and Pirog-Good (1990), in a study of students, found that men were no more likely than women to attempt control in the sense of managing or regulating the partner's thoughts, feelings, or actions. Women who attempted to control and men who successfully controlled were more likely to inflict and sustain minor aggression. Perhaps surprisingly, women were responsible for more severe aggression than men, but the data indicated that women used aggression to gain control, men to maintain it, and other studies indicate that aggressiveness is more closely related to gender than to sex (cited Wood, 1993). Christopher, Owens, and Stecker (1993), studying a sample of 184 male students, found that individuals low in empathy were likely to have violent attitudes and to be easily angered, and that violent attitudes were also positively linked to anger through hostility to women. Having violent attitudes and sexual promiscuity both had a direct link to premarital sexual aggression. Aggression was also linked to anger through past negative relational experiences.

Not surprisingly, high scores on a hostility scale have been associated with self-reported anger and overt hostility in marital discussion, especially in men. Such men also blamed their spouses for the disagreements (Smith, Sanders, & Alexander, 1990). Mason and Blankenship (1987) assessed the needs for power, affiliation, and activity inhibition from the protocols of a thematic apperception test. Men, but not women, with a high need for power were especially likely to inflict abuse. Amongst women, those who were stressed, had a high need for affiliation, and low activity inhibition, were most likely to be abusive.

Studies of student samples could be interpreted on the view that one partner was high on trait aggression, or that the dating relationship involves situations where passions are especially likely to erupt into violence. However it must not be forgotten that the tendency towards violence may be more a part of the relationship than of either participant as an individual. Bugental et al. (1993) provide evidence that abusive parents hold threat-oriented relationship schemata which indicate to them that negative interactions with the child are controlled by the child and not by themselves. This, in an interaction with the child, may trigger a sequence of cognition, affect, and behaviour that perpetuates the schema (see also Gergen & Gergen, 1988).

SUMMARY

1. Some degree of conflict is almost inevitable in a close relationship. Defence processes may operate to suppress conscious awareness of the conflict.
2. Conflict can be constructive.
3. Conflicts may concern immediate goals, but most involve (also) incompatible long-term issues, such as the conflict between autonomy and connectedness.
4. Conflict is associated with a number of personality and situational factors.
5. Jealousy is a potent source of relationship conflict.
6. The possibility of resolution is influenced by the partners' attitudes to conflict and by the attributions that they make. Distressed partners are liable to see negative behaviour as reflecting global characteristics, positive behaviour as due to temporary or situational factors.
7. Methods of dealing with long-term conflict issues can be categorised as selection, separation, neutralisation, and reframing.

8. Some ways of describing behaviour in conflict situations are discussed. The female demand/male withdraw pattern is both common and ineffective.
9. The strategies used in conflict situations vary with the personalities of the individuals involved, and the stage and nature of the relationship.
10. Conflict behaviour in distressed and non-distressed marriages are compared.
11. The relations between conflict and satisfaction may be affected by other aspects of the relationship, and changes with the stage of the relationship.
12. Conflicts sometimes lead to violence. This is not always resented.

11 Conflict and Power: Power

In general, people like to feel in control of the situations which they are in. When the degree of control that they perceive themselves to have falls below a desired level, the discrepancy causes anxiety and they seek, perhaps without conscious intent, to increase their control. The means by which they do this may be subtle. In this chapter we consider the nature of power and its relation to control. We shall see that it is a more slippery concept than might appear at first sight.

POWER AND CONTROL

When the goals of the two participants in a relationship do not coincide, it is natural to ask whether, and to what extent, the behaviour of one partner is controlled by that of the other—who holds the power? However we shall see that, while the concept of "power" has an obvious value in some contexts, its usefulness is limited.

Although there is little agreement about how "power" should be defined (Murstein & Adler, 1995), we may take Thibaut and Kelley's (1959) definition of power as a starting point—Person A has power over B to the extent that by varying his behaviour he can affect the quality of B's outcomes. With dyads such as teacher–pupil, officer–soldier or doctor–patient it is obvious, at any rate at first sight, where the main power lies. But the ability of A to affect B's outcomes by no means rules out the possibility that B can affect A's.

Power is in fact rarely absolute: it usually involves at most an influence by one partner on the relative probabilities of actions by the other. Indeed, the exercise of power is usually limited by the controlled party: the worker can strike, or seek employment elsewhere. Even in the parent–child relationship, where the parent seems to hold the power since he controls the tangible resources, the child can in fact control the parent in many ways— by creating a disturbance, by eliciting care-giving behaviour, or even by punishing himself by self-inflicted injury or starvation. In most close relationships one partner has power in some contexts and the other in others, the power distribution being the result of negotiation between them (cf. discussion of complementarity in Chapter 9). These two latter points indicate that power is a property of the relationship and not of one or other individual.

TYPES OF POWER

It will already be apparent that the ways in which "power" may operate in a relationship may be diverse, if only because of the varied natures of the resources involved. We may take as a starting point a classification of types of influence due to French and Raven (1959), which recognises five categories:

(i) *Reward Power*. This depends on A's potential for providing rewards to B. Any type of resource may be involved. In general, reward power may influence any aspect of B's behaviour that involves dependence on A, but it is unlikely to be effective for actions that B believes will remain unknown to A.

(ii) *Coercive Power*. This depends on A's capacity for punishing B. Punishment here includes not only physical punishment, but also the removal of resources. One form of coercion whose importance in intimate relationships has been neglected is silence: the power of non-disclosure will be familiar to the parents of teenagers. However we saw in the last chapter that withdrawal seldom provides a long-term solution.

As with reward power, any type of resource may be involved. However the exercising of coercive power is apt to be more difficult (and thus more costly) than that of reward power, since B is prone to display actions that he or she believes will be rewarded but to hide actions that he or she believes will be punished (Thibaut & Kelley, 1959). Furthermore the consequences of coercive power may be complex. Pain inflicted as punishment, and frustration induced by the non-availability of resources, may have complex consequences, including aggression directed towards the supposed frustrating agent or redirected elsewhere (Dollard et al., 1939; Ulrich & Symannek, 1969).

In most cases, of course, the effectiveness of a reward or punishment depends on the previous experience of the individual concerned. Very often, rewards and punishments are symbolic.

(iii) *Expert Power*. This depends on special knowledge or skill, possessed by A, on which B depends in some way. It is obviously characteristic of relationships such as that between doctor and patient or teacher and pupil. Its effectiveness depends not only on B's dependence on A's knowledge or skill, but also on the esteem in which B holds A relative to other potential sources of expertise. Often expert power involves the dispensation of information, as in the teacher–pupil case. However in this and other cases its effectiveness may depend on further, perhaps more tangible, resources that thereby become available to B. The patient values the doctor not only because he wishes to cease to be ill, but because he values the opportunities that health will bring.

Apart from fatigue, time, and the opportunity to obtain other rewards, the exercise of expert power may involve A in little cost. However it must be remembered that in exercising it A may diminish his ability to influence B in the future: the ill patient is more dependent on his doctor than the healthy one; and the more a teacher teaches his pupil, the less the pupil needs him.

(iv) *Legitimate Power*. This refers to the exercise of power by A over B by virtue of B's acceptance of A's authority, often as a consequence of conventions current in the society. Thus it may be usual to accept the authority of A because of his age, his relationship to B, or his status in society. The extreme case is of course acceptance of the power of a supernatural being.

Acceptance of A's status by B may depend on expectations of future rewards or escape from future punishment consequent upon the relationship. Thus in multiplex relationships status may bring legitimate power even to situations in which that status is irrelevant, as when teacher meets pupil out of school. In other cases legitimate power can be ascribed to B's satisfaction consequent upon behaving in a manner congruent with his own values and norms. To the extent that A can evoke such norms, he is asserting power over B.

This form of power is of special importance in the relations between the sexes. Traditional norms have given a higher power status to the male in heterosexual relationships, and are still accepted by both partners in many couples, give rise to conflict in some, but are being increasingly disregarded in an increasing number of others.

(v) *Referent Power*. This is based on the identification of B with A. B is attracted to, admires, or envies A, and therefore models himself on A and is influenced by A's behaviour. Referent power may develop out of reward power, perhaps because the exercise of reward makes A more attractive to B. It may also arise from the need for consensual validation: if B sees A as similar to himself, or desires to see himself as similar to A, he may imitate his behaviour and use him as a model with which to interpret his own experiences. It is also possible for A to exert negative referent power over B: if B finds A distasteful, he may attempt to behave in ways different from him.

Referent power usually involves no cost to A. Indeed it may occur in A's absence, and even continue for years after his or her death. It may operate even in the absence of any awareness by A or B that it is doing so.

French and Raven's classificatory system considerably extends the notion of power, as used in everyday life, to encompass a much wider range of influences exerted by one individual on another. Kelvin (1977) points out that the five forms of power fall into two groups whose psychological characteristics are quite different. Reward and coercive power are rooted in sanctions and lead to *compliance*. Expert and referent power, by contrast, depend on *acceptance*: an expert is not an expert unless he is accepted as such. Legitimate power also involves acceptance by the less powerful of the right of the more powerful to influence him, though indirect sanctions may operate. Homans (1976) had made a similar point in distinguishing between power and authority. In the latter case A has control over B's outcomes, but only because B believes that obedience will bring favourable outcomes from the external social or physical environment.

Operation of the different types of power is however related to the probability of open conflict. The more reward and coercive power the participants in a relationship have over each other, and the smaller the discrepancy between their power over each other, the more likely is "autistic" conflict (see p.154) to develop. Where there is a large power difference, it seems that guilt on the part of the more powerful tends to reduce "autistic" conflict. Expert and referent power, by contrast, are often associated with mutual respect, and thus the probability of "autistic" conflict is reduced. Legitimate power tends to reduce conflict because of the associated norms specifying the rights and duties of the parties (Holmes & Miller, 1976).

In any case, the exercise of power is usually limited by the emergence of norms. If a powerful partner A threatens to use his power, B may appeal to a norm of fairness. Or B may threaten to leave the relationship, whereupon A may appeal to a norm of loyalty (e.g. Thibaut 1968). Limitations on the use of power are reviewed by Gruder (1970).

POWER AND THE RESOURCES EXCHANGED

While French and Raven's categories of sources of power appear clear-cut, their applicability to close relationships raises some further issues. But first we may ask how they relate to exchange theories (see Chapters 19 and 20).

In terms of exchange theory, A's power over B will be determined primarily by the resources that A controls and B dependence on those resources. B's dependence will depend in part on the availability of those resources elsewhere. However this will not be the only issue, for A's power will also be affected by the costs he incurs in transferring the resources to B. Here, however, the issues differ somewhat with the type of resource in question. Foa and Foa (1974) pointed out that the various resources transferred in personal relationships have different properties. If A influences B by transferring goods or money (reward power), A will consequently have less. If A imparts information to B (expert power), B may become better informed and A therefore less able to influence him in the future. But A may also acquire information, in the sense of increased understanding, in the process of teaching. If A gives status to B (legitimate power), he may thereby diminish his own superiority or increase his own inferiority, but he may also strengthen his relationship with B and hope to gain therefrom in the future. If A gives services to B, he may or may not limit his capacity to help B in the future. But if A gives love to B, he may thereby augment his own resources, for giving pleasure to a loved one adds to one's enjoyment. The important point that Foa and Foa have made here does not depend on the precise details of their classification of resources: the nature of the change in the donor's resources, consequent upon giving, depends on what has been given.

The point must be taken even further. Another cost of resource exchange concerns the time involved. Performing a service for another involves time that could have been spent in other ways. Actions falling within the Foas' category of love, and to a lesser extent many of those classed as involving status, may be peculiar here also. For whilst the cost in time of giving most resources involves the time involved in the transaction and the time involved in acquiring (or replacing) the resource, the giving of love (or status) may involve commitments of time extending into the future.

The Foas emphasised that resources differ on a dimension of particularism: the value of money is the same whatever its source, but the value of love depends critically on who gives it. This dimension of particularism introduces a further consideration. In principle, whilst any type of resource could be available elsewhere, transactions with any particular supplier often tend to increase the probability that future transactions will involve the same individual. This is the case even with non-particularate resources like money—we tend to go to the bank clerk we know. In so far as B has a tendency to return to the same supplier, that supplier's power over B is increased even if alternative sources of reward are available, for by making use of those alternative sources B would be incurring extra costs. This is of course even more the case with particularate resources, such as love—especially when the exchange of love involves commitment. Furthermore sanctions imposed by society, or by individually held beliefs about monogamy, limit some transactions to particular individuals. In such cases the nature of the relationship makes alternative relationships less desirable.

In summary, then, the issues that actually arise over the power in relationships vary with the resource in question.

POWER IN CLOSE RELATIONSHIPS

The distribution of power is always an issue in close relationships, though the distribution may not be equal, and inequality may be accepted and does not necessarily detract from satisfaction in the relationship.

Even in a society with egalitarian ideals, men often have more power in premarital heterosexual relationships than women. Although not all the evidence is in harmony with this conclusion, there are a number of reasons why it might be so. Considerable evidence suggests that men tend to be less motivated towards intimate relationships (e.g. McAdams, 1988), or at least to intimacy within relationships: since intimacy (as the term is usually used) is usually mutual and reciprocal, the partner to whom it matters less is likely to set the pace of relating. In addition, traditional sex roles have left a legacy of male power even in close relationships (Rosenbluth & Steil, 1995; Wood, 1993). However, the evidence for a similar conclusion about marriage is less clear-cut (Murstein & Adler, 1995), and the issue presumably depends primarily on the norms of the sub-culture, though in most cases male power is still the norm. The distribution of power may also depend on the context in which power is assessed and the precise questions asked in any assessment (see pp.147–148).

Even in premarital heterosexual relationships, it is not always the case that men tend to hold more power. In a study of 272 dating individuals, Stets (1993) found that women controlled more than men over everyday issues. It is salutary to compare possible explanations for this with those given for male power (see earlier). Thus it has been suggested that women's greater control could be understood in terms of the evidence that women have more control over love—men fall in love more; that the woman's involvement is a better predictor of the health of a heterosexual relationship than the man's; that more relationships are ended by women than by men; and that the ending of a relationship tends to be more traumatic for the male partner (e.g. Hill et al., 1976). High conflict in a relationship, or lack of perspective taking, can give rise to a perception of loss of control.

Perhaps because they have more power, when their control is threatened women feel that they have more to lose, and therefore may step up their control. It is also possible that, in dating relationships, men seek to please, conceding power in the hope of future favours.

However, it is somewhat revealing to ask how far the French and Raven classification applies to close relationships. In the first place, in relationships in which it may seem obvious at first sight where the power lies, the impression may be deceptive. The means whereby power is exerted are often very subtle—the complaining of the hypochondriac, exploitation of the partner's anxiety or solicitude, the "I'm upset" routine, the nurturant care which cannot be refused without offending the barriers of convention.

Second, the French and Raven classification might be seen as implying an equality of power between the two participants apart from the source of power specified—the more powerful individual is so only because he or she holds the means to reward, punish, or teach. Power may, however, be largely determined by personal characteristics—some individuals seek to dominate and have characteristics that enable them to do so, others tend to be submissive, nurturant, and so on. Seen from this perspective, the French and Raven categories become tools for exerting power rather than sources of power.

Third, even if one of these categories does apply, it is likely to be limited to particular types of interaction, and not to the whole relationship.

Fourth, the role of legitimate power in marriage is changing in the Western world. That of referent power is more difficult to specify: in the paradigmatic romantic relationship, each partner may idealise the other, so that each holds referent power. In the real world, in so far as the partners are to be seen as constructing a common narrative, doing what the other wants becomes a goal in its own right, and power is not an issue.

That, perhaps, brings one to the nub of the matter. The French and Raven classification could imply that relationships are merely strings of interactions—a view certainly not applicable to close relationships. And in the real world, in so far as the partners are to be seen as constructing a common narrative, doing what the other wants becomes a goal in its own right, and power is irrelevant. Nevertheless, as we have seen (Chapter 10), some degree of conflict is almost inevitable—the incompatibilities between autonomy and connectedness, self-disclosure and privacy, and so on, must be resolved. And although the giving of love may involve no depletion of resources (see earlier), it can itself be a source of power, in that it may be seen to create an obligation for connectedness (cf. p.442). The romantic ideal of loving for love's sake and expecting nothing in return is incompatible with our ideas of fairness. Being loved can therefore be seen as a denial of autonomy, of being in the other's power, and in the extreme case of being smothered. And the feeling of a loss of autonomy can conflict with the desire to please the partner. Thus, while power over specific issues can be a useful concept for understanding close relationships, a more detailed examination of where power lies leads one into considerable difficulties. The power that comes with loving does not fit easily into any of the French and Raven categories.

POWER TACTICS

The means whereby power is exerted vary widely, and some of the more subtle ways were mentioned earlier. Some techniques, such as the use of threats or promises, inducing guilt, or passive manipulation may have adverse effects on the relationship in the long term if not immediately, because they are based on the view of only one participant (Rubin & Rubin, 1993). We may consider some examples in which the tactics used were shown to be related to personal or relationship characteristics.

By asking subjects to write an open-ended essay describing how they "got their way" with their partners, and coding the resulting data, Falbo and Peplau (1980) listed 13 categories of "power strategy" used by the subjects. These were: Asking, Bargaining, Laissez-faire, Negative affect, Persistence, Persuasion, Positive affect, Reasoning, Stating importance, Suggesting, Talking, Telling, and Withdrawal. Analysis (Multidimensional scaling) showed that these fell into two dimensions: one, going from indirect to direct approaches, was labelled as "Directness"; the other, going from interactive strategies to those in which one person takes unilateral action, was labelled as "Bilaterality" (See also Steil & Weltman, 1992, cited p.182). The Directness dimension was associated with satisfaction with the relationship, and Bilaterality with preferences for autonomy. The sample included homosexual men and lesbian women, but only amongst the heterosexuals was there a gender difference in the strategies employed. Male heterosexuals tended to report using Bilateral and Direct strategies, female heterosexuals Unilateral and Indirect ones. It is somewhat surprising that the males tended to use techniques conducive to relationship satisfaction more than the women: the authors ascribe this finding to the fact that the men saw themselves as influencing their partner from a position of relative strength and, expecting compliance, used Bilateral and Direct strategies.

In a study of women in heterosexual and lesbian couples, Rosenbluth and Steil (1995) found that in both groups Relationship Intimacy (based on a 60-item scale assessing Romantic love, Supportiveness, and Communication ease) was related to the use of Direct/Bilateral strategies in both groups, and argue that this suggests that equality of power between partners facilitates feelings of intimacy. In this study the woman's Self-esteem and "Capacity for intimacy" were also measured, the latter by a scale containing 28 two-choice comparative value judgements. For women partnered with women, high Self-esteem and high Capacity for intimacy predicted relationship intimacy, but this was not the case for women in heterosexual relationships. The authors suggest that this was because power is usually unequally distributed in heterosexual couples for the reasons mentioned earlier.

In a study of homosexual and heterosexual couples, Howard, Blumstein, and Schwartz (1986) identified six types of influence tactics—Bargaining, Manipulation (drop hints, flatter, etc.), Autocracy (insist, claim knowledge), Disengagement (sulk, make guilty), Supplication, and Bullying, their frequencies decreasing in that order. The subjects' gender, structural power (e.g. income, age, attractiveness) and personal power (commitment to and dependence on the relationship) were also assessed. The weaker influence tactics of manipulation and supplication were used to men and by those weak on structural or personal power. The neutral tactics of disengagement and bargaining were used more by men, but the strong tactics of autocracy and bullying showed few relations with the individual characteristics assessed.

NON-VERBAL CONCOMITANTS OF POWER

One rather subtle indicator of power in a relationship is worth noting in that it depends on what the individuals feel, rather than on their actual abilities to influence each other's outcomes. It is the ratio of the amount an individual looks at the partner while he/she is speaking to the amount he/she looks while listening. This ratio tends to be higher in individuals with higher social power. Dovidio et al. (1988) showed further that, with no power differential the ratio tended to be higher in men than in women.

THE USEFULNESS OF THE CONCEPT
OF POWER

A number of authors have expressed reservations about the usefulness of the concept of power (e.g. Cromwell & Olson, 1975; Rollins & Bahr, 1976; Safilios-Rothschild, 1970; Sprey, 1972; Turk, 1974). These mostly stem from the difficulties of measuring power, and these in turn come from the very nature of relationships—what A does depends at least to some extent on B, so one must ask whether A exerts power over B or B elicits dominant behaviour from A. And beyond that, we have already seen that it is necessary to discriminate between who makes decisions and who decides who should make decisions (pp.147–148). Furthermore it is not usual for power to be absolute, for it may differ according to the nature or context of the interaction, and B may have alternative sources of supply. Thus A may have more power than B in some contexts, while B has more than A in others. The power structure may then depend on complex and continuing negotiation on a number of levels in the different but inter-related areas of the relationship.

But the fact is that many individuals in relationships do feel that they are controlled by their partners, and it is what they feel that matters, however difficult it is to evaluate it or assess its bases. One may speculate that this has at least two sources. First, as noted earlier, social norms have long assumed male control in many aspects of heterosexual relationships, though with the growth of feminism more and more people are challenging this convention. Second, we have seen that in heterosexual relationships there is a tendency for women to feel a greater need for connectedness than men. They are therefore likely to be less willing to do anything that might disturb the relationship. The fact that anything they did might upset the relationship could, of course, be a consequence of male pride or stubbornness. Nevertheless, as a result women may feel that their autonomy is constrained, and suffer stress or other costs.

SUMMARY

1. Power involves the ability to control another's behaviour. It is rarely absolute.
2. Power has been categorised as Reward, Coercive, Expert, Referent, and Legitimate power.
3. In terms of exchange theory, the utility of these categories is influenced by the nature of the resource exchanged. If A gives B money, A has less; but if A gives B love, A may have more.
4. The concept of power, most easily applicable to interactions, runs into difficulties in the study of close relationships. This is partly due to the fact that loving involves a desire to please the loved one, so that power is irrelevant, and partly because the perception of being loved carries with it a perceived obligation to reciprocate, and this can be seen as involving a loss of autonomy.
5. Tactics used to exert power vary widely.
6. Whilst the bases of power are often difficult to specify, it is common for one partner to feel controlled by the other.

B4 Closeness

In Chapters 4–6 we discussed what the participants in a relationship do together, and how they do it, and we were mostly concerned with interactions seen as separate units by an external observer. In considering the frequency and patterning of interactions in Chapter 7, and even more with the pattern of reciprocity vs. complementarity, and conflict and power in Chapters 8–11, the focus was less on the individual interactions, and more on the relations between the parts within the whole sequence of interactions. Now Chapters 12–15 focus on the relationship as a whole, and on its more subjective aspects. For instance, how far do the participants reveal themselves to each other? (Chapter 12). Do they understand each other? (Chapter 13). These issues contribute, directly or indirectly, to the participants' satisfaction with the relationship (Chapter 14) and to the extent to which they dedicate themselves to its success (Chapter 15).

12 Self-Disclosure and Privacy

The issues that we shall discuss here are not equally important in all relationships. For some formal relationships they would be irrelevant, but for close relationships the extent to which the participants reveal themselves—experiential, emotional, and physical aspects of the self, hopes, beliefs, fears, failures, successes—to each other is of great significance. Through such revelations each builds up a knowledge of the other as a total person—knowledge which extends far beyond the interactions between them and has the potential for affecting future interactions in fundamental ways. As noted in Chapter 4, self-disclosure is thus an important component of intimacy or closeness. Self-revelation by one partner in a relationship permits more effective incorporation of aspects of the relationship into the self-system of the other. Beyond that, self-revelation to another may contribute to self-realisation, helping one to understand oneself better—or at least to construct a new narrative better suited to current circumstances. Thus self-revelation can itself be an instrument of change. Dindia (1994) has suggested that we should think in terms of an intrapersonal–interpersonal dialectical process of self-disclosure.[1]

---

[1] Self-disclosure is often equated with Intimacy (e.g. Altman & Taylor, 1973; Hinde, 1979). As discussed in Chapter 4, however, Intimacy has also been used to cover a number of other dimensions which may or may not include self-disclosure.

SELF-DISCLOSURE AS AN INDIVIDUAL OR RELATIONSHIP CHARACTERISTIC

Early attempts to measure self-disclosure treated it as an individual characteristic, and attempted to characterise individuals along a scale from "disclosers" to "non-disclosers". Thus Jourard (1971), in a number of pioneering studies, used a Self-Disclosure Questionnaire of 60 questions in each of six content areas—attitudes and opinions, tastes and interests, work, money, personality, and body. Subjects were asked to indicate on three-point scales to what extent each type of information had been revealed to father, mother, same-sex best friend and opposite-sex best friend. Not surprisingly, such an instrument is a poor predictor of self-disclosure to a stranger in an experimental situation: what one person tells another depends on who the other is and on the situation.

The extent to which one individual confides in another could be influenced by his/her tendency to confide in people in general, by the tendency of the recipient to act as a confidant(e), and by the nature of the relationship between them. These can be separated by the Social Relations Model (see pp.206–207). Using this approach, Kenny and La Voie (1984) assessed how much individuals felt they had disclosed to other members of their groups. The tendency of the actor to disclose to people in general accounted for 39% of the variance, the tendency of the partner to receive confidences for 15%, and the relationship between them for 46%. Of prime interest in the present context, therefore, is the assessment of self-disclosure in specific relationships.

However the necessity for a distinction between self-disclosure as an individual characteristic and as a relationship characteristic depends partly on the topic discussed. Miller (1990), using a sample of women students, found that disclosure of relatively superficial topics appeared to be an individual characteristic, but for "high intimacy" topics it was characteristic of the relationship. Furthermore, the nature of the relationship may dictate the nature of the disclosures that are made. In a study of parent–adolescent conversations, Spencer (1994) found that both parties were more likely to disclose feelings about the adolescent rather than about the parent—presumably the parents were prone to be judgemental.

ASSESSMENT OF SELF-DISCLOSURE

An important landmark in the assessment of self-disclosure was provided by the work of Altman and Taylor (1973). Their approach was based on a picture of the personality as the systematic organisation of the individual's ideas, beliefs, feelings and emotions. This organisation involves the arrangement of items into areas such as sex, family, or work. This is entirely compatible with the models of the self-system discussed in Chapter

3. For heuristic purposes, they found it convenient to picture the personality as an onion, composed of successive layers of skins. The content areas, such as those listed, are defined on the surface, where relatively superficial items, such as specific biographical facts, are located. The inner layers contain progressively fewer and more fundamental items, involving "basic core feelings about life, trust in others, and the nature of one's self-image" (pp.25–31) (see also Levinger & Snoek, 1972). These more central areas may affect numerous peripheral areas, but they are more vulnerable and less accessible than the external layers.

Disclosure between two individuals can thus be assessed in terms of breadth—that is, how many of the other's surface areas each contacts—and depth, how far penetration proceeds. As a relationship develops, each individual exposes more areas to the other, and penetration in each area becomes deeper. To pursue the onion analogy, as a relationship grows, many wedges are cut into the onion, each becoming wider and deeper.

To assess degree of self-revelation in a quantitative way, Altman and Taylor collected 671 items relevant to self-disclosure, either by taking them from existing tests or by inventing them intuitively. These items were rated by one group of judges for depth, while another classed them in *a priori* topical categories. Thirteen categories were identified, including "Own marriage", "Family", "Love–dating–sex", "Relationships with others" and so on. Each item acquired an intimacy scale rating from 1 to 11 based on the judges' ratings.

On this basis, two aspects of breadth could be measured. Breadth category was simply the number of categories (out of 13) the individual revealed. Breadth frequency was measured either by the total number of items revealed, or by the number per category. Various temporal measures, such as "total time talked per category", were also possible. Measures of depth were obtained from the scale values of the statements used in interaction. Of course, the scaling of the items in such an instrument is liable to change with time and to differ between sub-cultural groups. It must thus be used with great caution.

Using techniques of this general sort, it has been possible to document the manner in which disclosure between college room-mates (Taylor, 1968), or between sailors confined together for 10 days (Altman & Haythorn, 1965), increases with time. In experimental situations it has been possible to show, for instance, that social approval contingent upon self-disclosure augments further disclosure (Taylor, Altman, & Sorrentino, 1969).

It will be apparent that such a method for assessing self-disclosure has a certain artificiality about it. It concerns the content of what is said, not its impact on the receiver. The receiver must understand and assimilate what is said, and defence and other mechanisms may stand in the way. Furthermore the impact on the receiver may depend on the style of the disclosure as well as on the content (Montgomery, 1988b). In addition, the criteria for assessing disclosure are culturally and contextually bound: what is not usually discussed in one society, or in one context within a society, may be in another. And what individuals talk about, and how they talk, will change as a relationship develops, so that what is considered as intimate at one stage may not be so later. In recent studies special instruments have often been designed to suit the problem in hand (e.g. Cline, 1989; Murstein & Adler, 1995).

An important issue concerns the extent to which the participants in a relationship disclose equally to each other. However the assessment of reciprocity is a matter of some complexity. This can be exemplified by a study by Miller and Kenny (1986). The authors distinguish three aspects of reciprocity or perceived reciprocity:

1. *Congruence*, or the relation between how much the subjects disclose to others and how much they believed those others disclosed to them (i.e. perceived reciprocity). Previous studies have reported high levels of congruence.
2. *Accuracy*, or the relation between what A says she discloses to others, and what others says A discloses to them. Again, previous reports indicated fairly high levels.
3. *Mutuality*, or the relation between what A says she discloses to others and what others say they disclose to A. While some previous studies provide evidence for mutuality, Miller and Kenny point out that apparent disclosure reciprocity may be due to a third variable. For instance both might be high (or low) on a general disposition to disclose their intimate thoughts to others. We must therefore also examine mutuality at the dyadic level—that is, the degree of disclosure reciprocity in the unique relationship between A and B after allowing for how much A and B typically disclose and receive disclosures.

Miller and Kenny therefore applied the Social Relations Model to distinguish these effects in a sample of college women. This permits a distinction between reciprocity at the individual level and the dyadic level. The individual level concerns, for instance, the correlation between the extent to which a person discloses in general and the extent to which he believes he receives disclosure in general. The dyadic levels concerns the extent of reciprocity unique to a particular relationship—is there reciprocity between A and B after accounting for the variances due to A's and B's readiness to receive and give disclosures generally to others?

Miller and Kenny found no evidence for mutuality or reciprocity of disclosing at the individual level. There was likewise no evidence for mutuality at the individual level for receiving disclosures. There was some evidence for congruence for topics of low intimacy, but none for accuracy, at the individual level.

However at the dyadic level, the model permits one to examine mutuality allowing for the individual's general levels of giving and receiving disclosures. At this level the coefficients for mutuality in giving and receiving disclosures, and also for congruence and accuracy, were consistently stronger than at the individual level, and significant in each case. The relationship component accounted for 61% of the variance in giving disclosure about low-intimacy topics (with the actor individual effect accounting for a further 38%), and for 86% with more intimate topics. Miller (1990) also found a mutual influence between disclosures given and liking for the particular partner.

BENEFITS AND COSTS: PRIVACY

Close relationships demand self-disclosure. Since most people want close relationships (e.g. Caldwell & Peplau, 1982; Weiss, 1974), and those who lack them may experience loneliness, leading to anxiety, depression, and perceived helplessness (e.g. Peplau & Perlman, 1982), it is to be expected that self-disclosure would have beneficial concomitants. We have seen that self-disclosure with another is necessary for validation of personal worth (Sullivan, 1953) and to confirm aspects of a person's construct system (Kelly, 1955; see Chapters 1 & 3), and to construct the shared meanings needed for a close relationship. It is related to satisfaction in dating partners (Berg & McQuinn, 1986) and married couples (Fincham & Bradbury, 1987a). Men with high intimacy "motivation" (readiness for experiences of warm, close, and communicative interaction with others) have been found to have better psychosocial adjustment in middle age (McAdams, 1988). In addition, self-disclosure may be used as a strategy to reach personal goals. Confidences may be shared in order to advance intimacy, or to enlist cooperation (Miller & Read, 1991).

This does not mean that the consequences of self-disclosure are always beneficial. In the first place, the nature of the disclosure makes a difference. Self-disclosure involves risk and increases the discloser's vulnerability, and may bring a loss of individuality. Secret desires might hurt if shared, and lay the discloser open to ridicule or exploitation. Extreme openness might increase the probability of conflict, and detract from rather than augment the mutuality of the relationship (Altman & Taylor, 1973; Altman, Vinsel, & Brown, 1981). Disclosure of an extra-relationship liaison may be seen as endangering genuine commitment to the continuity of the existing relationship. Information may also be withheld out of a desire not to hurt the partner—for instance opinions about in-laws (Goffman, 1959).

Psychological well-being may be affected by problems stemming from intimate disclosure (Rook, 1988), and married couples who define their relationships in an emotionally somewhat distanced manner may find disclosure disturbing (Fitzpatrick, 1987). Too much or inappropriate disclosure can bring hostility (Miell, Duck, & La Gaipa, 1979). Intrapersonal conflict between openness and protecting the self is thus common, especially when it is a question of exposing stigmatising conditions, such as AIDS (e.g. Dindia, 1994). Retzinger (1995), pointing out that the emotion of shame always involves self-in-relation-to-others, suggested that it often guards the boundaries of privacy, and may involve anything from social discomfort to humiliation. Some areas of the personality may become "sealed off" by mutual agreement, in order to avoid such risks or the possibility of disruptive experiences, or because cultural convention decrees what is appropriate in the particular roles the participants see themselves as playing.

Disclosure may also be limited by the conflict between the needs for autonomy and connectedness in close relationships (see pp.157–160), for self-revelation may involve relinquishing some autonomy. Couples may opt for one or the other, but most close relationships fluctuate between periods of mutual accessibility and periods of relative inaccessibility (Altman et al., 1981). In either case, the retention of areas of privacy may have a subtle importance. Schwartz (1968) and Kelvin (1977) stress that areas of privacy are areas in which the individual is not exposed to the power or influence of others. In Kelvin's view, an individual sees himself as the agent of his own actions in so far as he sees his actions as not governed by social constraints. His sense of continuity across roles and across situations provides him with a view of himself as a unique person, and this sense of uniqueness in turn derives from the areas of privacy that he carries with him wherever he goes. Kelvin admits that evidence for such a view is hard to find, but points to the way in which lack of privacy in total institutions, such as armed forces and prisons, leads to loss of the sense of being oneself.

But at the same time, as we have seen, each individual's concept of self can only be validated by others, and this must apply even to those central areas of privacy. Here, Kelvin argues, lies one of the essential tasks of love. The privacy of these central areas becomes a shared privacy, maintaining the continuity of a shared self. On such a view the others with whom an individual forms intimate relationships become a part of his perceived world, and in so far as the construction and validation of his own self depends on them, part of his self. Because they come to define his position in the world, they have power over him. He is vulnerable to their criticisms or rejection, because they could undermine the beliefs that he holds about himself. But at the same time it is only to them that he can open up the most intimate areas of himself, only with them that he can validate the most essential aspects of his being (Kelvin, 1977). (There are, of course, possible points of contact here with the view that the formation of a close relationship involves including the other in the self—see Aron et al., 1991, cited p.59.)

The ways in which privacy may be violated have been studied by Burgoon et al. (1989) in a wide range of relationships. Analysis of questionnaire data gave five categories—psychological and informational; nonverbal interactional (e.g. standing too close, touching, and verbal invitations to disclose); verbal interactional (violations of conversational norms); physical violations; and impersonal violations (e.g. traffic noise). These authors also detailed techniques used to restore privacy. They emphasise that what is seen as an intrusion on privacy depends on the nature of the relationship. For instance privacy is much more readily invaded in a teacher–pupil relationship than in a spousal relationship. One might add that the degree of privacy normally expected in any role relationship is partly determined by cultural convention (e.g. considerable self-disclosure is expected between spouses) and partly by needs inherent in the relationship in question—for instance adolescents may need to erect barriers round themselves in order to permit the development of autonomy. Furthermore, within any type of relationship there may be wide variations in intimacy—siblings are an obvious example. Diverse tactics are used to protect individuals' intimacy requirements, including deception. Metts (1989) found that avoiding hurt to the partner was the most frequently given justification for deception (see pp.92–93).

Self-disclosure may be limited by the placing of a taboo on particular topics. In a study of an undergraduate population Baxter and Wilmot (1985) found that quite a wide range of topics were regarded as taboo in close relationships. The more important ones could be described in six groups—the state of the relationship, extra-relationship activity, relationship norms, earlier relationships with members of the opposite sex, conflict-inducing topics, and negatively valenced self-disclosures. The relative frequency of these categories, and the reasons given for avoiding the topics, are shown in Table 12.1. Whether or not such taboos are conducive to a healthy relationship is an open issue—La Follette and Graham (1986) make a strong case for the importance of honesty in close relationships.

Some secrets are family matters—private either to the whole family, to a group within it, or to an individual. Vangelisti (1994) found that they could be categorised as taboo topics (e.g. marital difficulties, substance abuse, physical/psychological abuse), rule violations (e.g. pre-marital cohabitation, drinking, disobedience of rules) and conventional secrets (e.g. physical health problems, religion, dating partners, school grades). Taboo topics were most often cited as whole family secrets, rule violations as individual secrets. The secrets were mostly concerned with negative events,

TABLE 12.1
Summary of Reasons Why Topic Categories are Taboo

I.	*The state of the relationship*	
	41.0%	Relationship destruction
	18.6%	Individual vulnerability
	16.9%	Effectiveness of the tacit mode
	13.6%	Futility of talk
	10.2%	Closeness cueing
II.	*Extra-relationship activity*	
	63.0%	Negative relational implications
	15.0%	Right to privacy
	11.1%	Negative network implications
III.	*Relationship norms*	
	55.0%	Negative relational implications
	32.0%	Embarrassment
IV.	*Prior relationships*	
	50.0%	Relationship threat
	27.0%	Irrelevance of the past
	14.0%	Impression management
V.	*Conflict-inducing topics*	
VI.	*Negative self-disclosure*	

The major six topic-categories are rank-ordered in terms of frequency, from most to least. Percentages reflect the proportion of respondents naming a given taboo who provided the listed reason for the taboo. Because respondents could provide multiple reasons, percentages do not total 100% within each topic category. (Baxter & Wilmot, 1985, *Journal of Social & Personal Relationships, 2*, 253–270. Copyright © Sage Publications Inc. Reprinted with permission.)

and had a protective function: Vangelisti notes that "protection" included avoidance of evaluation, avoiding being taken advantage of, and maintaining a loving family environment. She does not mention protection of individual autonomy, perhaps because respondents would find some other reason for justifying secrecy maintained for that purpose. The more family secrets, relative to those believed to be held by other families, the lower was family satisfaction—though satisfaction was not linked to the actual number of secrets believed to be held by the family: it was the comparative level that mattered. Taboo topics held as secrets from other family members were associated with lowered satisfaction with family relationships.

In less close relationships, social norms may dictate the level of self-disclosure seen as appropriate. There is good reason for this if continuity in the relationship is necessary for social reasons, for matters likely to be disruptive to the relationship may thereby be avoided. While we can agree to disagree with others on issues that seem minor to us, we often find it difficult to get on with people with whom we disagree on major issues. So when we have to get on with others with whom we might disagree on important issues, it is perhaps better to avoid controversial topics such as religion or politics and to use "polite conversation" which implicitly acknowledges the relationship but avoids those topics on which disagreement might be disruptive. The assumption often seems to be that if you have to be colleagues or neighbours or acquaintances, or have to eat together in the same college, it may be better not to know each other's opinions in case disagreement on issues not relevant to the context of the relationship should be a cause of friction. Whether the assumption is correct is another issue.

In such a case, a move towards greater disclosure would be met by withdrawal. More usually, however, self-disclosure breeds self-disclosure— a matter to be discussed in Chapter 22. Whether self-disclosure has a positive or negative effect on the relationship depends, as might be expected, on the content and on the meaning ascribed to the move towards intimacy by the individuals involved. Using Morton's (1978) distinction between self-disclosure about facts and self-disclosure about feelings about one's life, Fitzpatrick (1987) found the latter to be more conducive to marital satisfaction. It is, of course, possible that in married couples most facts are known anyway.

DISCLOSURE, VULNERABILITY, AND TRUST

Because self-disclosure involves an increase in vulnerability, it requires trust, in the sense of "confident expectations of positive outcomes from an intimate partner" (Holmes & Rempel, 1989, p.188). To earn trust, an individual must be perceived as motivated to dilute their own self-interest in order to respond to the needs of the perceiver (Holmes, 1981). Readiness to trust is partly, but only partly, a personal characteristic. Individuals, describing themselves as "secure" in the Hazan and Shaver (1987) Attachment Styles questionnaire (p.389), also see themselves as trusting. However Holmes and Rempel (1989) report that extreme trust correlates negatively both with desire for extreme intimacy (i.e. those who love too much) and (in men) with a measure of fear of closeness, and positively with a desire for some autonomy, but not with the defensive self-sufficiency of defensive individuals. Thus extreme motivation for either connectedness or autonomy tend to be negatively associated with trust. However, as we might expect, measures of generalised trust have little predictive value for particular close relationships, because trust depends on both partners.

CHARACTERISTICS OF SELF-DISCLOSERS

In so far as the tendency to share information about the self with others is an individual characteristic, we may ask what sort of people are likely to be ready disclosers.

There is evidence (pp.180–181) that dyadic relationships are in many ways more important to women than to men, and it is popularly supposed that women are more prone to disclose than men. Some studies do indeed show greater disclosure by women than by men (e.g. Dolgin, Meyer, & Schwartz, 1991; Sherrod, 1989; Taylor & Hinds, 1985), and Reis, Senchak, & Solomon (1985) have suggested that this is because men genuinely prefer less intimate interactions with same-sex friends than do women. As assessed on a Thematic Apperception Test, women are somewhat more strongly motivated to disclose than men (McAdams, 1988). Jourard (1971) suggested that men are less willing to reveal their feelings because this would be incompatible with the traditional male role, and might be taken as a sign of weakness. However androgynous men are said to disclose more to a best friend than other men, and as much as women disclose to their best friends (LaVine & Lombardo, 1984); and other studies have found little or no gender difference in self-disclosure (Dindia, 1994; Pearson, 1981; Sherrod, 1989), though this could be because a norm of reciprocity prevails.

The situation becomes clearer if relationship and context are taken into account. Cline (1989) cites evidence that females disclose less in mixed-sex dyads than in female–female dyads, that both males and females tend to disclose more to females than to males, and female–female dyads disclose more than male–male ones (Cline, 1986; Cozby, 1973).

In addition, the content of what is disclosed tends to differ. Women describing close relationships tend to focus on intimate feelings, men on shared activities (Caldwell & Peplau, 1982). In a study involving disclosure to a confederate of the experimenter, Shaffer, Pegalis, and Cornell (1991) found that femininity was related to more disclosure in socially expressive contexts (as determined by the confederate), but inhibited such exchanges in an instrumental context (see also Murstein & Adler, 1995).

Naturally, disclosure tends to increase as individuals get to know each other. However, in the very early stages of acquaintance a reversal of the usual sex difference has been found. In an experimental study Derlega et al. (1985) found that on an initial encounter men may disclose more to a female partner than to a male and than a female to a partner of either sex. They ascribe this to a cultural prescription that males should take the first move in developing a male–female relationship. It could also be a consequence of a male tendency to try to impress a potential partner.

A further complication arises with the finding of gender-differences in the effects of the anticipation of future interaction. Shaffer and Ogden

(1986) report that male subjects were more intimate if they expected future interaction with a newly-encountered same-sex partner, but females became less so.

Between spouses, there is evidence that wives disclose more than husbands (Hendrick, 1981), but the situation is complicated because reciprocity of disclosure may become less important as the relationship acquires a norm of trust, and autonomy needs are recognised: in such a relationship one partner's failure to disclose may not impair closeness (Morton, 1978). In any case, spouses tend to overestimate how much they agree with and understand their partners (Sillars et al., 1994) implying some concealment of areas of disagreement.

The gender difference in a tendency to disclose personal information is coupled with a parallel difference in impact on the partners. In an experimental situation, highly disclosing males were less liked, and evaluated as having poorer psychological adjustment, than highly disclosing females, but the opposite was found for low-disclosing males and females (Caltabiano & Smithson, 1983; Derlega & Chaikin, 1976). However, again, this effect is influenced by the topic discussed. Kleinke and Kahn (1980) presented subjects with messages purporting to come from a male or a female discloser, whose photograph was presented. Messages disclosing intimate information about a parental suicide or about sex, coupled with a picture of a female discloser, were preferred over medium- or low-intimacy disclosures by a female, but less when the disclosure concerned aggressive feelings of competitiveness. High disclosures by presumed males were not preferred to low disclosures on any topic. In addition, physical attractiveness increased liking of the discloser.

Turning to issues less related to gender, individuals who are prone to disclose to others tend to express more trust and concern for friends, have more effectively positive thoughts, are seen as more likeable by others, report greater marital enjoyment than low disclosers, etc. (McAdams, 1988).

Craig, Koestner, and Zuroff (1994) examined the relations between implicit and self-attributed intimacy motivation. (In explanation of those terms, self-attributed motives—assessed by self-report—differ from implicit motives—thematically assessed—in that they are more cognitively elaborated and less directly tied to natural incentives and emotions. They are also more likely to lead to behavioural self-regulation which requires phenomenal self-awareness and is oriented towards maintaining consistency between behaviour and self-image.) McClelland, Koestner, and Weinberger (1989) found that implicit motives better predict behaviour over time, self-attributed motives better predict immediate responses; implicit motives are more easily aroused in the process of performing an activity, self-attributed motives by external expectations or demands; and implicit motives are based on early affective experience rather than explicit teaching.

Craig et al. assessed implicit intimacy motivation from stories written by subjects about four pictures resembling those used in Thematic Apperception Tests, self-attributed intimacy motivation from a self-report questionnaire concerned in part with striving to obtain friendship and in part with affect and communication in social situations. The student subjects also kept a record of their social interactions over a period of a week. It was found that the two sorts of intimacy motivation were not significantly correlated, and were associated with different sorts of social interaction. High implicit intimacy motivation was associated with a high proportion of dyadic interactions, a high proportion of dyadic interactions with women, and high levels of self-disclosure to close friends. High self-attributed intimacy motivation was associated with a high total number of social interactions, and high self-disclosure when the situation explicitly called for it.

Presumably because disclosure entails vulnerability, individuals who perceived a high risk in close relationships (as assessed by a "Risk in Intimacy Inventory") reported fewer close relationships, less trust in others, and more hesitant approaches towards committing themselves than those with lower scores. They also had less rewarding social lives (Nezlek & Pilkington, 1994).

There is perhaps a relation between the gender difference in disclosure and the fact that disclosure yields a degree of power to the partner, for women interacting with men are said to tend to yield behavioural control whereas men tend to try to establish dominance (Henley, 1977; see pp.180–181). Cline (1989) studied the relation between sex and willingness to yield to influence attempts in interaction. Using a questionnaire to distinguish internally evaluative people (i.e. those whose behaviour is regulated by their own expectations and standards) from externally evaluative individuals (influenced by others), Cline assessed the amount of self-disclosure achieved in arranged interviews between mixed sex dyads. The results (Fig. 12.1) showed that externally evaluative individuals altered their behaviour according to the partner's locus of evaluation, the males disclosing more with external partners and the females less. Internally evaluative individuals failed to adjust their behaviour in accordance with the partner's locus of evaluation. Males disclosed less than females: Cline regards this masculine reluctance to disclose as a device to maintain and exert power (see earlier). However the receptivity of the partner may also play a part in determining the extent of disclosure. In any case, Murstein and Adler (1995) found power to be independent of disclosure of feelings in married and dating couples, though high-power men and women tended to disclose more about their accomplishments. The authors suggest that before marriage the more powerful partners seek to impress, but after marriage there is less need to do so. (These data are in harmony with those obtained by Swann, de le Ronde, & Hixon, 1994; see Fig. 13.1).

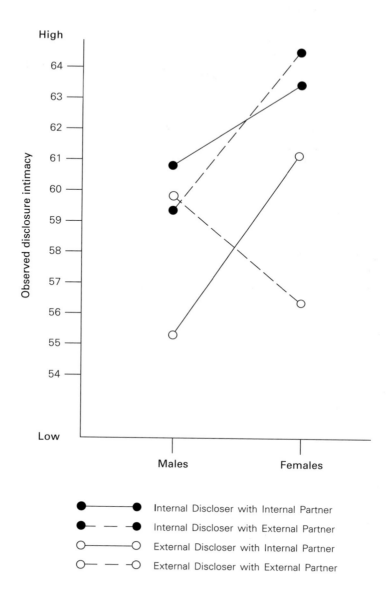

FIG. 12.1 Disclosure intimacy: interaction between gender and locus of evaluation of discloser and partner. (From Cline, 1989, *Journal of Social & Personal Relationships*, 6, 5–20. Copyright © Sage Publications Inc. Reprinted with permission.)

Perhaps not unrelated to the difference between internally and externally evaluative individuals is the characteristic of private self-consciousness, the tendency to focus attention on the more private aspects of the self. Assessing this with a 10-point subscale of a self-consciousness scale, Davis and Franzoi (1986) found clear evidence that greater private self-consciousness leads to greater self-disclosure to peers. It is suggested that individuals high on private self-consciousness have more self-knowledge to share and are more willing to share it.

Individual characteristics may affect not only whether individuals disclose, but also what they disclose. Shaffer, Ogden, and Wu (1987) found that high self-monitoring individuals (see p.117) were attentive to situational cues in deciding what to disclose, while low self-monitors were more reliant on personal thoughts and feelings.

There also appears to be a relation between an individual's general tendency towards intimacy and the defence mechanisms they employ. Sharabany (1994) cites evidence that subjects scoring highly on a (same-sex friend) intimacy scale used "reaction formation" (i.e. seeing the positive aspect of even unhappy events) as their dominant defence mechanism. Those with lower intimacy scores tended to use "turning against others" (i.e. projection, blaming others). (The intimacy scale used here included diverse aspects of closeness.)

THE NATURE OF THE RELATIONSHIP

The amount and consequences of disclosure are likely also to vary with the nature of the relationship. If it is non-existent, as in an encounter with a stranger, there is no question of future vulnerability and disclosure can occur readily—the "stranger on the train" phenomenon. In an experimental situation Shaffer, Ogden, and Wu (1987) demonstrated that the prospect of future interaction had an important influence on the tendency to disclose intimate information to a confederate of the experimenter. However individuals who do not have a close primary relationship may disclose equally to strangers and friends. It is of course possible that a failure to discriminate strangers from friends is responsible for their lack of a close relationship.

Disclosure tends to increase as a relationship develops, though in a study of friendship formation it was found to reach an asymptote as early as six weeks into the formation of a new relationship (Hays, 1984, 1985).

At any stage in a relationship, its nature will influence the consequences of disclosure. Both the occurrence of disclosure and its impact are likely to be less if the recipient is perceived to be uninterested (Reis & Shaver, 1988), and acknowledgement and sympathy may produce more liking of the recipient than reciprocal self-disclosure.

As mentioned already, self-disclosure may be used strategically to achieve personal goals, and it should therefore be considered in terms of mediating cognitive structures (goals, beliefs, resources, etc.). But the maintenance of power may depend on what is disclosed: Murstein and Adler (1995) point out that disclosure of one's own accomplishments might serve to impress the partner, while disclosure of feelings of weakness and inadequacy might put one in a position of vulnerability. (In either case, of course, the response might be just the opposite.) However Murstein and Adler's data (from married and dating couples) indicated that women revealed more about feelings and weakness than men, though this was not related to a lack of perceived power.

One might expect disclosure to decrease in relationships in the course of dissolution. Tolstedt and Stokes (1984) predicted that the breadth and depth (see above) of disclosures would decrease, and their valency would become increasingly negative. Analysing audio tapes of couples discussing problems, they confirmed the prediction for breadth and valency, but found that the depth increased. In such circumstances some of the constraints on disclosure are removed—couples may become more honest with each other in the hope of saving the relationship, or because hurt to the partner no longer matters.

THIRD PARTIES

Self-disclosure within a relationship may be affected by the possibility of leakage to third parties. In an interview study Tschann (1988) found that married men disclosed less to their friends than unmarried men and also less than married or unmarried women. The effect was not found with married women, whose disclosure to friends was moderately high and in some cases as high as to their spouses.

A related issue concerns the extent to which the participants in a relationship reveal or conceal the fact or extent of their involvement with each other from their peers. Sometimes people feel impelled to discuss their relationships with outsiders because of a previous relationship with the outsider, or because they want support, or simply because of a desire for emotional expression. On the other hand they may feel inhibited from doing so for fear of a negative reaction. The latter is especially the case in concealment from parents (Baxter and Widenmann, 1993).

PHYSICAL SELF-DISCLOSURE

The vulnerability and protection that self-disclosure brings raises the question of the relation between cognitive and physical self-disclosure. While Erikson (1963) regarded true intimacy as including mutually gratifying sexual activity, Sullivan (1953) regarded it as a separate issue (Tesch,

1985). Kelvin (1977), stressing the enormous power of physical intimacy, compared lovers' exploration of each other's body images with the exploration of their self-concepts. Each involves both positive gains on the one hand and increased vulnerability on the other. Although Kelvin does not take it that far, one is led to speculate that, at least for people with traditional norms, the vulnerability consequent upon physical self-disclosure may be ameliorated by trust, and that trust occurs more readily with cognitive disclosure.

While the general issue of reciprocity in disclosure will be considered elsewhere (Chapter 22), we have already noted that disclosure can lead to reciprocal disclosure, or it can provoke distancing on the part of the recipient. There is some evidence that the same is true for physical intimacy.

Some studies suggest that changes in physical intimacy elicit compensatory responses, such that a preferred level of overall "intimacy" is maintained. For instance, increased proximity may lead to decreased eye contact (Argyle & Dean, 1965). Other studies indicate the opposite—for instance, touching by a confederate elicited increased self-disclosures from a subject (Jourard & Friedman, 1970). Patterson (1976) suggests that such apparently contradictory findings can be reconciled on the supposition that changes in perceived intimacy produce changes in arousal levels, which may be evaluated as positive or negative emotional states. Negative emotional states produce compensatory behaviour tending to restore the initial level of intimacy, while positive emotional states lead to reciprocity and greater intimacy. Whether this gets one much further is not clear.

SUMMARY

1. Self-disclosure can be assessed by comparison of speech content with a standard, but conclusions about the depth of self-disclosure will always be culture-specific.
2. The tendency to reveal information about oneself is only partly an individual characteristic, and depends primarily on the relationship in question.
3. Close relationships demand self-disclosure, but self-disclosure involves relinquishing some autonomy and increased vulnerability. There is also a need to protect one's privacy. Diverse tactics are used to protect privacy. Partners may recognise a taboo on particular topics.
4. Self-disclosure requires trust.
5. Gender and various other personal characteristics may affect the tendency to disclose.
6. The nature of the relationship, and the possibility of disclosure to third parties, are also important issues.

13 Interpersonal Perception, Accounts, and the Perception of Relationships

INTERPERSONAL PERCEPTION AND ITS ASSESSMENT

The extent to which partners agree about the external world, and the extent to which each sees the other as he is, or as he sees himself, may have many effects on their relationship. At the lowest level, behavioural meshing (see p.61) would not be possible unless each partner's view of the other were reasonably close to reality. Their feelings about each other may affect and be affected by the extent to which they agree, or perceive that they agree, about the rest of the world (pp.129–130). Understanding another individual, the ability to predict and mesh with his/her behaviour, to share feelings and meanings, to "read his/her mind', to facilitate his/her goals, requires the ability to take the other's perspective and point of view. If B believes that A's view of her is different from her (B's) own view of herself, she (B) will feel misunderstood (e.g. Cahn, 1990). Individuals develop more satisfying relationships if they feel they understand how their partners see them and their desires for stability or change (Neimeyer & Neimeyer, 1985). Of course A may understand B better than B understands A, but differences in their perspectives, if recognised, may provide a source of motivation for the partners to resolve their differences (Dixson & Duck, 1993).

For one cause or another, individuals may misperceive themselves and each other: this may have an important influence on the nature of their relationships. The perceptions or misperceptions of partners form the bases of the accounts that they make of their relationship, and thus affect its

219

future course. Interpersonal perception is thus of crucial importance for the dynamics of close relationships (e.g. Long & Andrews, 1990).

Although interpersonal perception is so important, finding out about another person is not always easy. People protect their privacy, and acknowledge that others might find enquiries intrusive. There are norms concerning the questions that can and cannot be asked, and anyway the asking of a question reveals ignorance and incurs vulnerability.

Indeed, we must here note a circular issue, for in forming impressions of other people we relate our perceptions of them to our perceptions of ourselves; while our perceptions of ourselves are formed from our perceptions of others and of the ways we perceive others to perceive us, and are structured in part round our relationships with others (Chapter 3). Although we have seen that different ways of looking at the nature of the self-concept are beginning to suggest similar conclusions, we are still a good way from understanding its complexity.

This chapter is therefore concerned with the views held by the participants in a relationship about each other, about their relationship, and also about objects and people outside their relationship. We shall ask, for instance, whether A sees A as similar to how B sees B; whether A sees A as similar to how A sees B (perceived similarity); whether A sees B as the sort of person B sees herself as (i.e. does A understand B?); and whether B feels that A sees B as B sees B (does B feel that A understands her?). Such issues are also closely related to the question of "satisfaction"—is B's view of A close to B's view of her ideal partner in the relationship in question? (see Chapter 14).

Assessing Interpersonal Perception

One group of methods involves self-reports in an imposed situation which are subjected to projective interpretation by a therapist. For instance a couple may be given a conjoint thematic apperception test, and the resulting stories then diagnosed. The validity of such methods is not easily assessed, and they will not be considered further here.

Of more interest are methods in which each member of the dyad answers a questionnaire and the responses to the test items are taken at their face value and used as data. Objective scoring is thus possible. A number of instruments have been standardised, e.g. the Interpersonal Checklist, Marital Communications Checklist, Family Relationships Inventory, etc. (earlier references in Cromwell, Olson, & Fournier, 1976).

The most interesting data have been obtained when individuals are asked to fill in a questionnaire from more than one point of view. In an early example which we may consider to illustrate the approach, Dymond (1954) asked each partner from 15 married couples to answer a true–false

TABLE 13.1
Hypothetical Set of Answers to MMPI Items Used in Assessing
Interpersonal Perception and Marital Happiness

Items	1	2	3	4	5
(1) Husband's answer	T	T	F	T	F
(2) Husband's prediction of wife's answer	T	F	F	T	T
(3) Wife's own answer	F	T	F	T	T
(4) Wife's prediction of husband's answer	T	T	T	F	F

(From Dymond, 1954. Copyright 1954, Canadian Psychological Association. Reprinted with permission.)

questionnaire made up of 115 items from the Minnesota Multiphasic Personality Inventory. Each individual was then asked to fill out another copy as he or she predicted his or her spouse would complete it. Thus each item was answered as True or False four times, as indicated in Table 13.1. Since predictions could reflect the ability to predict not the answer of the spouse but those of most of the subjects' acquaintances, all items marked similarly True or False by more than 66% of a group of subjects were dropped. From the answers, scores were obtained for *similarity* by comparing rows 1 and 3 (three out of five items in the Table); for *understanding* by comparing rows 2 and 3 or 1 and 4 (three out of five); and for *assumed similarity* by comparing rows 1 and 2 and rows 3 and 4 (three out of five and one out of five respectively). The couples were divided into happy and unhappy ones—in part on their own assessment and in part on that of the experimenter. The data indicated that the happy couples had more understanding of each other, and were more like each other in their self-descriptions, than the unhappy ones. There was no indication in this study that perceived similarity was related to happiness, though later studies indicate that that is the case.

As another example, we may consider Drewery's (1969) interpersonal perception technique. This is based on a standardised instrument for assessing personality traits, the Edwards Personal Preferences Schedule, designed to measure 15 traits by a questionnaire method. The subject is presented with 255 paired statements, and required to select one from each pair. The two statements in each pair are designed to be equal in social desirability, but concern different traits. The pairings are such that a statement about each trait is combined with one about each other in two pairings. Thus if the statements concerning a particular trait were selected every time, that trait could score a maximum of 28 points, and no other traits could score more than 26. When used for studying a dyadic relationship, say that of a married couple, each member answers the schedule three

TABLE 13.2
Use of the Edwards Personal Preference Schedule

(a) Husband's protocol	Respondent asked to describe	Wife's protocol
A	Myself as I am	B
A_1	My spouse as I see him/her	B_1
A_2	Myself as I think my spouse sees me	B_2

(b)	Husband's expectations	Wife's expectations
	B vs. A_1	A vs. B_1
	B_1 vs. A_2	A_1 vs. B_2
	A vs. A_2	B vs. B_2
	A vs. B	

(a) The six schedules. (b) The correlations used by Drewery and Rae (see text). (From Drewery & Rae, 1969, *British Journal of Psychiatry*, *115*, 287–300. Reprinted by permission of the Royal College of Psychiatry.)

times—on one occasion describing her or himself, on another describing the spouse, and on yet another describing how she (or he) believes the spouse perceives her (or him). Thus the pair completes six schedules in all, as indicated by the letters in Table 13.2a.

A number of comparisons between these protocols can be made. Thus Drewery and Rae (1969) calculated seven correlation coefficients for each couple, as shown in Table 13.2b. The size of these coefficients indicate, for example, whether the husband sees himself as the wife sees him ($A–B_1$), or whether the wife sees herself as she thinks her spouse sees her ($B–B_2$). In a comparison of marriages having an alcoholic member with non-psychiatric marriages Drewery and Rae found that the correlations for patients were consistently, and usually significantly, lower than those for the controls. For example, the correlation for A vs. B1 was 0.26 for controls and –0.32 for patients. Normal men's views of their wives accorded only poorly with their self descriptions (A1 vs. B, r = 0.48), but the wives did rather better (B_1 vs. A, r = 0.64). How far the quantitative side of such questionnaires can be pushed is an open issue, for there may be problems concerning the degree of independence between the items.

Using a basically similar approach, Laing (1969; Laing, Phillipson, & Lee, 1966) has tackled further complexities. It is necessary to say a few words about his system. Laing explicitly emphasised how relationships are experienced by the people involved. He thus used the term "relationship" in a rather different sense from that used elsewhere in this book. For a dyadic relationship (in our sense) between A and B, Laing distinguishes A's relationship with B from B's relationship with A. Both A and B will have views of each of these. Furthermore, A has views about his (or her) relationship with himself (or herself), and about B's relationship with himself (or herself), and similarly for B. Thus at the level of direct perspective there are eight possibilities: A's views of A's relationship with A, of B's relationship with B, of A's relationship with B and of B's relationship with A, and similarly for B.

Now A will also have a view on, for instance, B's view of A's relationship with A, etc. This is the level of metaperspective. For example, I may feel disappointed with myself for giving a poor lecture. If one of my colleagues knows that I am disappointed with myself, that is metaperspective. It will be apparent that, for each of the four possible views of A at the level of direct perspective, B may have a view at the level of metaperspective. For each of those A may have a view at the level of meta-metaperspective. Laing has used this sort of analysis of interpersonal perception to examine the extent to which:

1. The two participants agree at the direct level—e.g. does A's view of the relationship (AB) agree with B's view of (AB).
2. They are aware of and understand the other's point of view—e.g. does A's view of B's view of (AB) correspond with B's view of (AB).
3. They feel understood—e.g. does A's view of B's view of A's view of himself (AA) agree with A's view of himself.
4. Each realises that the other understands him—e.g. does A's view of B's view of A's view of himself correspond with B's view of A's view of himself.

This leads to a number of possibilities. For example A and B agree about, let us say, A's relationship with B at the direct level. But while A may understand B's view of A's relationship with B, B may not understand A's. And if A does understand B's view of A's relationship with B, B may or may not realise that he does. Laing has attempted to evaluate agreement, understanding, and realisation of understanding in six areas of interpersonal perception—it will be apparent that this is a not inconsiderable task. Alperson (1975) has shown that Boolean algebra can provide a rigorous language for interpreting this and other comparable tests. Whether the level of meta-metaperspective is useful either clinically, or for understanding the dynamics of relationships, is doubtful (see Monsour, Betty, & Kurzweil, 1993).

FACTORS AFFECTING
INTERPERSONAL PERCEPTION

On Acquaintance

There is an extensive literature on the ways in which newly acquainted individuals form impressions of each other. Much of this involves laboratory experiments, of more relevance to the appraisal of strangers than to interpersonal perception in relationships, and only a few points will be made here (see Chapter 25).

A number of studies are concerned with the surprising accuracy, or at least inter-individual agreement, that is found in assessments of another individual, even after a quite brief exposure. Individuals assess another's personality using just those behavioural cues most likely to be valid for the personality dimension in question (Funder & Sneed, 1993). Naturally, some characteristics, especially those related to extroversion, are more easily judged than others—possibly because of their relation with physical attractiveness (Albright, Kenny, & Malloy, 1988; Ambody & Rosenthal, 1993; Berry, 1991; Borkenau & Liebler, 1992; Frey & Smith, 1993; Kenny et al., 1992; Park & Judd, 1989; Watson, 1989). However, Paunonen (1991) has sounded a note of caution, pointing out that many such experiments depend on comparing the average assessments made by a number of judges with self-reports by the subject: in such circumstances a small number of accurate judgements among a number of random ones can produce substantial overall correlations.

Others have analysed the cues that are used: many of them may be used unconsciously or half-consciously, such as dress or age-related qualities of gait (Montepare & Zebrowitz–McArthur, 1989).

However no-one, except possibly personality psychologists, runs through a series of personality traits when sizing up another individual. Usually the issue that matters is whether one likes them or not, and "likeability" depends on (usually subconscious) weighting of a number of different characteristics. Park and Flink (1989) noted that, as might be expected, judges tended to agree well on likeability about targets who were rated high or low in an experimental situation, but much less well about those in the middle. They showed that the lack of agreement was due both to how the targets were perceived (is this person honest?) and to differences in weighting the traits that contribute to liking (is honesty more important than friendliness?). The attributes that contributed to liking in this study were extroversion and intelligence/responsibility/honesty, physical attractiveness and perceived similarity to self (see also Park, DeKay, & Kraus, 1994).

In making inferences about others, we compare them with ourselves (see pp.25–26, 228–229) and with others we have known or categories of others we have known. Perception of similarity between a newly encountered other and either a known individual or a set of features representing a category of individuals, may permit inferences about the stranger, though of course such inferences may not be correct. Andersen and Cole (1990) compared the manner in which representations of others significant to the subject are stored with the representations of non-significant others. When subjects were asked to list the features of significant others, non-significant others, stereotypes of types of individuals, and types of person describable by a particular adjective, they listed more attributes for significant others. Furthermore the features of significant others, although more numerous, could be retrieved more rapidly than those of the other categories, implying greater cognitive accessibility. They also showed experimentally that the assimilation of an unknown individual into the representation of a significant other permitted more inferences about him/her than assimilation into another category. This study is of special interest in that it provides a parallel to the process of transference in psychoanalysis, as when the properties of a significant other are transferred on to the analyst.

Differences in Behaviour by the Person Perceived

We have seen that individuals behave differently according to whom they are with. This of course, leads to different perceptions of their personalities. In the terminology of Goffman and of the symbolic interactionists, we see others in the identity or role they display in their relationship with us (Chapters 1 and 3). Thus individuals may try actively to manipulate what others think of them. In interactions and relationships people present themselves not only in a manner that they believe will be acceptable to the partner, but also with the image they would like to present (see Backman, 1985, 1988, cited pp.28–29). On the whole, people want to be seen in a good light and like people who praise them. Sometimes however, it is preferable to be seen as one really is—perhaps to avoid dissonance and to promote coherence with past experience, or perhaps because it is then possible to interact with the other in a more straightforward and honest way. Swann et al. (1994) arranged that members of married and dating couples should make independent assessments of themselves, and their partners, and also rate their satisfaction/intimacy. For dating couples, satisfaction/intimacy was least if the partner's appraisal were less positive than the subject's rating of him or herself, increased if the partner's appraisal were equal to the subject's own, and increased still more if it were greater. For married couples, however, an inverted U relation appeared, satisfaction/intimacy being low if there were a large discrepancy between the partner's appraisal and the subject's self-rating. This was the case both for subjects with generally positive self-views and for those with generally negative ones (Fig. 13.1). In other words, dating individuals were

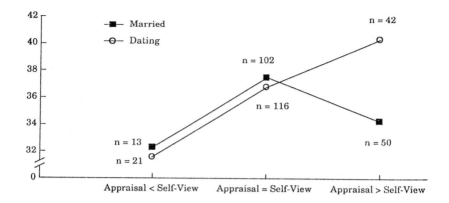

FIG. 13.1   Disclosure and self/other discrepancy in married and dating couples (From Swann, de la Ronde, & Hixon, 1994. Copyright by the American Psychological Association. Reprinted with permission.)

more intimate if their partner viewed them favourably, married individuals if their partner's view coincided with their own. The authors explain these results on the view that courtship is a period in which people evaluate each other and want to be seen favourably, while married partners prefer that their partners see their weaknesses as well as their strengths, because this puts them in a better position to develop their unique potentials. Recent data suggest a route for further analysis: Murray and Holmes (1996) found that married as well as dating individuals were more satisfied in their relationships when they perceived their partners to have positive qualities that their partners did not perceive in themselves.

Sometimes individuals try deliberately to lower the opinion of others. Thus high-anxiety individuals, doubtful of their own abilities, may perform poorly in a way that lowers the expectations of others, so that they will then be seen by others as they see themselves (see also Baumgardner & Brownlee, 1987; Darley & Fazio, 1980; McNulty & Swann, 1994; Snyder 1984; Swann, 1987).

How do individuals attempt to present the image that they wish to be perceived? A number of devices are available. First, individuals tend to associate with others who see them as they wish to be seen, or who imply to others that they have properties that they would like to be seen as having. Second, they display cues to the identity they wish to present in dress and behaviour. Third, and of greater interest in the present context, they can channel the behaviour of the partner so that it confirms their expectancies or desires, thereby promoting appropriate feedback and assuring themselves that the partner is perceiving them as they would wish. That such efforts are often successful has been demonstrated in numerous studies. Individuals who see themselves as likeable will behave in a way that promotes liking, self-disclosing more, speaking more positively, disagreeing less—behaviours that are reciprocated by the partner (Curtis & Miller, 1986). The process can be circular: people who believe an individual to be attractive induce her to behave in a friendly and sociable way (Snyder, Tanke, & Berscheid, 1977). Similarly, those who see themselves as leaders behave in a way that creates that impression (Swann & Hill, 1982; see also Clark, Pataki, & Carver, 1996; Forgas, 1996).

Such devices may fail, but, as we have seen (Backman, 1988, cited pp.28–29), individuals may yet protect their self-concepts by attending preferentially to aspects of the partner's behaviour that seem to provide confirmation of their self-image. They are more likely to endorse the validity of the feedback they receive if it confirms their views of themselves.

Thus, as we saw in Chapters 1 and 3, the partners in a social interaction or relationship construct their own social reality by negotiating social identities. Each attempts to display the image she or he wishes to display, to channel the behaviour of the other to confirm that image, and to convince him or herself that he or she has done so.

DIFFERENCES BETWEEN AND INFLUENCES ON JUDGES

The same individual may be perceived differently by several others not only because he behaves differently, but because judges differ in their sensitivity and in the manner in which they assess others. We shall consider here some biases and influences that operate on most judges, and some generalisations about differences between judges.

Congruency of Dimensions

The dimensions by which we assess others are social constructions. They are based on our experiences in our families of origin and throughout our subsequent development, on discussions with others, on the books we have read and the tales we have heard. We may tolerate a good deal of incongruity between the various dimensions that we use to describe a person, but our impression of others is influenced by our beliefs about the compatibility of traits. Trait adjective pairs that are descriptively and evaluatively incongruent (e.g. kind and cold) are less likely to occur together in the description of a given target individual than congruent ones (Casselden & Hampson, 1990). Behaviours that are conceptually related (e.g. aggression, dominance, disagreeing, and criticising) are likely to be recalled during judgements of another individual as though they co-varied (Riesmann & Angleitner, 1993; Schweder, 1982).

Cultural Stereotypes

Preconceptions about which characteristics are likely to go together are much influenced by cultural stereotypes. Such stereotypes may also be of crucial importance developmentally. For example, mothers' perceptions of their children's abilities in various domains are influenced by their stereo-typic beliefs about the relative abilities of boys and girls (Jacobs & Eccles, 1992). Furthermore, parents' perceptions about what children *ought* to be like may affect their behaviour towards their children. Thus Stevenson-Hinde and Hinde (1986) found that mothers had better relationships with moderately shy 4-year-old girls than with non-shy girls, but the opposite was true for boys. The difference seemed to be due to maternal values— it was seen as proper for a little girl to be shy but not a little boy.

Self-perception and Other-perception

How one individual perceives another may be influenced by how he sees himself. We have already seen that knowledge about the self and about others are interdependent, and that the self may provide a reference point for perceptions of others (Chapter 3). We may assess others in part in terms of how much they resemble, or differ from, our views of ourselves, picking out dimensions that are salient in our own self-images by which to assess others. Often, there is an irrational assumption of similarity with the other ("false consensus" or "projection") which may augment or distort our judgement. Or we may contrast too strongly our own firmly held attitudes with those who appear to disagree. Of course such processes are not ubiq-uitous: the relative influences of the stimuli from the other person and the relevant aspect of the self-concept presumably depend on their salience (Markus, Smith, & Moreland, 1985. See also Aron et al., 1991; Reis & Knee, 1996).

We may also note that our own views of ourselves may influence not only our own views of others, but also our views of how others perceive us (Lewis and Brooks-Gunn, 1979).

Relevance to Self

Individuals tend to focus or to judge more accurately traits that are important to them than those that are of less importance (Gangestad et al., 1992). For this and other reasons there is an eye of the beholder effect: there may be more overlap in the dimensions used by one judge in describing two targets than there is in those used by two judges describing one (cf. Park, DeKay, & Kraus, 1994). Bugental et al. (1993) observed women in simulated teaching interactions with children. The subjects had previously been classified into those who attributed low control to self and high control to the child, and those who attributed high control to self or low control to both. Those women who saw themselves as power-disadvantaged reacted strongly to power-related cues in the teaching situation, showing exaggerated responses to the unresponsiveness or responsiveness of the trainees. They thus reacted more strongly to an issue important to their self-image.

Similarity

Similarity between self and other may affect appraisal in a number of ways. As one example, dysphoric women detected sympathy from a dysphoric stranger more accurately than did non-dysphoric women, while non-dysphoric women detected sympathy more accurately from a non-dysphoric stranger. However such differences may depend on the nature of the interaction: in this case the difference emerged only after disclosure of a personal problem, when they may have felt especially vulnerable and needed to detect the partner's sympathy (Pietromonaco, Rook, & Lewis, 1992; see also Murray & Holmes, 1996).

The circumstances in which status or achievement differences between self and other may affect appraisal are discussed on pp.140–141.

Relevance to Significant Others

A judge may attribute traits of a significant person in his life to a stimulus person who resembles the significant other in other ways (Andersen & Cole, 1990; see p.228).

Pragmatic Implications

In assessing another person, individuals do not merely respond directly to what they see or hear, but focus on its pragmatic implications, asking why was this or that information conveyed? (Wyer et al., 1994). Judges agree better when targets are evaluated with respect to a particular role (e.g. room-mate) than in the abstract (Park & Flink, 1989).

Influence of First Encounter: Polarisation

The first encounter may create an impression that is hard to erase, in part because there is always a tendency to regard the personalities of others to be unchanging over time (e.g. Park et al., 1994). In addition, people are more ready to accept evidence that confirms beliefs that they already have than evidence that contradicts them.

Furthermore, given an initial attitude to an object, the more the person thinks about that object, the more polarised will both attitude and affective reactions become (Tesser, 1978). For example, Tesser and Paulhus (1976) found that feelings of love for a dating partner caused individuals to think about the date, and this further enhanced love. However actual contact with the dating partner might constrain this distortion of feelings, so that love decreased. Tesser and Danheiser (1978) further suggested that the direction in which thought polarises attitudes depends on the "cognitive schema" being applied to the partner at the time—for instance is he/she seen as trustworthy or unfaithful? Experimental data in which the schema applied to a potential partner were manipulated confirmed the suggestion (see also Hill et al., 1989). However behaviours seen as inconsistent with a general impression may be remembered better than consistent behaviours (Belmore & Hubbard, 1987).

Context

When one individual meets and seeks to understand another, the first step is to categorise the behaviour the latter shows. He or she may, for instance, be smiling or weeping copiously or talking assertively. The second stage involves attributing to the actor a trait based on the behaviour observed. He or she may be seen as a happy, sad, or assertive individual. However in a third stage this attribution may be corrected by taking the situation into account. As we have seen (pp.86–88) some expressive facial expressions and gestures may indicate a range of internal states, and contextual cues are required for their interpretation. Thus the person concerned may just have won a lottery or be attending a funeral, or be arguing with someone who has just run into his parked car. This last stage may require close attention, without which correction may be inadequate (e.g. Gilbert, Pelham, & Krull, 1988; Gilbert et al., 1992; Trope, 1986).

In general, context may have two kinds of effects on evaluative judgements: (a) *Contrast*. A face may be judged as less attractive if it is preceded by a very attractive face. (b) *Assimilation*. A judgement is displaced towards a contextual standard. Thus an individual may be judged as more attractive if seen to be associated with another attractive individual (e.g. Martin & Seta, 1983). These two effects are, of course, potentially conflicting.

The way in which contextual information is integrated varies with the nature of the judge (Wedell, 1994). Judges often overestimate the importance of stable personality traits and underestimate situational effects (Park et al., 1994; see later). Graziano et al. (1993) found that women were influenced by peers in judging the attractiveness of both males and females, though there was no comparable evidence for men.

Judges' Sensitivity: Masculinity/Femininity

Sensitivity to the characteristics and feelings of others is, of course, an individual characteristic: common experience indicates that some individuals are more sensitive than others.

Traditional stereotypes suggest that women are more sensitive than men and some studies are in harmony with this. Thus Long and Andrews (1990) used three measures of perspective-taking—in general social interaction, perspective-taking of the self (e.g. "Before criticising my partner, I try to imagine how I would feel in her place"), and perspective-taking of the spouse. In all these, women scored more highly than men, and all three were positively related to marital adjustment.

However not all studies point in the same direction. In a study of empathic accuracy in perceiving a friend's conversation, Hancock and Ickes (1996) found no sex difference. And where there is a difference, it may be an issue not of an inherently greater sensitivity in women, but because they more often occupy a subordinate position. In a study involving male and female students playing boss and employee roles (Snodgrass, 1992), the subjects were asked to assess their feelings about their partner and about themselves. Sensitivity of those in a subordinate role to how the leaders felt about them was greater than the sensitivity of the leaders to the subordinates. Snodgrass points out that this could be due either to the greater need of the subordinate to know what the boss is feeling, or to the greater tendency of the boss not to reveal his or her feelings. The leaders were, however, more sensitive to how the subordinates felt about themselves than vice versa, perhaps because the boss needs to know how the employee feels about his/her work or the employee must reveal feelings to obtain guidance from the boss. In accordance with her hypothesis, Snodgrass found no significant sex difference.

There is also evidence that masculinity/femininity may affect gender-relevant responses. Lobel (1994) showed masculine, feminine, androgynous, and undifferentiated preadolescent boys videotapes of boys behaving in various ways, and asked for assessments of their gender style. While the cognitive stereotypic inferences were similar in all four groups, and accorded with the gender-stereotypic nature of the behaviour observed, the affective judgements (e.g. liking the subject) of the feminine males showed a pattern that differed from and was often the reverse of the other groups.

Judges may also be sensitive to different aspects of information about others—for instance they may be interested in what another is really like, or merely in what third parties would think about that other. They may also differ in their biases, in the sorts of issues on which they make their judgements, in their readiness to ascribe relevance to events, and so on.

Vorauer and Ross (1996) have described the diverse ways in which individuals gain information about others.

Mood

Judgements made of another may be influenced by one's mood (Forgas, 1996). Forgas and Bower (1987) required subjects who had been artificially made happy or sad to make judgements about persons from information containing positive and negative details about them. The subjects spent longer learning about mood-consistent details but were faster in making mood-consistent judgements than mood-inconsistent ones. Happy subjects made more favourable judgements than sad ones. There is some evidence that the effect of mood on judgements of others may be stronger for positive moods than for negative ones (Clark & Reis, 1988). Forgas (1991, 1992, 1994) has shown that mood affects not only the kind of information people attend to when making a judgement, but also how that information is processed.

Longer-term states also may influence interpersonal perception. For example, Thompson, Whiffen, and Blain (1995) found that dysphoric students perceived both themselves and their partners as behaving more coldly than did non-dysphoric students.

In a slightly different vein, attraction to a person of the opposite sex may be enhanced by arousal, especially if that person is attractive (Allen et al., 1989; White, Fishbein, & Rutstein, 1981).

Simultaneous Cognitive Operations

Judgements may be affected by other cognitive operations going on simultaneously. Thus linguistic cues are more easily disrupted by another simultaneous task than are non-linguistic cues, so that the non-linguistic judgements may be more accurate (Gilbert & Krull, 1988). And we have seen (p.230) that when one assesses another individual engaged in an activity one must ask successively "What is he doing?", "What does the action imply?", and "What situational constraints may have caused the action?", and that the last is most easily disrupted by other cognitive tasks.

Mutuality

Perhaps most important of all, in forming a relationship we are usually assessing another in an interactive situation, in which we are simultaneously being assessed. The target may dress or behave in order to create a particular impression: for instance one study found that women ate less when taking a meal with an attractive male partner than when with a less attractive man or a woman (Mori, Chaiken, & Pliner, 1987). But the issue is likely to be two-way, with each partner in an interaction endeavouring to impress and to make the other behave in a way that will confirm his own expectancies. They may overestimate their success. In a round robin experiment in which subjects were asked to report on their partner's likeability and competence, and on the impressions they believed they had conveyed to the partner, subjects were reasonably accurate in telling how they were assessed by different partners, but not at perceiving differences in how their partners perceived them, believing they conveyed similar impressions to all partners (DePaulo et al., 1987; see also Snyder, 1984; Swann, 1987).

Length of Acquaintance

Not surprisingly, the accuracy of one's perceptions of another increases with acquaintance (Funder & Colvin, 1989; Paulhus & Bruce, 1992). Individuals in long-term relationships tend to judge their partners more or less as the partners judge themselves, and the partners know how they will be judged (Malloy & Albright, 1990; but see earlier). Whether the memories of the partner's past behaviour are stored as separate memories of the various incidents, or as summary representations of traits formed by abstraction from observation of specific behaviours, or a combination of the two, is a matter of dispute (Fletcher & Thomas, 1996; Klein et al., 1992; Reis & Knee, 1996).

Misperception

Finally, individuals sometimes strive to find out all they can about a partner (Vorauer & Ross 1996), and at other times misperceive their partners and thereby reassure themselves. They may tend to see their partners as better than their partners view themselves, and use a number of techniques to ward off doubts about them. They may deny that any negative behaviour reflects an underlying disposition, attributing it to circumstances; minimise the significance of faults by finding excuses for the partner; mask faults by emphasising virtues; and, valuing the relationship, meet the partner's negativity with positive responses.

In a study of married and dating couples, Murray and Holmes (1996) found that individuals perceived their partners with a mixture of illusion and reality. Their data showed that the couples' ideals were closely related to their own self-perceptions, standards for an ideal partner being higher the more positively they felt about themselves. However their ideals bore little relation to their partner's actual qualities. Their views of their partners were related to how the partners saw themselves, but were also influenced by their ideals: the higher their ideals, the more idealised their impression of their partners. Among dating couples, impressions of the partners also showed some positive influence from their self-impressions.

INTERPERSONAL PERCEPTION IN ON-GOING RELATIONSHIPS

Perceived Similarity and Understanding

There are a number of reasons why persons in satisfactory long-term relationships are likely to show an increase in perceived similarity and mutual understanding (Lewis & Spanier, 1979). First, if an individual likes someone but perceives him to have different attitudes from himself, he may change his own attitude, or attempt to change the other's attitude, so that similarity increases; or misperceive the other's attitudes as being more similar than they are, so that at least perceived similarity increases (Heider, 1958; Newcomb, 1961; see Chapter 18). Furthermore, if an individual is forced to interact with another who at first sight is seen as unattractive or undesirable, she may paradoxically come to like the other more—apparently in an attempt to balance the situation. This is especially the case with individuals who are prone to cope with threat by denial or by directing their attention elsewhere: persons who cope with threat by exaggerating it may come to dislike the unpleasant stranger even more (Graziano, Brothen, & Berscheid, 1980).

Second, partners in a close relationship must communicate with each other. Communicating enhances interpersonal perception, which in turn facilitates better communication. This may enhance both perceived similarity and understanding (White, 1985).

Third, in the course of continued interacting, the partners in a close relationship construct a common viewpoint on the world, and thus each is likely both to see the other as similar to herself, and to understand the other (Berger & Luckman, 1966; Lewis & Spanier, 1979).

One might expect that a couple who saw themselves as similar to each other would also understand each other. However, White (1985), using a Laing-type method (see pp.222–223), found that the relation between perceived similarity and understanding varied with the salience of the issue. When all items were considered together, there was little support for a relation between perceived similarity and understanding. However when items assessed by the subjects (perhaps surprisingly) as of high salience for the marriage (i.e. family size, child discipline, leisure time, and work) were considered separately from those of low salience (economic contribution, chores, who gives more in the relationship, and women's rights), some interesting differences emerged. Overall, husbands tended to perceive interspousal similarity more accurately than did wives, wives tending to perceive more similarity than the husbands. This may indicate greater positivity towards the relationship by the wives. The discrepancy between husband and wife was small for high-saliency issues, the wife becoming more accurate at perceiving similarity when the issues were important.

However the wives' understanding of the husbands was more accurate than the husbands' understanding of the wives—a difference perhaps understandable in terms of the power difference found in many marital relationships, since it may be more important for the subordinate to understand the dominant than vice versa.

It is indeed generally the case that perceived similarity between spouses or friends tends to be greater than actual similarity. Byrne and Blaylock (1963) obtained ratings for husbands and wives on a scale for dogmatism, and also assessed each partner's view of the other on the same scale. The results showed that each saw the other as more like him or herself than the other really was. Murstein (1967a) found that the perceptions that members of 99 University couples (engaged or going steady) had of each other were not significantly more similar than were those of randomly selected couples, though the subjects perceived that there was more homogamy than was actually the case. Similarly Monsour, Betty, and Kurzweil (1993) found that perceived agreement and understanding between cross-sex friends was greater than actual agreement and understanding.

Misperception of similarity may contribute to the maintenance of the relationship. Perceived similarity in attitudes and preferences is a better predictor of marital satisfaction than is actual similarity (Byrne & Blaylock, 1963). Levinger and Breedlove (1966) found that spouses who scored highly on a marital satisfaction index tended to overestimate their similarity, while spouses who scored low tended to underestimate it. Spouses tend to perceive their behavioural styles in conflict situations to be more similar than they actually are (Acitelli et al., 1993; see also McFarland & Miller, 1990).

Studying conflict in newlyweds, Acitelli et al. (1993) found that the husband's marital well-being was greater the more frequently he reported using constructive behaviours and the less both partners reported using destructive behaviours. The wife's marital well-being, however, was more related to how her perceptions related to her husband's—for instance it was better the more she understood her husband and saw him as similar to herself, and the more she understood his (reported) destructive behaviours.

Nevertheless understanding between partners is often surprisingly low. Berger (1993) cites evidence that couples showing a direct style of communication show no greater understanding of each other than those who have an evasive style.

Interpersonal Perception and Empathy

Empathy requires interpersonal perception, but of course that is not sufficient. Empathy can be seen as involving three facets—perspective-taking (i.e. taking the point of view of the other), empathic concern, and personal distress. While the first two are directed towards the other, the personal distress involves self-oriented emotions (Davis & Kraus, 1991).

Misperception

It will be apparent that there are many routes by which misperceptions may arise. First, there may be genuine difficulties in communication arising from differences in accepted norms—for instance across the generations (Weigel & Weigel, 1993).

Second, at a global level, our own notions about how people function, and about how different traits are interrelated—our so-called "implicit personality theories"—may blind us to the way that individuals actually behave (Bruner & Tagiuri, 1954).

Third, misperception may arise because partners interpret actions differently. For instance, one partner's care-giving and solicitude may be interpreted by the other as excessive control.

Fourth, individuals may be misperceived because they are seen as concealing their "true" attitudes, dissembling, constrained by social pressures, attempting to please us, and so on. Of course they may really be dissembling, or they may be perceived incorrectly to be dissembling because their behaviour does not conform to the perceiver's expectations or desires. In the case of deliberate deception of the partner, the factors influencing the latter's ability to detect the deception have been studied by a number of workers (Ekman, 1985). McCornack and Parks (1986) suggested that as degree of involvement in the relationship increases, confidence in ability to detect the partner's deception increases. This leads to a "Truth bias", which reduces the ability to detect deception.

Misperception may be important for the progress or stability of a relationship (Murstein, 1971c). For example, early in a romantic relationship the partners may see nothing but good in each other (e.g. Holmes & Rempel, 1989). However as the relationship develops, more opportunities for each partner to display negative qualities arise. If the participants have some degree of commitment to the relationship, evidence for potentially negative dispositions must be countered. Defence mechanisms operate (Murray & Holmes, 1996, cited above).

ACCOUNTS

The importance of the accounts of their lives and relationships that people construct has been emphasised already, but it is appropriate to return to the issue again here because accounts may influence interpersonal perception and interpersonal perception may influence the accounts that are made.

A number of different and independent lines of research have contributed to the recognition of the importance of accounts (e.g. Bruner, 1990). Harvey, Agostinelli, and Weber (1989) see them as explanations for past actions and events which include characterisation of self and of others, enabling individuals to make sense of past events. They argue (1989, p.40) that "accounts develop over a period of time, are rehearsed and periodically elaborated in front of audiences varying in size (from oneself to a set of close others), are triggered by a variety of stimuli including many emotionally relevant sights and sounds, and endure in varied forms until our deaths." The accounts an individual constructs are based on past events and influence how the present is construed, but the reverse is also true, the present affecting memories of the past (Holmberg & Veroff, 1996).

The account an individual makes about a relationship resides in the first instance in his or her head. It is a way of understanding the relationship, of coming to terms with its growth, of dividing up its stages, of perceiving the participant's role in it, of placing it in perspective with the rest of the world. The account may be individually constructed, or elaborated in the course of conversation with the partner, or in conversation with outsiders, or all three. Accounts involve selecting some aspects of what has happened, rejecting or de-emphasising others, making attributions about causes, distorting, rearranging and so on. They may have a degree of flexibility: as presented to the self or to another they will be affected by the individual's mood, tailored to the recipient or situation, and so on. There will be redefinitions, excuses, explanations. To cite but one example, stories of the wedding and honeymoon collected shortly afterwards were similar in couples who experienced a large fall in marital well-being over the next two years and in more stable couples. However, the former's memories of the wedding, collected at the end of the two-year period, were much more negative than those of the happy couples (Holmberg & Veroff, 1996).

How all this is achieved may be an individual matter, and will be influenced by experience in the relationship and in other relationships. Ross (1989) has suggested that people fill in the gaps in their memories by constructing likely scenarios from their views of how things are now and how they are likely to have changed. Thus if an individual is happily married now and believes that happy relationships are stable, she will record the past as being like the present. But if she believes that relationships become more satisfying with time, she may recall the past more negatively.

Accounts may also be influenced by myths prevalent in the culture: Sternberg (1995), discussing ideas of love, sees the notion of ludic (game-playing, see p.434) love as derived from Ovid's poetry, and romantic love to be influenced by Tristan and Isolde or by Romeo and Juliet.

While some accounts are imparted to, and indeed designed for, particular individuals, others may be kept private. The latter may form an overview or master account of the individual's life-story (see also Antaki, 1987). If this master account tends to conform to the norms and rules of the groups to which the individual belongs, it may serve to maintain self-esteem and, if imparted, to win approval from others. Harvey et al. (1989) emphasise that not only does account-making help to justify actions to oneself and to others, but may serve to enhance a personal sense of control, provide emotional release, and satisfy the "sheer desire to understand". Accounts may make the present more meaningful by facilitating under-standing of the past. Accounts may affect the future encoding of informa-tion, the anticipation and reconstruction of events, and actual behaviour in interaction (see also Baldwin, 1995; LaRossa, 1995).

Thus coming to terms with self and partner may be accomplished through the development of story-like representations which help to dispel any feelings of doubt about the future (e.g. Murray & Holmes, 1993; 1996). Where these stories concern apparent defects in the partner, they may be much more than simple excuses and involve a complex interweaving such that the meaning of potential faults is interpreted in the light of surround-ing virtues. A variety of devices may be employed. First, faults may be interpreted as virtues, as when stubbornness is interpreted as integrity. Second, positive attributes may be exaggerated so that they overshadow negative ones. Or third, the importance of the faults may be minimised or the faults rationalised. In studies involving deceiving dating individuals to believe that some of their partner's qualities were faults (with subsequent supposedly adequate debriefing), Murray and Holmes demonstrated these processes, and also the poetic licence that would be involved in the re-construing of events in the relationship. They suggest that the narratives produced provide a cognitive structure supportive for the effective care of the relationship.

Given the ubiquitous importance of such constructed narratives, it must be the case that the data provided by the instruments described earlier in this chapter are abstracted from the accounts the individuals have made about their partner and the relationship.

PERSONAL CONSTRUCT ANALYSIS AND THE PERCEPTION OF RELATIONSHIPS

So far we have considered how the partners in a relationship perceive them-selves and each other. As Laing's approach (pp.222–223) emphasises, people also have perceptions of their relationships, and these may be im-portant for their future course. Cate (cited Acitelli, 1993) found that the more individuals reminisced about their relationship, and the less they engaged in thinking evaluatively about it, the more satisfied they were. The cause–effect relation could be either way, but the data suggested that thinking about their relationship augmented satisfaction by reducing their uncertainties. Acitelli also cites evidence that "tacit relationship awareness"—taking the perspective of the dyad, as in the use of the first person plural—is related to satisfaction. During interviews with married couples, Acitelli found that wives talked about the relationship more than did husbands, and that wives' marital satisfaction was positively related to how much their husbands talked about the relationship. The converse was not true for husbands (see also Acitelli & Young, 1996).

Talking about the relationship may also play a part in problem-solving. In a disagreement, distressed couples tend to focus on an issue or on one or other partner, while non-distressed ones can switch to the relationship and discuss the communication between them. Acitelli also cites experimental data indicating that individuals perceive that talking about a relationship is likely to make the partners feel better than not talking about it. Interestingly, men felt better about relationship talk in unpleasant situations than in pleasant ones, apparently seeing it as instrumental, while women felt equally good about it in either case. Relationship talk is satisfying or useful when used to reminisce about pleasant situations or analyse unpleasant ones, but can be destructive if it involves reminiscing about unpleasant situations or analysing pleasant ones.

In Chapter 8 we saw how the technique of personal construct analysis could be used to assess the importance for friendship of similarity in the ways in which individuals see the world. The technique can also be used to assess how individuals perceive their relationships. Here the elements in the repertory grids are relationships between individuals. For example, Ryle and Breen (1972) studied heterosexual couples, some of whom were known by independent criteria to be maladjusted. Lists containing a number of constructs (e.g. Is affectionate to, Is submissive to, Is dependent upon) were made up, some being supplied by the experimenter and others elicited from the subjects. The experimenters, in consultation with the subjects, also selected a set of dyads of importance to the subject—e.g. self to partner, self to father, father to mother. Each member of each couple was then presented with two grids, the constructs being arranged along one edge and the dyads along another. They were asked to rate each relationship for each construct on a seven-point scale, first according to their own views, and second as they predicted that their partner would do it. The construct space provided by the first two factors from a principle components analysis of the resulting scores was then plotted. The closeness of two elements (dyads) in the construct space then implies perception of role similarity. When two lines joining a dyad are parallel, this represents a similar role relationship. The data showed that the maladjusted couples were more likely to see their relationship with their partner as like their relationship with a parent, and their own role as like that of a child, than were the

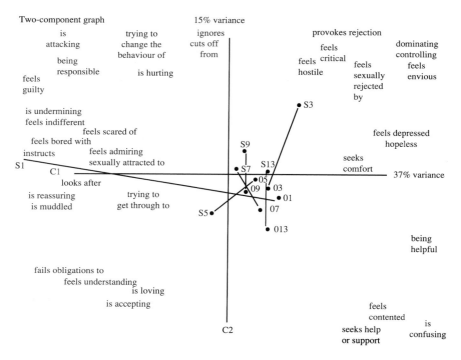

FIG. 13.2   The course of marital therapy as shown by the reconstruction grid of the wife in terms of the first two components. Every second session is shown. S indicates self-to-other; O indicates other-to-self. (From Ryle & Lipshitz, 1975, *British Journal of Medical Psychology*, *49*, 281–285. Reprinted by permission of the British Psychological Society.)

controls; and that when the relationship was going badly they perceived their own role as more child-like, while that of their partner became less parent-like (see also Ryle & Lunghi, 1970).

A related example is provided by Ryle and Lipshitz's (1975, 1976) use of a "reconstruction grid" to plot the course of marital therapy. A list of 18 constructs describing behaviour of one partner to the other and 15 describing feeling towards or about the other was presented to the couple. The couple were asked to rate these 33 constructs on 11 occasions, giving each item two scores, one representing the relationship of husband to wife and the other that of wife to husband. The resulting 33 × 22 grid was then subjected to a form of principal components analysis. The progress of the therapy could be seen by plotting every second (to save congestion) occasion on a plot of the two principal dimensions to emerge. Figure 13.2 shows the successive positions that the couple occupied.

Ryle and Lipshitz (1975) state:

In the wife's reconstruction grid ... it is seen that she-to-him moved initially from being extremely, but ambivalently, negative (bored, indifferent, scared of, but also reassuring and respecting) to being rejected, rejection-provoking, dominating and hostile on the third occasion. Thereafter she moved towards the seeking comfort and reassurance and being contented and accepting area. She saw less change in him-to-her than in herself-to-him, locating him in the more accepting, helpful and confusing quadrant throughout. The husband's reconstruction grid followed a similar pattern in that he saw himself as moving from an ambivalently attacking and undermining position through being hostile, anxious, depressed and critical to a final position in which self-to-other and other-to-self are both in the contented but also dominating quadrant. By the end of therapy, therefore, they agree in seeing their relationship as much more similar than had been the case before treatment.

SUMMARY

1. The perceptions that individuals have of themselves, their partners and their relationships, and their understanding of each other, are crucial to the nature of their relationships.
2. A variety of methods are available for assessing interpersonal perception.
3. Some factors affecting interpersonal perception are reviewed. These include both the appearance and behaviour of the person perceived, and various aspects of and influences on the perceiver.
4. Partners in long-term relationships are likely to show an increase in interpersonal perception and understanding. However there is a persisting tendency to perceive greater similarity than is actually the case.
5. Misperception may have a variety of causes. It may facilitate or hinder progress or stability in the relationship.
6. The partners' perceptions of each other form the bases of the accounts that they make (separately or together) of the relationship.
7. People's views of their relationships can also be assessed by a repertory grid technique.

14 Satisfaction

We inevitably tend to make global assessments of our relationships, and the nature of those assessments may affect behaviour both within and outside the relationship. The nature of the assessment is important for each partner's immediate well-being as well as for the longer-term course of the relationship. But although we make global assessments, many individual aspects of a relationship can contribute to those assessments, and many can detract from it. Satisfaction thus has many determinants, including individual characteristics of the participants, the nature of the relationship, contextual factors, and the relations between all of these.

Furthermore, how any particular aspect of the relationship contributes to satisfaction, or how any event within it is evaluated, will depend both on societal norms and on the idiosyncratic expectations of each participant. A couple who desire a very close relationship, and a couple who each prefer considerable autonomy, may be equally satisfied with their relationships. And the nature of relationship satisfaction must differ between cultures—for instance between marriage in polygamous vs. monogamous societies, or societies with arranged marriages vs. those where partners choose their mates. Even in our own society, in the last few decades the feminist movement has highlighted the contrast between expectations in traditional and non-traditional marriages, and within each of these there is almost infinite diversity. And in any type of marriage, what the wife wants and expects may differ from what the husband wants and expects:

to say that both partners in a marriage are equally satisfied does not mean that they are satisfied in the same way (Peplau, 1983).

The nature of satisfaction also differs considerably according to the nature of the relationship. The bases of satisfaction in a marital relationship, where issues of sharing chores and child-care enter in, may be very different from those in friendship or dating relationships. There is also evidence that the partners in dating relationships like to be seen in the best possible light, while marital partners tend more to like to be seen as they really are (pp.225–226): this also implies differences in the criteria of satisfaction. Unfortunately research on relationships has seldom faced up to this issue. Most of the work discussed here refers to dating or marital relationships.

MEASUREMENT AND RELATED PROBLEMS

The complexity of the concept of "satisfaction" is indicated by the number of semi-alternative terms (relationship "quality", "adjustment", "stability", etc.) which have been used by research workers in this context, so that it is hardly surprising that measurement has posed a problem (Sabatelli, 1988). Studies using a variety of these dependent variables are discussed in this chapter, but caution is necessary: for instance, while it might seem reasonable to suppose that satisfaction and relationship stability would be related, the evidence is not substantial (White, 1990), and Eddy (1991) emphasises that the much-used Dyadic Adjustment Scale does indeed measure primarily "adjustment", with "satisfaction" accounting for only about 25% of the variance. Newcomb and Bentler (1981) emphasise the distinctions between satisfaction, stability, lack of tension, companionship, consensus, cohesion and so on. Measurement techniques have also been varied: while retrospective accounts and questionnaire methods have been used most (e.g. Locke & Wallace, 1959; Snyder, 1979; Spanier, 1976), a variety of other techniques have also been employed (reviews by Glenn, 1987; Harvey, Hendrick, & Tucker, 1988; Newcomb & Bentler, 1981; Sabatelli, 1988).

Part of the measurement problem stems from the ease with which satisfaction or marital quality is seen solely as a state or consequence of the relationship—in other words as a dependent variable. (The Dyadic Adjustment Scale in fact refers both to the process of adjustment and to its outcome.) But satisfaction feeds back into the intimacy, love, investment, commitment, and other variables that promote it. The partners in a loving relationship love each other in part because they find satisfaction in the relationship, and they find satisfaction in part because they love each other. Kurdek (1990) has argued that newlyweds' evaluations of their spouses' positive attributes, and their evaluations of the positivity of their interactions, are both part of a single dimension of relationship quality.

Satisfaction implies some standard or ideal, and a number of studies have shown it to be related to the discrepancy between the perceived situation and a norm or ideal. Thus satisfaction in heterosexual relationships has been found to be negatively related to the discrepancy between perceived global quality and ideal quality, or to the discrepancy between expectations of parenting and household chores before the birth of a baby and perceptions of actual responsibilities afterwards (Belsky, 1985; Hackel & Ruble, 1992). Satisfaction with the parenting role in both biological and step-parents has been shown to be related to the discrepancy between parents' appraisals of their parenting performance and their assumptions about what most parents do or what parents ought to do (Fine & Kurdek, 1994). Similarly Levinger (1966) found that marital satisfaction was related not to the frequency of sexual intercourse, but to the discrepancy between desired and actual frequency. Sternberg and Barnes (1985) investigated whether satisfaction was related to an individual's actual feelings about the partner, their imagined feelings towards an ideal partner, their perceptions of the partner's feelings about them, or their perceptions of the feelings of an imagined ideal partner. They found that both the absolute levels of feelings, and the comparison between those levels and the ideal, affected satisfaction independently. Feelings about the partner were more predictive of satisfaction than feelings about an ideal partner; and feelings towards and perceived feelings by the partner were almost equally important. The authors suggest that actual feelings and feelings relative to ideals are inextricably interwoven in a person's emotional make-up, and that neither the actual nor the ideal other is the key to satisfaction, but rather the perceived other. More recently Murray and Holmes (1996) reported that the more idealised were individuals' constructions of their partners' qualities (controlling for their actual attributes), the greater was their satisfaction.

Thus a considerable number of studies confirm that the critical issue is not what the partner is actually like but the idealised perception of the partner, or the relation between perception and ideal; not what actually happens in a relationship but the relationship as experienced in relation to hopes and expectations (see also Fincham & Bradbury, 1987a; Schaefer & Burnett, 1987). Of course an ideal relationship—say an ideal marriage— may be very different in one culture from what it is in another, and even between one sub-culture and another. Indeed in any one culture what women want and expect from their relationships differs from what men want.

A central and controversial issue is whether "satisfaction" is to be seen as an overall evaluative judgement of the relationship, or whether satisfaction in different aspects of the relationship should be evaluated independently. Fincham and Bradbury (1987a, p.800) advocate the former:

"Global evaluations of the marriage, rather than self-reports of any behaviour or cluster of behaviours, are likely to represent the final common
pathway through which marital maladjustment is expressed." Scales that
include items concerned with diverse aspects of the relationship leave open
the question of how the several items should be weighted, so that the total
derived from them is inevitably arbitrary.

Others take a different view. Drigotas and Rusbult (1992) argue that a
global assessment of satisfaction cannot lead us directly to its sources.
Furthermore, although a global assessment may be a useful predictor of
further interaction, it begs the question of what standard the participants
are using—is the relationship being assessed with reference to what the
respondent would like, or what the respondent thinks is typical of other
relationships, or what the respondent thinks is proper and correct (cf.
Goodnow, 1988)? Drigotas and Rusbult therefore advocate the use of a
construct termed "need satisfaction dependence". This can be assessed
from data concerning how important each of several needs is perceived to
be, how well satisfied each is in the relationship, and the extent to which
each would be satisfied in an alternative relationship.

Some workers have combined global and analytic approaches. Thus
Huston and Vangelisti (1991) and Huston and Chorost (1994) used a
Marital Opinion Questionnaire, adapted from a measure of life satisfaction,
which was weighted heavily by a single item concerned with overall satisfaction. Blais et al. (1990) used several instruments including a Marital
Happiness Scale assessing nine aspects of marital relationships on ten-
interval scales, but including also a global assessment.

Another approach, currently insufficiently evaluated, consists in evaluating positive and negative dimensions of marital quality independently.
Johnson et al. (1986) found that factor analysis of data from a large sample
of couples yielded two dimensions, one consisting of scales of marital
happiness and interaction, the other of disagreements, problems, and instability. These were found to have different relations to the several aspects
of family life, and the authors comment that any combination of measures
from the two dimensions is likely to yield ambiguous results. Although
Glenn (1987) pointed out that the two dimensions might not be independent, happiness being affected by disagreements, a related approach has been
developed independently by Fincham, Beach, and Kemp-Fincham (in
press). They suggest that marital evaluations should be seen as involving
two dimensions—"Positive marital quality" (PMQ) and "Negative marital
quality" (NMQ). This permits a more differentiated view of those who are
assessed as intermediate on a single bipolar dimension of marital quality,
who might be either indifferent (caring little about either pole) or ambivalent (caring equally about both). Instead of a distressed versus non-
distressed dichotomy of marital quality, this offers a four-category

typology—Happy (high PMQ, low NMQ), Distressed (low PMQ, high NMQ), Indifferent (low on both), and Ambivalent (high on both). Fincham et al. present empirical data in support of this approach.

A further issue arises from the fact that individuals may respond to questions about their relationship in a manner influenced by their dominant sentiment about it ("sentiment override"), and the extent to which this is the case differs individually. Fincham et al. point out that this may have important implications for data on the correlates of marital quality obtained by self-report measures.

Although direct questioning about satisfaction or its determinants is most often used, other methods may be possible. Levenson and Gottman (1983, 1985) assessed a number of physiological indices and self-reported affect during interchanges between partners. Both negative affect and more reciprocity of negative affect, and in one study a measure of the physiological "linkage" between the partners, were related to current satisfaction. The more aroused the couple were, the greater the decline in marital satisfaction when they were assessed three years later. Dissatisfaction on the first occasion and the decline in satisfaction were predicted by the husbands' emotional withdrawal and greater reciprocity by the wives to the husbands' negative emotions.

In a later study of older couples (40–50 and 60–70 years), Levenson, Carstensen, and Gottman (1994) found that marital interaction was accompanied by less physiological arousal in the older couples. Marital dissatisfaction was again associated with less positive and more negative affect, and greater reciprocity in the latter. Physiological arousal was associated with negative feelings in the husbands but not in the wives.

CONSISTENCY

This, like most aspects of satisfaction, has been studied primarily in marital relationships. A number of studies indicate that marital satisfaction tends to decline in the first few years of marriage (e.g. MacDermid, Huston, & McHale, 1990). Some studies report a rise later, perhaps when the children grow up. Schumm and Bugaighis (1986) also found an initial decline in marital quality (assessed by three global questions), but showed that it represented not a mild problem in most cases but a severe one in some— namely a group of low-income mothers who were employed full time and were finding too little time to discuss daily matters with their husbands, though they saw their husbands as just as caring as did the less-stressed wives.

There is some evidence that the finding of a decline in marital quality may depend on the sampling technique (cross-sectional or longitudinal studies, cohort differences) or on the method of assessment: Vaillant and Vaillant (1993) studied a sample of college men from around 1940. Global measures of marital satisfaction were made in 1954, 1967, 1974, 1983, and 1989, and for the wives in 1967, 1975, and 1987. This approach showed little change in marital satisfaction. Husbands (in 1979) and wives (in 1987) also completed a retrospective chart of marital satisfaction in five-year periods. This indicated a weak curvilinear pattern of satisfaction with time (i.e. a gradual decrease with a low point at about 20 years, followed by gradual recovery). Further progress in this field may demand more sophisticated methods of data analysis: Karney and Bradbury (1995a) advocate the use of multiple longitudinal assessments to estimate parameters of change within individuals which are then used to account for variability in patterns of change between individuals.

The changes that do occur may result from particular stresses occurring in the first few years. Suitor (1991), examining satisfaction with the division of labour between husband and wife over time, itself related to marital quality, found that wives' satisfaction did follow a U-curve, being lowest when their contribution was greatest. Husbands were more likely than wives to report themselves as satisfied with the division of labour, and did not change over the life cycle. An explanation in terms of temporary stresses, affecting marriages differentially, is in keeping with the fact that consistency in the early years is relatively low: one study found correlation coefficients for satisfaction of only .34 for wives and .51 for husbands over the first two years of marriage (Huston & Chorost, 1994), compared with stability coefficients of .96 and .81 over a three-year period for partners married about 4 and 24 years (Gottman & Krokoff, 1989).

Satisfaction also declines after the birth of the first child. Although MacDermid et al. (1990) warn that this should be seen against the background of the general decline in marital satisfaction in the early years of marriage, it is a robust finding (e.g. Belsky, Rovine, & Fish, 1989; Cowan & Cowan, 1988). Furthermore it depends on the nature of the marriage and on expectations about what life would be like after the baby was born. Thus Hackel and Ruble (1992) showed that the more negative feelings about marriage were associated with the disconfirmation of expectancies about the sharing of child-care and household responsibilities after the baby was born. The birth usually leads to less sharing of chores than the wife had expected, and thus to decreased satisfaction. A few wives, however, showed an opposite effect—more satisfaction was associated with doing more chores than had been expected: this was especially the case with couples scoring low on an adaptability scale and with more traditional wives. In their study MacDermid et al. (1990) found that the couples most at risk for marital difficulties were those with traditional attitudes who take on more egalitarian roles, and they therefore emphasise the importance of congruence between sex-role attitudes and the post-natal division of labour.

Although there is less systematic research on the matter, chores connected with the arrival of the baby are certainly not the only issue. A husband may fear that the baby competes for his wife's affections, the wife may fear for her looks, there may be sexual problems, and so on. Conversely, in many cultures the birth of a baby cements the marriage and enhances the wife's status.

FACTORS AFFECTING SATISFACTION

Introduction

We have seen that the abilities of partners to support and extend one another's construct systems plays an essential role in the development of close relationships, and this issue is likely to play a critical role in satisfaction. If the partners can provide each other with continued validation of progressively more fundamental levels of their construct systems, they are likely to experience happiness and satisfaction with the relationship. Life events, such as spousal infidelity, children leaving home, deaths of close relatives, or (as just discussed) the birth of a child, demand a revision of one's system of constructs, perhaps a new account of one's life, and both construct validation by the partner and commitment to the relationship may be necessary. Many of the issues that affect relationship satisfaction can be seen as operating through the partners' construct systems (Neimeyer & Hudson, 1985; Neimeyer & Neimeyer, 1985). These in turn are affected by the day-to-day interactions within the relationship and the attributions that are made in consequence.

In Chapter 19, in the context of exchange and interdependence theories, we shall discuss how satisfaction relates to the dynamics of relationships. Here it is appropriate to emphasise that satisfaction is related to a wide variety of variables—demographic, socio-cultural, psychological, and interpersonal—though rather few studies have addressed the issue of compatibility in personal characteristics between the partners.

Among the diverse issues found to be related to relationship satisfaction, some are discussed elsewhere in this volume (e.g. communication and its effectiveness, pp.95–97; attributions about responsibility for marital problems, pp.319–331; and physiological arousal, p.247). The relation of satisfaction to exchange variables is discussed in Chapter 19. Additional issues are discussed by Bradbury and Fincham (1989) and Kurdek (1989). In what follows the division between personal characteristics and properties of the relationship is only an expository device.

Personal Characteristics

General. In considering the impact of personal characteristics, it is important to distinguish between characteristics facilitating or hindering the establishment of new relationships, such as shyness or assertiveness, from those that contribute to satisfaction with existing relationships. It is also necessary to note that the impact of a particular characteristic may change over a relationship's history. Here discussion is limited to a few aspects of the impact of personal characteristics and of patterns of inter-action.

Gender and Expressivity. Most studies have found little difference in satisfaction between husbands and wives. Where a difference has been found, it has favoured husbands. Thus Fowers (1991), using a scale that differentiated a variety of areas of marriage, found husbands to be more satisfied: the difference, though highly significant with the large sample size (N = 7261), does not appear to have been very great. Feeney (1994), in a more detailed study, also found a small difference in favour of husbands.

Nevertheless the masculinity/femininity of the participants does have an important influence on relationship satisfaction. As we have seen, it is now recognised that masculinity and femininity are independent constructs, and individuals high on both are known as androgynous (Spence & Helmreich, 1978). In general, satisfaction in short-term interactions is higher if one or both of the partners are high on femininity or androgyny (Ickes, 1985). While some studies indicate that both femininity and androgyny are associated with marital satisfaction (e.g. Kurdek & Schmitt, 1986a), the most consistent finding in North American studies is that satisfaction is associated with high levels of emotional expressivity or femininity in both husbands and wives (King, 1993; Lamke, 1989). The importance of femininity is in harmony with Peplau's (1978) finding that lesbian couples tend to report high relationship quality.

In long-term and marital relationships, emotional responsiveness and support is more important than in short-term interactions and, since a number of studies indicate that androgyny and femininity are associated with marital adjustment, it has been suggested that expressiveness is the immediate issue. The evidence is in harmony with this view, expressiveness being clearly associated with marital adjustment but instrumentality barely so. In a study of 102 rural families in Alabama, Lamke (1989) found the husbands' expressiveness was the sole predictor of both husbands' and wives' marital satisfaction. He noted that a number of previous studies had shown correlations between wives' expressiveness and the husbands' marital adjustment, but his regression analysis indicated that in his study female expressiveness did not contribute significantly to the husbands' marital adjustment.

King (1993) not only confirmed that husbands' emotional expressiveness was positively related to relationship satisfaction, but also that husbands' ambivalence over their emotional expressiveness (i.e. how comfortable they felt with their own style of emotional expression) was negatively related to their own and their wives' satisfaction. The expressiveness of the husbands could be a cause or a consequence of their marital satisfaction. The common male conflict strategy of withdrawal (see pp.180–181) may be a consequence of internal ambivalence in response to external conflict, while absence of conflict permits release of their expressiveness. King found the wives' perception of the husbands' expressiveness was positively related to their own satisfaction.

It is thus important to note that the relations between satisfaction and femininity or expressiveness are likely to be two-way. Expressiveness may increase satisfaction, but satisfaction may also permit or enhance expressiveness. Furthermore it must be remembered that the data on the importance of femininity in both wives and husbands comes from the Western world in the late twentieth century: whether such a generalisation is or would have been ubiquitously valid is an open issue. Our view about expressiveness and caring in close relationships is coloured by our culturally constructed notions of what expressiveness and caring involve. Wood (1993) emphasises that we tend to value the feminine techniques of talking about issues, disclosing feelings, and engaging in conversation more than the masculine approach which involves doing things.

Although a considerable number of studies indicate the importance of feminine characteristics for marital quality, aspects of masculinity may also be important. In a longitudinal study Bradbury, Campbell, and Fincham (1995) found that wives' marital satisfaction declined to the extent that they described themselves as having desirable masculine traits and their husbands described themselves as having fewer desirable feminine traits. In a second study, after the self-esteem of both spouses was controlled for, wives' satisfaction declined if the husbands described themselves as having undesirable masculine traits and (in marriages of at least five years' duration) as having fewer desirable masculine traits. Masculinity, as well as femininity, was also related to behaviour in problem-solving discussions, but sex role and behaviour in discussions made independent contributions to changes in wives' satisfaction.

But it may be that the individual sex-role attitudes of husband and wife matter less than the relation between them (Peplau, 1983). Li and Caldwell (1987), studying a mid-western USA sample, found that the extent to which the husband was more egalitarian than the wife was associated with positive adjustment, but if the wife was more egalitarian than the husband, adjustment tended to be poorer.

A number of the studies cited indicate that the determinants of marital happiness differ in some respects between husbands and wives. Acitelli and Young (1996) review studies indicating that wives' well-being is related to relationally oriented perceptions (relationship thinking and talking, wives' understanding of husbands, wives seeing their husbands as similar to themselves, wives giving support to and receiving support from their husbands), while such relationship perceptions are not related to husbands' well-being. They link this to the greater importance of relationship factors in women's self-concepts.

The relations between the use of constructive/destructive behaviour and marital well-being also appears to differ between husbands and wives. Acitelli et al. (1993) found that husbands reported more marital well-being the more often they reported using constructive tactics, and the less often both spouses reported using destructive ones. This is as might be expected. However for wives the relations between the partners' perceptions seemed to be more important, marital well-being being related to the degree to which they understood their husbands and their husbands' destructive behaviour and saw their husbands as similar to themselves.

Dating relationships might be thought of as intermediate between marital and non-intimate relationships. In a detailed study of 174 dating student couples Lamke et al. (1994) confirmed the associations between self-reported femininity and expressive behaviours and between masculinity and instrumental competence. Perceptions of the partners' femininity by females was predicted by both males' and females' self-perceived femininity, while for males perception of the partner's femininity was predicted by male's self-perceived masculinity and female's self-perceived femininity. In turn, perception of the partner as feminine was directly related to satisfaction for both males and females. Furthermore, perception by females of themselves as feminine and capable of self-disclosure and of giving emotional support was also related to feeling satisfied. Surprisingly, the partner's expressive competence did not predict satisfaction: possible reasons (some artefactual) for this are discussed. Their path model indicated that instrumental competence tended to enhance expressive competence and (for men only) vice versa. Although the variance in satisfaction accounted for by femininity was not large, this study is of special interest in showing how levels of expressive competence mediated between femininity and satisfaction (see also Siavalis & Lamke, 1992).

An interesting study by Rosenbluth and Steil (1995) must be mentioned here, though the variable at issue was termed not "satisfaction" but "Relationship Intimacy". It was assessed by summing the scores on three dimensions—Romantic Love, Supportiveness, and Communication ease.

The special interest of the study stems from the finding of a difference in the relations between personal characteristics and relationship intimacy according to the nature of the relationship. Capacity for Intimacy, assessed on a scale designed for that purpose, and self-esteem were related to relationship intimacy for women in lesbian couples, but not for those in heterosexual couples. There were no significant differences between the two groups in these individual characteristics themselves. The authors suggest explanations in terms of the lower motivation for close relationships in men, who therefore are likely to set the pace for intimacy, and their greater power as compared with the more egalitarian relationships of lesbian women.

Attachment Style.   Attachment style, as assessed by Hazan and Shaver's (1987) three-item instrument (see Chapter 21), appears to be related to the quality of romantic experiences and beliefs about relationships. Secure individuals tend to report happy, trusting experiences, avoidant individuals tend to fear intimacy, and ambivalent subjects to be preoccupied by relationships. Bartholomew (1990) suggested that marital relationships may be affected by the interaction patterns associated with different combinations of attachment styles. A number of studies have shown this to be the case. For example Senchak and Leonard (1992) assessed the attachment styles of both partners. Using instruments to assess aspects of marital functioning likely to be related to satisfaction, they found that couples in which both partners were secure showed better marital adjustment than those in which one or both were insecure (see Chapter 21).

Given such data, one must ask just how security leads to satisfaction. Assessing security in terms of high "comfort with closeness" and low "anxiety over relationships" in established married couples, and satisfaction on a six-item global measure, Feeney (1994) found that security of attachment was related to own satisfaction, though for husbands the main factor was a negative correlation between anxiety over relationships and satisfaction. Husbands were also the more satisfied, the lower their wives' anxiety. The relation between satisfaction and attachment for wives was largely mediated by the nature of the communication patterns (mutuality, coercion, destructive processes and post-conflict distress): mutually constructive communication was the strongest correlate of satisfaction for both partners.

Of special interest in this study was an apparent interplay between gender roles and the attachment dimensions in predicting satisfaction. Wives' anxiety was associated with the dissatisfaction of both parties only if the husband was uncomfortable with closeness: Feeney suggests that the clinging demanding style associated with anxiety conforms to the female gender-role stereotype. However husbands' anxiety was associated with low satisfaction for both partners, perhaps because it violates gender stereo-types (see also Noller, 1996).

Characteristics Linked to Aspects of Behaviour or Perception. A number of studies have linked individual characteristics to aspects of behaviour or perception, and those to satisfaction. The studies by Lamke et al. and by Feeney (see earlier) exemplify this. As another example, Blais et al. (1990) reviewed evidence that intrinsic motivation (i.e. motivation involving activity that is an end in itself, Deci & Ryan, 1985) to maintain the relationship leads to greater feelings of love and faith in the relationship than extrinsic motivation (which involves activities engaged in for instrumental purposes, such as to gain a desirable end or to avoid negative situations). The type of motivation influences the type of behaviour shown, and hence the partners' perceptions of each other's behaviour and their happiness in the relationship. Data from a questionnaire study confirmed this model (see also Broderick & O'Leary, 1986).

As another case, Davis and Oathout (1987) showed that empathy (assessed in terms of perspective-taking, empathic concern, and personal distress in the presence of distressed others) in one partner of a hetero-sexual couple was related to a variety of types of dyadic behaviour in that individual, which in turn were related to the partner's perceptions, and these to the partner's satisfaction. The effect of female empathy on female behaviour was stronger than that of male on male behaviour. The authors explain the gender difference in terms of the greater relevance of empathy to the traditional role for women as the partners especially responsible for emotional needs in relationships. For both men and women satisfaction was enhanced by perceptions of partner warmth and positive outlook, and decreased by perceptions of partner possessiveness and untrustworthiness. Partner insensitivity and even temper were not found to have a significant effect on satisfaction. Surprisingly, and in disagreement with data from other studies, perceived positive behaviour in the partner was found to have a greater effect than perceived negative behaviour.

Another study linking an individual characteristic through behaviour to satisfaction concerns private self-consciousness or self-awareness—that is, the disposition to focus attention on the more private and covert aspects of oneself. As noted on p.216, Franzoi and Davis (1985) found that individuals high on this characteristic tend to be more prone to self-disclose to peers. This is probably because their more accurate self-understanding makes them better equipped to self-disclose to others, though the authors raise the interesting possibility that the reverse may also be true—namely that disclosing intimate thoughts and feelings may lead to greater attentive-ness to one's intimate thoughts and feelings, and provide more self-knowledge to share (Davis & Franzoi, 1986). In turn, self-disclosure to others is linked to less loneliness amongst adolescents. Franzoi, Davis, and Young (1985) extended this study to student couples, showing that private self-consciousness affected relationship satisfaction through its effect on self-disclosure. Capacity for perspective-taking had an independent effect on relationship satisfaction which did not operate through disclosure, but was associated with better social skills. Self-disclosure may augment satisfaction also because the receiver feels trusted as a target for the disclosure (Derlega & Grzelak, 1979).

Another study of 144 married individuals and 18 cohabitors found wives' marital satisfaction to be related to perceptions of the husbands' sensitivity, shared spirituality, physical affection, honesty, and joint activities (Bell, Daly, & Gonzalez, 1987).

Interpersonal Perception. We have already seen that interpersonal perception may be important for marital satisfaction, especially for wives (see Chapter 13). In addition, as discussed on p.236, individuals tend to see their partners in more rosy terms than the partners see themselves. Those in intimate relationships often construct idealised accounts that obscure each other's faults and embellish each other's virtues. This appears to increase the satisfaction of both parties (Murray & Holmes, 1996). Presumably the cause–effect relations may act in both directions, satisfaction enhancing idealisation as well as vice versa.

Type A Characteristics. These have been linked to lowered marital dissatisfaction, but the correlations tend to be low and inconsistent. MacEwen and Barling (1993) suggested that that was because two dimensions of Type A—Achievement striving and Impatience/Irritability—have different effects on mediating variables and should be considered separately. Impatience/ Irritability is associated with increased negative interactions by men, with a negative effect on marital satisfaction, and also with depression and reduced sexual behaviour. Achievement striving, however, has a negative effect on depression and hence may be associated with enhanced sexuality and marital satisfaction.

Properties of the Relationship

Birth of a Baby. We saw earlier that the birth of a child may have a profound effect on marital quality. However the effects may differ according to the nature of the relationship. Fitzpatrick (e.g. Fitzpatrick et al., 1994) assessed three dimensions of marriage and categorised couples as having Traditional, Independent, and Separate Relationships, and those in which the couples had discrepant orientations towards the relationship (Mixed) (see pp.63–65). They explored the extent to which beliefs about the criteria for marital satisfaction differed according to the nature of the relationship, focusing on the changes that occur during pregnancy. This is a time when there are marked adjustments in the degree and nature of interdependence between husband and wife, the quality of emotional communication may wane and, after the birth, some women feel overburdened and unfairly treated. In a detailed study, Fitzpatrick et al. (1994) found that both husbands and wives reported giving and receiving more nurturance during this period, but the main effect was that husbands noted greater increases in giving nurturance, and wives in receiving it. Assessment of satisfaction was based on three questions concerned with satisfaction with marriage, spouse, and relationship. Wives in Traditional marriages tended to be more satisfied than those in most others; husbands in Separate/Traditional and wives in Separate marriages reported less satisfaction than most others. Wives in Independent marriages reported receiving less nurturance during pregnancy than wives in most other marriage types, and felt that the change in nurturance received had had a less positive influence on their relationships. Fitzpatrick et al. noted that this might seem surprising, given the high levels of interdependence and sharing of Independent couples. However, pregnancy also makes the needs of Independent couples for autonomy more salient. It is also possible that the high level of sharing found in Independent couples precludes increases in needs for nurturance. The authors comment that, in any case, the type of interdependence experienced by Independent couples may be different from that in other couple types.

Other studies of satisfaction after the birth of a baby emphasise the extent to which the mother had visualised herself as a mother during pregnancy (Alexander & Higgins, 1993), and the extent to which expectations about the sharing of chores and child-care between spouses were realised (see pp.248–249). One might suspect that the greater satisfaction found in traditional marriages might be related to the closer match between what the spouses had been socialised to expect and the reality. Expectations have been changing rapidly, and an individual's current orientation to relationships, as assessed by interview or questionnaire, may not mesh happily with more deep-seated prejudices.

Marital Style.   In another study, Aida and Falbo (1991) found that married couples who saw themselves as equal partners were more satisfied than those who saw their marriage as following the traditional pattern (cf. Fitzpatrick et al., cited earlier). Equal partners used fewer strategies to get their way, dissatisfaction being associated particularly with the use of indirect strategies (see p.182). The traditional wives used more strategies than traditional husbands. No doubt whether traditional or egalitarian marriages bring greater happiness depends on how the partners were socialised and on the current mini-cultural climate.

Negativity. Studies assessing the qualities of interactions also indicate that negative ones can have a greater influence on satisfaction than positive ones, at any rate in the short-term. This in no way denies the fact that conflict, coupled with commitment, can sometimes lead to improvement in a relationship. But a number of studies indicate that negatively valued behaviours are associated with lower levels of marital satisfaction at the same time and also over time (e.g. Gottman & Krokoff, 1989; Huston & Vangelisti, 1991).

However, as discussed earlier, the relations between spouses' socio-emotional behaviour and satisfaction may be complex, and may differ between husband and wife. Huston and Vangelisti found that negativity by either husband or wife was associated with low satisfaction, while receiving and giving affection was associated (especially for husbands) with satisfaction. The relations between negativity and satisfaction over the first two years of marriage were complex. The husband's negativity early in marriage was associated with lower wife's satisfaction two years later but early indices of the wives' socio-emotional behaviour did not predict the husbands' later satisfaction. It thus seems that the husband's socio-emotional behaviour may have a powerful effect on the marriage. Early satisfaction did not predict the later socio-emotional behaviour of the same individual. However, husbands who were initially satisfied showed affection, and their wives maintained fairly high levels of affectional expression: if wives were less satisfied early on, both partners were more negative, and the husbands became increasingly negative. Negativity of the wife early in marriage was not significantly related to a change in the husband's satisfaction. On the basis of these and other data, the authors suggest two possible cycles: the husband's negativity increases the wife's dissatisfaction which increases the husband's tendency to behave negatively; or the wife's dissatisfaction increases the husband's negativity which increases the wife's dissatisfaction. Although such hypotheses might suggest that the wife's negativity is unimportant, Huston and Vangelisti (1991, p.731) point out that wives' negativity early in marriage predicted declines in their own satisfaction, and this may encourage negativity in the husband, which increases the dissatisfaction of the wife. "These results provide evidence that the spouses' attitudes and behaviour operate as a complex, integrated whole. Each spouse both influences and is influenced by the other, either directly or indirectly." (See also Levenson et al., 1994.)

Furthermore, negativity becomes increasingly strongly connected with negativity as time goes on. One possibility is that affectionate behaviour and commitment early on buffer the effects of negative behaviour, but that these decrease with time. If negative behaviour were coupled with attempts by the couple to come to terms with problems, this could at least ameliorate the effects of the negative behaviour on satisfaction (Gottman &

Krokoff, 1989), and one theory of marital breakdown is based on the view that what matters is the ratio of cumulative positivity to negativity (Gottman, 1994).

In a study designed to assess the influence of affectionate and friendly behaviour, and of behaviour aimed at meeting each other's needs and the maintenance of the relationship, on the impact of negativity on satisfaction, couples were interviewed (so far as possible independently) face-to-face and at times by telephone over a two- to three-week period, and again two years later. The data showed virtually no effect of husband's negativity on the wife's satisfaction (assessed by the Marital Opinion Questionnaire) if the husband's level of affectional expression was high, but a marked effect if his affectional expression was low, though this buffering effect was present only when they were recently married. Much the same was true of maintenance behaviours: the effect of the husband's negative behaviour on the wife's satisfaction was ameliorated if he were open and accommodating, and this was the case both early in marriage and two years later. None of these findings was true for wives. Furthermore, the affectionate behaviour of the newlywed husbands reduced the predicted value of their early negativity on the wives' satisfaction two years later, but the reverse was not the case (Huston & Chorost, 1994). The latter is hardly surprising, in view of the lack of evidence from the same sample (see earlier) that wives' negativity affects husband's satisfaction. The authors suggested that, because wives engage in more maintenance behaviour than husbands early on, this buffers the effects of their negativity. They point out that their data do not show whether husband's affectionate behaviour affects how wives experience negativity—for instance whether their perception is affected by the socio-emotional atmosphere of the relationship. This study is noteworthy in that the data on negativity and affectional expression came from the spouse, while the maintenance behaviour and marital satisfaction data came from self-reports. Thus respondents' biases cannot account for the relations between maintenance behaviours and satisfaction.

Other studies have linked negativism to the attributions made by the partners. If negative behaviour by the partner receives non-benign attributions, marital satisfaction a year later is likely to be lower: the data indicate a causal connection (Fincham & Bradbury, 1993). Karney et al. (1994) assessed cross-situational negative affectivity (i.e. the cross-situational tendency to experience and express negative thoughts and feelings), and found that individuals high on that measure tended to offer maladaptive attributions for marital events, though the attributions made by one spouse were not related to the negative affectivity of the other. Negative attributions detracted from marital satisfaction, and this relation was shown not to be simply a manifestation of general negativity.

Relational Awareness and Understanding.   Satisfaction depends in part on "relational awareness", the extent to which the partners think and talk in relationship terms (Acitelli & Young, 1996). Cate et al. (1995) suggest that relational thinking should be categorised as "relationship enhancing", "distress maintaining", or neutral, and showed that these were respectively positively and negatively related to relationship satisfaction in the dating relationships of college students, and to the quality of their subsequent interactions.

Mutual understanding is also linked to marital satisfaction. Acitelli et al. (1993) found that the marital well-being of wives was linked to the wives' understanding of the husband, while that of the husbands was more closely linked to the spouses' self-reports of their own behaviour: husbands' understanding of wives did not predict husbands' well-being. This is in keeping with other studies, and is compatible with the view that the wife understands the husband better than vice versa, possibly because she has less power, and the person with less power needs to understand the person with more power.

In a study of married couples, de Turck and Miller (1986) used a questionnaire that distinguished between individuals who saw their spouses as unique individuals rather than as undifferentiated incumbents of roles, and found greater satisfaction among the former.

Interdependence in Friendship.   Considering some data on non-marital relationships, interdependence, including mutual assistance and companionship, seems to embrace the critical provisions that contribute to stability in friendship (Hays, 1988). While it is generally true that women show greater intimacy, trust, and communal orientation in friendships than do men, Jones (1991) found no clear sex difference in the contribution of these variables to satisfaction: self-disclosure, trust, a low endorsement of an exchange orientation, and companionship and enjoyment of the relationship were related to satisfaction in both men and women. As in many other studies (see earlier), negative relationship characteristics were found to be more effective in detracting from satisfaction than positive ones in adding to it. In this study of introductory psychology students, mutual assistance was not found to contribute significantly to satisfaction.

Time and Activities Together.   Some evidence comes from a comparison between students in premarital romantic relationships whose partners did or did not live close enough to be seen every day. Self-reported levels of relationship satisfaction, intimacy, trust, and relationship progress did not differ between the two groups. Guldner and Swensen (1995, p.313) comment that the data suggest "that the amount of time a couple spends together does not itself play a central role in relationship maintenance", (though it might be supposed that the couples who were in relationships in spite of living far apart may have had more going for them in other ways). Thus in general these data indicate that time spent together is an inadequate predictor of the quality or future of a relationship (see also Surra & Longstreth, 1990).

However a number of studies have shown a relation between the time a couple spend together and marital satisfaction (e.g. Hill, 1988). One study found that happy couples were together more in their homes, but less in public places, than unhappy couples. Furthermore, when together the happy couples more often performed recreational activities, and were less often in conflict, blaming their spouses for negative feelings less than distressed spouses (Kirchler, 1988).

Although it may be that time spent together enhances companionship and communication, and thus satisfaction with the relationship, it is also possible that causation operates in the other direction, the more satisfied couples spending more time together (e.g. White, 1983). In a study based on three telephone interviews with each of 1341 respondents over eight years, Zuo (1992) obtained evidence that causation indeed operated both ways. In an experimental situation no convincing evidence either way was obtained, but the data threw some doubt on the view that time together by itself enhances satisfaction (Reissman, Aron, & Bergen, 1993; see also later).

But it is not only time together but what the partners do and why that matters. With respect to the former, Reissman et al. (1993) found that exciting activities had a greater impact on satisfaction than pleasant ones. But more importantly, satisfaction is likely to be greater if the activities undertaken together are undertaken because they are chosen by each partner as satisfying in themselves ("intrinsically motivated") rather than for instrumental purposes ("extrinsically motivated") (e.g. Rempel, Holmes, & Zanna, 1985). This, however, is a relatively crude distinction and it is more useful to distinguish several types of motivation differing in levels of experienced self-determination or autonomy:

(a) *Amotivation*, similar to learned helplessness (Seligman, 1975), where the individual feels unable to control life.
(b) *External regulation*, where the individual seeks to maintain the relationship for the security or social recognition it brings.
(c) *Projected regulation*, where behaviour is motivated internally (e.g. guilt or feelings of obligation).
(d) *Identified regulation*, where the individual values the activities that the relationship makes possible.
(e) *Integrated regulation*, where the activity is chosen and endorsed, and the regulation is consistent with the self-concept.

Motivations of types (a) to (c) were decreasingly negatively correlated with measures of the quality of the relationship, and (d) to (e) increasingly positively correlated. The more self-determined both partners' motivational styles, the greater their perceptions of positive dyadic behaviour and the greater their happiness with the relationship (Blais et al., 1990).

Finally, perhaps the most important aspect of doing things together is the communication involved. Time spent communicating is more important than mere time together (Holman & Jacquart, 1988). Acitelli (1992) found that wives' marital satisfaction was related to the amount of time husbands spent talking about the marital relationship.

Expectations and Beliefs: Love Styles.   In this section we are concerned with a variety of expectations about marriage and other cultural beliefs.

Satisfaction, we have seen, is linked to the discrepancy between what an individual expects of a relationship and what is actually experienced. Kelley and Burgoon (1991) found that agreement between spouses on what they expected from the relationship did predict satisfaction, but the discrepancy between expectation and experience was more powerful. Beliefs about what is important in a relationship moderate the relations between an individual's perception of a relationship and its perceived quality. For instance, subjects who had strong beliefs about the importance of passion made decisions as to whether belief-relevant adjectives described their own intimate relationship almost equally fast whether or not they were asked to perform a concurrent memory task, but weak-belief subjects were significantly slower in the concurrent memory task condition (Fletcher, Rosanowski, & Fitness, 1994).

As might be anticipated, much depends on the "style of loving" that the partners expect. This has been most studied in the context of the six love styles differentiated by Hendrick and Hendrick (1986), as discussed in Chapter 24. A number of studies (e.g. Hendrick, Hendrick, & Adler, 1988) have shown that individuals who endorse Eros (passionate love) and to some extent Agape (selfless love) and reject Ludus (game-playing love) report themselves as more satisfied with their relationships. Ludus (game-playing love) and instrumentality (manipulative sexuality) were negatively related to satisfaction. (Satisfaction was assessed here by the Dyadic Adjustment Scale and the Relationship Assessment Scale.) Couples whose relationships continued differed from the others on Eros, Ludus, self-disclosure, self-esteem, commitment, investment, and satisfaction.

In a study of 186 students and their dating partners, Morrow, Clark, and Brock (1995) assessed love styles as predictors of satisfaction, commitment, and associated variables according to the Rusbult model (see pp.348–351). The relations between self-reported love styles and relationship properties were generally similar for men and women, with those reporting

Eros and Agape reporting higher satisfaction, investment, and commitment. The relations between Eros and investments and commitments, and those between Agape and rewards, commitment and (negatively) availability of alternative partners, were significantly higher for men than for women. Morrow et al. comment that this could be due to the women, as the relationship specialists, reinforcing passionate or selfless behaviour in their partners, leading to greater satisfaction in the latter, or to men becoming more erotic or agapic as their relationship improves: the causal sequence could thus be in either direction, and one might think it is probably in both.

In this study, respondent's scores on Eros, Ludus, and Agape were related to relationship characteristics, but Pragma and Mania showed less clear relations to the relationship variables considered. (It must be noted that the authors comment that the Pragma and Storge scales used in this study may have been deficient.)

Morrow et al. also showed that satisfaction may be related also to the love styles endorsed by the partner. Thus for both sexes, satisfaction was correlated positively with the partner's Eros and negatively with the partner's Pragma. For women it was also related positively to the partner's Agape and negatively to the partner's Ludus. The data suggested that differences between the partner's love styles were more important for women than for men.

At this point it is as well to emphasise that data from such studies may depend critically on the age, stage, circumstances, and personalities of the individuals involved. Morrow et al., were fully aware of this problem, emphasising for instance that scores on Eros and Mania decrease with age. However it is worth emphasising again that what is important in a close relationship to a 20-year-old is not the same as what is important to a 40- or 80-year-old. Indeed, what is important to some 20-year-olds may not be important to others.

Using the distinction between companionate and passionate love (pp.429–430), Aron and Henkemeyer (1995) studied couples in a student housing project who had been married for a mean of eight years. They examined the relation of the Dyadic Adjustment Scale and of a Passionate Love Scale to six measures indicative of marital satisfaction, one a global measure. Both husbands and wives who scored highly on the DAS tended to score highly on the satisfaction scales. However only wives, and not husbands, who scored highly on the PLS scored highly on satisfaction.

Frazier and Esterley (1990) used questionnaires to assess the relation of satisfaction to beliefs about relationships (romanticism versus pragmatism), experience of relationships and love styles in subjects between 19 and 47 years of age, three quarters of whom were single. (Since many subjects had no partners, and some were dating more than one, it is unfortunately not always clear what relationship satisfaction was assessed.) For both men and women, scores on Agape, Eros and romanticism, and expressivity were positively related to satisfaction. Pragmatism was related to less satisfaction for men but not for women. Manic beliefs were associated with more satisfaction for women but not for men. Economic dependence was negatively related to satisfaction for women but not for men. Placing importance on sex was negatively related to satisfaction in men but not in women—perhaps because men who were very high on this measure failed to meet women who matched their expectations.

For dual-career families, the distribution of domestic chores and child-care is a crucial issue. Yogev and Brett (1985) studied spouses in 136 dual-earner and 103 single-earner marriages, assessing perceptions of the sharing of chores and child-care each with a single question asking whether the respondent felt he/she was doing much less, less, a fair share, more than, or much more than his/her share. For dual-earner husbands and single-earner wives, those who saw the spouse as doing more than his/her share and self as doing less were the most satisfied (i.e. an exchange model would fit). For dual-earner wives and single-earner husbands, marital satisfaction was correlated with perceiving self and spouse as doing a fair share of the work (i.e. an equity model fits best—see pp.347–348). However Benin and Agostinelli (1988), studying 160 dual-employed couples in Arizona, found that husbands were most satisfied with an equitable division of labour, wives if the division favoured them (i.e. they did less).

In a study with a more sociological bias in Israel, where some of the marriages were arranged, Shachar (1991) found that the husband's liberalism and desire to marry augmented the satisfaction of both spouses. The wives' desire to marry did not influence satisfaction, and husbands were most satisfied if they were liberal and the wives conservative. Schnacher interprets this in terms of the difficulty for a husband who, though having liberal views, desires a traditional family and must come to terms with the egalitarian expectations of his wife. No difference in satisfaction was detected between the arranged and free-choice marriages in this study, though such a difference was found in China (Xiaohe & Whyte, 1990).

Several studies have been concerned with the relations between religious beliefs and happiness in marriage in the USA. In general, strong convictions and church attendance seem to be conducive to a happy marriage. Homogamy is also an issue: the more different the denominational affiliations of husband and wife, the greater the chance of unhappiness (Ortega, Whitt, & Williams, 1988). However Shehan, Bock, and Lee (1990) found that religious heterogamy was not related to marital unhappiness in a sample of Catholics, perhaps because husband and wife shared other activities together. However, religiosity (i.e. frequency of attendance at religious services) was related to happiness in homogamous Catholic marriages. Heaton and Pratt (1990) assessed denominational homogamy, church attendance, and belief in the Bible. Only the first of these was strongly related to marital happiness, with church attendance weakly so. The authors note that denominational homogamy is a relatively external character, and might be thought less relevant to the more intimate aspects of the marital relationship: they suggest, however, that it may have far-reaching correlates in other aspects of the marriage.

Sexual satisfaction.   In marital relationships overall satisfaction is likely to be related to sexual satisfaction, and vice versa (see reviews by Lawrence & Byers, 1995; Sprecher & McKinney, 1993). Feelings of adequacy as a marital partner may be linked to feelings of adequacy as a sexual partner.

Much of the research on the sexual aspects of marriage can be criticised for using frequency of intercourse or orgasm as measures of sexual satisfaction (Perlman & Abramson, 1982), whereas the relation between overall sexual satisfaction and frequency of intercourse is at best weak. Noting that people generally make independent evaluations of the positive and negative aspects of a relationship (see pp.246–247), Henderson-King and Veroff (1994) made separate assessments of the extent to which individuals married for between one and three years felt that sex was justified and felt upset about sex, about their feelings of affirmation in the relationship (feeling good about oneself, valued, and cared for) and the incidence of tension and arguing. Feelings of affirmation were found to be associated positively, and tension negatively, with sexual satisfaction for black and white women and men. However the relations between sexual satisfaction and several dimensions of marital well-being were complex and differed between race and gender groups. Cupach and Comstock (1990) found that ease of communication about sexual matters was linked to sexual satisfaction and to measures of marital satisfaction and adjustment. They interpret the data as indicating that sexual communication leads to sexual satisfaction, and that that contributes to dyadic adjustment.

In a study of respondents in long-term sexual relationships but heterogeneous in age and marital status, Lawrence and Byers (1995) found that the difference between the perceived rewards and costs of sexual interaction when entered first into a regression analysis accounted for 72% of the variance in sexual satisfaction. The addition of the difference between the perceived rewards and costs available elsewhere, and equality in rewards, also contributed uniquely to sexual satisfaction. Overall relationship satisfaction was found to contribute to sexual satisfaction, and the data suggested that the effect was a two-way one.

Extra-relationship Factors

Satisfaction with a relationship may be affected not only by interactions within the relationship but also by the consequences of life transitions or external events. For instance, young children may both decrease opportunities for marital interaction and lead to or exarcebate perceptions of marital inequity over chores, or they may bring an increase in closeness and joy in the family (see earlier; Lee, 1988; White, Booth, & Edwards, 1986).

Employment, enrolment in a university or caring for an elderly relative may have similar effects. Emotional support by the spouse can have a marked ameliorating influence on the relationship satisfaction of a partner caring for an elderly relative, while attitudes or behaviour of the spouse that hinder care-giving can have a negative effect (Suitor & Pillemer, 1992). The experience of receiving social support is more important than the extent of the social network (Stemp, Turner, & Noh, 1986).

In addition, the resources available to the couple may have a marked effect on their satisfaction with their relationship. Resources can affect satisfaction either directly, or by facilitating the avoidance of conflict. This may happen in a variety of ways—some tangible, like purchasing help with chores or enabling the couple to go on a holiday together, and some intangible, like supporting comparisons in social status with others. Kamo (1993) found income to make a less important contribution, and romantic involvement a more important one, to marital satisfaction in a USA sample than in a Japanese one, while age (or time since marriage) was negatively related to satisfaction in the USA but not in Japan.

CONCEPTUAL MODELS OF THE BASES OF SATISFACTION

In the previous section a number of variables that affect marital satisfaction were reviewed. Several conceptual models to describe the manner in which they operate have been proposed (cf. Kurdek, 1991a):

(a) *The Interdependence and Investment models.* In exchange theory terms, satisfaction is seen as derived from the perception of rewards received and costs incurred, relative to internally derived standards. The level of outcomes individuals believe they deserve may be influenced by past experience, observation of others' relationships, and comparison with the partner's outcomes (Thibaut & Kelley, 1959; Rusbult, 1983; Rusbult & Buunk, 1993). Further discussion is best postponed to Chapter 19.

(b) *The contextual model.* Bradbury and Fincham's (1989) model of relationships was discussed in Chapter 3 (see Fig. 3.3). It distinguishes a "proximal context" of momentary thoughts and feelings which provides an immediate environment that qualifies the processing of events, from a "distal context" which includes individual difference variables (e.g. personality traits), relationship variables, learning histories, etc. The elements in the distal context influence both the variables in the proximal context and the processing of information. Satisfaction is altered by behaviours that alter the proximal context in the course of interaction, and by appraisals that occur between interactions. In turn satisfaction affects the responses to the partner's behaviour. The distal context (e.g. attachment style) thus filters and assists in the evaluation of information from proximal contexts. Bradbury and Fincham showed that marital satisfaction is related to higher levels of femininity in the partners, lower levels of unrealistic beliefs about how relationships should function, and less benign attributions. While it might be thought that the effects on satisfaction of long-term, stable variables, such as beliefs about relationships, were mediated by the proximal content, such as attributions for specific events in the relationship, Bradbury and Fincham showed this not to be the case. Rather these proximal and distal variables seemed to have discrete effects, and the authors speculated that the association between femininity and satisfaction arises because feminine individuals behave in ways that promote marital happiness. Lamke et al. (1994) suggest that these may involve intimate self-disclosure and emotionally supportive behaviour (see p.252).

It will be noted that the contextual model suggests that appraisals of satisfaction are related to individual difference variables at two levels— proximal and distal. The interdependence model focuses on the appraisals of rewards and costs, alternatives, and investments in particular relationships. In a study of gay and lesbian relationships Kurdek (1992) found that variables from both the contextual (personality traits) and the interdependence model discriminated between stable and unstable couples. In general interdependence variables were found to mediate the effects of the contextual variables.

(c) *The Problem-solving Model*. Marital satisfaction is predicted from problem-solving strategies and communicative skills used in conflict situations (e.g. Gottman, 1979). High conflict engagement tends to be associated with low satisfaction, but may be predictive of an increase in satisfaction so long as it does not involve defensiveness, stubbornness, and withdrawal (Gottman and Krokoff, 1989; see Chapter 10).

SUMMARY

1. Satisfaction, though usually treated as a consequence of relationship behaviour, is also a cause. It implies a standard, and has been assessed both in terms of a global judgement, and in terms of the extent to which a variety of separate needs are met. Satisfaction may be influenced by

properties of the relationship, perceived (and often idealised) properties of the partner, expectations, and discrepancies from expectations.

2. The evidence suggests that marital satisfaction decreases in the early years and then rises again. There is often a decline after the birth of the first child.

3. Satisfaction may be affected by personal characteristics and by properties of the relationship. Femininity is of special importance, but masculinity also plays a role. The determinants may differ between husbands and wives, and the associations of own characteristics with satisfaction may differ from those of the partner's. A secure attachment style is related to marital satisfaction. A number of studies have explored how the relations between characteristics and satisfaction are mediated by behaviour.

   Negative interactions have a greater effect on satisfaction than positive ones. Time spent together, activities performed together, general expectations and beliefs, and love styles have all shown relations to relationship satisfaction. Extra-relationship factors also play a role.

4. Several conceptual models of how such factors affect satisfaction have been elaborated.

15 Commitment

One of the most important aspects of a close relationship concerns the extent to which each participant is committed to it. Commitment plays a role in every relationship in which the successive interactions are not due to mere chance. In an elementary form it can be seen even in relatively trivial relationships, such as loyalty to one of a number of alternative bank cashiers. Efforts by a manufacturer to maintain a relationship with a retailer, or by a retailer to maintain a relationship with a customer, involve commitment. Indeed, commitment may also be present in relationships with an enemy or rival, in that rivals may know exactly how to irritate each other, and maintain their relationships in order to provide opportunities for so doing. But commitment becomes of special importance in relationships from which the participants could opt out but in fact see themselves as a dyad, differentiated from other dyads—friends, lovers and married couples: it then implies incorporating part of the self into the relationship—or the relationship into the self. It is with such relationships that most research has been conducted.

DEFINITION

Definitions of commitment differ considerably. Kelley (1983) pointed out that the term has been applied to actions, processes, states, and dispositions. Rosenblatt (1977) defined commitment as an avowed intent of a person to maintain a relationship, and Michaels, Acock, and Edwards

(1986, p.162) define it as "one's desire and intent to maintain, rather than terminate, a relationship". Lund (1985) put the emphasis not on the desire for the relationship to continue but on the expectation that it would. Her instrument included judgements of the partner's commitment and the person's expectation of forming another relationship. Michaels et al. (1986) measured commitment in terms of the partners' estimates that the relationship would terminate. However desires, intents, or expectations can have little effect unless translated into action. Hinde (1979) used commitment to refer to situations in which one or both parties either accept their relationship as continuing indefinitely or direct their behaviour towards ensuring its continuance or towards optimising its properties. Sternberg (1986), writing about loving relationships, emphasised that commitment involves both a short-term decision that one loves, and a long-term one to maintain it. Rusbult and Buunk (1993, p.180) combine intent and action: "a subjective state, including both cognitive and emotional components, that directly influences a wide range of behaviors in an on-going relationship". Rusbult and Buunk (1993) and Lin and Rusbult (1995), with an eye on the role of commitment in the dynamics of a relationship, emphasised that commitment subjectively "summarises" the degree of dependence on a relationship and promotes behaviour that maintains it (see pp.348–350).[1]

Erikson (1963, p.263) used "intimacy" in a sense approximating to the capacity for "commitment". Thus he defined intimacy as "the capacity to commit (oneself) to concrete affiliations and partnerships and to develop the ethical strength to abide by such commitments even though they may call for significant sacrifices and compromises." Erikson argued that intimacy (in this sense) demanded a firm sense of separateness or identity, for without it the experience of partial fusion with another individual is frightening and not gratifying. As Levitz-Jones and Orlofsky (1985) point out,

---

[1] Rusbult's discussion of the concepts of commitment and satisfaction link to the discussion of the difficulty of finding the correct level of analysis in studying relationships, as discussed in Chapter 4. Both may be global constructs, and may equate to subjective assessments by which participants label their relationships. Drigotas and Rusbult (1992) argue that although commitment is to be seen as a global, subjective mediator of factors influencing stay vs. leave decisions, it is not equivalent to dependence, which is related to specific determinants of those decisions. Thus it is necessary to assess the degree to which the relationship satisfies each of several needs. Drigotas and Rusbult point out that the available alternatives are too often assessed in terms of a single alternative partner, whereas in fact different needs may be satisfied by different partners: therefore dependence must be assessed by the extent to which the most important needs are better satisfied in the current relationship than elsewhere, whether by a single or by multiple partners, or by none. See Chapter 19 for discussion in the context of exchange theories.

when two individuals have resolved their own separateness, and feel secure and confident as individuals, closeness and commitment can be sought because they pose no threat to autonomy, mutual growth as separate individuals does not awaken fears of loss and abandonment, and the partners' real qualities and limitations can be accepted (cf. Bowlby, 1973, 1980).

Discussion of definitions is often boring, but it is important in the present case because of the differing techniques used for assessing commitment. As we have seen, some workers use instruments that put the emphasis on, or at least include, the expectation of how long the relationship would last (e.g. Drigotas & Rusbult, 1992; Lund, 1985; Michaels et al., 1986). (Where individuals are asked retrospectively to assess the chance of marriage as it was perceived at particular points in the development of their relationship, e.g. Surra, 1985, a considerable possibility of retrospective distortion must be present.) However the inclusion of expectations implies that commitment involves something more than desire or intent, because expectations about the durability of a relationship are likely to be influenced by the desirability and availability of possible alternatives. It also involves recognition that the chances of continuity may be influenced by factors external to the relationship, including social pressures one way or the other, or discrepant career ambitions. Of course such outside forces may be internalised: the moral sense of obligation, mentioned by Kelley (1983) as one of the forces leading to commitment, may have external origins.

Because studies of commitment have been concerned with courtship and marriage in Western societies, two important distinctions are often disregarded (Hinde, 1979). First, commitment may be concerned either solely with the maintenance of a relationship over time, or with optimising its quality, or with both. Ruth's promise to Naomi, "Where thou goest, I will go" (Ruth, 1:15) was a promise to maintain the relationship whatever its nature and included a willingness to change with her and even to share her grave. On the other hand a householder's relationship with his neighbour may involve commitment to maintain goodwill, but indifference to the neighbour's moving away. Of course most personal relationships involve commitment for both continuity and for optimising content, each being a means to the other. In some circumstances commitment for continuity and for consistency may be in conflict: people change, and continuity may only be possible if the partners can adjust their patterns of interacting so that the relationship is preserved.

A second important distinction is between exogenous commitment, where the continuity or the desire for continuity is imposed from outside or arises as a consequence of outside forces, and endogenous commitment, which arises from within. Arranged marriages and blood relatives in most societies are obvious examples of exogenous commitment: the partners are bound into the relationship by forces often outside their control, though exogenous commitment to continuity may, and often does, lead to endogenous commitment to quality. Conversely endogenous commitment may lead to exogenous commitment, as when courtship leads to ties supported by public sanctions. Commitment is of course especially important in an endogenous relationship when continuity is desired but far from assured, as in the early stages of courtship: the relationship itself then becomes a goal, and ensuring adequate rewards for the partner, thereby reducing the attractiveness of other relationships for him or her, may become more important than short-term personal satisfaction.

A similar distinction has been made by Kelley (1983) and by Stanley and Markman (1992). The latter see commitment as encompassing two related constructs—"personal dedication", or the desire to maintain or improve the quality of the relationship for the joint benefit of the participants, and "constraint commitment", referring to external or internal pressures favouring stability. They cite studies showing the value of both concepts.

Johnson (e.g. 1982) earlier distinguished commitment as referring to the determination to follow a particular line of action, referred to as "personal commitment", and commitment as referring to social constraints—"I promised my colleagues, so I must." The latter is referred to as "structural commitment". Personal commitment, according to Johnson (1982), has three aspects: satisfaction derived from the rewards and costs involved; definition of the self in terms of the relationship; and an internalised sense of moral commitment to the maintenance of the relationship. Structural commitment includes events or conditions that constrain the individual to continue the relationship once it has been initiated, regardless of personal commitment. These include, first, the investments that would be irretrievable if the relationship were to break down. Many of these are social, and would require a re-modelling of the social network. Second, the ways in which the relationship affects others, as when divorce affects the lives of children. Third, the availability of alternatives: if acceptable alternatives are lacking, the decision to leave a relationship is less likely. Fourth, the procedures, social and/or legal, that would have to be gone through to terminate the relationship. In this usage both personal and structural commitment would seem to embrace factors that contribute to the desire or intent to continue the relationship. However Johnson rightly points out that the literature on the dissolution of relationships has emphasised "dissatisfaction" and underestimated the role of constraints, primarily because satisfaction is a factor that changes, while the constraints tend to be continually on-going. In a longer perspective, changes in divorce rates over time and differences between cultures indicate the importance of structural constraints.

COMMITMENT AND AUTONOMY

Commitment to a close relationship does not mean abandoning autonomy (see pp.157–158). We shall see later (Chapters 19 & 26) that the success of close relationships often involves replacing personal goals with joint goals, and giving a high priority to spending time in helping the partner towards his or her goals. This does not mean a loss of autonomy in the sense of a loss of control over one's own actions, because the choice has been made in accordance with one's own needs and values.

DETERMINANTS OF COMMITMENT

We shall return to a more detailed discussion of the determinants of commitment in Chapter 19 in the context of Interdependence theory and the Investment Model, where it is seen as a summary of the factors influencing the decision to stay or leave (Drigotas & Rusbult, 1992; Lin & Rusbult, 1995; Rusbult & Buunk, 1993). To summarise the issues briefly, an individual is more likely to strive to continue or to enhance the quality of a relationship, the greater is:

(i) Satisfaction with the relationship. This in turn increases with the rewards received from the relationship, decreases with the costs entailed, and increases with the extent to which the quality of the relationship exceeds generalised expectations.
(ii) Dependence on the relationship, as determined by the availability of attractive alternatives in the sense of other relationships or activities, solitude, etc.
(iii) Investments in the relationship. These may include intrinsic investments (e.g. time spent, vulnerability incurred by the relationship) and extrinsic investments (mutual friends, shared associations and possessions) which would be lost if the relationship were abandoned.
(iv) Centrality of the relationship, or the extent to which it is important in bringing meaning to an individual's life and is linked to personal identity.

COMMITMENT IN UNSATISFYING RELATIONSHIPS

Most studies of commitment involve dating or married partners who are already at least moderately satisfied with and invested in the relationship. But sometimes individuals feel committed to a relationship when the costs are great and in the face of considerable adversity, and here the issues may be rather different. One possible explanation lies in the difficulty of recognising that what one has invested in a relationship has become valueless—"I must love him because I have looked after him all these years". In other cases, internalised values or external pressures may maintain the relationship: Lauer and Lauer (1986), in a study of long-term happy and unhappy marriages, found that commitment to the spouse or to the institutions of marriage was given as one of the most important reasons for marital stability. A similar conclusion was reached by Heaton and Albrecht (1991), who also found that age, lack of prior marital experience, lack of social activity, and a feeling of lack of control over life were also associated with the continuation of unhappy relationships.

Support for the view that internalised values might be especially important in such cases is found in a laboratory study of commitment to tasks. Lydon and Zanna (1990) suggest that it is when people see a task as diagnostic of their fundamental values that they feel committed in the face of adversity. They argue that the values serve as the standards by which people assess their experiences in relation to fundamental concerns about the integrity of the self. In a task involving questions about real-life projects on which the subjects were engaged, the relevance of the task to basic values was unrelated to commitment under low adversity, but was related to it under high adversity. In another long-term study of students engaged in a project, value relevance at the outset predicted commitment in the face of adversity. Thus this experimental study is in harmony with the view that commitment such as that found by Heaton and Albrecht may be related to basic values stemming from belief in marriage as an institution (see also Lin & Rusbult, 1995).

Another example is provided by the partners of frequently violent addicts: the persistence of relationships in which one partner is persistently abusive is far from uncommon. Although the threat of losing the investments already made, or the lack of an alternative partner, may make the option of leaving less attractive, these hardly provide a full explanation. Wright and Wright (1995) have described two categories of individuals who are prone to enter and maintain such a relationship. The first involves people whose socialisation has emphasised the importance of loyalty and commitment to relationships. This may be augmented by the advice of outsiders—the abused wife who is told by her mentor to endure and pray that her husband will improve. The second group includes those with negative self-perceptions who have distorted ideas of what relationships should be like. Negative self-views could also make an alternative partner seem unattainable.

BELIEF IN THE PARTNER'S COMMITMENT

Commitment of one participant in a relationship is much influenced by her or his perception of the partner's commitment—an issue too often neglected in studies in this area. In a traditional marriage the woman must be satisfied that she will not be left without resources, the man of the woman's fidelity: it can be argued that these propensities stem from our biological heritage. The very formation of a long-term heterosexual relationship depends on each partner becoming satisfied that the other is committed. Buss (1994) lists a variety of ways in which individuals signal commitment or the potential for commitment during courtship—persistence in courtship, demonstrations of affection and kindness, generosity, denigrating alternative partners, and so on. No doubt subtle nuances of non-verbal communication as well as explicit avowals and public behaviour all play a role, with the signs differing to some extent between cultures.

The importance of belief in the partner's commitment in on-going relationships involves a number of further issues. First, from an exchange or interdependence point of view (Chapter 19), each partner provides the other with rewards in the hope of future reciprocation. If that hope is to be realised, continuity is essential, and continuity depends on the partner's commitment. Second, the development of a relationship may involve giving precedence to the partner's rewards over one's own, for thereby the partner is less likely to see other relationships as more attractive. This would be folly if the partner were not seen as committed. Third, building a relationship involves laying oneself open to hurt—hurt resulting from the possible exploitation of revelations, as well as from possible desertion and loss of investments. Such eventualities are less likely with a committed partner. Fourth, as a relationship proceeds, the participants come to see the dyad as a unit: this is made possible if each sees the other's goals as similar to his or her own. Fifth, individuals have a need for autonomy as well as for relationships with others (see pp.157–158). Autonomy could be interpreted as signifying a decrease in the importance of the relationship, so faith in the partner's commitment may be necessary for the assumption or granting of a degree of autonomy. Finally, individuals must be free to develop, but personal growth may involve change in an individual's relationships. Faith in the partner's commitment is necessary for the relationship to have the flexibility to accommodate change.

Given that commitment, and the self-disclosure that almost inevitably goes with it in close relationships, involves increased vulnerability, this will be acceptable to the extent that the partner is perceived as benevolent and honest (see e.g. Johnson-George & Swap, 1982). Early in a relationship, a degree of dispositional trust must be important, but trust in the specific partner depends on learning experiences in the course of the relationship. Agreement about control, autonomy vs. connectedness, and other potential sources of conflict should also augment trust, because it gives rise to clear expectations and agreement about goals (Canary & Cupach, 1988). Furthermore, experimental evidence shows that the building up of trust may involve a degree of positive feedback: a highly trusting individual can assimilate negative information about the partner without impairment of their trust or of the relationship. Indeed such information may actually increase trust and increase positive feelings about the partner. Contrariwise, an individual lacking in trust will tend to discount positive information (Holmes & Rempel, 1989; Murray & Holmes, 1993).

INDIVIDUAL CHARACTERISTICS
AND COMMITMENT

We saw in Chapter 3 that even pre-school children differ in the extent to which they form relationships with others: some have close friends, whereas others may be very sociable, but play with whoever happens to be available. In adulthood, also, there are considerable individual differences in the tendency to become committed to a close relationship. High self-monitoring individuals (that is, those who say they guide their behaviour in accordance with the demands of the situation) choose friends as activity partners on the basis of their particular skills in the activity domain, whereas low self-monitors rely on general feelings of attraction. High self-monitoring individuals are not only attracted to external characteristics of others, as opposed to low self-monitors who pay more attention to psychological characteristics, but are more promiscuous in their sexual behaviour. High self-monitors adopt a more uncommitted attitude to dating relations, and are more ready to have sexual relations with someone to whom they are not psychologically close. The basic issue may be that high self-monitors like to be the centre of attention (Snyder, Simpson, & Gangestad, 1986).

Lin and Rusbult (1995) examined the impact of a number of personal dispositions on commitment, and found that their effects were indirect—femininity seems to promote feelings of satisfaction as well as tendencies to invest in a relationship, and lower self-esteem was found to be associated with perception of poorer alternatives, and thus with enhanced commitment.

SUMMARY

1. Commitment has been defined in a variety of ways. It is used here to refer to situations in which one or both partners in a relationship direct their behaviour towards ensuring its continuance or optimising its properties.
2. It is useful to distinguish commitment for continuity from commitment to quality, and endogenous from exogenous commitment.
3. Commitment does not necessarily mean abandoning autonomy.
4. Commitment is likely to be greater the more satisfied the individual is with the relationship, the greater the dependence on the relationship,

the greater the investments that have been made in it, and the more central the relationship is to the individual's life.

5. Commitment is often strong, even in unsatisfying relationships.
6. Belief in the partner's commitment may be critical for the maintenance of a relationship and for the personal growth of the participants.
7. Commitment is a relationship characteristic, but individual characteristics may affect its extent.

C Further Principles for Understanding Relationship Processes

While the search for understanding the dynamics of relationship processes should properly proceed from description to analysis of process, the very fact that relationships are dynamic means that description must involve reference to process. Some of the characteristics discussed in the previous section could in fact also be described as processes playing an integral part in the dynamics of relationships. This section focuses on some further issues involved in the dynamics of relationships. All of these principles play some part in practically every relationship, but none is likely to be universally applicable: some of their limitations will become apparent in these chapters and in the following sections.

16 Individual Characteristics

INTRODUCTION

The relations between personality and behaviour in relationships pose special problems (Auhagen, 1994; Auhagen & Hinde, in press), many of which relate ultimately to the nature of the self (see Chapter 3). We all have a feeling of on-going identity—that we continue to be the same person in different contexts. At the same time we know that we behave differently according to whom we are with. While much of the variance in many individual characteristics can be traced to genetic factors (Goldsmith, 1983; Loehlin, Willerman, & Horn, 1988; Plomin, 1990), personality is shaped by experience, especially in early childhood (Bowlby, 1969/82, 1973, 1980; Plomin, 1990). And while measures of individual characteristics show reasonable temporal continuity, they can be changed by life events (Goodyer, 1990; Paykel, 1983; Wink & Helson, 1993). We must therefore recognise from the start the importance of the dialectical relations between the individuals and their behaviour on the one hand and the relationships with which we are concerned on the other (Frontispiece).

Since Mischel (1968) criticised the extent to which traditional personality theories emphasised stable internal psychological structures, such issues have been met by an acceptance that behaviour is controlled by person characteristics, situation characteristics, and by interaction between them (Endler & Magnusson, 1976; Magnusson & Endler, 1977). For present purposes, the most important part of the context is the relationship in which the individual is involved. Kenny's Social Relations Model (e.g.

Kenny & LaVoie, 1984), mentioned on pp.206–207, uses a round robin design to apportion the variance of any particular behaviour into that due to actors, to partner differences in eliciting the behaviour in question, and to relationships (which remains after controlling for the other sources of variance). As an example, Ingraham and Wright (1987) used this social relations model to show that an individual may be anxious because he/she is disposed to be anxious in any situation, or because of the particular relationship in which he/she is involved.

But any science of relationships must face three issues: (i) How do relationships affect individual characteristics? (ii) How do individual characteristics affect relationships? (iii) Do individuals differ in their adaptability to situational demands? This chapter exposes the nature of these problems, but does not provide solutions. First, however, we must consider the distinction that is often made between personality characteristics and traits.

PERSONALITY AND TRAITS

The term personality, often used broadly, usually refers to a rather limited set of dimensions. In the more influential approaches, these are usually derived by some form of factor analysis of questionnaire or observational data. The number of dimensions that is optimal or necessary is a controversial issue. Cattell (e.g. 1965, 1985; Cattell & Dreger, 1977), using oblique solutions to factor analyses, identified 16 first-order traits. Eysenck (1947, 1975), using orthogonal axes, emphasised the importance of two—Extroversion/Introversion and Neuroticism/Stability—but later included Psychoticism as a third. Recently, attention has been focused on the "Big Five" of Extroversion vs. Introversion, Neuroticism vs. Stability, Friendliness, Conscientiousness, and Openness to experience (e.g. Costa & McCrae, 1989; John, 1990). Held by many to cover the basic motivational, emotional, and interpersonal styles of individuals (Botwin & Buss, 1989), this approach has nevertheless been criticised by Block (1995a, b—see reply by Costa & McCrae, 1995).

The means by which such dimensions are obtained guarantees that each will be applicable to a wide range of behaviours, but cannot be expected to predict any one type of behaviour precisely. To some extent, this can be ameliorated by using combinations of two (e.g. Kiesler, 1983; Wiggins, 1982) or even five dimensions (Hofstee, de Raad, & Goldberg, 1992), which can then be related to a much larger number of behavioural styles. We have seen an example in the Interpersonal Circumflex (see Figure 8.1). In any case the behaviour shown in any particular context also depends on situation-dependent motivational variables, socially determined roles, and mood or emotional states influenced by the situation (Cattell, 1985).

Other workers prefer to work with lower-level constructs or traits, involving particular aspects of psychological functioning such as assertiveness, trait anxiety, dependency, shyness, and so on. This is likely to be profitable but, as noted already, the development of a science of relationships has been handicapped because the relations between the characteristics of individuals and of relationships, and the extent to which the characteristics overlap, have been insufficiently specified. Furthermore, attempts to represent characteristics of psychological functioning in terms of a number of dimensions, whether these be few or many, inevitably involve compromise: the fewer the dimensions used for understanding differences in psychological functioning, the more intermediaries may have to be introduced to relate them to the actual behaviour of individuals. But the fewer the instances of behaviour that the trait accounts for, the more the concept becomes merely descriptive of behaviour rather than explanatory.

THE INFLUENCE OF RELATIONSHIPS ON INDIVIDUAL CHARACTERISTICS

The developmental influences of early social relationships on personality is referred to incidentally in this book, but in general is outside its scope (see Engfer et al., 1994). Rather the focus is on how relationships can promote both stability and change in individual characteristics.

As we have seen in Chapter 3, in developing their Interpersonal Congruency Theory, Secord and Backman (e.g. 1974) initially laid emphasis on the ways in which social interactions and relationships maintain individuals' dispositions. They distinguished two issues. One involves institutional and sub-institutional sources of reinforcement, such as those obtained in the sociometric or status structure of groups. Ichheiser (1970) points out that some of the characteristics we ascribe to others are merely qualities that they are permitted to lay some claim to by virtue of the positions that they hold. We tend to regard politicians as successful, doctors as having good judgement, and so on, and the individuals concerned identify with the characteristics they are deemed to have, and claim them because of the positions they hold. Indeed you can be a doctor or a politician only if you behave as the incumbents of those offices are supposed to behave.

The other way in which relationships maintain individual dispositions involves intra- and inter-personal processes that stabilise people's self-perceptions and facilitate the maintenance of "congruency". These were discussed on pp.28–30. To summarise, individuals are seen as seeking congruency between particular aspects of the self-concept, their behaviour with respect to those aspects, and relevant perceptions, feelings, or behaviours of other persons. Congruency is achieved for much of the time because people tend to form relationships with others who will allow them to behave in a self-confirming way, or to be seen as having the characteristics that they ascribe to themselves. Once formed, congruent relationships tend to stabilise self-conceptions because intimates tend to discuss discrepant assessments by an outsider, but accept each other's because each has supported the other's self-concepts in the past (Backman, 1985, 1988).

Secord and Backman suggested that the experience of congruency is positive because it indicates an ability to deal with others in pursuit of one's own goals. People do not like to change their self-views because they feel that they might then get into situations with which they cannot cope, and disappoint partners with whom they have an established relationship. There is thus a tendency to maintain the self-concept (Snyder, 1984; Swann, 1987; Tesser 1978, 1988).

However, there may be changes in both the self-concept and in individual characteristics. As individuals develop or change, they attempt to present themselves in ways that will achieve congruency with their new views of themselves (or of what they want to become), thereby attempting both to bring others' views into line with their self-perceptions and confirming to themselves that they are the sorts of persons that they see themselves as being or becoming.

While politeness usually requires us to confirm others' views of themselves, there are circumstances in which this is not the case. Thus if someone asks for an honest view of his/her behaviour, or shows behaviour so abhorrent that we cannot restrain ourselves, we may say what we really think. If our attributions produce incongruency, and if the other party cannot restore congruency in one of the ways noted earlier, then, Backman suggests, they may produce change. However the outcome will be a dialectical product of the attempts of both partners to use processes that produce congruence in the total situational context.

Conflict in a relationship may result in a change in behaviour, self-perception, or perception of the partner which may have ramifying consequences. A traditional husband accused of not taking his share in cooking may invoke traditional cultural norms, exaggerate what he actually does, create an impression that he cannot cook, and so on. But if, for instance, he agrees to take turns, this may result in a change in his self-image.

Any such change may have ramifying repercussions. If an individual changes his or her behaviour or self-concept as a result of the perceived attributions of one partner, this may lead to incongruencies in interactions with others. Appointment to high office may require the display of leadership qualities to subordinates in the organisation, and a change in self-image, but if these spill over into relationships with peers outside, there may be problems: the new personality may be incompatible with the old relationships.

Backman (1988, p.256) summarises thus:

> Personality is conceptualized as a unique product of both relationship partners' attempts to create, maintain and at times change the terms of their relationship and who they are in that relationship. What kind of a person each person becomes is a unique product of all those processes, factors and vicissitudes that have affected the development of the relationships they have with others.

This account, of course, emphasises the actual or potential flexibility that a person may show. It still remains the case that there are limits to that flexibility, limits that differ between individuals, and these affect the course of relationships.

THE INFLUENCE OF INDIVIDUAL CHARACTERISTICS ON RELATIONSHIPS

Individual development involves a continuing interplay between the person at each moment in time and the environment experienced (see e.g. review by Engfer, Walper, & Rutter, 1994). In discussing aspects of relationships elsewhere in this book, some representative studies of how they are related to individual characteristics are cited (see also Clark & Reis, 1988), and discussion here is limited to some studies indicating the complexities of the issues involved.

First, a given individual characteristic may affect relationship behaviour by a number of routes. Thus Bolger and Schilling (1991) suggested that neuroticism could give rise to day-to-day stress because: (a) it leads people to become more exposed to stressors; (b) it results in stressors causing greater upset; and (c) it leads people to become more distressed for reasons other than (a) and (b). Their research produced clear evidence for (a) and (b).

As another example, the need for structuring the world in a fairly simple way may influence how a person understands, experiences, and interacts with others. Such an individual is likely to organise social and non-social information in less complex ways, stereotype others, and so on (Neuberg & Newsom, 1993; see also Moskowitz, 1993). Again, high "self-monitoring" individuals strive to be the kind of person called for by each situation in which they find themselves. They generally adopt an orientation towards maintaining less close and less exclusive relationships. Low self-monitors attempt to display what they see as their own personal dispositions and attitudes in every situation, and seek to establish relatively close and exclusive relationships. High self-monitors tend to be less committed to their relationships than low self-monitors, have a more unrestricted attitude to sexual relations, and lay more emphasis on physical characteristics in choosing a partner. They perceive themselves to have a wider network of available partners, and have fantasies about interactions with alternative partners more than do low self-monitors (Snyder & Simpson, 1987).

Other examples, taken from a rather different research tradition, are provided by intimacy (in the sense of a recurrent preference for warm, close, and communicative exchanges with others) and power motivation. McAdams (1985) assessed these in Thematic Apperception Tests and showed that individuals scoring highly on intimacy motivation spend more time thinking about people and relationships, engage in more conversations and write more letters, and express more positive affect in interpersonal situations, than those with lower scores. In addition women (but interestingly not men) high on intimacy motivation described their friendships as more deeply satisfying and meaningful. Those high on power motivations tend to see friendships as opportunities to take a dominant, controlling, organisational or supporting role.

Second, individual characteristics may affect each other. To take a relatively simple case, the work of Reis et al. (1982) strongly suggests that physical attractiveness may affect psychological characteristics. They arranged that senior students should keep daily records of their interactions with others, and assessed various aspects of those interactions. Amongst the findings was evidence that attractive males were more assertive, and lower in fear of rejection by females, than less attractive males, while attractive females were less assertive and less trustful of males than less attractive females. Although the evidence does not show this directly, it is a reasonable assumption that physical attractiveness, influencing interactions with others, had different long-term consequences on males and females. It also seems likely that causation may operate in the opposite direction, psychological characteristics affecting behaviour and thus attractiveness.

Third, the influence of any one characteristic on behaviour is likely to be mediated or moderated by others. Thus in the study by Reis et al. (1982) just cited, social competence mediated the influence of attractiveness on the men's interaction patterns, but social competence in women had the opposite effects from attractiveness.

Again, Cheek and Buss (1981) assessed shyness (self-consciousness, low self-esteem, awkward feelings with others) and sociability (preferences for being with others). In free interaction, subjects who were sociable but shy talked less, averted their gaze more, and automanipulated more than those who were not shy and, interestingly, more than those who were shy but not sociable. Thus the quality of interaction was less for people who were shy and wanted to be with others than for those who were shy but did not want to mix (see also Stevenson-Hinde & Shouldice, 1995).

Another example, mentioned in Chapter 10, may be repeated here (Zuroff and de Lorimer, 1989). Dependency and self-criticism were assessed in women students, who were also asked to rate three characteristics of their ideal male friends—intimacy, achievement, and masculinity. As predicted, high dependency in the women was linked to an ideal of intimacy, but the magnitude of the effect increased with concomitant self-criticism. Women who were both dependent and self-critical desired higher levels of intimacy than some who were dependent but not self-critical. The authors suggest that dependent but self-critical women desire intimacy but feel unworthy and unable to receive it. Highly self-critical, low dependent women had ideal partners who were low in intimacy, as though they were saying "I want to be alone". Highly self-critical, high dependent women wanted men with high achievement motivation, perhaps hoping that such partners could bring them rewards that they felt unable to achieve themselves.

Fourth, and related to the last, a given characteristic may be seen differently in different relationships. "Integrative complexity" assesses the extent to which individuals dislike ambiguity and dissonance and make rapid judgements of others, as compared with those who recognise and allow for inconsistencies, mixed motives and so on. Either of these extremes can be seen as desirable according to the situation and personal values of the observer (Tetlock, 1991). Tetlock, Peterson, and Berry (1993) indeed found that the correlates of integrative complexity differed according to the method of assessment. On self-report measures, complex persons were higher on openness and creativity, lower on social compliance and con-scientiousness. On personality ratings made by faculty members, graduate students, etc. in informal social settings, they were seen as narcissistic and antagonistic. On ratings for likely success in a managerial position, made by business school faculty members in formal tasks, they were higher on initiative and self-objectivity; and on semi-projective measures as high on power motivation.

Fifth, the relations between individual characteristics and relationships depend also on the partner's characteristics. In every relationship the behaviour of each partner affects that of the other and, if the relationship is to be successful, their behaviours must be compatible. A number of studies concerned with compatibility were cited on pp.141–142, and others concerned with the conditions necessary for successful social support on pp.143–149. As another example, Hill (1991) assessed the personality dis-position of "Affiliative need", using subscales of the Interpersonal Orien-tation Scale, a self-report questionnaire designed to measure interest in various social incentives. The readiness of the subjects to seek support from a bogus stranger described either as extremely warm and empathetic or as less so was then assessed. Those who had a high affiliative need expressed strong interest in the warm and empathetic bogus stranger, but tended to avoid interaction with the less warm stranger. Individuals with a lower affiliative need showed no preference. Thus the outcome depended on the characteristics of both partners.

ADAPTABILITY

Every person is likely to be involved in many relationships, so the extent and manner in which individuals can adjust to different situations is an important but somewhat neglected individual characteristic (Paulhus & Martin, 1988). Adaptability is not unrelated to social skill, since adaptable people are likely to be able to introduce themselves to strangers, etc. (Shaver, Furman, & Buhrmester, 1985). It is less necessary, and thus consistency in behaviour is more marked, across situations with similar psychological meanings or demands (Krahe, 1990; Shoda, Mischel, & Wright, 1993), and this depends also on the domain of behaviour (Pawlik & Buse, 1990). Adaptability may be partly a matter of cognitive competence. Shoda et al. predicted that children high on a measure of cognitive social competence which assessed their ability to discriminate situations, would show behaviour that varied across situations, while those low on this measure would show more rigid responding. Their prediction was confirmed for cognitively mediated social behaviour but not, as expected, for the relatively impulsive aggressive behaviour.

Important in this context is the characteristic of ego-resiliency (Block & Block, 1980). Block and Kremen (1996) have pointed out that adaptability requires more than the replacement of untamed impulsivity with rigid impulse control. Rather control must be modulated: lack of ego-resilience implies less control than is adaptively effective or greater flexibility than is necessary. People low on ego-resilience tend to be susceptible to anxiety and to overly predetermined response patterns, lack of behavioural flexibility, and inability to engage in positive exploration of the environment. Block and Kremen have shown that individuals high on ego-resilience (assessed on a 14-item scale) tend to be oriented towards and competent in the world of personal relationships. Individuals high on raw intelligence may be very effective in the world of work, but tend to be uneasy with affect and unable to realise satisfying personal relationships.

SUMMARY

1. Individuals behave differently according to whom they are with. Individual characteristics affect the nature and course of relationships, and relationships affect individual characteristics.
2. Although the distinction is far from absolute, some of the research in this area concerns personality characteristics, of which relatively few are

usually postulated, while other research concerns traits. There is almost no limit to the number of the latter, but not infrequently those used overlap with each other.

3. Individuals use their behaviour in relationships to maintain consistency in their self-image and facilitate the maintenance of congruency, or to achieve change.

4. The relations between individual characteristics and behaviour are complicated in a number of ways. First, a given individual characteristic may affect behaviour in diverse ways. Second, different individual characteristics may affect each other. Third, characteristics may interact in their effects on behaviour in relationships. Fourth, a given characteristic may be seen differently by others in different relationships. Finally, the behaviour in an interaction depends on the behaviour of both participants.

5. The capacity to adapt to different situations and relationships is an important individual characteristic.

17 Social and Other Extra-Dyadic Influences

We have seen that every relationship influences and is influenced by the social situation or group in which it is embedded, by the socio-cultural structure of norms, beliefs, values, and institutions, and also by the physical environment (Frontispiece). A comprehensive review of social influences on relationships is beyond the reach of this book, but a few issues must be mentioned briefly.

INFLUENCES FROM THE PHYSICAL ENVIRONMENT

In the shorter term, the availability of an appropriate environment (Hall, 1966) or the precise arrangement of physical features may affect the course of interactions. For instance it has been claimed that interaction is more likely between individuals sitting on either side of the corner of a table than in other positions; that people in a competitive interaction choose to sit opposite to each other (Sommer, 1965); and that subjects forced to sit close to others or to intrude on their space respond more negatively than controls (Dabbs, 1971). Goffman (1959) has provided a penetrating analysis of the manner in which aspects of the physical environment (objects, clothes, and so on), as well as of the person himself, are used as "fronts" to help define the situation (see p.8). In a multiplex relationship, the physical and behavioural context may influence the content of the interactions that occur and differences in the context may serve to insulate interactions that would otherwise be incompatible.

Although undue crowding can engender or augment negative behaviour, we have already seen that propinquity can foster the formation of relationships. That relationships once formed may be affected by their physical environment is well illustrated in the clinical literature. For instance a family's life circumstances and social class have consistently been found to be associated with the incidence of psychiatric disorders (e.g. Kolvin et al., 1971). In a US sample depressive symptoms were more common in low-income groups (Schwab et al., 1976), and Richman (1974, 1977) found that women living in flats in London were more prone to depression and loneliness than women living in houses. In some of these cases, at least, there were strong reasons for believing the external factors to be causal.

Barker (1978a, b) has embraced many aspects of the influence of the physical environment in his concept of "behavior settings". These are "ecological" units, including both human and physical components, and embracing a number, often a large number, of "behavior episodes". "Behavior episodes" are molar units of behaviour with the characteristics of constancy of direction, equal potency throughout their parts, and limited size range. Barker points out that the same people behave in different ways in different "behavior settings", and different sets of people behave in similar ways in the same setting. For example, academic communities incorporate different and idiosyncratic individuals, year after year, into the characteristic patterns of their several "behavior settings". Barker cites Rausch, Dittman, and Taylor's (1959) study of a therapeutic community as finding more variation on the hostility–friendliness and dominance–passivity dimensions in the behaviour of the same boys in different settings than there were with different individuals in the same setting. There are clear parallels here with the earlier emphasis that people behave differently according to the situation they are in, and with the concept of "role identity" (pp.9–11).

RELATIONSHIPS AFFECT RELATIONSHIPS

Virtually every dyadic relationship is nested within a network of other relationships, and will both influence and be influenced by them. A close relationship may be in competition with the participants' other relationships: time spent together is not time spent with others. As courtship proceeds, partners tend to interact less with outsiders (Milardo, Johnson, & Huston, 1984), and newlyweds may need a degree of isolation to cement their bond.

But at the same time the viability of one relationship may be augmented by others in which the partners are involved: a relationship may be strengthened by recognition from third parties, or maintained because its continuation ensures rewards outside it. Murstein (1972, 1977) has likened courtship to a slowly accelerating conveyor belt leading to matrimony, in order to convey the potency of the social pressures that make it progressively more difficult to get off. Furthermore, attempted interference with the progress of a relationship by an outside party can have the effect of strengthening it. Correlational evidence suggests that parental interference can strengthen the relationship between an engaged couple though, as the authors point out, other explanations are possible (Driscoll, Davis, & Lipetz, 1972; Rubin, 1974). Such a finding could be understood in terms of Brehm's (1976) generalisation that individuals act to protect their freedom of action. On this view, if an option is threatened the individual becomes more likely to exercise it, especially if the option is important to him.

Another route by which one relationship may be affected by another concerns the accounts that the participants give themselves or each other about the relationship (see pp.236–238). These may be influenced by outsiders, or by the supposed views of outsiders, and thus affect the relationship. They may even be shared with an outsider, and if they are adjusted to make them more acceptable to the outsider in the telling, the new version may influence behaviour in the relationship.

A number of workers have studied the effects of children on the nature of a marriage. Though there are differences of opinion as to the generalisations that can be made, and the extent of their cross-cultural validity, it is clear that the effects may be crucial. There is general agreement that the arrival of the first child can have a profound effect on the marriage (e.g. Cowan & Cowan, 1978), and a considerable number of studies have demonstrated that tensionful parent–child relationships are associated with poor marital relationships (Belsky, 1984; Easterbrooks & Emde, 1988; Engfer, 1988; Katz & Gottman, 1995; Meyer, 1988).

Such correlational studies do not show whether the marriage is affecting the parent–child relationship or vice versa. Probably both effects occur, though there is clearer evidence for the former. For instance temporary absence of the father or divorce (Hetherington, 1988; Hetherington, Cox, & Cox, 1982) may affect the mother's attitudes to the children. However, the data are more complex than appears at first sight, and the effects for very distressed families may be different from those within the normal range, for mothers and for fathers, for different socioeconomic groups and so on (e.g. Dunn, 1988; Radke-Yarrow et al., 1988).

There are also multiple influences between other relationships within a family (e.g. Hinde & Stevenson-Hinde, Eds., 1988). To cite a now classic example, Dunn and Kendrick (1982) studied 41 families in Cambridge, from the mother's second pregnancy until the second child was about 18 months old. With the birth of the sibling, there were changes in almost all aspects of the mother–first-born relationship. At the behavioural level, the diversity, quality and relative frequency and patterning of the interactions all changed—in part because the mother was busy, preoccupied, and often over-tired, and in part perhaps because she saw the new baby as having the greater need. Confrontations between mother and first-born became more frequent, and the latter tended to regress in some respects. At the same time there were often signs of increased maturity and self-awareness, negative and positive changes often going together. The first-born's response to the new sibling might involve care, interest, and concern on the one hand and hostile behaviour or teasing on the other.

Clearly, changes in the mother–first-born relationship at many levels were involved. These could include changes in the self-perception of the first-born. Dunn and Kendrick suggest that "the arrival of the new sibling would involve a new dimension of self-awareness, a re-categorization of self, on the part of the first child. Now he is the big one, not the small; the elder, not the younger; the boy, not the girl, and so on". At the same time, however, the first-born may be comparing his lot with the baby's, the maternal attention he receives now with that he used to receive. No doubt much depends on the mother's sensitivity to the changes in the first-born's life resulting from the baby's arrival. On the one hand she may succeed in bringing him in as a partner in coping with the baby, so that he sees himself as "the big one" and on the mother's side. Or the contrast between his and the baby's relationship with the mother may alienate him, and he may even use the baby as a model and regress. The changes that occur will of course depend on the first-born as well as on the mother and the relationship, and will certainly be complex.

And this only just scratches the surface of the problem. The new baby is likely also to have direct effects on mother–father and father–first-born relationships, and these also may have ramifying secondary consequences (Stevenson-Hinde, 1990). Within a family, any triad is liable to differentiate into a pair of allies and an isolate, and this may be crucial in the development of family relationships (Schazer, 1975). The ramifications of the effects of change in one focus on the rest of the family is exemplified by Burton's (1975) study of the consequences for the family of a chronically sick child (see also Gath, 1973).

Parke, Power, and Gottman (1979) have set out a scheme for conceptualising influences within a family triad which can encompass both face-to-face interactions and influences exerted over time. Figure 17.1 shows the possible types of influence exerted by A on B and C. Single arrows represent behaviours or cognitions involving or directed at another individual. For example, A → B could represent the attitude of A to B, a specific item of behaviour directed by A to B, or the style of A's interactions with B over a period. The double arrows indicate the consequences of such directed behaviours or cognitions. So a direct influence A → B ⇒ B → A, represents a situation where the consequence of A's actions or attitudes to

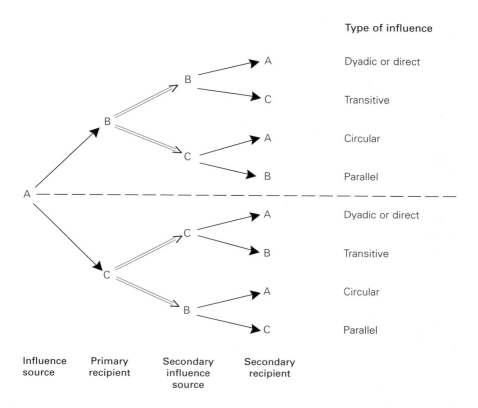

FIG. 17.1   Model of influence patterns within a triad. A is the individual whose influence is being studied. (From R.D. Parke, T.G. Power, & J.M. Gottman. Conceptualizing and quantifying influence patterns in the family triad. In M.E. Lamb, S. Suomi, & G. Stephenson (Eds.) *Social interaction analysis: Methodological issues.* © 1979 Madison: University of Wisconsin Press. Reprinted by permission of the University of Wisconsin Press.)

B is an action or attitude of B to A—for instance a mother smiles at her infant and the infant smiles back. Transitive influences involve mediation by one individual of an influence on another—for instance, the father kisses the mother and the mother then nestles the infant. In a circular influence the same individual initiates the sequence and is the secondary recipient after mediation by the others—for instance father tickles infant, infant vocalises, and then mother smiles at father. Finally, in a parallel influence the primary and secondary recipients are the same individual—for instance the father tickles the infant and then the mother imitates him by tickling the infant, or the father ignores the infant's vocalisation and so the mother responds to it in an exaggerated fashion.

Although the examples given all involve short-term interactions, the categories have much wider applicability. Thus an example of a circular influence might be the finding that boys in mother-dominant families are more likely to imitate their mothers than their fathers ($M \rightarrow F \Rightarrow I \rightarrow M$). Parke et al. illustrate their scheme with numerous examples drawn from family interaction patterns. Although, as the authors point out, it has some difficulties with family members' perceptions of relationships between other family members, or of the family as a unit, the scheme undoubtedly represents a useful way of picturing the effects of relationships on relationships (see Barrett & Hinde, 1988).

The effects of one relationship on another may have ramifying consequences through the family or group. Thus Christensen and Margolin (1988) showed that in distressed families the marital alliance was often weak, with the two parents treating the children differently. Cross-generational alliances were often formed, and conflict moved readily from one part of the family to another.

An important issue concerns the extent to which family members perceive the family as a unit, and this requires a rather different sort of approach. A promising conceptual scheme is provided by Wertheim's (1975a, b, c) treatment of the family as an open system, including its individual members as subsystems and itself embraced within supra-systems, such as the community. The family is seen as having a degree of stability, but also an ability for adapting to changes in the intra- and extra-familial environment. Of special interest in the present context is Wertheim's analysis of family patterns in terms of hierarchies of rules. First, "ground" or "first-order rules" refer to concrete action and contain specific behavioural prescriptions, such as "In our family, we don't fight". These are governed by "meta-rules", or rules about the ground rules. These reflect the moral code of the family, regulating behaviour accordingly. Different meta-rules might lead to different sorts of stability and/or change in the family structure. "Family members should never quarrel" implies a rigid, unchanging system. "If people are angry, it's best to talk it through", involves more flexibility to meet a threat. And "If people don't get on, it's best to get advice from someone more experienced" implies the possibility of change as a result of outside intervention. Meta-rules may be guided by meta-meta-rules, such as "Only kinsfolk have to be protected, there is no loyalty to strangers", and these to an even smaller number of meta-meta-meta-rules, and so on. (There is a similarity here to Thibaut and Kelley's 1959 analysis of the behaviour of dyads and groups in terms of "norms" and "meta-norms", the latter specifying the domains of applicability of and priorities between norms.)

Wertheim emphasises that the degree of family integration can be assessed only at the level of meta-rules. For example, the ground rule "In this family everyone comes and goes as he or she pleases" may be qualified by a meta-rule such as "A family should enable its members to develop fully as individuals". Individuals can then "come and go" only so long as this is seen by everyone to be conducive to individual development. Thus each individual rule derives its meaning from the network of systemic rules of which it is part.

Wertheim suggests that the organisation of these rules can be understood in terms of two principles—the principle of hierarchical linkage, as outlined earlier, and the principle of functional linkage. The latter defines functional connections within and between the structural levels. It is suggested that intellectually and psychosocially adequate family systems differ from inadequate ones in having a reasonably complex, differentiated, integrated, and internally consistent rule network. The scheme represents a reasonably objective method for tackling the way in which relationships may be affected not only by third parties but also by the social system in which they are placed.

Various types of family systems approach provide also a necessary corrective to the tendency to regard either individuals or dyads as entities independent of the environment in which they function (e.g. P. Minuchin, 1985; S. Minuchin & Fishman, 1981), and are of great importance clinically: links with attachment theory (Chapter 21) are beginning to be helpful in treatment (Bretherton, 1990; Byng-Hall, 1990; Stevenson-Hinde, 1990). For instance, one study has shown that insecure attachment may provoke family interactions that involve "capturing" an attachment figure, turning to an inappropriate attachment figure, responding inappropriately to attachment behaviour, or anticipating loss similar to loss experienced in the past (Byng-Hall & Stevenson-Hinde, 1991). There are, however, some problems in deciding whether some properties, such as the homeostatic properties of the system, should properly be ascribed to the system as a whole, to relationships, or to individuals (e.g. Hinde, 1989).

Other influences on group cohesion may involve mutual "felt obligations" involving expectations for appropriate behaviour from others (Stein, 1993). These may be based on cultural conventions which may become socially and individually elaborated. Families can also be seen as having family scripts. These are modes of behaviour, derived from the family of origin or constructed in the current family, often retained unconsciously, and re-enacted from time to time. When partners in a relationship or family members have different scripts, problems can arise if the situation is not understood (Byng-Hall, 1995).

In addition, families and other groups often have rituals—either daily, as the evening meal together, or on special occasions, which help to integrate the members. Their incidence is associated with greater marital satisfaction (Fiese et al., 1993). Presumably causation acts both ways, with rituals more likely to occur in, and being more enjoyed by, happy families, and also augmenting that happiness.

As indicated by the earlier reference to scripts originating from the family of origin, influences of relationships upon relationships within the family may cross successive generations. In some cases this involves negative characteristics in an individual leading to non-optimal parenting and thus the development of negative characteristics in the next generation (e.g. Caspi & Elder, 1988; Patterson & Dishion, 1988). In other cases the effect may be positive: thus mothers who report negative relationships with their own siblings tend to have children who interact more positively with each other, apparently because the mothers select better child-rearing strategies (Kramer & Baron, 1995).

THE DYAD AS A UNIT WITHIN A GROUP

Outsiders may affect the dynamics of a dyadic relationship in another way—namely by causing the participants to feel and/or behave as a unit, distinct from and in some cases set in opposition to the others. Here we are concerned with dyads in which mutual commitment has some importance. To the extent that the dyad has a structure of beliefs based on the idea that the formation of alternative liaisons is undesirable, difficult, or impossible, it can be considered as a (minimally sized) group. Such a dyad may behave as a unit to others, treating them as though they were in some degree outsiders (Tajfel, 1978). Secrets within a relationship, and even more the secrecy of a relationship, may add to its attraction (Wegner, Lane, & Dimitri, 1994).

THE SOCIAL NETWORK

The participants in a relationship are prone to talk to outsiders about their relationship, or about each other: as we have seen, this may cause problems, but it may also add to their store of shared knowledge about each other. Outsiders may also satisfy needs that are not met within the relationship: here again, the effect on the relationship may be positive or negative.

The interface between the dyad and the social networks of the partners has been discussed by Klein and Milardo (1993). They initially pointed to two dimensions along which the "relationship competence" of individuals could be assessed—the extent to which they are guided by norms or traditions as opposed to individual interests; and the extent to which they are guided by the awareness of the perspectives of one or both partners. Following that, they suggest that the influence of third parties on a relationship may differ along similar dimensions—the extent to which they encourage focus on conventional norms as opposed to individual needs, and the extent to which one or both partner's needs are considered.

The importance of influences external to the relationship can be illustrated by studies on social networks. It is useful here to distinguish "interactive networks", constituted by all those with whom the individual interacts, from "psychological networks" which comprise persons who are close and important to her (Surra & Milardo, 1991). Unfortunately, many studies do not make this distinction.

The classic study of 20 families by Bott (1957) showed that the extent to which husband and wife shared activities, interests, and decisions was related to the social network in which the family was embedded. Families in a "close-knit" network, in which the various friends and relatives knew each other, tended to have segregated husband and wife roles. Where the network was "loose-knit", with friends and relatives not knowing each other, husband and wife tended to depend more on each other and to have joint roles.

In a more recent study (Stein et al., 1992) spouses in 49 families in Ohio were asked to name the people important in their lives. These were divided into "shared family network" (number of family members listed by both spouses); "shared friend network"; "husband's separate family network" (family members listed by husband only); "husband's separate friend network"; and wife's separate family and friend networks. The number of shared friends turned out to be small: a clustering procedure then gave a four-cluster solution:

1. Small shared family network, husbands with large separate family network and wives with moderate family and friend network (nine couples).
2. Medium-sized shared family network, large separate friend network for both spouses (six couples).
3. Large shared family network, separate networks with balanced numbers of family and friends for both spouses (17 couples).
4. Small shared family network, with similar-sized networks of family and friends for both spouses (15 couples).

This, of course, is only one way of dealing with the data (see e.g. Milardo, 1992), but it did yield some correlations with marital satisfaction. Type 2 was highest in marital satisfaction for both partners, but the husbands scored highly and the wives low on a depression rating. Type 4 was lowest on satisfaction and the wives highest on depression. Of course, these correlations tell one nothing about the direction of causation, and they might be quite different in a different culture.

The latter point is emphasised by Wellman and Wellman (1992), who note that the kin-centred networks studied by Bott in the 1950s in the UK differ from those found now in North America, which differ again from the networks in many Third World countries which are crucial to economic and political survival. In their own work in Toronto they found that the network is household-centred and wife-operated, with community ties used almost entirely for domestic concerns. Engagement with the network is influenced by the presence and age of children and by the wives' employment.

Although relationships with others in an individual's social network are generally held to be supportive and to ameliorate stress, that is not always the case, and relationships can also induce stress. For example there may be conflict between pressure to conform to public conventions and the desire to create a private bond. Networks can lead to an obligation to invest time and energy in relationships (role-overload), and thus to increase stress (Leslie, 1989), and young mothers may experience difficulties with their male partners, differences of opinion with their mother or mother-in-law, conflicting demands from their peer-group, and so on (see e.g. Rhodes, Ebert, & Meyers, 1994).

There is an apparent contradiction between the views that the closer a relationship, the smaller will be the social networks of the participants, and the evidence that friends may intensify a personal bond. Burger and Milardo (1995) point out that the benefits of social ties may increase with network size up to a point, but that beyond that point the demands of the network may detract from the relationship. Furthermore, the effects may depend on the nature of the network and differ between husbands and wives. In a study of 25 couples who had been married 5–10 years and lived in central Maine they found no overall relationship between network size and interdependence (assessed by a questionnaire assessing love; maintenance and communication; conflict; and ambivalence about continuing the relationship). For husbands, involvement with friends was not related to interdependence, but husbands with kin (especially fathers) in their networks reported greater love for their wives. Wives showed very different associations: wives with many kin (especially brothers-in-law) reported higher marital conflict, greater ambivalence about their marriage, and less love. The friendships of wives had no effect on their own levels of interdependence, but were related to reports of more conflict and ambivalence by the husbands. As the authors point out, such correlational studies raise challenging questions about the direction of causation; and the possibility is raised that the husbands feel they can have friends but do not want their wives to have them.

A number of studies have traced relations between work-engendered mood or fatigue on subsequent mood and marital interaction at home, and between mood at home and subsequent mood at work. Although there are some differences in detail, there is strong evidence for influences in both directions. Furthermore, if both spouses work there may be a cross-over effect—spouse's work-mood and fatigue on partner's reactions at home, and home effects on partner's work mood (Bolger & Kelleher, 1993; Chan & Margolin, 1994).

SOCIO-CULTURAL INFLUENCES

Every aspect of human behaviour is subject to cultural influences. These are conveyed through narratives and folk tales, which may be secular or religious, by novels and plays, by traditional epic poems, by games, through the media, and by many other routes. In addition cultural norms are soaked up through observation of others—their gestures, actions, the objects they use, and the way that they use them, as well as the admonitions that they make. Development itself involves participation in socio-cultural activities, and a growing individual's changing roles involve dynamic cultural processes (Rogoff et al., 1995). The influences are two-way—the culture influences how people behave and how people behave influences the culture (Frontispiece). And in so far as people share beliefs, values, and norms, the society gains coherence, for shared knowledge structures are essential for adequate social functioning.

In the same way, every human relationship is influenced in fundamental ways by the culture in which it develops. In so far as adult participants in a relationship share cultural norms, the basic structure of their relationship will be influenced by those norms. They will agree that theirs is a relationship of a particular type, and expect it to have certain properties. They may half hope that the narrative they are creating will unfold in the ways that the folk tales suggest: a fairy godmother might come, a toad might turn into a prince. But they are likely also to have been subjected to different influences by virtue of class, wealth, religion, opportunity, or peer-group, so that the premises and expectations they bring to the relationship are far from identical. In this section we shall consider the nature of some of these cultural and sub-cultural influences.

Cultural Influences on Emotion and Psychological Functioning

The course of any close relationship is influenced by the nature of the emotions expressed by the participants. The extent to which emotional expression is culturally influenced has been a matter of considerable debate, with some inclining towards the view that much emotional expression involves pan-cultural hard-wired patterns (e.g. Eibl-Eibesfeldt, 1972), while others argue that what a person experiences depends on physiological arousal and how he or she has learned to label the situation (e.g. Schachter & Singer, 1962). On the latter view, when a child hears his mother say "Don't be shy", the child may learn that the emotion one feels in the presence of strangers is called "shyness". The current view is that the primary emotions (see pp.87–88) show striking cross-cultural universality in patterning, but cultural differences in elicitation, regulation, symbolic representation, and social sharing (Ekman, 1992; Scherer & Wallbott, 1994). However for all emotions individuals tend to acquire socially constructed scripts: it is because the knowledge structures are shared that they are effective (see e.g. Clark, Pataki, & Carver, 1996; Forgas, 1996).

In addition to aspects of emotion, experience may result in many other aspects of cognitive functioning differing between cultures. For instance, in explaining behaviour Americans make greater reference to general dispositions or less to contextual factors than do Hindus or Chinese (Miller, 1984; Morris & Kaiping Peng, 1994). The differences increase in development, and Miller suggests that they derive from different conceptions of the person.

Changing conditions within a society may also lead to temporal changes in psychological functioning. For example Doherty and Baldwin (1985) assessed locus of control in working men and women in the late 1960s through to the late 1970s. (Locus of control concerns the extent to which individuals attribute the causes of events to themselves or to outside factors.) They found no change in the 1960s and early 1970s, but in the late 1970s the evidence indicated that women were tending to make more external attributions. The authors suggest that at that time women became more aware of the external constraints on their ability to meet their goals in the labour force and in other settings.

In the same vein, Goodwin (1995; Goodwin & Emelyanova, 1995) has investigated changes in self-disclosure and family relationships in Russia, where the roles of the individual with respect to the collective and to authority are in a state of flux. In doing so, he drew on Douglas's (1982) proposal that individuals have a range of world-views with ramifying effects on their way of life. These world-views can be classified along two dimensions—group orientation (roughly comparable to the individualistic–collectivist dimension) and the "grid preference" or extent of regulation sought in particular social settings. In so far as individuals share a world-view, it may be characteristic of a family, group, or whole society. This world-view may affect behaviour in close personal relationships and, of course, vice versa. To cite but one of the findings, manual workers found it difficult to discuss the family, while entrepreneurs found it difficult to discuss sex and love.

Not surprisingly, moral judgements are also affected by cultural forces. For example, some Indian cultures favour a broader and more stringent view of social responsibilities than does American. Miller, Bersoff, and Harwood (1990) found that Indians from Mysore regarded failure to help another, whatever the situation, as a moral issue. Americans from New Haven did so only over life-threatening issues or in cases of parents responding to the moderately serious needs of their children (see also Haidt et al., 1993; Schweder, 1991).

More recently Miller and Bersoff (1995) have reported that, while Americans emphasise the building of relationships and expressing emotion in family life, Hindu Indians stress the importance of individuals subordinating their own desires to those of the family as a whole. To the Indians, acting out of duty is essential to family life and brings its own reward.

It goes without saying that the study of cultural differences faces formidable difficulties, not the least of which is the difficulty of knowing what is a representative sample of individuals or relationships. Another is that the terms used to characterise relationships in one culture may not be equally applicable in another. Hooley and Richters (1995) review studies showing that "expressed emotion" (assessed by the extent to which family members of a psychiatric patient express criticism or hostility to him or her) has a much greater incidence in the United States and Europe than in Mexican-American or Hindi-speaking Indian families, but point out that this could indicate either a real cultural difference in the tendency to be critical, or a difference between cultures in the validity of the method used to assess "expressed emotion" (see also Chao, 1994).

Roles

The term "role" has had a confused history in the social sciences, and has carried a wide spectrum of meanings (Linton, 1936; Newcomb, 1952; Hinde, 1978a). The narrow usage, in which "role" refers to the rights and duties imposed on the incumbents of certain positions within a society, characteristic especially of the anthropological literature, grades into a much wider usage among some social psychologists. In this section we shall first consider its narrower usage, though later in the chapter we shall be concerned with its wider (and looser) implications. Even here, however, it is necessary to make some further terminological points.

The term "role" is usually used in relation to behaviour—or expectancies about behaviour or criteria relevant to behaviour (Kelvin, 1970)—associated with a position or status in the society. We may speak of the role of Prime Minister, doctor, traffic warden, or good neighbour. The behaviour in question is that normally or ideally shown by the diverse incumbents of the position, and does not refer to their individual idiosyncrasies. The behaviour is usually described in terms of certain of its effects on others—

the rights and duties of the incumbent. "Role" is thus not a category at the data level with absolute properties, but a concept that may or may not be useful in coming to terms with specified problems. It is usually used with respect to two problems: (a) that of the determinants of behaviour in the individual and (b) that of the way in which individual behaviour contributes to the structure of relationships, groups, or societies. As used here, "role" is closely linked to the concept of "institution". Thus marriage is an institution, with "husband" and "wife" as roles; "sovereignty" is an institution, with "king" and "subject" as roles. An institution involves one or more positions with recognised rights and duties: "role" can refer either to determinants of the behaviour of the incumbents of these positions, or to the manner in which their behaviour contributes to the institution.

If the role concept is to be useful with reference to the *determinants* of social action (i.e. the factors because of which this social action differs from that), it must differentiate one set of determinants from the many others that affect behaviour. That set must surely be the goals and limits that individuals set themselves in relation to their position in society. For example, the difference between the behaviour of boys and girls can be regarded as due to interactions between differences in their biological make-ups (biological constraints and predispositions), differences between the ways in which others treat them (social constraints and pre-dispositions), and differences in their own ideas about the behaviour that is appropriate to the gender they see themselves as having (goal constraints and predispositions). It need hardly be said that the important word here is "interaction"—biological factors affect social ones, and social ones bio-logical; and the subject's own goals are derived from those of other indi-viduals, and influence and are influenced by how he is treated by others. Within all this complexity, the role concept is usefully applied to a subset of determinants—namely those that constitute the culturally shared goals (conscious or unconscious) of the subject defined in respect to the relevant real or imagined effects of his behaviour on others.

On this view, not all the determinants of social behaviour can be described in role terms. A baby's behaviour is determined not at all by his own concept of how a baby should behave—he has not yet reached a stage of development where he could have one. Furthermore his behaviour only gradually comes to be shaped by those around him; the role concept is irrelevant to the determinants of his behaviour. In the same way the behaviour of invalids, or old men, is to be understood only partially in role terms: inherent constraints on behaviour are more conspicuous than those that arise from their socially determined roles. With healthy adults the latter are usually more conspicuous. The behaviour of a king, *qua* king, can be described to a considerable extent in role terms. But even a king acts out his role in an idiosyncratic way: if it were possible to place two individuals on the same throne at the same time, they would carry out their duties differently. Thus to attempt to account for all the behaviour of a king while acting as king in role (*sensu stricto*) terms would be a mistake; other determinants not necessarily wholly compatible with the kingly role, such as personal ambition and indigestion, may also operate.

The use of the role concept in reference to the socially relevant *consequences* of behaviour may be quite unrelated to its use with reference to *determinants*. Thus a baby plays a large role in the family even though the determinants of its behaviour are not usefully considered in role terms. The structure of relationships within a hospital is determined in part by aspects of patients' behaviour, the causation of which cannot usefully be described in role terms (i.e. in terms of the goals or limits patients set themselves). And much of the behaviour of individuals in organisations may be determined by factors, such as personal ambitions, quite different from their role in (i.e. consequences for) the organisation. The determinants of the actions of a soldier in battle may be related not at all to the strategic plan of the commander-in-chief. The soldier may be ignorant of that plan, and yet the consequences of his actions play a crucial role in it. Again, role as a determinant of behaviour may involve goals that are never attained. Parents may strive to create a parent–child relationship of the type most valued in their culture, but the consequences of their behaviour may never match up to the goals they set themselves.

While roles as determinants of behaviour and roles as consequences of behaviour are thus in principle separable, in practice they are often closely linked. This comes about in two ways. First, the goals that act as determinants often are closely related to the consequences which result. If a chairman successfully guides a discussion to a sound decision acceptable to all, the most important determinant of his behaviour, namely the goal towards which it was directed, and its consequences, are identical. Second, when the social goals are not achieved, social sanctions may result. Anticipation of such sanctions may form an additional determinant.

Now social roles are usually defined in terms of the content of the interactions involved. Thus husband, mother, doctor, manager, and employee are necessarily involved in certain relationships, and their "rights and duties" in those relationships are defined in terms of the content of at least some of the interactions. Some of these rights and duties concern interactions that are to be included in the relationship, others those that are to be excluded.

Some such labels for relationships refer to only one type of interaction, or to a small group of related interactions. To be a manager, it may be necessary only to manage in a certain limited range of contexts; to be an employee it may be necessary only to do certain kinds of work. But more usually rights and duties are multiple. The explanatory power of the role label will of course increase with the extent to which that is the case. If the only difference between other ranks and commissioned officers in an old-fashioned army was that the former saluted the latter we would have no need for a concept of commissioned rank, though we might usefully classify soldiers into saluters and salutees. In practice, individuals occupying different ranks were obliged to interact in some ways, for example by condescension/obedience, and not to interact in others, such as eating at the same table. Furthermore the diversity of interactions between them was limited, certain qualities of interaction were proscribed, their interactions were by definition complementary, and their intimacy was likely to be limited. Thus a difference in rank implied both that some interactions were possible, and that they would have certain properties, whilst other interactions were not.

The importance of culturally recognised roles is brought home by the impact of their absence, or by situations where roles conflict. Part of the difficulties experienced by the children of divorced parents and their step-parents stems from the ambiguity of their respective roles.

Both the number and the nature of recognisable roles differ between societies. For instance, in many societies a male has a special relationship with his mother's brother (Goody, 1959), but such a relationship is not so emphasised in our own. Conventions also influence the sort of individual to be preferred in most of the role relationships specified in the culture.

Conventions may also decree which role relationships are (more or less) indissoluble, and which can be vacated at will. This has important influences on the dynamics of the relationships. If either partner can opt out at will, there is always the possibility that other relationships will seem more attractive: it therefore behoves each participant to ensure that the relationship remains sufficiently attractive to the other to ensure that he or she remains within it (Thibaut & Kelley, 1959; see Chapter 19). But to some role relationships, the participants are inevitably committed. Kinship ties, for instance, are a part of life, and must be accepted. This has two consequences. First, it makes possible the unlimited exploitation of one partner by the other. This is one argument against social practices imposing permanence on relationships of particular types. But second, it may also facilitate the development of trust: each partner may be the readier to dispense rewards now, knowing that the other will be there to help in the future (see pp.274–276).

Roles and Rules: Non-obligatory Rights and Duties

While some relationships, like that between commissioned officer and soldier, involve diverse obligatory rights and duties, specifying many or all dimensions of the relationship, in other cases some may be obligatory and others merely expected. For instance, in the husband–wife relationship, (public) commitment is, in most societies, part of the definition of the role. In addition certain types of interaction may be obligatory. But other aspects of the relationship, such as the degrees of intimacy and the pattern of reciprocity vs. complementarity, will, to extents that differ between societies and even between different locations in one society, be expected rather than obligatory (Rosenblatt, 1974). Again, a teacher is obliged to teach, but there may be considerable latitude in the degree of control/ permissiveness expected of him. Within any society the various types of role relationship differ in the extent to which the partners' behaviour is regulated by external forces (Marwell & Hage, 1969), and within any one type of relationship, the duties may not be expected all the time, but vary with time and place (Reno, Cialdini, & Kallgren, 1993).

There have been a number of attempts to formulate these non-obligatory duties in terms of sets of rules applicable to particular relationships. Thus Harré and Secord (1972) pointed out that there are rules which generate social behaviour and explain how others act in particular types of social situation or social relationship. These may depend on more basic rules which are relevant to a wider range of social situations and determine courses of action within the constraints of the surface rules (e.g. Midwinter, 1992; see also Wertheim, cited p.296).

The most ambitious attempt to specify such rules is due to Argyle and Henderson (1985), who have produced lists of "rules" which operate in each of a wide range of relationships. Table 17.1 shows their rules for employers and employees: their rules for friends are listed in Chapter 27. They refer to behaviour seen by most people in the culture as appropriate for the relationship in question. Of course, these rules are not laid down in black and white: they are often absorbed through the skin in the course of living in a particular culture. Nevertheless Argyle and Henderson suggest that such rules, concerned primarily with interpersonal relations and rewards and with the tasks expected of participants, help to ensure that the relationship will meet the needs of the participants. If they are broken, the relationship is likely to be disturbed or disrupted.

Some rules are applicable to a wide range of relationships, others only to relationships of particular types. They may be prescriptive, proscriptive, or permissive, and some or all of them may not be accepted by particular dyads. But they are to be seen as both influencing and influenced by the behaviour of individuals: individuals or dyads may or may not accept particular rules, and may create further rules either deliberately or by the way in which they behave.

There are, however, difficulties with the concept of "rule", which stem in part from the difficulty of determining whether a rule is merely descriptive, or whether it actually influences behaviour. Collett (1977) distinguished four senses in which an individual can be said to know a social

TABLE 17.1
Rules for Employers

1.	Plan and assign work efficiently.
2.	Keep subordinates informed about decisions affecting him/her.
3.	Respect the other's privacy.
4.	Keep confidences.
5.	Consult subordinates in matters that affect him/her.
6.	Encourage the subordinate's advancement.
7.	Advise and encourage subordinates.
8.	Fight for subordinate's interests where necessary.
9.	Don't be jealous of the subordinate's ability.
10.	Don't give commands without explanation.
11.	Be considerate regarding the subordinate's personal problems.
12.	Look the subordinate in the eye during conversations.
13.	Don't criticise the subordinate publicly.
14.	Don't visit the subordinate socially, unannounced.
15.	Don't supervise too closely.
16.	Don't engage in sexual activity with the subordinate.
17.	Repay debts, favours, and compliments.
18.	Don't discuss personal finances with the subordinate.

(Argyle & Henderson, 1985. By permission of the author.)

rule—being able to verbalise it; being able to recognise an infringement; by application of a sanction (which may be just embarrassment); and by observation of behavioural regularity. But Ginsburg (1988) points out that it is in practice difficult to know whether a person "knows" a rule, and even more difficult to establish a link between rule knowledge and behaviour, and prefers to see them as features of the social world rather than items of knowledge. Whether this really surmounts the problem seems doubtful.

Many of the rules listed by Argyle and Henderson show considerable cross-cultural generality, but others clearly do not. Indeed it will be apparent that the various rules cannot have equal generality, since the applicability of some will depend on the precise situation and on the personality of those involved. Furthermore, they change with time. For instance college students are likely to hold much more egalitarian values now than a few decades ago. Margolin (1989) even found more support for female autonomy than for male, though interestingly this was significant only in non-sexual spheres. Again, 50 years ago Komarovsky (1946) found that girl students interacting with men tended to play down their academic qualities: they tried to adopt the persona which at that time was believed to be (and perhaps often still is) most attractive to men. They were in fact behaving towards a stereotype of the male student as they saw him. And

Peplau (1976) compared women with "modern" and "traditional" sex-role attitudes when in a competitive situation. Traditional women performed less well when competing against their boyfriends than when working with them. For women with more "modern" attitudes the reverse was the case. The difference in attitude affected the relationship even in the artificial test situation.

Roles and rules thus cover a wide spectrum including both obligations and expectations, and the distinction between the two can never be a precise one. But the continuum can be traced by the extent to which sanctions are imposed. For instance, in a study of changing family styles in the USA, Nye (1974) identified the existence of roles by asking both whether a person occupying a given position (e.g. husband or wife) has a duty to enact the role, and whether there are sanctions if he or she did not. But sanctions could involve little more than disapproval. Perhaps the minimum requirement is that, if rights are infringed or duties unfulfilled, the injured party may appeal to the convention, and the transgressor shows guilt (cf. Thibaut & Kelley, 1959).

Cultural differences in non-obligatory role expectations have been studied especially in the mother–child relationship. Whilst interactions within that relationship that are closely related to the infant's basic biological needs are relatively invariant across cultures, other aspects of the relationship vary considerably. Caudill and Weinstein (1969) compared the mother–infant relationships in 30 families in the USA with those in 30 Japanese ones. They found that the US mothers had a more lively and stimulating approach to their babies, as indicated by a number of variables, and their babies were more happily vocal and active, and explored more. The Japanese mothers did more lulling, carrying, and rocking, and tried harder to soothe and quiet their babies. The investigators felt their data to imply that the mothers tended to rear the babies they wanted, the babies learning even in the first 3–4 months to behave in culturally appropriate ways.

This theme has been greatly extended in a series of studies by Bornstein and colleagues (e.g. Bornstein, 1993), which revealed both consistencies and differences in mother–child interaction across cultures. Some measures of infant or mother behaviour, and of the relations between them, showed little cross-cultural variation. However while American mothers induced their infants to attend to the environment more than Japanese mothers, Japanese mothers caused their infants to attend to themselves more than American mothers (see also Fernald & Marikawa, 1993). These and other data are in harmony with the popular conception that American mothers encourage exploration while Japanese mothers encourage closeness.

Such modulatory influences may be very persistent. Connor (1974) found similar differences between US families and Japanese families which had lived in the USA for three generations. Comparable inertia in the face of pressure for change was found by Van der Geest (1976) in a study of marital roles in the Kwatu area of Ghana. Though she may wield considerable social power, the wife is traditionally deferent to her husband. Schoolchildren's answers to questions showed that they evaluated positively the possibility that a man should eat together with his wife, and he should help her grind *fufu*. But in spite of these expressed preferences amongst the young, role segregation was still considerable.

What is "culturally appropriate" in this case can be related to broader issues. Triandis (1991) has contrasted the individualism of the West with the collectivist societies in the East. The collectivist ideology militates against great intimacy between husband and wife because of the prior bonds to parents and family of origin, loyalties running vertically through families taking precedence over horizontal ones. Individualism is compatible with seeking self-fulfilment in a close relationship, though within an individualistic society autonomy (see Deci & Ryan, 1987, cited pp.157–158) may militate against closeness (Dion & Dion, 1994). However a comparison of student couples in North Carolina and Taiwan produced "little evidence that culture interacted with other variables in predicting commitment or other features of relationships" (Lin & Rusbult, 1995, p.23). (Of course, as the authors would certainly recognise, there is not only the difficulty of proving the null hypothesis, but also that of knowing that student cultures in these two societies really did differ in relevant ways.)

Finally, it must be noted that behaviour that stems from a cultural difference may not only be seen as strange, but also interpreted as indicative of a personal characteristic: this lies at the root of many of the difficulties in inter-cultural relationships.

Temporal Changes in Roles and Rules

We have seen that roles and rules change with time, but the changes are not necessarily simple. "Modern" sex role attitudes are related to the autonomy that was emphasised (perhaps falsely) in the 1960s: "Be yourself, man" (or woman). But at the same time there has been a growing emphasis on intimacy in close relationships (Montgomery, 1988a), perhaps resulting from the greater equality between the sexes. Thus both poles of the autonomy–connectedness dimension have been emphasised.

It is probably usual for changes in behaviour to lag behind changes in role attitudes (see Van der Geest, 1976, cited earlier). On the basis of questionnaire data obtained from 1154 married men and women, Araji (1977) believed that many showed incongruence between their attitudes and behaviour. Both men and women had egalitarian role attitudes which were not reflected in behaviour. This may lead to problems.

However it may also happen that circumstances force a change in behaviour which is not accompanied by a change in attitudes. This is illustrated by a study of families in Cambridge and Budapest carried out in the early 1990s and mentioned briefly earlier (Gervai, Turner, & Hinde, 1995). As expected, in both samples the data showed that the traditionality of parents' attitudes concerning behaviour in social situations were similar to those concerning marriage, and individuals with more traditional views on adult relations between the sexes had more sex-biased expectations of their children. Traditional attitudes were also related to involvement in stereotypically sex-appropriate household tasks. Budapest mothers were an exception here, their involvement in household chores and child-care being unrelated to their attitudes. The latter finding was probably due to the Budapest mothers' necessary involvement in full-time work and inability to shape their own lives according to their preferences (while only 9% of the Cambridge mothers worked full time, 53% of the Budapest mothers did so, and virtually all the Budapest mothers who were not working at least part-time were normally employed but on temporary maternity leave). However, the more traditional the father's attitudes, the more gender-typed was the mother in her role behaviour. Fathers tended to be more sex-biased in parenting expectations, and more traditional in their attitudes towards social interaction with the other sex than mothers.

There were, however, some surprising differences between the two samples. Contrary to expectations, although the Budapest parents (of necessity) were less traditional in what they did in the house and with the children than the Cambridge parents, they were more traditional in their attitudes about social interactions and marital roles, and more sex-biased in their expectations about their children. This could be a reaction against the constraints which they perceived to determine their lives, many Budapest mothers saying they would prefer to work part-time, or to a deep-rooted conservatism comparable to that found in Germany and Austria, where economic constraints are less marked (Tóth, 1991).

Overlapping Categories

As these examples suggest, each individual brings to his relationships presuppositions derived not only from the society as a whole, but also from many overlapping categories to which he (or she) sees himself (or herself) as belonging within the society. "I am a girl (or a boy)", "A modern woman", "A member of the younger generation", "Liberal", "Academic", and so on. Actions are fundamentally influenced by perceived membership of such categories, and by the perceived structure of relations between them: in appropriate contexts category members are differentiated from outsiders; and the outsiders, and even the members, are seen as stereotypes.

And both what individuals expect from their relationships, and how they behave within them, will be affected by the promises and expectations they have acquired from, and associate with, these various overlapping subdivisions of the society as a whole (cf. Tajfel, 1978).

At this point it is necessary to refer back to the anthropological use of the term "role" for behaviour associated with a position or status in the society. Each such "role" is associated with specific rights and duties, and involves "norms", deviations from which provoke sanctions. Such a concept is appropriate when we are concerned with differences between societies— for instance how the recognised rights and duties of the Head of Government, or of Wives, in the relationships relevant to their positions, differ between this society and that. But from that we have gone on to consider differences between sub-cultures within a society—between Japanese and Caucasian families in California, for instance. Once again norms, enforced by sanctions of some degree, operate. And beyond that, each individual belongs not to one but to many groups within the society, deriving expectations from each of them with respect to certain types of relationship. Norms by definition are shared with others, but while some are common to a large society, others may be shared only by small sub-groups within that society, and be subject to constant renegotiation between and within those sub-groups. Now, having moved as it were from anthropological to sociological and social psychological usage, we must go one step further and consider expectations about behaviour more or less specific to dyads or to individuals within a relationship. Thus Thibaut and Kelley (1959, p.147) define a norm as "a behavioural role that is accepted to some degree by both members of a dyad". Since each individual may belong to many sub-groups, his repertoire of norms is likely to be idiosyncratic. And individuals also acquire idiosyncratic expectations as a result of their own life histories. One aspect of this is discussed in the next section.

Cultural and Social Influences in the Development of Particular Relationships

Just because cultural conventions are acquired by individuals especially from others significant in their lives, it is often difficult to draw a line between those properties of relationships that are seen as desirable through general cultural conventions and those seen as desirable through the influence of one or more others significant in an individual's life. While the general nature of each type of role relationship may be assimilated from the culture, the particular way in which an individual behaves in each role that he occupies is idiosyncratically coloured by the significant others with whom he has interacted (Lewis, 1975). For example Teevan (1972) found norms and values relating to premarital sexuality to be much influenced by the peer group. The attitudes of young married students to their roles as husband and father are similarly influenced by important figures in their lives (Hutter, 1974). Such influences may not be consciously recognised. As another example, Toman (1971) has suggested that adult social relationships have more chance of success, the more they resemble early intra-familial ones. To be more specific, he suggests that sibling positions tend to determine "role" preferences in later social contexts. Thus, considering only two-child families, an elder brother with a younger sister would be used to a senior position and to close interaction with a girl, and a younger sister with one elder brother would be used to the junior position with an elder brother. Such a couple would on this thesis be deemed compatible. By contrast a boy with a younger brother would be incompatible with a sister with a younger sister. A survey of 2300 families and 108 divorced couples provided some support for this view.

The quality of a woman's relationships with her various family members provide further evidence for this principle. Uddenberg, Englesson, and Nettelbladt (1979) compared the descriptions of their parents given by 69 women with their reports about their partners and children, and with independent data from the latter. The women's relationships with opposite-sex partners and sons, but not with daughters, were related to their perceived relationships with their fathers. Thus the father–daughter relationship appears to influence the daughter's way of relating to other significant males.

More recently VanLear (1992) obtained data from 171 couples from 58 families of origin in the USA. The effects were of several kinds. The marital styles of the grown-up children resembled those of their parents in certain respects, though there was a general change away from traditionalism in accord with the general cultural change. In general, similarities in styles of relating were greater with the mother than with the father, though they resembled their fathers more in sharing. The similarities tended to be greater if the parents were satisfied with their marriages. Thus it seems that the children did not blindly repeat their parents' styles, but were more prone to do so if their parents were happy. The young husbands tended to rebel against the parents' conflict style, using a style in conflict situations different from their fathers, and marrying wives with conflict styles unlike their mothers'.

Another more subtle influence on subsequent behaviour involves the names that individuals are given. People tend to "live up to their names". An interesting example is provided by the influence of the given name. Ashanti children were given, as one of their names, the name of the day of the week on which they were born. Amongst male children, particular personality types were traditionally associated with being born on certain days. In particular Monday boys were supposed to be retiring, quiet, and peaceful, and Wednesday boys to be quick-tempered, aggressive troublemakers. Jahoda (1954) compared the frequency distribution of the day-names between the boys in a school and the delinquents in the law courts. Monday children were markedly under-represented in the latter sample. For offences against the person, Wednesday children were over-represented. This is in harmony with the view that Ashanti beliefs influence the course of social development. In like vein, there is some evidence that nicknames or assumed names of children (Harré, 1975) and adults (Seeman, 1976) can influence the personality of the person concerned. Liddell and Lycett (in press) have data on the relations between the names (African or European) of South African children and their school performance.

Norms of Behaviour in the Development of Relationships

Norms of behaviour will also affect the various moves in the development of a relationship. As we shall see in Chapter 26, each partner must work out with the other an agreed definition of the relationship. In doing so, each will make moves and use symbols, whose meanings may be idiosyncratic but are more often the result of a consensus of opinion within the society. Often an essential contribution to a definition of the situation comes from preliminary moves such as those involved in greeting. Greeting ceremonials or specified sequences of behaviour are an essential preliminary to further interactions in many contexts (e.g. Goody, 1972; Harré, 1974; Kendon & Ferber, 1973). In the longer term there may be socio-cultural rules about the steps to be followed in establishing a relationship. In heterosexual relationships, for instance, there are cultural and sub-cultural differences in who should take the first step, and in the significance of asking the partner to one's home (e.g. Cook, 1977; Honeycutt, Cantrill, & Greene, 1989). And there may be special rituals for cementing relationships, such as having a beer together, or for maintaining a degree of distance in a relationship whose continuity is enforced, such as cutting (e.g. Harré, 1977). Usually there are sanctions against infringement—though often the embarrassment felt as a consequence of infringing such a convention is itself a sanction (Collett, 1977). Many of these micro-sociological issues have been documented by Goffman (e.g. 1963, 1967), Argyle (e.g. 1975), Harré (1977) and others. Finally, as the relationship develops, the partners will develop their own "norms". Each will come to expect the other to behave in particular ways, and deviances will demand explanation.

General

Thus the social influences on the behaviour of an individual in a given relationship come from: (a) expectancies concerning obligatory properties of the type of role-relationship in question. In some formal relationships these may be all-important, in some personal relationships much less apparent. They may be shared with all other members of the society, or with more limited sub-groups within it; (b) expectancies concerning similar but less obligatory properties; (c) social influences from significant others affecting behaviour in general or behaviour in particular relationships; and (d) experiences in earlier stages of the relationship, themselves affected by social conventions but often involving dyad-specific norms. Thus the norms that determine behaviour within relationships must be seen as varying along (at least) two dimensions—the extent to which they are obligatory, and the extent to which they are shared with others both within and between relationships.

Role Conflict

Most roles are complementary to some other role or roles. Husband and wife, doctor and patient, trawler skipper and crewman, each occupies complementary roles, and each has legitimate expectations about the behaviour of the other to him or her. These expectations will include culturally valued norms of fairness (Blau, 1964). It will be apparent that conflict may arise in a number of ways. One may not live up to the expectations of the other. Or the participants may hold different views about the behaviour expected from people in such a relationship. Or one or both may fail to understand how the other interprets his role, or the extent to which he or she believes that he adequately fills it. The consequences of such role conflict may be apparent in nearly all dimensions of the relationship.

The nature of role conflict is likely to differ from that of conflict arising from other sources. For example, a husband who did not earn his living would in many circles be considered not to be fulfilling his role, but a husband who could not play badminton would not, however frustrating this might be to his wife.

The term "role conflict" has been used deliberately broadly here, to embrace all causes of conflict caused by departures from role expectations. Role conflict can of course also occur within an individual who finds himself in situations where he has to face up to two or more conflicting expectations simultaneously.

How do Social Forces Affect the Individual?

Finally a fundamental issue, implicit in the preceding discussion, must be made explicit. How are we to relate the cultural forces, the social institutions that shape the nature of relationships, to the psychological forces guiding the behaviour of the individual? We have seen that the whole problem not only of socialisation but of personality development is involved here. For some purposes "definition of the situation" and "definition of the relationship" (see p.7) are useful conceptual tools. Individuals perceive and define situations in terms determined by their past history. In seeking to reach mutually agreed definitions of their relationships they are influenced by that history, including the norms they have acquired, and by the current situation. Many influences from their past history will be shared with all or most other individuals growing up in the same culture. Others will be specific to the individual or to the relationship.

The definitions of the situation and of the relationship will include expectancies about how the individual and others should behave. It will involve specification of the relative rewarding values of different possible outcomes, which may lead to the formulation of plans of action, and thus determine subsequent behaviour. Thus the way in which the actor defines the situation and in particular the relative values he has acquired, form a link between the social and the psychological forces determining the nature of relationships (cf. Stebbins, 1969; Tajfel, 1978).

However if the concept of the "definition of the situation" embraces diverse expectations and values placed on different types of behaviour within a relationship, we must ask at what level of analysis it should properly be applied. Is it just the sum of its component parts, or does the concept imply the existence of emergent properties, or of a whole whose perception as such is an important determinant of the behaviour of the participants? Such concepts are useful in part because of their flexibility, but they need to be given edges before much further progress can be made.

We have seen that the course of a relationship may be affected by influences from the physical environment, by the immediate impact of other relationships, and by a variety of cultural and social influences. In conclusion it must be emphasised that, if we wish to describe these influences in any detail, assess their distribution, or estimate their potency, we must do so against a background of an adequate description of the relationships themselves.

SUMMARY

1. Relationships affect and are affected by the physical environment.
2. Within any group, relationships may affect relationships. Group or family rules may be an important key to interaction patterns within a group.
3. The social networks of the partners in a relationship may affect its nature, and vice versa.
4. Relationships affect and are affected by the socio-cultural structure. Culture affects emotional and psychological functioning, and cultural values affect relationships.

5. The concept of role refers to the rights and duties associated with the incumbency of particular positions within institutions. These rights and duties are not necessarily obligatory.
6. The rights and duties associated with roles, and the behaviour expected from participants in particular types of relationships, may change with time.
7. Individuals bring to their relationships presuppositions derived from the many overlapping groups to which they see themselves as belonging.
8. Behaviour in relationships is thus influenced both by culture and by individual experience, and it is often difficult to separate the two.
9. Roles may conflict.

18 Dissonance, Balance, and Attribution

DISSONANCE AND BALANCE

We have seen that it may be rewarding to find that others share our views. The suggestion was that people need to assess social reality correctly, and many of our beliefs can be validated only by other people: when others provide confirmation of our views ("consensual validation"), we may feel positive affect and be attracted to them. But what if we discover that a colleague we think highly of holds opinions different from our own on an important matter? The immediate outcome is likely to be experienced anxiety—anxiety which may be accompanied by physiological arousal (Elkin & Leippe, 1986) and may choke or disturb the relationship at that point (Sullivan, 1953). Furthermore, our beliefs and attitudes not only require validation from the external world, they also need to have some degree of consistency with each other; and it is more disturbing to find that one disagrees with someone one admires than with someone for whom one has little respect. Of course we may not recognise inconsistency, but if we do, it must be put right. We may decide that we do not think so highly of our colleague after all, or change our own opinion, or disbelieve the news—"he can't really think *that!*".

A number of related theories involve this general view. Items of knowledge, opinion or belief that individuals have, if not irrelevant to each other, may be consistent or inconsistent with each other, and may affect each other. For example, how we see ourselves behaving towards another person may influence our feelings towards him (e.g. Festinger, 1957). In accordance with equity theory (pp.344–348), an individual who harms another may convince himself that the victim deserved what he got. He is more likely to do this, the more highly he thinks of himself (Glass, 1964), perhaps because it is then more "dissonant" for him to accept blame himself. Of course these are not the only escapes open to the harm-doer; he may accept responsibility and attempt compensation, deny responsibility, or minimise the harm he has done (Brock & Buss, 1962). Again, belief that a man is a scoundrel and news that he has recently wronged a friend would be consistent, whilst the same belief would be inconsistent with news that he had helped a friend at great personal sacrifice. In the latter case, tension will be felt and some change is likely to occur. We might change our view of the individual in question, or disbelieve the news (e.g. Heider, 1958; Kelley, 1971; Newcomb, 1961).

Some of the theories in this area lay emphasis on consistency between cognitive elements (attitudes or beliefs), others on consistency between attitudes and the self-image, and yet others on consistency between attitudes and behaviour (e.g. Aronson, 1969). In so far as what is important about an actor's behaviour is what he believes himself to have done, and in so far as the self-image involves beliefs about the self, we need not, for present purposes, be too concerned about the differences between these possibilities. Let us consider how the extent to which we share opinions with others may affect our feelings about them, or vice versa.

Newcomb (1961) supposed that individuals form positive and negative attitudes towards objects (physical and social) in the world. If two individuals like each other and perceive each other to have similar attitudes towards an object (which may be another person), a state of "balance" will exist. However imbalance occurs if they like each other but see each other as having dissimilar attitudes, or dislike each other and see each other as having similar attitudes. In the former case, at least, there will be a tendency to restore balance if the partners expect their relationship to be a continuing one. One or both will change either his feelings towards the object or towards the other individual. The object concerned may be external to the dyad. Thus A, who likes watching football, is more likely to like B if he perceives that B likes watching football. Furthermore A will like B the more, the more important watching football is to A. This could be because A looks forward to enjoyable discussions with B about football, but it could also simply be because positive views about another football-lover are consistent with his own positive views about himself— "He must be another good chap like me". Alternatively, if A likes B but perceives that B does not like football, he may decide that after all watching football is a waste of time, or that he does not like B after all, or he may misperceive B and decide that B does like football, "really". People are more likely to change their views to accord with those of a liked partner than with a disliked one, and more likely to change their views to differ from a disliked one (Sampson & Insko, 1964).

In other cases the object may concern characteristics of one of the individuals involved. A, who is proud of his badminton skills (i.e. A likes A in this respect) is more prone to like B if A perceives that B appreciates his (A's) skill (i.e. if B also likes A in this respect). Alternatively, A, liking B, might come to believe that B appreciated his skill at badminton or, knowing that B was uninterested in badminton, that badminton does not matter all that much anyway.

In a classic study, Newcomb (1961) studied students, initially strangers to each other, living together near the university campus. At the start of term, the students were given several attitude and personality inventories, and their values in a number of important life areas were assessed. At intervals the students were asked to estimate the attitudes of other students, various measures of friendship were taken, and a few simple experiments were conducted. It was found that the students were attracted to others with the same values or who liked the same people as themselves. Agreement on attitudes led to the gradual development of friendship, as might be expected from the attractiveness of similarity (Chapter 8). But as friendships developed, agreement between them increased. Experiments employing an outside stooge also showed that attraction increased agreement. All these findings are in accordance with balance theory (see also Kenny & Kashy, 1994).

One result of special interest concerned the effect of the personality of the subjects on the way balance was obtained in Newcomb's study. The students had previously been assessed on a scale for authoritarianism. Since authoritarian individuals are more rigid than non-authoritarian ones, and tend to interpret the world in terms of their own preconceived notions, they would be expected to be less good at perceiving other peoples' attitudes. This was the case. So, although both groups were equally likely to achieve balanced relationships, they did it in different ways. Non-authoritarians became attracted to people who agreed with them, whilst authoritarians achieved balance by misperceiving other peoples' attitudes.

In a similar vein, Byrne and Wong (1962) found that white subjects scoring high on prejudice on a denigration scale assumed greater attitude dissimilarity between themselves and a black stranger than between themselves and a white stranger. They also assumed greater dissimilarity between themselves and a black person than did subjects low on prejudice.

Balance theories have been applied to many other aspects of interpersonal relationships. For instance they would predict that perceived similarity in a positively affiliative relationship would be greater than the actual similarity as measured by the differences between the partners' self-concepts (e.g. Murstein, 1967a). Again, balance theories have been cited in relation to the view that relationships are seen as better, the more effort that is put into them. Shortcomings of the relationship are inconsistent with the effort put in, and will be minimised, whilst desirable qualities will be consistent, and therefore maximised—"I must love him if I have looked after him all these years". Similarly, personal commitment (see Chapter 15), as well as depending on a positive evaluation of the partner, is likely to enhance it. Once A is committed to B, negative qualities in B will be inconsistent and positive qualities consistent; attention will be focused on the latter, and the former may be seen in a more favourable light.

Of course, within a dyadic relationship, balance may exist for A but not for B. A may perceive that B's attitudes towards object O are the same as he has, but B may perceive A's attitudes to differ from his own. It must be remembered that balance depends on perceived, not actual, similarity: A and B may like each other and perceive each other to have similar attitudes or personalities, when in fact their attitudes differ. This is probably common, since engaged and married couples see each other as having attitudes more similar to their own than is actually the case (Chapter 13).

Newcomb pointed out that different balanced states are not equivalent to each other. For example, there are differences between an approximately balanced state when A likes B and one when A does not like B. The latter is more unstable, and involves less marked tendencies towards balance. Newcomb ascribes this to the intrusion of forces other than those towards balance—for instance, ambivalence about both positive and negative reciprocation from a disliked person, and the limited involvement of A with a person for whom he has no regard. If A likes B he is likely to assume that B likes him, but if A dislikes B he may neither assume that B dislikes him nor care whether he does.

There is also another problem. We have seen that balance theories would predict that A would be attracted towards another individual B who had attitudes similar to A's own not only about objects in the external world, but also about himself. And this should hold for both positive and negative evaluations—we should be attracted not only to others who recognise the good points that we know we have, but also to others who perceive the weak ones (Deutsch & Solomon, 1959). In his classic studies of the formation of relationships amongst students, Newcomb did indeed obtain some evidence that a student tended to be attracted to another whom he saw as seeing him in the same way as he saw himself, even where undesirable characteristics were concerned (see pp.451–452). However, balance theory generally receives less support in situations involving dislike than it does in situations where the feelings towards the other person are positive. In the former type of situation it seems that a need to be liked by others, however poorly one may view oneself, overrides the effect of consistency or balance.

Of course positive evaluations from others are subject to the effects of a variety of qualifying influences, including the subject's perceptions of the validity of the evaluation and of the evaluator and his intent, the subject's need for positive evaluations, and the nature of preceding interactions (Mettee & Aronson, 1974). But the view that people are attracted to those who evaluate them as they evaluate themselves is generally supported more where the evaluations concern specific attributes of the subject rather than global assessments (Stroebe, 1977; see also Curry & Emerson, 1970). It may also depend on the state of the relationship (see Fig. 13.1).

Early balance theories also tended to be over-simplistic in their dependence on overall assessments of "attraction" or "liking". As argued here in a number of contexts, such global assessments are useful in some cases, but can require further analysis. Newcomb (1961) takes up this issue in reply to a previous criticism of balance theory—its apparent inability to cope with the case of the triangle Joe loves Ann, Ann loves Harry, does Joe like Harry? Balance theory suggests that he should, but if Joe sees Harry as a rival, commonsense suggests that he will not. Newcomb argues that attraction is not unitary, and will vary with the role perceptions of the individuals involved. Joe may perceive Harry sometimes as a male friend and sometimes as a rival: it is a commonplace that we can be attracted to a person in some contexts and not in others. On this view a tendency towards "balance" is not ubiquitous (see also Murstein, 1971b), but a principle which provides a handle on certain aspects of interpersonal relationships.

Indeed, it is important to remember that imbalance depends on how the participants perceive the total situation (e.g. Abelson, 1959). Agreement with someone we do not expect to meet matters much less than agreement with a person we shall see shortly (Insko et al., 1974). Imbalance matters only if it is thought about: we accept but neglect some features in our friends that we would find unpleasant in others. And a friend's discordant view may be seen as based on sound motivation (e.g. friendly criticism), or "understood" as part of other more desirable characteristics ("the defects of his qualities").

As these examples indicate, one of the qualities, and one of the defects, of balance theories is their flexibility. Although theories of dissonance and balance have been stated much more precisely than this brief summary might indicate, it is clear that, if used descriptively, they could rather easily be used to explain almost anything.

Furthermore, alternative explanations of some of the phenomena are possible. For example Bem (1967, 1972) suggested that people generally do not know their own attitudes, but infer them from their behaviour. Thus while dissonance theory postulates that an unpleasant motivational state arises from dissonance between attitudes and behaviour, and that this state can be reduced by an attitude change, Bem argues that a person's attitudes come to be compatible with his behaviour because they are inferred from it. It appears to be very difficult to design a definitive experiment to decide between the two views (Bem & McConnell, 1970).

Because of these reservations, it is clear that we should use theories of dissonance and balance with circumspection, though they do provide a valuable framework for thought.

ATTRIBUTION

People are always trying to understand what is happening around them, with social events being especially salient and social events that concern them even more special (Berscheid et al., 1976). And understanding often implies assigning causes to events. We are therefore concerned here with how people assess or attribute the causes of changes in the behaviour of others, especially those with whom they have a close relationship. Attributions of causes may be implicit and relatively superficial (e.g. "Boy, he is angry") or more thoughtful and explicit (e.g. "He is angry because of X"). Baucom (1987) stresses that both may be important in close relationships. But we shall see later that we must go farther than the mere attribution of causes and consider how perception of the current situation influences, and is influenced by, the accounts which are constructed of the past.

Heider (1958) argued that a primary distinction must be whether a given action or change in action is due to something internal to the actor, or to something external. For instance, if a friend is late for an appointment, is it the friend's fault (laziness, tardiness, other preoccupations) or something that could not be helped (the friend's car broke down, or was held up by traffic)? Kelley (1971) extended this by specifying the three sources of information which make it possible to attribute causation. Suppose we wish to explain why A hit B, these sources would be:

(a) *Distinctiveness.* Does A hit other people?
(b) *Consensus.* Do other people hit B?
(c) *Consistency.* Does A always hit B when he gets a chance?

Thus if A often hits other people, other people do not hit B, and A often hits B, we might conclude that the problem lay with A and label him as a bully. If A does not hit other people, others do hit B, and A often hits B, we might conclude that B elicited hitting, perhaps because he was obnoxious in some way. And if A does not hit other people, other people do not hit B, and A does not usually hit B, we might attribute the conflict to the situation.

Earlier studies of the processes involved in attribution usually involved single individuals in controlled laboratory situations. In real life there may be no opportunity to make multiple observations to assess consistency or consensus, as in the example just given, and attributions must be made on the basis of a single instance. In such cases attributions are based on previously held beliefs, theories, or preconceptions which provide causal schemata with which the current situation can be compared and integrated. Kelley (1972) has postulated a number of principles to account for how this occurs. For instance, if a possible cause for an event is conspicuous, other possible causes may be discounted; or the importance of a possible cause may be emphasised more if apparently inhibitory factors are present.

While Kelley's approach is valuable for indicating the sorts of attribution people make, especially under experimental conditions, it still underestimates the complexity of the psychological processes involved (e.g. Hewstone & Antaki, 1988). Attributions may be influenced by the expectation of future interactions, by the attributor's view of the other's view of her, and so on. It is important to study the dynamics of attributions in real life as well as in the laboratory. We shall return to this shortly.

Factors Influencing Attribution

Individual Characteristics and Mood.   Making an attribution about the cause of an event gives one a sense of understanding and thus a feeling that one can control one's environment. In harmony with this view, Burger and Hemans (1988) found that individuals high in a general need for control were especially prone to engage in attributions.

Happy and satisfied individuals tend to make attributions to stable internal causes when things are going well, and to unstable external causes when they are not, thereby enhancing the quality of their relationships. Distressed and depressed subjects tend to do the opposite, and are usually less likely to give the partner credit for positive events (Baucom, 1987; Baucom, Sayers, & Duke, 1989; Fletcher, Fitness, & Blampied, 1990; Forgas, Bower, & Moylan, 1990). The effect of mood on attribution is likely to be of major importance. It is greater for serious conflicts than for minor ones, apparently because of the greater cognitive processing time required (Forgas, 1994). Alden (1987) tested anxious and non-anxious subjects in an experimental situation, requiring subjects to initiate interactions with a confederate and receiving social feedback indicating either continuous success, improvement, deterioration, or continuous failure. With improving feedback the anxious subjects made attributions most strongly to internal factors—but to their own efforts rather than to personal ability. With consistent success the anxious subjects made more attributions to external factors like luck than did the non-anxious ones, who accepted personal responsibility for the consistent success.

Comparable findings have been found with subjects who differed in self-esteem. Individuals who think well of themselves show a self-serving bias in causal attributions by attributing success to themselves and failure to external sources. They rate positive outcomes as more important than negative ones. Tennen and Herzberger (1987) found self-esteem to be a better predictor of such effects than depression. Baumgardner, Kaufman, and Levy (1989) found individuals with high self-esteem, receiving negative feedback, were often less critical of the source in public than in private. Those with low self-esteem reacted in a self-enhancing way when under public scrutiny, complimenting those who liked them and derogating those who did not. Such a pattern seemed temporarily to raise their self-esteem. The authors suggest that everyone wants to enhance their view of self: those with high self-esteem enhance or maintain a positive self-image privately, but those with low self-esteem may compensate in other ways. For instance those with low self-esteem might also acquire impediments to performance that would excuse failure, fail early on in the tests to create low expectations, or affiliate with less fortunate others (see also Wheeler & Miyake, 1992).

Two further individual factors that affect attributions have been identified by Fincham and Bradbury (1989b). One is the extent to which the individual has dysfunctional or unrealistic beliefs about relationships: an individual who expects too much is likely frequently to find his expectations violated and thus to perceive the behaviour of the partner as negative and due to stable and global dispositions. The other is the degree to which the individual uses complex attributional schemata: this includes such issues as a preference for multiple-cause explanations, awareness that behaviour is a function of interaction with others, and so on. In a study of 43 married couples, Fincham and Bradbury found these two factors to be related to the tendency of spouses to ascribe negative events to stable and global characteristics of their partners. Perspective-taking did not contribute to this tendency.

We have noted elsewhere how gender orientation may affect attributions (see Lobel, 1994, and p.258), and how the way in which individuals perceive themselves influences the way in which they perceive others (see Bugental et al., 1993, and p.228).

Actor versus Reactor.   Kelley (1979) has presented data on conflicts between dating couples showing how the one who is at fault tends to make attributions about the situation ("I was late because there was an accident on the road and I was held up"), while the partner makes attributions about the actor's attitudes or character ("You were late because you don't really care about me any more") (see also Weiner et al., 1987). It has been suggested that this is because actor and observer have different information—the observer did not know about the accident. However there is more to it than that. When partners in a close relationship are in disagreement, attributions are coloured by intention and anticipation (Orvis, Kelley, & Butler, 1976). Attribution in conflictual situations is embedded in a process of re-evaluating the partner and the relationship, of restructuring the relationship, of making a new account. It is affected by the supposed blame-worthiness of the action (see earlier and Alicke, 1992). And after a "sin", actors have been found to give longer and more complex accounts after sins of commission than after sins of omission: offenders try to redefine themselves as less blameworthy. Interestingly, accounts given by women imagining themselves to be a guilty party tend to be more complex than those of men (Gonzales, Manning, & Haugen, 1992; Hill et al., 1976). Attributions may thus form a basis for a new evaluation and structuring of the relationship. They are also used to air feelings—for instance saying that your partner's actions were influenced by her/his mother may be another way of saying "get weaned" or of insulting the mother-in-law.

Attributions in Relationships

Because attributions give a sense of control, it is not surprising that attempts to explain relationship events are more common in the early stages of a relationship, when there are choice points or changes in the relationship, and when the relationship is perceived to be unstable (Baucom, 1987; Fletcher et al., 1987). And since negative events tend to be more salient than positive ones, individuals tend to notice and assign causes to negative behaviour by the partner, while positive behaviour including tokens of affection may go unnoticed.

The attributions made may enhance the quality of a relationship. Thus some individuals idealise the attributes of their spouses, and this may be self-serving, involving a concern for maintaining the relationship and hopes for future rewarding interaction (Lavin, 1987; Murray & Holmes, 1996). In a study of married or divorced students, Schriber, Larwood, and Peterson (1985) detected a "responsibility bias" in both distressed and non-distressed marriages—that is, a tendency for individuals to assume more than their objective responsibility for an event. There was also an "unrealistic optimism" that future outcomes would be positive: this was lower in couples with a high level of conflict. Attributions may be used to ameliorate threats to the relationship or to the self, so that if one partner becomes less affectionate, the other may attribute it to pressure at work. Or an individual may protect him or herself from jealousy by not paying attention to possible signs of infidelity—a course which may, or may not, be in the long-term interests of the relationship. Again, a spouse may exercise "secondary control" by bringing his or her expectations in line with reality: a wife who says "He never remembers my birthday" is thereby not hurt when no gift is forthcoming (Baucom, 1987).

As a result of misattributions, partners may think that they agree about sources of conflict, when in fact they do not (Harvey, Wells, & Alvarez, 1978). Harvey et al. argue that it is not agreement between partners that facilitates the maintenance of relationships, but the perception of agreement. It seems that, in times of conflict, attribution is concerned with protection or illusion as much as analysis. As noted earlier, misattribution may ameliorate the perception of a threat to the relationship (Harvey et al., 1982).

If conflict becomes more severe, however, illusion is checked, and partners seek the causes of the conflict, perhaps each justifying his or her own course of action or blaming the other. Divergencies in attributions, if not discussed and reconciled, can lead to a gradual distortion of the relationship. If things get worse, each partner may justify his or her own course of action, or blame the other. While non-distressed spouses tend to make benign attributions about the behaviour of their partners, distressed spouses make negative ones (Baucom et al., 1989; Bradbury & Fincham, 1988; Fincham, Beach, & Baucom, 1987; Fincham, Beach, & Nelson, 1987). Fincham and Bradbury (1987a, b) have suggestive evidence that the attributions influence the level of satisfaction in marriage rather than satisfaction leading to positive attributions. Attributions that serve as excuses tend to refer to external, uncontrollable, and unintended events, but causal attributions to internal and controllable factors tend to be withheld (Weiner et al., 1987).

Attributions are also used tactically between individuals. Weber and Vangelisti (1991) used a questionnaire to elicit tactical and non tactical attributions from 214 college students. Tactical use was especially prevalent when the attribution was used as an excuse for behaviour acknowledged as wrong ("I got low marks in the test because the examiner did not like me") and when used as a means of affiliation. Tactical attributions then tended to focus on positive events or behaviours, and to emphasise interpersonal stable sources.

BEYOND ATTRIBUTION

People are not merely naive scientists, as a superficial reading of G.A. Kelly might suggest. They are not concerned solely with cognitive coherence, nor with assigning responsibility or blame for events. They also seek to maintain their self-esteem, and support their self-image. They try to discern meaning in events, interpreting situations both cognitively and emotion-ally, and in doing so use both automatic and controlled processing. The cognitive interpretations and emotions lead to action (Rusbult, Yovetich, & Verette, 1996).

Thus Fincham and Bradbury (1987c; 1989a, b; 1992) point out that it is important to distinguish between attributions concerning the cause of a given event and those concerning responsibility for it. Responsibility implies intent, and the ascription of responsibility will depend on judge-ments that the actor could have foreseen that a given action might lead to conflict or harm, or knew of other possible courses of action and had the ability to carry them out. Fincham and Bradbury suggest that such issues as the criteria for responsibility and the capacity of the individual to act otherwise will all influence the attribution of responsibility, and that that in turn influences the assignment of blame. Further considerations may affect the expectation that the conflict can be resolved. Attribution of blame may lead to anger.

As an example of the complexity of the issues involved, in one study subjects gave autobiographical accounts of conflicts in which they had angered someone else or of conflicts in which they had themselves been angered. The behaviour that initiated the conflict was usually seen by the perpetrator as meaningful and comprehensible, but by the victim as arbi-trary, gratuitous, and incomprehensible. Victims tended to describe a series of provocations or grievances, and sometimes noted how they had stifled their anger on earlier occasions. Thus the perpetrator might at first not have realised that offence was being caused, and repeated the provocation until the victim expressed the accumulated anger. The perpetrator might then have seen the anger as unjustified by the single event to which it was expressed, and felt himself to be victimised. Furthermore perpetrators tended to see the incident as closed, while victims saw it as having lasting implications of continuing harm (Baumeister, Stillwell, & Wotman, 1990).

In real life attributions may be immediate and virtually automatic, but even then they are likely to depend in part on past experience involving both cultural conventions and individual memory (Fletcher & Fitness, 1993). And in real life attributions are not necessarily made to single causes, but involve the elaboration of complex causal accounts (Howe, 1987).

The pursuit of meaning which is involved is subject to many influences. The mood of the individual, and the emotional response engendered by the event or situation, will affect the attributions made. How they affect them will in turn depend on the emotional script elicited (e.g. Forgas, 1992, 1996). Furthermore appraisals concerning relationship events will be influenced by self-appraisals, such as the power that the appraiser sees her-self to have in the situation (e.g. Fitness, 1996). And the situation must be assimilated into the individual's knowledge structure, which must accommodate accordingly.

Classic attribution theory is thus too narrow to cope with the complexity of the causal attributions made in real life. Planalp and Rivers (1996) prefer to describe the processes involved in terms of "explanatory coherence", suggesting that the new knowledge being processed activates related knowledge systems, including relational schemata, and the most coherent set of modes is chosen as an explanation on the basis of such criteria as parsimony, breadth, absence of contradiction, and analogy (Thagard, 1989). This implies that the self-system is equipped with an interwoven network of knowledge available for explaining events and constructing new schemata as necessary. While recognising the value of laboratory experiments for addressing precise questions about the cognitive processes involved in explanation, Planalp and Rivers have turned to the analysis of accounts of real incidents in order to obtain a broader picture of what goes on in real life. In their work they found that explanation-seeking was instigated especially by unexpected events of a negative character and involving an important relationship. It often involved extensive gathering of data (for instance by discussion with the partner or with third parties) and testing out the hypotheses formed. As in classical attribution theory, emphasis was placed on consistency in and distinctiveness of the available data. Sometimes several explanations were given, either as alternatives or as necessary sequelae to the initial explanation. The explanations accepted could change with time and be influenced by the situation. Assigning responsibility was often evident.

Thus, in seeking explanation for a surprising event, subjects did not merely add qualifications to existing knowledge, but used more complex and sophisticated explanation-seeking procedures. The sort of explanations that people ordinarily give for events within relationships are not limited to the person, situation, etc. categories discussed by attribution theorists, but may involve new knowledge structures that explain the existing knowledge together with the new and apparently inconsistent information in a completely new framework. This model of cognitive functioning is clearly more flexible and can account for a wider range of phenomena than traditional attribution theory: a problem may be that this view will not be easily falsifiable.

But cognitive changes are not merely passive, imposed on people by events. True, the attributions studied most often, and perhaps those that occur most often, concern unexpected and especially negative events. But seeking for information, for causes, for meaning, is not limited to such occasions. Vorauer and Ross (1996) stress that individuals try to discover the truth about their relationships, actively searching for information and devoting considerable energy to the scrutiny of events and behaviours.

Indeed the desire for information about issues that matter to them may lead them to attribute significance to ambiguous events. Within relationships they may exaggerate the extent to which they are the target of the partners' actions, especially where there are strong feelings of mutual interdependence. They may then interpret minute details as relevant to their own goals. They may even use the effect of an event on themselves to ascribe meaning to the event. Vorauer and Ross suggest that informational goals heighten the accessibility of relevant knowledge structures, so that stimuli that would not otherwise activate those knowledge structures can do so. At the same time the informational goals motivate people to examine their own and others' behaviour.

SUMMARY

1. Individuals strive to perceive that they assess social reality correctly, and that their perceptions are compatible with each other and with the perceptions of others whom they like or respect. They may distort their perceptions in order to achieve compatibility. Thus if A likes B but disagrees with B's views about X, A may change his own views about X, or change his views about B, or disbelieve that B's views are different from his own.
2. Individuals make attributions about the causes of events or changes in their relationships, and these attributions may affect the relationship's future course.
3. A variety of factors affect the attributions made. These include individual characteristics and mood, the role the perceiver had in the incident in question (actor or reactor), and aspects of their relationship. Attributions are often associated with assignment of responsibility.
4. The search for meaning implies more complex cognitive processes than traditional attribution theories suggest.

19 Exchange, Interdependence, Equity, and Investment Theories

Classical learning theories have been used to a limited extent to account for aspects of interpersonal attraction and interactions within relationships. For example Lott and Lott (1974) applied a classical conditioning paradigm to a study of children. The children were divided into groups of three, and each group played a game in which one or more members were rewarded whilst others were not. Each child was then asked which children he or she would like to take along on their next family holiday. Children who had been rewarded were more likely to choose members from their own group than children who had not. The data were explained in terms of association between the reward and other members of the group.

As an example of the use of an operant paradigm, Patterson (e.g. 1982) explained the use of coercive types of behaviour by children in terms of their sequelae in the family situation.

But it is apparent that such paradigms are inadequate. For both of the examples cited they suffice only at a descriptive level, and Neisser (1976) argued that the laboratory experiments on which the classical learning theories were based hardly provide an adequate basis for a theory of human cognition. The social learning theorists therefore invoked a range of cognitive concepts (e.g. Bandura, 1977).

However, relationships exist over time and involve sequences of interactions between participants. It is the additional problems that these issues raise that exchange and interdependence theories have tried to meet. That exchange theories are diverse will become apparent shortly, but they share the assumption that social behaviour is in large measure determined by the rewards and costs, or expectations of rewards and costs, consequent upon it. That is not to say that *all* social behaviour is to be seen in terms of exchange, though theorists differ in how widely they cast their nets. In any case most theorists emphasise that relationships do not depend on the mere sum of reciprocated giving of rewards and incurring of costs, for additional issues arise from the fact that the giving and taking constitute an exchange occurring in time and within a social context. And this social context may involve the expectation that people should be rewarded in relation to the costs they have incurred, and/or that people observe a norm of reciprocity in their dealings with each other—i.e. that what I do for you should be, roughly and in the long run, commensurate with what you do for me. This has required exchange theorists to move progressively farther from their early learning theory origins.

DEFINITIONS

The present discussion has the limited aim of establishing the place of exchange theories within the general framework presented in this book. It is first necessary to introduce, in terms sufficiently broad to permit general discussion, a few concepts used in most variants of exchange and interdependence theories.

(a) *Reward.* In laboratory studies of learning, stimuli that increase the probability of recurrence of a response are usually referred to as "rewards" or "reinforcers" (Kling & Schrier, 1971). Of the two terms, "reinforcer" is generally preferred because it carries no necessary implication that the stimulus is pleasant to the recipient. Exchange theorists, concerned with interactions between adult human beings, more often use "reward", and this is in keeping with its generally looser and less sophisticated usage, and with the fact that the primary emphasis is on the *perception* by the recipient that it is valuable or pleasant. What is perceived as valuable or pleasant will in turn be influenced by the individual's values and expectations, and these may differ between the sexes and between individuals.

(b) *Cost.* This refers to the extent to which an activity is punishing, including the extent to which its performance results in alternative rewards being foregone. Included here are physical or mental fatigue and embarrassment or anxiety etc. incurred through the behaviour. (It may be noted that minimisation of costs may form one basis for attraction. Thibaut and Kelley, 1959, cite the case of a stutterer who said she liked a friend because the latter thought stuttering cute.)

(c) *Resource*. This is sometimes used as synonymous with reward—e.g. sometimes by Foa and Foa (1974), cited in Chapter 20. However it often refers to the attributes by virtue of which P *could* modify the rewards and costs experienced by another person. This may include material goods that he possesses, skills and expertise, and social characteristics (sex, age, etc.) which he or she brings to the situation and which may be valued by the other. The skills and social activities are often referred to as his or her "investments", in the sense of that with which he or she is invested.

(d) and (e) *Value and Dependency*. A given resource is not of equal value to all individuals: indeed its value to any one may vary with time and situation. The value of a given resource to B is usually spoken of in terms of the need for or dependency of B on A or on the particular resource in question.

(f) *Profit*. This refers to the rewards less the costs for engaging in an activity.

(g) *Alternative sources of reward*. The extent to which A can influence B will depend not only on the value to B of A's resources but also on the alternative sources of such rewards available to B.

Within these broad definitions, the emphases are placed rather differently by different theorists. As examples we shall consider briefly certain aspects of the classic approaches of Homans and of Thibaut and Kelley. We shall then examine the basic propositions of Equity theory, derived from these and from the work of Adams (1965) and formalised by Walster et al. (1978a), and the Investment model of Rusbult (e.g. Rusbult & Buunk, 1993). We shall then be in a position to consider some of the problems faced by, and the limitations of, exchange theories.

HOMANS

Homans (1961, 1974) attempted to build up a logical theory by deriving hypotheses to explain actual behaviour from a small number of explanatory propositions. The initial propositions were intended to be closely related to those of operant theory, reward being used in much the same way as reinforcement. They concerned stimulus generalisation (responding to stimuli similar to stimuli associated with behaviour that was rewarded); value and frequency of reward (the more and the more often behaviour is rewarded, the greater the frequency with which it will appear); and satiation (rewards become less valuable with repetition). In addition Homans introduced a concept of distributive justice, suggesting that an individual expects to receive rewards in relation to his costs, and will show anger if he does not. From his basic propositions Homans derived additional propositions and corollaries with which to explain everyday behaviour.

A central issue, both in Homans's theory and in other comparable theories, concerns the manner in which individuals assess the rewards and costs they obtain. The Law of Distributive Justice describes the manner in which individuals expect to receive rewards commensurate with the costs incurred in an interaction and a profit in line with the investments they bring to it. What counts as an investment is to a large degree culture-specific, though such things as age, maleness, beauty, seniority, wealth, wisdom, and acquired skills contribute in many societies. People appraise the rewards they receive and the costs they incur in relation to those received and incurred by comparable others in comparable situations. As Homans (1961, p.76) puts it, "For with men the heart of these situations is a comparison". If the rule of distributive justice is not seen to be met, Homans postulates that the individual concerned will show anger. In his (1976) view, what is compared is not the subjective values and costs of the rewards and contributions, but rather the outward and visible amounts of the rewards and contributions, as perceived by all the parties concerned. "Thus workers in a factory compare their earnings but not how much these earnings 'mean' to each of them" (1976, p.232). It is implied that a party to a dyadic relationship will see justice to have been done if he perceives the ratio of his rewards to his costs to be similar to those he perceives his partner to obtain, and to those he sees comparable others obtain in comparable situations.

Homans also discussed the problem of choice, suggesting that the decision between alternative actions depends in each case on the product of the value of the outcome and the probability of getting it. Probability of outcomes may, of course, be assessed over a long timespan, and there is no implication that the individual will necessarily be right in his assessment.

Thus Homans had attempted to demonstrate the possibility of arriving at a rigidly deductive scheme, defining his concepts reasonably precisely and discussing the extent to which the variables could be measured. The latter, as we shall see, poses some difficulties, especially when it comes to measuring "value" and comparing the values of different resources (e.g. Abrahamsson, 1970). Though setting out from a traditional learning theory position, Homans employed, especially in relation to the notion of distributive justice, cognitive and emotional concepts such as value, anger, and choice. While some have argued that such concepts reduce the elegance of his scheme, they enormously increase the possibility of providing plausible explanations of real-life social behaviour. Indeed some have argued that Homans did not go far enough in this direction (e.g. Stebbins, 1969; Davis, 1973). However Homans's aim (Homans, 1976) was to derive principles of social behaviour from more general propositions valid for social and non-social behaviour.

THIBAUT AND KELLEY:
INTERDEPENDENCE THEORY

Thibaut and Kelley (1959; Kelley & Thibaut, 1978; Kelley, 1979) emphasised social interdependence rather than mere exchange, and have had a
major influence on research on relationships. Like that of Homans, their
approach is based in learning theory, but they lay even more emphasis on
the cognitive operations that guide each participant's choice of action,
supposing for instance that each individual maintains a "set" or plan of
action which is evaluated in terms of the outcomes produced. They stress
especially the interdependency inherent in any relationship. This interdependency arises from each partner's ability to influence the behaviour of
the other by determining his rewards and punishments. Successful interaction must involve the continuity of the relationship, and this depends on
the satisfaction of both parties concerned. In effect, this emphasis on interdependency involves a greater recognition of the continuity of the relationship in time. For A to maximise her outcomes she must consider not only
the rewards and costs to her that are consequent upon her actions, but
also the consequences for B: A must try to maximise B's profit as well as
her own, or B may opt out of the relationship.

Thibaut and Kelley also emphasise that every relationship is embedded
in a network of other relationships, both actual and possible. The participants compare their outcomes within the relationship, defined as the ratio
of perceived rewards to perceived costs, with the outcomes they have
experienced in the past, and with those they might expect in other relationships, by means of two comparison levels. One is the minimum level of
possible outcomes that A feels he deserves (actor's comparison level CL),
and is based on the average value of past outcomes in relation to the actor's
present situation, qualifications, and so on. The second is A's view of the
alternative outcomes open to him in other situations or relationships
(alternatives comparison level CLalt), or more precisely the lowest level of
outcomes A will accept in the light of available alternative opportunities.
Thibaut and Kelley suggest that A evaluates the outcomes he actually
receives in a relationship relative to these two levels. Comparison with the
actor's comparison level determines his satisfaction with the relationship,
while comparison with the alternatives comparison level determines his
dependence on it. If outcomes are lower than the alternatives comparison
level, the actor will be inclined to abandon the relationship.[1]

---

[1] We may note here that the concept of comparison level may be too simple. Comparisons
are likely to operate over multiple dimensions of individual characteristics, with the outcome
depending on individual expectations and relationship prototypes (Fletcher & Thomas, 1996).
However it is useful at this stage of analysis.

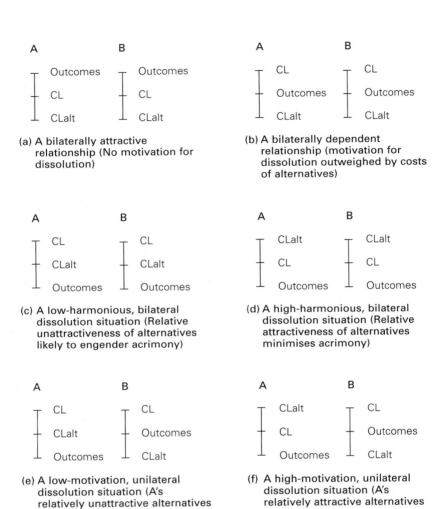

FIG. 19.1 Some possible exchange alternatives in a relationship between A and B. (Miller & Parks, 1982. Reprinted by permission of Academic Press, London.)

Figure 19.1, due to Miller and Parks (1982), illustrates six of the many possible alternatives for a dyadic relationship. In Fig. 19.1a, both participants have outcomes that exceed their comparison levels (CL), and the perceived alternatives (CLalt) do not exceed their CLs. Both should be happy. In Fig. 19.1b, outcomes fall below CL but remain above CLalt— both partners would do best to remain in the relationship in the absence of alternatives, even though they are not getting what they feel they deserve. They may complain about each other in attempts to increase their outcomes. In Fig. 19.1c, neither participant is getting what he/she feels he/she deserves, but all available alternatives fall below CL, so that both are doing better than they could in any situation perceived as a possible alternative. They may then agree to part, but with mutual discontent. By contrast, Fig. 19.1d illustrates a situation in which both partners will wish to dissolve the relationship, as both can see alternatives acceptable in being above their CLs. The alternative is not necessarily another available partner, but could consist in a belief that autonomy is preferable to a debilitating relationship. Figs. 19.1e and f represent situations in which A wishes to dissolve the relationship and B wishes to retain it, even though B is not obtaining the outcomes he/she thinks he/she deserves. A can decide to withdraw unilaterally, and will be especially motivated to do so if the CLalt is greater than CL, but may incur heavy social costs in doing so. Or A may try to persuade B by attempting to raise B's CLalt above B's outcomes.

Miller and Parks's (1982) scheme thus illustrates how interdependence theory can be used to understand relational dynamics. They point out that, of course, it involves considerable oversimplification. The analysis in Figs 19.1c–f focuses on the partner who is likely to want to dissolve the relationship, whereas in fact the outcomes of the two partners are interdependent. B may resist A's tactics, and make counter-moves. And there are obvious difficulties in assessing CLalt. While CLalt is usually thought of in terms of currently available alternatives, we have seen that one of these may be independence from any close relationship. Furthermore there may be costs in finding or being accepted by another partner (Simpson, 1987), and the different needs satisfied in the present relationship (e.g. emotional involvement, companionship, security) could be satisfied either in one or in several others (Drigotas & Rusbult, 1992; see later).

Some of the research to which Thibaut and Kelley's work initially gave rise has involved outcome matrices in game-like situations (e.g. Kelley & Thibaut, 1978). This can be seen as a way of abstracting the essential elements from real-life situations and investigating their consequences. The most frequently used models were based on the Prisoner's Dilemma. This game consists of a series of choices made by each partner in the absence of any knowledge of the partner's current choice. The outcome each gets depends both on his own choice and on that of his partner. In Fig. 19.2a

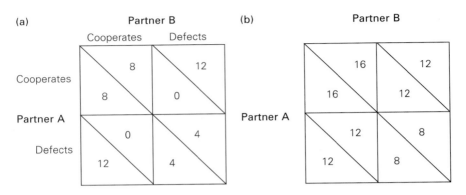

FIG. 19.2 (a) Given matrix for Prisoner's dilemma. (b) Transformation of matrix to maximise joint outcomes. (Redrawn from Kelley, 1979.)

each player has a binary choice. The outcome for B for each combination is shown in the upper right triangles, and that for A in the lower left triangles. Each is told the results of his own and his partner's choice but, in the classic form of the game, they are not otherwise allowed to communicate. Since, on every turn, each partner has to predict his partner's choice as well as making his own, data on how cooperative each perceives the other to be, how accurate each is at predicting the other's moves, and what each does when he believes his partner will cooperate, are available.

Figure 19.2a represents a hypothetical matrix. Figure 19.3a shows some data obtained in a more real-life situation (Kelley, 1979). Members of young heterosexual couples were asked "Assume that you and your partner share an apartment. Cleaning is a disagreeable job, but it has reached the point where it has to be done. Each of you has other time-consuming things to do... Rate each of the following events as to the degree of satisfaction or dissatisfaction you would feel". The four events were (1) Both clean; (2) You clean and your partner does other things; (3) Your partner cleans and you do other things and (4) You both do other things. Ratings were from −10 (very dissatisfied) to +10 (satisfied). It will be apparent, for instance, that female partners are on average very satisfied if both clean, pretty dissatisfied if neither do, and have more strong feelings than the males in either case.

The variance in an outcome matrix of the type shown in Fig. 19.3a can be analysed into three components. The first, termed "Reflexive Control", concerns the extent to which each partner can influence his or her own

(a)

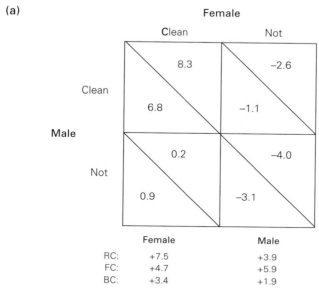

(b)

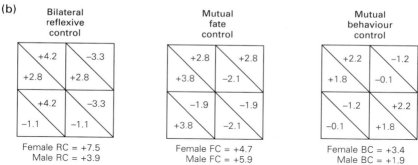

FIG. 19.3 (a) Mean ratings of satisfaction for various combinations of self and partner cleaning apartment. Data for females shown in upper portion of each cell, males in lower. (b) Various components for cleaning the compartment. (Redrawn from Kelley, 1979.)

outcomes. Thus for the female this is a column effect, showing how much on average she can affect her own satisfaction by varying her own behaviour. The second, termed "Fate Control", is a row effect for the female, and concerns how much on average her satisfaction is affected by her partner's behaviour. The third "Behaviour Control", is a column-by-row effect reflecting how much on average her outcomes are affected by combinations of her own and her partner's actions. This measures the satisfaction that she gets if both do the same (or different) things.

These components are shown in Fig. 19.3b. It will be seen that the woman on average gains 4.2 units when she cleans or loses 3.3 when she does not; gains 2.8 or loses 1.9 according to what her partner does; and gains 2.2 or loses 1.2 if they do the same or different things. The combinations of the partner's reflexive, fate, and mutual fate control are termed "Bilateral reflexive control", "Mutual fate control" and "Mutual behaviour control" respectively. The matrices show that the female exercises 7.5 (i.e. the difference between 4.2 and –3.3) reflexive control and the male 3.9 (the difference between 2.8 and –1.1).

The female in fact is subject to more reflexive control than the man (she cares what she does more than he cares what he does); the man is more subject to fate control (he cares what she does more than she cares what he does); and she is subject to more behavioural control than he is (she cares more that they should both do alike).

As another (hypothetical) example, consider what might happen to a married couple in which the husband likes playing tennis and the wife likes to go to art museums. Whether or not they played tennis would depend on the resultant of the husband's desire to play tennis, the wife's desire to play (or dislike of playing) tennis, and their desire to do things together. If they both had an overriding desire to do things together they could alternate between tennis and museums or, if they valued autonomy over connectedness, they could go their own ways in their spare time. Thus what we are talking about is the degree of interdependence between the partners, or the factors that determine how they coordinate their behaviour (Thibaut & Kelley, 1959).

Returning to the Prisoner's Dilemma type games, many variants of the outcome matrix shown in Fig. 19.2a are possible. The values in the cells can be varied, so that the temptation to defect changes: for example in "Chicken" the values in the bottom right-hand triangle could be –4. The participants may be allowed to communicate only by the moves they make, or by non-verbal or verbal means. Again, one of the participants may be bogus, passing pre-programmed responses to the subject. By using such games to study the processes of exchange and negotiation in a two-person situation, Kelley and Thibaut (1978; Kelley, 1979) and others attempted to abstract laws of general validity. It is argued that real-life relationships can often profitably be seen as posing to each participant the problem of choosing a course of action in order to maximise what he or she sees as profit, when which choice he or she should make depends in part on the choice being made by the other, and in part also on the other's probable outcomes. Whilst there has been some dispute over the extent to which specific research findings derived from this approach can be generalised, the use of outcome matrices has been productive of ideas about the course of social interaction, the nature of power, negotiation, etc.

Of course, as Thibaut and Kelley point out, people do not always assess situations dispassionately or act accordingly. Furthermore, people do not act solely to maximise their own outcomes in the given matrix, but take account of the other person's as well. They may direct their behaviour so that their joint outcomes are maximised, or to do their partner down at some cost to themselves, or in many other ways. In a close relationship, the partners may relinquish self-interest and act so as to benefit the partner or the relationship. Or again, the interests of the partners may become intertwined, so that the positive experiences of one are vicariously rewarding for the other. Such situations can be conceptualised as transformations of the given matrix. For instance, decisions to maximise the joint outcomes of both participants in Fig. 19.2a yields the matrix shown in Fig. 19.2b: in this case the use of such a transformed matrix by both participants would yield greater given outcomes. Many types of decision would of course be possible—for instance to maximise one's own relative outcomes, or the difference between own and other's outcomes. In every case the outcomes yielded would depend on the decisions made by both partners.

Such decisions can be regarded as in part the consequences of dispositions to be cooperative, competitive, loyal, and so on. Each partner attributes such dispositions to the other on the basis of his or her observed behaviour, and such attributions may or may not be reassuring about the future of the relationship. But beyond that, while each partner's decisions will be influenced by his own nature, they will also be affected by the dispositions he attributes to his partner, so that each partner's actual and perceived dispositions will affect the direct outcomes each obtains. In addition to the direct outcomes as specified in the given matrix (e.g. Fig. 19.2a), an individual may obtain (and affect the partner's ability to obtain) symbolic, abstract outcomes from displaying dispositions (for instance, to be cooperative) that he likes to see himself as having. Conceivably satisfaction at the dispositional level (i.e. seeing oneself as cooperative) can compensate for poor (though perhaps more tangible) outcomes at the direct level. However if living up to principles involves poor direct outcomes the relationship may be impractical, while adequate direct outcomes obtained with poor dispositional ones may be unfulfilling—as when a competitive individual gets what he wants too easily (Kelley, 1979; Kelley & Thibaut, 1978).

The implications of these ideas have been worked out in considerable detail (e.g. Kelley, 1979; Kelley & Thibaut, 1978). That they fit many of the facts about personal relationships, and provide a framework against which the data can be examined, cannot be doubted.

EQUITY THEORY

Having much in common with the two preceding approaches, equity theory was applied initially by Adams (1965) and his colleagues in situations where rewards and costs could be measured with reasonable objectivity. Adams, like Homans and Thibaut and Kelley, emphasised the importance of processes of social comparison in perceived equity. A person perceives an interaction or relationship to be equitable provided that he sees his rewards to be proportionate to his costs, in comparison with his partner or with comparable others. The more A sees himself as putting into an activity, in comparison with what he sees another to put in, the more he feels he should receive in return. An equitable relationship between A and B is said to exist if

$$\frac{(O_A - I_A)}{(|I_A|)^k{}_A} = \frac{(O_B - I_B)}{(|I_B|)^k{}_B}$$

I represents the participant's inputs to the exchange which are seen as entitling him to reward or cost. They may involve assets (high rank, beauty, labour, kindness), which entitle him or her to rewards, or liabilities (e.g. incompetence, drunkenness) which entitle him to costs. What counts as input may depend on individuals persuading others that the inputs they happen to possess are relevant and important. $|I_A|$ and $|I_B|$ represent the absolute values of the Inputs, disregarding sign. O represents the Outcomes or Profits the participant is perceived as receiving, that is, rewards less costs. Both I and O presume a scrutineer, who may be external to the relationship or one of the participants. In the latter case, a relationship may be perceived by one to be equitable but not by the other (Walster, Walster, & Berscheid, 1978a).

(O – I) represents the gain of each individual, and may be either positive or negative. Equity occurs if the ratios of gains to inputs are equal. Inequity arises if one participant finds that the relative gain is small compared with the other's, in which case she finds the situation to be unjust, or too great, when guilt is experienced. k may be +1 or –1, depending on the sign of the individual's inputs and outputs (k_A = sign $|I_A|$ × sign [O_A – I_A]).

Equity theory has been extended into a general theory of social psychology by relating it to the theory of social norms, and to dissonance theory, and by formalising it in a series of propositions (Walster, Berscheid, & Walster, 1976; Walster et al., 1978a). The first proposition merely states that individuals try to maximise their outcomes. However, it is pointed out that if everyone did this, chaos would result and all would suffer. Groups must therefore work out compromise systems for "equitably" apportioning rewards and costs among members, and for inducing their members to accept such systems (Proposition IIA). This will generally be achieved by rewarding those who treat others equitably and punishing those who do not (IIB). In assessing equity, outcomes (rewards – costs) are defined as the consequences a scrutineer perceives the participant to have incurred.

Further propositions state that individuals finding themselves to be participating in inequitable relationships become distressed (III) and will then attempt to restore equity (IV). The perceived inequity produces arousal, and attempts to restore equity are made if the arousal is attributed to the inequity. Restoration of equity can be achieved in a number of ways. First, "actual equity" can be restored by appropriate alteration of the participant's own outcomes by manipulation of either rewards or costs, or those of the other participant. Alternatively a participant can restore "psychological equity" by appropriately distorting his perception of his or his partner's outcomes. Here equity theory assimilates attribution theory (Hassebrouck, 1987).

These principles can be illustrated from research on the relationship between harmdoers and their victims. Applied in this context, the principles indicate that a harmdoer may either compensate a victim, or he may convince himself that the victim deserved what he got, or did not really suffer, or that he (the harmdoer) was not really responsible. At this point, equity theorists are obliged to predict which course of action will be taken when. In practice it is possible to classify the response of a harmdoer as involving either compensation or justification, and then to work out the variables that predispose towards one or the other. Considering not only the harmdoer but also the victim and outside agencies, Walster et al., (1976) have summarised research on the variables affecting the steps taken to restore equity.

Walster et al. (1978a) listed some of the difficulties of applying equity theory to intimate relationships. Some of these have been addressed by Interdependence theorists: thus we have seen that in close relationships the participants see themselves as a couple, so that one's gains are not the other's losses (i.e. the matrix is transformed). Other possible problems are considered later in this chapter and in the next. However, Walster et al. (1978a) claim not that equity theory is adequate to explain all aspects of intimate relationships, but that it can provide important insights. In a balanced discussion, they acknowledge possible limitations of their theoretical approach for relationships of this type.

Support for the application of equity theory to close relationships comes from studies in which individuals or couples are asked to assess their inputs, outputs, and outcomes in their relationships. It is not immediately obvious that an individual will feel anxious if he is profiting more from a

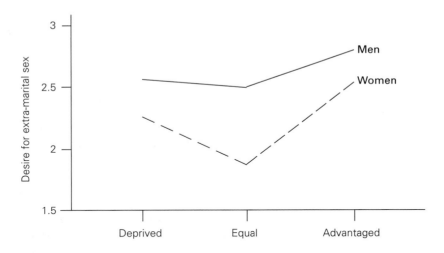

FIG. 19.4   Desire for extra-marital sex as a function of perceived equity. (From Prins, Buunk, & Van Yperen, *Journal of Social & Personal Relationships*, *10*, 39–53. Copyright © 1993 Sage Publications Inc. Reprinted by permission.)

relationship than his partner and, as we shall see, the issue is still controversial. However studies on diverse types of relationship, and on the early stages of close relationships, have supported the view that over-benefited as well as under-benefited partners feel less satisfaction than those who feel that they are equitably benefited. To cite one example, Walster et al. (1978b) categorised the participants in dating relationships as perceiving themselves to be under-, equitably-, or over-benefited. Equitable relationships were found to be more stable and to be characterised by greater sexual involvement. Over-benefited individuals felt about the same degree of satisfaction as, and considerably more guilt than, the under-benefited ones (see also Utne et al., 1984).

Another example is shown in Fig. 19.4. A sample of Dutch men and women (mean age 41) were recruited through a newspaper advertisement (Prins, Buunk, & Van Yperen, 1993). Assessments were made of their perceptions of equity in their marriage, their marital satisfaction, and their desire to engage in extra-marital sex. As the Figure shows, both women who felt themselves to be deprived and those who felt themselves to be advantaged showed stronger desires for extra-marital sex than those who felt themselves to be in an equitable relationship. The actual number of the women's extra-marital relationships were related to inequity in a similar way. The authors comment that the direction of causality cannot be determined from their data (see also Buunk et al., 1993; Hatfield et al., 1985; Van Yperen & Buunk, 1990).

Interestingly, although men were inclined to extra-marital affairs more than women, especially if they were dissatisfied with their marriage, their actual extra-marital involvement was, somewhat surprisingly, independent of marital or sexual satisfaction. The relation between perceived equity and extra-marital sex for men was not significant. The authors comment that, for men, extra-marital desires seem to be more or less independent of the way they feel about their marriages: the difference in the importance of inequity for men and women could be due to a greater exchange orientation and thus a greater salience of inequity for women, perhaps as a result of the women's movement.

Studying student relationships, Sprecher (1986) similarly found that over-benefiting as well as under-benefiting detracted from the relationship satisfaction of dating couples. Global impressions of inequity explained more variance in men's than in women's emotions. Hatfield et al. (1985) found that women are more distressed with being over-benefited in close relationships than men are, while men are more distressed by under-benefit. In an experimental situation Sprecher (cited Acitelli & Young, 1996) found that women not only felt more distress about inequity involving either over- or under-benefit, but were more prepared to do something about it. Acitelli and Young relate this to a difference in self-concepts between men and women, relationships playing a more important role in those of women.

All benefits do not contribute equally to perceived rewards. Van Yperen and Buunk (1990), studying married or cohabiting couples, found that the most important positive contributions were commitment, being sociable and pleasant to be with, leading an interesting and varied life, and taking care of the children. On the other side, the most negative items were being suspicious and jealous, and being addicted to tobacco and alcohol. Van Yperen and Buunk found that individuals tended to weight different rewards differently and some women considered themselves to be equitably treated even though they contributed more to the relationship than their partner, because they compared themselves with other women. Van Yperen and Buunk also had some evidence that equity was a better predictor of satisfaction than vice versa.

Similar principles have been shown to apply in the workplace. Buunk et al. (1993) showed that relationships between equals were seen to be equitable more often than relationships with superiors, where a high proportion of subjects felt over-benefited. Departures from equity caused greater distress in subjects high in exchange orientation or low in communal orientation (see p.355). Uehara (1995) has summarised considerable evidence that individuals avoid being over-benefited, or avoid perceiving themselves to be over-benefited: many of her examples concern social support or elderly individuals.

However the prediction that over-benefited individuals would feel less satisfaction than those who felt their relationship to be equitable is not intuitively obvious, and under-benefit is more strongly linked to dissatisfaction than over-benefit. It may be that the issue depends on the characteristics of the participant or the relationship.

And not all studies support that view. Feeney, Peterson, and Noller (1994) review a number of studies in which the predictive power of equity for satisfaction was compared with that of other predictors, such as equality of outcomes, or their absolute level, or the availability of alternatives, and the evidence for equity theory was far from clear-cut. Some studies indicated that equity was unrelated to satisfaction, or that reward level may be a more important determinant of satisfaction than equity (Berg & McQuinn, 1986; Cate et al., 1988). In addition, there may be gender and cultural differences.

In a cross-sectional study of 373 Australian couples who were either pre-parental, rearing children, in the stage of launching their children, or with all offspring independent, Feeney et al. (1994) assessed perceptions of global equity. As shown in Table 19.1, from child-rearing onwards husbands tended to experience over-benefit, wives under-benefit. Over the whole cycle, over-benefited spouses reported more marital satisfaction than under-benefited ones, but equity also made an independent contribution to satisfaction. However the effect varied with the stage of the marriage, equity contributing to satisfaction in the pre-parenthood and child-rearing phases, but not significantly during launching. In the empty-nest phase equity alone predicted satisfaction. Apparently spouses' views of their gains from and equity in the marriage change when the children leave home.

Again, using perceived probability that they would break off their relationship in the near future as a measure of the commitment of dating students, Michaels et al. (1986) found that commitment varied directly with relationship outcomes, with outcomes relative to alternatives, with satisfaction, and with duration, but not with equity. They regarded their findings as consistent with research indicating that an inequitable relationship is maintained as long as the outcomes exceed those expected from the best alternative.

THE INVESTMENT MODEL

Interdependence theory has been extended in the Investment model of Rusbult (1980), Drigotas and Rusbult (1992) and Rusbult and Buunk (1993). This extends the principles of Interdependence to provide a powerful tool. It emphasises, first, the contrast between the satisfaction an indi-

TABLE 19.1
Numbers and Percentages of Husbands and Wives Experiencing Over-benefit,
Under-benefit, or Equity in Marriage

	Global Equity Category					
	Over-benefit		Equity		Under-benefit	
Family Stage	Husbands	Wives	Husbands	Wives	Husbands	Wives
Pre-parental						
N	10	18	20	23	8	12
%	26	34	53	43	21	23
Child-rearing						
N	47	14	27	43	14	26
%	53	17	31	52	16	31
Launching						
N	11	7	12	14	3	13
%	42	21	46	41	12	38
Empty Nest						
N	12	2	7	14	3	6
%	54	9	32	64	14	27

(Feeney et al., 1994. By permission of Cambridge University Press.)

vidual may feel about a relationship and his or her dependence on it. In Interdependence theory terms, individuals evaluate their relationships in terms of their comparison levels (CL), which depend on their experience in previous relationships, observation of peers' relationships, and comparison with the partner's outcomes. Because individuals' expectations differ between the various aspects of a relationship (autonomy, sex, etc.), CL is usefully conceived of as a qualitative expectation. If outcomes are greater than or equal to the CL, the individual feels satisfied. However dependence on the relationship depends on CLalt—the lowest level of outcomes acceptable in the light of other available opportunities. As we have seen in Fig. 19.1, a variety of relations between CL and CLalt are possible.

It is further argued that commitment is a psychological state that represents the experience of dependence and directly influences a wide range of behaviours in the relationship. Commitment is seen as depending in part on satisfaction (which may depend on both own and partner's outcomes), and thus on the individual's CL and, in harmony with equity theory, on comparisons of the input/output ratio with that of the partner. In addition, commitment depends on the quality of alternatives that the individual perceives as being available. Quality of alternatives is assessed in terms of the degree to which the individual sees that important needs could be met outside the relationship but, as we have seen, this would not necessarily involve another relationship. This is in harmony with the fact that divorce becomes more frequent if women's economic, social, and legal power approaches that of men. The perception of alternatives is also influenced by personal characteristics: individuals with high self-esteem, and those with a strong need for autonomy, may be more ready to leave a relationship.

A third contribution to commitment is provided by the resources invested in the relationship. These may include time and emotional energy, mutual friends, shared confidences and the resultant vulnerability, and abandoning an aspect of personal identity as a result of the merging of selves inherent in a close relationship. Lund (1985) pointed out that investments, unlike most costs, involve actions over which the person has control, and that the effect of a behavioural investment is to create a cognitive shift so that expectations about the future of the relationship are strengthened. In a study of 129 students Lund found that investment strengthened commitment (assessed partly in terms of expectations of continuity), and was associated with greater subsequent longevity of the relationship. Social norms, whether or not internalised, and social pressures may also enhance commitment. A fourth contribution to commitment has been identified by Lin and Rusbult (1995)—the extent to which the relationship has become central to the individual's personal identity. Thus commitment results both from forces that make the individual want the relationship more, and forces that make it undesirable to leave (see also Johnson, 1991). The latter may include social pressures.

This model has been applied to a variety of relationships, including a seven-month longitudinal study of dating relationships which had lasted for durations of two to eight weeks, in which the variables mentioned earlier were assessed by questionnaires. The data showed that increases in rewards did indeed lead to greater satisfaction, which was unaffected by the costs in the early stages of the relationship but was diminished by costs later. Commitment again showed the relations predicted by the model—it was related positively to satisfaction and investment, negatively to the availability of alternatives. (Lloyd, Cate, & Henton, 1984, failed to find the last of these relations.) Furthermore, changes over time in commitment differentiated between enduring relationships, abandoned individuals, and those who left relationships voluntarily. Rusbult and Buunk (1993) cite a number of other studies supporting this model and demonstrating its validity for homosexual relationships as well as for heterosexual dating relationships and marriage.

However the link between satisfaction and commitment is not of the same strength in all types of relationship. In a later study of undergraduates in Taiwan and the USA, Lin and Rusbult (1995) found it to be stronger for dating relationships than for cross-sex friendships. They also found that the link between commitment and the availability of alternatives was present in dating relationships but not in cross-sex friendships, though it was present in "best" friendships.

A number of other studies support, with minor variations, these conclusions, though it is important to note that the criteria for commitment differed between studies. For instance Sabatelli and Cecil-Pigo (1985) found that commitment (measured by six items, concerned with both the degree of cohesion felt in the relationship and the extent to which other relationships were monitored) was related to high satisfaction, the experience of equity and also the presence of barriers to dissolution.

GENERAL ISSUES

Since the present aim is not so much to analyse as to provide an overview, these brief summaries will perhaps suffice to indicate the general nature of the principal exchange theories. While these theories provide a useful perspective on relationships, some of the predictor variables exert weak influences, and there are considerable gender differences in their effectiveness (Heaton & Albrecht, 1991). On the other hand the Investment model combines new insights into the dynamics of relationships with old ones, and has received a not inconsiderable amount of empirical support. We may now discuss some general issues relevant in greater or lesser degree to all exchange theorists.

The Problem of Measurement

The problem of measuring the rewards exchanged and costs incurred in real-life situations is crucial for exchange theorists. If they are to proceed beyond a qualitative approach to real-life problems, they must find a way of assessing profits and costs. The matrices used by Thibaut and Kelley and other theorists may be filled with numbers that are useful for illustrating theoretical points, but the actual measurement of values in real life, and especially in real-life close relationships, presents a problem. For some types of relationship, such as that between employer and employee, it is possible to assess the several rewards and costs involved (wages, hours of work, fringe benefits) against a common yardstick. It was for just this reason that exchange theorists first concentrated on monetary exchanges. But if one is dealing with personal relationships where social approval, understanding, or intangible services are at issue, how can one make measurements adequate for scientific enquiry? The problem is exacerbated by the facts that the value of a particular reward differs between the sexes and between individuals, and changes with time for any one—not just as a consequence of satiation, but through changing contextual factors.

In addition, an emphasis on rewards minus costs implies equivalence between an activity bringing high rewards with high costs and another bringing the same profit with less effort. In practice high rewards and high costs seem likely to be associated with conflict, in a psychological sense, and thus to require qualitatively different treatment.

But there is yet hope for limited progress if we do not aim too high. For many purposes an equal interval scale is not necessary—we need only one in which the rewards and costs can be ordered in degree of effectiveness. And it is the meaning of the rewards and costs to the individuals concerned that matters, not their extent as measured on some absolute scale common to all individuals. The value of social approval, or of gestures of affection and love, depends on their being seen as genuine and not too freely given, on the relationship context, and on the personalities of those involved. Although this makes rewards and costs more intangible, at least one can ask people what they feel about their outcomes and inputs, what rewards they feel they have received and provided (see e.g. Walster et al., 1978a). And it is what they feel that is likely to influence the future course of the relationship.

This, of course, raises further problems: biases and defence mechanisms may affect a respondent's assessments of her relationships. Here one could take the argument one stage further and say that it is not what individuals feel about their outcomes but what they think that they feel—though one must still worry whether what they say is what they think they feel. Another difficulty is that a respondent's response to a question about outcomes is not independent of her response to other questions about the relationship—questions about satisfaction or commitment, for instance. This, however, is a problem common to many studies of relationships.

Overall, then, the problem of measurement, though formidable, can be seen as merely one making difficulties for the exchange theorists, and by no means insuperable.

However here another problem arises. In the study of Van Yperen and Buunk (1990), cited on p.347, two measures of equity were used. One was a global measure, in which partners were simply asked for a subjective overall rating of the fairness of the relationship on a scale from extreme under-benefit to extreme over-benefit. The other involved an apparently more sophisticated approach in which the participants made independent ratings on 24 separate relationship elements of their own and their spouses' contributions and outcomes. The data for each exchange element was weighted by its subjective importance to the respondent, and summed across the elements. The global measure supported the predictions of equity theory, at least for wives. Equitably treated wives were more satisfied than inequitably treated ones though, amongst those who were inequitably treated, over-benefited wives were happier than under-benefited ones. However the more detailed measure failed to give support for equity theory's predictions. Indeed the global and the more detailed measures were negatively correlated. Feeney et al. (1994) suggest that a global assessment tends to be based on a few key socio-emotional elements, giving scope for one or a few elements idiosyncratically to outweigh others, and thus provides a more valid measure of perceived equity.

Justice, or What is Fair?

Criteria of Fairness.   How can one assess what is fair? As we have seen, in answer to this question Homans invoked the "law of distributive justice", and Thibaut and Kelley used a comparison level concerned with satisfaction with the relationship. Since for Homans the costs of engaging in an interaction include the rewards forgone by not engaging in other possible interactions, his proposal and that of Thibaut and Kelley are in fact compatible (Homans, 1974). In neither case, of course, is there any necessary implication either of conscious decision, or that justice implies equality. But some difficulties arise. For one thing, the participants are likely to have different values and different standards about what is fair. In so far as "fairness" requires that A should see not only his own outcomes as fair, but also those of B, it involves considerations of interpersonal perception (Chapter 13). Another point, recognised by Homans, stems from the fact that relationships are extended in time. What is considered "fair" nearly always involves expectations about the future, so that assessment at any one time is bound to involve a degree of arbitrariness.

This problem of uncertainty was emphasised early on by Blau (1964). He took the view that social exchange differs from economic exchange in that it does not necessarily involve attempts to obtain the greatest material profits and in that it entails unspecified obligations. When an individual buys a house, a precise sum of money is paid. But if A does a kind turn for B he creates a diffuse obligation to reciprocate without specifying precisely what would be a fair exchange. In Blau's view (p.95) this is not a mere methodological problem, but a substantive fact: "It is not just the social scientist who cannot exactly measure how much approval a given helpful action is worth; the actors themselves cannot precisely specify the worth of approval or of help in the absence of a money price."

Nor, often, can they bargain about the returns to be made—a norm of trust is essential. The fact that we can and do specify how much gratitude we expect for a service rendered, albeit only in round terms, is not the issue here: the point is that such thanks can be seen as acknowledgement of unspecified future indebtedness. Indeed "intrinsic" rewards can often not be separated from the extrinsic ones: one may gain friendliness from an interaction as well as more tangible rewards. In any case love, respect, and many other social rewards are spontaneous expressions of feelings, and cannot (in Blau's view, though see Chapter 20) be said in any meaningful way to be used in bargaining. Furthermore, "fairness" does not necessarily operate at the conscious level.

Given that some standard operates, other workers have distinguished a variety of criteria for "fairness" (Clark & Reis, 1988). Lerner (1974) emphasises that, in any one society, a number of different rules of justice may develop. These are applicable in different situations. Sometimes notions of "equality"or parity prevail—everyone deserves equal outcomes. In others equality is subordinated to "equity"—each person's outcomes should be related to what he has put in—either to his costs in the endeavour in question, or to his investments, where the latter includes also the skills, expertise, social status etc. with which he is equipped. Disproportionate outcomes may be aversive to both parties, as when only one receives a high level of rewards in relation to costs (e.g. Fig. 19.4). Several studies have been concerned with the factors that determine whether equality or equity will prevail. There is some evidence that equality is paramount amongst younger children and that the importance of equity increases with age (e.g. Leventhal & Lane, 1970). Lerner (1974) suggests that equality is more likely amongst close friends and Pataki, Shapiro, and Clark (1994) report that elementary schoolchildren who are friends tend to share earned rewards equally, while acquaintances use an equity norm.

A third form of justice, "social justice", encompasses the view that each deserves outcomes in proportion to his needs. Lerner suggests that this is most likely to apply when the subject identifies in some way with the needy other. This happens especially inside families. Outside the family it is perhaps most often found when people have been hit by unavoidable catastrophe ("It could have been me"), and when they are seen to have deserved better than they have got. In the latter case, considerations of equity also enter. It would seem that, almost by definition, social justice is most likely to apply in the context of complementary interactions.

Another form of justice discussed by Lerner (1974) is the justice of "legitimate competition". This seems most likely to apply when resources are limited and A has negative or neutral feelings for B, and is thus less relevant to close relationships.

In the context of the present discussion, it will be apparent that the special importance of Lerner's approach lies in his emphasis on the way in which participants' definitions of the nature of the relationship may determine what is considered fair. For this purpose, he suggests, relationships can be seen as varying along two dimensions. The first concerns their closeness—do the partners identify and empathise with each other, or do

TABLE 19.2
Forms of Justice in Different Types of Relationship

| | | Perceived Relationship | | |
		Identity	Unit	Non-unit
Object of relationship	Person	Perception of O as self	Perception of similarity with or belonging with O	Perception of contrasting interests
		Needs (Social Justice)	Parity (Equality)	Law, Darwinian justice
	Incumbent	Perception of self in O's circumstances	Perception of equivalence with O	Scarce resources, with equally legitimate claims
		Entitlement, Social obligations	Equity	Justified self-interest

(Modified from Lerner et al., 1976.)

they merely have a less close bond involving similar circumstances or some degree of promotive interdependence, or are they in an antagonistic or competitive relationship? The second dimension concerns whether the other person is seen as an individual person or as the incumbent of a position in society. Table 19.2 (Lerner, Miller, & Holmes, 1976) shows the types of justice associated with relationships of each of the possible six types. A positive personal bond favours justice determined either by needs or by considerations of equality according to the closeness of the relationship, while a role relationship favours some form of equity (see also Walster et al., 1978a).

These distinctions can be compared with that between what Mills and Clark (1982) call "exchange relationships",[2] as exemplified by relationships between acquaintances and business contacts, and communal relationships, such as family relationships, friends, and lovers. In the former there is no obligation to look after the other's welfare: benefits are given in reciprocation for benefits received in the past or anticipated in the future. In

[2] Quotation marks are used here because many would see both "exchange" and communal relationships as involving exchange, with the norm governing exchange of benefits being equity in one case and need in the other. (See Chapter 20.)

communal relationships there is an obligation or desire to look after the other's welfare. Accordingly, participants in "exchange relationships" keep track of benefits they dispose, while in communal relationships record-keeping is unnecessary because benefits are given more according to need (cf. Table 19.2). In an experiment involving a bogus stranger presented as being either in a potentially communal or potentially "exchange" relation, Clark, Mills, and Powell (1986) verified that subjects were more likely to keep track of the other's needs if they desired communal rather than "exchange" relationships. Similarly Clark and Waddell (1985) found that failure to offer repayment for a benefit was perceived as exploitative and decreased attraction for the partner in the context of a presumed "exchange" relationship, but not in a communal one (see also Deutsch, 1985).

That raises the question of what it is about communal relationships that mitigates the need for reciprocity. Several factors contribute to the acceptance of imbalance (O'Connell, 1984):

(a) *Kinship and Friendship Licence.* It may simply be accepted that reciprocity is inappropriate in such relationships. There are two ways of accounting for this. First, it may be that we are predisposed biologically to act in this way—to exchange with relatives because thereby we are helping the propagation of genes similar to our own (Hamilton, 1984), and with friends because we expect reciprocation at a later date. The second explanation is that these are long-term relationships, and so participants can delay reciprocation into the indefinite future.

(b) *The Need Norm.* It is assumed that one helps those in need. There may be an assumption that help given to one in need will be returned if the helper later finds him or herself in need.

(c) *The Norm of Non-instrumental Concern.* The assumption that altruistic help is part of relationships of certain kinds. This is in harmony with Kelley's (1979) view of interdependence between the partners in a relationship: the matrix may be transformed so that one partner may feel rewarded if the other is.

It will be apparent that these factors overlap, but involve to different extents an assumption of eventual reciprocation. Another view, involving the suggestion that communal relationships do involve the exchange of resources, though those resources are intangible and have special properties, is discussed in Chapter 20.

However fairness does not operate in all personal relationships (see earlier). Cate et al. (1988) found not only that rewards were more important than fairness in predicting satisfaction in dating relationships, but also that over time fairness declined and rewards improved as predictors of involvement (assessed by uniqueness, disclosure, outcome correspondence, and emotional caring).

Relationship Norms of Fairness.   It is necessary that a relationship should be regulated by "norms"—that is, behavioural rules that are more or less accepted by both members. As we have seen, norms may be shared with other members of the society, but they may also be more or less specific to the dyad. They may regulate not only what the participants do and how they do it, who takes which decision and how conflicts are resolved, but also what are to be counted as rewards and costs, what values are to be placed on various types of behaviour, and what ratio of rewards to costs is to be accepted by each partner. If the norms are agreed upon and adhered to, conflict may be reduced. But the participants may not agree. While parents may allocate resources amongst their children according to need, the children may be quick to spot departures from equality in their outcomes. A teenage daughter seeking an advance on her allowance from her father might stress her needs, thereby favouring social justice, whilst the parent might ask what she had contributed to the relationship, favouring equity. Or different rules may be followed in different types of interaction within the relationship. Husband and wife might operate on equality over food delicacies, but justice over the use of the joint resources for clothes.

Again, norms of fairness may differ with the context: people expect to profit more in the workplace than in their personal relationships (cf. exchange vs. communal relationships, discussed earlier). Major, Bylsma, and Cozzarelli (1989) found that both sexes were more likely to prefer their outcomes to exceed their inputs in work domains than in personal relationships. In a communal relationship, a favour performed for a friend is perceived as more valuable than a similar favour performed by a friend. This may not matter between friends, as full reciprocity is not expected in communal relationships (Beach & Carter, 1976). However in unfriendly exchanges, resources are also perceived as more valuable when lost than when received, so that equity may be difficult to achieve (Foa, Megonigal, & Greipp, 1976; see also Tornblom, 1992).

But where norms of fairness exist and are recognised, where do they come from? A dominant view has been that they are the product of power-seeking by individuals, though this may be hidden behind religious precepts or cultural norms. Walster et al. (1978a) argue that individuals will try to maximise their own outcomes by persuading others to accept norms of fairness that will be beneficial to the persuader. Thus in a work group the most productive worker would argue for pay in proportion to productivity, older workers would argue for years of service, junior workers for equality, and workers with large families for need to be the criterion. Those who are most powerful are likely to decide what is fair to their own advantage, unless the social group imposes criteria of fairness that further its (collec-tive) goals (Austin & Hatfield, 1980). Lerner (1981, p.21), however, believes that the self-seeking basis of justice has been over-emphasised: "Rather than being an instrumental device to facilitate the acquisition of desired resources, justice appears as the guide for assessing what 'resources' are available." Instead of assuming that standards of justice emerge from the power motivation of individuals, Lerner proposed that they develop in the child as an interactive effect of cognitive structure and environmental con-tingencies (see later).

Some Variations in Norms of Fairness.   First, we must note that the norm of reciprocity is much less prominent in some societies than in others. For example, Indian subjects allocated money to hypothetical recipients more on the basis of need and less on the basis of merit or equality than did American respondents (Murphy-Berman & Berman et al., 1984).

Of particular interest is the influence of gender on exchange. As we have seen, Hatfield et al. (1985) found that, while men were more distressed by being under-benefited than by being over-benefited, women were more distressed by being over-benefited. And women perceive their relationships with other women to be more equitable than men perceive their relation-ships with other men (Berg, 1984). Of course this does not mean that their relationships are more equitable in an absolute sense: the perception of equity depends on expectations, and women may expect less.

A number of studies of exchange in the workplace show that women do in fact, at least in that situation, consistently pay themselves less than men do when allocating rewards between themselves and others. Several differ-ent explanations have been offered (Major, McFarlin, & Gagnon, 1984):

1. Women have lower expectations because of their history of wage discrimination.
2. Women tend to compare their outcomes with those of other women, rather than with men's. Because women tend to be paid less, they evaluate their outcomes against a lower reference group standard. (In some contexts, this may be less plausible than it was in the early 1980s.)
3. Women may value money less, and relationships more, than men do.
4. Women devalue their inputs relative to men, and hence under-reward their work.
5. Women see less of a connection between work and pay than men do, as the result of sex-role socialisation.

Probably, multiple factors are at work. In their own study Major et al. confirmed that women perceived less money as fair pay for their work than men, despite similar perceived work inputs; and women worked harder and longer, and more efficiently than men, for a given amount of pay. The data indicated that comparisons with the rewards currently obtained by others contributed to these differences. Women worked longer for a fixed amount of pay when their pay was monitored than did men, suggesting that impression management is more important for women than for men. No support was found in this study for the views that an individual's past pay history or women's lower evaluation of money played a role. There was some evidence that they undervalued their work. But Major et al. placed most weight on the view that people determine whether an outcome is fair primarily by comparison with the outcomes of "generalised others", thought to be typical of a class of individuals similar to the self, if salient others were not available for comparison.

The way in which rewards are apportioned in task situations may also depend on assessment of the partner's generosity, and on the participants' self-esteem. Brockner et al. (1987) arranged that subjects should take part in a creativity task with a bogus partner. Rewards were allocated alternately by the subject and the bogus partner, who might behave in an equitable, egalitarian, selfish, or generous manner. Subjects were sometimes led to believe that they had performed better, and sometimes less well, than the bogus partner. Thus a subject's cues for allocating resources came from her performance relative to her partners' and the partners' behaviour in allocating rewards to her. The participants rewarded themselves better when they thought they had performed better than the bogus partner, and vice versa. However they also tended to match the allocations made by the partner, making the largest allocations to themselves when they believed the partner to be selfish, and so on. These effects were moderated by their self-esteem. Those with low self-esteem were more likely to imitate the partner's behaviour, while those who thought well of themselves were more likely to allocate rewards on the basis of presumed performance.

Other aspects of the personality also affect what is seen as an appropriate balance. We have seen that exchange in close relationships must be seen in temporal perspective: benefits bestowed now repay benefits received in the past or increase credit for benefits to be received in the future. Thus at any one time there is likely to be an imbalance, and individuals differ in the sort of imbalance they prefer. Two extreme types have been recognised. Some follow a "creditor ideology", returning greater benefits than had previously been received. Such individuals recognise that they have a power advantage over those who are indebted to them, and may be disinclined to yield that advantage unless their need for assistance is great. The other extreme involves "reciprocation wariness". Individuals behaving in this way suspect the motives underlying the other's help, and exercise caution in returning help because they are afraid that they will be taken advantage of (Eisenberger, Cotterell, & Marvel, 1987).

We have seen that the importance of equity in marital relationships changes with the stage of the relationships (p.349). The criteria of fairness may also change with the stage of other relationships. In a study of college room-mates Berg (1984) found that at first balancing the total amount of rewards received mattered, but later meeting each other's needs became more important.

People tend to judge fairness either by comparison with the behaviour and outcomes of those about them, or by internal standards derived from past experience. Messé and Watts (1983) found, in an experimental study, that the relative importance of these two sources of standards depended on the conditions in which the judgements were made. Social comparison operated to make subjects feel they were treated unfairly by being paid a low amount, but did not operate appreciably if they received what they considered to be fair.

None of this should be taken as implying that fairness of one sort or another is bound to prevail. As we have seen, because the participants strive to maintain a balance between their inputs and outputs there will be a tendency towards fairness, often described as a "strain towards reciprocity". But because each also strives to accumulate a balance in his favour there will also be a "strain towards imbalance" (Blau, 1964; Cate et al., 1988). In Blau's view this may be true even of the relationship between two lovers, for each may, for example, act in order to obtain credit or to avoid debt in the future. But the tendency of each participant to maximise his gains must be weighed against a need to help the other involved in the relation (Thibaut & Kelley, 1959). A detailed example, concerning the relations between a trawler skipper and his crew, has been worked out by Barth (1966).

Why Does Fairness Matter?

We must ask not only what is considered to be fair, but also why fairness matters. Some tendency towards reciprocity may come from each partner's tendency to reward the other in order that the partner should provide rewards in his turn. But beyond that, why should the participants in a relationship think that fairness matters?

A number of answers are possible, but most involve the view that individuals expect to be rewarded for being fair. On this view the rewards stemming from an exchange that is seen to be fair are greater than those inherent in the exchange itself, for there is also a reward in being fair. The latter can be taken as an assumption, or derived from more basic postulates. Thus if failure to achieve equity brings anger or distress (see p.345), and if it is rewarding to avoid these states, fairness will be sought in addition to the reward itself. Equity theory suggests that society offers rewards for fairness. If these are internalised in the course of socialisation, fair exchange may bring high self-regard.

Of special interest here is Lerner's (1974) suggestion that belief in a just world is necessary for adequate social functioning. If we all believed that rewards and punishments arrived randomly, we should be incapable of effective action. Lerner thus pictures individuals as making, in the course of socialisation, "Personal Contracts" with themselves to give up immediate rewards in their own longer-term interests (Lerner, 1974; 1981). Present-day costs are seen in the first instance as an effective route to future rewards. But individuals are also seen as recognising a degree of equivalence between themselves and others. That being so, if an individual perceives that others do not get what they deserve, he may regard this as a threat to his getting what he sees as his own just desserts. He is therefore motivated to behave fairly to others as a means of maintaining the premises on which his own personal contract was founded. On this view, then, exchange of resources with another is seen not so much as important in its own right, but as a means of maintaining a personal contract that is essentially independent of the current relationship. Evidence in favour of the view that considerations of reciprocity are more to do with a moral obligation to avoid being over-benefited than with self-interested concerns for reciprocity is discussed by Uehara (1995).

Finally for a number of reasons, most of which have been mentioned already, the continuation of a relationship does not necessarily depend on each partner believing that the other is providing him with as much as he deserves (Murstein, 1977; Thibaut and Kelley, 1959). For one thing, neither member is likely to dissolve the relationship unless a more viable alternative exists. For another, a relationship may bring rewards, or its dissolution costs, from sources other than the partner: an employee may continue to work for a disliked boss because he likes his workmates. Third, rewards may be accepted, although of small immediate value, as symbols of future rewards. Fourth, members of the couple may be governed by attempts to emulate an internal model, or by prior commitment (see Chapter 15). There is thus need to specify not only where the various possible types of justice are involved, but also where justice is of secondary importance.

Nature of Distress

Whilst equity theorists have postulated that inequity results in anger or "distress", little effort has been put into the study of this supposed state. Adams and Freedman (1976) point out that an attack on its nature, an investigation of the extent to which it should be pictured as varying along one, two (guilt and anger), or more dimensions, the nature of its determinants, and the effectiveness of various measures in reducing it, would be important avenues for extending existing knowledge. Furthermore how individuals perceive injustice has many determinants—some may see it as their own fault, others as chance, others as deliberate malpractice by the partner (Utne & Kidd, 1980; see also attribution, Chapter 18).

Interpersonal Perception and Exchange Theories

As we have seen, equity theorists forge links with sociology by their treatment of fairness as a socially induced norm and with balance theory by suggesting that injustice can be either rectified in fact, or misperceived. But there are also links with studies of interpersonal perception. If a relationship is to continue, each participant must direct his behaviour in such a manner that the other sees himself to be fairly treated. If A is to achieve this, A's view of B's view of the relationship must resemble B's view of the relationship. And beyond this, at least in personal relationships, B's behaviour, for instance his tendency to leave the relationship, will be affected by his assessment of A's intentions. If B perceives himself to be unfairly treated, but believes that A was genuinely misled in believing that B felt himself to be fairly treated even though B did not, he will be much less likely to leave or seek reprisals than if he believes that A was deliberately profiting at his expense.

Interdependence and the Content of Interactions

In a study of dating student couples, Surra and Longstreth (1990) examined the extent to which each partner's preference for various activities, and the similarity in their preferences (weighted by the liking for the activity in question) would predict participation. In general, they found that the success of the relationship depended on how far individual preferences were satisfied through joint activities. Similarity in activity preferences and relatively few conflicts were associated with happier, enduring relationships. However preferences for activities did not affect satisfaction directly, but through their impact on joint behaviours and on conflict. Partners did not restrict their activities to domains that were free of conflict, and increased participation in some activities was associated with increased conflict, and thus with reduced satisfaction with the relationship. In general, the data were in harmony with previous studies in indicating that activities and similarity in activity preference was more important for men than for women (p.414), that men were more responsive to given outcomes than women and that women's experiences predicted the breakdown of the relationship more than did men's (p.506). Although activity participation is important to women, their evaluations of their relationship are more broadly based, depending also on judgements of how cooperative, moral, and compatible the partnership is.

However the nature of interdependence varied with the particular activities that were the focus of attention. Surra and Longstreth (1990) discuss three categories:

1. Some activities lend themselves to turn-taking, so that partners can coordinate with each other to receive their best outcomes at different times. Each partner may engage in activities selected by the other, with reciprocity later. Leisure activities, because of their voluntary nature, are often used in this way.

2. Some activities involve unresolved competition. Thus the men in the Surra and Longstreth study preferred sexual activities and sport more than did the women, while women had stronger preferences for activities involved in relationship maintenance. For the partner who liked such an activity most, the preference of the other predicted participation. Participation in such activities may be associated both with more conflict and with better relationship outcomes. Surra and Longstreth note that unresolved competition may be characteristic of activities essential to relationships. Relationship maintenance and sex must be performed with a partner (preferably *the* partner), and turn-taking is not possible. They are also activities with strong gender-related preferences, yet partners must tolerate unresolved competition because they are essential to the relationship.

3. Some activities are associated with cooperation, like food-related activities and errands. Here the outcomes are similar for both partners, and this facilitates cooperation.

Altruism and Intimate Relationships

One of the most difficult issues that the exchange theorist has to face is the fact that social exchange sometimes is, or at least has the appearance of being, altruistic. Individuals often provide others with rewards with no expectation that those others will reciprocate. This principle is exemplified equally by the uncountable little acts of kindness performed daily to strangers as by the dramatic acts of heroism in war or peace-time rescues. Friends and family members do not always seek to maximise their gains from a narrowly egocentric point of view (Levinger and Snoek, 1972). Experimental studies on the readiness of strangers to provide help ranging from the gift of a penny to a bone marrow transplant have been reviewed by Berkowitz (1972). As he stressed (p.67), "Many persons do help their fellow men even when there are no obvious material benefits to be gained from this action." While the possibility that hope of some future reward operated cannot be ruled out from field data, it is minimised in many laboratory studies (Berkowitz, 1972; Staub, 1974). Whether genuine altruism ever occurs is a question that requires further research (Fultz &

Cialdini, 1991). One can erect a definition of altruism such that any given action can be placed on an altruistic–non-altruistic continuum (Swap, 1991), but what probably matters most is that we have the *idea* of altruism and can use it in ordering our actions and organising society (Heal, 1991).[3]

It will be apparent that exchange theories can cope with supposed altruism. Homans (1961, 1976) argued that the profit gained depends on what people value. They may value the success of their children or their view of themselves as self-sacrificing humanitarians (see Kelley, 1979, cited p.343). Lerner's "personal contract" is clearly also relevant here.

A common approach is to suppose that people follow rules internalised in childhood in order to avoid guilt feelings or social disapproval. Thus such behaviour is seen as controlled by internal factors rather than by the hope of external rewards. But here two difficulties arise. First, whilst the concept of "self-reinforcement" can be treated in a hard-headed fashion (e.g. Bandura, 1977), it is also easy to use it loosely. Great care is needed to ensure that "empathic reinforcement" does not become an explanation that will explain anything. Second, the importance of internalised influences is not static and constant, but depends on a host of situational determinants. According to Berkowitz (1972, p.106), these may affect "the extent to which the individual is aware that someone is dependent upon him, recalls the pertinent social ideals, believes that this dependency is proper or improper, and is willing to accept the psychological costs of being helpful." The variability in the effectiveness of supposed internalised moral standards is clearly liable to detract greatly from their explanatory value (see also Asch, 1959).

The approach of Kelley and Thibaut (1978; Kelley, 1979) meets many of these difficulties. As we have seen, they focus on the interdependence of the two partners over time, rather than short-term exchange. Each partner responds to a pattern of outcomes, and to his predictions about the nature of that pattern in the future: these predictions depend in part on attributions he makes about his partner. Furthermore each individual is responsive not only to his own outcomes, but also to the other's. This is a function not only of the need to keep the partner involved, but of the acquisition of potential rewards at the dispositional level—each partner may seek to see him or herself as a considerate, tender, forgiving etc., lover, showing qualities he has been socialised to value, as well as obtaining immediate rewards.

---

[3] Sociobiologists would not expect family members always to behave selfishly with each other. Their explanation of altruism would concern the manner in which the consequences of altruistic behaviour contributed to inclusive (genetic) fitness. But in the present context we are concerned with its proximate causes.

Another approach is to argue that altruistic behaviour in close relationships is not really incompatible with equity theory predictions because it often leads to hostility, humiliation, and alienation (Walster et al., 1978a; see also discussion of social support, pp.143–144). Whilst the evidence that both benefactor and recipient may feel ill at ease in relationships involving altruism is considerable, it is of course impossible for the exchange theorists to prove that ambivalence is always present, or for their opponents to prove that it is ever absent.

EXCHANGE THEORIES OF THE DYAD AND THE SURROUNDING GROUP

It is important to stress here again some of the issues mentioned in Chapter 17. Whilst in this chapter exchange theories have been discussed in relation to the dyad, exchange theorists have pointed out that equity may be achieved in a transrelational manner—if A finds his relationship with B to be inequitable, and cannot restore balance in that relationship, he may compare himself also with another individual C, or with other people in general, so overall he feels justice to have been done (W. Austin, cited Walster et al., 1978a).

Beyond that, Blau (1964) has emphasised that the dynamics of the dyad can often not be understood without reference to the group. This is not merely that the investments and needs of each individual may be affected by position in the group, nor that each member of the dyad has other relationships, interactions, or potential interactions which may affect his dependency on the other. Intra-dyadic interactions may be affected also by the manner in which one member sees the other interacting with other individuals. Extra-dyadic interactions by the partner may elicit admiration, disgust, or jealousy. Furthermore we have seen that intra-dyadic exchange may depend on group norms. As an obvious example, norms may prevent competitive interactions between the workers in a group. More importantly, norms of obligation to members of the group may permit unbalanced exchanges within dyads: an individual may give more than he gains in one relationship, but be compensated in other relationships or through membership of the group as a whole (Blau 1964; Thibaut & Kelley, 1959).

CONCLUSION

Are exchange theories to be seen as potentially ubiquitously applicable, unifying all aspects of social interactions and relationships? Or is their scope more limited? In the first place, they do not pretend to explain the ups and downs of relationships. Fairness is what is fair over a span of time: all exchange theories recognise that exchange cannot be fair all, or even much, of the time. Blau's view was that attempts to apply them too widely would only detract from their value. Men may be physically coerced to act, they may act for fear of supernatural beings or of other men, for conscience, or perhaps altruistically: in these areas the concept of social exchange is not useful. Perhaps it is valuable only *between* the area of economic transaction where profit and loss can be calculated precisely and these other areas where it is not applicable. Berkowitz's (e.g. Berkowitz & Friedman, 1967) postulation of a norm of social responsibility also places limits on the value of a simple-minded exchange theory approach (see also Hoffman, 1975; Schwartz, 1977). However Kelley's emphasis that it can be rewarding to behave in ways that confirm the characteristics we attribute to ourselves goes a long way to meet the difficulties: rewards are obtainable at the dispositional as well as the direct level. And even those who emphasise the difficulties of applying exchange theories in a quantitative manner must agree that they can provide an important and useful framework for studying relationships, though they may need to be buttressed by considerations of criteria of fairness, changing social conventions, and individual idiosyncrasies. Further issues are raised by considerations of the differing properties of the resources exchanged: this is discussed in the next chapter.

SUMMARY

1. Exchange theories share the assumption that social behaviour is in large measure determined by considerations of rewards and costs.
2. In Homans's theory, individuals expect to receive rewards commensurate with their costs and a profit in line with the investments they bring to the situation.
3 Thibaut and Kelley emphasised the interdependence of the partners. They proposed that partners assess their outcomes both in terms of what they feel that they deserve and in terms of the outcomes available elsewhere. However individuals do not always act so as to maximise their own outcomes, but take account also of their partners'. They may also experience positive outcomes from their perception of their own behaviour as generous, etc.
4. Equity theorists suggest that individuals avoid both being under-benefited and being over-benefited, and feel discomfort if either is the case. Some but not all studies support the view that over-benefited individuals feel discomfort.
5. The investment model emphasises the distinction between satisfaction with and dependence on a relationship. Satisfaction depends on comparison with previous relationships, with observations of other's relationships, and with the partner's outcomes. Commitment depends

in part on satisfaction, on the quality of available alternatives, on the resources invested in the relationship, and on the extent to which the relationship is central to the individual's identity.

6. Some potential obstacles to the application of exchange theories include difficulties of measurement, and the differing standards of what is fair.

20 The Categorisation of Resources

Any attempt to understand the role of learning in interpersonal relationships must sooner or later employ a concept of reward, reinforcement, or incentive. The exchange theories discussed in the last chapter inherited much of their structure from Hullian or from operant theory. But the concept of reinforcement, although used in a hard-headed way in laboratory experiments is, as we have seen, liable to be somewhat diluted in studies of complex human actions. In this chapter we shall consider how some of the difficulties that arise might be met.

REINFORCEMENT IN LEARNING THEORY AND REAL-LIFE REWARDS

Traditional theories of learning were based on experiments in which food was used as a reinforcer for hungry animals. Many laboratory experiments on learning used animals whose body weight had been lowered by starvation and were therefore highly motivated. Furthermore we know that, within limits, the effectiveness of food as a reinforcer varies with the period for which the animal has been deprived of food. It is therefore possible to control motivation rather precisely.

But food is relatively rare as a reinforcer in interpersonal relationships. Even in the early mother–infant relationship, where food was earlier thought to be critical, it is now apparent that its importance was overrated (Bowlby, 1969/82; Harlow and Zimmermann, 1959). And whilst there are still dreadful exceptions in some classes and some parts of the world, food as such is often important in adult relationships in most of the Western world as a symbol as well as for its need-reducing properties. The rewards important in interpersonal relationships are in fact diverse, ranging from tangible goods and services, through items primarily of symbolic value like money, to the expression of intangible emotions such as love.

We must therefore ask whether the properties of these varied types of social rewards are necessarily similar to those of food. Are exchange theorists misled in attempting to apply a theory drawn from studies of the effects of food on hungry animals to the subtleties of interpersonal relationships? In particular, are we dealing with individuals as highly motivated for, say, social approval as a pigeon starved to 80% of its body weight is motivated to feed? And can we assume that changes of the sort that occur in the effectiveness of food with deprivation occur also with other rewards?

We may consider these questions in the context of work on "social approval", a category of reward frequently used in studies of social interaction and interpersonal attraction. That social approval is a potent reward was demonstrated by Verplanck (1955). Individuals, who did not know they were being used as subjects for an experiment, increased the rate at which they made statements of opinion when these were followed by social approval from the experimenter, and decreased the rate when approval was withheld.

But this does not mean that all subjects need social approval in the way that a partially starved pigeon needs food. In fact people differ markedly in their long-term need for social approval. This need has been measured in a variety of ways, one of the more usual being a questionnaire consisting of items which could be answered in a more or less socially desirable way. Individuals who give socially desirable answers are supposed to have a high need for social approval. Such individuals did indeed respond to approval from the experimenter—for instance by increasing the frequency of plural nouns used when these were followed by an approving "mm-hmm" and a nod of the head from the experimenter. Subjects who scored lower on the questionnaire showed only a transient increase in the use of plural nouns (Crowne & Marlowe, 1964). In other words, social approval resembles food as a reinforcer in that it is more effective with subjects having a high need for it (assessed by an independent means), but not all subjects do have a sufficiently high need for social approval of this type to maintain its effectiveness.

Turning to the question of whether short-term deprivation influences the effectiveness of social approval in the same way that hunger influences that of food, some evidence suggesting that preceding satiation or deprivation can influence its effectiveness as a reinforcer has been brought forward. For example Gewirtz and Baer (1958) claimed that approval was a more effective reinforcer for children who had received no social approval during a pre-experimental period of over 20 minutes than for children who had (see also Landau & Gewirtz, 1967). However other studies show that the effectiveness of social reinforcers depends much more on longer-term needs for social rewards than on the immediately preceding conditions of satiation or deprivation (e.g. Berg, Balla, & Zigler, 1976; Zigler, 1964). Furthermore, even if deprivation/satiation of social rewards does influence their effectiveness for children, it may not do so in adults. Walters and Parke (1964) found that social isolation had a greater effect on the responsiveness of children to social reward than on that of adolescents (see Mettee & Aronson, 1974, for a further review). Intuition strongly suggests that the independent variables influencing the effectiveness of social rewards are very different from those operating in the case of food. For instance the distrust engendered by excessive social approval is surely different from the disgust produced by excessive food.

The power of the reinforcement concept in the laboratory also depends in part on our ability to predict which events will and will not have reinforcing properties. In non-social learning situations such predictions are often possible, but it has now been recognised that a given event may be reinforcing for one response but not for another, and that the effectiveness of potential reinforcers is influenced by a variety of constraints (Hinde & Stevenson-Hinde, 1973; Seligman & Hager, 1972). The effectiveness of "social approval", for example, varies enormously with the social situation, and depends on its being accepted as genuine, and on the frequency with which the individual in question is known to bestow his approval (Blau, 1964; Stroebe, 1977). In some contexts it may even be aversive.

But if we cannot predict in advance which events will have reinforcing properties and which will not, explanations of behaviour based on the reinforcement concept will be circular. There is a danger that rewards will be postulated *ad infinitum* and thus explain anything. The situation here is just that which bogged down instinct theory 50 years ago: instincts were postulated to explain each type of behaviour observed, and therefore explained nothing (see e.g. Blau, 1964). It is of course here that a proper integration of personality theory with studies of interpersonal relationships is especially needed: specification of what is reinforcing in what circumstances demands understanding of the differences between individuals.

THE CLASSIFICATION OF RESOURCES

One path towards ameliorating these difficulties might be to categorise the rewards under study. Perhaps, if we could divide the rewards into classes, we should be able to distinguish between the properties of the members of those classes. This might even help us to predict when particular events would or would not be rewarding by reference to the class to which they belong. It is in fact the case that different exchange theorists have concentrated on exchanges involving different types of resource (La Gaipa, 1977). Homans (1974) and Blau (1964) were concerned largely with exchanges involving social approval and information relating to skills and expertise, Altman and Taylor (1973) with information of a more personal kind, Adams (1965) with pay or money. La Gaipa (1977) points out that this has affected their theorising, in that different mediating variables tend to be postulated to explain reciprocity—exchanges of goods and services are said to be based on "obligation", but exchanges of "information" on "liking".

Homans did in fact recognise differences between physical goods and other social rewards, but saw this as no obstacle to theory building. Blau went a good deal further: his classification of social rewards called attention to a shortcoming in the label "exchange theory", namely that social rewards have many properties different from those of economic ones. Blau also pointed out that, while some rewards are clearly detachable from their source, this also is a matter of degree. Advice, assistance, and compliance are valuable both in their own right and also because they come from a particular other. This is yet another reason for distinguishing social from economic exchange—"The impersonal economic market is designed to strip specific commodities of these entangling alliances with other benefits..." (Blau, 1964, p.96). However such issues can be fully accommodated by Interdependence theory, since vicarious and dispositional rewards can lead to "transformation of the matrix" (see pp.337–343).

More detailed suggestions for the classification of rewards come from the work of Foa and Foa (1974), and their scheme is beginning to have influence amongst exchange theorists. Using data drawn primarily from questionnaires given to adult subjects in a variety of cultures, and also ideas arising from developmental and other studies, these authors have constructed a far-reaching theory concerning the resources used in interpersonal exchange. It will become apparent that the types of argument and the nature of the data used by Foa and Foa are very different from those discussed elsewhere in this book. And we shall see that further research may require many modifications to the scheme they propose. But their conclusions appear to provide a basis on which it will be profitable to build. Let us consider those conclusions first, and return to the difficulties later.

Foa and Foa suggested that the resources used in interpersonal exchange can conveniently be classified into six categories:

(a) *Love or positive affect*—that is, expression of affectionate regard, warmth, or comfort (e.g. "your company is pleasant"; "you are charming").

(b) *Status*—evaluations conveying prestige, regard or esteem (e.g. "well done"; "I am honoured by your presence").

(c) *Information*—opinions, advice, instruction, etc. (e.g. "It is five o'clock").

(d) *Goods*—tangible objects.

(e) *Services*—activities that affect the body or person of another.

(f) *Money*.

These classes are classes of meaning assigned to actions, so that each class covers numerous actions conveying resources of the same general kind. In recognising these categories, Foa and Foa emphasised that the distinctions between them are not absolute; indeed we shall see that their thesis depends in part on the view that some of these categories are more closely related to each other than are others.

Considering the categories first from a developmental viewpoint, they argued that an infant at first perceives an undifferentiated bundle of love and services: differentiation between them becomes possible only when he can do some things for himself, so that the mother can give him the one without the other. Subsequently the child differentiates goods from services and status from love. The former is possible only when the child realises that some objects disappear (e.g. "dinner all gone"), whilst others can be used again and again. The differentiation of status from love depends, of

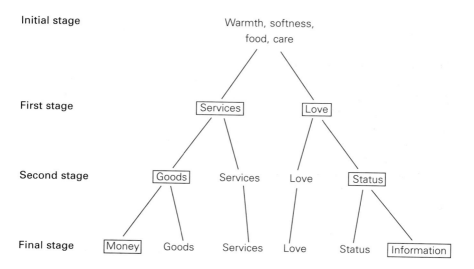

FIG. 20.1 The ontogenetic differentiation of resource classes. Newly differentiated classes are indicated by a box. (Foa & Foa, 1974.)

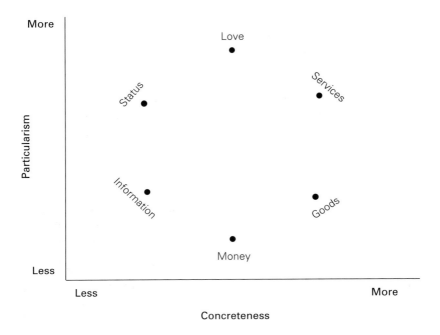

FIG. 20.2   The cognitive structure of resource classes. (Reprinted with permission from Foa, 1971, *Science*, *171*, 345–351. Copyright 1971 American Association for the Advancement of Science.)

course, on the development of language. Finally money is differentiated from goods and information from status. Money is at first treated merely as an object, its exchange potential being realised only gradually. Information from parents, or requests for information from parents, are initially closely associated with praise from the parent, and praise is one form of giving status; only later does a child encounter other criteria for status, such as physical strength. Thus the Foas' view of the gradual differentiation of resource classes can be illustrated as in Fig. 20.1. Though based largely on anecdotal impressions, the sequence seems fairly reasonable. It is relevant since differentiation is not necessarily complete, and the "permeability" of the boundary between any two categories will depend on the sequence. Thus Foa and Foa argued that resources that are close together in this sequence are more related, are more likely to occur together, and will tend to be perceived as more similar than resources remote from each other. They suggested that services and status are more closely related to love than is money, while services and money are more closely related to goods than to status. On these latter points they presented evidence of quite different kinds, to be mentioned in a moment.

If the resources are to be ordered with respect to their similarity, it is proper to ask, similar in what respects? Two dimensions are of special importance. The first, which the Foas called particularism, concerns one aspect of the context defining the effectiveness of the resource in question. The value of love depends on whom it comes from, but the value of money does not (see also Blau, 1964). In operant terms, this dimension concerns "the extent to which variables associated with the agent of reinforcement are important discriminative stimuli affecting the salience of the reinforcer" (Foa & Foa, 1974, p.81).

The second dimension is concreteness. Services and goods are regarded as concrete. By contrast status and information, typically conveyed by verbal or non-verbal behaviour, are primarily symbolic. Love and money, so the Foas argue, are exchanged in both concrete and symbolic forms and thus occupy an intermediate position on this coordinate. The argument here depends on the view that the classes are not discrete, the boundaries are permeable, so that actions in one class may have more or less affinity with those in neighbouring classes. A verbal expression of love resembles the conveyance of status rather than services, and tends towards the "symbolic" end of the continuum, whilst kissing and touching are closer to services than to status, and are regarded as more concrete (in the current sense) ways of expressing affection.

Thus these two dimensions provide the structure of resource classes shown in Fig. 20.2. It will be noted that the order of the classes is the same as that given by developmental considerations.

In harmony with this categorisation of resources, Lloyd, Cate, and Henton (1982) found that receipt of status predicted satisfaction in casual friendship, but information and love, not status, were (not surprisingly) important in romantic relationships. Berg and McQuinn (1986) showed that exchange of particularistic and symbolic resources increased as romantic relationships progressed.

Another approach adopted by the Foas was to test the perceived similarity between the resource classes empirically. Subjects were given a series of messages each of which represented a particular resource class (e.g. Money, "Here is your pay"; Services, "I repaired it for you"; Love, "I care about you"). They were asked to return, from a selection provided by the experimenter, the messages that they considered most similar to (or most dissimilar from) the one they had been given. At each trial they were provided with five messages from which to select their answers, one from each resource class other than that of the message given to them on that trial. Table 20.1 shows the percentage frequency with which the various resources were returned as most like the resource received. The order of

TABLE 20.1

Percentage Frequency of Resource Returned Being *Most Like* Resource Received

Resource Received	Resource Returned						
	Love	Status	Information	Money	Goods	Services	All Resources
Love	—	65	10	0	2	23	100%
Status	62	—	20	10	3	5	100%
Information	17	34	—	11	24	14	100%
Money	0	16	8	—	60	16	100%
Goods	6	5	21	55	—	13	100%
Services	41	18	7	16	18	—	100%
All Resources	21	23	11	15	18	12	100%

(Foa & Foa, 1974.)

resources given in Fig. 20.2 would predict that the highest frequencies should lie nearest to the diagonal: with few exceptions, this is the case. The predicted pattern of the smallest percentage near the diagonal was likewise obtained in nearly all cases for the most dissimilar resource.

In a second type of test, concerned with the degree of boundary permeability between resource classes, subjects were presented with a situation in which they were supposed to be providing a resource to another individual, and asked which resource they would prefer to receive in exchange. For example the subject might be told "You convey to a person that you enjoy being with them [*sic*] and feel affection for them" (Love), or "You are helping a person by providing certain services for them" (Services). Examples of the items to be rated as desirable in return are "The person gives you some merchandise" (Goods) or "You receive affection from the person". Table 20.2 shows the relation between the preference for receiving status when various resources are given. For example, the figure of 0.61 indicates the correlation between the desire to receive status when love is given and the desire to receive status when status is given. The prediction was that resource classes postulated as close together in the structure in Fig. 20.2 should receive higher intercorrelations than those that are more distant, and the relative sizes of the coefficients were (more or less) in line with this prediction (see also Converse & Foa, 1993).

It is important to note that similarity between resource classes lies in the meaning behind the behaviour, rather than the behaviour itself. Furthermore in real life the value of a given resource may depend on the individual's perceptions. For instance, people may modify their valuation

TABLE 20.2
Intercorrelation Among *Preferences for Status*
When *Different Resources* are Given

	Love	*Status*	*Information*	*Money*	*Goods*	*Services*
Love	—	61	40	29	46	52
Status	61	—	52	26	54	45
Information	40	52	—	42	56	51
Money	29	26	42	—	66	57
Goods	46	54	56	66	—	69
Services	52	45	51	57	69	—

(X 100) (Foa & Foa, 1974.)

of a resource by taking into account its availability (Brinberg & Castell, 1993; Brinberg & Ganesan, 1993).

Although some studies show the ordering of the resource categories to be invariant across cultures (Foa et al., 1993b), there may be some differences in their relative importance in particular relationships between cultures. Thus Kamo (1993) found that expressive aspects of marriage were more important in the United States of America than in Japan, while socioeconomic aspects were more important in Japan.

Furthermore the relative need for the several resource classes may change with age. Foa and Bosman (1979) found that the perceived need for more love decreased with age, while that for money increased. Teichman, Glaubman, and Garner (1993) found that adolescents display greater needs for resources than adults: this was the case across most resource classes but was especially marked for status—perhaps reflecting a special problem of adolescence.

It will be noted that the sources of a given resource, as well as the resource itself, may vary along the particularistic–universalistic dimension. Tornblom and Nilsson (1993) showed that even universalistic resources are regarded as contributing more to satisfaction if they come from someone close to the recipient.

The value placed on some resources may depend on their source in another way. In a study of the social support given to cancer patients, Dakof and Taylor (1990) found that some potential providers of social support feel a degree of aversion and tend to withdraw, while some employ over-cheerful, over-optimistic tactics. Not surprisingly, perhaps, what the patients found helpful varied with the provider. Physicians and other cancer patients were especially likely to provide both helpful and unhelpful information about cancer. The spouse, other relatives, and friends were valued for esteem and emotional support, while the information and tangible aid that they provided was less often seen as helpful.

A further important difference between the resource classes must be mentioned. The Foas argued that, if one gives money to another, one is simultaneously taking it away from oneself. However this is not necessarily true of all resources. At the other extreme, they suggested that if one gives love to another, one simultaneously increases the amount one has oneself (see also Blau, 1964). Similarly, if an individual quarrels with another (which the Foas describe as taking love away), he simultaneously reduces the amount of love he has for himself. They proposed in fact that the structure of resource classes also indicates the relationship between giving to other and what is left for self. For love, and to a lesser extent for status, this relationship is positive. Giving information to another usually does not affect the amount possessed: in some circumstances it may increase it, as when teaching increases understanding, and in others it may diminish the value of the information possessed. Giving money or goods reduces the amount possessed by the giver. For services the relationship is also usually negative.

It is worth noting that these differences in the consequences of giving are not incompatible with interdependence theory. When Foa and Foa claim that one can gain love by giving love, Kelley might say that the matrix was transformed so that joint rewards became prominent. And the man-in-the-street would say that it pleases you to please her whom you love (see Chapter 29).

What we have here is an attempt to make sense of the wide range of resources used in interpersonal exchange. Given some such means of classifying resources, it is possible to ask not only whether their properties differ, but also whether we can find principles determining where each is most likely to be effective. Can the different classes of resource be related to the different conditions under which social exchange takes place? Here the Foas considered two sets of such conditions, one concerning the motivational states of the participants, and the other the appropriateness of the environment. With regard to the first they propose that for each resource class there is an optimal range. When the amount of the resource classes falls below a minimum value it is felt as a need, and when the upper limit is exceeded one is motivated to "get rid of" some of that resource. On merely intuitive grounds it is suggested that the range between upper and lower limits is larger for resources that can be stored outside the body, and that for money the amount that can be stored is infinite. Certainly not everyone would agree with this aspect of their scheme, and especially with the view that it is easy to have too much love, but the issue is not important for the main thesis.

At first sight the notion of an optimal range provides an easy explanation for differences in motivation. If an individual is below the optimal range for a given resource he will have a need to acquire it, and if above he will have a need to give. But the latter view is incompatible with the assumptions in previous paragraphs. In the case of particularistic resources, like love, the Foas proposed that giving love to other is associated with giving love to self, and so will not result in depletion. And with non-particularistic resources like money the upper limit is so high that there is seldom or never a surfeit. But this difficulty disappears if giving is a device for getting needed resources—it is nearly always part of an exchange.

Because the resource classes are related, the need states related to them are also likely to be related. For example, a person exposed to loss of love will also feel some need for status. This makes intuitive sense and is supported by test data.

The classification of resource types also provides a classification of types of power—each of the six types of resource can be either given or taken away (see pp.195–196). And the structure of resource categories provides suggestions about the relations between types of power—money can buy goods or information, possibly status and services, but not love.

We may now consider how the properties of the response classes are related to the conditions under which exchange takes place. We have already seen that giving love to others also involves giving love to self, whereas giving money involves taking money from self. A further proposal is that the degree of ambivalence in a transaction follows the same order: one can love and hate (i.e. give and take away love from a person) simultaneously, but one cannot, or at any rate does not, give and take away money at the same time. For these reasons the rules of exchange that apply to money transactions will apply to a lesser degree or not at all to other resource classes: one can simultaneously give love and have more, and one can simultaneously give love and take it away.

Four other properties may be mentioned briefly. First, it was suggested that verbal language is more suitable for transactions involving money or information, non-verbal for love or services. Second, the more particularistic a resource, the more likely that exchange will take place within a resource category: we may exchange money for goods, but usually exchange love only for love. Third, and related to the last, the more particularistic the resource, the narrower the range of other resources with which it can be exchanged. Finally, the more particularistic resources are more likely to require a face-to-face exchange.

Turning now to the manner in which the appropriateness of the environment affects exchange, the Foas suggested that money can be exchanged quickly, love takes time. In a busy environment, the more particularistic resources are likely to receive lower priority. In an environment where most encounters are with strangers, the less particularistic resources are more likely to be used. Thus the rewards of an exchange of love are likely to be reaped only after several encounters, while money can bring immediate reward. Finally, the Foas suggested that small group size favours the more particularistic resource categories.

Given these differences in the manner in which resource classes are related to the conditions under which exchange takes place, it seems possible that the laws of exchange for the more particularistic resources need be no less hard-headed and respectable than those for the laws of exchange of money and goods. The Foas described a number of investigations concerning not only such questions as, "Given a particular resource, what sort of resource does a subject prefer in exchange?"; and "If a particular resource is removed, how would the subject choose to retaliate?"; but also "How does cognitive distance between the resource category of which a subject has been deprived and the resources available for retaliation affect the intensity of his response?"; "Does deprivation affect the probability of occurrence of positive and negative behaviour?" and so on. These studies involved questionnaires or experiments with confederates, with all the dangers attendant thereon. Space does not permit the detailed exposition which would be necessary to enable the reader to evaluate them: the reader is referred to the Foas' book (1974) and to the later edited volume (Foa et al., 1993a).

The Foas thus supported their proposed structure of resource classes with evidence drawn from considerations of development, from the nature and properties of the resources themselves, and from evidence on perceived similarity and perceived equivalence drawn from studies of adults. Their classification seems to make sense of a number of aspects of the ways in which rewards operate, including some admittedly rather gross generalisations about the environmental contexts in which they are efficacious.

Commentary

It is of course possible to make many comments. As the scheme is in part intuitive, it is fair to criticise it on the same grounds. In general, the approach tends to neglect the relationship context: the meaning of resources exchanged in interactions depends critically on the relationship of which the interaction is part. Although the Foas emphasised that they were concerned with the meanings ascribed to actions, their experimental technique was not consistent with this. Consider first the categories themselves. Might there not be other ways to carve up the resources used in interpersonal exchange in ways that would fit the data even better than that proposed? Did not the Foas come near to reifying each class when they write of "a wide range of actions each conveying the same resource"?

Did the Foas stick to their definition of the classes as classes of meaning assigned to actions? For instance, what are the properties of tangible goods given as tokens of love? Is the acquisition of status easily separable from that of other attributes? And could some of the apparent differences between the categories be due to the particular way in which the resources have been categorised, rather than to intrinsic properties of the "meanings assigned to actions"? For instance, love is heterogeneous and can be expressed in many ways, whereas money passes in relatively few. Is not that reason enough why love is often exchanged for love, but not money for money?

Perhaps the greatest difficulties arise with the category of information. Information may concern the external world and be valued because it may enable the recipient to acquire more tangible rewards at a later date. Surely such information is more closely related to the response class to which it may later give access, than to its neighbours in the Foas' scheme? Take for instance the issue of reciprocation. If I moved to a new town and asked my neighbour where the post office was, it would not be inappropriate for him to ask me to post his letters as well as my own (services); but if he told me where I could pick blackberries (goods), I might well bring him a box in gratitude.

Another type of information may also concern the external world, but be of importance to the hearer because he sees it as agreeing or disagreeing with opinions he holds himself. This will be relevant in the context of consensual validation, and thus pertinent to the perceived status of the hearer.

Yet another type of information may concern the speaker. Here it may be relevant in relation to consensual validation, or it may be interpreted by the hearer as love, or as directly providing status, or as evidence that the speaker may render him services in the future. Or it may provide the hearer with guidance in a situation that is potentially stressful or in which he is unsure of his abilities (Wheeler, 1974). How the hearer interprets it may depend crucially on the sort of relationship he already has with the speaker. Consider, for instance, how the statement "I am devoted to you" could be interpreted in any of the above ways. The meaning of a piece of information will thus be affected by contextual cues, and may have primary relevance to any of the other resource classes.

This last point applies not only to information. Items in any one of the resource classes may be valued because they give access to others. Their meaning may change with the personality and temporary needs of the recipient, and even with the stage of the relationship.

Again, is not the evidence supporting the developmental sequence a little thin? What role does socialisation play in the differentiation of resource classes? Is it really the case that love is intermediate between status and services on a dimension of concreteness? Is it really so easy to have too much love? And if love does indeed have a narrow optimal range, and the way to get rid of a surfeit is by taking love away from other (and thus also from self), would not one expect lovers' quarrels to be much more common than they are? In any case, how far should one generalise about interpersonal relationships from experiments carried out mostly with students?

And how much value should one attach to this sort of questionnaire data about perceived similarity, equivalence, and boundary permeability? Although the classes of resources are said to be classes of meaning assigned to actions, has not meaning somehow been left behind?

What all this amounts to is that the properties of a given reward may depend on the nature of the interaction and relationship in which it is exchanged. That rewards should be classified is essential, but the classification required is one that will interdigitate with a classification of relationships. The Foas do not sufficiently emphasise that the meaning attached to one of their resource category labels will vary with the context. To continue the examples given earlier, what A would expect in return for services would depend on whether those services involved A scratching B's back or changing a wheel on his car. And if it were back-scratching, the expected return would differ if A were scratching his wife's back from if Mata Hari were scratching the back of an important general, while if A was changing a wheel it would depend on whether the car were her neighbour's or a stranger's.

We may pursue this question of the relation between a classification of rewards and a classification of relationships a little further. We have seen that there are differences in what individuals expect from the relationships in which they are involved. In exchange theory terms, the ratio of rewards to costs expected in a given sort of relationship varies between individuals: some expect more, others less. And what any one individual expects from one relationship is not what he expects from another, even when he can measure both in the same currency. Thus we cannot study how the value of a reward changes with the context in which it is exchanged until we can describe and classify relationships. If exchange theorists are to generalise about the difficult problems which arise from the different properties of rewards, adequate classifications both of relationships and of rewards are essential.

It is in fact the case that practically any one of the statements that the Foas used in their questionnaires could take on diverse meanings according to the context of the relationship in which it was given. The words "I love you" could mean something different in parent–child, sibling, or peer–peer relationships (i.e. in relationships of different content); they would be almost meaningless in a uniplex relationship; and their value changes with the degrees of self-disclosure, interpersonal perception, and commitment that characterise the relationship. In the latter cases their value might well change in a complex way, perhaps first increasing with increasing intimacy and then decreasing. The value of money or goods would also vary with the content of the relationship, with many of its qualities, with the relative status (financial and otherwise) of the participants (i.e. complementarity), and again with self-disclosure, interpersonal congruency, and commitment.

However that is not all. The interactions and relationships between two individuals cannot be seen as the mere sum of giving and receiving rewards. As we have seen, were each participant to be concerned merely with maximising his own rewards and minimising his costs, with no thought for his partner, that partner might soon find a better option elsewhere. He must, therefore, consider not only his own probable rewards and costs, but also those of his partner (Thibaut & Kelley, 1959). The issues again depend on the characteristics of the relationship. If the relationship is uniplex and involves reciprocal interactions it may in theory be a relatively straightforward matter, for each partner's gains and costs are measurable in the same currency. If the relationship is uniplex and complementary, the situation is a little more complex because, although gains and losses occur in the same interaction, they differ in kind: what a teacher gains from teaching is not the same as a pupil gains from learning. If the relationship is multiplex, the issue is one of extraordinary complexity, and must involve assessing one's own gains and one's partner's losses on the swings against one's own losses and one's partner's gains on a multiplicity of roundabouts. Thus the properties of the relationship will affect the nature and meaning of the exchange that takes place.

One possible solution to these problems is to subdivide further the categories of resources. Buss (1983) has suggested finer distinctions among the social rewards, listing four "Process rewards"—presence of others, attention from others, responsivity by others, and initiation by others, each of which forms a dimension with the optimum in the middle (i.e. isolation–crowding; shunning–conspicuousness; boredom–over-arousal; and no interaction–intrusiveness). In addition he lists four "Content rewards"—deference, praise, sympathy, and affection. However it is not clear that this takes us a lot further.

What general conclusion can be drawn? On the one hand, we must be wary of theories seeking to extract principles about relationships without asking whether similar conclusions would have been reached with a different type of relationship or a different type of reward. On the other hand, the Foas' view that resources exchanged are more likely to come from resources classes that are neighbours in their scheme (Fig. 20.2) than from more distant ones, must also take into account the fact that equivalences may change with the nature of the relationship. What is needed therefore is not only an adequate classification of relationships and an adequate classification of the rewards used in interpersonal exchange, but further research to marry the two.

From another point of view, the Foas' contribution can be seen as an attempt to build a bridge between the current use of exchange theories and their bases in the learning theories of the 1950s. In practice, the development of interdependence and equity theories and the investment model (Chapter 19) have rendered the links to the learning theories obsolete, though the insistence that resource classes differ in their properties is still salutary.

It thus seems likely that substantial modification to the Foas' present scheme will be required. However this does not greatly diminish its value in emphasising that the several rewards used in interpersonal exchange differ in their properties, and that such differences must be taken into account if interpersonal relationships are to be understood.

SUMMARY

1. Traditional learning theories become inadequate in studies of relationships even at the behavioural level because their dynamics depend on the effects of interactions on interactions over time.
2. The resources exchanged in relationships have different properties. Foa and Foa emphasised particularly their "concreteness" and "particularism". The latter refers to the extent to which it matters from whom the resource is received.
3. Differences in the properties of the resources lead to differences in the consequences of giving. Thus the Foas suggest that, whereas if A gives B money, A has less, but if A gives B love, A has more.
4. However, a number of problems remain.

21 Attachment Theory

ATTACHMENT IN CHILDHOOD

An approach to the relations between individual characteristics and relation-ships, which has become increasingly prominent in recent years, has been developed from Bowlby's (1969/82, 1973, 1980, 1991) attachment theory. Originally formulated to account for the effects of maternal deprivation on personality development, the essence of attachment theory is that the parent (or other primary caregiver) provides a secure base from which the infant can set out to explore the world, but to which he or she can return if distressed, tired, etc. Bowlby's work started from the observation that delin-quency in adolescent boys was associated with a history of early separa-tions from the mother. He therefore suggested that maternal deprivation, or the lack of a secure base, especially during the first few years of life, put children at risk for the development of both mental and physical illness.

Drawing concepts from ethology, Bowlby pointed out that many of the features of the parent–child relationship were shared with our non-human relatives. For instance the so-called "irrational fears of childhood"—fears of darkness, of falling, of being alone, etc.—would have contributed to survival in our environments of evolutionary adaptedness. He assimilated experiments showing that "contact comfort" between mother and infant rhesus monkey was critical (Harlow & Zimmermann, 1959); replaced the libido energy model of his psychoanalytic background with a control systems approach; and stimulated experiments with rhesus monkeys that showed that a few days' separation between mother and infant could produce effects detectable months and even years later (Hinde & McGinnis, 1977).

In Bowlby's scheme, behaviour that predictably results in attaining or maintaining proximity to or communication with some other preferred individual is called "attachment behaviour". Such behaviour is particularly likely to occur under conditions of fear, uncertainty, fatigue, etc. Over the first half-year of life attachment behaviour becomes organised into a goal-corrected behaviour system. A "behaviour system" is a set of alternative behaviour patterns with some common causal factors leading to an outcome that normally decreases the activation of the system in question (Baerends, 1976). In this case, the behaviours are such as promote proximity to or communication with the attachment figure. A complementary parental behaviour system is also postulated.

As discussed earlier, Bowlby also suggested that the child forms an "internal working model" of the relationship with the caregiver—a mental representation portraying both the self and the caregiver (Bretherton, 1990; Bretherton et al., 1990). This model is supposed to guide future relationships (see pp.31–36 for a discussion of the relation of this to other models of cognitive functioning.) Attachment theory recognises that an individual may become attached to a number of individuals (mother, father, grandparent, sibling, etc.), but it is assumed that attachment to the principal caregiver has an overriding influence on personality development and on subsequent relationships. The working model of the caregiver becomes internalised and allied with the self-system, so that attachment as a property of the relationship becomes an individual characteristic. The critical feature of the attachment relationship is the "felt security" provided by the caregiver. Thus while attachment theory is entirely compatible with the notion that the self-view is determined in large measure by the individual's view of others' perceptions of him/her, it lays emphasis on the relationship with the primary caregiver, the self-image being strongly influenced by the sensitivity in responsiveness of the caregiver in that relationship. The child may, of course, form other relationships and other working models concerned with issues other than, or in addition to, security of attachment.

Bowlby's theory was put on a more quantitative base by Ainsworth, who devised the "Strange Situation" test for assessing the infant–mother relationship (Ainsworth et al., 1978). This is an experimental procedure, with a series of episodes involving the mother's temporary absence and subsequent return, designed to activate the attachment behaviour system. How the infant organised his/her attachment behaviour to the mother-figure, particularly following the stress of a brief separation, fell into three main patterns of attachment, to which a further category of "disorganised" was later added by Main (Main & Solomon, 1990). These categories can be characterised as follows:

Secure. Typically the infant uses the parent as a secure base from which to explore the room, is distressed when she leaves, but on her return shows positive affect, interacts calmly, and is readily soothed, indicating an intimate and special relationship.

Avoidant. Typically the infant is little distressed by the parent's departure, and avoids contact on reunion, responding minimally.

Ambivalent. The infant behaves as if preoccupied with the caregiver. On reunion the infant shows angry whiny dependence, often with resistance to physical proximity or contact.

Disorganised. These infants, initially difficult to classify, show stereotyped, undirected behaviour, which may indicate underlying fearfulness.

These categories of attachment are related to maternal behaviour as observed in the home. Mothers of securely attached children are consistently available and sensitively responsive to their needs. Mothers of avoidantly attached children deny their infants' requests for comfort and provide little close bodily contact, but may interact intrusively when they do. Mothers of ambivalently attached infants tend to be inconsistent, sometimes unresponsive and sometimes intrusive. Finally, mothers of children in the disorganised category are usually depressed, and either frightened or frightening (e.g. Ainsworth et al., 1978; Egeland & Farber, 1984; Grossman et al., 1985; Isabella, 1993; Stevenson-Hinde & Shouldice, 1995).

Bowlby was careful to say that by mother he meant the primary caregiver, though that was usually the mother. Children tested with their fathers in the Strange Situation often fall into a category different from that when tested with the mother (e.g. Main & Weston, 1982), suggesting that the postulated early working models formed by the child must be specific to particular relationships.

The attachment pattern is usually stable over the first few years of life, but can change if the family's social circumstances change (Egeland & Farber, 1984). Although the strange situation was originally devised for 1-year-olds, coding systems for older ages have now been devised (e.g. Cassidy & Marvin, 1989/92). In the absence of major life events, concordance of over 80% from 1 to 6 years in the attachment category has been demonstrated in stable families (Main & Cassidy, 1988). But the changes that do occur indicate that the pattern of attachment is susceptible to change if there is an alteration in life circumstances or in an important relationship.

The supposition is that the attachment category indicates the nature of the internal working model formed by the child. Thus though the category is initially a property of the child–parent relationship, it becomes a characteristic of the child. Patterns of attachment predict concurrent and later behaviour. For instance Sroufe (1983) showed that children classified as securely attached at 12 months had better relationships with peers in pre-school than children who were insecurely attached (see Bretherton, 1987; Shulman, Elicker, & Sroufe, 1994). Use of the coding system devised for older children has also permitted the demonstration of relations between contemporaneous attachment classification and other aspects of behaviour (review by Shaver, Collins, & Clark, 1996). Turner (1991) showed that gender differences in the behaviour of pre-school children are largely due to the insecure children, securely attached boys and girls behaving similarly.

ADULT ATTACHMENT

The Strange Situation procedure is applicable only to infants and young children, and attachment in adulthood is likely to differ in a number of ways from attachment in infancy. Most importantly, it may involve a reciprocal relationship with each partner providing security to the other, rather than the complementary parent–infant relationship where it is primarily the parent providing security for the infant. In addition, physical proximity becomes less important, psychological availability often being adequate for the provision of security (e.g. Hazan & Shaver, 1994). However, in both children's and adult's attachment relationships, attachment behaviour is elicited in conditions of stress, there are analogies in the attachment behaviours shown in the event of separation, and in both the behaviour and feelings are centred on a particular provider of security. Thus it should be possible to apply attachment theory to behaviour in adulthood. Two principal routes to this end have been developed.

First, Main has developed an "Adult Attachment Interview" with which it is possible to categorise the adult's present state of mind with respect to his or her childhood relationships as "autonomous", "dismissing", or "pre-occupied". Each of these is divided into several sub-categories. The coding of the interview depends not only on what the interviewee says, but also on how he/she says it, and thus attempts to make allowance for un-conscious processes (George, Kaplan, & Main, 1985). Those who report their early experiences in a coherent and balanced manner ("autonomous") tend to have infants who are securely attached to them. However those who dismiss the relevance of early relationships ("dismissing"), and those who are unduly "preoccupied" with them, tend to have infants who are insecurely attached (e.g. Benoit & Parker, 1994; Fonagy, Steele, & Steele, 1991; Grossman et al., 1988). This instrument has been shown to have considerable predictive validity (van IJzendoorn, 1995).

The second route for applying attachment theory to adults was due initially to Hazan and Shaver (1987), who devised a simple questionnaire (Table 21.1) for distinguishing three categories of "attachment style", secure, avoidant, and anxious/ambivalent, by translating Ainsworth et al.'s

TABLE 21.1
Questionnaire Used for Assessing Adult Attachment Types

Question: Which of the following best describes your feelings?

Answers and percentages:

Secure (N = 319; 56%):   I find it relatively easy to get close to others and am comfortable depending on them and having them depend on me. I don't often worry about being abandoned or about someone getting too close to me.

Avoidant (N = 145; 25%):   I am somewhat uncomfortable being close to others; I find it difficult to trust them completely, difficult to allow myself to depend on them. I am nervous when anyone gets too close, and often, love partners want me to be more intimate than I feel comfortable being.

Anxious/Ambivalent (N = 110; 19%):   I find that others are reluctant to get as close as I would like. I often worry that my partner doesn't really love me or won't want to stay with me. I want to merge completely with another person, and this desire sometimes scares people away.

The figures in brackets indicate the frequencies in a newspaper sample. (From Hazan & Shaver, 1987. Copyright © 1987 by the American Psychological Association. Reprinted with permission.)

(1978) descriptions of infants into terms appropriate to adult love. The three adult attachment styles occurred in about the same proportions as Ainsworth's three categories of infant–mother relationships. Hazan and Shaver also produced a 12-item "Love Experience" instrument by factor analysis of the replies of 620 respondents to a 56-item questionnaire. Individuals who classified themselves in each of the Hazan and Shaver attachment categories indicated that their love experiences were consistent with their categorisation. The secure individuals said they had happy and trusting love experiences. Avoidant individuals often feared intimacy, had pessimistic views about relationships, and were often judged by peers to be hostile; and ambivalent ones had experiences of a rather obsessive, fluctuating form of love, falling in love easily but showing indiscriminate and often inappropriate self-disclosure, jealousy, and low self-esteem (Hazan & Shaver, 1994).

Hazan and Shaver's concept of attachment differs somewhat from that of Bowlby, and at first sight it seems almost unbelievable that such a simple instrument could probe very deeply. The use of a questionnaire approach assumes that individuals can accurately report their feeling and experiences, an assumption not made by Main's interview technique. The classifications it (and other self-report instruments) yields appear to hold little correlation with those obtained with the Adult Attachment Interview (Steele, Steele, & Fonagy, 1996). It must be noted that much of the support for the Hazan and Shaver instrument comes from studies in which self-categorisation for attachment style was shown to be correlated with data from other self-reports.

Nevertheless it is the case that the Hazan and Shaver instrument has yielded correlations with a number of aspects of adult behaviour. For instance, self-reported attachment styles were related to the individuals' history of and beliefs about relationships, to descriptions given by the subjects of their current romantic partners (Feeney & Noller, 1990, 1991), and in heterosexual couples secure attachment was associated with more trust, love, satisfaction, and commitment. Individuals with a secure style experience more positive emotion and less negative emotion in their relationships than insecure individuals (Simpson, 1990). Secure adults tend to regard others in general as well-intentioned, while avoidant individuals see others as untrustworthy (Collins and Read, 1990).

Again, a secure style (as assessed on the Hazan and Shaver instrument) predicts positive relationship characteristics and constructive approaches to conflict, whereas the other two styles predict negative characteristics (Levy & Davis, 1988). Fuller and Fincham (1995), studying a sample of distressed and non-distressed married couples over a two-year period, assessed the affect experienced by husbands and wives before discussion of a problem-oriented issue. Secure husbands reported more positive affect, and the secure wives more positive and less negative affect and less anxiety, than avoidant or ambivalent individuals (see also chapters in Sperling & Berman, 1994).

There is also evidence from a study of long-term dating relationships that individuals classified as secure tend to maintain relationships with others similarly classified, and some tendency for avoidants to associate with individuals categorised as anxious/ambivalent. There were no anxious/anxious or avoidant/avoidant pairs (Kirkpatrick & Davis, 1994; Table 21.2; see also Feeney, 1994). The avoidant/anxious pairing is to be expected, because anxious individuals expect partners to avoid intimacy and be rejecting; while avoidants are too much concerned about intimacy and un-easy about commitment. However, while the relationships of anxious women and avoidant men were surprisingly stable over three years, those of anxious men and avoidant women were likely to break up. Secure individuals reported most satisfaction and least conflict in their relationships. In view of the possibility that the attachment style as assessed by a questionnaire is concerned primarily with a current relationship (see later), these cross-sectional data do not provide evidence that the attachment style was present before the relationship started (Bartholomew, 1994; cf. Simpson, 1990). However, some evidence is contradictory: using rating scales to measure aspects of attachment in students and their dating partners, Whisman and Allan (1996) found no significant correlations between the partners' scores.

TABLE 21.2
Relations Between the Attachment Styles of Partners in Long-term
Dating Relationships

Male partner's attachment type	Female partner's attachment type		
	Avoidant	Secure	Anxious
Avoidant	0	25	9
Secure	28	138	12
Anxious	7	21	0

(Modified from Kirkpatrick & Davis, 1994.)

In spite of its successes (see also Shaver, Collins, & Clark, 1996), there is still doubt about the validity of the Hazan and Shaver instrument. The self-reported categorisation depends on a global orientation to relationships, but if the Hazan and Shaver instrument is presented in the context of specific relationships, individuals may classify themselves differently (Krojetin, cited Berscheid, 1994). The procedure has therefore been criticised in that it assesses attachment styles in relation to current experiences and expectations, so that the data may be ephemeral (Bartholomew, 1994). Attachment style so assessed has only limited temporal consistency, as might be expected if the attachment style as assessed by the questionnaire reflects a current relationship (Simpson, 1990). In one study where adults were assessed three times in a year, nearly a quarter of them had changed their classification, and the changes seemed to be related to recent romantic experiences incompatible with the self-concepts they had previously held (Shaver & Hazan, 1993). A third of the married individuals studied by Fuller and Fincham (1995) changed their categorisation over a two-year period, in keeping with changes in the mental model of the spouse, and they suggest that this finding is in harmony with Baldwin and Fehr's (1995) view that attachment styles are to be seen as relationship schemata that can vary over time, reflecting the current relational schema, rather than as stable personality traits. Baldwin and Fehr found that about 30% changed their attachment style classification over a timespan ranging from a week to several months, and cite comparable data from other studies. Even Kirkpatrick and Hazan (1994), who regard attachment styles as "highly stable" over a four-year period, found that 30% changed category. The changes could largely be ascribed to changes in the respondents' relationships. Commentaries on Hazan and Shaver's (1994) review of adult attachment revealed considerable unease.

This view, that attachment styles are mutable, and the view of Rholes, Simpson, and Blakely (1995) that relationship styles concern global "core" features that affect functioning in different kinds of relationship, are not easy to reconcile. The implicit suggestion that individuals have a single personality style seems to neglect the complexity of particular relationships and the differing ways in which an individual may behave in her or his several relationships. Attachment style must be seen as causing experience, giving meaning to experience, and being caused by experience, and all three must be taken into account.

The Hazan and Shaver description of each category refers to several relational dimensions, and yet it is an all-or-none measure which does not assess differences within each category. Several workers have therefore developed instruments that assess the attachment categories in terms of dimensions, though these instruments differ from each other in important ways (Bartholomew, 1994; Collins & Read, 1990; Simpson, 1990). Fuller and Fincham (1995) found that attachment category was not significantly related to marital satisfaction for either husbands or wives, though a dimensional measure of attachment did show a significant relation for wives. Whisman and Allan (1996), using an instrument measuring aspects of adult attachment on rating scales, found some relations with aspects of social cognition.

The relations between Main's Adult Attachment Interview and Hazan and Shaver's questionnaire have been discussed by Bartholomew (1990, 1993). She pointed out that Main's dismissive group involves defensive exclusion from awareness of negative feelings or attachment needs. In contrast, Hazan and Shaver's avoidant group consciously hold a negative view of themselves, reporting low self-confidence and feelings of being unacceptable to others. Bartholomew therefore suggested that the two instruments identify two overlapping but somewhat different groups, each capturing a different aspect of adult avoidance.

In line with this view, Bartholomew devised the four-category scheme shown in Fig. 21.1. This involves an elaboration of the Bowlby concept of an internal working model to distinguish individuals' views of themselves from their expectations of others. Her scheme thus involves the two dimensions, one of positivity of the model of the self and the other of positivity of expectations of others. Individuals with a positive self-image will be less dependent on others for self-validation; individuals with positive models of others are likely to seek out intimacy and support in close relationships, while negative models of others lead to avoidance of intimacy. The scheme thus differentiates two patterns, in each of which the individual has a hesitancy about becoming intimate with others—a fearful style in which the individual desires social contact but fears rejection, and a dismissing style with a positive self-image but a defensive denial of the

MODEL OF SELF
(Dependence)

	Positive (Low)	Negative (High)
Positive (Low)	**CELL 1** SECURE Comfortable with intimacy and autonomy	**CELL II** PREOCCCUPIED Preoccupied with relationships
Negative (High)	**CELL IV** DISMISSING Dismissing of intimacy Counter-dependent	**CELL III** FEARFUL Fearful of intimacy Socially avoidant

MODEL OF OTHER
(Avoidance)

FIG. 21.1   Styles of adult attachment. (Bartholomew & Horowitz, 1991. Copyright © by the American Psychological Association. Reprinted with permission.)

desire for social contact. Those with a negative self-view but a positive view of others show a preoccupied style in which they strive to find self-validation and fulfilment in intimate relationships, while those with positive models of both self and others (secure style) can form intimate relationships with others and enjoy autonomy (Bartholomew, 1993).

The four patterns shown in Fig. 21.1 can be reliably assessed by semi-structured interviews. Like Main's technique, the interpretation of these interviews goes beyond the mere content of what is said (Bartholomew & Horowitz, 1991). Indeed, Bartholomew (1990) emphasises the possible confounding effects of defence mechanisms in self-reports. More importantly, subjects can be rated for the degree to which they correspond to the prototypes of each pattern, and thereby located on a two-dimensional space according to the positivity of their models of self and other. This is potentially much more sensitive to the complexity of individual differences: while the Hazan and Shaver categorization approach might seem to provide a welcome simplicity, Bartholomew's goes farther towards recognising the complexity of real-life relationships.

Latty-Mann (see Latty-Mann & Davis, 1996) identified a number of subjects who endorsed both of the Hazan and Shaver insecure types as descriptive of themselves: these subjects, whom she called "Ambivalent" were aware of their own tendencies to want closeness, but also feared the consequences, so that ambivalence was at the very heart of their approach to relationships. This group were predicted to overlap with Bartholomew's Fearful-Avoidant type, and this was confirmed in that data showed not only a strong correlation between the two styles, but also that each correlated similarly with six dimensions supposedly underlying attachment (Frustration with partner, jealousy, ambivalence, trust, self-reliance, and proximity-seeking). A relation to the Disorganised pattern of Main and Solomon (1990) was suggested.

Bartholomew (1993) claims that the four-category model is applicable to both peer and family attachment relationships, and predicts individual's self-concepts and interpersonal functioning. In a later paper Griffin and Bartholomew (1994) assessed the two dimensions of the model by self-reports, friend-reports, romantic partner reports, trained judges' ratings of peer attachment, and trained judges' ratings of family attachment, establishing their convergent and discriminant validity. They showed individuals' models of themselves converged with direct measures of the positivity of their self-concepts, and their other-models with the positivity of their interpersonal orientations (see also Bartholomew & Perlman, 1994). Bartholomew's model also accounts for anomalies in the relations between attachment style and the individual's view of the partner as trustworthy, found by Fuller and Fincham (1995).

Furthermore, while Rholes, Simpson, and Blakely (1995), using a two-dimensional variant of the Hazan and Shaver instrument assessing avoidant versus secure and high versus low anxious ambivalence, found that insecure individuals, especially avoidant ones, have a more negative orientation towards children and the parental role, some aspects of their data could be better understood on the Bartholomew model. Their avoidant/secure dimension is related to Bartholomew's "model of other" axis, and the high/low anxious-ambivalence reflects Bartholomew's "model of self" axis. Rholes et al. point out that the secure vs. avoidant differences that they found are in harmony with Bartholomew's positive vs. negative orientation to relationships, the more avoidant individuals having more negative attitudes about having children. Their results for anxious/ambivalent individuals were not so clear-cut: mothers' levels of ambivalence were associated with feelings of closeness to the child, but the direction of the effect depended on the quality of their marriage. Highly ambivalent women reported more closeness to their children when their marriages were negative than when they were positive, but less ambivalent women reported the opposite. However, they did find that anxious/ambivalent individuals expressed reservations about their ability to be a good parent—a finding compatible with the view that they have negative self-views.

Attachment as assessed on these principles is related to satisfaction with the relationship. Feeney (1994) used an instrument to assess security of attachment involving the two dimensions termed "comfort with closeness" and "anxiety over relationships". These two dimensions are compatible with the Bartholomew four-category system: the comfort dimension separates the dismissing and fearful groups from those low in avoidance; and the anxiety dimension, reflecting dependence on others for a sense of self-worth, separates preoccupied and fearful groups from the others. In a study of 361 married couples she found that security was associated with the subject's own relationship satisfaction, though in the case of husbands the relation was principally with the anxiety dimension. Wives' anxiety was associated with low satisfaction for both spouses, especially if the husband was uncomfortable with closeness. The relations between attachment and satisfaction were mediated by communication variables, especially for wives.

The relation of these two dimensions to expressing emotion was further studied in 72 dating couples (Feeney, 1995). Comfort was inversely related to the subject's own control of negative emotions and to perceptions that the partner wished the subject to control his/her negative emotions. Anxiety was associated with perceptions that the partner controlled sadness and wanted the subject to control his/her anger and sadness. The data were consistent with the view that avoidant individuals tend to avoid acknowledging distress and seeking support from attachment figures. Feeney stresses that it may be important to distinguish between the several negative emotions.

This is clearly a rapidly developing area of research, but it is as yet too early to be certain how far the available instruments, and their three or four major category systems, will be successful in accounting for aspects of adult relationships. More validation studies of the questionnaire instruments that do not involve comparison between self-reports from the same subject are highly desirable. But it is important to recognise that one criticism sometimes made is invalid: no variant of attachment theory claims to account for all aspects of all relationships. It is concerned with relationships in which one or both partners provide, or are expected to provide, felt security to the other.

SUMMARY

1. Attachment theory was originally developed to highlight the importance of a caregiver providing a "secure base" in early childhood. It is supposed that the child develops a "working model" of itself, its caregiver, and the relationship between them. This model tends to form the basis of subsequent relationships, but can be modified to some extent in the light of subsequent experience.

2. Attachment, initially a property of the relationship, thus becomes a characteristic of the individual.

3. Main has developed an interview for assessing attachment in adulthood. Mothers who are "secure" ("autonomous") tend to have children who are securely attached to them.
4. Hazan and Shaver have developed a simple questionnaire also to assess the attachment style in adulthood. This has had some considerable successes, but recent data indicates that it reflects the individual's current attachment status rather than a longer-term individual characteristic.
5. A related approach, postulating two dimensions (positivity of the model of self and positivity in expectations of others), and thus giving a four-category scheme, is showing considerable promise.

22 Negative and Positive Feedback

INTRODUCTION

Some interpersonal relationships retain many of their characteristics over a long period, or change only gradually. Others, having remained stable for a period, are suddenly disrupted or undergo metamorphosis. Stability of a relationship in spite of changes in the participants or external stresses could be due to compensatory interactions within the relationship. In such a case, negative feedback could be said to operate. And where slight change leads to gradually accelerating change and metamorphosis or disruption, the sequence could be described in terms of positive feedback.

Although we can use the language of control systems in a qualitatively descriptive way here, it requires caution; the veneer of sophistication it provides can easily obscure the complexity of real-life relationships. For one thing, the same course of action can have both positive and negative feedback effects depending on the dependent variable examined—when a parent encourages independence in an adolescent daughter, he/she may be diminishing commitment for consistency (positive feedback) but promoting it for continuity (negative feedback).

However such concepts can be useful at both the individual and relationship levels. At the former, Bandura (1977), taking a social learning theory approach, has argued that self-regulatory processes operate on the participants in interactions, people responding to their own actions in self-rewarding or self-punishing ways. Thus some individuals, who have adopted codes involving a high evaluation of aggressive behaviour, feel better as a result of physical conquests, and become subsequently more likely to indulge in further aggression. But other individuals have personal standards which condemn aggression: for them, aggressive acts are followed by self-condemnation, and anticipated self-condemnation may serve to reduce potential aggression. Such regulatory mechanisms can be augmented or rendered less effective in a variety of ways—Bandura discusses, for instance, moral justification, euphemistic labelling, dehumanisation of the object, and similar processes. It will be apparent that a delicate balance may control whether positive or negative feedback effects occur (see Backman, 1988, cited pp.28–29).

In dyadic relationships the issues are even more complex. However, in spite of this complexity, a distinction between positive and negative feedback provides a framework for discussing the long-term patterning of interactions within a relationship.

NEGATIVE FEEDBACK

Theorists with widely differing orientations have argued that a stabilising tendency is intrinsic to many relationships. Amongst equity theorists (Chapter 19), the view that participants in a relationship actively seek a balance between their outcomes is basic. That dyadic relationships and families have powers for self-regulation has been emphasised for many years by clinicians (e.g. Watzlawick et al.,1967; Wertheim, 1975c; P. Minuchin, 1985; S. Minuchin & Fishman, 1981): negative feedback produces stability within a defined range whilst, in healthy families, permitting limited change in specified directions (see p.297). Psychiatric illnesses are seen by some as means for maintaining certain aspects of the status quo. Whilst processes describable in terms of negative feedback are thus widespread, it is important to remember that either the continuity or the consistency or both of many relationships may also be ensured by external constraints, such as physical propinquity, convenience, or social forces. In such cases stabilising mechanisms internal to the relationship are unnecessary.

The nature of the changes necessary for a relationship to accommodate external stresses or changes in the participants will depend on the nature of that relationship. Small changes in the behavioural propensities of one partner require different changes in the other according to whether the relationship is predominantly reciprocal or complementary. Where reciprocal interactions are involved, if one partner changes, the other should change in a similar fashion to preserve stability. Thus with two peers, if one changes in such a way that he wants to play more, the other should change in a similar fashion. By contrast, the mother–infant relationship is predominantly complementary and, if one partner changes in one direction (e.g. the infant becomes more demanding), stability may be best preserved if the other changes in a complementary fashion (the mother becomes more accommodating). We may note here that special problems are perhaps liable to arise with relationships that are in some contexts reciprocal and in others complementary: changes in either partner must be met by appropriate changes in appropriate areas by the other.

In either reciprocal or complementary interactions there is a third way of coping with change that must be mentioned: if change occurs in one partner, it may be altered or reversed if the other fails to produce an appropriate change. Thus if an infant becomes more demanding, the mother might ignore its demands. This would be the equivalent of an extinction procedure, and may be a powerful way to decrease the frequency of an operant response, even in a social situation. However extinction may have far-reaching effects on other aspects of the relationship, including the induction of aggressive behaviour. Thus, whilst the infant's demands may disappear if they are ignored, the relationship may also be changed in other, perhaps undesirable, ways. Furthermore, extinction may be ineffective: Ainsworth and Bell (1974) claim that their data indicate that infants whose mothers most frequently ignored their crying in one quarter-year were likely to be amongst the most frequent criers during the next quarter-year (though see Gewirtz & Boyd, 1977). Similar considerations apply to punishment (Feshbach, 1989).

The existence of stabilising tendencies is of crucial importance for studies of child development. Absence or excessive presence of a so-called "normal" aspect of the parent–child relationship may lead to divergence or disruption, or it may be adequately compensated by stabilising mechanisms (Bateson, 1976; Dunn, 1976). We cannot tell, without empirical data, what aspects of a relationship are essential for continuity: indeed, the answer to that question is liable to depend on circumstances. And where stabilising mechanisms operate, we must expect them to operate only so long as the divergence lies within certain limits—small divergencies may be unnoticed, and moderate ones adequately compensated, whilst larger ones are disruptive. Furthermore the consequences of a given degree of disruption may depend on the impact of other variables on the system: regulation may occur in some circumstances but not others (e.g. Bateson, 1976; Sameroff & Chandler, 1975).

Stabilising mechanisms may act to maintain a relationship in the short term, yet permit gradual changes on a longer timescale. This is especially evident in relationships where the behaviour of one participant is directed towards supporting or inducing change in the other. In teacher–pupil and parent–child relationships, teacher and parent strive to maintain the relationship in the short term, but in the long term to produce change which will be incompatible with the initial nature of the relationship. Much unhappiness could perhaps be prevented if it were more clearly recognised that such relationships contain the seeds of their own disruption or transmutation.

POSITIVE FEEDBACK

Bateson (1958) pointed out that both reciprocal and complementary interactions may have a built-in tendency to escalate. Thus if boasting by A induces boasting by B, and this induces more boasting by A, boasting will tend to escalate. If A is assertive, and B replies with submission, this may reinforce A's assertiveness. A may then become more and more assertive and B more and more submissive (see the interpersonal circle, Figure 8.1). The extent to which each partner confirms or disconfirms the other's claims will determine the degree and duration of feedback.

In practice positive feedback can operate to hinder or help the future course of a relationship. As a short-term example of the former, if one partner in a marriage is unwilling to interact in a particular way, the other may show frustration-induced anger and aggression, and this may enhance the uncooperativeness of the former. As another, paranoid beliefs can lead to mutual rejection, and feed the paranoia.

Anger may be invoked also by separation from a parent or loved one. Bowlby (1973) suggests that such anger is usually functional in (a) assisting the separated individual to overcome obstacles to reunion and/or (b) discouraging the loved one from going away again. Negative feedback thus operates. However if separation or threats of separation invoke intense, frequent, or persistent anger, the affectional bond between the partners may be weakened and alienation occurs. Thus such dysfunctional anger, whose effects can be described in terms of positive feedback, occurs because separations, especially when prolonged or repeated, have a double effect. On the one hand anger is aroused, and on the other love may be attenuated. Similar considerations can apply to infidelity.

An example showing the subtlety of the factors determining the balance between negative and positive feedback is provided by a sensitive analysis of the "melancholy marriage" by Hinchliffe et al. (1977, p.140). On the basis of tape and videotape recordings of patient and wife interacting, they write:

> In a good relationship the wife would respond to the distress of her husband by being reassuring and protective. In many instances this would be effective, but when the stress increases or when the wife is unable to respond in a manner which meets his needs he may develop depressive symptoms. The failure to meet his needs can also be understood in terms of the shift in roles

which occurs ... ; as the wife becomes more caring and mother-like the husband comes child-like and dependent. The system becomes less stable at this point and psychological symptoms emerge which further constrain or regulate the pattern of the interaction. The husband becomes ambivalent about his needs, since he has on the one hand the security and comfort of the regression and dependence, while on the other he experiences the pain and discomfort of his impoverished self-image and loss of self-esteem. His behaviour can be confusing to his wife as he emits cues suggesting a dependency need and at the same time rejects her. As she fails in her efforts to meet his distress she becomes envious, irritable, frustrated and depressed and begins to feel alienated. Any motivation for a change in his behaviour would depend on his tolerance of the altered equilibrium.

Further examples of positive feedback leading to a gradual deterioration of a relationship are discussed in Chapters 27 and 28. Turning to cases of positive feedback acting to facilitate the course of a relationship, one case has already been mentioned (Chapter 15). The belief that effort has been put into a relationship is dissonant with its dissolution, and conducive to further effort. Commitment to the relationship is consistent with seeing its good aspects, and with dispensing rewards in the expectation of future returns.

When Liking leads to Liking

It seems likely that the development of dyadic relationships often depends on positive feedback consequent upon the initial dyadic attraction. Liking may lead to being liked and this to increased liking (e.g. Newcomb, 1961). This effect of perceiving that one is liked can operate even when one is initially prejudiced against one's evaluator (Byrne, 1971).

The means by which liking may lead to liking are certainly diverse. At a simple level, liking may lead to greater proximity in terms either of immediate interpersonal distance or of frequency of encounters. Proximity enhances familiarity, which in turn increases liking (see also Homans, 1961). Indeed even the anticipation of future interaction can, in some circumstances, induce liking (Darley & Berscheid, 1967).

An effect of being liked on liking would be predicted by balance theory (Chapter 18). If A likes himself, and A perceives that B likes A, a balanced state in which A likes B will be facilitated. It would also be predicted by reinforcement theory: B's esteem is rewarding to A, and increases A's liking for B. It will be noted that the latter prediction is independent of A's own self-esteem. By contrast, balance theory would predict that, if A does not like himself, perception by A that B likes him would make A less likely to like B in return. As discussed earlier, the evidence here is in harmony with the view that both the reward value of B's esteem and the congruency of

B's perceived evaluation of A influence A's feelings about B (Deutsch & Solomon, 1959). If A does not think highly of himself, B's esteem will induce less liking of B than if A has high self-regard.

A number of other conditions influence the effectiveness of positive evaluations in producing liking. Whether a positive evaluation that is believed to be inaccurate produces liking for the evaluator depends on the precise meaning ascribed to it by the evaluatee (Stroebe, 1977). As discussed earlier, evidence that temporary deprivation of esteem from others will increase its effectiveness is not conclusive. However evaluations that change from negative to positive are, in some circumstances at least, more effective than evaluations that are consistently positive (Aronson & Linder, 1965).

The effect of being liked on liking may be further augmented in another way. Equal sharing of scarce resources may induce or augment friendship, and friends are more likely to share equally (Lerner, 1974). If we like someone we may be willing to do things for them, even without expectation that the favours will be returned. And a person who does favours without expectations of recompense tends to be liked. There are thus considerable possibilities for positive feedback. For example, in one study it was found that receiving led to liking, liking led to giving, and giving led to liking. In another, children were more prone to share possessions with children they liked than with children they disliked (Staub & Sherk, 1970). Furthermore there is considerable experimental evidence that people tend to help those who help them, harm those who harm them, and confide in those who confide in them (see later). Just how far such studies can be generalised is, as usual, open to question: there are circumstances in which subjects think less highly of donors when there is no requirement to reciprocate than when there is. And of course, it may be that the children in the study cited were more willing to lend their things to those who could be relied on to return them, or who might lend them their things in return. It could even be that they lent because they wanted to be liked by those they liked.

Such data do not necessarily mean that a "reciprocity norm" is ubiquitous: the questions of how far the postulation of such a norm is useful as either a descriptive or an explanatory device, and what its bases may be, are still open (see p.106). If people are guided by social conventions dictating that they should reciprocate benefits received, the force of those conventions certainly varies with a number of factors such as the needs of the recipient, the resources of the donor, and the motives imputed to him. Furthermore it is not clear under what circumstances or in what kinds of relationships it is necessary to invoke a norm of reciprocity as a causative agent. If the fact of reciprocity can be explained in terms of intervening variables, such as effects of giving and receiving on liking, it could be that there is no need to postulate anything else (Altman & Taylor, 1973).

Be that as it may, the very act of behaving generously, or of believing that one has behaved generously, can provide further opportunity for feedback. One likes oneself for having behaved generously, and attributes to oneself liking for the person to whom one has been generous (Chapter 19). Thus liking induces generosity and generosity induces liking. But generosity induces liking only when it is perceived as generosity. If A confers favours on B that B feels were owed to him, there will be no inducement for B to like A, and if B saw A's favours as constraining his own freedom of action, he might even resent them.

Self-disclosure, Reciprocity, and Liking

Yet another issue here involves the relation between self-disclosure and liking. Intuitively it seems that we are more likely to reveal ourselves to those we like, and that we like those who are open with us. In exchange theory terms, disclosure can be seen as a resource, which provides the partner with a benefit. Benefits are more likely to be bestowed on individuals who are liked, and the recipients of benefits are prone to like the donors. Thus an exchange between self-disclosure and liking is to be expected. But an exchange theory approach can easily over-simplify the issues. Thus revealing oneself to another person may increase liking for oneself (Jourard, 1971), possibly because one likes oneself for being honest, or sees oneself as more trusting, or understands oneself better, and liking self induces liking for the person to whom one has revealed oneself. In any case, disclosers disclose because they want to: the act of disclosure may itself be rewarding or cathartic. And if B has some positive feeling for A already, A's disclosures may be additionally rewarding to B because they mark B as worthy to share intimate information. In the same way, an individual induced to help another in the context of a communal relationship may feel better and evaluate themselves more positively as a result (Williamson & Clark, 1989).

It is also important to remember here that any exchange may involve the return of a different resource (see Chapter 20). Disclosure may call not for reciprocated disclosure but for concern. And if it does involve reciprocal self-disclosure, that may involve intimate facts, emotions, or judgements, and may or may not address the same topic as that addressed by the initial discloser (Berg & Archer, 1982). In any case, disclosure may not elicit any positive response if the disclosure casts a bad light on the discloser or the recipient does not want to be involved.

There are other reasons why the bases of reciprocity are not straightforward. First, as we have seen, spouses or room-mates may believe that what they give and receive is correlated to a greater extent than is actually the case: the degree of reciprocity as measured by a third party may be considerably less than that which the partners believe to be occurring. La Gaipa (1977) thus proposed that there is a "bias" towards perceiving that social relationships are reciprocal. La Gaipa found that members of a dyad each expected the same degree of reciprocity in intimacy from the other: this index of the perceived likelihood that the other would reciprocate in self-disclosure was predictive of growth in the relationship over time.

Second, although a degree of reciprocity has been found in a number of laboratory experiments on self-disclosure, the generality of any "norm of reciprocity" for intimacy must be questioned. Most experimental studies of reciprocity of self-disclosure have used subjects who were initially strangers to each other, and there is evidence that reciprocity within any one encounter is more usual in encounters between strangers than in those between friends (Altman & Taylor, 1973; Derlega & Chaikin, 1976; Thibaut & Kelley, 1959), though the evidence is not all one-way (Dindia, 1994). Furthermore, in a laboratory context special factors may act to enhance reciprocity. Two people confined together quickly reach levels of self-disclosure that in ordinary circumstances would be achieved only by very close friends (Altman & Haythorn, 1965). And the subjects in shorter-term laboratory experiments may not be sure how they should behave, and look to each other for cues. Reciprocity is thus enhanced by modelling. One study (Davis, 1976) found that subjects did indeed disclose information about themselves to similar extents, but not as a result of mutual reciprocity. Rather one partner assumed responsibility for prescribing the level of intimacy, and the other then reciprocated.

In longer-term relationships confidence is selective; we are more likely to be intimate with some people than others, in some situations than others, and about some things than others. Spouses tend to reciprocate high-intimacy disclosures within conversations but not low-intimacy revelations—perhaps because the latter do not count as disclosures in long-term relationships, where the partners already know a great deal about each other anyway (Dindia, 1994).

Another issue is that, while there is good experimental support for the view that liking leads to disclosure (Worthy, Gary, & Kahn,1969), it is less clear that disclosure leads to liking of the discloser by the person with whom the secret is shared. While a positive effect has been found, other studies have found no effect, or a curvilinear relationship with most attraction at moderate levels of disclosure. In the latter case, very intimate disclosure may be interpreted by the recipient as indicative of a personality problem (reviewed Cozby, 1973; La Gaipa, 1977; Ajzen, 1974; Rubin, 1975). Sex differences may also be important here. For at least some subjects in some circumstances revelation of intimate information by women is indicative of better adjustment than is absence of self-disclosure, but for men the reverse is the case (Derlega & Chaikin, 1976).

The issue here is similar to that discussed in the context of the effect of similarity on interpersonal attraction. Presumably what matters is not how much is disclosed, but to whom, what, when, and why. Ajzen (1977) reports a study in which students were shown a set of statements purporting to come from a fellow student, and asked to evaluate her. The statements varied in the intimacy vs. superficiality and the desirability vs. undesirability of the information conveyed. Desirability of the information had a significant effect on liking, but its intimacy did not. However there was an interaction. Attraction was greater when the information concerned undesirable items and was intimate than when it was undesirable and superficial, perhaps because the hypothetical stranger was then viewed as honest: there was virtually no effect of intimacy with desirable information.

Again, Altman and Taylor (1973) emphasise that progressive disclosure requires mutual trust and rewarding exchange. They thus picture a sequence of mutual trust, rewarding exchange, projected future trust, and anticipated positive outcomes as necessary for the cycle to continue. But self-disclosure by A will not prompt reciprocation by B if B perceives that A's self-disclosure was motivated by self-interest, or that it was the product of an unsound mind. B's interpretation of the meaning of A's behaviour, or the information contained in the self-disclosure, is crucial. Such facts indicate that attempts to treat mutual self-disclosure in terms of exchange theory, with disclosure as a reward, are likely to need qualifications specifying when it is rewarding and when it is not in terms of the meaning ascribed to the disclosure (see also Dindia, 1994).

The preceding discussion of the manner in which liking, rewards, disclosure, and/or services may be reciprocated indicates some ways in which positive feedback could occur, and provides some (not necessarily incompatible) suggestions as to the mechanisms involved. Comparable data showing an influence of hate on hating could no doubt be obtained.

As yet, however, little is known about circumstances in which feedback does and does not occur. Laboratory experiments, often rather contrived, can provide very interesting data about what can happen, but more natural history-type description is necessary to indicate when it will. We have seen that the meaning attached to a gift, to an evaluative statement, or to a confidence, may be a crucial determinant of its potency for inducing reciprocation, and this will depend on the nature of the relationship (e.g. Davis & Martin, 1978). For example, a crucial issue may well be the stage of the relationship; not only may the explanatory value of exchange theory be reduced in relationships of long duration, but the rules of reciprocity may also be quite different.

Finally, in real life many of the processes mentioned earlier may operate together and mutually sustain each other. This will already have become apparent from the preceding discussion, and may be especially important in the process of "falling in love". Tesser and Paulhus (1976) have suggested that love increases dating frequency and dating frequency increases love by a number of interrelated mechanisms. These include exposure learning, classical conditioning resulting from the good times experienced together, enhanced similarity in attitudes and values as a consequence of shared experiences, rationalisation justifying the time and energy spent in meeting, and private and public commitment. Although some of the assumptions in their empirical work have been questioned (Smith, 1978) their conclusions probably stand.

SUMMARY

1. Processes that may be described as negative feedback sometimes operate to maintain the characteristics of a relationship. The nature of the changes required depend on the nature of the relationship. Such processes may operate to produce stability in the short term but permit longer-term development.
2. Processes that may be described as positive feedback may operate to produce progressive change. Diverse mechanisms are involved. Of special significance in the current context are the variety of ways in which liking can elicit liking in return, and the relations between self-disclosure and liking.

D Friendship and Love

Section B was concerned primarily with the description of relationships: particular aspects were abstracted from the whole and their properties examined. Some of these aspects concerned process, and Section C focused on some additional psychological processes involved in the dynamics of relationships. But in life these aspects and processes are interwoven and relationships must therefore be seen as wholes. This section goes a little way towards putting that right, examining the concepts of friendship and love. Further steps in the same direction are taken in Section E, which deals with temporal changes in relationships.

23 Friends (and Enemies)

WHAT IS FRIENDSHIP?

In the Western world, friendship is one of the few types of relationship that is not defined in terms of what the participants do together.[1] Of course it may be that two individuals are friends in part because they like doing the same things but, so far as defining friendship is concerned, it does not matter what those are. So-called dating relationships also involve activities of many sorts, and may evolve out of friendship (see Davis & Todd, 1985, cited later). And kin relationships in general are also not defined in terms of the content of the interactions, but the individual has no choice as to his/her relatives, while choice is the essence of friendship. Since friendship is little institutionalised and is usually not marked by public ritual, since the benefits it brings are diverse and perhaps peculiar to the particular relationship, and since it may be relatively uninfluenced by social pressures, one quality is essential for its cohesion—a degree of affection between the participants. When friends come together it is out of choice—they enjoy each other's company and the activities they share (Auhagen, 1991, 1993).

Although no form of activity is obligatory, one activity is highly characteristic of most adult friendships—namely talking (e.g. Aries & Johnson, 1983; Duck & Wright, 1993; Gottman & Parker 1986). Friendship

---

[1] A recent synthesis of work on adult friendship is provided by Blieszner and Adams (1992).

depends on a pool of shared knowledge, and it is often an essential element of friendship that the two partners keep up to date with each other's doings. It is the shared knowledge which makes it possible for them to understand each other's problems, to connect what happens with what happened before, and so on (Planalp & Garvin-Doxas, 1994). Beyond that, friendship is characterised by a number of features such as self-disclosure, trust, interpersonal perception, and commitment, which may be present to different degrees and in different proportions in different friendship relationships. In popular speech friendship implies more than mere acquaintance but need not necessarily imply great intimacy. It does not have the passionate aspect that is usually conspicuous in romantic love, but it is likely to involve *"amae"*—the readiness to ask for, or accept, help from the partner—which is not necessarily conspicuous in love. Even in young children it involves what Sullivan (1953) called "chumship"—an interest in augmenting the well-being of the partner (Schneider, Wiener, & Murphy, 1994). There is evidence that the total amount of resources exchanged, especially if they are particularistic ones (see Chapter 20), is related to intimacy in friendship (Berg, Piner, & Frank, 1993).

Perhaps the essence of friendship is the feeling of comfort, of freedom and naturalness of emotion. This depends on and creates comparable feelings in the partner, and initiates a dynamic process which leads to expectations of mutual responsibility. Interaction between friends creates and sustains a mutual reality in which each partner's identity confirms that of the other. But the expectations of trust and support that are central to friendship must be seen against the fragility engendered by the facts that it is voluntary and has no formal societal support (Wiseman, 1986).

Friendship is thus not easy to define, and indeed is seen somewhat differently in different cultures, by men and women, and even by individuals in any one culture. Yet some definition is helpful if we are to have an ordered body of knowledge about relationships. Hays (1988, p.395), in an extensive review, defined friendship as involving "voluntary interdependence between two persons over time, that is intended to facilitate socioemotional goals of the participants, and may involve varying types and degrees of companionship, intimacy, affection and mutual assistance." Auhagen (1991, p.17) sees it as a dyadic, personal, informal relationship, involving reciprocity and mutual attraction, and which is voluntary, longlasting, positive in nature and does not involve explicit sexuality. Others advocate treating sexuality as a dimension of friendship which may or may not be present (e.g. Wood, 1995).

Davis and Todd (1985) prefer to define the category of friendship in terms of a paradigmatic case. This has the great merit of recognising the fuzziness of the borders of the concept of friendship. Their paradigmatic case would involve two individuals recognising each other as friends and participating in a relationship which is mutual and reciprocal, involving equal participation and eligibility, mutual enjoyment, trust, assistance, acceptance and respect, spontaneity, understanding, and intimacy. Of course, real cases of friendship may not have all these characteristics: some may be missing or only partially present, but that would not require the relationship to be ruled out as not involving friendship. Unlike Auhagen, Davis and Todd do not exclude relationships involving physical intimacy. They regard friendship as differing from romantic relationships in lacking the characteristics of fascination and exclusiveness and having less demanding criteria of loyalty and willingness to help.

Wright (1984; see also Lea, 1989) has a more complex approach, based on a penetrating analysis of what friendship involves. While it brings many benefits in both the short and long term, Wright argues that friendship quality is not just a matter of more or less tangible rewards. Rather friendships are more than superficial and become ends in themselves: "...they involve persons whose participation as unique and irreplaceable individuals equals or transcends the importance of any specifiable set of rewards" (Wright, 1984, p.115, see also Wiseman, 1986). Friendships are rewarding but, in Wright's view, the rewardingness follows from the ability to show behaviour related to the self and its attributes. Individuals use their perceptions of themselves as reference points for experience, and are therefore motivated to behave in ways that promote the worth and well-being of the self. The two basic criteria of friendship are seen as "voluntary interdependence", or the extent to which two persons commit time for interaction in the absence of external pressures and constraints; and the "person-qua-person" factor, or the extent to which a relationship is "characterized by a mutual personalized interest and concern as reflected in the degree to which the partners react to one another as unique, genuine and irreplaceable in the relationship" (Wright, 1984, p.119). In addition, friendships are formed to fulfil other needs, such as providing:

(i) *Ego support value*—helping the subject to maintain an impression of the self as a competent worthwhile person.
(ii) *Self-affirmation value*—behaving in ways that facilitate the expression and recognition of one's more important attributes.
(iii) *Stimulation value*—capable of fostering positive elaboration of the self.
(iv) *Security value*—being safe, non-threatening, trustworthy.
(v) *Utility value*—helpfulness and cooperation in meeting one's day-to-day needs.

Wright (1982, 1984) thus emphasises that friendship is both voluntary and unconstrained, and involves interactions in which the participants respond to one another as unique individuals rather than as packages of discrete attributes.

Friendship implies trust, defined by Boon (1994, p.88) as "the confident expectation that a partner is intrinsically motivated to take one's own best interests into account when acting". Thus trust involves risk-taking, and is a crucial element in friendship. The self-disclosure intrinsic to friendship brings vulnerability (Chapter 12), and this also requires trust. And trust usually requires a belief in the partner's commitment matching one's own.

Although the content of the interactions in friendship are undefined, friendship does involve expectations about the quality and other aspects of the interactions. These are referred to as the rules of friendship by Argyle and Henderson (1985), and their list is shown in Table 23.1.

It is as well to note two things that friendship is not. Friendship is not the same as popularity: thus sociometric measures depending on questions of the type, "Whom would you most like to be with?" may be quite un-related to friendship. And having one or more friends is not the same as being sociable: even 4-year-olds may have friends but not be sociable, while others may be sociable (in the sense of interacting frequently with others) but promiscuously so (Hinde, 1978b). And one may add that friendship does not necessarily involve frequent interaction; it can endure long separations.

All of this requires two qualifications. First, because friendship is de-fined in terms of positive qualities, that does not mean it is free from ten-sions. The conflictual issues mentioned in Chapter 10 may be, and usually are, present in friendship as in any other close relationship. The second qualification lies in the introductory words of this chapter, "In the Western world". In other societies (and sometimes in the West) friendship is institutionalised, and may be marked by ritual (e.g. blood brotherhoods) and require even more lasting commitment.

ASSESSMENT OF FRIENDSHIP QUALITY

While friendships clearly differ in closeness in a general sense, to measure the intensity of friendship along a linear scale inevitably neglects quali-tative diversity. Most attempts to assess friendship use a number of scales which assess distinct but related domains. For example Hays (1984), basing his work on Altman and Taylor's Social Penetration Theory (pp.204–206), measured depth of friendship (superficial, casual, or intimate) and breadth (companionship, communication, consideration, and affection). Bukowski, Hoza, and Boivin (1994; see also Bukowski, Hoza, & Newcomb, 1994), measuring friendship quality during adolescence, used five scales—companionship, conflict, help/aid, security, and closeness. Sharabany (1994) used eight scales for intimate friendship—Frankness and Spontaneity;

TABLE 23.1
Rules for Friends

---

1. Volunteer help in time of need.
2. Respect the friend's privacy.
3. Keep confidences.
4. Trust and confide in each other.
5. Stand up for the friend in his/her absence.
6. Don't criticise each other in public.
7. Show emotional support.
8. Look him/her in the eye during conversation.
9. Strive to make him/her happy while in each other's company.
10. Don't be jealous or critical of his/her other relationships.
11. Be tolerant of each other's friends.
12. Share news of success.
13. Ask for personal advice.
14. Don't nag.
15. Engage in joking or teasing with the friend.
16. Seek to repay debts, favours, and compliments.
17. Disclose personal feelings or problems to the friend.

(Argyle & Henderson, 1985. Reprinted by permission of the author.)

Sensitivity and Knowing; Attachment (feeling close); Exclusiveness; Giving and Sharing; Imposition (ability to count on the partner); Common activities; and Trust and Loyalty. Each of these scales involved four questions, and the overall friendship score was obtained by adding all eight scales, which intercorrelated with coefficients between .41 and .63. The relative importance of the scales changed with age. Davis and Todd (1985), using the paradigmatic criteria listed earlier and a combination of empirical, conceptual, and statistical arguments, showed that seven global scales (Viability of the relationship; Support; Intimacy; Enjoyment; Stability; Spontaneity; and Overall success) could discriminate between different types of friendship (e.g. best friend, acquaintance, former friend) and between relationships that had been terminated by violation of one of the norms and those where the participants had just drifted apart.

An instrument based on Wright's approach to friendship (see earlier), known as the Acquaintance Description form, also incorporates a number of other variables. It involves five main categories—Relationship strength (Voluntary interdependence and Person-qua-person), Interpersonal Rewards (Utility, Ego-support, Stimulation, Self-affirmation, and Security), Tension or Strain (Maintenance difficulty), Response bias (Global favourability), and Relationship differentiation (Exclusiveness, Salience of emotional expression, Social regulation, and Permanence). It probably goes further than any other in capturing the complexity of friendship (Lea, 1989; Wright & Keple, 1981).

An instrument designed to assess "friendship-based love" in heterosexual relationships (Grote & Frieze, 1994), and assessing affection, enjoyment of mutual activities, companionship, shared laughter, trust, etc., is discussed in Chapter 24. The assessment of friendship in children and adolescents is discussed by Hartup (1995).

GENDER DIFFERENCES IN FRIENDSHIP

From pre-school onwards, and perhaps earlier, children tend to make friends with same-sex partners. This is probably related to activity preferences: rough-and-tumble play and manipulative play is seen more in boys, doll play and art in girls (e.g. Turner, Gervai, & Hinde, 1993). Girls' friendships tend to be more intimate and close than those of boys (Maccoby, 1990).

In adulthood, a considerable literature attests to the statistical significance of differences in the nature of friendship between men and women. For instance women tend to be more emotionally expressive (Williams, 1985), intimate (in the sense of self-disclosure) (Reis, Senchak, & Solomon, 1985; Sherrod, 1989), and to have friendships that are emotionally richer (Booth, 1972). Reis et al. have experimental evidence suggesting that the differences are not a consequence of a lesser capacity for interacting intimately amongst men, but rather in large measure to a preference for not doing so. Women place more emphasis on intimacy as a basis for friendship, men on shared activities (Caldwell & Peplau, 1982; Sapadin, 1988), and social support plays a greater part in women's friendships than in those of men (Auhagen, 1991). The lesser expressiveness of men in same-sex friendships has also been ascribed to a fear of being or being seen as homosexual (Lewis, 1978), to their giving career responsibilities greater priority and, in Western societies, to their greater competitiveness (Reisman, 1981), but it could also be a facet of more basic differences between the sexes. Middle-aged men tend to have more numerous but less intimate friends than women (Fischer & Oliker, 1983 cited in Adams & Blieszner, 1994; see also Auhagen (1991, 1996) for a comprehensive review of these and other issues).

In harmony with such data, some studies have shown women's friendships to be more satisfying than those of men. In a study of professional men and women, Sapadin (1988) found that, although both sexes viewed the characteristics of an ideal friendship similarly, women rated their same-sex friendships higher than cross-sex friendships for overall quality, intimacy, enjoyment, and nurturance. Men, by contrast, rated their cross-sex friendships higher, except on intimacy where there was no difference. By these criteria, then, women make better friends. In the same vein Elkins and Peterson (1993) found that friendships that involved one woman were more satisfying than male–male friendships, though women's friendships with women were not more satisfying than those with men.

In a study which included high school students and adults in the USA and Hungarian college students, Reisman (1990) also found that women rated their same-sex friendships as more disclosing and close than did men. The data from this study did not support a suggestion that men felt their same-sex friendships to be as intimate as did women: rather they indicated that men turn to cross-sex friendships for intimacy and are not concerned by its absence from same-sex friendships (see also Barth & Kinder, 1988; Jones, Bloys, & Wood, 1990).

However, judgements in the studies just cited may often depend on the criteria used for closeness, intimacy, or satisfaction. Closeness is often judged in terms of feminine expressivity, and it has been argued that close- ness in friendship can be confused with the expression of closeness. Male friendships may be close in a different way, the closeness being made explicit in action rather than in expressiveness (Duck & Wright, 1993; Wood, 1993). In heterosexual relationships, especially, it is claimed that men tend to assess intimacy in terms of its physical manifestations, women in terms of verbal ones. However, in a study of a student sample, Burleson et al. (1996) found that both men and women rated affectively oriented communication skills as more important than instrumental ones, though women rated the former more highly than men, and vice versa, in both friendship and romantic relationships.

In any case the sex differences in behaviour with friends, though statis- tically significant in many studies, are often small and must not blind us to the extensive overlap between the sexes. There are considerable similari- ties in the ways in which men and women perceive intimacy in close relationships (Monsour, 1992). Parker and de Vries (1993) also found similarities in the perceptions of their friendships by men and women. Same-sex friendships seemed to be more durable than cross-sex friendships, though relationships between men were less reciprocal than those between women, and men's same-sex friendships had less giving and receiving than women's (see also Auhagen, 1991; Helgeson et al., 1987; Peplau, 1983; Reisman, 1981). In aspects of conflict and sexuality, Nardi and Sherrod (1994) found few differences between lesbians and gay men in their approach to friendship.

Even if some aspects of behaviour are, or are regarded, as more characteristically masculine and others as more characteristically feminine, the degree of masculinity/femininity expressed may nevertheless depend on the sex of the partner. Vonk and van Nobelen (1993) found that both men and women tended to mention more masculine attributes and fewer feminine attributes when describing their "Self-in-general" than when describing "Self-with-(opposite sex) Partner" or the Partner. The data suggested that people behave in a more feminine way towards their intimate partner than to others, and that this is beneficial for the relationship. (See also Parker & de Vries, 1993; Reis et al., 1985).

In any case dimensions of gender are likely to be more important than a dichotomy of sex (Jones et al., 1990; Williams, 1985; Wood, 1993). On such grounds Wright (1982, 1988), while acknowledging that women's friendships tend to be "face to face" while men's are "side by side", cautions against the tendency to be misled by social stereotypes into over-emphasising the importance of what are often quite small differences.

These issues have been taken up by Duck and Wright (1993) in analysing a form assessing various aspects of the strength and quality of same-sex friendships. On the average, women responded more positively, and reported investing more in and gaining more from their same-sex friend-ships, than did men. Their relationships, within the same level of friend-ship, did tend to be more expressive than those of men, though they were no less instrumental. But there were also other differences that did not fit easily into an expressive vs. instrumental dichotomy. The authors note that since women's friendships seem to be stronger than men's, it is possible that some of the differences reported in previous studies between women's and men's "best friends" may be differences in strength of friendship. They emphasise further that both women and men are attuned to the caring, supporting, encouraging, and other socio-emotional aspects of their friend-ships. The feminine ways of expressing closeness explicitly may have been misinterpreted as closeness itself, and the masculine methods by instru-mental acts discounted. Clearly there are conceptual as well as methodo-logical problems to be faced before these issues can be resolved.

CROSS-SEX FRIENDSHIPS

The boundary between friends and lovers will always be difficult to define. Physical intimacy may be present in many degrees, and the desire for physical intimacy may colour a relationship when it is not overtly present. In any case most lovers are also friends (Hendrick & Hendrick, 1993).

However, cross-sex friendships (without physical intimacy) are not so common as same-sex friendships, though in adolescence they may serve as a bridge between same-sex friendships and sexual relationships (Block, 1980; Gaines, 1994; Parker & de Vries, 1993). Amongst the possible reasons for their relative rarity, an important one is probably the hostile social pressures that cross-sex friendships encounter. Not only are they seen as threatening by existing partners, and presumably for that reason are even less common amongst married persons, especially wives (Booth & Hess, 1974), but also they are constrained by conventions and norms which see cross-sex relationships as inevitably or potentially sexual, with resultant suspicions by co-workers and others.[2] This is probably exacerbated by the current salience of the sexual harassment issue. In addition, opportunities for men and women to meet on equal terms are less common than for same-sex encounters—most cross-sex interactions in workplaces still involve a difference in status (O'Meara, 1994).

There are also problems in conducting cross-sex friendships. It is necessary to circumvent the culture-bound tendency to see members of the opposite sex as sex objects, and the perceptions of outsiders that sexual attraction is basic to the relationship. There may also be anxieties about an existing partner's jealousy. Beyond that, it is necessary to overcome traditional male–female ways of relating if a relationship between true equals is desired.

Partly because cross-sex friendships are less common than same-sex friendships, they have been much less studied. And those studies that have been carried out have tended to treat same-sex friendships as the norm, contrasting cross-sex friendships with them. This has had two results. First, although most studies find few differences between cross-sex and same-sex friendships, it is the areas where differences do occur that tend to get highlighted (Rawlins, 1994). Second, closeness, as a salient character of (at least women's) same-sex friendships becomes a focus of interest in studies of cross-sex friendships, with the implication that the closer a relationship, the more support, rewards, and enjoyment it will offer. Cross-sex friendships, even in the absence of a sexual element, may be just as close, in a loose sense, as same-sex ones, but the resources exchanged may differ: in particular, men and women who are friends may reciprocate respect rather than affection (Gaines, 1994). However Lin and Rusbult (1995) found that dating relationships were characterised by more satisfaction, investment, and centrality than cross-sex friendships.

Sapadin (1988) found that adult women tended to find their cross-sex friendships less intimate and satisfying than same-sex friendships, while men rated cross-sex friendships more highly. Men characterised cross-sex friendships as reciprocally nurturant, but women felt more nurtured by their women friends. Especially for women, but also for men, sexual tensions ranked highest for what was disliked about cross-sex friendships, though men made less distinction between friendship and sexual relationships than did women. In slight contrast to this, a study of cross-sex friendships in college students indicated that good friends understood each other well and agreed on the amount of sexual and romantic undertones in the relationship (Monsour et al., 1993).

---

[2] Just why outsiders should react strongly to the knowledge or suspicion that a cross-sex friendship involved a physical element is itself an interesting issue, and seems to imply an ultimate basis in reproductive competition.

CULTURAL VARIATIONS

In the West, friendship is only loosely institutionalised. Friendships are diverse, and although they must be seen as involving dialectical relations between the socio-cultural structure and the psychological dispositions of the participants in the context in which they are living (Adams & Blieszner, 1994), the constraints are not as rigid as in some other relationships. There are rights and duties associated with the status of friend (see Table 23.1; Argyle & Henderson, 1985), but it is doubtful if any are ubiquitously essential. A different selection of the rules is seen as essential in different cases. Nevertheless, cultural influences are not unimportant. The precise nature of friendship has changed over the centuries in both East (McDermott, 1992) and West (Contarello & Volpato, 1991) and differs between cultures (Adams & Blieszner, 1994; Schneider et al., 1994). Sapadin (1988) has suggested that friendship in the West used to be based on male values like loyalty, duty, heroism, and bravery, but there is now more emphasis on the female values of trust, caring, and intimacy.

The cultural norms for friendship can change even over a few decades. In an analysis of popular American magazine articles in the 1970s and 80s, Prusank, Duran, and DeLillo (1993) found that earlier emphases on the performance of behaviours that would please the partner or oneself, and avoidance versus openness in communication, have changed to emphasis on the unity of the partners and on shared goals and needs.

FACTORS CONDUCIVE TO FRIENDSHIP

Individuals differ greatly in the number and closeness of their friends. While some of this variation is due to differences in opportunity, much also depends on social skills: individuals differ in their abilities to make friends. But beyond that, there are also differences in motivation: having friends is more important to some people than to others. Using stories written in response to Thematic Apperception Test pictures, McAdams (1985, 1988) has described an "intimacy motive", involving a recurrent preference or readiness for warm, close, and communicative interactions with others. In a series of studies McAdams found that intimacy motivation was related to positive peer ratings; themes of warmth, love, etc. in autobiographical recollections; memory for story themes concerning personal interaction; self-disclosure with friends; and frequent thoughts about friends and relationships. Some comparable data have been obtained with pre-adolescent children (McAdams & Losoff, 1984).

Friendship, however, can have many qualities, and other aspects of the personalities of the participants may affect its nature. McAdams also investigated the effect of power motivation on friendship. Persons high in power motivation may see friendships as opportunities for self-assertion and display, though taking the lead may involve giving advice or help.

Friendship is a relationship. If some people are perceived as more friendly than others, and some people are more prone to see others as friendly, the question arises whether, within a particular relationship, the partners would perceive the partner as more friendly than would be predicted either from their general tendency to see others as friendly or from the partners' general friendliness. As we have seen, Wright and Ingraham (1986a) separated these issues using the Social Relations Model of Kenny and LaVoie (1984, see pp.206–207). They arranged that students reasonably well acquainted with each other should rate each other on affiliation. The data showed that, within specific relationships, an individual's feeling of being appreciated was positively correlated with the other's, over and above their respective tendencies to elicit appreciation and to feel appreciated. In other words, friends are special.

In older individuals a number of individual characteristics have been linked to friendship formation—e.g. level of moral judgement; ability to interpret behaviour of others; and lack of egocentricity. Individuals with an internal locus of control perceive their social relationships as being established and maintained by their own efforts and abilities, and Lefcourt et al. (e.g. 1985) therefore predicted that individuals with an internal locus of control for affiliation would have more effective social skills: in laboratory studies they found that internality was associated with greater social perceptiveness, and with a variety of conversational and other social skills.

Individual characteristics also influence the sort of friends that are made, as might be expected. High self-monitors, who try to adapt to whatever situation they are in and see themselves as sensitive and responsive to social cues, tend to partition their social worlds so that they engage in particular activities with particular partners, and tend to choose friends as activity partners in particular domains. Low self-monitors prefer a homogeneous social world in which they spend time with people who are globally similar, and tend to choose friends on the basis of general feelings of liking (Snyder, Gangestad, & Simpson, 1983; data obtained from students).

Friendship depends on compatibility between the partners. The development of friendship therefore usually requires a prolonged period of probing the characteristics of the potential partner (Miell & Duck, 1986; Rose & Serafica, 1986; see also Chapters 25 & 26). Behaviour involved in the development and maintenance of friendship has been documented by Auhagen (1991) by requiring both parties to complete diaries about events relevant to their relationship—a method likely to bring new insights into the nature of friendship.

AGE CHANGES

Since friendship is not necessarily centred round any particular activity, and is only loosely constrained by rules (see Table 23.1), the participants' conceptions of what friendship should be like plays an important part in its development and maintenance. However even toddlers can show considerable commitment to relationships with friends. Friendship pairs choose each other, prefer each other, try to be like each other, and may be devastated by separation (Whaley & Rubinstein, 1994). Some 4-year-olds who choose to spend much time close to each other may nevertheless seldom interact overtly, suggesting that at this age co-construction through talk is less important than later (Hinde, 1978b).

The model of friendship may evolve from the working model of relationships formed earlier with the caregiver (see p.386). The affection and identification with friends shown by adolescent girls has been found to be positively related to their affection and intimacy with their mothers (Gold & Yanof, 1985), as Bowlby would have predicted. In addition, the children of mothers who have high-quality friendships tend also to have good friends (Doyle, Markiewicz, & Hardy, 1994).

However expectations are influenced by cultural norms. A conception of what friendship should be like develops gradually in children (Bigelow, 1977). Schneider, Wiener, and Murphy (1994) found propinquity of residence or school and shared activities to be important for friendship for 4-year-olds. Similarity in age, race, physical attributes, and activity preferences, important early on, tended to decline in importance with age, while that of similarity in attitudes and interests increased. Tangible support, self-disclosure, trust, and reciprocity were also seen to be important.

There is evidence from kibbutzim that the extensive exposure to peers and reduced adult supervision reduces the incidence of intimate friendship in children. In addition, the lower-class Israeli children showed more intimate friendship than middle-class children, but differentiated less clearly between best and other friends (Sharabany, 1994).

Much of the research on friendship has been concerned with children or young adults, but the friendships of older adults have many of the same properties (Reisman, 1981). Shea, Thompson, and Blieszner (1988; Blieszner & Adams, 1992) provide evidence that older people desire to contribute to relationships, and not just to benefit from them; that persons who feel themselves to be over-benefited feel uncomfortable (see pp.345–347); that friends who are emotionally and physically close are most likely to exchange resources; and that issues of equity (see p.354) are more salient in less close relationships. However one of the most outstanding characteristics of the friendship of elderly adults is the importance of duration: individuals preferred existing friendships to the prospect of new ones, and could not imagine that new ones would ever be the same as the established ones.

FRIENDSHIP AT WORK

The benefits of friendship are a matter of common experience, and may radiate beyond the dyadic relationship. For instance the quality of friendship at work is related to job satisfaction. Studying the staff at two universities, Winstead et al. (1995) found that the quality of the best friendship at work was predictive of an overall measure of satisfaction at work. The relations with other measures, such as satisfaction with people on the job or the opportunities for promotion, were much smaller, supporting the general conclusion.

FRIENDS AND THE SOCIAL GROUP

Friendship is usually a dyadic relationship, though three or more can be mutual friends. However, beyond that most friendships both influence and are influenced by the group in which they are embedded. Although we tend to think of friends meeting and doing things together, often this is in the company of others—other friends or other couples. Furthermore, especially among adolescents, the very fact of having one or more friends may bring status in the group. Even if one discounts the manipulative use of friendship to gain advantage, it may do so adventitiously. In addition, there may be negative effects—jealousy by other group members, for instance (Allan, 1993; Milardo, Johnson, & Huston, 1984). Some causes of conflict between dyads and the surrounding network are mentioned on pp.300 and 473.

THE FRAGILITY OF FRIENDSHIP

In a sensitive essay based on interviews with subjects ranging widely in age, Wiseman (1986) has emphasised the fragility of friendship. It is unlike most other relationships in lacking external forces tending to maintain its quality. Thus marriage partners may make a home, have children, attempt to please relatives and so on—all actions that tend to cement the bond between them quite apart from the legal and social pressures. Friendship, by contrast, has no role or task around which it can reform itself if stressed, and no societal mechanism to encourage reconciliation. And it contains the seeds for its own potential destruction in the contradictory pressures for autonomy and intimacy.

Friends tend to be clear about the traits in their friends on which they depend, but much less clear about those traits in themselves on which their friends count. They are aware that their friends have both desirable and undesirable traits, but tend to overlook the latter, perceiving the other as the other would like to be perceived. However if they perceive a new trait in the other, this may cause their whole view of the other to be re-cast. And friends may change or appear to change just because they do not realise what it is that is important about them to the other: this is the more likely if friends do not discuss each other or their relationship. It may be difficult to allow for a friend's right to change, or to cope with change that results from a change in life circumstances. As we have seen, this is where commitment becomes crucially important, though with friend-ship there may be no outside forces to maintain commitment.

The very fact of the mutual trust inherent in friendship carries with it the possibility of betrayal, and the danger that adverse attributions about the partner will be made for transgressions that were unavoidable (see pp.326–327). Expectations for specific actions in specific circumstances, which may develop autonomously within the relationship or be imported from other relationships or cultural norms, form an intrinsic part of friend-ship, but such expectations may be disappointed. Friends who enjoyed similar attitudes to people or institutions external to their relationship may come to find that they differ, and experience dissonance.

Thus friendship, with its voluntary nature and generating its own ex-pectations, and its undiscussed reliance on unwritten contracts to offer and receive aid, can easily run into problems. Wiseman (1986, p.210) concludes by saying "given these built-in pitfalls, the social miracle is that, for the most part, friends do manage the balancing act for which the position calls ... they do fulfil expectations a great deal of the time; they do not overdo demands". Perhaps the very absence of social norms leads to the bounds of friendship being appreciated even more, leading to more self-correction.

There is another danger, emphasised by Davis (1973), in friendships that become extremely close. The partners' conceptions of self may come to overlap so completely that each sees his or her individuality threatened: this may lead to behaviour that decreases the closeness of the relationship.

While all these issues are intrinsic to the nature of friendship, it is also important to remember that friendship may face external threats. The exclusivity of friendship means that closeness to one person militates against closeness to another. For that reason, marital partners are espe-cially likely to see a spouse's friend as a threat.

THE PERSISTENCE OF FRIENDSHIP

Given these hazards, the persistence of the relationship between friends may require that the partners work at it, sustaining their interest in and involvement with each other (Rose & Serafica, 1986). What factors are conducive to the survival of friendship after disruption?

Griffin and Sparks (1990) carried out a study of non-sexual friendship at college and four years later. Of the eight measures used in the initial phase when the subjects were still in college, none was significantly related to closeness four years later (measured by the sum of five characteristics of the relationship plus the degree of proximity) in female–female or platonic cross-sex friendships. For male–male friendships, five measures were significantly related to closeness:

(a) Status similarity, the sum of measures of intellectual ability, social skills, physical attractiveness, physical coordination, spiritual maturity, and financial resources. The authors ascribe this to comparison leading to self-depreciation by an inferior partner.
(b) Competence in a linguistic game that depended on the two members of the dyad sharing a universe of discourse.
(c) Having been room-mates.
(d) Current proximity.
(e) Protection of the partner, in that few topics had to be avoided in conversation.

ENEMIES

Wisemen and Duck (1995) have recently called attention to the dearth of studies on the relationships between enemies. In so far as each interaction is influenced by preceding ones and perhaps by the expectation of further interactions in the future, enemyships certainly count as relationships as defined here. Unlike friendships, however, they do not necessarily involve participants who are ready to incur costs just for the sake of sharing each other's company. More usually enemyships involve individuals who are constrained to associate as members of the same institution, and merely needle each other as opportunity arises. There may be commitment to maintain the (negative) quality of the relationship, but not for continuity (see Chapter 15). Analysing data from a pilot study, Wiseman and Duck found that most respondents reported a desire to stay out of the way of their enemies—a tendency fully understandable in view of the often expressed feeling that the enemy possessed power over the respondent.

Most respondents reported that the state of enmity emerged unexpectedly: Wiseman and Duck suggest that this may have been because trivial actions, such as unintended slights or thoughtless remarks, by their respondents had led cumulatively to negative feelings in the "enemy"—feelings which built up gradually and then became apparent more or less suddenly. In general one must suppose that enemyships start from some infringement of status, competition, rivalry, or frustration.

The respondents in this study also reported a feeling that enemyships were less fragile, more stable, than friendships. This is the more surprising in that enemyships involve no socially sanctioned rights and duties, and usually no social pressures to stay involved, as do many other relationships. Possibly relevant in this context was the further finding that the enemyships could be especially frightening if they were covert, without open conflict, denying the participants opportunity to express their points of view. Their stability implies either inability to resolve the bases of difference, or a degree of dependence on the relationship, even though that dependence may involve only the desire to be free, or to see oneself as free, from the other's power. That this dependence can go to extremes is suggested by Maugham's (1976) story of two enemies confined together in a sanatorium who missed no opportunity to irritate or insult each other. When one of them died, the other started to go downhill, feeling that his principal source of pleasure had disappeared.

One possible source of this dependence concerns the need to define and protect the integrity of the self (see Chapter 3). While conversation with someone who thinks exactly as one does oneself can be boring, conversation with someone who thinks slightly differently can be stimulating. Its value comes in part from the opportunity it provides to clarify one's position to oneself—to define the precise nature of one's own views. The definition of a boundary requires reference to what is outside as well as to what is inside. Perhaps, therefore, part of the fascination of an enemy is that the enemy calls into question part of one's self-image, and one seeks opportunity either to justify oneself in open discussion or conflict, or to denigrate the enemy. This, however, is speculation.

Many enemyships are not simply individual matters, but involve a social context. When enemies do seek each other out in order to joust with each other, there is often an ancillary motive involving a real or imagined audience—for instance when it is a matter of revenge, or honour is at stake.

SUMMARY

1. Friendship, unlike most other relationships, is not defined by the content of the interactions. It is a voluntary and positive relationship.
2. Assessments of friendship quality employ somewhat diverse criteria of desiderata.
3. The evidence indicates that, on the whole, women's friendships are more satisfying than those of men, though this conclusion depends in part on the criteria of satisfaction used.
4. Cross-sex friendships face special problems.
5. Friendship shows considerable cultural diversity.

6. A variety of factors influence the nature of friendship, including the skills, motivational and other characteristics of the participants.
7. The nature of friendship changes with age.
8. Friendship both influences and is influenced by the social group or groups to which the participants belong.
9. A variety of factors influence the nature of friendship, including the skills, motivational and other characteristics of the participants.
10. Although friendship lacks some of the factors that support the continuity of other relationships, it often shows surprising persistence.
11. Enemyships can be quite intense relationships, even though the participants do not usually seek each other out. Their attraction may lie in part in the opportunity they provide for self-definition.

24 Love and Romantic Relationships

In the expanding literature on human relationships, a high proportion of studies have been concerned with "romantic" or "dating" relationships or marriage. Romantic relationships are presumably to be identified by the fact that the participants experience, or hope to experience, "love", but "love" means many different things to different people. The love felt by young adults in a romantic relationships bears some resemblances to, but in other respects is very different from, the love felt by a long-term married couple, and both differ according to the age and other characteristics of the participants, as well as between cultures. Love is also an important element in, for instance, parent–child and sibling relationships, and in friendship. Each of these has other properties associated with it— nurturance and security, mutual support, companionship, and so on, the relative importance of which differs between relationships of the different types. For instance, a comparison of the relevance of trust, need, and care indicated that care predominated in subjects' conceptions of love, trust in those of friendship, and need in those of attraction (Steck et al., 1982). We must therefore ask whether love is the same sort of thing in different types of relationships.

If we are to understand romantic and married relationships, and the relevance of conclusions that can be drawn from their study to other types of relationships, some exploration of the concept of love is clearly essential. What the young adults, with whom most of the work has been done, think and feel is important, and may have repercussions throughout their lives

(Hendrick & Hendrick, 1989), but it may be necessary to exercise care in generalising data from studies in which they were subjects. The nature of people's conceptions of love is therefore a major theme in this chapter: other aspects of relationships characterised by love are discussed elsewhere (especially Chapters 12 to 15).

WHAT IS LOVE?

More has been written about the nature of love than any other aspect of social relationships, and many of the insights come from outside social psychology. To survey the literature here would be impossible, but it is necessary to sketch briefly the perspective used in this book.

To discuss whether love is pancultural and fundamentally biological, or whether it is culturally created, would be sterile. It is both. The pride, tenderness, and love of a mother with her baby, and the love and longing between man and woman, clearly have biological bases, but the way each is expressed differs greatly between cultures. As we shall see later, cultural differences are very considerable, and the very notion of a romantic relationship is to a considerable extent a Western peculiarity that would be incomprehensible to many in other parts of the world.

To a lay-person in the Western world love can be seen as a useful label for a complex of relationship characteristics—a complex which differs between individuals and even in the same individual at different times— and especially for the feelings that accompany such relationships. The everyday concept of love has fuzzy borders, yet it has sufficient coherence for colloquially recognised types of love (maternal, romantic, self-love, affection, etc.) to be ranked as poor or good examples of love (Fehr & Russell, 1991). To the social psychologist love could be seen as an hypothetical construct, or perhaps better as an intervening variable (MacCorquodale & Meehl, 1954) with which to describe or explain certain aspects of some close relationships. As such, it is the more useful, the more consistent those properties are across the relationships in question. The properties include behaviour involved in the expression of love, affective experience in the relationship including the enjoyment of being with the partner, and thoughts about the relationship, including thoughts about the future (e.g. Noller, 1996). In what follows, we are concerned principally with love in close relationships between non-related adults. An important distinction often overlooked is that between "loving" and "being in love"; the latter involves affect, behaviour, and thoughts and is to be seen as a relationship characteristic, while "loving" can refer just to the subjective experience (Berscheid & Meyers, 1996).

In practice, close loving relationships differ greatly in their characteristics, and their variability stems in part from cultural influences. In every society people are acculturated to accept that certain types of relationship, including a wide variety of loving relationships, have certain properties. Individuals recognise that their relationship is a loving relationship because it resembles what they believe a loving relationship to be like; and their recognition of, and desire for, that resemblance leads them to experience their relationship as a loving one and to behave appropriately.

Differences between loving relationships also stem from differences in motivation and circumstances which affect the way in which the partner is perceived (see later). Even amongst the relationships of, say, young adults, there are great individual differences. Sternberg (1996) sees love as a story developed and held by the individual, and with which he tries to match his experience. These stories vary greatly—Sternberg presents a taxonomy of 24 types with labels like "Addiction", "Fantasy", "Science fiction", and so on. For instance, "Love as science" implies a rational approach to love.

Recognisable differences between types of loving relationship pose the question of whether love does in fact have a unitary coherence, or whether the meaning of love changes with the object to which it is directed. One way to approach this is to investigate the way in which lay-people talk and think about love. A variety of ways for doing this have been reviewed by Berscheid and Meyers (1996). Fehr (1994) asked student subjects to name types of love, and then used 15 of these types in a study of their validity and relations to psychologists' conceptions of love: these were friendship, maternal, sisterly, parental, familial, brotherly, committed, affectionate, platonic, romantic, sibling, passionate, infatuation, puppy, and sexual love. Features of each of these prototypes were obtained from another group of subjects, and further groups of 160 subjects (80 dating couples involving students) and 227 students were asked to rate their similarity to their own view of love. The prototypes were placed (in different assessments) roughly in the above order, with friendship most similar and sexual least. The prototypes were then compared with the results of a factor analysis of a variety of love scales as used by psychologists, and this indicated that the prototype measures had convergent and discriminant validity and could be used for assessing people's views of love.

A cluster analysis of the similarity ratings in this study showed that the prototypes were related to each other in meaningful ways—for instance puppy love and infatuation clustered together, and were then joined by sexual and passionate love prototypes. The two final clusters contained passionate love and companionate love groupings, in keeping with the distinction frequently made by psychologists (Hatfield & Walster, 1978). Friendship and familial relationships fall within the companionate group. However Berscheid and Meyers (1996), also studying lay theories of love, doubted the validity of the companionate grouping, which often contains a high proportion of family members. Analysing the difference between "loving" and "being in love", they found that most of the people whom subjects saw as being in the latter category were also seen in the former, though being in love was much more likely to be seen as involving sexual desire (see also Reis & Shaver, 1988; Sternberg, 1995).

To return to the issue of romantic love, this came fairly low down on the Fehr and Russell (1991) typicality ratings referred to earlier, with passionate love, sexual love, and infatuation near the bottom. Romantic love has been characterised in a number of ways, but they mostly include idealisation of the partner who is regarded as unique and special, physio-logical arousal, sexual implications, commitment, longing for the partner during separation, concern for the partner's well-being, and so on. Romantic love can be regarded as overlapping more with "being in love" than with loving. Other labels for related types of love in current English-speaking societies involve stress on one or other of these properties—for instance passionate love implies an emphasis on arousal and usually also on the sexual implications, infatuation on the longing.

Perhaps because most research has been done in cultures with a stereo-type of romantic love, and much of the work has been concerned with young people, many definitions or measures of love seem to emphasise what the lover feels about the loved one. Yet one of the essential qualities of more mature love involves much less of the idealisation of the loved one than the romantic view of love suggests. Stepping outside the academic traditions, it is salutary to consider Tweedie's (1979, p.135) remarks, made with reference to a mature adult relationship:

> Love, used in a romantic or a passionate context, is merely a licence for indulgence of our own needs and fantasies, a prop for our weaknesses and an accessory for our shaky egos. True love is, above all, an emanation of reason; a rational apprehension of another human being and a logical assessment of his or her particular needs, virtues and failings, in the light of reality.

The contrast between romantic love and Tweedie's description of ma-ture love is dramatic, and perhaps this overstates it. Whilst it has been generally supposed that mutual attraction and passion are most intense early in a relationship, the extent to which the partner supplies comfort and emotional support becoming gradually more important later (Reedy, Birren, & Schaie, 1981), Aron and Henkemeyer (1995) found considerable levels of "passionate love" in both men and women in long-established marriages, "passionate love" being measured on a widely used, 15-item "Passionate love scale". The principal difference between "romantic" and "mature" love thus seems to lie not in a decrease in passion but rather in a change in the defence mechanisms to allow more recognition and acceptance of the partner's perceived deficiencies. Acceptance of the partner for what he is has been seen as part of love by a number of authors (Noller, 1996), and the earlier and longer version of Rubin's Love scale differed from the Liking scale in involving recognition that the loved one might not be perfect. Acceptance is crucial if it is to be possible for one individual to open up his most intimate areas to another, and thereby validate his essential core self (Kelvin, 1977; see pp.208–209).

It is helpful to look at the difference between romantic and "mature" love from a functional perspective. We have seen that young couples often believe that they know more about each other than is actually the case (pp.233, 236), and their relationship may seem to be held together in a very tenuous fashion. Romantic relationships form part of the process of family formation and reproduction, and it seems that societies have developed two routes to ensuring this development in the early stages. One involves the socially constructed convention of arranged marriages with sanctions against their disruption. The other, equally socially constructed, involves romantic love, which can serve as temporary scaffolding while trust and a more (though still incompletely) objective view of the relationship can be built up. Thus Noller (1996) points out that the views that romantic love is blind, externally imposed, and uncontrollable, with exaggerated views about what love will bring, and that love is volatile, are not conducive to stable relationships. But perhaps they are conducive to initial bonds— if love is blind, it is no good trying too hard to see what is going on; if love is uncontrollable, best submit; and so on.[1]

Be that as it may, neither romantic love nor mature love are always of a common pattern. Even within those categories, there are diverse ways of loving and diverse beliefs about love. We shall see some of these later.

ASSESSMENT OF LOVE

A considerable number of instruments have been devised to assess both love as a whole and its several aspects (see e.g. reviews by Hendrick & Hendrick, 1989; Shaver & Hazan, 1988; Sternberg & Barnes, 1988). Some of these were intended primarily to assess the intensity of the experience,

---

[1] In an important paper Leckman, Mayes, and Insel (personal communication) have called attention to the similarities between romantic love and the early stages of parental love—the altered mental state, intrusive thoughts and images associated with a heightened awareness of the other, and a complex behavioural repertoire leading to the formation of an intense interpersonal tie. They suggest that romantic and parental love may share certain "evolutionarily conserved" mechanisms, including central oxytocin pathways. On the view advanced here, romantic love would involve the cultural exploitation of these mechanisms primarily serving parental attachment.

TABLE 24.1
Shortened Self-report Scales for Loving and Liking

LOVE SCALE

1. I feel I can confide in ____ about virtually everything.
2. I would do almost anything for ____.
3. If I could never be with ____, I would feel miserable.
4. If I were lonely, my first thought would be to seek ____ out.
5. One of my primary concerns is ____'s welfare.
6. I would forgive ____ for practically anything.
7. I feel responsible for ____'s well-being.
8. I would greatly enjoy being confided in by ____.
9. It would be hard for me to get along without ____.

LIKING SCALE

1. I think that ____ is unusually well-adjusted.
2. I would highly recommend ____ for a responsible job.
3. In my opinion ____ is an exceptionally mature person.
4. I have great confidence in ____'s good judgement.
5. Most people would react favourably to ____ after a brief acquaintance.
6. I think that ____ is one of those people who quickly win respect.
7. ____is one of the most likeable people that I know.
8. ____is the sort of person whom I myself would like to be.
9. It seems to me that it is very easy for ____ to gain admiration.

From Rubin (1974).

like Rubin's (1974) scales which distinguished liking and loving . Table 24.1 shows a much used shortened version of this scale: it is to be expected that any such scale would be in some degree culture-specific. More recent approaches have attempted to differentiate between different forms, components, or styles of loving, or ways of expressing love. Consideration of the following instruments may provide further insight into the ways in which research workers construe love, though the focus of most research has been on love between young adults.

(i) Jeffries (1993), in one of the relatively few studies not concerned with heterosexual love, distinguished between love based on the perception of gratifications which may be received from the relationship and love involving attempts to further the welfare of the other. Although these tend to be associated with each other because seeking to benefit others enhances positive feelings towards and from them (see Foa & Foa, 1974), they were shown to be separate dimensions on a factor analysis of students' replies to a questionnaire which assessed love for parents and perceived love of parents for them.

(ii) Sternberg and Grajek (1984) enumerated a number of facets of love present to differing degrees in relationships between parent and child, lovers, siblings, friends, etc.—namely, understanding of the other, sharing of ideas and information, sharing of personal ideas and feelings, receipt and provision of emotional support, mutual facilitation of personal growth, mutual help, mutual feelings of needing the other, and giving and receiving affection. Sternberg (1986) later proposed that nearly all types of love could be understood as combinations (in differing proportions) of three constructs—Intimacy (defined as closeness, connectedness, emotional investment); Passion (a motivational component including arousal which may or may not be sexual); and Commitment (a cognitive component). Different weightings of these three components can give rise to different qualities of loving: thus "infatuated love" would involve only passion, and "fatuous love" passion and commitment but no intimacy. The three components vary systematically across relationships of different types. The statistical bases of Sternberg's instrument have been assessed by Whitley (1993).

(iii) Based on an earlier qualitative study, Hecht, Marston, and Larkey (1994) used factor analysis of a questionnaire to identify different aspects of the experience of being in love. They see these as combined in different ways in different individuals, and yet in each individual giving a holistic experience which is recognised as being in love. These five aspects, which they term "love ways", are:

(a) *Intuitive love*, expressed largely through non-verbal means (physical contact, non-verbal expression, sexual activity);
(b) *Companionate love*, concerned with togetherness, communication, and support, and expressiveness;
(c) *Secure love*, concerned with security and need;
(d) *Traditional love*, involving a strong emotional component and notions of love as engendering both warmth and anxiety; and
(e) *Committed love*, involving commitment and planning for the future.

In two studies, each with subjects who had had longer relationships and many of whom were somewhat older than the all-student subjects used in many comparable studies, they found that *individuals* experiencing committed love were the most likely to perceive their relationships as being of high quality (as assessed by another instrument). Whether this was because commitment is more likely to be experienced in a high-quality relationship, or because a feeling of commitment is in line with implicit theories of what love should be like, could not be determined.

They also found that *couples jointly experiencing* high levels of companionate love tended to perceive their relationships as of higher quality than those jointly experiencing high levels of other forms—presumably because companionate love emphasises connectedness and communication. In addition, couples whose members experienced similar levels of secure love and similar levels of companionate love tended to see their relationships as of higher quality than those experiencing similar levels of other forms of love. Security reflects in part on dependence, and thus this finding suggests that symmetry in either dependence or independence is important for quality in relationships. Hecht et al. (1994) also note that the two aspects associated with relationship quality (committed and companionate love) both emphasise verbal communication.

(iv) Lee (1973), on the basis of interviews with adults about their love relationships, postulated three primary love styles—Eros, Ludus and Storge. These could be combined to form three further styles, Mania (eros and ludus), Pragma (ludus and storge), and Agape (storge and eros). These six styles have been studied extensively by Hendrick and Hendrick (e.g. 1986, 1990) and may be defined roughly as follows:

Eros. Physical; intense emotion; strong commitment
Ludus. Love as a game, with little depth of feeling. Manipulative. No commitment.
Storge. Love as friendship; solid, down-to-earth, with little passion.
Pragma. Rational, calculating.
Mania. Emotional, irrational, involving uncertainty but intense feelings.
Agape. Altruistic, non-demanding love.

These emerged clearly as distinct styles in a factor analysis of a 42-item questionnaire, accounting for 44% of the variance—though Shaver and Hazan (1988) point out that eros and agape are correlated with each other in most studies. Hendrick and Hendrick have shown that the six styles are related to individual characteristics (gender, ethnicity, current love status, previous love experiences, and self-esteem) in predictable ways. For instance, those "in love now" endorsed eros, storge, mania, and agape more strongly, and ludus less strongly, than those not in love. The findings were confirmed in a second study. In a later study, the endorsement of eros and agape by students and their partners was related to various aspects of satisfaction, the relation of own love style to satisfaction being stronger than that of the partner (Morrow, Clark & Brock, 1995; see also Bettor, Hendrick, & Hendrick, 1995).

The Hendrick and Hendrick (1990) Love Attitudes Scale is rather specific to young adults, and has been revised by Grote and Frieze (1994) to increase its applicability to married adults in lengthy relationships. The most extensive changes concerned storge, which was renamed Friendship-based love. This is defined as a "comfortable, affectionate, trusting love for a likeable partner, based on a deep sense of friendship and involving companionship and the enjoyment of common activities, mutual interests and shared laughter". Friendship-based love was found to be distinct from, but often associated with, erotic or passionate love, and strong in the relationships of both young dating and middle-aged married couples. It was more closely related to a number of variables, including relationship satisfaction, than were the revised Eros and Ludus scales. Middle-aged married women scored more highly than men on friendship-based love, but did not differ from them in ludic love. In dating young adults, men scored more highly than women on ludic love, but did not differ on friendship-based love.

Hazan and Shaver's (1987) theory of love has already been mentioned in relation to Bowlby's theory of attachment. In its dispositional aspects, love between adults is seen as resembling in some but not all respects the relationships between infants and their caregivers (see Chapter 21).

TRAIT OR STATE?

The experience of loving must be specific to a particular relationship, yet individuals may seem to show a similar love style in their different relationships. This raises the question, how far is love style to be seen as a disposition, characteristic of the individual, and how far as a state specific to the situation? Just because love is an aspect of a relationship, this is a difficult issue to assess. The natural approach would be to assess the love styles of individuals in their different (or successive) love relationships: if an individual's style were similar across relationships, this could be taken as evidence for a disposition. However individuals choose their partners, and the relationship depends on both. A given individual is likely to choose partners who, at least to a limited extent, resemble each other. Thus similarity across relationships could be due to similarities in the partners. Furthermore, recollections of past relationships are subject to many forms of bias. Aware of the impossibility of surmounting these and other difficulties, Amelang (1991) has nevertheless produced evidence that the love styles of Eros, Storge, and perhaps Ludus are dependent on the partner, while Pragma, Mania, and Agape show more trait-like properties.

INDIVIDUAL CHARACTERISTICS AND BELIEFS ABOUT LOVE

In so far as love has dispositional properties, one must expect the capacity for and experience of love to be related to other individual characteristics. Indeed Fromm (1956) argued that one must love oneself before one could love another.

A number of studies indicate that women value and convey intimacy in close relationships more than do men (see pp.212–213; Reis, Senchak, &

Solomon, 1985). Hendrick and Hendrick (1986; see also Hendrick et al., 1984) compared males and females on their six love styles (see earlier). Males were significantly more ludic than females, females more storgic, pragmatic, and manic than males. Hatkoff and Lasswell (1979), studying an American sample with a wide age-range, had obtained rather similar findings for the love styles, and in addition found males to be more erotic.

Frazier and Esterly (1990), however, studying beliefs about love in a sample with a wider age-range (19–47 years), obtained rather different data. Males were more ludic but also scored more highly on agape, and women were not significantly more pragmatic, storgic, or manic than men. Furthermore the relations between gender-related personality attributes and beliefs about love differed in some respects from what might have been expected. For example, high agape scores were associated with being male and, somewhat surprisingly, with being expressive, usually considered a feminine trait. Expressivity was, however, more strongly associated with relationship beliefs than instrumentality. Thus expressive individuals reported passionate, selfless, and friendship-based beliefs about love, while less-expressive individuals were more likely to be game-playing. An important aspect of these data concerned age-changes in beliefs about love. With age and experience women tended to become less romantic and selfless and more pragmatic—perhaps indications of becoming more realistic.

In a more recent study, Taraban and Hendrick (1995) assessed the personality traits that students perceived to be associated with each of the six love styles. The subjects perceived different personal characteristics to be associated with each of the six love styles. For example, the two traits seen as most important for each love style were: Eros, sexual and exciting; Ludus, inconsiderate and secretive; Storge, honest and loyal; Pragma, family-oriented and planning; Mania, jealous and possessive; Agape, committed and giving.

Other workers have examined not sex differences in love styles but their relations to gender role orientation. Coleman and Ganong (1985) found androgynous students to score more highly than masculine ones on awareness of love feelings, expression of love, non-material evidence of love, tolerance of faults, and total expression; and more highly than feminine subjects on awareness, willingness to express feelings, and toleration of faults.

The experience of love depends in part on one's beliefs about what love is or should be like. Sternberg's conception of love as a story has already been mentioned. Amongst other approaches to this issue, the Relationships Belief Scale (Fletcher & Kininmonth, 1991) assesses the factors that respondents believe would produce a successful and loving heterosexual relationship. In a student sample, analysis revealed four factors which were labelled Intimacy (e.g. honesty, mutual respect, communication, confronting conflict, support, love); External factors (individual backgrounds, over-lapping social networks, sharing beliefs and values); Passion (e.g. sexual relations, excitement); and Individuality (e.g. right to privacy, sharing of chores). Fletcher and Kininmonth found relations between the beliefs that an individual held and relationship satisfaction. For example, subjects who believed strongly in the importance of intimacy showed stronger links between self-reported levels of satisfaction and self-reported levels of intimacy than subjects who had weaker beliefs about the importance of intimacy. (Although the correlations depended on two self-reports, it is not unreasonable to suppose that satisfaction depends on the relation between what the individual aspires to and what he or she experiences, but it is also not unlikely that satisfaction may affect beliefs.)

Sprecher and Metts (1989) developed a Romantic Beliefs scale by a factor analysis of questionnaire data which gave a four-factor solution, named "Love finds a way"; "One and only"; "Idealisation"; and "Love at first sight": the titles are self-explanatory. In harmony with previous research, they found that being feminine in gender role orientation was associated with endorsement of the ideology of romanticism, and that men were more likely than women to have romantic beliefs. The greater romanticism of men is ascribed to the fact that they have or are expected to have roles that give them greater economic security than women—even though these role differences are now changing. The relation of femininity to romanticism is explained in terms of the traits that have been seen to con-tribute to the assessment of femininity—affectionate, childlike, loyal, etc.—which are likely to be associated with an idealistic view of love. Androgyny, found in previous studies to be associated with being more loving and holding fewer dysfunctional beliefs than other gender role orientations, explained little further variance when entered after masculinity and femi-ninity in a multiple regression analysis.

Moving beyond differences due to gender orientation, Hendrick and Hendrick found relations between love style and self-esteem: eros and ludus were positively correlated with self-esteem, mania was negatively correlated. Dion and Dion (1979, 1988) used their Romantic Love Questionnaire to assess various parameters of love including the frequency, duration, and intensity of experience of love. They found:

(a) Subjects with an internal locus of control (i.e. who tend to view events that affect them as being under their own control) were less likely to report having experienced romantic love, and described their experiences of love as being more rational and less volatile than those with an external locus of control. They were also more opposed to an idealistic view of love. This fits with the view of romantic love as an experience in which one loses control.

(b) The relations between experiences of love and self-esteem were in some respects more complex than those of Hendrick and Hendrick (see earlier), in that they depended on the individual's defensiveness. Those with high self-esteem and low defensiveness experienced love most frequently. However persons with low self-esteem reported more intense experiences of romantic love and described them as less rational. Dion and Dion suggest that those low in self-esteem are less skilled socially and thus less adept at entering loving relationships, but once in a loving relationship appreciate it and their partners more than those high in self-esteem; while defensive individuals avoid close relationships in order to protect their vulnerable self images, and are liable to feel distress if they feel they are losing control.

(c) Self-actualisation was measured by an instrument designed to reflect an individual's degree of positive mental health and the extent to which he or she was fulfilling his or her potential, and especially autonomy from external pressures. Individuals high on self-actualisation reported a richer, more satisfying love experience than did those who were lower, but tended to be less idealistic and more pragmatic in their attitudes towards love. They seemed to be more involved in love as a fulfilling personal experience than as involving interdependence with another person, with less love for the partner (see also later).

Another characteristic linked to love as a disposition is anxiety. Hatfield, Brinton, and Cornelius (1989) found significant positive correlations between both trait and state anxiety and scores on a love scale in young adolescents.

Beliefs about love are also related to the adult attachment style (Table 21.1), itself related to experiences in childhood. In general, those self-classified as secure described their most important love experience as happy and trusting. They were more likely to believe that romantic feelings could from time to time reach the intensity experienced early in the relationship, and that romantic love need never fade. Those with an avoidant style were characterised by fear of intimacy and jealousy. They were more inclined to believe that romantic love does not exist in real life, that romantic love seldom lasts, and that it is rare to find someone you can really fall in love with. Anxious/ambivalent subjects experienced love as involving obsession. They claimed that it was easy to fall in love, but that they rarely found true love (Hazan & Shaver, 1987). (It must however be noted that these results involve the comparison of self-reports, and that not all differences were significant on a second replication.)

Attachment style has been linked to love style in a cross-cultural study of European-, Japanese-, and Chinese-Americans and Pacific Islanders, all at the University of Hawaii, by Doherty et al. (1994, see later). In all groups

Anxious subjects were most likely to be in love and scored highly on a passionate love scale, whereas Avoidant subjects scored lowest. The Secure subjects scored highest on a scale of companionate love.

CULTURAL DIFFERENCES

Just because love involves intense subjective experience, the ideology of romanticism, if prevalent in the culture, is likely to play an important part in determining individuals' orientations towards love (cf. Sprecher & Metts, 1989). The claim that romantic love is found in virtually all cultures rests largely on a finding that at least one indicator of romantic love (e.g. longing, elopement) was found in ethnographic material from a sample of 166 societies (Jankowiak & Fischer, 1992). However romantic love involves a spectrum of characteristics and cannot be identified by the presence of only one; love songs and folk lore are not necessarily closely related to personal experience; and there are certainly some societies in which romantic love is effectively absent (Dion & Dion, 1996). Conceptions of love are related to societal conceptions of the nature of humanity (Beall & Sternberg, 1995), and romantic love is emphasised much more in some cultures than in others (Berscheid & Walster, 1974a).

Even in Europe and North America adolescents often have only vague notions as to how love should be identified. Whether or not adolescents label their feelings as "love", and whether or not they act out the role of romantic lover, is likely to depend on the cultural climate. The more the culture idealises the lover, the more will they be rewarded for labelling their feelings as love and for acting as lovers are expected to act. Furthermore, in a culture that emphasises the value of particular attributes, such as physical beauty, manliness, or docility, for inducing love in an opposite-sexed partner, an individual will be more likely to seek out such a partner and more likely to label his feelings as love and to act as a lover when he finds one. The culture will affect the emotions individuals feel or express, and the sorts of relationships they form.

Furthermore, the ways in which culture decrees that we label feelings, and thus the nature of the relationships in which we are involved, may depend in part on contextual cues (Berscheid & Walster, 1974a). It appears, for instance, that American young adults are more likely to use "romantic love" to refer to relationships with the opposite sex that are in progress, but "infatuation" for those that have been terminated. If this is so, the distinction can be made only in retrospect.

There have been differences of opinion about the cultural correlates of romantic love. Oppong (1979), reviewing data from several societies, has emphasised that sexual and erotic bonds, psychological bonds of affection and empathy, and legal and economic social bonds, do not necessarily go together (see also Williams, White, & Ekaidem, 1979). There are also differences in views about the relations of love to marriage. Rosenblatt (1974) found romantic love to be more prevalent in societies where the young couple lived with one of their kin groups, where it would help to maintain the relationship in the face of outside pressures (Driscoll, Davis, & Lipetz, 1972). Love also appears to be more important as a basis of marriage in societies where economic dependence between the spouses is weak, and where there is a marked imbalance in the levels of food production by men and women. Goody (1973) has pointed out a correlation between female property inheritance, monogamy, and the concept of conjugal love. A number of other studies demonstrating societal differences in views about the importance of romantic love are reviewed by Dion and Dion (1996).

Comparisons between the orientations towards love of American, Russian, and Japanese university students have been made by Sprecher et al. (1994a). Although there were many similarities, there were also differences, including differences of opinion about the importance of love in marriage: the authors suggest some of these may be related to cultural differences in security of attachment (Chapter 21). In addition, Japanese students tended to be less romantic—possibly a consequence of the collectivistic orientation, or to the lack of the Western tradition of romantic love.

Differences between collectivist and individualistic orientation at both cultural and individual levels do indeed appear to be important in relation to the emphasis on romantic love. Societies in which romantic love is seen as less important for marriage tend to be collectivistic, such as China and India. Western cultures tend to emphasise the freedom of the individual to seek personal gratification and development through relationships, and to pay great attention to the emotions experienced in them. In many non-Western societies, by contrast, family networks and inter-connected relationships are stressed, with arranged marriages or pragmatic selection of partners being obvious correlates (Dion & Dion, 1996; Triandis, 1991). Thus the notion of romantic love fits less well in collectivist societies, where individuals are expected to place a high priority on obligations to others, while romantic love fits with a more individualistic orientation. But there are exceptions to every generalisation: although the ethnic groups in Doherty et al.'s study (see earlier) differed in individualism vs. collectivism, they did not differ in the likelihood of being in love, or in the intensity of their feelings. The authors point out that differences might be found if societies that were modern, urban, and affluent were compared with ones that lacked these characteristics.

However, while the experience of romantic love is seen as providing an important basis for successful marriage in Western societies, the seeking of individual fulfilment may make that more difficult. Dion and Dion (1996) emphasise this paradox, and point to the importance of distinguishing between the societal levels and the psychological levels of individualism and collectivism. Within Canada they found that psychological individualism (assumed to be related to "self-actualisation") was associated with less deep and less tender love for the partner, and with a ludic attitude to love (Dion & Dion, 1991, 1994, 1996). Diversity exists in both individualistic and collectivist societies, and in the latter is increasing under Western influence. Some have claimed that romantic love is decreasing in Western societies, and an increase in individualism may be responsible. An increase in individualism and belief in self-fulfilment may also be related to the increase in divorce (Hinde, 1979; Dion & Dion, 1996), though over-emphasis on the view that love is essential for marriage would also lead to the same result.

The personality differences found by Dion and Dion (see earlier) to be important in the experience of love could also be important here. They point out that Japanese has a word *"amae"* for dependence on and presumption of another's benevolence. This has positive connotations for the Japanese, but is incompatible with Western individualism. In Japan, *amae* links dependency with the desire to be loved, whereas self-actualised persons (see earlier) do not need the partner in the same way.

PASSIONATE LOVE IN YOUNG CHILDREN

Hatfield et al. (1988) found that even 4-year-olds may report that they have experienced passionate love, in the sense of intense longing for a boy- or girl-friend. It is, of course, difficult to know how to interpret this, even though the investigators took great care to make their procedures suitable for young children. However the authors point out that only a few hundred years ago (and currently in other societies) children were seen as miniature adults, and so it is not so surprising that they should experience similar emotions. Of course what they experience as romantic love may be shaped by cultural stereotypes both before and after this age.

THE ROMEO AND JULIET EFFECT

Love may be augmented by obstacles placed in its way. Driscoll et al. (1972) found strong evidence that perceived parental opposition can intensify romantic love in both unmarried and married couples. The authors ascribe this effect to the motivating effects of goal frustration and reactance. However, while interference increased feelings of romantic love, it was also associated with decreased trust, increased criticism of the partner, and more negative behaviour. The decrease in trust may be a consequence of greater dependence on the partner and/or reduced certainty about the relationship. The other sequelae may represent intense involvement based on external opposition rather than on solid friendship, or perhaps on aggression redirected from the parents to the partner (see also Sprecher et al., 1994b).

IS THERE A NEGATIVE SIDE TO LOVE?

Love, usually seen as wholly positive, may have some negative aspects. All love involves costs. Sedikides, Oliver, and Campbell (1994) arranged that students (with experience of romantic relationships) should rank order the benefits and costs of romantic involvement. Companionship, happiness, and feeling loved or loving another were among the most important benefits. The more serious costs included stress and worry about the relationship, sacrifices made on its behalf, and increased dependence on the partner. While females regarded loss of identity and loss of innocence about relationships and love as more important costs than did males, males saw monetary loss as more important than did females.

The exaggeration of particular aspects of love can give it a destructive character. Some aspects of romantic love, which Noller (1996) describes as "crushes", may be harmless enough at the appropriate time, but can lead to family disruption if experienced later. Infatuation involves focusing on limited aspects of the partner, and can easily lead to disillusionment. Again, it has been argued that the Western emphasis on female expressiveness in love and the downgrading of masculine ways of expressing loving is associated with more rigid and stereotyped gender roles, conflict, and inadequate support between married partners. Excessive dependency can lead to inordinate possessiveness and jealousy, and have a negative impact on self-fulfilment (Noller, 1996).

This last issue is, of course, an aspect of the conflict between autonomy and relatedness (pp.157–158). The lover is likely to feel a desire to fulfil the desires of the loved one. So long as this springs from the heart, representing "reflective autonomy", there is no problem, but if it is a consequence of culturally imposed beliefs about what the concomitants of love should be, or of demands by the partner, the issues may be different. For many, total inclusion of self in other (see p.50) is unlikely to be viable as a long-term arrangement. Overemphasis on closeness when it is not appropriate and other aspects of the romantic love stereotype can lead to much unhappiness (e.g. Tweedie, 1979).

There may also be negative aspects to being loved which are insufficiently recognised in a culture with a romantic stereotype about love. An individual who feels loved, may feel also an obligation to behave in ways that the lover would wish. Raz (1994, pp.12–13) has argued that there should be no obligation to love in return, because the very nature of love is that it is spontaneous and unfettered (at least as perceived in our society); "...at its core love speaks of a spontaneous, unplanned response to another ... a duty of reciprocity destroys the very attitude it seeks to extend". But the loved one may nevertheless feel an obligation to reciprocate in other ways, and the more the lover has sacrificed for the loved one, the greater the latter feels obligation. Thus loving imposes a form of control on the partner, constraining autonomy. This is an issue little studied by psychologists, but well known to playwrights, novelists, and other students of human behaviour.

SUMMARY

1. Ideas about the nature of love are socially constructed, and differ between cultures, with age, and with the nature of the relationship. Love is an aspect of many familial and friendship relationships: however, much, though not all, of the work in social psychology has concerned the romantic love of students. While the beliefs of young adults about love are important, they may be very different from those of long-married couples, and generalisations must be made with caution.
2. A variety of instruments for assessing attitudes and love styles are available. Distinctions between love styles known as Eros, Ludus, Storge, Pragma, Mania, and Agape have been much used.
3. The experience of loving must be specific to a particular relationship, but individuals may show a similar style of loving in different relationships.
4. Differences in attitudes to love and in love styles may be related to gender-role orientation and various individual characteristics.
5. The ideal of romantic love is present to different extents in different cultures. Attitudes to love may be related to other aspects of the culture, such as individualism versus collectivism.
6. Young children can seem to experience passionate love.
7. Love may be enhanced by obstacles placed in its way.
8. Love can have a negative side. It may be associated with jealousy, and it may place constraints on the loved one.

E Relationship Change

A relationship is a process, not an entity. But even that is misleading, because the process itself involves many interdependent strands. Affective, cognitive, and behavioural processes are involved, and each of these has intra-individual, inter-individual, and social aspects. What is more, while all relationships must have a beginning and many end, the course from beginning to end is seldom smooth. Partners become acquainted, become closer, recede, and approach in a never-ending fluctuation of states. Consciously or unconsciously, they continually assess the state of the relationship, examining their emotions, updating accounts of how they got to where they are and why they feel as they do, sharing these accounts, aligning or contrasting them. They consider what others think about the relationship, whether it conforms to their internalised norms and to the norms of their social group, what impact it has on that group. They may discuss it with others. Of course, there may be long-term trends in the state of the relationship, the partners becoming gradually closer or more distant, but these are the result of a continuing dynamic. And if the relationship does end, it may leave traces which are never erased.

Because of this continuing flux, attempts to divide a relationship into temporal stages tend to be no more than a fiction—though sometimes a convenient one (e.g. Dindia & Baxter, 1987). Of course, there may be real markers, as when heterosexual partners go public and announce their "engagement", thereby opening their relationship to new (or augmented) influences from outside. But by-and-large all we can say is that there are positive tendencies early on, there may be negative ones later, and there is usually a period in between when the two are, over a span of time, more or less in balance.

Throughout, some similar things are going on, but there are likely to be major differences between the period of early growth and any subsequent period of decline. In the early stages of a close relationship, the potential partners are guided by expectations and hope; but if decline seems inevitable, retrospection and perhaps recrimination take their place. At first, positive emotions predominate, not so in decline. Early on the partners gather information about each other and about the relationship, constructing new cognitive schemata; in decline they still gather information but fit it into different schemata and make different attributions. And while the growth of a relationship is often tentative, the partners making small moves and behaving ambiguously in order to protect themselves from disconfirmation, decline is likely to be unambiguous and may be precipitate (Duck, 1982b).

There is some justification, therefore, provided we are constantly aware of the underlying flux, of segmenting our discussion into phases—Acquaintance, Growth, Maintenance, and Decline. While this is primarily an heuristic device, it may be a little more than that, its convenience stemming in part from the ways in which our own memories are structured in terms of prototypical types of behaviour that occur in close relationships (Honeycutt, 1993). Particular types of behaviour are stored together and provide a basis for labelling stages. The meta-memory (p.33) can be seen as storing expectancies of what should happen in the various stages of different sorts of relationships. (But, of course, the dialectic will operate; if we discuss relationships in terms of stages here, we shall be more likely to think of them in those terms in future.)

25 Acquaintance

INTRODUCTION

Some relationships start adventitiously. One moves to a new town, buys bread at a local shop, chats with the shopkeeper and gradually gets to know him or her better. But most research on the development of relationships has been concerned with close relationships—friends or romantic partners—where there is some degree of initial choice and successive interactions are usually actively sought for their own sake. It is with such that we are concerned in these chapters.

Just because relationships involve properties which must be assessed along diverse dimensions (Chapters 4–15), development cannot be seen as a smooth progression. Although earlier characterisations of relationship development suggested that it involved three levels—awareness, surface contact, and mutuality (Levinger & Snoek, 1972)—the issues are clearly more complex than such a description implies: the various aspects of a relationship develop at different relative speeds in different relationships. Furthermore we are concerned all the time with dynamic processes, with inputs from other levels of social complexity (Frontispiece), processes that may go in fits and starts, backwards, forwards, and even sideways. But in general, progress depends on the participants perceiving successive criteria to be met. While these vary between individuals, they move from the fairly concrete issues of physical appearance, overall interactional style, apparent status, and so on, to attitudes and traits, and to progressively more abstract characteristics including the way in which the potential friend or partner construes the world (Duck, 1973b; Duck & Craig, 1978; Duck & Miell, 1986). This does not mean that characteristics important early on become totally irrelevant. For instance, physical attractiveness may remain important in marriage (Margolin & White, 1987). But all the way along, an important criterion is likely to be the extent to which each partner perceives the other as able to support aspects of his or her self-concept.

PHYSICAL ATTRACTIVENESS

Some relationships, at least, are initiated as a consequence of physical attraction between the potential partners. Although what makes for attractiveness differs between cultures and between men and women, and may even change within a culture as a matter of fashion, certain physical characteristics seem to be fairly generally attractive (Buss, 1994). Women like men who are big, strong, and healthy. In an American study, Cunningham, Barbee, and Pike (1990) found evidence in harmony with the view that women were attracted to a combination of features eliciting nurturance and indicative of sex and dominance, and to men who were seen as sociable, approachable, and of high status. High status is presumably indicative of being a good provider. The neotenous feature of large eyes, the mature features of prominent cheekbones and a large chin, and a big smile were found to be attractive (see also Mueser et al., 1984; Sprecher, Sullivan, & Hatfield, 1994b).

Physical characteristics are more important to men than to women (Berscheid & Walster, 1978; Feingold, 1990, 1992). Men are especially likely to be attracted by women somewhat younger than themselves, healthy, with a waist-to-hip ratio between 0.67 and 0.80 (Singh, 1993; see also Furnham, Hester, & Weir, 1990). It is suggested that such features are attractive because they are indicative of high reproductive potential (e.g. Buss, 1994).

Men and women also differ in their beliefs about other factors conducive to sexual desire. Both male and female psychology students studied by Regan and Berscheid (1995) perceived female sexual desire to depend on interpersonal and relationship factors, male sexual desire on intraindividual and erotic environmental factors. Both sexes saw physical attractiveness as the most important issue in sexual desire. However, women but not men saw femininity as a sexually desirable female characteristic, men but not women saw power and status as sexually desirable male characteristics.

However it is important to distinguish between characteristics eliciting sexual desire and characteristics used to select a long-term partner (e.g. Deaux, 1976; Peplau & Gordon, 1985). The features that men in general find attractive for a short-term liaison with a woman are not the same as those that are attractive for a long-term relationship (e.g Kenrick et al., 1993). For the latter, characteristics indicative of fidelity, reliability, and good mothering become important.

In any case, there are cultural differences in the characteristics deemed to be attractive. Ford and Beach (1951) reported that, whereas men in many cultures prefer large firm breasts, there are some where long, pendulous breasts are seen as more attractive. And from time to time in our own society flat-chestedness is seen as desirable (see also Buss, 1994). Within Western cultures personality factors may affect the importance placed on physical attractiveness: high self-monitoring individuals tend to place emphasis on physical attributes, low self-monitoring ones on psychological characteristics (Snyder, Berscheid, & Glick, 1985).

Particular physical characteristics are not to be considered in isolation, for assessments based on one characteristic may be influenced by others: when shown a display including the face of another, and simultaneously hearing the other's voice, judges' assessments of vocal attractiveness were influenced by facial attractiveness, and vice versa (Zuckerman, Miyake, & Hodgins, 1991).

Physical characteristics have an importance beyond immediate attractiveness: interactions with an attractive other are reported as more rewarding and intimate than those with a less attractive other (Reis et al., 1982). Individuals who are physically attractive tend to be credited with more positive attributes than people who are less attractive (Berscheid & Walster, 1974b; Dion, Berscheid, & Walster, 1972), and may show different behavioural propensities. Especially important in the formation of relationships is the role of physical attractiveness on fear of rejection by the opposite sex: Reis et al. (1982) found the two to be negatively correlated in men, though not in women.

SELECTION

The extent to which people are attracted to others depends not only on physical appearance but also on their psychological characteristics. These are assessed in the course of interaction, in which each partner hints at his or her goals and probes the other's (see pp.7–8). But with respect to psychological characteristics, what exactly are they looking for? This will, of course, depend on who they are and the sort of relationship that is anticipated. It is also an issue that is not easy to investigate, for at least four reasons: (a) Individuals have different needs, and are most likely to attempt to form a relationship with someone whom they expect to satisfy those needs (Graziano & Musser, 1982); (b) People also differ in their views as to what liking, loving, or falling in love entail (Chapter 24); (c) The features that are relevant for evaluating a relationship change as the relationship develops. People may not be conscious of what initially attracted them to another person; and (d) The use of retrospective accounts is problematical, as matters that might seem mundane, and motivations that might seem socially undesirable, may be suppressed. Nevertheless the principal issues can be categorised as follows:

(i) Characteristics generally recognised as socially desirable, such as physical attractiveness (see earlier) and certain aspects of personality, such as considerateness, honesty, and openness (Goodwin, 1990). Of particular importance are characteristics related to ease of communication. Individuals who are expressive (presumably within limits) are seen as more attractive, perhaps because expressiveness facilitates interpersonal perception and negotiation (Sabatelli & Rubin, 1986). Of course mere expressiveness may not be enough. People require their partners to attend to them, to understand them, and to be responsive (Davis & Perkowitz, 1979).

There is also evidence that women seen as moderately "hard-to-get" are seen as more attractive than women who are less selective or extremely selective. In an experiment assessing undergraduates' responses to descriptions of a bogus woman stranger, Wright and Contrada (1986) found that moderately selective women were seen as more intelligent, physically attractive, and sociable than non-selective women, and very selective women as more conceited and less likely to be sociable and intelligent than moderately selective ones.

(ii) Similarity. The role of similarity to self in attractiveness, and the reasons why it is attractive, were discussed in Chapter 8. We have seen that similarity in activity preference is as or more important as a basis of friendship than similarity in attitudes or personality for men and for high self-monitors (Jamieson, Lydon, & Zanna, 1987; Werner & Parmelee, 1979). And similarity may not have an overriding influence: in an analysis of questionnaire data on the initiation of friendship and falling in love, Aron et al. (1989) found similarity to be less important than perceiving the other as having desirable characteristics and as liking oneself.

Given that there is a general expectation that attitudes will be similar, there may be occasions on which differences have a special salience, for instance in giving scope for "expansion of the self" (Aron & Aron, 1986, 1996; see pp.134, 453). It has also been suggested that, in real-life relationship formation, people may rely initially on negative factors such as dissimilar attitudes, negative personal evaluations, and physical unattractiveness to exclude others; but later, in the reduced field of eligibles, rely increasingly on positive factors (Byrne, Clore, and Smeaton, 1986).

(iii) Dominance. Dominant behaviour has been found to increase the attractiveness of males to both males and females, but not that of females. This effect was found in the responsiveness of students to actors or actresses playing the roles of interviewer and interviewee, or to descriptions of hypothetical persons. The attractiveness of dominance was not shared by related characteristics such as aggressiveness or being domineering, and was limited to sexual attractiveness, and not to general liking (Sadalla, Kenrick, & Vershure, 1987). Jensen-Campbell, Graziano, and West (1995) found that dominance enhanced the attractiveness of men to women only when the men were agreeable.

(iv) Need fulfilment and complementarity. Although it explains nothing, and in this context is no more than a figure of speech, we can assume that an individual forming a relationship with another is trying to fulfil a need or needs. What those needs are, and at what level we should try to describe them, no doubt differs between relationships and with the sort of issue with which we are concerned. However a basic need is for security of attachment, and there is evidence that individuals with a secure attachment style are preferable to insecure individuals (Latty-Mann & Davis, 1996; see Chapter 21).

A global approach might postulate needs to retain or augment one's positive evaluation of the self, and to feel effective in dealing with the world (Graziano & Musser, 1982). The relation between self-esteem and experiencing love was mentioned on pp.437–438, where it was noted that the issues are complicated by an interaction with defensiveness. Support for the need to feel effective comes from the finding that individuals with an internal locus of control were less likely to report having experienced romantic love—presumably because romantic love is seen as a powerful external force (Dion & Dion, 1973). However here again there were complications in the details of the data, including sex differences.

One is more inclined to feel effective in dealing with the world if one's view of oneself is confirmed by other people. Thus self-verification can be seen as a need in its own right. For people with a poor opinion of themselves, this may bring self-verification into conflict with the need to augment one's self-esteem. Swann et al. (1992a) examined what subjects said as they chose interaction partners. The bases of choice appeared to differ between those who had positive views of themselves and those who viewed themselves negatively. The former were guided by both self-verification and positivity to choose partners who viewed them favourably. Those with negative self-views also tended to choose partners on the basis of self-verification, though pragmatic concerns and a desire for a perceptive partner also contributed. Apparently it is so important to individuals to confirm their perceptions of the social world that confirmation of one's negative views of oneself may not be totally unacceptable (see also p.322).

In any case, it is clear that issues important to self-esteem, and the matters over which effectiveness is important, differ markedly between individuals. And the fulfilment of many other needs may be important in partner choice. As we have seen (Chapter 9), complementarity in need satisfaction is now seen as less important as a basis for friendship and marital relationships than it was formerly, though it sometimes plays a part even in close relationships, and there are many relationships in which need fulfilment is basic (McAdams, 1988). Indeed complementarity may be not only a matter of choosing a partner who fulfils one's own needs: perception that one can provide another with something that he or she needs can form a basis for liking or loving.

(v) Compatibility. Clearly, if a relationship is to be successful, the participants must be compatible one with the other. Two dominant individuals may be similar, but may or may not find each other compatible (see later). Cappella (1984) has suggested that compatibility may be important even in the early stages of acquaintance, arguing that people react to one another's actions rather than to characteristics presumed to be behind those actions. He has thus investigated the extent to which it is possible to assess an individual's conversational style, and the extent to which two individuals' styles mesh.

(iv) Being liked. It is no good fostering a developing relationship if it is apparent that the potential partner does not like you. Perception that one is liked can make an important contribution to one's attraction to another person (Jones & Archer, 1976; Shaver et al., 1987; Walster & Walster, 1963; see p.131).

(vii) Social desirability. Approval by parents, peers or others may be important in some cases (e.g. Parks, Stan, & Eggert, 1983).

Naturally, the relative importance of these issues differs with the type of relationship and the nature of the individuals involved. A study by Aron et al. (1989) assessed the relative importance of a variety of issues for "falling in love" and for "falling in friendship", with both seen as involving strong feelings. Although the data were based on retrospective accounts, and thus subject to distortion, some interesting differences emerged. Falling in love was often preceded by the other appearing to have desirable characteristics and to like the self, moderately often with one of the variables traditionally associated with falling in love (such as readiness for a relationship and a feeling of arousal or unusualness), and rather less often by the perception of similarity and having spent time with the other.

Friendship was also preceded by the perception of desirable characteristics in the other and a feeling of being liked, though less often than falling in love. Perceived similarity and propinquity were mentioned more frequently for friendship than for falling in love, but the traditional love variables were rarely cited except for arousal/unusualness. The relative insignificance of similarity and propinquity for falling in love, although they appear frequently in the literature of attraction, is perhaps surprising—the authors suggest that they may be considered too mundane to be mentioned, or belong to a different stage of relationship formation.

Aron et al. (1989; Aron & Aron, 1996) suggest that the importance of desirable characteristics and reciprocal liking for falling in love are in keeping with the self-expansion model (Aron & Aron, 1986) which holds that individuals strive to enhance their efficacy by incorporating the resources of another in the self. An individual with desirable characteristics would provide an opportunity to expand the self, and being liked would indicate the possibility of forming a relationship.

Of special importance in this study is the authors' discussion of the several ways in which the use of retrospective accounts could have influenced their findings. For instance, the rather small emphasis placed on similarity and propinquity, variables emphasised in other studies, may have been because they play a role at a different stage in relationship formation—perhaps in determining the field of eligibles before falling in love. Fulfilling needs were seldom mentioned, perhaps because the respondents did not like to invoke a selfish motive for falling in love. Social influences may have been downplayed because respondents wanted to attribute responsibility for a successful relationship to themselves, and/or because it might appear unromantic. The authors comment (Aron & Aron, 1986, p.254), "We have no doubt that these accounts represent as much construction as description ... Further, these reports are no doubt influenced by the particular self-presentational context in which they were collected."

NON-CONSCIOUS PROCESSES IN SELECTION

The preceding paragraphs must not give the impression that interpersonal attraction is a totally rational matter. Not only do conscious and unconscious biases operate all the time, but psychological processes operate to increase the chances of needs being satisfied or of an appropriate partner being selected. Thus individuals tend to respond selectively to situations likely to satisfy their needs, and relevant aspects become salient. A girl standing at a bus stop might catch the eye of a young man looking for an attractive partner, and he might see her as more attractive than longer acquaintance would confirm (Berscheid et al., 1976).

But the issue does not stop there. Once one has an attitude, the more one thinks about the matter, the more polarised one's attitude and effective response becomes. Thus the more our young man thinks about the girl, the more gorgeous she seems (see Tesser, 1978; Tesser & Paulhus, 1976). And if he approaches her, his manner may induce her to behave even more attractively than she might otherwise do (Snyder et al., 1977).

In any case, unconscious biases influence judgement. Wheeler and Miyake (1992) assessed the use that students made of comparisons in their accounts of their lifestyles and assets. Students with a negative mood tended to notice, select, perceive, and/or interpret others as superior, and thus make upward comparisons. This decreased their subjective well-being. Individuals with high self-esteem used more self-enhancing comparisons.

FIRST JUDGEMENTS

When we make an acquaintance, we are likely to make a quick judgement as to whether we like or dislike him or her, or are simply not interested (Rodin, 1982). Liking may embrace any of a large number of features, but the overall judgement is important because it influences the future course of the relationship.

Rodin (1982) emphasised that liking in this global sense is not just the opposite of disliking. There is an asymmetry: we may concede that disliked others have likeable qualities, but liked others very rarely have unpleasant ones. Rodin argues that this does not mean that all the people one likes are perfect: if we hear something bad about someone we like we may approve of them a little less, but that may make us even more attached to them—"Old Jack always had a weakness for...". And some people whom we do not like we simply disregard. This means that we eliminate them from the list of potential relationship partners—we may still notice them in a behavioural sense and behave politely to them. The criteria for disregarding a person vary with the relationship in question.

In Rodin's scheme, we don't necessarily follow up on all the people that we like. We may feel well-disposed towards them, but are not especially attracted to them. Whether we seek further acquaintance with someone we feel we like depends on our readiness to enter a new relationship, its probable costs, and the effort required. However, if one individual believes that another is attractive and would meet his or her needs, he or she will process information selectively so that it tends to confirm the schema that has been formed, and behave in a way that will elicit the desired behaviour from the partner (Graziano & Musser, 1982; Snyder et al., 1977).

At present, it seems as though a considerable proportion of men welcome the initiation of a heterosexual relationship by a woman, but such relationships tend to be less successful. Apparently this is partly a matter of social skill, and partly due to conflict between the imagined attractiveness of female assertiveness and the male's perceived threat to his dominance (Kelley & Rolker-Dolinsky, 1987).

ACQUAINTANCESHIP

The preceding sections indicate that the processes of forming an acquaintance and developing an acquaintanceship into a friendship or other close relationship are essentially interactive. Much of the experimental work on attractiveness depends on the presentation of pictures, screen images, or non-reactive actors: although this does not invalidate them, it involves situations that are impoverished compared with the early stages of acquaintanceship in real life. When would-be friends or partners first meet, the interchange between them is perhaps best described in terms of Goffman's (1959, 1961, 1963, 1967) dramaturgical perspective and the approach of the symbolic interactionists (e.g. G.J. McCall, 1970, 1974; McCall & Simmons, 1966; M. McCall, 1970). In Chapter 1 we saw how Goffman emphasised that, in addition to conveying information in the conventional sense, an individual "gives off" messages that convey impressions of what sort of person he or she is. Others use that information to "define the situation", so that they can surmise what to expect of the speaker and what he expects of them. If a relationship is to develop, the participants must define the situation similarly. This involves agreement about the content of and priorities within the relationship, and has implicit reference to some or all of the characteristics of the relationship described in earlier chapters. It may involve agreement not only about what the participants in the relationship should do together, but also what they should not do together, and perhaps about what each should and should not do with outsiders. It will involve rules of conduct, and agreement concerning which rules of etiquette or civil proprieties, potent in the society at large, do and do not apply within the relationship (Denzin, 1970). Many of the difficulties in the earlier stages of a relationship, even with primarily formal relationships such as that between secretary and employer, can be seen as involving the reaching of an acceptable agreed definition of the relationship. Many of the traumatic aspects of the relationships between parents and adolescents stem from the difficulties of changing the definition of the relationship—that is, of maintaining continuity but changing content.

The definition is usually worked out progressively as the relationship develops—not necessarily explicitly, but as each accepts or denies the claims the other makes in each interaction. The critical role played by conversation has already been emphasised. It is here that the dramaturgical approach, introduced in Chapters 1 and 3, becomes useful. The symbolic interactionists define a "character" as a person with a distinctive organisation of personal characteristics, and a "role" as a plausible line of action truly expressive of the personality of a character. A person's "role identity" is seen as the way he likes to think of him or herself as the occupant of a particular social position. Each person may have many "role identities", which are seen both as emerging as a consequence of inter-action and as having a causal function in behaviour, providing both plans for action and the criteria by which action is evaluated.

A person's "role identities" are seen as hierarchically organised, with some more prominent than others. It will be apparent that this approach is not incompatible with the emerging picture of the self-system (pp.25–35): role identities could be seen as related to hierarchically-arranged knowledge structures. In each encounter with another individual, a person endeavours to display a selection of his "role identities", and these will constitute the character he there assumes. The other party may, however, give differential support to the several "role identities" displayed, and thus play a part in determining their relative prominence. The consequent inter-actions involve bargaining between two individuals. A tries to perceive the character underlying the set of "role identities" that B displays, and devises a "role" for himself that can best make use of B's "role" and character. This of course is a two-way process, and continuation of the interaction demands some mutual accommodation such that each improvises a "role" roughly in line with that of the other.

Here, perhaps, this approach does not go quite far enough. When two individuals come together in a close relationship, they change. There is more to a relationship than the selection of roles—it is a process of cre-ation. Furthermore, it is not only how each person wants to be seen, but also what her expectations are, that matters. Sometimes an acquaintance-ship is expected to blossom quickly, sometimes one does not care, some-times one expects it to wither: such expectations have a way of being self-fulfilling.

Whether or not a relationship continues will, in McCall's view, depend on how reliably each provides the other with the rewards he needs or desires, and at what costs. But amongst the most important of these needs, in many cases, is that of providing "role support"—that is, confirmation of each other's "role identity". This involves more than support for the particular place in society, with its attendant rights and duties, that the other wishes to occupy, and more than social approval or esteem. The important issue is that it should tend to confirm the person's individual view of himself and of how he should behave. There is a link here with the G.A. Kelly/Duck view that similarity in construct systems may facilitate friendship because each partner provides the other with confirmation of his view of himself and of the world (see pp.122–123). Even more relevant is the parallel with H.H. Kelley's emphasis on the importance of each individual's ability to express his own preferred dispositions, and of the extent to which he facilitates or inhibits the expression of his partner's (see pp.46 and 342–343).

The symbolic interactionist approach is not well buttressed by empirical data. It is perhaps better seen as a way of describing how relationships work than a theory of their dynamics, and it could be argued that the concepts used require more rigid specification. However it emphasises an important issue—the need for the two participants in a relationship not only to have compatible views about themselves and each other, but to see their relationship, present and future, in a similar way. An individual's satisfaction with a relationship will depend on the difference between how he sees the behaviour of his ideal self and of an ideal partner in that relationship and how it works out in actuality. His view of the behaviour of an ideal partner will depend in part on his view of himself. All four perceptions—of himself, of his ideal self, of the ideal partner, and of the actual partner—may be modified in the course of the relationship.

INTERACTIONAL SKILLS

The successful development of a relationship depends not only on the partners having characteristics that appeal to each other, but also on their having the skills to overcome the problems intrinsic to relationship formation and development (Planalp & Garvin-Doxas, 1994). Interpersonal competence and social skills have been shown to be important for success in a variety of relationships across the lifespan. However competence is a global concept, and competencies of different sorts are required in relationships of different types and at different relationship and life stages (e.g. Carpenter, 1993; Levenson & Gottman, 1978).

In the earlier stage, shyness or "reciprocation wariness" may make it difficult to strike up an acquaintance or to proceed to the formation of a relationship (Cotterell, Eisenberger, & Speicher, 1992; Garcia et al., 1991). These early stages are inevitably accompanied by fears and fantasies about the future (Duck & Miell, 1986), and further development can be seen as a process of anxiety reduction and reassurance (Berger, 1988).

But reassurance is only part of the problem. Buhrmester et al. (1988) used a questionnaire to assess the competence of students in relationships with same-sex friends and with romantic partners. Five domains of competence were recognised—Initiating interactions and relationships; Assertion of personal rights and displeasure with others; Self-disclosure; Emotional support of others; and Management of interpersonal conflicts. There were some sex differences, but the several competencies were related in meaningful ways to reported frequency of dates, initiation of dates, and perceived popularity, and in a second study with masculinity and femininity, self-esteem, loneliness, and social desirability. Relationship satisfaction with new friends was best predicted by initiation competence, while satisfaction in friendships was most closely related to social support competence. Thus the validity of these five domains of competence in these relationships was established: as the authors point out, other types of competence may be important in other relationships (see also Trower, 1981).

Some authors make a distinction between social skills, embracing characteristics that can be exercised in diverse relationships, and "relational competence", which is immediately socially constructed and context-specific. In "relational competence" the identification of the problem at issue, the tactics, and the evaluative criteria to be used, occur in partners who may have a long history of interaction, who may embue each other's actions with unique meaning, and who may be influenced by third parties. Relational competence is seen by Klein and Milardo (1993) as involving two dimensions. One runs from competence based on norms and traditions to that based on individual needs. For example heterosexual friends going out for a picnic might see responsibility for the provision of food according to traditional sex-divisions of labour, or in terms of the partners' choices and talents. The second dimension concerns the extent to which one or both of the partners' views is taken into account. The nature of the relational competence conducive to a successful relationship would, no doubt, be influenced by the personalities of the participants.

One issue that may go to the heart of the matter concerns individuals' "interpersonal projects", such as their relationship goals and how their likely success in their projects is appraised. Salmela-Aro and Nurmi (1996), studying women undergraduates mostly in their twenties, found that those who rated their interpersonal projects in uncertain and negative terms had lower self-esteem and were more depressed and lonely than those who showed confidence. This effect was present only for single women, not for those who had a boyfriend or spouse. In that the assessments were contemporaneous, causation could be acting either way. However the uncertain women tended to become more depressed by the transition to university, suggesting that the project appraisal affected subsequent well-being.

Lack of social skills and lack of friends may mutually reinforce each other, leading to the phenomenon of loneliness. Jones et al. (1985), reviewing the literature on loneliness, describe lonely individuals as self-absorbed, non-responsive, negativistic, and ineffective in their interactions with strangers. They go on to emphasise, however, that loneliness is usually at least partly due to external circumstances (see also Peplau and Perlman, 1982).

SUMMARY

1. The development of relationships seldom proceeds smoothly.
2. Physical attraction may play a part initially. It is more important for men than for women. Characteristics conducive to sexual desire differ from those seen as desirable in a long-term partner.
3. Certain psychological characteristics then come to the fore. Their relative importance varies with the individuals concerned and the nature of the relationship, but compatibility is of course crucial.
4. Selection may be in part unconscious.
5. First judgements may be unduly important.
6. The formation of an acquaintanceship involves processes of negotiation in which each probes the role identities of the other.
7. Individuals differ in their interactional skills.

26 The Development of Relationships

No two relationships develop in quite the same way, so generalisations are dangerous. Nevertheless it is possible to make some broad generalisations about how close relationships develop. We have already seen some of the issues that promote the early stages of commitment (Chapter 15): here we extend that discussion.

The development of a relationship can be seen as a process of uncertainty reduction—uncertainty about that individual as a potential partner, and uncertainty about the relationship (Berger & Bradac, 1982). Perhaps initially it may be better described as a process of reduction in the uncertainty of whether or not a relationship exists (Duck, 1995), and then of increasing agreement as to its nature. At any stage things may go wrong, leading to the cessation of development, regression, or termination. In this chapter, however, we shall be concerned primarily with relationships that do progress.

THE GROWTH OF UNCONSCIOUS COMMITMENT

Endogenous commitment usually develops gradually. Once a relationship has started, there are a number of reasons why it might be preferable to a novel one:

(a) The current partner is known, with behaviour somewhat predictable. The relationship has its accepted norms. A new partner might bring fewer rewards and greater costs.

(b) The current relationship may be secondarily rewarding by association with past happiness. Reminiscing about shared experiences by the partners plays a part here.

(c) Resources will have been invested in the current relationship, with the expectation of future gains: the investment would be wasted if the relationship ceased (see Chapter 19). Seen from another theoretical perspective, any uncongenial aspects of the relationship are inconsistent with the expectations of gains consequent upon the costs already incurred in the relationship. It is perhaps partly for that reason that the past is often misperceived in terms more rosy than reality, terms that augur well for the future (Murray & Holmes, 1993; Veroff et al., 1993a, b).

Thus each partner is likely to have something to gain by staying in the relationship, and in making sure that the partner does likewise. This may involve incurring further costs in order to provide the partner with benefits without concern for present or even for ultimate reciprocity.

COGNITIVE EXPLORATION

Forming a close relationship necessarily involves changes in the self; one becomes, or one sees oneself as becoming, a different person. In harmony with the view that individuals seek to expand the self, and that forming a relationship involves including the other in the self (Fig. 4.1), Aron and Aron (1996) report that the number of content domains (e.g. social status, family relationships, major emotions) that students used in self-descriptions increased as a consequence of falling in love. There were also increases in self-esteem and self-efficacy.

But changes in the self occur with respect to the partner. In a developing relationship individuals are strongly motivated to find out as much as they can about the partner. Each assesses how her behaviour compares with that of the other, how the other affects her own behaviour, and so on, and interprets and judges her reflections in the light of relationship schemata already acquired (Surra, 1996; Vorauer & Ross, 1996).

As we have seen, it is necessary that the partners in a relationship should define that relationship similarly, and the definition is usually worked out progressively as the relationship develops. Each probes the other, using a variety of strategies to detect the other's intentions (Baxter & Wilmot, 1985). Early on, this probing involves the acquisition of relatively superficial factual issues about the other. The recognition of shared values, likes, and dislikes, also soon comes to the fore. But for this to happen, the participants must exchange views, interacting and negotiating, and come to recognise the existence of similarity. They may employ a variety of strat-

egies for finding out about each other and about the state of the relationship (Baxter & Wilmot, 1984; Vorauer & Ross, 1996). Some of the knowledge may come from outsiders, but most will be conveyed in the course of
conversation (Planalp & Garvin-Doxas, 1994; Spencer, 1994). Politeness,
equivocation, or downright deception may impede the growth of real intimacy, which is reached mainly through conscious or unconscious disclosure
through talk (Duck & Barnes, 1992). Perhaps it is as well to remember
here that, in trying to analyse relationships, it is very easy to intellectualise
them. Sometimes a great deal of understanding can be achieved without
the aid of verbal intermediaries. And there is evidence that men are less
likely than women to use gossip to foster solidarity in same-sex friendships (Leaper & Holliday, 1995).

The partners must also acquire similarity in the organisational structure
of meaning—and the importance of similarity in any particular aspect will
depend on the extent to which it is indicative of broader areas of psychological similarity (Duck, 1994b). The discovery of successive layers of similarity, and the acceptance of dissimilarities, paves the way for the formation
of a relationship schema (Monsour, 1994). Progressively the partners must
come to define the relationship in ways that are not necessarily identical
but must not be incompatible with each other's definitions. At the same
time the recognition of differences may help to confirm the identity of each
individual and reinforce the relationship through the mutual recognition
of each partner's selfhood.

The dynamics of the relationship may come to depend in part on idiosyncratic conventions concerning what is done and when, with turn-taking,
with communication, and so on, conventions which may be derived in part
from the culture, often via the peer group, but may be entirely idiosyncratic.
This may involve agreement about areas of discourse that will be excluded.
As each partner adjusts to the other, he becomes less able to find the support
he needs elsewhere. Each step in this process can be regarded as a private
pledge to continue the relationship (see also Berger, 1993).

Growth of a relationship depends in large measure on what the partners
do together and especially on what they say to each other and how they say
it (Duck, 1995). But it does not depend solely on what happens in interactions. The partners probably spend more time apart than together, and
while apart they reflect on what has been happening and perhaps discuss it
with outsiders. This also affects the course of the relationship (Berger, 1993).

PHYSICAL SIGNALS

In relationships with a sexual component, physical gestures of affection
both demonstrate the actors' feelings and, if welcomed, augment those of
the recipient. "Unobtrusive behavioural observation" of couples in public

places by Guerrero and Andersen (1991) indicated that touching increased in the earlier stages of heterosexual relationships, but subsequently decreased as the relationship became stable. They suggest that the decline is due not to a decline in relational closeness, but to a reduced need to communicate closeness behaviourally in public. It perhaps also suggests that touching is in part manipulative, in that it is intended to elicit reciprocation, as well as expressive. Another study found that women's perceptions of how much their partners touched them increased and then levelled off in the seriously dating, engaged, and married stages. Men's perceptions of how much their partners touched them decreased after the seriously dating stage (Emmers & Dindia, 1995). Christopher and Frandsen (1990) report a detailed study of the diverse strategies used by students to influence the course of sexual intimacy.

IDENTIFICATION WITH THE PARTNER

The processes by which commitment becomes explicit are diverse, and may involve not only genuine expressions of feelings but also manipulative attempts by one partner to induce commitment in the other (Miell & Duck, 1986; Tolhuizen, 1989). Major issues are the performance of activities costly to the performer but rewarding to the partner, and acknowledgement that there is pleasure in "doing it together", no matter what it is (Blau, 1964).

As commitment proceeds, each partner's feelings about her or himself may be transferred to the partner, so that the more they think well of themselves, the more they will tend to think well of the partner (Darley & Berscheid, 1967; Murray & Holmes, 1996). Furthermore, through identification with the partner, each vicariously shares the other's happiness and enjoys the other's success by processes basically similar to those underlying the emotions of a football supporter when his team wins. As we have seen, there is, of course, a danger here: if the partner's success is in a domain where success is relevant to the individual's own self-definition, he or she will be tempted to make comparisons and may feel diminished by the partner's success. But if it is in a more or less irrelevant field the other can glory in it—as it were expanding his own success into a new arena (Tesser, 1980, 1988).

As we have seen, Aron and Aron (1986, 1996) regard relationship formation as including the other in the self, and thus expanding the self. Cognitive merging of self with other may involve the ability to feel the presence of the other in his or her absence, the sense that each is "inside" the other's world, and the feeling that their relationship is a new creation in its own right (Register & Henley, 1992). The cognitive merging of self with other is also in harmony with another language for describing increasing commitment, one that comes from interdependence theory

(Chapter 19). Kelley (1979, 1983) pictured increasing closeness as involving transformation of each person's outcome matrix so that they have a pattern of perceived interdependence and see partner's and joint benefits as ultimately benefiting self (see also Borden & Levinger, 1991).

These metaphors of "cognitive merging" and "inclusion of other in the self" provide valuable insights into the processes of relationship formation, but must not be over-interpreted. To state the obvious, the individuals remain individuals, even if their thoughts and desires are focused on the partner. Each continues to discuss with him- or herself the nature and intentions of the partner, what is to be expected in the relationship, and the discussions that go on *between* them are partly dependent on the discussions that continue *within* each of them (Berger, 1993). Indeed conversations between partners may seem disjointed to an outsider not only because they know each other well enough to leave much unsaid, but also because every utterance reflects an intrapersonal discussion.

The understanding engendered as commitment develops makes it possible for the individuals concerned to give each other more emotional and informational support (Hays, 1985). Exchange factors are monitored less closely, and the participants become less sensitive to costs and more to the benefits received. What is important for the partner or for the relationship becomes more salient (Kelley, 1979). As time goes on, the resources exchanged become more particularistic (see Chapter 20) and symbolic (Berg & McQuinn, 1986).

Yet another theoretical language, which may provide additional insights into the nature of commitment, comes from the psychology of groups, of which the dyad is the smallest possible representative (McCall, 1970). Tajfel (1978) uses the term "Social identity" to refer to that part of an individual's self-concept (i.e. that part of A's view of A) that derives from his knowledge of his membership of social groups, together with the value and emotional significance attached to that membership. In the case of the dyad, not only the rewards which the participants exchange but also the membership of the dyad may have an important influence on their behaviour towards each other and towards outsiders. The partners tend to reciprocate each other's levels of affectionate and respectful behaviour (Gaines, 1996). As they become committed, members of a dyad come to favour each other over outsiders, to show a united front to outsiders and even to differentiate less amongst outsiders than they had done previously. Furthermore, recognition of the dyad as a unit by the participants and by outsiders will affect the future course of the relationship. In so far as each participant perceives that dyad membership contributes positively to the way he sees himself and brings him other rewards, he will act to further the existence of the dyad as a unit. (In the language of interdependence theory, this involves a transformation of the matrix—Borden & Levinger,

1991; Kelley, 1979). Social situations that force the participants to act as members of the dyad will enhance the extent to which they identify with it, and the more they identify with it, the more they will perceive social situations as requiring them to act as a dyad. The possibilities for positive feedback are considerable—see Tajfel's (1978) discussion of the processes of differentiation between groups.

TRUST

Trust is essential to the development of a relationship. It promotes self-disclosure, permits open communication and the voicing of needs, and facilitates effective problem-solving (Holmes & Rempel, 1989; Reis & Shaver, 1988). Some individuals are more trusting than others: individuals lacking in trust tend to encounter problems in their relationships—competitiveness, envy, resentfulness, vindictiveness, and lack of feelings towards others (Gurtman, 1992). But trust within a relationship is a property of that relationship, though its basis and nature changes. Early on it may be mainly a matter of blind hope, based perhaps on idealisation of the partner and denial of doubts. As the partners evaluate each other more effectively, imperfections appear, but by then there is scope for an empirically based sense of trust. Trust becomes more securely based, with (ideally) both partners directing their efforts towards its creation. Growth of the relationship is fostered if the partners cease to doubt and act consciously as though trust in the partner were rightly deserved (Boon, 1994; Holmes & Rempel, 1989).

COMPARISON WITH OUTSIDERS

In an increasingly close relationship, the partners tend to devalue alternative partners (Buss, 1994; Eidelson, 1981; Johnson & Rusbult, 1989). Comparison with others can also help to develop and enhance positive views of oneself, one's partner, and one's relationship. In harmony with this, Buunk and Van Yperen (1991) found that most people see their own marriage as better than those of comparable peers, and that perceived superiority of one's own relationship is greater for relationships that persist than for those that subsequently dissolve. Furthermore, earlier commitment predicts the later perceived superiority of one's own relationship. The relations between the perceived superiority of one's own relationship, satisfaction and commitment are in harmony with the view that perceived superiority enhances satisfaction, which enhances commitment, which further enhances perceived superiority (Rusbult & Buunk, 1993).

EARLY STAGES PREDICT LATER ONES

There is considerable evidence that the viability of friendships (Berg, 1984) and dating relationships (Berg & McQuinn, 1986) is predictable quite early on. College room-mates made the decision to stay together quite soon after coming together, and first impressions were very important. Couples who were still dating four months after being initially contacted demonstrated greater love, evaluated their relationship more highly and did more to maintain it, and self-disclosed more when first assessed, than did those couples who later broke up (see also Hays, 1985; Kurdek, 1991b, 1993; Schaefer & Burnett, 1987; Surra & Huston, 1987; Surra, Arizzi, & Asmussen, 1988).

CREATING AN ACCOUNT

Mutual understanding and similarity in cognitive structures becomes progressively more important (Duck, 1977b) and this is facilitated by small talk and discussion (Duck et al., 1991). The partners must explain to themselves and to each other the successive decisions they take (Surra, 1985), and make a joint account of the relationship and a joint memory of its history that presupposes agreement between them. These accounts of the relationship are made both independently and in the course of mutual discussion ("Do you remember when we..."), and indicate the meaning that the couple is deriving from their relationship. The account an individual makes as a relationship develops is not concerned solely with the past. It will contain expectations about the future, expectations that will influence current behaviour. Each partner needs both to make an account that is compatible with his or her self-image, and to construct a reality that is shared with the other. To this end they use metaphors to make sense of what is happening to them (Sternberg, 1995).

Baxter (1992b), analysing undergraduates' accounts of their relationships, identified three root metaphors of major importance—relationship development as work (e.g. "It was hard getting into the groove of being together"); as a journey of discovery ("I really liked the fact that he was from a different culture"); and as an uncontrollable force ("It was like I was drugged or something"). Four others of lesser importance were relationship development as danger, as organism, as economic exchange, and as game (see also Berger, 1993; Harvey, Weber & Orbuch, 1990).

The narrative accounts of their courtships given by newlyweds are related to their well-being. Collecting data from newlyweds over four years, Veroff et al. (1993a, b) found that a focus on the couple as a unit or on the nature of their relationship was indicative of marital well-being.

Accounts concerned with individual experience were less so. Accounts involving affect, especially when given by men, reflect a depth of caring about the other that communicates marital well-being. Some particular themes in the accounts furnished had different meanings for black and white couples (see also Fletcher et al., 1987). Highly romantic reconstructions do not predict marital well-being, but stories with a general positive tone without romanticism do (Orbuch, Veroff, & Holmberg, 1993).

TABOO TOPICS

The growth of closeness in a relationship implies self-revelation: mutual intimacy fosters and is fostered by the development of the relationship. Of course, this is not true of all relationships—a relationship with a colleague or neighbour with whom it is necessary to remain at least on superficially good terms may involve progressively more concealment of what one really thinks and feels about the other. But if a relationship is to become close, it must become progressively more sharing and understanding. But, as we have seen, self-revelation increases vulnerability. Thus there may be taboo subjects.

In the early stages of a relationship a high proportion of complaints may not be expressed verbally to the partner (though there may be non-verbal communication of irritation). Cloven and Roloff (1994) found the proportion to decrease as the relationship progressed up to a point, but was then no longer related to the closeness of the relationship. Cloven and Roloff ascribe this change to a variety of processes. In the early stages of a relationship, controversial topics are avoided as inappropriate to a relationship that has not yet achieved much closeness, and the participants may also feel that the relationship is not worth the effort that would be involved in discussing the problems that arise. They may be afraid of nipping the growing relationship in the bud; or they may be inhibited by the social circumstances of the interaction (VanLear, 1987, 1990). These issues become less important as a relationship develops, and the participants tend to become more communicative (Altman & Taylor, 1973).

However increasing intimacy includes the possibility of criticism and conflict (Cate & Lloyd, 1992; Christopher & Cate, 1985), and while increasing commitment may require the participants to get problems out into the open, there are also reasons why it might be as well to conceal them. For one thing, as the relationship becomes more valuable, partners will be less willing to expose disagreements if they think it would be destructive (e.g. Baxter & Wilmot, 1985). For another, the value of the relationship may enable the participants to regard irritations as unimportant in the context of a satisfying relationship. Cloven and Roloff's (1994) data support the relevance of such factors, and they regard changes in decisions to conceal irritations as due to changes in balance between such motives.

Rather surprisingly, one study of dating couples (Baxter & Wilmot, 1985) found that couples often had an unspoken agreement not to talk about the state of their relationship. While it may be wise not to dig up bulbs that you have planted to see if they are growing, such an embargo would hardly seem conducive to the construction of a joint account or to the growth of intimacy.

THE MINICULTURE

People entering a relationship are guided to some degree by a cultural blueprint of what the relationship should be like, including the various stages through which it may be expected to pass. Members of the same cultural group share this picture, including its detailed structure, acquired partly by word of mouth and partly by vicarious experience (Honeycutt et al., 1989). Of course the nature of the cultural blueprint changes with time: for instance it is now much more acceptable for unmarried heterosexual couples to live together than was the case a few decades ago.

This view of what a relationship should be like or is normally like plays a part in determining its course. But in every particular relationship the participants modify that cultural definition to suit their own temperaments, aspirations, and circumstances. In doing so they create a miniculture with its own values, meanings, rituals, traditions and so on (Bell & Healey, 1992). This miniculture emerges from their interactions and changes as they interact. It is characterised, for instance, by the use of the pronouns "we" and "our", by attempts to differentiate the relationship from others by the sharing of secrets, and by the elaboration of private signs, idioms, and languages (Goffman, 1959; Hopper, Knapp, & Scott, 1981). The idioms include words, phrases, and gestures with meanings unique to the relationship. Their use is an index of positive affect, and the closer the relationship, the more extensive and diverse are the idiomatic codes. Codes used by two friends may be shared by a third, but this is less common in marriage. In friendship a relatively small proportion of the idioms are used in private situations, but in dating and marital relationships the proportion is much higher (Bell & Healey, 1992). Pet names may be developed, and these again help to cement the bond, their use by outsiders being seen as intrusive. However their use seems to decline with time (Bruess & Pearson, 1993), and Berger (1993) suggests that the evidence for secret codes and idioms has been overstated.

Another way in which the partners construct meanings in a developing relationship is through play. Play can indicate intimacy; moderate conflict and tensions; act as a safe communication strategy, as when playfully declaring emotional feelings to see if the partner feels likewise; serve as an outlet for individual expression so that individuals can celebrate their own qualities while remaining in the relationship; provide a richer repertoire for communication; and promote intimacy as well as reflecting it. Baxter (1992a) has produced a typology of play, and shown that it correlates with the closeness of same-sex and opposite-sex romantic relationships. The different forms of play seem to serve different functions. For instance playful idiomatic expression is a strong indicator of intimacy. Role-playing and gossiping enable the participants to distance their behaviour from the self, so that they can say and do things with diminished accountability.

MONOGAMOUS COMMITMENT

None of this implies that commitment to one relationship necessarily involves the exclusion of others. In some cultures, for some types of relationship, and for some individuals, increasing commitment to build up one relationship may be seen as implying a willingness to forgo others, and there may be practical reasons why that should be so, but that is not a necessary implication of the term "commitment" as used here. Of course, where fidelity is regarded as important by the individuals concerned, it becomes paramount.

THE SOCIAL NETWORK

In the case of personal relationships, commitment developed privately may be symbolised by public acts, such as appearing in public together, or by the giving of a ring or brooch. An essential characteristic of such acts is that they involve others, so that the participants' view that they are a pair is reinforced by that of outsiders (Surra & Huston, 1987). The network then takes on a new significance. The partners may receive support or disapproval from other members of their network, and must assess the nature of the response that news of their liaison is likely to elicit, and reveal or conceal it accordingly. Social support may assist the development of the relationship (Sprecher & Felmlee, 1992)—but social norms in some societies may decree that certain kinds of relationship (e.g. across social divides or races) are unacceptable. Not only will the network members affect the relationship, but the relationship may have repercussions on the participants' relationships with others in the network, and the effects may ramify (Parks & Eggert, 1991).

The social network may modify the expectations and norms that the partners entertain, and in doing so the network members may be influenced by their own interests. Reciprocally the partners' liaison may affect the network, and the partners may influence each other and their relationship by their attitude and involvement in their networks (Klein & Milardo, 1993). Such potential tensions between dyad and group parallel some of those between the individuals in a dyad. Thus Baxter (1993) calls attention to: (a) Inclusion versus seclusion, the tension between the partners' involvement as a couple and their isolation from others (cf. Autonomy versus connectedness, pp.157–158); (b) Conventionality versus uniqueness, the tension between conventional and idiosyncratic ways of relating (cf. Predictability versus novelty, pp.158–159); and (c) Revelation versus concealment, the tension over the extent to which the relationship is made public (cf. Disclosure versus privacy, p.159).

The social networks of the partners may overlap to varying degrees. If the overlap is small, the partners are likely to become progressively more involved in each other's networks (Kim & Stiff, 1991; Surra & Huston, 1987). The direct role of the social network tends to decrease as courtship proceeds, the couple gradually withdrawing from their contacts with outsiders. Surra (1985) differentiated several types of courtship on the basis of retrospective accounts according to the rapidity with which they approached marriage—accelerated, accelerated-arrested, intermediate, and prolonged. Involvement in the network decreased fairly rapidly in the first two cases. Withdrawal was especially pronounced for the accelerated-arrested group, perhaps because network members opposed their relationship. Those with a prolonged courtship remained active in their networks for much longer.

Young people are more likely to tell peers than parents about a nascent relationship (Baxter & Widenmann, 1993). In a study of 159 college students, Leslie, Huston, and Johnson (1986) found that the more committed the dating relationship, the more likely were the participants to tell their parents, and to try to influence their parents' opinions. Parents were more likely to give the relationship their support, the more committed they perceived their children to be, but their support did not predict the young adults' involvement in their relationships. The authors suggest that the range of parental reaction was relatively limited, perhaps because the range of people with whom their children were likely to become involved at this university would nearly all be likely to be seen as suitable.

THE PUBLIC PLEDGE

Involvement of others becomes even more important in the rituals and ceremonies which, though not ubiquitous, accompany marriage in most cultures. These may involve not only commitment by the marriage partners, but also by members of their families. Such ceremonies may not only provide powerful social forces for the maintenance of the relationship, but also cause the partners to believe that their bond is blessed, divine, or in some other way likely to succeed (Rosenblatt, 1974).

Of course rituals signifying commitment to a relationship are not limited to marriage. "Blood brotherhoods" are of this nature, and one consequence of many initiation ceremonies is a commitment to a relationship or group. In the latter case public commitment may occur in the absence of any personal attachment.

Such public ceremonies are of course of even greater significance in those cultures where husband and wife are virtually unacquainted with each other at the time of the marriage, or have no personal ties to bind them. Even in Europe and North America, engaged couples may know relatively little about each other. Murstein's (1971a) data on this have already been mentioned. Each member of 99 university dating couples were asked to fill in a modified version of the Edwards Personal Preference Schedule on behalf of self, ideal self, fiancé(e), and ideal spouse. Although in the eyes of each individual the partner was quite close to the ideal spouse, there was a near zero correlation between the self-concept of one member of the couple and the ideal spouse of the other. On the assumption that the self-concept bears some resemblance to reality, one wonders how such relationships could be viable. It seems likely that commitment, and playing the social role of the engaged couple, must provide a necessary glue in the early stages. Murstein predicted that the self-concept should move closer to the ideal desired by the partner as the individual strives to meet the aspirations of the partner and as the partner lowers his ideal to approximate more closely to reality. Some disappointment is likely to occur, but private and public commitment may be important in keeping the couple together during the development of their relationship.

In later stages, there is likely to be a positive feedback relationship between culturally held conventions about the immutability of the marriage contract and the incidence of divorce. An increase in divorce will affect the plausibility of the conventions and thus the perceived immutability of the contract, and thus the incidence of divorce.

Public commitment is important not only because a pledge is made public, but also because outsiders may then contribute to the relationship. The mutual interdependence for role support will involve the maintenance of each other's role identities not only in their own eyes, but in the eyes of third parties. And to the extent that the partners treat themselves as a dyad, outsiders will do so too and thereby contribute to their commitment.

Public re-commitment is an issue in the renewal ceremonies which are apparently becoming increasingly frequent amongst US married partners. Three features are of special interest here. The data suggest that the ceremonies tend to be of greater significance if planned to be uniquely meaningful to the particular marriage. Second, they are public, in the sense that witnesses are present, though these may be just intimates. And third, artefacts (rings, photographs, etc.) are often woven into the ritual (Braithwaite & Baxter, 1995). The celebration of anniversaries may play a similar role.

CONFLICT IN DEVELOPING RELATIONSHIPS

The preceding account of the development of commitment emphasised positive growth, and could give the impression that the course of true love always runs smoothly. Of course that is far from the case.

In the very early stages of a relationship, the participants may feel that the relationship could be dropped at any time (Surra & Huston, 1987), or think solely about its potentially rewarding consequences (Rusbult, 1983). If they are carried along by perceptions of positive feelings in the partner they may be optimistic, trusting both partner and the future (Larzelere & Huston, 1980). Quite soon, however, they may start to think about the risks they are taking and the costs they are incurring. They may have to face the difficulty of finding a fully reciprocal intimate relationship, as well as cope with conflict between the developing relationship and other aspects of their lives (Cantor, Acker, & Cook-Flannagan, 1992). Such anxiety in the pursuit of intimacy is found especially in those with an anxious-ambivalent attachment style as assessed by the Hazan and Shaver instrument (see p.389) (Collins & Read, 1990).

Even in these days of frequent divorce, many people feel "premarital anxieties". In a study of college students Zimmer (1986) found that these involved anxieties over the security of the proposed marriage, anxieties concerned with fulfilment in marriage, and anxieties concerned with possible boredom in the relationship. The data clearly showed that many subjects felt that marriage inevitably involved tension between security and excitement. Interestingly, although the instrument used was based on discussions with married and unmarried individuals, nearly all the items referred to anxieties about the rewards that might be received or costs incurred in marriage, and not about personal inadequacies in the respondents that might militate against its success. The impact of anxiety may be ameliorated by optimism: in one study optimism about future love relationships was found to be related to experience in previous dating relationships, while optimism about marriage was related to the parents' relationship with each other (Carnelley & Janoff-Bulman, 1992).

Conflict may arise through the presence of potential alternative partners. Committed individuals may protect their relationship by wearing symbols of their commitment (e.g. a ring), behaving coolly to third parties, or by derogating possible alternative partners (Buss, 1994; Johnson & Rusbult, 1989; Simpson, Gangestad, & Lerma, 1990). Jealousy about possible or actual infidelity tends to be greater, the greater the dependence on the partner (e.g. Buunk, 1995), but a committed couple adopts or develops rules and norms to govern extra-dyadic involvements.

Of course third parties are not the only external force threatening the development of a relationship. Amongst at least some students, the workload may be an obstacle. Zvonkovic, Pennington, and Schmiege (1994) found that those whose dating relationships ended perceived their work differently from those whose relationships continued; women's academic results were negatively related to the extent that they loved their partner; and there were relations between the workload and aspects of the relationship. For women, a high workload was associated with more conflict, while with men it was associated with less. The authors interpret this on the view that women are under pressure to put their romantic relations before their academic work, whereas men can more easily withdraw from the former to get on with the latter.

The attributions each makes about the other both affect and are affected by the progress of the relationship. In an experimental study, Manusov (1990) arranged that 63 married or romantically involved couples should be videotaped while playing a game, one being instructed independently to "act positive" or "act negative" (*sic*) from time to time. Negative behaviours of the confederate were seen by the partner as more intentional, stable, and controllable, and positive behaviours to be more externally determined, unstable, and specific, the less satisfied the partner was with the relationship. Satisfied participants were more likely to ascribe neutral motives to their partners' negative behaviours than were non-satisfied ones. This is in harmony with the data cited earlier (Chapter 10) that negativity has a greater impact on a relationship than positivity.

If all goes well, with the greater knowledge of the partner and mutual understanding that comes with a close relationship, the partners become better able to attribute any little unpleasantness to transitory causes, and to dismiss any negative qualities of the partner as something they are willing to put up with (Hays, 1989). But at the same time more frequent contact, greater investment, and the greater potential costs if the relationship should fail, may cause an increase in conflict and emotional ambivalence (Hays, 1985). One partner's dependency may surpass the other's willingness for commitment, or fail to meet expectations.

While such uncertainties may fuel passion (Berscheid, 1983), when perceptions of unequal involvement come to the fore, trust becomes more and more necessary. If it is a romantic relationship, individuals may think that the more they allow it to matter to them, the more they could lose (Hays, 1989). The feeling of being loved may bring fears about the loss of autonomy. Vulnerability increases, and a firm basis of trust becomes necessary. This can be achieved by mutual reassurance and exchange of resources, tangible and intangible (Holmes & Rempel, 1989; Kelley & Thibaut, 1978). Especially important here is the perception that the partner too is willing to take risks, so that belief in the partner's commitment is enhanced (see pp.274–276).

However uncertainties may persist, and the course of time (McCarthy & Duck, 1976) or external circumstances (Hill et al., 1976) may bring a special need to review the relationship. Accounts fabricated independently but coalesced in discussion, may play a role here.

RATE OF DEVELOPMENT

Some attention has been paid to the rate at which courtship develops into marriage. Surra et al. (1988) asked spouses (married 8–39 months) separately about changes in the "chances of marriage" during their courtship, and the reasons for those changes. The reasons given (retrospectively) involved 14 sub-categories of four major categories—(a) Interpersonal normative reasons, in which aspects of the self, partner, or relationship were evaluated against a normative background; (b) Dyadic reasons, concerned with their interaction; (c) Social network reasons concerned with individuals outside the dyad, including third parties; and (d) Circumstantial reasons, referring to external events.

Inferences made about improvement in the chances tended to concern the nature of the relationship itself. Most of those that concerned evaluation of the self, the partner, or the relationship against some ideal or normative standard, and those concerned with the social network or circumstances, referred to negative turning-points. The authors conclude that inferences about causality may contribute to the way commitment develops. Accelerated relationships may involve partners predisposed towards marriage in the first place, or occur because they are convinced that the time is propitious and the partner the right one. Those that develop more slowly are more affected by the partner's beliefs about their life circumstances.

Individual courtships often had themes, with the same type of reason for a change in commitment recurring. The type of reason predominating was related to the course of the courtship. For example, those in type (a) and some in type (c) were associated with short and direct courtships, while reasons concerned with alternative partners and circumstantial issues with extended ones.

The couples were interviewed again with the Dyadic Adjustment Scale to assess marital happiness when they had been married on average 4.4 years. Not surprisingly, reasons for commitment changes during courtship relating to third parties or network interaction were related to low marital happiness. Those high in marital happiness had reported reasons concerned with behavioural interdependence and disclosure. The authors discuss the complexity of the reasons given for changes in commitment, and indicate that even their sub-categories failed to capture the diversity. But in general, commitments that were event-driven, perhaps because they arose from simplistic decisions based on salient happenings, tended to lead to a less happy marriage than those that were relationship-driven. Although the sample was predominantly Mormon, the authors consider the results to be corroborated by other studies (see Chapter 28).

The stage of a relationship at which more intimate sexual activities occur is partly a matter of social norms, which have changed dramatically in recent years, and partly of idiosyncratic preferences. Christopher and Cate (1985), on the basis of a cluster analysis of data from 54 dating couples, identified four types of couple—"rapid-involvement", "gradual-involvement", "delayed-involvement", and "low-involvement". The degree of sexual involvement on the first date during casual dating, when considering becoming a couple, and being one, was progressively less in each of these types.

SUMMARY

1. The growth of commitment depends in part on processes intrinsic to the development of the relationship.
2. Cognitive integration proceeds. Each probes the other, and changes in the self occur with respect to the partner. The partners come to define the relationship similarly, and to recognise similarities and differences between them.
3. Physical signals may play a part.
4. The partners gradually identify with each other: several theoretical languages can be used to describe the processes involved.
5. Trust, initially based on inadequate and insecure knowledge, is essential.
6. Comparisons with outsiders may help to consolidate the bond. The couple see their relationship as superior to that of outsiders.
7. The success of a relationship may be predictable from its very earliest stages.
8. The partners construct their own and a joint account of their relationship.
9. Self-revelation is essential, but it may be limited and certain topics may become, by mutual agreement, taboo.
10. The partners develop a miniculture, devising their own norms and conventions.
11. The social network, and the making of a public pledge, may have an important influence on the relationship.
12. Some conflict is likely.
13. The rate at which relationships develop is variable.

27 Maintenance

STABILITY AND CHANGE

We have seen that a relationship is best viewed not as an entity but as a process in continuous creation through dialectical relations with other levels of social complexity (Frontispiece). Here we are concerned primarily with the dialectical relations with the interactions within the relationship. Each interaction, as we have seen, is affected by past interactions and by expectations of future ones: thus the nature of the relationship affects the interactions within it, and those interactions affect the future of the relationship, though what happens between interactions may also play a role.

Just because the history of previous interactions is different for each interaction that occurs, relationships are likely to change with time. In addition, and perhaps even more important, the participants in a relationship are likely to change with time, either through natural processes of growth, development, and decay, or as a consequence of events within the relationship, or as a consequence of events outside it, the latter including interactions in other relationships in which they are involved. Some degree of conflict is usually present (see Chapter 10)—not necessarily overt, but perhaps contributing to a feeling of unease. All this implies that relationships are virtually never static, that a changing pattern of interactions is likely to be the rule rather than the exception, and that such stability as they have is essentially dynamic in nature (see Montgomery, 1993).

If it is unusual for the properties of a relationship to remain constant over time, what do we mean by a "stable" relationship? Most relationships change progressively, or vary whilst remaining within certain limits, or change from one temporarily more or less constant state to another. Such changes or variations may be anything from trivial to so great that the new relationship has little in common with the old. An example of the latter would be a parent–child relationship. This starts with one set of interaction types, marked complementarity related to the gross differences in moral and cognitive levels, and gradually changes to something more like a peer–peer relationship with a different set of interactions, more reciprocity and even reversed complementarity, and much greater similarity in moral and cognitive levels. There may be periods of discord and apparent change, but what emerges is in some ways a new relationship and in others still the same one. Clearly, then, stability is a relative matter, and how much change we allow without describing the relationship as a new one is an arbitrary matter.

Furthermore, "stability" depends on the time-frame with which we operate, and the relationship characteristics that we choose to observe. A relationship is constantly changing, but smoothing across a number of interactions, it may seem to be unchanged. And changes in the details of interaction may not affect their basic form and pattern (Baxter & Dindia, 1990). Changes in interaction may be fluctuating, perhaps swinging about a mean level (some would say cyclical, but that seems to be going beyond the evidence). Thus the partners may alternate periods of autonomy and periods of connectedness: they may, but need not, coordinate their fluctuations (Altman, Vinsel, & Brown, 1981; Montgomery, 1993; VanLear, 1991). The fluctuations may take place within an encounter, or over periods of days or weeks or longer.

Such stability as a relationship has over time is of two types—consistency, implying constancy of content, and continuity, in the sense of continued association. For many of the relationships in which we are involved, continuity is assured by external factors. We may have little choice but to visit the grocer at the end of the street, or may be powerless to determine who lives next door. In such cases continuity is not an issue, but consistency will be, for each interaction will affect the nature of future interactions. Institutions in the sociological sense may play a similar role: in societies where marriages are arranged and divorce impossible or unthinkable, continuity is unlikely to be an issue for marriage partners. In other cases continuity may be at issue, but consistency of little importance because the nature of the interactions is in large measure predetermined: one may have to choose between two doctors, though the broad outlines of the doctor–patient relationship are set by convention.

Although for Darby and Joan consistency and continuity were synonymous, for developing close personal relationships they are almost incompatible. If courtship is to progress, the nature of the relationship must change, so there must be continuity without consistency. In most teacher–pupil relationships, change in content, and even in continuity, is itself a long-term goal, or is at least seen as an inevitable consequence of the short-term goals of the participants. And even where continuity is assured, personal growth may demand changes in content or other properties: the development of an individual who cannot change the relationships most important to her may be stifled. The conventional wife of a domineering husband or bachelor son of a demanding mother seem to be cases in point, but it must be remembered that their tragedy resides in the fact that inability to change the relationship is a product of both parties. The costs to wife or son of breaking or changing the current relationship might well include damage to their own integrity, and be severe (cf. Black, 1975).

In discussing the stability of relationships, it is useful to make some gross distinctions between different types of stability, and control systems analysis provides some guidelines (Hinde & Stevenson-Hinde, 1976). Where the partners in the relationship strive to approach a goal or ideal no matter what the current parameters may be, the situation can be described as involving *global stability*. Thus marriage partners may strive towards an ideal relationship, and parents may try to build ideal relationships with their children. Such ideals are often encapsulated in the so-called norms that govern behaviour in given roles in the society. Of course some goals may be peculiar to the dyad, differing in some degree from those held appropriate for the corresponding "formal" relationship—husband and wife may strive for goals that differ from those of the ideal marriage in their society. At one level, this contradicts the view of some authorities, who claim that "the dialectics of social phenomena assume no ideal end state" (Montgomery, 1993, p.210). At the relationship level, persons often do have an idea of the sort of relationship they would like to have, and guide their actions accordingly for at least some of the time. But not for all: influenced by the many contradictory desiderata in any relationship, behaviour may swing this way and that.

Usually, however, the partners strive only so long as the ideal seems attainable, or only so long as the present state is within certain limits: marriage partners may strive towards an ideal marriage only so long as their relationship retains certain properties. If commitment is lost, the relationship almost inevitably becomes more distant. Such cases, in which the state heads for a goal only when it is in a specifiable region near the goal, can be described as involving *asymptotic stability*. The greater the availability of divorce, the more do marriages depend on asymptotic and the less on global stability.

In both of these cases, a goal must be postulated. We have seen that these goals are often determined in large part by the culture: the participants may seek to build a marriage or a parent–child relationship that their society will view with approval. But in many relationships stability seems to depend not on seeking for an ideal, but rather on the opposite—on the active avoidance of undesirable states. One can then postulate a *stability boundary*, as when marriage partners retreat from states that make divorce a real possibility. Another example, on a shorter timescale, is the avoidance of excessive escalation in parent–infant interaction. Such a mechanism could permit considerable flexibility in the content of the relationship. For example, relationships between parent and adolescent child sometimes seem to depend on the avoidance of interactions that could terminate the possibility of future interactions, and not on consistency of content.

Yet another possibility is that one or both participants should attempt to keep a relationship more or less within bounds, there being limits both to the increased closeness and to the amount of drifting apart that would be tolerated. Such relationships can be seen as having a stability area (see discussion of autonomy vs. connectedness, p.172).

Many relationships in our societies involve acknowledged goals or boundaries of these types. As indicated earlier, one aspect of the term "commitment" is the acceptance of such goals and/or boundaries. But it is not necessary that they be either culturally determined or consciously recognised. For instance, individuals may be so constituted as automatically to avoid states in which aggression between them is probable.

Furthermore, mechanisms involving goals or boundaries are not the only means whereby relationships are maintained. The constituent interactions may serve continuity, in the absence of any long-term goal. In addition, each relationship is set in a nexus of other relationships, and is inevitably affected by them: powerful social forces may contribute to the stability of individuals' relationships.

MAINTENANCE PROCESSES INHERENT IN A POSITIVE RELATIONSHIP

A number of psychological processes seem almost inevitably to contribute to the maintenance of a close relationship once formed. The attractive aspects of the partner are selectively perceived, things relevant to the relationship are remembered with special vividness, and there is a tendency for persons in a happy heterosexual relationship to see opposite-sexed persons outside their relationship as less attractive than they are seen by others (Graziano & Musser, 1982; Simpson, Gangestad, & Lerma, 1990).

A study of both dating and married couples showed that people view their partners with a mixture of illusion and reality. Murray and Holmes (1996) showed that:

(i) Individuals' ideal partners were closely related to their self-perceptions. The better they felt about themselves, the higher were their standards.

(ii) The reality of their partners' qualities bore little relation to the nature of their ideal partner.

(iii) Individuals tended to see their partners as the partners saw themselves.

(iv) How they saw their partners was also affected by their idea of their ideal partner. Higher ideals predicted more idealised impressions of the partner.

(v) Dating, but not married, partners' self-perceptions also influenced their perceptions of their partners.

These findings could not be accounted by a general tendency to idealise everything. The data also showed that both dating and married individuals evaluated their partners more positively than the partners evaluated themselves.

An individual's views about a partner seem to have a resistance to change, perhaps because changing a schema requires effort. Furthermore, information about the partner is processed selectively to confirm existing schemata, and the individual may behave in ways that elicit the required behaviour from the partner (Graziano & Musser, 1982; see Snyder et al., 1977). Commitment to one relationship tends to be associated with negative views about other relationships and people tend to hold more positive and less negative views about their own relationship than about those of others (Rusbult & Buunk, 1993).

Involvement in the maintenance of a relationship is likely to depend on the values of the relationship to the individual and expectations about the future. Graduating students, about to be separated from their friends, reported greater emotional involvement with close friends compared with acquaintances, as compared with students not facing separation (Frederickson, 1995).

ATTRIBUTION

In any relationship, new information may become available which throws a surprising light either on one of the participants or on a third party. If this is negative information, it can override preceding impressions with considerable ease. It is then necessary for the participants, both individually and as a pair, to assimilate the new information. Attributions must be made (Chapter 18). One partner may conclude that the other was not the sort of person they considered him or her to be, and that it is necessary to adjust or terminate the relationship. Or they may decide that circumstances were against the partner, so that help and understanding are called for. If the problem is to be resolved and a common view achieved, a good deal of discussion may be necessary (see Ruscher & Hammer, 1994).

MAINTENANCE STRATEGIES AND BEHAVIOURS

Both intrapersonal and interpersonal processes contribute to the maintenance of a relationship. Partners seldom behave as an ideal partner might, and conscious or unconscious efforts to "see the best" may come into play. Defence mechanisms (p.32) may ensure that good motives are attributed to misdemeanours, benefits are magnified and costs are overlooked. The partners may each think about past interactions, and resolve or discuss how to do better in future (Acitelli & Holmberg, 1993).

Some of the studies on this issue concentrate on "maintenance strategies", with an apparent implication that they were used with some conscious intention of sustaining the relationship. For instance, an analysis of the responses of 956 married or romantically involved subjects by Stafford and Canary (1991) yielded five categories of proactive approaches to the maintenance of romantic involvements:

(i) *Positivity*: cheerful optimism, compliments, adding to the partner's self-esteem.
(ii) *Openness*: self-disclosure or intimacy.
(iii) *Assurances*: emphasising affection or love for the partner.
(iv) *Network*: spending time with common friends and creating a support network.
(v) *Sharing tasks*: taking equal responsibility for the tasks and responsibilities inherent in the relationship.

The extent to which the partner was seen to use these strategies varied with the stage of the relationship. Engaged and seriously dating partners perceived greater partner positivity and openness than dating or married partners. Married, engaged and seriously dating partners perceived more use of assurances and sharing tasks than those who had just begun dating, and married persons perceived their partners to use the social network to maintain the relationship more than individuals at other stages. The various strategies had differential relations to the several characteristics of the relationships (see also Canary & Stafford, 1992). They are also more frequent in relationships that escalate or remain stable than in deteriorating or terminating relationships (Guerrero, Eloy, & Wabnik, 1993).

Buss (e.g. 1994), using student questionnaires, experiments, and literature data, has also reviewed tactics used in relationship maintenance, some
of which are rather more negative:

(i) *Fulfilling the partner's desires.* This involves acts of love and commitment, providing resources (especially by men) and enhancing
physical appearance (especially by women).

(ii) *Using emotional manipulation*—for instance weeping or making the
partner feel guilty, self abasement, and provoking jealousy.

(iii) *Keeping competitors at bay.* Buss includes here public displays of
affection, public signals in dress, maintaining vigilance, and guard-
ing the spouse.

(iv) *Destructive measures.* Derogation of potential competitors, punishing the partner for (potential) infidelity, and aggression towards
rivals.

However much behaviour that contributes to a relationship is of a routine nature, and is not undertaken with the deliberate intent of fostering it.
Small-talk plays an important role, but many activities of an apparently
mundane and trivial nature may contribute (Duck et al., 1991). Accordingly Dainton and Stafford (1993) developed a taxonomy of maintenance
behaviours from open-ended questions given to couples in midwestern
USA. The most commonly reported category was the sharing of tasks, and
this in spite of the fact that the questions concerned maintaining a relationship and not a household: this is, of course, in keeping with the view that
much communication in close relationships is routine. Among other
frequently reported items were sharing time, proactive social behaviour, and
self-disclosure. The sample used by Dainton and Stafford included both
married and dating couples but, apart from a lower frequency of sharing
tasks in the latter, there was little difference between them in the maintenance behaviours used, although some studies had found such a difference
(Stafford & Canary, 1991; see earlier). The two partners in each couple
tended to use similar behaviours, though women reported the use of more
positivity and openness, and more general talk. They also tended to use
behaviours that would generally be considered antisocial, such as manipulation and jealousy, more than the men.

Most of the maintenance behaviours revealed in the Dainton and
Stafford study are of types that would be expected. One further issue of a
rather different kind may provide a partial answer to the fact that during
the early phases of marriage there is often a decline in satisfaction. This
has been ascribed to a decline in love due to habituation, or to a decline
in the opportunities for uncertainty reduction as the partner becomes more
and more familiar, or as disillusionment through the breaking down of the

idealisation of early love. A more challenging proposal is inherent in the self-expansion perspective of Aron and Aron (1986). As we have seen, these authors propose that many aspects of behaviour can be understood on the view that people have a motive to expand the self, in the sense of enhancing their potential efficacy. Relationships expand the self because the other person is incorporated in the self, so that his or her resources, perspectives and characteristics become in some sense available. Once that is achieved, however, further opportunities for expansion diminish, and boredom may ensue. One solution to this is to engage in exciting and stimulating activities. Consistently with this hypothesis, Reissman, Aron, and Bergen (1993) found that married couples instructed to engage in exciting activities over a 10-week period showed greater marital satisfaction than couples instructed to engage in activities that were merely pleasant, and than controls with no special instructions. Whilst, as the authors point out, there are other explanations, this study provides some evidence in favour of the self-expansion hypothesis, and also of the importance of the novelty–boredom contradiction discussed by Baxter (1988; see p.159). Dindia and Canary (1993) also comment on the extent to which actions designed to produce novelty, stimulation, and variety are often used for maintenance.

We have seen that the state of a relationship is seldom constant for long periods, and periods of closeness may be interspersed with periods when the participants feel not so close. That being so, the timing of maintenance activities may be crucial. This is especially the case when the participants meet incompatible needs by alternating between the two poles, for instance spending time doing things with the partner alternating with autonomous activities. Baxter and Simon (1993) obtained evidence that a proposal to swing away from one pole to the other was most acceptable when the relationship was already at the former. For example, contact with the partner was more effective in autonomy-dominated moments than in connection-dominated ones.

There is some evidence that masculine individuals are less inclined to put effort into the maintenance of relationships than feminine ones. They tend to see the relationship more as a goal to be achieved. Once there is a satisfactory degree of intimacy they tend to relax, whereas feminine individuals seek to sustain the relationship through introspection and discussion (Duck, 1990; Wood, 1993).

However it must be remembered that it is not what the partners actually do that matters, but the impact on the partner. Oggins, Veroff, and Leber (1993, p.507), on the basis of interview material with a wide range of black and white families, suggest that "affirmation of one's identity in a relationship may be the underlying psychological process that provides marital interactions with their special meaning for marital well-being ... whether the affirmation is expressed directly in words or individually in positive sexual relations". The authors emphasise that positive sexual inter-action may be viewed differently by men (who tend to see it as an affirma-tion of marriage) and women (who link it with positive orientation to spouses sharing time and interests), and that the meaning of marital inter-action must also be interpreted within the cultural context.

Finally, the importance of rituals and celebrations in the maintenance of relationships is not to be underestimated. Birthday celebrations, wedding anniversaries, Christmas dinners, and comparable occasions play an important part in reaffirming and maintaining relationships. Werner et al. (1993) emphasise that in these ceremonies individual, group, and dyad explore, develop and celebrate their unique and collective identities simul-taneously.

CONTINUITY OF UNHAPPY RELATIONSHIPS

Some relationships continue even though the partners are far from happy. Some possible explanations were discussed on pp.273–274.

SUMMARY

1. The properties of a relationship are liable to change with time. Stability may involve consistency in content and quality, or continuity over time, or both.
2. Behaviour-enhancing stability may involve striving for an ideal, striving only when the relationship is reasonably near a goal-state, or striving only so long as it is within a certain stability area.
3. Certain processes inherent in a positive relationship enhance its stability. Some of these can be described as involving the wearing of rose-tinted spectacles.
4. Various strategies and behaviours are used more or less consciously. These may involve both pleasing the partner and denigrating outsiders. Celebrations and social occasions may be important.

28 The Decline and Dissolution of Relationships

PHASES OF DECLINE

Here we turn to the declining stages of a relationship, and must immediately face some terminological distinctions. Duck (1982b) has advocated the terms "dissolution" and "termination" to refer to the permanent dismemberment of a relationship, "decline" to a reduction in closeness, and "breakdown" to refer to turbulence or disorder in a relationship which may or may not lead to dissolution. These conventions are followed here.

As with the development of relationships, it is tempting to see the decline and dissolution of a relationship as involving a series of stages. Of course no two relationships are alike, and any attempt to squeeze all relationships into a common pattern is bound to fail. Nevertheless, such an approach helps to categorise the data. Perhaps the most useful of such attempts is due to Duck (1982b), who describes four phases—an intrapsychic phase, in which one of the participants reflects on the causes of his or her dissatisfaction; a dyadic phase of confrontation and negotiation; a social phase concerned largely with the consequences of the decline on the social network outside the dyad; and a "grave-dressing" phase of readjustment (Fig. 28.1). In each of these phases, the person initiating the decline has certain goals and concerns. These are shown for the dyadic phase in Fig. 28.2. We may consider these phases in turn.

(i) *The intrapsychic phase.* Here one partner has become aware of dissatisfaction which may lead to a desire to improve the relationship, to live

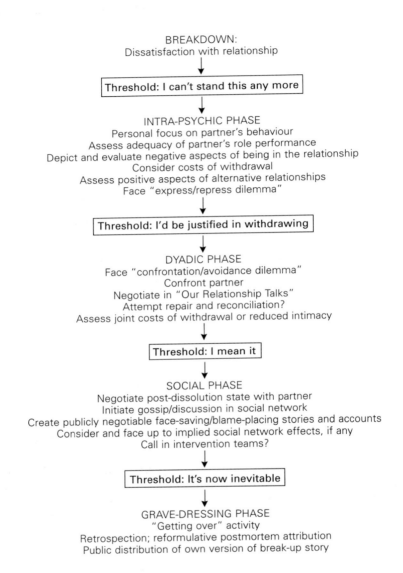

BREAKDOWN:
Dissatisfaction with relationship

↓

Threshold: I can't stand this any more

↓

INTRA-PSYCHIC PHASE
Personal focus on partner's behaviour
Assess adequacy of partner's role performance
Depict and evaluate negative aspects of being in the relationship
Consider costs of withdrawal
Assess positive aspects of alternative relationships
Face "express/repress dilemma"

↓

Threshold: I'd be justified in withdrawing

↓

DYADIC PHASE
Face "confrontation/avoidance dilemma"
Confront partner
Negotiate in "Our Relationship Talks"
Attempt repair and reconciliation?
Assess joint costs of withdrawal or reduced intimacy

↓

Threshold: I mean it

↓

SOCIAL PHASE
Negotiate post-dissolution state with partner
Initiate gossip/discussion in social network
Create publicly negotiable face-saving/blame-placing stories and accounts
Consider and face up to implied social network effects, if any
Call in intervention teams?

↓

Threshold: It's now inevitable

↓

GRAVE-DRESSING PHASE
"Getting over" activity
Retrospection; reformulative postmortem attribution
Public distribution of own version of break-up story

FIG. 28.1 Four phases of relationship decline. (Duck, 1982b.)

GOALS

Confronting partner
Gaining compliance from partner
Redefining relationship
Repairing/dissolving relationship

MAJOR SPECIFIC CONCERNS	RESEARCHABLE MANIFESTATIONS AND CONSEQUENCES
To confront partner with person's dissatisfaction	Hostility; negative communication style
To present own view of relationship	Guilt; anxiety; stress
To express discomfort directly to partner	Increased private discussion with partner
To assess costs (to partner) of own views	Withdrawal from other contacts, temporarily
To evaluate partner's view of relationship	Anger
To cope with partner's rejoinders	Experimental withdrawal/experimental repair
To weigh up relationship together	Increased fantasising about future form of the relationship
To consider alternative or ideal forms of the relationship under review	
To choose between repair and dissolution	

FINAL OUTCOME
Resolve to dissolve/repair the relationship

FIG. 28.2   Dyadic phase of relationship decline. (Duck, 1982b.)

with it, or to terminate it. During this period he or she will be reflecting on the merits and costs of the relationship, wondering whether they have been assessed correctly, pondering on what the partner may be thinking, and considering the consequences of withdrawal from the relationship and the possibilities of alternatives. There may be consultations with outsiders. Although the dissatisfaction is not communicated verbally to the partner, the felt dissatisfaction is bound to influence behaviour, so that the partner may become aware that all is not what it seemed. Behaviour is likely to fluctuate between attempts to rejuvenate the relationship and recrimination, but in due course a decision to terminate may be taken.

(ii) *The dyadic phase*. Here, the desire of one partner to terminate the relationship is communicated to the other. This may be a consequence of a change in the dissatisfied partner's behaviour, or of a direct confrontation or, most hurtful of all, of information from an outsider (McCall, 1982). A great deal of discussion will follow, in which the initiator will give accounts of the relationship to the partner which focus on the partner's failings. The course that this phase takes will then depend largely on whether the partner also already had, or had acquired, a desire to terminate the relationship. Further fluctuations between attempts at reconciliation and withdrawal may follow. Baxter (1984) has summarised the dyadic phase of the break-up of 92 romantic relationships in a flow chart (see later).

(iii) *Social phase.* It is likely that outsiders will have noticed that all is not well in the dyadic phase, but if a final decision for termination has been taken, it can be publicly acknowledged. This will bring a new set of forces into play, involving judgements by outsiders, and attempts to reconcile the partners or to persuade them to get on with the separation. The partners, probably individually, may amend their accounts of what has happened for public consumption.

(iv) *Grave-dressing.* Once separation has occurred, both participants must come to terms with it, and with the distress that they may feel, and amend yet again the accounts that they give to themselves and to outsiders (McCall, 1982). These come to involve comprehensive descriptions of the antecedents and consequences of the dissolution, more or less acceptable to the person concerned and/or to the social network, to whom they may be transmitted by gossip (La Gaipa, 1982).

Duck's perceptive scheme for tracing the course of the breakdown of relationships has great heuristic value, and it is no criticism of it to make three points which must be borne in mind. First, as with all stage models, one must remember that the stages overlap. In real life, social concerns will enter in from the start of the intrapsychic phase. As Duck points out, partners prefer to ease themselves out of a declining relationship, and insults and negative communication are less common than one might expect: one reason for this is likely to be the social sanctions of the surrounding network. Again, self-questioning usually continues until, and after, the final dissolution. A second issue is that, as set out, it applies primarily to the initiator of the decline: the perspective of the partner is there only by implication. A third problem is the emphasis on cognition: the self-questioning is not just a matter of cold calculation, but is driven by what the person feels, and the cognitive processes involve attempts to come to terms with and justify feelings (Graziano & Musser, 1982). The preparation of accounts, for consumption by the self and by outsiders, is a critical part of the process, but they too are emotion-driven. These issues are explicit in Duck's discussion of his model, but need to be emphasised because simplified schemes, while heuristically valuable, too easily create a false impression. What is important about the scheme is the suggestion that several psychological and social thresholds must be crossed in sequence, from the initial dissatisfaction to private and public acceptance.

ASPECTS OF BREAKDOWN

Attribution and Accounts

It will be apparent from the above that a critical part in the dissolution of a relationship is played by the accounts that the participants give, to themselves, to each other, and to outsiders (cf. Duck, 1981). Impressions and attributions about the partner or about the relationship usually form the basis of the initial dissatisfaction and lead to the desire for dissolution, but then the cause of the breakdown is attributed to one or other or both partners, or to outside pressures. Attributions made may mis-identify or excuse the cause of the problem, leading to efforts to repair the relationship, fix blame unfairly on one partner, etc. They may either retard or accelerate the decline in the relationship, moderating or mediating the supposed cause(s) of the decline.

Certain regularities are found in the attributions made during relationship decline. Hill et al. (1976), studying the breakdown of dating relationships, found that women tended to probe the causes of the breakdown more deeply, and to terminate the relationship more readily, than men. The partners tended to agree on the influence of external factors on their problems, but not on differences between them or on factors internal to their relationship. Individuals tended to claim that they had initiated the dissolution, and those who felt they had initiated it suffered less distress. Orvis, Kelley, and Butler (1976) also found many areas in which the attributions made by the two partners in a romantic relationship were likely to disagree.

A study by Sprecher (1994) involved 101 young adult dating couples, 60 of which broke up over an approximately six-month period. While Hill et al. had found that individuals were more likely to say that they had initiated the break-up than that the partner had, Sprecher and other more recent studies found that about equal numbers of subjects assigned responsibility to themselves and to the partners. However Sprecher differentiated between who was responsible for the decline in the relationship and who initiated the dissolution. Women tended to see their partners as responsible for the problems leading to the breakdown, but to say that they were responsible for terminating the relationship. The most common reasons given for the decline were different interests and communication problems, followed by one partner wanting to be independent or becoming bored. There was moderate agreement on living apart as a reason for the decline, and for all the dyadic reasons involving differences or conflict, but lack of agreement or disagreement over reasons referring to the self or to the partner.

In a study of retrospective attributions made about retrospectively perceived changes in the chances of marriage in serious relationships that were eventually broken off, Lloyd and Cate (1985b) distinguished between (a) Dyadic attributions, rooted in interactions within the relationship and including redefinitions of the relationship, conflict, etc.; (b) Individual attributions that emanated from an individual's belief system, standards, etc.; (c) Network attributions that related to interactions or anticipated interactions with others; and (d) Circumstantial attributions referring to matters over which the partners had no control. Attributions referring to interactions within the relationship were most common in the casual acquaintanceship and couple phases, but became less so as the relationship deteriorated. Individual attributions became especially common in the later stages before break-up. The latter trend could represent an increase in introspection, or a desire to feel in control as the relationship disintegrated.

Where a turning point was in a positive direction, dyadic attributions were most common, but where the change was for the worse, individual attributions were. Network attributions were relatively uncommon when changes were in a positive direction, but common when the chances of marriage were seen as little affected or deteriorating. Circumstantial attributions were most commonly associated with moderate decreases in the chances of marriage. Males gave more dyadic reasons and fewer individual reasons for a decrease in the probability of marriage than did females. Finally, individuals involved in mutual break-ups and individuals whose partner broke off the relationship gave more dyadic and fewer individual reasons for a change than did those who initiated the break-up themselves (see also Surra et al.,1988).

Causal analysis continues even after a close relationship has been terminated: the former partners continue to ruminate, assign blame, re-evaluate each other, and so on. Harvey et al. (1982, p.119) comment that "Relationships are as much symbolic events and images to the involved parties as they are interactional episodes or histories", and these images stay in partners' minds even after they have separated. In a deteriorating relationship the partners may engage in what seem to be tripartite discussions—the two partners and "our relationship". The disappearance of the latter must be dealt with, and each partner makes attributions about what has happened and about the partner.

Naturally, the nature of the attributions change as the decline progresses. After dissolution, the attributions often involve rationalisations and justifications for each partner's role, fixing blame, and re-evaluating both self and partner (Weiss, 1975). Harvey et al. (1982) found that such ruminations might go on for months, and even be a hindrance to recovery.

Communication

During the growth and continuation phases, the balance of communicative acts is inevitably positive, but during the declining phases of a relationship there are clear changes. These have been reviewed by Miller and Parks (1982), and include the following:

(i) *Global interaction characteristics.* There is a general diminution in communication between the two partners.

(ii) *Communication network characteristics.* The partners have less mutual interaction with outsiders. Communication with outsiders about the relationship or the partner becomes more negative.

(iii) *Non-verbal communication characteristics.* Physical proximity, the amount the partners touch each other, the ratio of leaning forwards to backwards and the amount of direct orientation towards the partner all increase with closeness in a relationship, and decrease as it declines. There are also changes in the frequency of body movements, in the facial expressions and features used, and in the amount of mutual gaze. The non-verbal characteristics of speech—its rate, tone, coordination between the partners, etc.—also change.

(iv) *Verbal communication characteristics.* As the relationship declines there are changes in the pronouns used, with fewer statements in the first person plural, fewer references to the future, and more ambiguous statements. There are of course also changes in the content of verbal messages, including a reduction in agreement, an increase in negative comments, an increase in the ratios of disagreements to agreements and of rejecting or coercive acts to reconciling and appealing ones.

During the dyadic and social phases of decline, many of the verbal interactions will involve attempts to obtain the compliance of the partner with particular courses of action. Basing their work on an earlier list of 16 strategies, Miller and Parks (1982) produced a four-category typology of compliance-gaining message strategies. The categories differed according to whether the onus is on the communicator or the recipient to take action, and whether carrot or stick is employed. Miller and Parks used this categorisation to propose hypotheses about the use of strategies in dissolution. For instance they suggested that initial attempts to dissolve a relationship will rely primarily on reward-oriented strategies, and that punishment-oriented strategies will be more commonly used by a partner seeking to dissolve a relationship in high motivation compared with low motivation unilateral dissolution, and in low-harmonious as compared with high-harmonious bilateral dissolution situations.

The Social Context of Dissolution

When a relationship breaks down, the former partners inevitably experience changes in their social networks. The partner's friends may be lost, solace may be sought elsewhere. The dissolution of a close relationship involves not only an emotional upheaval, but also a loss of part of one's identity, manifested most clearly when a role status like "husband" or "wife" is also lost. There may also be a need to come to terms with changes in the patterns of daily living (Hagestad & Smyer, 1982). In addition to the use of attributions and the construction of accounts about the dissolution, the social network may be used to cushion the impact. The shortcomings of the partner are discussed, and anger and grief expressed. Friends may try to help by denigrating the former partner or distracting the sufferer (Harvey et al., 1982). The accounts that are made up must be guided by the culturally accepted norms for the relationship in question, and outsiders may have a role to play in limiting the defamation of character that may go on.

Gossip may be important in the dissolution process, helping to establish a negotiated account of what has happened (La Gaipa, 1982). There are rules to gossip—make sure you are going to get the sort of response you want; use gossip to reduce the credibility of an opponent, but do so with care; don't be too extreme, or you will be labelled a slanderer; and so on. Gossip can become ritualistic, emphasising the maintenance of sacred values, norms, and ideals. There may be direct references to ideals, or they may be implied by the description of departures from them. Semi-fictionalised accounts of the breakdown, known to be false or exaggerated, may be accepted in an attempt to protect a supposedly innocent victim.

Cultural Determinants in Dissolution

The incidence of marital break-up both affects and is affected by social attitudes to divorce. White and Booth (1991) have argued that the threshold of marital unhappiness necessary to prompt divorce is lower than it used to be. Cultural norms may also operate in another way. Expectations about marriage have changed, especially amongst women, and may not be met by traditionalist spouses: marriages may therefore be less happy than they used to be.

Just as those entering a relationship have shared views about how relationships normally develop or ought to develop, so do those who see their relationship to be deteriorating. Honeycutt, Cantrill, and Allen (1992) showed that these were, to a considerable degree, shared among the members of a cultural group by asking students to list 20 actions believed to be typical in breaking up a romantic relationship. These were coded into 21 categories of actions (of which 11 were seen as prototypical), which represented six clusters—Decrease intimacy, Aversive communication, Decrease contact, Re-evaluate relationship, Comparison with alternatives, and Termination of relationship. Subsequent studies found that students showed considerable agreement in arranging the prototypical items in a logical order. However the expectancies for de-escalating actions were more individually variable than those for escalating ones. That there are cognitive structures for escalation and de-escalation helps explain why people are not surprised at break-ups: people have stage-appropriate communication strategies.

FACTORS MAKING FOR A DECLINE

If the basis for a decline is internal to the relationship, it is likely to evoke dissatisfaction in one or both partners. This may involve dissatisfaction with the partner because of new knowledge or changed perceptions: sometimes the very characteristics that were attractive in a potential dating partner become aversive (Felmlee, 1995). Or there may be growing dissatisfaction with the relationship because the costs come to outweigh the rewards: for instance, after relocation of one partner, the costs of keeping contact may escalate. Or the relationship may outlive its usefulness, as when teacher–pupil relationships cease after a while.

In this section we shall consider some general issues concerning factors that lead to dissatisfaction in relationships, and then consider the three cases of decline in friendship, pre-marital romantic partners, and marriage. The following overlapping categories embrace many of the factors making for a decline in relationships of all sorts.

Predisposing Personal Factors

This includes individual characteristics that make it difficult for the individual to form or maintain relationships of any sort, such as an unstable early environment (Tizard & Hodges, 1978; see also Chapter 21), neuroticism, or lack of social skills (Trower, 1981); characteristics that give an individual difficulty in some sorts of relationships but not others; and characteristics and needs that are incompatible with characteristics of particular others. Duck (1981) points out that, in so far as adolescent friendships are based on consensual validation, they may break down because the partner fails to supply support for those parts of the individual's personality system that need it most, or because the partners lack the skills to reveal the similarities that are present.

External Factors

Some relationships come to an end because a participant moves away or finds new employment. Others because of interference by third parties (parental disapproval may be potent), the disappearance of a source of support outside the relationship, or the appearance of a rival. And of course one of the participants may die. In general, the longer a marriage has lasted, the stronger are the external barriers to divorce and the poorer are the alternatives. Thus marital satisfaction is likely to be more closely related to the possibility of divorce in longer marriages (White & Booth, 1991).

Change in a Participant

People change, and what they need from their relationships changes. For that reason, the very success of some relationships is conducive to their own demise or metamorphosis, as with parent–child or teacher–pupil relationships. Duck (1981) suggests that adolescent friendships may break down because the individual's personality system develops and overtakes the requirement for similarity in regions where it was previously present.

Changes in the Relationship

Partners may find themselves to be suited to each other in the early stages of a relationship, but decreasingly so as it progresses. They may find satisfying similarities early on, but discover that they lack the deeper points of contact necessary for a close relationship (see pp.122–123). Or the relationship may take off, becoming too much for them, or fail to take off, disappointing their expectations. Another possibility is that the comparative position between the partners may change: while able to share vicariously in each other's successes in different fields, they may become competitive if the fields come to overlap (see pp.140–141 and Tesser, 1980, 1988).

Cultural Norms

The importance of cultural norms must not be forgotten. As noted above, the increase in the rate of divorce in recent decades has been affected by (and has affected) a lowering of social barriers to divorce and an increase in alternatives to marriage (White & Booth, 1991).

Internal Factors

Whatever the causes, doubts about the partner's ability to meet hoped-for standards may mount up, and may overcome any defence mechanisms that may operate. A variety of mechanisms that diminish interdependence may then operate. The doubting individual may acquire a defensive pessimism, expecting the worst and being prepared for further disappointments. This may lead to negative distortions in perceptions of the partner's behaviour. There may also be increased attention to the keeping of an account of costs and benefits and a focus on whether they do indeed balance (Boon, 1994; Holmes, 1981).

THE DECLINE OF FRIENDSHIP

Depending on the intensity of the relationship, the termination of friendship may be accompanied by a certain amount of distress, or the friends may just drift apart and the relationship slowly wane.

Rose (1984) described four patterns of friendship dissolution in young adults. First, one partner may cease to like or grow to dislike the other. This might be because the friend behaved in an unexpectedly conflictual way, perhaps violating a previously accepted rule of friendship; or one of the partners changed her needs or her expectations about how a friend should behave, so that she no longer matched up or ceased to provide consensual validation; or new circumstances arose demanding qualities the former friend could not provide; or, for other reasons internal or external to the relationship, it no longer seemed worthwhile (see also Rodin, 1982). Second, a new friend may come to replace the old. Third, physical separation might cause the relationship to wane simply because of the difficulties in interacting, as in a school-to-college or post-college transition: Rose found this to be especially the case with men. Or, in some cases and especially in women, a romantic involvement intervened. However Rose found that few friendships ended in "breakdown", and in most cases there was little emotional response and little or no negotiation about the demise of the relationship—even though nearly half of the respondents said they wished the relationship had continued.

THE DECLINE OF ROMANTIC RELATIONSHIPS

The termination of a romantic relationship differs in a number of ways from that of friendship. Unlike friendships, there is likely to be a good deal of negotiation and/or recrimination between the partners, and there is almost inevitably distress on the part of one or both. There is also likely to be more involvement of the social network.

Baxter's (1984) study, based on 92 retrospective accounts of students who had experienced the break-up of romantic relationships, led to the recognition of a series of stages based on, but more elaborate than, those suggested by Duck (see earlier): Stages 3–5 and 6–7 are alternatives:

1. *Onset.* Either an accumulation of problems, or a critical incident involving one major one, led one of the participants to come to the view that the relationship might end.

2. *Decision to end the relationship.* This may be unilateral (68% of the cases studied) or bilateral.

3. *Initiating unilateral dissolution.* This involves communication of the desire to leave the relationship. This could involve:

(a) Indirect communication (76%). This might involve Withdrawal (e.g. using excuses not to see the partner); Pseudo-de-escalation (a false declaration of a wish for a relationship of reduced closeness); or Cost-escalation (Increasing the costs of the partner).

(b) Direct communication (24%), which might involve a direct confrontation with a statement that the relationship was over; or a statement of a desire to leave in the context of a bilateral discussion.

4. *The initial reaction of the broken-up-with party.* Unilateral direct approaches were more likely (.66) to gain initial acceptance than indirect ones (.22). Usually, the other party resisted the termination, either by offering the terminator rewards or by threatening costs, and only 35% resulted in acceptance of the initial disengagement bid.

5. *Ambivalence and repair scenarios.* If the initial attempt was unsuccessful, the terminator may persist, usually using indirect means. In a few cases, however, the terminator might have a change of mind, and this could lead to a continuation of the relationship. Where this did not happen, one or more repeat bids at termination followed until the situation was accepted.

6. *Initiating bilateral dissolution.* This may involve indirect communication, such as agreement, perhaps unspoken, that the relationship was over, or mutual pseudo-de-escalation with both parties pretending some continuity but intending termination. Or direct communication could involve either conflict or a negotiated farewell. Direct and indirect initiations were equally frequent.

7. *Ambivalence and repair.* Even after the decisions had apparently been accepted, there was sometimes a change of mind by both parties and attempts were made to repair the relationship. However this was successful in only one case out of twelve.

Baxter emphasises the large number of possible trajectories that the dissolution of a relationship could take. The most frequent trajectory was unilateral and indirect, requiring a number of attempts by the initiator and no attempted repairs: however only 30% of the dissolutions were of this type.

Among other interesting data reported by Baxter (1985) was an increase in the variety of strategies used with age; a tendency of pre-adolescents to use more direct strategies (perhaps through lack of awareness of the impact on the other's self-esteem); a tendency of androgynous persons to use direct negotiation; and tendencies for more direct strategies to be used in closer relationships.

Baxter (1986) also extracted the "rules" implicated in the dissolution of heterosexual relationships from the accounts of 157 respondents who had taken the initiative in the dissolution process. (Ginsburg, 1988, points out that these are grounds for dissolution, and thus rules only in the sense that their violation justified termination.) The primary rules were: obligation to grant autonomy outside the relationship; expectation of similarity; obligations to be supportive, to be open, to be loyal; expectations of shared time, of equity, and of some magical quality in the relationship.

A number of other authors have investigated factors predictive of the dissolution of premarital relationships. Some of the earlier work (Burgess & Wallin, 1953) emphasised extra-relationship factors, such as parental opposition, and circumstantial issues, such as prolonged separation, as well as personality problems and cultural differences. Differences between the partners in age, educational goals, intelligence, and physical attractiveness, as well as lack of intimacy and unequal involvement, were found to be important by Hill et al. (1976) (see also Felmlee et al., 1990).

Drigotas and Rusbult (1992) used a construct which they termed "need satisfaction dependence" to predict relationship dissolution (see Chapter 19). This assesses the extent to which each of a number of needs is important and effectively satisfied in the current relationship, and the extent to which better alternatives are available. Dependence measures obtained in this way successfully differentiated student relationships that persisted over a six-week period from those that ended.

Many of the respondents in Sprecher's study of dating couples (reported earlier) said that they felt distress on dissolution. The most common negative emotions were hurt, frustration, depression, and loneliness. For some respondents, positive emotions predominated, love for the other and relief being the most frequent. Women and men were about equally likely to feel distress, but women were more likely to report positive emotions. There were positive associations between the emotions felt by the two partners in a relationship, except for negative correlations for guilt, resentment, and loneliness. The more men felt themselves to be responsible for the break-up, the more guilt they felt, but this was not the case for women. More distress was felt if the partner was perceived to have control over the decline, and especially if the partner became interested in someone else.

Distress on the break-up of dating relationships has been investigated also in a number of other studies. Simpson (1987) found that the amount of distress experienced was related to the duration and closeness of the relationship, and to the availability of alternative partners, but not to satisfaction with the relationship. Frazier and Cook (1993) found that both factors related to commitment to the relationship (satisfaction, duration, closeness, and perceived alternatives) and coping factors (perceptions of the controllability of the break-up, social support, and self-esteem) were related to distress. The former are more closely related to initial distress, the coping factors to subsequent recovery. The relation between prior closeness and distress may reflect not only the extent of the loss suffered, but also the vulnerability resulting from the knowledge and experiences shared with a partner whose discretion is no longer certain.

Many of the studies of the factors leading to the breakdown of romantic relationships rely on data from only one partner, but Attridge, Berscheid, and Simpson (1995) showed that rather little predictability was gained by using data from both.

Finally, one study indicates that students' romantic relationships could be important as learning experiences. Harvey et al. (1989) asked undergraduates to explain why a significant close relationship had broken up, and to list their expectations about current and future relationships. There was a considerable degree of correspondence between their views about the past and their expectations for the future. For instance, those who had identified a communication problem as the reason for the break-up, tended to list expectations that could be described as involving "working at the relationship". Harvey et al. therefore suggest that, if one can identify a solvable problem in a past failed relationship, this may affect one's behaviour in the future.

The attributions made are likely to be related to the possibility of love being replaced by friendship. Amongst students, this appears to be less likely if the partners were not friends before becoming romantically involved, if the withdrawing partner used withdrawal strategies and felt as if he or she had been taken advantage of in the relationship, and if the other partner used manipulation and not positive strategies (Metts, Cupach, & Bejlovec, 1989).

Unrequited Love

In romantic relationships, the issue of unrequited love is perhaps an extreme case. Distressing to both parties, each is unable to comprehend the other's actions. The rejected lover suffers more intensely than the rejector but, so long as the situation remains unresolved, has at least a possibility of happiness to strive for. The rejector must face guilt and distress, or tolerate an unenjoyable relationship, and thus can have no positive outcome in view. Why then do individuals tolerate such a situation? Aron and Aron (1996) suggest three possibilities, based on the view that motivation for the relationship depends on three factors—the desirability of the relationship (and especially the possibility for self-expansion, see pp.464–465), its probability, and desiring the culturally scripted role of lover without actually wanting the relationship. Thus it could be that the rejected one wants the relationship very much but recognises its improbability; or feels certain that love is returned but later discovers it is not; or simply desires the state of being in love. The data supported this model. Individuals classed as Avoidants by the Hazan and Shaver technique (p.389) were especially likely to fall into the third category: they could experience being in love without the risk of a relationship.

Those involved in such relationships must incorporate them into an account. Based on an analysis of autobiographical accounts of past events, which presumably involved considerable interpretation by the parties concerned, Baumeister, Wotman, and Stillwell (1993) found that rejected lovers remembered both positive and negative emotions, and that they tended to believe that attraction had been mutual and that the rejection had never been communicated directly. Their accounts were constructed to re-build self-esteem, depicting the rejectors as inconsistent and mysterious. Rejectors gave almost wholly negative accounts, feeling guilty but also regarding their pursuers as intrusive and annoying. Their accounts were constructed to reduce their guilt, their would-be lovers being seen as self-deceptive and unreasonable.

THE BREAKDOWN OF MARITAL RELATIONSHIPS

Marital breakdown is not an event, but a "multifaceted process of multiple social and psychological ceasings" (Hagestad & Smyer, 1982, p.187). Marriage is a public commitment, and for that reason the course and consequences of marital decline involve social factors much more than does the decline of a romantic relationship.

Predictors of Breakdown

There are obvious difficulties in assessing the ultimate causes of marital dissolution, in that the events that are usually blamed for the breakdown may be merely symptoms of disaffection that has earlier roots. Extra-marital sexual involvement, alcohol abuse, and money problems are often cited in divorce courts, but it has been pointed out that they do not always lead to dissolution, and when they do they may be merely precipitating events for an already weakened marriage, or even caused by the un-satisfactory marital relationship. Extra-marital liaisons may even be used to escalate the tensions in an unsatisfactory marriage and bring matters to a head. Newcomb and Bentler also point out that divorced persons not surprisingly complain more about events that were under voluntary control (e.g. bickering) than about issues like ill-health, which are not. There is some evidence that women are more likely to be dissatisfied with their relationships than men.

The earlier literature was summarised by Newcomb and Bentler (1981; see also Kitson, Babri, & Roach, 1985): more recently Karney and Bradbury (1995b) have reviewed a large number of longitudinal studies.

These authors found that most of the variables that have been studied have similar effects on marital satisfaction and stability, a notable exception being marital duration. Antecedents that have been linked to marital breakdown can be categorised as follows:

Demographic Factors.   Both satisfaction and stability are related to age, but this is confounded by marital duration. Marital satisfaction may decrease with time since marriage, at any rate in the early years (p.247), but marital stability tends to increase.

Husband's employment and income enhance stability, but the opposite is (at present) true for wives. It is not known whether the effect of wife's income operates through a decrease in marital satisfaction, or by enhancing the possible alternatives.

Lack of education is also associated with breakdown.

Cohabitation before marriage is often associated with marital instability, but this effect disappears if allowance is made for the total time that the couple have lived together (Teachman & Polonko, 1990).

Children may decrease satisfaction but also decrease the likelihood of marital dissolution.

Individual Characteristics.   Aspects of past relationship history may hazard the probability of marital stability—a history of divorce, brief acquaintanceship, pre-marital sexual experience, and other variables indicative of low commitment, and pre-marital or step-children (e.g. Booth & Edwards, 1992).

Marital breakdown has been related to a wide range of personality factors. Karney and Bradbury (1995b) aggregated the 56 traits that have been examined in longitudinal studies into five, and found that neuroticism had the greatest impact on marital stability. In a study in which couples were followed over nearly 50 years, Kelly and Conley (1987) likewise found that neuroticism of both spouses and husband's impulsivity predicted later breakdown. Other factors that have been implicated include a rigid defensive style, masculinity, achievement motivation, competitiveness, individualism, and ambition. Presumably some of these operate through lowered commitment to the marriage. Constantine and Bahr (1980) found internal orientation on the leadership subscale of a measure of locus of control to be important. There are also differences between men and women: men who are introverted, invulnerable, and with a high need for orderliness, but women who perceive themselves as ambitious, intelligent, liberal, and unstable, have been found to be more prone to divorce in American samples (Bentler & Newcomb, 1978).

Kurdek (1991b) compared the individual characteristics of 23 married couples who separated before their first anniversary with 353 couples who did not. The former scored higher on external motivation (e.g. He/she is someone of whom my parents would approve), dysfunctional relationship beliefs, and global severity of psychological distress, and lower on satisfaction with social support, all measured a month or two after marriage.

Differences in Age, Race, Religion, Personality and Marital Expectations. Such issues were discussed on pp.115–117. However Karney and Bradbury (1995) note that many of the studies of attitude and personality homogamy did not control for the initial levels of the variables in question, and it is therefore necessary to be cautious before concluding that heterogamy is associated with reduced stability or satisfaction.

Relationship Factors. Satisfaction is more positively related to marital stability than most other variables, but dissatisfaction is not strongly predictive of dissolution. This is in keeping with the view that commitment to a relationship does not depend solely on satisfaction, but also on the resources invested in the relationship, the extent to which it is central to the individual's identity, and the availability of alternatives (see pp.348–350). Of course a variety of factors contribute to satisfaction (pp.249–265).

The incidence of conflict is also of major importance, negative interactions decreasing stability and (in most studies) satisfaction. Conflict over basic issues like child-rearing (Block, Block, & Morrison, 1981) and poor problem-solving skills may increase the probability of dissolution (Markman et al., 1992). The characteristics of distressed couples discussed on pp.94–97 are associated with later dissolution. Filsinger and Thoma (1988), studying pre-marital couples, found that affect reciprocity, as well as the extent to which the woman interrupted the man, predicted relationship instability five years later.

In a recent study Gottman and Levenson (1992) studied 73 couples with a laboratory interview and physiological assessment. These were divided on interview data into 42 "regulated" and 31 "non-regulated" couples in terms of the cumulative difference between the positive and negative remarks made by the spouses: in regulated couples the difference was consistently positive. Non-regulated couples were more conflict-engaging, defensive, stubborn, angry, whining, and withdrawn, and less affectionate, interested in their partners, and joyful, than regulated couples. The non-regulated couples reported more negative marital problems, and were more negative in the interview. They were in poorer health than the regulated couples. There were also some physiological differences, though an earlier finding that a high level of physiological arousal during interaction predicted a decline in marital satisfaction (Levenson & Gottman, 1985) did not receive strong support. They were also more likely to have considered dissolution or separation than the regulated couples.

External Stress. Although data are scarce, it is likely that external factors may affect marital satisfaction and stability.

Of course, listing variables associated with marital breakdown tells one little about the dynamics of the processes involved. In a study of married couples, 538 of which were followed over one year and 241 over five years after marriage, Kurdek (1993) assessed the role of demographic, individual difference, interdependence, and spousal discrepancy variables in marital dissolution. The individual difference variables of dysfunctional beliefs about relationships and neuroticism were associated with subsequent dissolution, but did not appear in the "best set" of early predictors of dissolution, being subsumed by combined effects of the other three sets of variables. Decreases in interdependence, and increases in the spouses' value of attachment, were larger in couples heading for dissolution. Kurdek concluded that dissolution is determined by relating stable individual and dyadic factors existing from the beginning with patterns of change in them that evolve over the course of the marriage.

Other studies also have indicated that precursors may be present long before breakdown is apparent. For example Schaefer and Burnett (1987) studied 51 women over a three-year period after their children went to kindergarten. Their perceptions of their husband's behaviour to them correlated with their self-reports of demoralisation three years later more strongly than with their contemporaneous demoralisation, suggesting that stable patterns of marital interaction may have cumulative effects on partners' adjustment (see also p.467).

A Model of Breakdown

To synthesise the various approaches to marital breakdown, Karney and Bradbury (1995b) have suggested the model shown in Fig. 28.3. This involves an influence of external stressful events (Path D) on adaptive processes, for instance on interaction between the spouses and their ability to provide each other with social support (Path A). These adaptive processes are also affected by enduring vulnerabilities (including those acquired in early childhood) (Path B), which may also affect the incidence of stressful events (Path C). The adaptive processes may, however, ameliorate the effects of the stressors (Path E), as shown by the effects of family factors on relapse in schizophrenia and depression. The adaptive processes affect (Path F) and are affected by (Path G) marital quality, which in turn affects stability.

While Karney and Bradbury acknowledge that this "stress–vulnerability–adaptation" framework emphasises broad outlines rather than detail, it

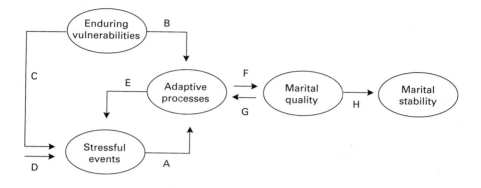

FIG. 28.3   The vulnerability–stress–adaptation model of marriage. (Karney & Bradbury, 1995b. Copyright by the American Psychological Association and reprinted with permission.)

integrates many of the known influences on marital breakdown, and indicates the need for longitudinal studies which assess the several predictor variables at a number of time points.

Distress

The distress accompanying and following marital breakdown is of course intense. It can be described in terms of the three phases of the mourning process, as described by Bowlby (1969; see also McCall, 1982). A phase of "protest" accompanied by much emotional expression, and associated perhaps with the dyadic and social phases in Duck's scheme (Fig. 28.1) is followed by a phase of "despair" or "disorganisation" characterised by indecision, loss of ambition, and depression. Eventually the threads of life are picked up again in a phase of reorganisation. It goes without saying that the experience of any divorce will differ between the two parties concerned, but each must realign his or her life and adjust his or her network of social relationships. In this phase, it is not simply the hate and anger that must be coped with, but also the attachment to the spouse that persists along with the negative feelings (Berman, 1988). The self that included the other must be reconceived as a new self—a new self which is compatible with the account of the marriage and its breakdown (Surra, 1996). The revising of accounts of the marriage and its decline must play a major role—accounts which are usually co-constructed with individuals outside the former marriage (see McCall, 1982). People with more active coping strategies tend to be less depressed after a break-up (Mearns, 1991).

In a number of studies commitment or its contributory variables have been found to be related to distress on the break-up of a marital or dating relationship (e.g. Bloom, Asher, & White, 1978; Simpson, 1987). In data obtained at one time point, Frazier and Cook (1993) found distress was related to satisfaction with the partner, the closeness of the relationship, and perception of difficulty in finding a replacement. However other variables were associated with recovery—perceptions of the controllability of the break-up, social support, and self-esteem.

Accounts

Not surprisingly, the accounts given by those who have suffered marital break-ups are more complex than those of persons who have separated before marriage. Cupach and Metts (1986) compared the accounts of the break-ups of 50 divorced persons with those of 50 students. The accounts of the previously married subjects involved more problems, and a more extreme tendency to blame the partner, than those of the unmarried. Sex differences were found in the pattern of attributions in the married, but not in the unmarried sample. Divorced men were less likely to blame themselves than divorced women, but more likely to assign responsibility to external factors. Efforts to repair the deteriorating relationship were attributed to the self more often than to the partner by the married respondents, but more often to the partner by non-marital respondents. The married sample also mentioned reasons for impeding dissolution more often than those who had not been married. All these differences are compatible with the view that marital partners are more interdependent, and constrained not only by concern for their children but also by other social and legal forces not present for those in a pre-marital relationship.

The vocabulary of motives used by those who initiated the divorce and by non-initiators do not match up to the complexities of the preceding marital situation, suggesting that they are rhetorical devices constructed after the divorce began (Hopper, 1993). Coping with marital break-up depends to a considerable extent on how the dissolution is appraised. Hill et al. (1976) found a general tendency for dating individuals to report that it was they who had most wanted to end the relationship, and speculated that this may have been a way of retrospectively taking control of the separation process (see earlier). Gray and Silver (1990), in a study of previously married respondents to a mailed enquiry, found that both ex-spouses agreed that the women were more likely to have had control over the separation process than the men, but confirmed Hill et al.'s suggestion in that the more control was attributed to the ex-spouse, the lower the level of psychosocial adjustment and resolution of the break-up. There was a general tendency for the respondents to regard the break-up in an ego-enhancing way, minimising their own responsibility, and seeing themselves as the victim.

Social Factors

After break-up, the erstwhile partners inevitably become more dependent for social support on their respective social networks. Milardo (1987) has suggested that marital norms tend to isolate women from their personal friends, so that after divorce they are somewhat isolated from the benefits that friends might bring, and more dependent on kin.

While parental cooperation after divorce is important where children are involved, too frequent contact may militate against adjustment to the divorce. Berman (1985) indicates that a quarter of the individuals involved in a divorce have difficulty in breaking the psychological bonds even after the legal proceedings are complete. But in the longer term, some even become friends (Masheter & Harris, 1986). While some parents maintain a mild attachment, the extent to which it is possible presumably depends on the tension surrounding and circumstances of the divorce. Cultural attitudes to divorce may also make a difference: where divorce is easier and more frequent, the rift may have been less deep. But in North America, and probably elsewhere, a great deal of hostility usually remains and post-divorce harmony is rather rare (Furstenberg, 1982; see also Ambert, 1988; Masheter, 1991).

Dissolution of a relationship by death also requires resolution through the elaboration of an account. There may be intermittent and devastating memories that disrupt normal functioning, and the bereaved person may follow routines formerly pursued with the deceased, with little thought about their current significance. Harvey et al. (1995) see recovery as involving the retention of memories but living in the present, and of having someone with whom those stories can be shared.

SUMMARY

1. The decline of a relationship can be seen as involving a series of stages—intrapsychic, dyadic, social, and grave-dressing.
2. Attributions and accounts play a critical role at all stages in the breakdown and in coming to terms with it afterwards.
3. The nature of the communication between the partners changes as the decline progresses.
4. Dissolution inevitably involves changes in relations with the social network. Cultural norms influence its occurrence and course.

5. Some of the major factors leading to dissolution are listed. They include individual characteristics, relationship factors, changes in the participants or in the relationship, cultural factors, etc.

6. The decline and dissolution of friendship may be accompanied by relatively mild distress.

7. The termination of a romantic relationship is likely to involve considerable negotiation and/or recrimination, and also distress. Unrequited love may involve distress on both sides, though differing in nature.

8. The breakdown of a marital relationship is a complex process in which social factors play a considerable role, and distress is likely to be acute.

29 A Programme for Integration

THE CURRENT STATE

The preceding chapters have presented the study of relationships as having a structure which, for heuristic purposes, can be seen as consisting of four stages. The first involves description of the phenomena and the identification of characteristics in terms of which relationships could be described and differentiated. The second phase involves discussion of the underlying processes, and the third recognition of the limitations of their relevance in relationships of different types. Since relationships are themselves processes, there is inevitably considerable overlap between these phases, but all are essentially analytical—relationships are analysed in terms of characteristics, and the characteristics are (partially) understood in terms of the processes that give rise to them. But we have seen that analysis is not enough and a fourth phase of re-synthesis is also necessary—we must see how the constituents contribute to give the whole.

Along the way the research has been heterogeneous, including experimental and survey approaches; interview, questionnaire, and observational techniques; problem-oriented research and theory-oriented research. Some students of personal relationships see the field as a "disorderly mix" (Peterson, 1994). As noted by many of those invited by Sarason, Sarason, and Pierce (1995) to contribute to a special section of the *Journal of Social and Personal Relationships*, we need an integrating framework, but it is not immediately clear where such a framework can be found.

Envying physics, some psychologists have yearned for an equivalent to the Laws of Motion, or Relativity. But psychology is not physics, and it is by no means clear that integration will be fostered by a search for a grand psychological theory, or even for a theory for the narrower field of personal relationships. Indeed, when one faces it, grand theory has not had a particularly good record in psychology. Psychoanalytic theory led to important insights, but it was never quite clear where metaphor stopped and reality began, and it was wrong in many of its particulars. The major learning theories guided research for several decades in the middle of the century, but it is by no means certain that the product was worth the effort. And the problems posed by personal relationships embrace both those that psychoanalysis and the learning theories were intended to cover and much else besides. Indeed, as we have seen, understanding personal relationships requires us to cross and re-cross between levels of complexity—intra-individual mechanisms, interactions, relationships, groups, and societies, with influences from and influences on the physical environment and the socio-cultural structure (Frontispiece).

Much of the progress that has been made has come from research guided by theories of more limited scope. These are not like the basic laws that explain diverse phenomena in the physical world, and not like the hypothetico-deductive systems of earlier learning theorists, but with more humility involve principles that integrate a limited range of phenomena. Principles such as those concerned with attribution; with equity, inter-dependence, and investment; with attachment; and others mentioned in preceding chapters have all provided fresh insights, have helped to inte-grate diverse phenomena, and have predictive value. All of these have been or are being modified as research progresses and as research workers strive to incorporate more of the complexities of real life in their approaches. Some have acquired sufficient sophistication to merit the name of theory, but none is universally applicable. Thus exchange theories apply differently in exchange and communal relationships; attachment theory is useful primarily for relationships involving "felt security"; love as a resource has properties different from money; what is seen as fair in a relationship depends on the attributions made. And ultimately each approach to description, explanation, or prediction must be aligned with our concep-tion of the self-system. But each goes some way towards "explaining" certain aspects of human relationships, and is perhaps essential on its own territory—though the limits of the territory need to be defined in each case.

That does not mean that progress should depend solely on studies that support, disprove, or extend our current approaches. These approaches will continue to be useful, but we need also new ones. At a general level, we urgently need progress in coming to terms with the emotions and motives, conscious and unconscious, that drive relationships. More important still, we need to focus on the *relations* between emotions, cognitions, and behaviour—relations which probably have a phyletic basis (Humphrey, 1992) and are to be found, perhaps, in the structure of the self-system (see Fletcher, 1996 and other chapters in Fletcher & Fitness, 1996).

At a more specific level, countless problems have been thrown up by the progress already made. To cite but a few examples arising from the issue of autonomy versus connectedness, we need to know how the need for autonomy may conflict with that for connectedness in different ways in relationships of different types and at different stages (pp.157–158); we need to know more about the ways in which different types of intra-dyadic conflict affect each other, as when seeking for autonomy leads to less self-disclosure; we need to know what, if anything, jealousy over a partner's autonomy has in common with jealousy over fear of loss (pp.163–165); and we need to know more about the relations between romantic love and the less idealising love of long-term relationships (pp.428–431). Such a list could be extended indefinitely.

In following new paths we must not be constrained by existing paradigms and principles, useful as they may be: each of them suggests avenues that must be followed, but we need above all to keep our eyes and ears open for what happens in real relationships in the real world, our own and those of others (see e.g. Planalp & Rivers, 1996). It is there that any shortcomings in our present tools may become apparent; there that we shall find new problems and new approaches.

Thus it is perhaps no bad thing that relationship research is producing a "disorderly mix" of description, problems, and theories. The issues that personal relationships pose demand eclecticism. But there is also a need for integration, and the integration we must seek is of more than one kind.

AGREEMENT OVER VARIABLES

First, at a rather mundane level, there is need for better agreement over the variables that are assessed, the relations between those variables, and the instruments used to assess them. The particular case of intimacy and closeness was discussed in Chapter 4. Fincham and Bradbury (1987a) have discussed the overlap between measures of marital quality and constructs examined in relation to marital quality, pointing out that this renders any association between them tautologous (see also Fincham et al., in press). In addition, some variables usually considered in terms of a single bipolar dimension may be better considered in terms of two or more: this is now accepted for masculinity/femininity (pp.138–139), and marital quality is another candidate (pp.246–247). Clearly agreement on such issues may not be easy to obtain: researchers, fortunately, have their own ideas, and do not like to be constrained. But a balance between creativity and discipline would surely facilitate progress.

INTEGRATION OF EXPLANATIONS

As a second route to integration, it will not have escaped the reader's notice that, in preceding chapters, a number of different descriptions/explanations, not necessarily incompatible with each other, have often been given for the same relationship phenomenon. Take, for instance, the fact that individuals like to do things for those whom they love, and the finding that the investment made in a relationship is related to commitment and continuity (pp.348–350). The lay view might be that of course one wants to do things for those whom one loves, and that one naturally strives to maintain a relationship with a person whom one loves. With a little more sophistication, the inherent circularity might be noted: you would not call it love unless you wanted to make your partner happy (p.430). Earlier exchange theorists might say that we make sacrifices in the expectation of future gains, to maintain the relationship so as not to lose what we have invested in it (p.462). More recently the interdependence theorists would see the rewarding nature of giving as a transformation of the matrix (pp.342–343). As an extension of exchange theories, resource theory would claim that in giving love one had more (p.378)—a view not incompatible with the picture of the formation of a close relationship as involving the inclusion of the other in the self (pp.464–465). Alternatively it might be argued that one likes oneself for putting effort into a relationship, and that liking oneself enhances liking of a partner who likes one (pp.320–321), and this contributes to the continuity of the relationship. Or putting in effort might cause one to misperceive the partner as a worthy recipient of that effort (p.233). Or the emphasis could be put on knowledge structures influenced by norms for loving relationships, norms which demand sacrifice and carry expectations of relationship longevity (pp.500–501). Or yet again, one may see the relationship as a two-person group, with the partner perceived favourably as a group member and a worthy recipient of one's efforts (p.466).

Other cases where similar phenomena have been explained in diverse ways have been mentioned in preceding chapters—for instance the diverse explanations of the attractiveness of similarity, at least some of which can be reduced to a common theme (Chapter 8), or the diverse ways of classifying behaviour in conflict situations (pp.171–179). It is not implied that one explanation or classificatory system will necessarily turn out to be right and the others wrong, though one may prove more useful than others. But such reflections do underline the need to integrate our perspectives on relationships, to see how theories are inter-related, to assess how far our current perspectives are compatible one with another, before setting up new paradigms. Creativity must not be stifled, but to build on what we have already, improving it where necessary, may advance knowledge more effectively than proposing new instruments or theories without specifying how they relate to current ones.

MODELS OF PROCESSES

A third sort of integration might lie at or near the phenomenological level. Of course, relationships are diverse. There is little in common between a doctor–patient relationship and one between lovers, except that in both each interaction is influenced by preceding ones—which is saying no more than that both are relationships. But an attempt at integration at the phenomenological level might involve drawing up a Table of what sort of characteristics are important in what relationships. We would see, for instance, that content is not an important characteristic for friendship, self-disclosure for some exchange relationships. But such a Table would require many reservations and would not advance research. Or we could draw up a Table showing what processes were important in what relationships, and would see, for instance that attachment and felt security were important in some relationships and not in others. But it is doubtful that that would advance understanding either.

But a degree of integration important for practical purposes can be achieved by assessing how phenomenological and process variables affect each other. Notable progress in this direction has been made for instance by Kelley et al. (1983) for close relationships in general (Fig. 3.2), by Fletcher and Fitness (1996) in their model of how knowledge guides action (p.35), and by Bradbury and Fincham (1989) (Fig. 3.3) and Karney and Bradbury (1995b) (Fig. 28.3) for marriage. More detailed models concern the relations between independent, intervening, and dependent variables, as in the study by Lamke et al. (1994; see p.252). Such models, and a number of others that have been referred to in preceding chapters, describe (it cannot yet be said that we understand) the relations between emotions, cognitions, behaviour, interactions, and relationships—though we must always be aware that analysis may support the operation of a one-way effect when real life would suggest that the effect is bidirectional. Clearly it is to this sort of integration that most of the studies cited in this book should lead, and which is most likely to be useful to lay person and clinician for understanding relationships.

INTEGRATION THROUGH DIALECTICS

Fourth, perhaps in the long term we can seek integration of an even more fundamental kind through further understanding of the dialectical relations between the successive levels of complexity shown in a simplified form in the Frontispiece. That, as Acitelli (1995) wisely remarks, requires us to become inter-disciplinary rather than merely multi-disciplinary. But even that will not be enough. The inter-relations shown in the Frontispiece are two-way, and we shall need to break into the continuously inter-reacting feedback loops. We shall need a starting point.

Here one can only try to look into the future, so what follows is speculative. Perhaps an heuristically useful first step, and we shall see later that it *is only* an heuristic device, is to think in terms of a continuum from psychological characteristics that are relatively stable to those that are labile. At the former end are the "Relatively Stable Characteristics" (RSCs), that is, aspects of structure or behaviour that are present to some degree in virtually all humans, or in all members of a given age/sex/class, though their expression may differ considerably between individuals (Hinde, 1987, 1991). Thus we all have noses, but no two noses are quite alike. In the same way, all humans have in common characteristics of perception, responsiveness to stimuli, motor patterns, motivations, cognitive processes, and so on, though in every case there is considerable individual variation. We all distinguish figure from ground, find circular shapes conspicuous, have somewhat similar smiles, and are willing to work for food. We all have at least some tendency to form relationships, which perhaps one day we will be able to explain in terms of more elementary tendencies such as the need for consensual validation (pp.129–130), or for security (p.395) or to expand the self (pp.464–465). This is not to suggest that these characteristics are "innate" or "genetically determined": all are influenced by "experience" during development, but in so far as they are similar across individuals, any environmental factors important in their development must be experienced similarly by all individuals.[1] It is usually reasonable to assume, though not essential to the present argument, that such characteristics evolved under the influence of natural selection during the course of evolution, or as a by-product of other characteristics that so evolved. One can refer to these characteristics as Relatively Stable Characteristics

---

[1] One could extend this concept of Relatively Stable Characteristics to refer to characteristics that have relative stability only within a particular culture, because of local experiential factors. An example is the ability to kneel and balance for long periods acquired by Mayan women in their very early years and subsequently essential for backstrap loom weaving (Greenfield & Childs, 1991; Maynard, Greenfield, & Childs, 1996).

(RSCs), or one can see them as based on "modules" (Fodor, 1983), though one thereby extends the use of the latter term (Sperber, 1994).

At the other end of the continuum lie labile characteristics, whose appearance depends critically on the environment of development. Shaking hands, a practice virtually ubiquitous amongst Europeans, is a labile characteristic: in many other parts of the world cheeks are kissed or noses rubbed in greeting instead.

However the need to do something on meeting an acquaintance would seem to be pan-cultural; the particular form the greeting takes in any society must depend on the dialectical relations between that need and the various levels of social complexity, including the socio-cultural structure. For the limited problem of advancing understanding of greeting, then, the need can be taken as an RSC, though it may itself be susceptible to further explanation in causal, developmental, or functional terms. Indeed, all human behaviour, relationships and institutions in all their complexity must depend on RSCs in this way.

The critical problem is thus to unravel the dialectical relations between RSCs and the successive levels of complexity. We must avoid the temptation, to which sociobiologists are exposed, of postulating an adapted "module" for every aspect of human behaviour that seems to favour survival or reproduction: such a course by-passes the developmental problem. Indeed we must account for the fact that much human behaviour is not such as to facilitate or enhance reproductive success. We make sacrifices for others, and send food to remote parts of the world. Much of our behaviour is coerced by others who, by one criterion or another, have established themselves in positions of power, perhaps controlling resources, perhaps having abrogated to themselves supposedly superior knowledge of what is right. We act as we do in part because of the two-way relations between individuals, their relationships, and the socio-cultural structure, itself both product and cause of the behaviour of individuals: it is upon these dialectical relations that all the complexity and diversity of the human condition depends.

To unravel that complexity we need a starting point, and therein lies the heuristic value of the Relatively Stable Characteristics. The suggestion is that the path to integration lies in unravelling the dialectical relations between the levels of social complexity, using RSCs as starting points. They can provide starting points for understanding the bases of higher levels of complexity—more complex individual propensities, interactions, relationships, groups, and the socio-cultural structure, all of which must arise from these RSCs. They can also provide a means for understanding the relations between more "basic" psychological/physiological processes. In other words, they provide a datum from which to analyse both "upwards" and "downwards".

Proceeding in this way would undoubtedly be facilitated if we could eliminate the redundancy inherent in our attempts to explain the phenomena of relationships—perhaps the multiple explanations of why we like to make those we love happy could be distilled down into a few core principles of wider explanatory value. But we must face a number of further problems which stem from the fact that, as emphasised earlier, the RSC concept is only an heuristic device. That brings us back to the identification of the RSCs. An immediately obvious problem is that of level of complexity. On the one hand, making fire or belief in the supernatural have been suggested as human universals, but it is by no means clear how long a group of children, isolated with no prior knowledge of fire or gods, would take to invent them. At the other extreme, the knee-jerk, sucking, or Moro reflexes, though clearly qualifying as RSCs, will not get us very far in explaining the complexity of human social life. What we are seeking must lie somewhere between these two extremes. We shall return to this issue later.

A second problem is that many of the RSCs important in the present context are somewhat intangible. It is one thing to say that all humans walk, seek food when hungry, cry out when in pain, or seek sex under appropriate circumstances. Everyone might agree that these are ubiquitous. But many of the issues that we have touched on in discussing the dynamics of relationships are not so clear-cut as these. For instance, it is well established in studies of other species that the genes, rather than determining aspects of development, influence propensities to develop in one way rather than another, or predispositions to learn this rather than that. Thus we have a predisposition to learn a spoken language not shared by our primate relatives which, it is reasonable to suppose, facilitates success in social living, a predisposition that is certainly multiply-determined but whose precise nature is a matter of considerable dispute.

Many other aspects of human behaviour can similarly be ascribed to predispositions to learn. For example, earlier chapters have referred repeatedly to gender differences which can be very roughly summarised by saying that males tend to be more individualistic and assertive, females more expressive and oriented towards relationships. There has been a long-standing and sterile dispute as to whether such gender differences in behaviour and relationships are due to nature or to nurture. As discussed elsewhere, this can be resolved on the view that the initial *development* of the differences is due in part to biological and in part to experiential factors; that the usual *direction* of the differences is due to slight differences in biological determinants, largely involving predispositions to learn one pattern rather than another; while the *extent and patterning* of the differences are due to learning from experience in the culture; and the *cultural differences* are associated with differences between societies in the relations between cultural elements (Hinde, 1991). (The evidence for a role of biological determinants comes both from genetic and physiological studies on the one hand, and comparisons with other mammalian species on the other.)

But many of the issues we have mentioned in discussing relationships are even more intangible than these. Take, for instance, the self-system, a metaphor basic to our discussion of the nature of relationships. A self-concept of some sort, giving a sense of continuity and control, but capable of limited modification by experience, must surely be a pan-cultural characteristic, however much self-concepts may differ between cultures and, indeed, between individuals—though we are still a long way from understanding the nature of what we call the self-system. It would be easy to suggest, though difficult or impossible to prove, that the human characteristic that we label as "Having a self-concept" had aided or does aid survival and reproduction. Its integrity must depend on a variety of processes including consensual validation, the avoidance of dissonance, the attribution of causes to events, and sometimes misperception. Its adaptive value may lie in the need to cope or to control, or to feel in control of, one's life and one's environment. To achieve that, one needs to monitor one's coping or control—so what is immediately important may be whether we feel we are coping, or the control we perceive ourselves to have. Having a sense of self, one can more easily guide one's behaviour appropriately in the circumstances in which one finds oneself—and perhaps even more appropriately if one's self-perception is influenced to a limited extent by the situation (pp.27–28). A need to cope or to feel in control would account for many aspects of the structure of the self-system, including the elaboration of internal working models (pp.31–33); the negative affect associated with cognitive dissonance (p.320); the needs for consensual validation (pp.129–130) and to achieve congruency (pp.28–29) (including the importance of similarity in non-verifiable beliefs, pp.129–130); the pains we take to act as naive (or sometimes far from naive and inappropriately biased) scientists (p.4) and attribute causes to events (pp.324–331); our sometimes contradictory needs to see ourselves as we really are (pp.225–226) and to maintain a high view of ourselves and of our relationships (pp.28, 236) and to see ourselves as liked (pp.130–131). The need to feel one is coping and in control accounts for the devastating effects of learned helplessness; our perception of our relationships as stable rather than dynamic (pp.42–44); the need to know all we can about our partners as well as the need to preserve some privacy; the potency of jealousy (pp.163–168) and the importance of the accounts we make (pp.467–468). The need to feel one is coping and in control may also be related to the need for "felt security" emphasised by the attachment theorists (p.395), and to a desire for equitable or advantageous exchange (pp.344–345). And the need to feel in control must also be related to the need for autonomy (p.157) and the importance of intrinsic motivation (p.158). It is related also to seeking for status—a human characteristic likely to have been (and still to be) important for survival and reproduction, and one that is responsible for much of the complexity of human society. That complexity is related also to characteristics of the dynamics of groups—the manner in which individuals tend to see members of their own groups as superior to those of out-groups.

Of course we must be careful here. Is postulating a need to feel in control or secure merely a device for tying together a number of facts about behaviour and about relationships? Presumably it has some sort of reality: one does not need the executive monkey or learned helplessness experiments to know that we like (or that it is rewarding) to feel in control. But is it a cause, in either an ontogenetic or an evolutionary sense, for the various facets of behaviour just mentioned? Or is it a consequence, an evolutionary synthesis of more elemental modules present in our mammalian ancestors? We cannot yet answer such questions: all that is suggested here is that for some purposes it is heuristically useful to treat the need to feel in control as an RSC.

We have mentioned a number of candidate RSCs—propensities to learn; the self-system; seeking for control, for status, for "felt security"; concomitants of gregariousness—though with considerable uncertainty as to the relations between them. There is, of course, no implication that this is more than a very small part of those that will be useful. But the suggestion is that such concepts will provide links between the characteristics and processes that we have found useful so far. As another example more closely related to the theme of this book, survival and reproduction depend on relationships with others, so a need for connectedness must be present. It is an open issue how far the processes that contribute to connectedness differ between relationships of different types, but it is reasonable to suppose that self-disclosure, interpersonal perception, and commitment contribute to connectedness in a wide range of relationships.

It will be apparent that we must return to the first problem—the level of analysis at which it is appropriate to postulate RSCs. The RSC, let us remind ourselves, is only an heuristic device, and what seem to be RSCs may not be unitary. Thus the propensity to learn a language, which certainly meets the necessary criteria for an RSC and which contributes to both connectedness and perceived control, undoubtedly depends on a variety of ancillary mechanisms. These include adaptations to the sensory and motor systems as well as (probably) specific mechanisms involved in the acquisition and use of language, and is also facilitated by, for instance, responsiveness to the mother's voice. Each of these could be seen as an RSC. Similarly the self-system is protected by defence mechanisms (p.32) and by the negotiations involved in conducting interactions (pp.36–37) and in establishing relationships (pp.455–456). And "felt security" and the concomitants of gregariousness are facilitated by the "fear of strangers" which children usually develop in the second half of the first year. Thus, as indicated earlier, we may be led to analyse the bases of the RSCs we pick on as well as using them to analyse more complex phenomena.

Two related points must be emphasised here. First, it will be apparent that the RSCs mentioned are inter-related. The self-system, seeking for control, status, and security depend on each other, and there is no present implication that one or other is primary. Indeed we must remember that these labels are only devices that we find useful in carving up reality, only useful tools: it remains to be seen how far they can be envisaged as entities in their own right.

Thus each of the aspects mentioned plays a part in many aspects of human behaviour. Consider the issue of fear of strangers. It can be assumed that, at an earlier stage in our evolution, it facilitated the maintenance of the mother–infant relationship and/or the relations between the infant and its natal group. It is involved in the differentiation of groups. It plays a part in gender differentiation: as children see themselves as members of one gender group they tend to denigrate the other ("Boys are dirty"; "Girls are sissy"). Its role in group differentiation has enormous repercussions on the structure of society. It is exploited in team games, by political parties, in the class system. It is used in war-time propaganda to denigrate the enemy, to portray them as dangerous and sub-human (Hinde & Watson, 1995).

Second, what have been described as "ancillary mechanisms" may be developmentally primary: fear of strangers develops before any tendency to denigrate the members of outgroups. Again, we may not have carved correctly: what we see as ancillary mechanisms might be better described as constituents of the RSCs.

It might seem as though the concept of RSC has been proposed as a starting point for unravelling the dialectical relations between levels of social complexity, and then immediately shown to be inadequate. But many concepts in science have a limited range of usefulness. Dalton's atomic theory led to great advances in chemistry, and the concept of the atom is still useful in many contexts, even though we now have much more sophisticated ideas. The concept of the molecule is still a useful one, even though it has limited applicability to solutions of electrolytes or crystal lattices. Indeed we are at an advantage over the earlier chemists in knowing the limitations of the concept from the start, and can be reasonably confident that such issues as the need to feel in control, the predisposition to learn a language, the fear of strangers, and other *relatively* stable characteristics form the building blocks for understanding the complexities not just of relationships but of all aspects of human behaviour, even though they are themselves complex.

It will be apparent that the road to integration is a long one, and at the moment it is not possible to be more than programmatic. To return to a comparison made earlier, in the social sciences integration of this degree is unlikely to involve a unifying equation or a handful of particles. Its probable course can more profitably be compared with chemistry. The first stage involves describing various types of relationship (analogous to elements) and their variants (isotopes) and assessing their properties. Then one may look for ways of grouping them—e.g. communal vs. exchange relationships, family relationships versus friendships, primarily complementary versus primarily reciprocal relationships: here the analogy is with the groups in the Periodic Table, but while one type of relationship can belong to several such categories, one chemical element is placed in only one group. The next stage is to search for the bases of their properties, for processes of relationship dynamics and knowledge of how those processes inter-relate (corresponding to, say, valency or chemical bonds), and then dig deeper for the ultimate entities—the RSCs and their immediate developmental sequelae (corresponding to protons, electrons, and neutrons), though recognising (as the physicists are now having to recognise) that these may themselves lead to still more elementary entities. But the nature of the RSCs and of the regularities in their interactions, must be sought in the Theory of Evolution by Natural Selection.

It is, of course, one thing to discuss in an abstract way how integration might be achieved, and another to follow the route designated. But the truly amazing increase in our understanding of what we call emotions, cognitive processes, and behaviour in close relationships, and especially our insights into the nature of the self, give plenty of cause for hope. And it is hope not just for an intellectually satisfying science of human relationships, but for an integrated body of knowledge that will make a real contribution to human happiness.

References

The following abbreviations have been used:

AdvExpSP—Advances in Experimental Social Psychology.
HCR—Human Communication Research.
JCCP—Journal of Consulting and Clinical Psychology.
JESP—Journal of Experimental Social Psychology.
J Mar Fam—Journal of Marriage and the Family.
JP—Journal of Personality.
JPSP—Journal of Personality and Social Psychology.
JSPR—Journal of Social and Personal Relationships.
PsychBull—Psychological Bulletin.
PsychRev—Psychological Review.
PR—Personal Relationships.

Where a number of chapters in an edited book are cited, reference is made to the book, which is listed separately.

Abelson, R.P. (1959). Modes of resolution of belief dilemmas. *Journal of Conflict Resolution, 3,* 343–352.

Abrahamsson, B. (1970). Homans on exchange: hedonism revisited. *American Journal of Sociology, 76,* 273–285.

Acitelli, L.K. (1992). Gender differences in relationship awareness and marital satisfaction among young married couples. *Personality and Social Psychology Bulletin, 18,* 102–10.

Acitelli, L. (1993). You, me, and us: perspectives on relationship awareness. In Duck (1993a), pp.144–74.

Acitelli, L. (1995). Disciplines at parallel play. *JSPR, 12,* 589–96.

Acitelli, L.K., Douvan, E. & Veroff, J. (1993). Perceptions of conflict in the first year of marriage: how important are similarity and understanding? *JSPR, 10,* 5–19.

Acitelli, L.K. & Duck, S. (1987). Postscript: intimacy as the proverbial elephant. In Perlman & Duck (1987), pp.297–308.

Acitelli, L.K. & Holmberg, D. (1993). Reflecting on relationships: the role of thoughts and memories. *Advances in the Study of Personal Relationships, 4,* 71–102.

Acitelli, L.K. & Young, A.M. (1996). Gender and thought in relationships. In Fletcher & Fitness (1996), pp.147–168.

Adams, J.S. (1965). Inequity in social

521

exchange. *AdvExpSP*, *2*, 267–299.

Adams, J.S. & Freedman, S. (1976). Equity theory re-visited. *AdvExpSP*, *9*, 43–90.

Adams, R.G. & Blieszner, R. (1994). An integrative conceptual framework for friendship research. *JSPR*, *11*, 163–184.

Aida, Y. & Falbo, R. (1991). Relationships between marital satisfaction, resources and power strategies. *Sex Roles*, *24*, 43–56.

Ainsworth, M.D.S. (1979). Attachment as related to mother–infant interaction. *Advances in the Study of Behaviour*, *9*, 2–52.

Ainsworth, M.D.S. & Bell, S.M. (1974). Mother–infant interaction and the development of competence. In K. Connolly & J.S. Bruner (Eds.), *The growth of competence*, London: Academic Press.

Ainsworth, M.D.S., Blehar, M.C., Waters, E., & Wall, S. (1978). *Patterns of attachment*. Hillsdale, NJ: Lawrence Erlbaum Associates Inc.

Ajzen, I. (1974). Effects of information on interpersonal attraction: similarity vs. affective value. *JPSP*, *29*, 374–380.

Ajzen, I. (1977). Information processing approaches to interpersonal attraction. In Duck (1977a).

Alberts, J.K. (1988). An analysis of couples' conversational complaints. *Communication Monographs*, *55*, 184–197.

Albrecht, T.L. & Halsey, J. (1992). Mutual support in mixed-status relationships. *JSPR*, *9*, 237–252.

Albright, L., Kenny, D.A., & Malloy, T.E. (1988). Consensus in personality judgements at zero acquaintance. *JPSP*, *55*, 387–395.

Alden, L. (1987). Attributional responses of anxious individuals to different patterns of social feedback: nothing succeeds like improvement. *JPSP*, *52*, 100–106.

Alexander, M.J. & Higgins, E.T. (1993). Emotional trade-offs of becoming a parent: how social roles influence self-discrepancy effects. *JPSP*, *65*, 1259–1269.

Alicke, M.D. (1992). Culpable causation. *JPSP*, *63*, 368–378.

Allan, G. (1993). Social structure and relationships. In Duck (1993c), pp.1–26.

Allen, J.B., Kenrick, D.T., Linder, D.E., & McCall, M.A. (1989). Arousal and attraction: a response facilitation alternative to misattribution and negative reinforcement models. *JPSP*, *57*, 261–270.

Alperson, B.L. (1975). In search of Buber's ghosts: a calculus for interpersonal phenomenology. *Behavioral Science*, *20*, 179–190.

Altman, I. & Haythorn, W.W. (1965). Interpersonal exchange in isolation. *Sociometry*, *28*, 411–426.

Altman, I. & Taylor, D.A. (1973). *Social penetration*. New York: Holt, Rinehart & Winston.

Altman, I., Vinsel, A., & Brown, B.B. (1981). Dialectical conceptions in social psychology: an application to social penetration and privacy regulation. *AdvExpSP*, *14*, 107–160.

Ambert, A-M. (1988). Relationship between ex-spouses: individual and dyadic perspectives. *JSPR*, *5*, 327–46.

Ambady, N. & Rosenthal, R. (1993). Half a minute: predicting teacher evaluations from thin slices of non-verbal behavior and physical attractiveness. *JPSP*, *64*, 431–41.

Amelang, M. (1991). Einstellung zu Liebe und Partnerschaft: Konzepte, Skalen, Korrelate. In M. Amelang, H.-J. Ahrens, & H.W. Bierhof (Eds.), *Attraktion und Liebe: Formen und Grundlagen partnerschaftlicher Beziehungen*, pp.153–196. Gottingen: Hogrefe.

Andersen, P.A. (1993). Cognitive schemata in personal relationships. In Duck (1993b), pp.1–29.

Andersen, S.M. & Cole, S.W. (1990). "Do I know you?": the role of significant others in general social perception. *JPSP*, *59*, 384–399.

Antaki, C. (1987). Types of accounts within relationships. In R. Burnett, P. McGhee & D. Clarke, (Eds.), *Accounting for relationships*, pp.97–133. London: Methuen.

Antill, J.K. (1983). Sex role complementarity versus similarity in married couples. *JPSP*, *45*, 145–155.

Antonucci, T.C., Fuhrer, R., & Jackson, J.S. (1990). Social support and reciprocity: a cross-ethnic and cross-national perspective. *JSPR*, *7*, 519–530.

Apfelbaum, E. (1966). Etudes experimentales de conflit: les jeux experimentaux. *L'Année Psychologique*, *66*, 599–621.

Araji, S.K. (1977). Husbands' and wives' attitude–behavior congruence on family roles. *JMarFam*, *39*, 309–320.

Argyle, M. (1975). *Bodily communication*. London: Methuen.

Argyle, M. & Dean, J. (1965). Eye-contact, distance, and affiliation. *Sociometry*, *28*, 289–304.

Argyle, M. & Henderson, M. (1985). *The anatomy of relationships*. London: Penguin.

Aries, E.J. & Johnson, F.L. (1983). Close friendship in adulthood: conversational content between same sex friends. *Sex Roles*, *9*, 1183–1197.

Aron, A. (1988). The matching hypothesis

reconsidered again: comment on Kalick & Hamilton. *JPSP, 54*, 441–446.

Aron, A. & Aron, E.N. (1986). *Love and the expansion of the self: understanding attraction and satisfaction.* New York: Hemisphere.

Aron, A. & Aron, E.N. (1996). Self and self-expansion in relationships. In Fletcher & Fitness (1996), pp.325–344.

Aron, A., Aron, E.N., & Smollan, D. (1992). Inclusion of other in the self scale and the structure of interpersonal closeness. *JPSP, 63*, 596–612.

Aron, A., Aron, E.N., Tudor, M., & Nelson, G. (1991). Close relationships as including other in the self. *JPSP, 60*, 241–253.

Aron, A., Dutton, D.G., Aron, E.N., & Iverson, A. (1989). Experiences of falling in love. *JSPR, 6*, 243–257.

Aron, A. & Henkemeyer, L. (1995). Marital satisfaction & passionate love. *JSPR, 12*, 139–146.

Aron, E.A. & Aron, A (1996). Love and expansion of the self: the state of the model. *PR, 3*, 45–58.

Aronson, E. (1969). The theory of cognitive dissonance: a current perspective. *AdvExpSP, 4*, 2–35.

Aronson, E. & Linder, D. (1965). Gain and loss of esteem as determinants of interpersonal attractiveness. *AdvExpSP, 1*, 156–171.

Aronson, E. & Worchel, P. (1966). Similarity versus liking as determinants of interpersonal attractiveness. *Psychonomic Science, 5*, 157–158.

Asch, S.E. (1959). A perspective on social psychology. In S. Koch (Ed.), *Psychology: a study of a science*, Vol. 3. New York: McGraw Hill.

Atkinson, J. & Huston, T.L. (1984). Sex role orientation and division of labor early in marriage. *JPSP, 46*, 330–45.

Attridge, M., Berscheid, E., & Simpson, J.A. (1995). Predicting relationship stability from both partners versus one. *JPSP, 69*, 254–268.

Auhagen, A.E. (1987). A new approach for the study of personal relationships: the double diary method. *German Journal of Psychology, 11*, 3–7.

Auhagen, A.E. (1991). *Freundschaft im Alltag. Eine Studie mit dem Doppeltagebuch.* Bern: Huber.

Auhagen, A.E. (1993). Freundschaft unter Erwachsenen. In Auhagen & von Salisch (1993), pp.215–234.

Auhagen, A.E. (1994). Personlichkeit und soziale Beziehungen: Unpersonliche Beziehungslosigkeit? In D. Bartussek & M.

Amelang (Eds.), *Fortschritte der differentiellen Psychologie und psychologischen Diagnostik*, pp.391–406. Gottingen: Hogrefe.

Auhagen, A.E. & Hinde, R.A. (in press). Individual characteristics and personal relationships. *PR*.

Auhagen, A.E. & von Salisch, M. (1993). *Zwischenmenschliche Beziehungen.* Gottingen: Hogrefe.

Auhagen, A.E. & von Salisch, M. (Eds.) (1996). *The diversity of human relationships.* New York: Cambridge University Press.

Austin, W. & Hatfield, E. (1980). Equity theory, power, and social justice. In G. Mikula (Ed.), *Justice and social interaction*, pp.25–62. Bern: Huber.

Backman, C.W. (1985). Interpersonal congruency theory revisited: a revision and extension. *JSPR, 2*, 489–505.

Backman, C.W. (1988) The self: a dialectical approach. *AdvExpSP, 21*, 229–260.

Backman, C.W. & Secord, P.F. (1962). Liking, selective interaction, and misperception in congruent interpersonal relations. *Sociometry, 25*, 321–335.

Baerends, G.P. (1976). The functional organization of behaviour. *Animal Behaviour, 24*, 726–738.

Bailey, R.C., Finney, P., & Bailey, K.G. (1974). Level of self-acceptance and perceived intelligence in self and friend. *Journal of Genetic Psychology, 124*, 61–67.

Baldwin, J.M. (1897). *Social & ethical interpretations in mental development.* New York: Macmillan.

Baldwin, M.W. (1992). Relational schemas and the processing of social information. *PsychBull, 112*, 461–484.

Baldwin, M.W. (1995). Relational schemas and cognition in close relationships. *JSPR, 12*, 547–552.

Baldwin, M.W. & Fehr, B. (1995). On the instability of attachment style ratings. *PR, 2*, 247–261.

Bandura, A. (1977). *Social learning theory.* Englewood Cliffs, NJ: Prentice Hall.

Bannister, D. & Fransella, F. (1971). *Inquiring man.* Harmondsworth, UK: Penguin.

Barker, R.G. (1978a). *Habitats, environments and human behavior.* San Francisco: Jossey-Bass.

Barker, R.G. (1978b). The stream of individual behavior. In Barker (1978a), pp.3–16.

Barrera, M. & Baca, L.M. (1990). Recipient reactions to social support: contributions of enacted support, conflicted support and network orientation. *JSPR, 7*, 541–51.

Barrett, J. & Hinde, R.A. (1988). Triadic

interactions: mother–firstborn–second-born. In Hinde & Stevenson-Hinde (1988), pp.181–192.

Barry, W.A. (1970). Marriage research and conflict: an integrative review. *PsychBull*, *73*, 41–54.

Barth, F. (1966). Models of social organization. *Royal Anthropological Institute Occasional Papers*, *23*, 1–33.

Barth, R.J. & Kinder, B.N. (1988). A theoretical analysis of sex differences in same sex friendships. *Sex Roles*, *19*, 349–364.

Bartholomew, K. (1990). Avoidance of intimacy: an attachment perspective. *JSPR*, *7*, 147–178.

Bartholomew, K. (1993). From childhood to adult relationships: attachment theory and research. In Duck (1993a), pp.30–62.

Bartholomew, K. (1994). Assessment of individual differences in adult attachment. *Psychological Inquiry*, *5*, 23–27.

Bartholomew, K. & Horowitz, L.A. (1991). Attachment styles among young adults: a test of a four-category model. *JPSP*, *61*, 226–244.

Bartholomew, K. & Perlman, D. (Eds.) (1994), *Attachment processes in adulthood*. London: Jessica Kingsley.

Bartlett, F.C. (1932). *Remembering*. Cambridge: Cambridge University Press.

Bateson, G. (1958). *Naven*. Palo Alto, CA: Stanford University Press.

Bateson, P.P.G. (1976). Rules and reciprocity in behavioural development. In Bateson & Hinde (1976), pp.401–422.

Bateson, P. (1996) Design for a life. In D. Magnusson (Ed.), *Individual development over the lifespan*. pp.1–20. Cambridge: Cambridge University Press.

Bateson, P. & Hinde, R.A. (Eds.) (1976). *Growing points in ethology*. Cambridge: Cambridge University Press.

Baucom, D.H. (1987). Attributions in distressed relations: how can we explain them? In Perlman & Duck (1987), pp.177–205.

Baucom, D.H., Sayers, S.L., & Duke, A. (1989). Attributional style and attributional patterns among married couples. *JPSP*, *56*, 596–607.

Baumeister, R.F., Stillwell, A., & Wotman, S.R. (1990). Victim and perpetrator accounts of interpersonal conflict: autobiographical narratives about anger. *JPSP*, *59*, 994–1005.

Baumeister, R.F., Wotman, S.R., & Stillwell, A.M. (1993). Unrequited love: on heartbreak, anger, guilt, scriptlessness and humiliation. *JPSP*, *64*, 377–394.

Baumgardner, A.H. & Brownlee, E.A. (1987). Strategic failure in social interaction: evidence for expectancy disconfirmation processes. *JPSP*, *52*, 525–535.

Baumgardner, A.H., Kaufman, C.M., & Levy, P. (1989). Regulating affect interpersonally: how low esteem leads to greater enhancement. *JPSP*, *56*, 907–921.

Baumrind, D. (1971). Current patterns of parental authority. *Developmental Psychology Monographs*, *4* (1 & 2).

Baxter, L. (1986). Gender differences in the heterosexual relationship rules embedded in break-up accounts. *JSPR*, *3*, 289–306.

Baxter, L. (1988). A dialectical perspective on communication strategies in relationship development. In Duck (1988), pp.257–274.

Baxter, L. (1990). Dialectical contradictions in relationship development. *JSPR*, *7*, 69–88.

Baxter, L.A. (1984). Trajectories of relationship disengagement. *JSPR*, *1*, 29–48.

Baxter, L.A. (1985). Assessing relationship disengagement. In Duck & Perlman (1985), pp.243–266.

Baxter, L.A. (1992a). Forms and functions of intimate play in personal relationships. *HCR*, *18*, 336–363.

Baxter, L.A. (1992b). Root metaphors in accounts of developing romantic relationships. *JSPR*, *9*, 253–275.

Baxter, L.A. (1993). The social side of personal relationships: a dialectical perspective. In Duck (1993c), pp.139–165.

Baxter, L.A. & Dindia, K. (1990). Marital partners' perceptions of marital maintenance strategies. *JSPR*, *7*, 187–208.

Baxter, L.A. & Simon, E.P. (1993). Relationship maintenance strategies and dialectical contradictions in close relationships. *JSPR*, *10*, 225–242.

Baxter, L.A. & Widenmann, S. (1993). Revealing and not revealing the status of romantic relationships to social networks. *JSPR*, *10*, 321–37.

Baxter, L.A. & Wilmot, W.W. (1984). Secret tests: social strategies for acquiring information about the relationship. *HCR*, *11*, 171–201.

Baxter, L.A. & Wilmot, W.W. (1985). Taboo subjects in close relationships. *JSPR*, *2*, 253–270.

Beach, L.R. & Carter, W.B. (1976). Appropriate and equitable repayment of social debts. *Organizational Behavior and Human Performance*, *16*, 280–293 (cited Converse & Foa, 1993).

Beach, S.R.H. & O'Leary, K.D. (1993). Marital discord and dysphoria: for whom does the marital relationship predict depressive symptomatology? *JSPR*, *10*, 405–420.

Beall, A.E. & Sternberg, R.J. (1995). The

social construction of love. *JSPR, 12*, 417–438.

Becker, W.C. (1964). Consequences of different kinds of parental discipline. In M.L. Hoffman & L. Hoffman (Eds.), *Review of child development research*, Vol. 1. New York: Russel Sage Foundation.

Bell, R.A. & Healey, J.G. (1992). Idiomatic communication and interpersonal solidarity in friends' relational cultures. *HCR, 18*, 307–335.

Bell, R.A., Daly, J.A., & Gonzalez, M.C. (1987). Affinity maintenance in marriage and its relationship to women's marital satisfaction. *JMarFam, 49*, 445–454.

Belmore, S.M. & Hubbard, M.L. (1987). The role of advance expectations in person memory. *JPSP, 53*, 61–70.

Belsky, J. (1984). The determinants of parenting: a process model. *Child Development, 55*, 83–96.

Belsky, J. (1985). Exploring individual differences in marital change across the transition to parenthood: the role of violated expectations. *JMarFam, 47*, 1037–1044.

Belsky, J., Rovine, M., & Fish, M. (1989). The developing family system. In M. Gunnar (Ed.), *Systems and development. Minnesota Symposia on Child Psychology, 22*. Hillsdale, NJ: Lawrence Erlbaum Associates Inc.

Bem, D.J. (1967). Self-perception: an alternative interpretation of cognitive dissonance phenomena. *PsychRev, 74*, 183–200.

Bem, D.J. (1972). Self-perception theory. *AdvExpSP, 6*, 1–62.

Bem, D.J. & McConnell, H.K. (1970). Testing the self-perception explanation of dissonance phenomena: on the salience of premanipulation attitudes. *JPSP, 14*, 23–31.

Bem, S. (1975). Sex role adaptability: one consequence of psychological androgyny. *JPSP, 31*, 634–643.

Bem, S.L. (1981a). Gender schema theory: a cognitive account of sex-typing. *PsychRev, 88*, 354–64.

Bem, S.L. (1981b). The BSRI and gender schema theory: a reply to Spence and Helmreich. *PsychRev, 88*, 369–71.

Benin, M.H. & Agostinelli, J. (1988). Husbands' and wives' satisfaction with the division of labor. *JMarFam, 50*, 349–361.

Benoit, D. & Parker, K.C.H. (1994). Stability and transmission of attachment across the generations. *Child Development, 65*, 1444–1456.

Benthall, J. & Polhemus, T. (Eds.) (1975). *The body as a medium of expression*. London: Allen Lane.

Bentler, P.M. & Newcomb, T.D. (1978). Longitudinal study of marital success and failure. *JCCP, 46*, 1053–1070.

Bentler, P.M. & Newcomb, M.D. (1979). Longitudinal study of marital success and failure. In M. Cook & G. Wilson (Eds.), *Love and attraction*, pp.189–194. Oxford: Pergamon.

Berg, B., Balla, D., & Zigler, E. (1976). Satiation and setting-condition components of social reinforcer effectiveness. *Child Development, 47*, 715–721.

Berg, J.H. (1984). The development of friendship between roommates. *JPSP, 46*, 346–356.

Berg, J.H. & Archer, R.L. (1982). Responses to self-disclosure and interaction goals. *JESP, 18*, 501–512.

Berg, J.H. & McQuinn, R.D. (1986). Attraction and exchange in continuing and noncontinuing dating relationships. *JPSP, 50*, 942–52.

Berg, J.H., Piner, K.E., & Frank, S.M. (1993). Resource theory and close relationships. In Foa et al. (1993a), pp.169–196.

Berger, C.R. (1988). Uncertainty and information exchange in developing relationships. In Duck (1988), pp.239–255.

Berger, C.R. (1993). Goals, plans, and mutual understanding in relationships. In Duck (1993b), pp.30–59.

Berger, C.R. & Bradac, J. (1982). *Language and social knowledge: uncertainty in interpersonal relations*. London: Arnold.

Berger, P.L. & Luckman, T. (1966). *The social construction of reality*. New York: Doubleday.

Bergman, I. (1974). *Scenes from a marriage*. London: Calder & Boyars.

Berkowitz, L. (1972). Social norms, feelings and other factors affecting helping and altruism. *AdvExpSP, 6*, 63–108.

Berkowitz, L. & Friedman, P. (1967). Some social class differences in helping behavior. *JPSP, 5*, 217–225.

Berman, W.H. (1985). Continued attachment after legal divorce. *Journal of Family Issues, 6*, 375–392.

Berman, W.H. (1988). The role of attachment in the post-divorce experience. *JPSP, 54*, 496–503.

Berndt, T.J. (1982). The features and effects of friendship in early adolescence. *Child Development, 53*, 1447–1460.

Berne, E. (1967). *Games people play*. Harmondsworth: Penguin.

Berry, D.S. (1991). Accuracy in social perception: contributions of facial and vocal information. *JPSP, 61*, 298–307.

Berscheid, E. (1983). Emotion. In H.H. Kelley et al. (1983), pp.110–168.

Berscheid, E. (1994). Interpersonal relationships. *Annual Review of Psychology, 45,* 79–129.

Berscheid, E., Dion, K.K., Walster, E., & Walster, G.W. (1971). Physical attractiveness and dating choice: a test of the matching hypothesis. *JESP, 7,* 173–189.

Berscheid, E., Graziano, W., Monson, T., & Dermer, M. (1976). Outcome dependency: attention, attribution and attraction. *JPSP, 34,* 978–989.

Berscheid, E. & Meyers, S.A. (1996). A social categorical approach to a question about love. *PR, 3,* 19–44.

Berscheid, E., Snyder, M., & Omoto, A.M. (1989). Issues in studying close relationships: conceptualizing and measuring closeness. In Hendrick (1989) pp.63–91.

Berscheid, E. & Walster, E. (1974a). A little bit about love. In T.L.Huston (Ed.), *Foundations of interpersonal attraction.* New York: Academic Press.

Berscheid, E. & Walster, E. (1974b). Physical attractiveness. *AdvExpSP, 7,* 157–215.

Berscheid, E. & Walster, E.H. (1978). *Interpersonal attraction.* Reading, MA: Addison-Wesley.

Bettor, L., Hendrick, S., & Hendrick, C. (1995). Gender and sexual standards in dating relationships. *PR, 2,* 359–369.

Biernat, M. & Wortman, C.B. (1991). Sharing of home responsibilities between professionally employed women and their husbands. *JPSP, 60,* 844–860.

Bigelow, B.J. (1977). Children's friendship expectations: a cognitive-developmental study. *Child Development, 48,* 246–253.

Billig, M. (1987). *Arguing and thinking: a rhetorical approach to social psychology.* Cambridge: Cambridge University Press.

Black, M. (1975). *The literature of fidelity.* London: Chatto & Windus.

Blais, M.R., Boucher, C., Sabourin, S., & Vallerand, R.J. (1990). Toward a motivational model of couple happiness. *JPSP, 59,* 1021–1031.

Blankenship, V., Hnat, S.N., Hess, T.G., & Brown, D.R. (1984). Reciprocal interaction and similarity of personality attributes. *JSPR, 1,* 415–432.

Blau, P.M. (1964). *Exchange and power in social life.* New York: Wiley.

Blieszner, R. & Adams, R.G. (1992). *Adult friendship.* Thousand Oaks, CA: Sage.

Block, J. (1995a & b). A contrarian view of the five-factor approach to personality description. *PsychBull, 117,* 187–215. See also *117,* 226–229.

Block, J. & Kremen, A. (1996). IQ and ego-resiliency: conceptual and empirical connections and separateness. *JPSP, 70,* 349–361.

Block, J.D. (1980). *Friendship.* New York: Macmillan.

Block, J.H. & Block, J. (1980). The role of ego-control and ego-resiliency in the organisation of behavior. In W.A. Collins (Ed.) *The Minnesota Symposia on Child Psychology, 13,* 39–101. Hillsdale, NJ: Lawrence Erlbaum Associates Inc.

Block, J.H., Block, J., & Morrison, A. (1981). Parental agreement–disagreement on child-rearing and gender related personality correlates in children. *Child Development, 52,* 965–974.

Bloom, B., Asher, S., & White, S. (1978). Marital disruption as a stressor: a review and analysis. *PsychBull, 85,* 867–894.

Bluhm, C., Widiger, T.A., & Miele, G.M. (1990). Interpersonal complementarity and individual differences. *JPSP, 58,* 464–471.

Bolger, N. & Kelleher, S. (1993). Daily life in relationships. In Duck (1993c), pp.100–109.

Bolger, N. & Schilling, E.A. (1991). Personality and the problems of everyday life: the role of neuroticism in exposure and reactivity to daily stressors. *JP, 59,* 355–386.

Bookwala, J., Frieze, I.H., & Grote, N.K. (1994). Love, aggression and satisfaction in dating relationships. *JSPR, 11,* 625–632.

Boon, S. (1994). Dispelling doubt and uncertainty: trust in romantic relationships. In Duck (1994), pp.86–111.

Booth, A. (1972). Sex and social participation. *American Sociological Review, 37,* 183–192.

Booth, A. & Edwards, J.N. (1992). Starting over: why re-marriages are more unstable. *Journal of Family Issues, 13,* 179–194.

Booth, A. & Hess, E. (1974). Cross-sex friendship. *JMarFam, 36,* 38–47.

Borden, V.M.H. & Levinger, G. (1991). Interpersonal transformations in intimate relationships. *Advances in Personal Relationships, 2,* 35–56.

Borkenau, P. & Liebler, A. (1992). Trait inferences: sources of validity at zero acquaintence. *JPSP, 62,* 645–657.

Bornstein, M.H. (1993). Cross-cultural perspectives on parenting. In P. Eelen, G. d'Ydewalle, & P. Bertelson (Eds.), *Psychology at the XXV International Congress.* Hove, UK: Lawrence Erlbaum Associates Ltd.

Bott, E. (1957; 2nd Edn 1971). *Family and social networks.* London: Tavistock.

Botwin, M.D. & Buss, D.M. (1989). Structure of act report data: is the five factor model of personality recaptured? *JPSP*, *56*, 988–1001.

Bowlby, J. (1969/82, 1973, 1980). *Attachment and loss*. [Vol. 1, Attachment (1969); Vol. 2, Separation: Anxiety and Anger (1973); Vol. 3, Loss: Sadness and Depression (1980).] London: Hogarth.

Bowlby, J. (1991). Ethological light on attachment problems. In P. Bateson (Ed.), *The development and integration of behaviour*, pp.301–314. Cambridge: Cambridge University Press.

Bradbury, T.N., Campbell, S.M., & Fincham, F.D. (1995). Longitudinal and behavioral analysis of masculinity and femininity in marriage. *JPSP*, *68*, 328–341.

Bradbury, T.N. & Fincham, F.D. (1988). Individual difference variables in close relationships: a contextual model of marriage as an integrative framework. *JPSP*, *54*, 713–721.

Bradbury, T.N. & Fincham, F.D. (1989). Behavior and satisfaction in marriage: prospective mediating processes. In Hendrick (1989), pp.119–143.

Bradbury, T.N. & Fincham, F.D. (1990). Attributions in marriage: review and critique. *PsychBull*, *107*, 3–33.

Braiker, H.B. & Kelley, H.H. (1979). Conflict in the development of close relationships. In R.L. Burgess & T.L. Huston (Eds.), *Social exchange in developing relationships*, pp.135–168. New York: Academic Press.

Braithwaite, D.O. & Baxter, L.A. (1995). "I do" again: the relational dialectics of renewal marriage vows. *JSPR*, *12*, 177–198.

Brehm, J.W. (1976). Responses to loss of freedom: a theory of psychological reactance. In J.W. Thibaut, J.T. Spence, & R.C. Carson (Eds.), *Contemporary topics in social psychology*. Morristown, NJ: General Learning Press.

Bretherton, I. (1987). New perspectives on attachment relations: security, communication and internal models. In I.D. Osofsky (Ed.), *Handbook of infant development*, pp.1061–1100. New York: Wiley.

Bretherton, I. (1990). Communication patterns, internal working models, and the intergenerational transmission of attachment relationships. *Infant Mental Health Journal*, *11*, 237–252.

Bretherton, I. (1995). Attachment theory and developmental psychopathology. In Cicchetti & Toth (1995), pp.231–260.

Bretherton, I., Ridgeway, D., & Cassidy, J. (1990). Assessing internal working models of the attachment relationship. In M.T. Greenberg, D. Cicchetti, & E.M. Cummings (Eds.), *Attachment in the pre-school years*, pp.273–308. Chicago: Chicago University Press.

Brinberg, D. & Castell, P. (1993). A resource exchange theory approach to interpersonal interactions. In Foa et al. (1993), pp.41–56.

Brinberg, D. & Ganesan, S. (1993). An application of Foa's resource exchange theory to product positioning. In Foa et al. (1993a), pp.219–232.

Bringle, R.G. (1995). Sexual jealousy in the relationships of homosexual and heterosexual men: 1980 and 1992. *PR*, *2*, 313–325.

Bringle, R.G. & Boebinger, K.L.G. (1990). Jealousy, and the "third" person in the love triangle. *JSPR*, *7*, 119–134.

Bringle, R. & Buunk, B. (1985). Jealousy and social behavior. *Review of Personality and Social Psychology*, *6*, 241–265.

Bringle, R.G., Renner, P., Terry, R., & Davis, S. (1983). An analysis of situational and person components of jealousy. *Journal of Research in Personality*, *12*, 354–368.

Brock, T.C. & Buss, A.H. (1962). Dissonance, aggression and evaluation of pain. *Journal of Abnormal and Social Psychology*, *65*, 197–202.

Brockner, J., O'Malley, M.N., Hite, T., & Davies, D.K. (1987). Reward allocation and self-esteem: the roles of modeling and equity restoration. *JPSP*, *52*, 844–850.

Brodbar-Nemzer, J.Y. (1986). Marital relationships and self-esteem: how Jewish families are different. *JMarFam*, *48*, 89–98.

Broderick, J.E. & O'Leary, K.D. (1986). Contributions of effort, attitudes, and behavior to marital satisfaction. *JCCP*, *54*, 514–517.

Brown, G.W., Birley, J.L.T., & Wing, J.K. (1972). Influence of family life on the course of schizophrenic disorders: a replication. *British Journal of Psychiatry*, *121*, 241–258.

Brown, J.D., Novick, N.J., Lord, K.A., & Richards, J.M. (1992). When Gulliver travels: social context, psychological closeness, and self-appraisals. *JPSP*, *62*, 717–727.

Brown, P. & Levinson, S. (1987). *Politeness: some universals in language use*. Cambridge: Cambridge University Press.

Brown, R. & Gilman, A. (1960). The pronouns of power and solidarity. In R.A. Sebeok (Ed.), *Style in Language*. Cambridge, MA: Technology Press.

Bruess, C.J.S. & Pearson, J.C. (1993). "Sweet pea" and "pussy cat": an examination of idiom use and marital satisfaction over the life cycle. *JSPR*, *10*, 609–615.

Bruner, J. (1990). *Acts of meaning*. Cambridge MA: Harvard University Press.

Bruner, J.S. & Tagiuri, R. (1954). The perception of people. In G. Lindzey (Ed.), *Handbook of social psychology*. Cambridge, MA: Addison-Wesley.

Bugental, D.B. & Love, L.R. (1975). Non-assertive expression of parental approval and disapproval and its relationship to child disturbance. *Child Development*, *46*, 747–752.

Bugental, D.B., Blue, J., Cortez, V., Fleck, K., Kopeikin, H., Lewis, J.C., & Lyon, J. (1993). Social cognitions as organisers of autonomic and affective responses to social challenge. *JPSP*, *64*, 94–103.

Buhrmester, D., Furman, W., Wittenberg, M., & Reis, H. (1988). Five domains of interpersonal competence in peer relationships. *JPSP*, *55*, 991–1008.

Bukowski, W.M., Hoza, B., & Boivin, M. (1994). Measuring friendship quality during pre- and early adolescence: the development and psychometric properties of the friendship qualities scale. *JSPR*, *11*, 471–484.

Bukowski, W.M., Hoza, B., & Newcomb, A.F. (1994). Using rating scale and nomination techniques to measure friendship and popularity. *JSPR*, *11*, 485–488.

Burger, E. & Milardo, R.M. (1995). Marital interdependence and social networks. *JSPR*, *12*, 403–415.

Burger, J.M. & Hemans, L.T. (1988). Desire for control and the use of attribution processes. *JP*, *56*, 531–546.

Burgess, E.Q. & Wallin, P. (1953). *Engagement and marriage*. New York: Lippincott (cited Simpson, 1987).

Burgess, E.W. & Locke, H.J. (1960). *The family from institution to companionship*. New York: American.

Burgess, R.L. (1981). Relationships in marriage and the family. In Duck, S. & Gilmour, R. (Eds.) (1981) *Personal relationships, 1*, London: Academic Press, pp.179–196.

Burggraf, C.S. & Sillars, A.L. (1987). A critical examination of sex differences in marital communication. *Communication Monographs*, *54*, 276–294.

Burgoon, J.K., Parrott, R., Le Poire, B.A., Kelley, D.L., Walther, J.B., & Perry, D. (1989). Maintaining and restoring privacy through communication in different types of relationship. *JSPR*, *6*, 131–158.

Burleson, B.R. & Denton, W.H. (1992). A new look at similarity and attraction in marriage: similarities in social-cognitive and communication skills as predictors of attraction and satisfaction. *Communication Monographs*, *59*, 268–287.

Burleson, B.R., Kunkel, A.W., Samter, W., & Werking, K.J. (1996). Men's and women's evaluations of communication skills in personal relationships: when sex differences make a difference—and when they don't. *JSPR*, *13*, 201–224.

Burton, L. (1975). *The family life of sick children*. London: Routledge & Kegan Paul.

Buss, A.H. (1983). Social rewards and personality. *JPSP*, *44*, 553–563.

Buss, D.M. (1987). Selection, evocation and manipulation. *JPSP*, *53*, 1214–1221.

Buss, D.M. (1991). Conflict in married couples: personality predictors of anger and upset. *JP*, *59*, 663–688.

Buss, D.M. (1994). *The evolution of desire*. New York: Basic Books.

Buss, D.M., Gomes, M., Higgins, D.S., & Lauterbach, K. (1987). Tactics of manipulation. *JPSP*, *52*, 1219–1229.

Buunk, B.P. (1995). Sex, self-esteem, dependency & extradyadic sexual experience as related to jealousy responses. *JSPR*, *12*, 147–153.

Buunk, B. & Bringle, R.G. (1987). Jealousy in love relationships. In Perlman & Duck (1987), pp.123–147.

Buunk, B.P., Doosje, B.J., Jans, L.G.J.M., & Hopstaken, L.E.M. (1993). Perceived reciprocity, social support, and stress at work: the role of exchange and communal orientation. *JPSP*, *65*, 801–811.

Buunk, B.P. & Van Yperen, N.W. (1991). Referential comparisons, relational comparisons and exchange orientation: their relation to marital satisfaction. *Personality and Social Psychology Bulletin*, *17*, 709–716.

Byng-Hall, J. (1990). Attachment theory and family therapy: a clinical view. *Infant Mental Health Journal*, *11*, 228–236.

Byng-Hall, J. (1995). *Rewriting family scripts*. London: Tavistock Clinic & Guilford Press.

Byng-Hall, J. & Stevenson-Hinde, J. (1991). Attachment relationships within a family system. *Infant Mental Health Journal*, *12*, 187–200.

Byrne, D. (1971). *The attraction paradigm*. New York: Academic Press.

Byrne, D. & Blaylock, B. (1963). Similarity and assumed similarity of attitudes between husbands and wives. *Journal of Abnormal and Social Psychology*, *67*, 636–640.

Byrne, D. & Clore, G.L. (1967). Effectance,

arousal and attraction. *JPSP, Monograph 6* (whole no. 638).

Byrne, D., Clore, G.L., & Smeaton, G. (1986). The attraction hypothesis: do similar attitudes affect anything? *JPSP, 51,* 1167–1170.

Byrne, D. & Griffitt, W. (1966). Similarity versus liking: a clarification. *Psychonomic Science, 6,* 295–296.

Byrne, D., Lamberth, J., Mitchell, H.E., & Winslow, L. (1974a). Sex differences in attraction. *Journal of Social and Economic Studies, 2,* 79–86.

Byrne, D., Nelson, D., & Reeves, K. (1966). Effects of consensual validation and invalidation on attraction as a function of verifiability. *JESP, 2,* 98–107.

Byrne, D. & Wong, T.J. (1962). Racial prejudice, interpersonal attraction, and assumed dissimilarity of attitudes. *Journal of Abnormal and Social Psychology, 65,* 246–253.

Cahn, D. (1990). Confrontation behaviors, perceived understanding and relationship growth. In D. Cahn (Ed.), *Intimates in conflict.* Hillsdale, NJ: Lawrence Erlbaum Associates Inc.

Cairns, R.B., Bergman, L., & Kagan, J. (Eds.) (in press), *The individual in developmental research: essays in honor of Marian Radke Yarrow.* Thousand Oaks, CA: Sage.

Caldwell, M. & Peplau, L.A. (1982). Sex differences in same-sex friendships. *Sex Roles, 8,* 721–732.

Caltabiano, M.L. & Smithson, M. (1983). Variables affecting the perception of self-disclosure appropriateness. *Journal of Social Psychology, 120,* 119–128.

Campbell, J.D. & Tesser, A. (1985) Self-evaluation maintenance processess in relationships. In Duck & Perlman (1985a), pp.107–136.

Canary, D.J. (1995). Mysteries of conflict in close relationships. *International Society for Study of Personal Relationships Bulletin, 11,* 3–5.

Canary, D.J. & Cupach, W.R. (1988). Relational and episodic characteristics associated with conflict tactics. *JSPR, 5,* 305–325.

Canary, D.J. & Stafford, L. (1992). Relational maintenance strategies and equity in marriage. *Communication Monographs, 59,* 243–267.

Cantor, N., Acker, M., & Cook-Flannagan, C. (1992). Conflict and preoccupation in the intimacy life-task. *JPSP, 63,* 644–655.

Cappella, J.N. (1984). The relevance of the microstructure of interaction to relationship change. *JSPR, 1,* 239–264.

Cappella, J.N. (1988). Personal relationships, social relationships and patterns of interaction. In Duck (1988), pp.325–342.

Cappella, J.N. & Palmer, M.T. (1990). Attitude similarity, relational history, and attraction: the mediating effects of kinesic and vocal behaviors. *Communication Monographs, 57,* 161–183.

Carnelley, K.B. & Janoff-Bulman, R. (1992). Optimism about love relationships: general vs. specific lessons from one's personal experiences. *JSPR, 9,* 5–20.

Carpenter, B.N. (1993). Relational competence. *Advances in the Study of Relationships, 4,* 1–28.

Caspi, A. & Elder, G.H. (1988). Emergent family patterns: the intergenerational construction of problem behaviour and relationships. In Hinde & Stevenson-Hinde (1988), pp.218–240.

Caspi, A. & Herbener, E.S. (1990). Continuity and change: assortative marriage and the consistency of personality in adulthood. *JPSP, 58,* 250–258.

Caspi, A., Herbener, E.S., & Ozer, D.J. (1992). Shared experiences and the similarity of personalities: a longitudinal study of married couples. *JPSP, 62,* 281–291.

Casselden, P.A. & Hampson, S.E. (1990). Forming impressions from incongruent traits. *JPSP, 59,* 353–362.

Cassidy, J. & Marvin, R.S. (1989/92). *Attachment organization in pre school children: coding guidelines.* Seattle: MacArthur Working Group on Attachment.

Cate, R.M., Koval, J., Lloyd, S.A., & Wilson, G. (1995). Assessment of relationship thinking in dating relationships. *PR, 2,* 77–96.

Cate, R.M. & Lloyd, S.A. (1992). *Courtship.* Newbury Park, CA: Sage.

Cate, R.M., Lloyd, S.A., & Long E. (1988). The role of rewards and fairness in developing premarital relationships. *J Mar Fam, 50,* 443–452.

Cattell, R.B. (1965). *The scientific analysis of personality.* Baltimore: Penguin.

Cattell, R.B. (1985). *Human motivation and the dynamic calculus.* New York: Praeger.

Cattell, R.B. & Dreger, R.M. (Eds.) (1977). *Handbook of modern personality theory.* Washington, DC: Hemisphere.

Cattell, R.B. & Nesselroade, J.R. (1967). Likeness and completeness theories examined by 16 personality factor measures on stably and unstably married couples. *JPSP, 7,* 351–361.

Caudill, W. & Weinstein, H. (1969). Maternal care and infant behavior in Japan and America. *Psychiatry, 32,* 12–43.

Chan, C.-J. & Margolin, G. (1994). The relationship between dual-earner couples' daily work mood and home affect. *JSPR, 11*, 573–586.

Chao, R.K. (1994). Beyond parental control and authoritarian parenting style: understanding Chinese parenting through the cultural notion of training. *Child Development, 65*, 1111–1119.

Cheek, J.M. and Buss A.H. (1981). Shyness and sociability. *JPSP, 41*, 330–339.

Chodorow, N. (1978). *The reproduction of mothering: psychoanalysis and the sociology of gender.* Berkeley: University of California Press.

Chown, S.M. (1981). Friendship in old age. In Duck & Gilmour (1981a) pp.231–46.

Christensen, A. & Heavey, C.L. (1990). Gender and social structure in the demand/withdraw pattern of marital conflict. *JPSP, 59*, 73–81.

Christensen, A. & Heavey, C.L. (1993). Gender differences in marital conflict: the demand/withdraw interaction pattern. In S. Oskamp & M. Costanzo (Eds.), *Gender issues in contemporary society*, pp.113–141. Newbury Park, CA: Sage.

Christensen, A. & Margolin, G. (1988). Conflict and alliance in distressed and non-distressed families. In Hinde & Stevenson-Hinde (1988), pp.263–282.

Christopher, F.S. & Cate, R.M. (1985). Premarital sexual pathways and relationship development. *JSPR, 2*, 271–288.

Christopher, F.S. & Frandsen, M.M. (1990). Strategies of influence in sex and dating. *JSPR, 7*, 89–106.

Christopher, F.S., Owens, L.A., & Stecker, H.L. (1993). Exploring the dark side of courtship: a test of a model of male premarital sexual aggressiveness. *J MarFam, 55*, 469–480.

Cicchetti, D. & Toth, S.L. (Eds.) (1995). *Emotion, cognition and representation.* Rochester, NY: University of Rochester Press.

Clark, M.S. & Mills, J. (1979). Interpersonal attraction in exchange and communal relationships. *JPSP, 37*, 12–23.

Clark, M.S., Mills, J., & Powell, M.C. (1986). Keeping track of needs in communal and exchange relationships. *JPSP, 51*, 333–338.

Clark, M.S., Pataki, S.P., & Carver V.H. (1996). Some thoughts and findings on self-presentation of emotions in relationships. In Fletcher & Fitness (1996), pp.247–278.

Clark, M.S. & Reis, H.T. (1988). Interpersonal processes in close relationships. *Annual Review of Psychology, 39*, 609–672.

Clark, M.S. & Waddell, B. (1985). Perceptions of exploitation in communal and exchange relationships. *JSPR, 2*, 403–418.

Clarke, D.D., Allen, C.M.B., & Salinas, M. (1984). Conjoint time-budgeting: investigating behavioral accommodation in marriage. *JSPR, 3*, 53–70.

Cline, R.J. (1986). The effects of biological sex and psychological gender on reported and behavioral intimacy and control of self-disclosure. *Communication Quarterly, 34*, 41–54.

Cline, R.J.W. (1989). The politics of intimacy: costs and benefits determining disclosure intimacy in male–female dyads. *JSPR, 6*, 5–20.

Clore, G.L. (1977). Reinforcement and affect in attraction. In Duck (1977a), pp.23–30.

Clore, G.L. & Byrne, D. (1974). A reinforcement–affect model of attraction. In T.L. Huston (Ed.), *Foundations of interpersonal attraction.* New York: Academic Press.

Cloven, D.H. & Roloff, M.E. (1994). A developmental model of decisions to withhold relational irritations in romantic relationships. *PR, 1*, 143–164.

Cole, T. & Bradac, J.J. (1996). A lay theory of relational satisfaction with best friends. *JSPR, 13*, 57–83.

Coleman, M. & Ganong, L.H. (1985). Love and sex role stereotypes: do macho men and feminine women make better lovers? *JPSP, 49*, 170–176.

Collett, P. (1977). *Social rules and social behaviour.* Oxford: Blackwell.

Collins, J., Kreitman, N., Nelson, B., & Troop, J. (1971). Neurosis and marital interaction. III Family roles and functions. *British Journal of Psychiatry, 119*, 233–242.

Collins, N.L. & Read, S.J. (1990). Adult attachment, working models, and relationship quality in dating couples. *JPSP, 58*, 644–663.

Colvin, C.R. (1993). "Judgeable" people; personality, behavior and competing explanations. *JPSP, 64*, 861–873.

Condon, J.W. & Crano, W.D. (1988). Inferred evaluation and the relation between attitude similarity and interpersonal attraction. *JPSP, 54*, 789–797.

Connor, J.W. (1974). Acculturation and family continuities in three generations of Japanese Americans. *J MarFam, 36*, 159–165.

Constantine, J.A. & Bahr, S.J. (1980). Locus of control and marital stability: a longitudinal study. *Journal of Divorce, 4*, 11–22.

Contarello, A. & Volpato, C. (1991). Images of friendship: literary depictions through the ages. *JSPR, 8*, 49–75.

Converse, J. & Foa, U.G. (1993). Some principles of equity in interpersonal exchange. In Foa et al. (1993a), pp.31–40.

Conway, J.K. (1995). Stages of a woman's life. *Bulletin of the American Academy of Arts and Sciences, 48,* 30–42.

Cook, M. (1977). The social skill model and interpersonal attraction. In Duck (1977a) pp.319–338.

Cook, M. (Ed.) (1984), *Issues in person perception.* London: Methuen.

Cook, M. & Wilson, G. (Eds.) (1979). *Love and attraction.* Oxford: Pergamon.

Cook, W.L. (1993). Interdependence and the interpersonal sense of control: an analysis of family relationships. *JPSP, 64,* 587–601.

Cooley, C.H. (1902). *Human nature and the social order.* Glencoe, Ill: Free Press.

Coombs, R.H. (1966). Value consensus and partner satisfaction among dating couples. *JMarFam, 28,* 166–173.

Cooper, J. & Fazio, R.H. (1984). A new look at dissonance theory. In L. Berkowitz (Ed.), *AdvExpSP, 17,* 229–262. New York: Academic Press.

Costa, P.T. & McCrae, R.R. (1989). From catalog to classification: Murray's needs and the five factor model. *JPSP, 55,* 258–265.

Costa, P.T. & McCrae, R.R. (1995). Solid grounds in the wetlands of personality: a reply to Block. *PsychBull, 117,* 216–220.

Cotterell, N., Eisenberger, R., & Speicher, H. (1992). Inhibiting effects of reciprocation wariness on interpersonal relationships. *JPSP, 62,* 658–668.

Cousins, P.C. & Vincent, J.P. (1983). Supportive and aversive behavior following spousal complaints. *JMarFam, 45,* 679–682.

Cowan, P.A. & Cowan, C.P. (1978). Changes in marriage during the transition to parenthood: must we blame the baby? In G.Y. Michaels & W.A. Goldberg (Eds.), *The transition to parenthood: current theory and research,* pp.114–154. New York: Cambridge University Press.

Cozby, P.C. (1973). Self disclosure: a literature review. *PsychBull, 79,* 73–91.

Craig, J.-A., Koestner, R., & Zuroff, D.C. (1994). Implicit and self-attributed intimacy motivation. *JSPR, 11,* 491–507.

Crohan, S.E. (1992). Marital happiness and spousal consensus on beliefs about marital conflict: a longitudinal investigation. *JSPR, 9,* 89–102.

Cromwell, R.E. & Olson, D.H. (1975). *Power in families.* New York: Halstead Press, Wiley.

Cromwell, R.E., Olson, D.H.L., & Fournier, D.G. (1976). Tools and techniques for diagnosis and evaluation in marital and family therapy. *Family Process, 15,* 1–49.

Crowne, D.P. & Marlowe, D. (1964). *The approval motive.* New York: Wiley.

Cunningham, J.D. & Antill, K.J. (1994). Cohabitation and marriage: retrospective and predictive comparisons. *JSPR, 11,* 77–93.

Cunningham, M.R., Barbee, A.P., & Pike, C.L. (1990). What do women want? Facialmetric assessment of multiple motives in the perception of male facial physical attractiveness. *JPSP, 59,* 61–72.

Cunningham, M.R., Roberts, A.R., Barbee, A.P., Druen, P.B., & Wu, C.-H. (1995). Their ideas of beauty are, on the whole, the same as ours. *JPSP, 68,* 261–270.

Cupach, W.R. and Comstock, J. (1990). Satisfaction with sexual communication in marriage: links to sexual satisfaction and dyadic adjustment. *JSPR, 7,* 179–187.

Cupach, W.R. & Metts, S. (1986). Accounts of relational dissolution: a comparison of marital and non-marital relationships. *Communication Monographs, 53,* 311–334.

Cupach, W.R. & Metts, S. (1995). The role of sexual attitude similarity in romantic heterosexual relationships. *PR, 2,* 287–300.

Curry, T.J. & Emerson, R.M. (1970). Balance theory: a theory of interpersonal attraction? *Sociometry, 33,* 216–238.

Curtis, R.C. & Miller, K. (1986). Believing another likes or dislikes you: behaviors making the beliefs come true. *JPSP, 51,* 284–290.

Dabbs, J.M. (1971). Physical closeness and negative feelings. *Psychonomic Science, 23,* 141–143.

Dainton, M. & Stafford, L. (1993). Routine maintenance behaviors: a comparison of relationship type, partner similarity and sex differences. *JSPR, 10,* 255–271.

Dakof, G.A. & Taylor, S.E. (1990). Victims' perceptions of social support: what is helpful from whom? *JPSP, 58,* 80–89.

Daly, J.A., Vangelisti, A.L., & Daughton, S.M. (1987). The nature and correlates of conversational sensitivity. *JMarFam, 14,* 167–202.

Danziger, K. (1976). *Interpersonal communication.* New York: Pergamon.

Darley, J.M. & Berscheid, E. (1967). Increased liking as a result of the anticipation of personal contact. *Human Relations, 20,* 29–39.

Darley, J. & Fazio, R. (1980). Expectancy confirmation processes arising in the social interaction sequence. *American Psychologist, 35,* 867–881.

Davis, D. & Martin, H.J. (1978). When pleasure begets pleasure: recipient responsiveness as a determinant of physical pleasuring between heterosexual dating couples and strangers. *JPSP*, *36*, 767–777.

Davis, D. & Perkowitz, W.T. (1979). Consequences of responsiveness in dyadic interaction. *JPSP*, *37*, 534–50.

Davis, J. (1973). Forms and norms: the economy of social relations. *Man*, *8*, 159–176.

Davis, J.D. (1976). Self-disclosure in an acquaintance exercise: responsibility for level of intimacy. *JPSP*, *33*, 787–792.

Davis, K.E. & Todd, M.J. (1985) Assessing friendship: prototypes, paradigm cases and relationship description. In Duck & Perlman (1985a), pp.17–38.

Davis, M. (1973). *Intimate relations*. New York: Free Press.

Davis, M.H. & Franzoi, S.L. (1986). Adolescent loneliness, self-disclosure, and private self-consciousness. *JPSP*, *51*, 595–608.

Davis, M.H. & Kraus, L.A. (1991). Dispositional empathy and social relationships. *Advances in Personal Relationships*, *3*, 75–116.

Davis, M.H. & Oathout, H.A. (1987). Maintenance of satisfaction in romantic relationships: empathy and relational competence. *JPSP*, *53*, 397–410.

Deaux, K. (1976). *The behavior of women and men*. Monterey, CA: Brooks/Cole.

Deci, E.L. & Ryan, R.M. (1985). *Intrinsic motivation and self determination in human behaviour*. New York: Plenum.

Deci, E.L. & Ryan, R.M. (1987). The support of autonomy and the control of behavior. *JPSP*, *53*, 1024–1037.

Dennett, D.C. (1991) *Consciousness explained*. Harmondsworth, UK: Allen Lane, Penguin.

Denzin, N.K. (1970). Rules of conduct and the study of deviant behavior: some notes on the social relationship. In G.J. McCall et al. (Eds.), *Social Relationships*. Chicago: Aldine.

DePaulo, B.M., Kenny, D.A., Hoover, C.W., Webb, W., & Oliver, P.V. (1987). Accuracy of person perception: do people know what kinds of impression they convey? *JPSP*, *52*, 303–315.

DePaulo, B.M., Stone, J.I., & Lassiter, G.D. (1985). Telling ingratiating lies: effects of target sex and target attractiveness on verbal and non-verbal deceptive success. *JPSP*, *48*, 1191–1203.

Derlega, V.J. & Chaikin, A. (1976). Norms affecting self-disclosure in men and women. *JCCP*, *44*, 376–380.

Derlega, V.J. & Grzelak, J. (1979). Appropriateness of self-disclosure. In G. Chalune (Ed.), *Self-disclosure*. San Francisco: Jossey-Bass.

Derlega, V.J., Metts, S., Petronio, S., & Margulis, S.T. (1993). *Self-disclosure*. Thousand Oaks, CA: Sage.

Derlega, V.J., Winstead, B.A., Wong, P.T.P., & Hunter, S. (1985). Gender effects in an initial encounter: a case where men exceed women in disclosure. *JSPR*, *2*, 25–44.

de Turck, M.A. & Miller, G.R. (1986). The effects of husbands' and wives' social cognition on their marital adjustment, conjugal power and self-esteem. *JMarFam*, *48*, 715–724.

Deutsch, F.M., Lussier, J.B., & Servis, L.J. (1993). Husbands at home: predictors of paternal participation in childcare and housework. *JPSP*, *65*, 1154–1166.

Deutsch, M. (1969). Conflicts: productive and destructive. *Journal of Social Issues*, *25*, 7–41.

Deutsch, M. (1985). *Distributive justice*. New Haven: Yale University Press.

Deutsch, M. & Krauss, R.M. (1965). Studies of interpersonal bargaining. *Journal of Conflict Resolution*, *6*, 52–76.

Deutsch, M. & Solomon, L. (1959). Reactions to evaluations of others as influenced by self evaluations. *Sociometry*, *22*, 93–112.

Dickens, W.J. & Perlman, D. (1981). Friendship over the life cycle. In Duck & Gilmour (1981a), pp.91–122.

Dindia, K. (1994). The intrapersonal-interpersonal dialectical process of self-disclosure. In Duck (1994a), pp.27–57.

Dindia, K. & Baxter, L. (1987). Strategies for maintaining and repairing marital relationships. *JSPR*, *4*, 143–158.

Dindia, K. & Canary, D.J. (1993). Definitions and theoretical perspectives on maintaining relationships. *JSPR*, *10*, 163–174.

Dindia, K. & Fitzpatrick, M.A. (1985) Marital communication: three approaches compared. In Duck & Perlman (1985a) pp.137–159.

Dinnerstein, D. (1976). *The mermaid and the minotaur: sexual arrangements and the human malaise*. New York: Harper & Row.

Dion, K.K., Berscheid, E., & Walster, E. (1972). What is beautiful is good. *JPSP*, *24*, 285–290.

Dion, K.K. & Dion, K.L. (1991) Psychological individualism and romantic love. *Journal of Social Behavior and Personality*, *6*, 17–33.

Dion, K.K. & Dion, K.L. (1993). Individualistic and collectivistic perspectives on gender and the cultural context of love and intimacy. *Journal of Social Issues, 49,* 53–69.

Dion, K.K. & Dion, K.L. (1996). Cultural perspectives on romantic love. *PR, 3,* 5–18.

Dion K.L. & Dion K.K. (1973). Correlates of romantic love. *JCCP, 41,* 51–55.

Dion, K.L. & Dion, K.K. (1979). Personality and behavioral correlates of romantic love. In Cook & Wilson (1979), pp.213–220.

Dion, K.L. & Dion, K.K. (1988). Individual and cultural perspectives. In R.J. Sternberg & M.L. Barnes (Eds.), *The psychology of love.* New Haven: Yale University Press.

Dion, K.L. & Dion, K.K. (1994). *Individual–collectivism and love.* Paper given at 7th International Conference on Personal Relationships, Groningen.

Dixson, M. & Duck S. (1993). Understanding relationship processes: uncovering the human search for meaning. In Duck (1993b), pp.175–206.

Doherty, R.W., Hatfield, E., Thompson, K., & Choo, P. (1994). Cultural and ethnic influences on love and attachment. *PR, 1,* 391–398.

Doherty, W.J. & Baldwin, C. (1985). Shifts and stability in locus of control during the 1970s: divergence of the sexes. *JPSP, 48,* 1048–1053.

Dolgin, K.M., Meyer, L., & Schwartz, J. (1991). Effects of gender, target's gender, topic and self-esteem on disclosure to best and middling friends. *Sex Roles, 25,* 311–329.

Dollard, J., Doob, L.W., Miller, N.E., Mowrer, O.H., & Sears, R.R. (1939). *Frustration and aggression.* New Haven: Yale University Press.

Douglas, M. (1982). Introduction to grid/group analysis. In M. Douglas (Ed.), *Essays in the sociology of perception,* pp.1–8. London: Routledge & Kegan Paul.

Douvan, E. & Adelson, J. (1966). *The adolescent experience.* New York: Wiley.

Dovidio, J.F., Ellyson, S.L., Keating, C.F., Heltman, K., & Brown, C.E. (1988). The relationship of social power to visual displays of dominance between men and women. *JPSP, 54,* 233–242.

Doyle, A.B., Markiewicz, D. & Hardy, C. (1994). Mother's and children's friendships: intergenerational associations. *JSPR, 11,* 363–378.

Drewery, J. (1969). An interpersonal perception technique. *British Journal of Medical Psychology, 42,* 171–181.

Drewery, J. & Rae, J.B. (1969). A group comparison of alcoholic and non-psychiatric marriages using the interpersonal perception technique. *British Journal of Psychiatry, 115,* 287–300.

Drigotas, S.M. & Rusbult, C.E. (1992). Should I stay or should I go? A dependence model of breakups. *JPSP, 62,* 62–87.

Driscoll, R., Davis, K., & Lipetz, M. (1972). Parental interference and romantic love: the Romeo and Juliet effect. *JPSP, 24,* 1–10.

DSM-1VTM (1994). Washington: American Psychiatric Association.

Duck, S.W. (1973a). *Personal relationships and personal constructs.* London: Wiley.

Duck, S.W. (1973b). Similarity and perceived similarity of personal constructs as influences on friendship choice. *British Journal of Social and Clinical Psychology, 12,* 1–6.

Duck, S. (Ed.) (1977a). *Theory and practice in interpersonal attraction.* London: Academic Press.

Duck, S.W. (1977b). Inquiry, hypothesis and the quest for validation: personal construct systems in the development of acquaintance. In Duck (1977a), pp.379–404.

Duck, S. (1981). Toward a research map for the study of relationship breakdown. In Duck and Gilmour (Eds.) (1981b), pp.1–56.

Duck, S. (Ed.) (1982a) *Personal relationships, 4: dissolving personal relationships.* London: Sage.

Duck, S.W. (1982b). A topography of relationship disengagement and dissolution. In Duck (1982a) pp.1–30.

Duck, S. (Ed.) (1988). *Handbook of personal relationships,* Chichester: Wiley.

Duck, S. (1990). Relationships as unfinished business: out of the frying pan and into the 1990s. *JSPR, 7,* 5–28.

Duck, S. (Ed.) (1993a), *Learning about relationships.* Newbury Park, CA: Sage.

Duck, S. (Ed.) (1993b). *Individuals in relationships.* Newbury Park, CA: Sage.

Duck, S. (1993c). *Social context and relationships.* Newbury Park, CA: Sage.

Duck, S. (Ed.) (1994a). *Dynamics of relationships.* Thousand Oaks, CA: Sage.

Duck, S.W. (Ed.) (1994b). *Meaningful relationships.* Thousand Oaks, CA: Sage.

Duck, S. (1995). Talking relationships into being *JSPR, 12,* 535–540.

Duck, S.W. & Allison, D. (1978). I liked you but I can't live with you: a study of lapsed friendships. *Social Behaviour and Personality, 6,* 43–47.

Duck, S.W. & Barnes, M.K. (1992). Disagreeing about agreement: reconciling differences about similarity. *Communication Monographs, 59,* 199–208.

Duck, S. & Craig, G. (1978). Personality similarity and the development of friendship: a longitudinal study. *British Journal of Social and Clinical Psychology*, *17*, 237–242.

Duck, S. & Gilmour, R (Eds.) (1981a). *Personal relationships, 2: developing personal relationships*. London: Academic Press.

Duck, S. & Gilmour, R. (Eds.) (1981b). *Personal relationships, 3: personal relationships in disorder*. London: Academic Press.

Duck, S. & Miell, D.E. (1986). Charting the development of personal relationships. In R. Gilmour & S. Duck, (Eds.), *The emerging field of personal relationships*, pp.133–143. Hillsdale, NJ: Lawrence Erlbaum Associates Inc.

Duck, S. & Perlman, D. (Eds.) (1985a). *Understanding personal relationships*, London: Sage.

Duck, S. & Perlman, D. (1985b). The thousand islands of personal relationships. In Duck & Perlman (1985a) pp.1–16.

Duck, S. & Pond, K. (1989). Friends, Romans, countrymen, lend me your retrospections: rhetoric and reality in personal relationships. In Hendrick (1989) pp.17–38.

Duck, S., Rutt, D.J., Hurst, M.H., & Strejc, H. (1991). Some evident truths about conversations in everyday relationships. *HCR*, *18*, 228–267.

Duck, S. & Wood, J.T. (Eds.) (1995a). *Confronting relationship challenges*. Thousand Oaks, CA: Sage.

Duck, S. & Wood, J.T. (1995b). For better, for worse, for richer for poorer: the rough and smooth of relationships. In Duck & Wood (1995a), pp.1–21.

Duck, S. & Wright, P.H. (1993). Re-examining gender differences in same-gender friendships: a close look at two kinds of data. *Sex Roles*, *28*, 709–727.

Dunkel-Schetter, C. & Skokan, L.A. (1990). Determinants of social support provision in personal relationships. *JSPR*, *7*, 437–450.

Dunn, J. (1976). How far do early differences in mother–child relations affect later development? In Bateson & Hinde (1976), pp.481–496.

Dunn, J. (1988). Connections between relationships: implications of research on mothers and siblings. In Hinde & Stevenson-Hinde (1988), pp.168–180.

Dunn, J. (1993). *Young children's close relationships*. London: Sage.

Dunn, J. & Kendrick, C. (1982). *Siblings*. Cambridge, MA: Harvard University Press.

Dunn, J. & Slomkowski, C. (1992). Conflict and the development of social understanding. In Shantz & Hartup (1992), pp.70–92.

Dunn, J. & Wooding, C. (1977). Play in the home and its implications for learning. In B. Tizard & D. Harvey (Eds.), *Biology of play*. London: Heinemann.

Dymond, R. (1954). Interpersonal perception and marital happiness. *Canadian Journal of Psychology*, *8*, 164–171.

Easterbrooks, M.A. & Emde, R.N. (1988) Marital and parent–child relationships: the role of affect in the family system. In Hinde & Stevenson-Hinde (1988), pp.83–103.

Easterling, P. (1989). Friendship and the Greeks. In R. Porter & S. Tomaselli (Eds.), *The dialectics of friendship*, pp.11–25. London: Routledge.

Eddy, J.M. (1991). An empirical evaluation of the dyadic adjustment scale: exploring the differences between marital "satisfaction" and "adjustment". *Behavioral Assessment*, *13*, 199–220.

Egeland, B. & Farber, E.A. (1984). Infant–mother attachment: factors related to its development and changes over time. *Child Development*, *55*, 753–771.

Eibl-Eibesfeldt, I. (1972). Similarities and differences between cultures in expressive movements. In Hinde (1972), pp.297–314.

Eidelson, R.J. (1981). Affiliative rewards and restrictive costs in developing relationships. *British Journal of Social Psychology*, *20*, 197–204.

Eidelson, R.J. & Epstein, N. (1982). Cognition and relationship maladjustment: development of a measure of relationship beliefs. *JCCP*, *50*, 715–720.

Eisenberger, R., Cotterell, N., & Marvel, J. (1987). Reciprocation ideology. *JPSP*, *53*, 743–750.

Ekman, P. (Ed.) (1982). *Emotion in the human face*. New York: Cambridge University Press.

Ekman, P. (1985). *Telling lies*. New York: Norton.

Ekman, P. (1992). An argument for basic emotions. *Cognition and Emotion*, *6*, 169–200.

Ekman, P. (1993). Facial expression and emotion. *American Psychologist*, *48*, 384–392.

Ekman, P. & Davidson, R.J. (1995). *The nature of emotion*. Oxford: Oxford University Press.

Ekman, P. & Friesen, W.V. (1969). The repertoire of nonverbal behavior. *Semiotica*, *I*, 49–98.

Ekman, P. & Friesen, W.V. (1975). *Unmasking the face*. New Jersey: Prentice Hall.

Ekman, P. & Friesen, W.V. (1978). *Facial Affect Coding System: a technique for the measurement of facial movement.* Palo Alto, CA: Consulting Psychologists Press.

Elkin, R.A. & Leippe, M.R. (1986). Physiological arousal, dissonance, and attitude change. *JPSP, 51*, 55–65.

Elkins, L.E. & Peterson, C. (1993). Gender differences in best friendships. *Sex Roles, 29*, 497–508.

Emmers, T.M. & Dindia, K. (1995). The effect of relational stage and intimacy on touch. *PR, 2*, 225–236.

Endler, N.S. & Magnusson, D. (1976). *Interactional psychology and personality.* Washington, DC: Halsted-Wiley.

Engfer, A. (1988). The interrelatedness of marriage and the mother–child relationship. In Hinde & Stevenson-Hinde (1988), pp.104–118.

Engfer, A., Walper, S., & Rutter, M. (1994). Individual characteristics as a force in development. In M. Rutter & D. Hay (Eds.), *Development through life*, pp.79–111. Oxford: Blackwell.

Epstein, E. & Guttman, R. (1984). Mate selection in man: evidence, theory and outcome. *Social Biology, 31*, 243–278.

Epstein, N., Pretzer, J.L., & Fleming, B. (1987). The role of cognitive appraisal in self reports of marital communication. *Behavior Therapy, 18*, 51–69.

Epstein, N.B. & Santa-Barbara, J. (1975). Conflict behavior in clinical couples: interpersonal perceptions and stable outcomes. *Family Process, 14*, 51–66.

Erikson, E. (1963) *Childhood and society.* New York: Norton.

Eysenck, H.J. (1947). *Dimensions of personality.* London: Routledge & Kegan Paul.

Eysenck, H.J. (1975). *The inequality of man.* San Diego, CA: Edits.

Falbo, T. & Peplau, L.A. (1980). Power strategies in intimate relationships. *JPSP, 38*, 618–628.

Fazio, R.H., Zanna, M.P., & Cooper, J. (1977). Dissonance and self-perception: an integrative view of each theory's proper domain of application. *JESP, 13*, 464–479.

Feeney, J.A. (1994). Attachment style, communication patterns, and satisfaction across the life-cycle of marriage. *PR, 1*, 333–348.

Feeney, J.A. (1995). Adult attachment and emotional control. *PR, 2*, 143–160.

Feeney, J.A. & Noller, P. (1990). Attachment style as a predictor of adult romantic relationships. *JPSP, 58*, 281–291.

Feeney, J.A. & Noller, P. (1991). Attachment style and verbal descriptions of romantic partners. *JSPR, 8*, 187–215.

Feeney, J., Peterson, C., & Noller, P. (1994). Equity and marital satisfaction over the family life cycle. *PR, 1*, 83–99.

Fehr, B. (1989). Prototype analysis of the concepts of love and commitment. *JPSP, 55*, 557–579.

Fehr, B. (1993). How do I love thee? Let me consult my prototype. In Duck (1993a), pp.87–120.

Fehr, B. (1994). Prototype-based assessment of laypeople's views of love. *PR, 1*, 309–332.

Fehr, B. & Baldwin, M. (1996). Prototype and script analyses of laypeoples' knowledge of anger. In Fletcher & Fitness (1996), pp.219–245.

Fehr, B. & Russell, J.A. (1991). The concept of love viewed from a prototype perspective. *JPSP, 60*, 425–438.

Feingold, A. (1990). Gender differences in effects of physical attractiveness on romantic attraction: a comparison across five research paradigms. *JPSP, 59*, 981–993.

Feingold, A. (1992). Gender differences in mate selection preferences. *PsychBull, 112*, 125–139.

Felmlee, D.H. (1995). Fatal attractions: affection and disaffection in intimate relationships. *JSPR, 12*, 295–311.

Felmlee, D., Sprecher, S., & Bassin, E. (1990). The dissolution of intimate relationships: a hazard model. *Social Psychology Quarterly, 53*, 13–30.

Fernald, A. & Marikawa, H. (1993). Common themes and cultural variations in Japanese and American mothers' speech to infants. *Child Development, 64*, 637–656.

Ferreira, A.J. & Winter, W.D. (1974). On the nature of marital relationships: measurable differences in spontaneous agreement. *Family Process, 13*, 355–369.

Feshbach, S. (1989). The bases and development of individual aggression. In J. Groebel & R.A. Hinde (Eds.), *Aggression and war*, pp.78–90. Cambridge: Cambridge University Press.

Festinger, L. (1957). *A theory of cognitive dissonance.* Evanston, Ill: Row, Peterson.

Fiese, J.H., Hooker, K.A., Kotary, L., & Schwagler, J. (1993). Family rituals in the early stages of parenthood. *JMarFam, 55*, 633–642.

Filsinger, E.E. & Thoma, S.J. (1988). Behavioral antecedents of relationship stability and adjustment: a five year longitudinal study. *JMarFam, 50*, 785–795.

Fincham, F.D., Beach, S.R., & Baucom, D.H. (1987). Attribution processes in distressed and non-distressed couples: 4 self–partner attribution differences. *JPSP, 52,* 739–748.

Fincham, F.D., Beach, S.R.H., & Kemp-Fincham, S.I. (in press). Marital quality: a new theoretical perspective. In R.J. Sternberg & M. Hojjat (Eds.), *Satisfaction in close relationships.* New York: Guilford.

Fincham, F.D., Beach, S.R., & Nelson, G. (1987). Attribution processes in distressed and non distressed couples. 3. Causal and responsibility attributions for spouses' behavior. *Cognitive Therapy and Research, 11,* 71–86.

Fincham, F.D. & Bradbury, T.N. (1987a). The assessment of marital quality: a re-evaluation. *J Mar Fam, 49,* 797–809.

Fincham, F.D. & Bradbury, T.N. (1987b). Cognitive processes and conflict in close relationships: an attribution–efficacy model. *JPSP, 53,* 1106–1118.

Fincham, F.D. & Bradbury, T.N. (1987c). The impact of attributions in marriage: a longitudinal analysis. *JPSP, 53,* 510–517.

Fincham, F.D. & Bradbury, T.N. (1989a). Perceived responsibility for marital events: egocentric or partner-centric bias. *J Mar Fam, 51,* 27–35.

Fincham, F.D. & Bradbury, T.N. (1989b). The impact of attributions in marriage: an individual difference analysis. *JSPR, 6,* 69–85.

Fincham, F.D. & Bradbury, T.N. (1992). Assessing attributions in marriage: the relationship attribution measure. *JPSP, 62,* 457–68.

Fincham, F.D. & Bradbury, T.N. (1993). Marital satisfaction, depression and attributions. *JPSP, 64,* 442–52.

Fine, M.A. & Kurdek, L.A. (1994). Parenting cognitions in stepfamilies: difference between parents and stepparents and relations to parenting satisfaction. *JSPR, 11,* 95–112.

Fischer, J.L. & Sollie, D.L. (1986). Women's communication with intimates and acquaintances. *JSPR, 3,* 19–30.

Fisher, J.D., Nadler, A., & Whitaker-Alagna, S. (1982). Recipient reactions to aid. *PsychBull, 91,* 27–54.

Fiske, A.P. (1991). *Structures of social life.* New York: Free Press.

Fiske, A.P. (1992). The four elementary forms of sociality: framework for a unified theory of social relations. *PsychRev, 99,* 689–723.

Fiske, A.R., Haslam, N., & Fiske, S.T. (1991). Confusing one person with another: what errors reveal about the elementary forms of social relations. *JPSP, 60,* 656–74.

Fitness, J. (1996). Emotion knowledge structures in close relationships. In Fletcher & Fitness (1996), pp.195–217.

Fitness, J. & Fletcher, G.J.O. (1983). Love, hate, anger, and jealousy in close relationships. *JPSP, 65,* 924–958.

Fitzpatrick, M.A. (1984). A typological approach to marital interaction: recent theory and research. *AdvExpSP, 18,* pp.2–47.

Fitzpatrick, M.A. (1987). Marriage and verbal intimacy. In V.J. Derlega & J. Berg (Eds.), *Self-disclosure: theory, research and therapy.* New York: Plenum.

Fitzpatrick, M.A. (1988). *Between husbands and wives: communication in marriage.* Beverley Hills, CA: Sage.

Fitzpatrick, M.A., Vangelisti, A.L., & Firman, S.M. (1994). Perceptions of marital interaction and change during pregnancy—a typological approach. *PR, 1,* 101–122.

Flannery, D.J., Montemajor, R., Eberly, M., & Torquati, J. (1993). Unraveling the ties that bind: affective expression and perceived conflict in parent–adolescent interactions. *JSPR, 10,* 495–509.

Fleming, J.H. & Rudman, L.A. (1993). Between a rock and a hard place: self-concept regulating and communication properties of distancing behaviors. *JPSP, 64,* 44–59.

Fletcher, G.J.O., Fincham, F.D., Cramer, L., & Heron, N. (1987). The role of attributions in the development of dating relationships. *JPSP, 53,* 481–489.

Fletcher, G.J.O. & Fitness, J. (1993). Knowledge structures and explanations in personal relationships. In Duck (1993b), pp.121–143.

Fletcher, G.J.O. & Fitness, J. (Eds.) (1996). *Knowledge structures & interaction in close relationships.* Hillsdale, NJ: Lawrence Erlbaum Associates Inc.

Fletcher, G.J.O., Fitness, J., & Blampied, N.M. (1990). The link between attribution and happiness in close relationships. *Journal of Social and Clinical Psychology, 9,* 243–255.

Fletcher, G.J.O. & Kininmonth, L. (1991). Interaction in close relationships and social cognition. In G.J.O. Fletcher & F.D. Fincham, (Eds.), *Cognition in close relationships,* pp.235–256. Hillsdale, NJ: Lawrence Erlbaum Associates Inc.

Fletcher, G.J.O., Rosanowski, J., & Fitness, J. (1994). Automatic processing in intimate contexts. *JPSP, 67,* 888–897.

Fletcher, G.J.O. & Thomas, G. (1996). Close

relationship lay theories. In Fletcher & Fitness (1996), pp.3–24.

Foa, U.G. & Bosman, J.A.M. (1979). Differential factors in need for love. In Cook & Wilson (1979), pp.287–293.

Foa, U.G., Converse, J., Tornblom, K.Y., & Foa, E.B. (Eds.) (1993a). *Resource theory*. San Diego: Academic Press.

Foa, U.G. & Foa, E.B. (1974). *Societal structures of the mind*. Springfield, Ill: Thomas.

Foa, U.G., Megonigal, S., & Greipp, J.R. (1976). Some evidence against the possibility of utopian societies. *JPSP*, 34, 1043–1048.

Foa, U.G., Salcedo, L.N., Tornblom, K.Y., Garner, M., Glaubman, H., & Teichman, M. (1993b). Interrelation of social resources: evidence of pan cultural invariance. In Foa et al. (1993a), pp.57–66.

Fodor, J. (1983). *The modularity of mind*. Cambridge, MA: MIT Press.

Fonagy, P., Steele, H., & Steele, M. (1991). Maternal representations of attachment during pregnancy predict the organization of infant–mother attachment at one year. *Child Development*, 62, 891–905.

Ford, C.S. & Beach, E.A. (1951). *Patterns of sexual behavior*. New York: Harper & Row.

Forgas, J.P. (1982). Episode cognition: internal representations of interaction routines. *AdvExpSP*, 15, 59–104.

Forgas, J.P. (1991). Affective influences on partner choice: role of mood in social decisions. *JPSP*, 61, 708–720.

Forgas, J.P. (1992). On mood and peculiar people: affect and person typicality in impression formation. *JPSP*, 62, 863–875.

Forgas, J.P. (1994). Sad and guilty? Affective influences on the explanation of conflict in close relationships. *JPSP*, 66, 56–68.

Forgas, J.P. (1996). The role of emotion scripts and transient moods in relationships: structural and functional perspectives. In Fletcher & Fitness (1996), 275–296.

Forgas, J.P. & Bower, G.H. (1987). Mood effects on person–perception judgements. *JPSP*, 53, 53–60.

Forgas, J.P., Bower, G.H., & Moylan, S.J. (1990). Praise or blame? Mood effects on attributions for success or failure. *JPSP*, 59, 809–819.

Forgas, J.P., Levinger, G., & Moylan, S.J. (1994). Feeling good and feeling close: affective influences on the perception of intimate relationships. *PR*, 1, 165–184.

Fowers, B.J. (1991). His and her marriage: a multivariate study of gender and marital satisfaction. *Sex Roles*, 24, 209–221.

Fransella, F. & Bannister, D. (1977). *A manual for repertory grid technique*. London: Academic Press.

Franzoi, S.L. & Davis, M.H. (1985). Adolescent self-disclosure and loneliness: private self-consciousness and parental influences. *JPSP*, 48, 768–776.

Franzoi, S.L., Davis, M.H., & Young, R.D. (1985). The effects of private self-consciousness and perspective taking on satisfaction in close relationships. *JPSP*, 48, 1584–1594.

Frazier, P.A. & Cook, S.W. (1993). Correlates of distress following heterosexual relationship dissolution. *JSPR*, 10, 55–67.

Frazier, P.A. & Esterly, E. (1990). Correlates of relationship beliefs: gender, relationship experience and relationship satisfaction. *JSPR*, 7, 331–352.

Frederickson, B. (1995). Socioemotional behaviour at the end of college life. *JSPR*, 12, 261–276.

French, J.R.P. & Raven, B.H. (1959). The basis of social power. In D. Cartwright (Ed.), *Studies in social power*. Ann Arbor, MI: University of Michigan Press.

Frey, K.P. & Smith E.R. (1993). Beyond the actor's traits: forming impressions of actors, targets and relationships from social behaviors. *JPSP*, 65, 486–493.

Fromm, E. (1956). *The art of loving*. New York: Harper & Row.

Fuller, T.L. & Fincham, F.D. (1995). Attachment style in married couples: relation to current marital functioning, stability over time, and method of assessment. *PR*, 2, 17–34.

Fultz, J. & Cialdini, R.B. (1991). Situational and personality determinants of the quantity and quality of helping. In Hinde and Groebel (1991), pp.135–146.

Funder, D.C. & Colvin, C.R. (1989). Friends and strangers: acquaintanceship, agreement, and the accuracy of personality judgement. *JPSP*, 55, 387–395.

Funder, D.C. & Colvin, C.R. (1991). Explorations in behavioral consistency: properties of persons, situations and behaviors. *JPSP*, 60, 773–794.

Funder, D.C. & Sneed, C.D. (1993). Behavioral manifestations of personality: an ecological approach to judgemental accuracy. *JPSP*, 64, 479–490.

Furnham, A., Hester, C., & Weir, C. (1990). Sex differences in the preferences for specific female body shapes. *Sex Roles*, 22, 743–754.

Furstenberg, F.F. (1982). Conjugal succession. In P.B. Baltes & O. Brim (Eds.), *Life-span development and behaviour*, 4. New York: Academic Press (cited Ambert 1988).

Gaelick, L., Bodenhausen, G.V., & Wyer, R.S. (1985). Emotional communication in close relationships. *JPSP*, *49*, 1246–1265.

Gaines, S.O. (1994). Exchange of respect-denying behaviors among male–female friendships. *JSPR*, *11*, 5–24.

Gaines, S.O. (1996). Impact of interpersonal traits and gender-role compliance on interpersonal resource exchange among dating and engaged/married couples. *JSPR*, *13*, 241–262.

Gambetta, D. (1988). *Trust*. New York: Blackwell.

Gangestad, S. & Snyder, M. (1985). To carve nature at its joints. On the existence of distinct classes in personality. *PsychRev*, *92*, 317–349.

Gangestad, S.W., Simpson, J.A., DiGeronimo, K., & Biek, M. (1992). Differential accuracy in person perception across traits: examination of a functional hypothesis. *JPSP*, *62*, 688–698.

Garcia, S., Stinson, L., Ickes, W., Bissonnette, V., & Briggs, S.R. (1991). Shyness and physical attractiveness in mixed-sex dyads. *JPSP*, *61*, 35–49.

Gath, A. (1973). The school-age siblings of mongol children. *British Journal of Psychiatry*, *123*, 161–167.

George, C., Kaplan, N., & Main, M. (1985). *The adult attachment interview*. Unpublished manuscript Berkeley, CA: University of California.

Gergen, K.J. & Gergen, M.M. (1988). Narrative and the self as relationship. *AdvExpSP*, *21*, 17–56 [and other contributions to this volume].

Gervai, J., Turner, P.B., & Hinde, R.A. (1995). Gender-related behaviour, attitudes and personality in parents of young children in England and Hungary. *International Journal of Behavioural Development*, *18*, 105–126.

Gerzi, S. & Berman, E. (1981). Emotional reactions of expectant fathers to their wives' first pregnancy. *British Journal of Medical Psychology*, *52*, 259–265.

Gewirtz, J.L. & Baer, D.M. (1958). Deprivation and satiation of social reinforcers as drive conditions. *Journal of Abnormal and Social Psychology*, *57*, 165–172.

Gewirtz, J.L. & Boyd, E.F. (1977). Does maternal responding imply reduced infant crying? A critique of the 1972 Bell and Ainsworth report. *Child Development*, *48*, 1200–1207.

Gilbert, D.T. & Krull, D.S. (1988). Seeing less and knowing more: the benefits of perceptual ignorance. *JPSP*, *54*, 193–202.

Gilbert, D.T., McNulty, S.E., Guilano, T.A., & Benson, J.E. (1992). Blurry words and fuzzy duds: the attribution of obscure behavior. *JPSP*, *62*, 18–25.

Gilbert, D.T., Pelham, B.W., & Krull, D.S. (1988). On cognitive busyness: when person perceiver meets persons perceived. *JPSP*, *54*, 733–740.

Gilbert, L.A. (1993). Studying personal relationships in two career families from a gender perspective. *Advances in Personal Relationships*, *4*, 139–164.

Giles, H. & Smith, P.M. (1979). Accommodation theory: optimal levels of convergence. In H. Giles & R.N. St. Clair (Eds.), *Language and social psychology*, pp.45–65. Oxford: Blackwell.

Gilligan, C. (1982). *In a different voice: psychological theory and women's development*. Cambridge, MA: Harvard University Press.

Gilligan, C. (1987). Moral orientation and moral development. In E.F. Kellay & D.T. Meyers (Eds.), *Women and moral theory*. Totowa, NJ: Rowman & Littlefield.

Ginsburg, G.P. (1988). Rules, scripts and prototypes in personal relationships. In Duck (1988), pp.23–39.

Glass, D.C. (1964). Changes in liking as a means of reducing cognitive discrepancies between self-esteem and aggression. *JP*, *32*, 531–549.

Glenn, N.D. (1987). Quantitative research on marital quality in the 1980s: a critical review. *JMarFam*, *52*, 818–31.

Goffman, E. (1959). *The presentation of self in everyday life*. New York: Doubleday Anchor.

Goffman, E. (1961). *Asylums*. Chicago: Aldine.

Goffman, E. (1963). *Behaviour in public places*. New York: Free Press.

Goffman, E. (1967). *Interaction ritual*. New York: Doubleday Anchor.

Gold, M. & Yanof, D.S. (1985). *Mothers, daughters and girlfriends*. *JPSP*, *49*, 654–659.

Goldsmith, H.H. (1983). Genetic influences on personality from infancy to adulthood. *Child Development*, *54*, 331–355.

Goldstein, J.H. (1986). *Aggression and crimes of violence*. Oxford: Oxford University Press.

Gonzales, R.H., Manning, D.J., & Haugen, J.A. (1992). Explaining our sins: factors influencing offender accounts and anticipated victim responses. *JPSP*, *62*, 958–971.

Goodnow, J.J. (1988). Parents' ideas, actions and feelings: models and methods from developmental and social psychology. *Child Development*, *59*, 286–320.

Goodwin, R. (1990). Sex differences among partner preferences: are the sexes really very similar? *Sex Roles*, *23*, 501–513.

Goodwin, R. (1995). The privatization of the personal? I. Intimate disclosure in modern-day Russia. *JSPR*, *12*, 121–131.

Goodwin, R. & Emelyanova, T. (1995). The privatization of the personal? II. Attitudes to the family & child-rearing attitudes in modern-day Russia. *JSPR*, *12*, 132–138.

Goody, E. (1972). "Greeting", "begging", and the presentation of respect. In J.S. Fontaine (Ed.), *The interpretation of ritual*. London: Tavistock.

Goody, E. (1978). Towards a theory of questions. In E. Goody (Ed.), *Questions and politeness*. Cambridge: Cambridge University Press.

Goody, J. (1959). The mother's brother and the sister's son in West Africa. *Journal of the Royal Anthropological Institute*, *89*, 61–88.

Goody, J. (1973). *The character of kinship*. Cambridge: Cambridge University Press.

Goodyer, I.M. (1990). *Life experiences, development and childhood psychopathology*. Chichester: Wiley.

Gottman, J.M. (1979). *Marital interaction: experimental investigations*. New York: Academic Press.

Gottman, J.M. (1982). Emotional responsiveness in marital conversation. *Journal of Communication*, *32*, 108–120.

Gottman, J.M. (1994). *What predicts divorce? the relationship between marital processes and marital outcomes*. Hillsdale, NJ: Lawrence Erlbaum Associates Inc.

Gottman, J.M. & Krokoff, L.J. (1989). Marital interaction and satisfaction: a longitudinal view. *JCCP*, *57*, 47–52.

Gottman, J.M. & Levenson, R.W. (1988). The social psychophysiology of marriage. In P. Noller & M.A. Fitzpatrick (Eds.), *Perspectives on marital interaction*, pp.182–202. Clevedon, UK: Multilingual Mothers.

Gottman, J.M. & Levenson, R.W. (1992). Marital processes predictive of later dissolution: behavior, physiology and health. *JPSP*, *63*, 221–233.

Gottman, J., Markman, H., & Notarius, C. (1977). The topography of marital conflict: a sequential analysis of verbal and nonverbal behavior. *JMarFam*, *39*, 461–478.

Gottman, J.M., Notarius, L., Gonso, J., &, Markman, H. (1976). *A couple's guide to communication*. Champaign, Ill: Research Press.

Gottman, J.M. & Parker, J.G. (1986). *Conversations of friends*. Cambridge: Cambridge University Press.

Gottman, J.M. & Porterfield, A.L. (1981). Communicative competence in the nonverbal behavior of married couples. *JMarFam*, *4*, 817–824.

Gray, J.D. & Silver, R.C. (1990). Opposite sides of the same coin: former spouses' divergent perspectives in coping with their divorce. *JPSP*, *59*, 1180–1191.

Graziano, W.G., Brothen, T., & Berscheid, E. (1980). Attention, attraction and individual differences in reaction to criticism. *JPSP*, *38*, 193–202.

Graziano, W.G., Jensen-Campbell, L.A., Shabilske, L.J., & Lundgren, S.R. (1993). Social influence, sex differences and judgements of beauty: putting the interpersonal back in interpersonal attraction. *JPSP*, *65*, 522–531.

Graziano, W.G. & Musser, L.M. (1982). The joining and parting of the ways. In Duck (1982a) pp.75–106.

Greenberg, M., Cicchetti, D., & Cummings, M. (1990). *Attachment in the preschool years*. Chicago: Chicago University Press.

Greene, J.O. & Geddes, D. (1988). Representation and processing in the self-system: an action-oriented approach to self and self-relevant phenomena. *Communication Monographs*, *55*, 287–314.

Greenfield, P.M. & Childs, C.P. (1991). Developmental continuity in biocultural context. In R. Cohen & A.W. Siegel (Eds.), *Context and development*, pp.135–159. Hillsdale, NJ: Lawrence Erlbaum Associates Inc.

Griffin, D. & Bartholomew, K. (1994). Models of the self and other: fundamental dimensions underlying measures of adult attachment. *JPSP*, *67*, 430–445.

Griffin, E. & Sparks, G.G. (1990). Friends forever: a longitudinal explanation of intimacy in same-sex friends and platonic peers. *JSPR*, *7*, 29–46.

Griffitt, W. (1974). Attitude similarity and attraction. In T.L. Huston (Ed.), *Foundations of interpersonal attraction*. New York: Academic Press.

Griffitt, W. & Veitch, R. (1974). Pre-acquaintance attitude similarity and attraction re-visited: ten days in a fall-out shelter. *Sociometry*, *37*, 163–173.

Grossman, K., Fremmer-Bombek, E., Rudolph, J., & Grossman, K.E. (1988). Maternal attachment respresentations as related to patterns of infant–mother attachment and maternal care during the first year. In Hinde & Stevenson-Hinde (1988), pp.241–262.

Grossman, K., Grossmann, K.E., Spangler, G., Suess, G., & Unzner, L. (1985). Maternal sensitivity and newborns' orientation responses as related to quality of attachment in Northern Germany. In I. Bretherton & E. Waters (Eds.), Growing points in attachment theory and research, *Monographs of the Society for Research in Child Development*, 50, 233–256.

Grote, N.K. & Frieze, I.H. (1994). The measurement of friendship-based love in intimate relationships. *PR*, 1, 275–300.

Gruber-Baldini, A.L., Schaie, K.W., & Willis, S.L. (1995). Similarity in married couples. *JPSP*, 69, 191–203.

Gruder, C.L. (1970). Social power in interpersonal negotiation. In P. Swingle (Ed.), *The structure of conflict*. New York: Academic Press.

Gryl, F.E., Stith, S.M., & Bird, G.W. (1991). Close dating relationships among college students: differences by use of violence and by gender. *JSPR*, 8, 243–264.

Guerrero, L.K. & Andersen, P.A. (1991). The waxing and waning of relational intimacy: touch as a function of relational stage, gender and touch avoidance. *JSPR*, 8, 147–166.

Guerrero, L.K., Eloy, S.V., & Wabnik, A.I. (1993). Linking maintenance strategies to relationship formation and disengagement: a reconceptualization. *JSPR*, 10, 273–283.

Guldner, G.T. & Swenson, C.H. (1995). Time spent together and relationship quality. *JSPR*, 12, 313–320.

Gurtman, M.B. (1992). Trust, distrust, and interpersonal problems: a circumplex analysis. *JPSP*, 62, 989–1002.

Hackel, L.S. & Ruble, D.N. (1992). Changes in the marital relationship after the first baby is born: predicting the impact of expectancy disconfirmation. *JPSP*, 62, 944–957.

Hadley, T.R. & Jacob, T. (1976). The measurement of family power: a methodological study. *Sociometry*, 39, 384–385.

Hagestad, G.O. & Smyer, M.A. (1982). Dissolving long-term relationships: patterns of divorcing in middle age. In Duck (1982a), pp.155–188.

Haidt, J., Koller, S.H., & Dias, M.G., (1993). Affect, culture, and morality, or is it wrong to eat your dog? *JPSP*, 65, 613–628.

Hall, E.T. (1966). *The hidden dimension*. New York: Doubleday.

Hancock, M. & Ickes, W. (1996). Empathic accuracy: when does the perceiver–target relationship make a difference. *JSPR*, 13, 179–200.

Hamilton, W.D. (1984). The genetical theory of social behavior. *Journal of Theoretical Biology*, 7, 1–52.

Harlow, H.F. & Zimmermann, R.R. (1959). Affectional responses in the infant monkey. *Science*, 130, 421–432.

Harré, R. (1974). The conditions for a social psychology of childhood. In M.P.M. Richards (Ed.), *The integration of a child into a social world*, pp.245–262. Cambridge: Cambridge University Press.

Harré, R. (1975). The origins of social competence in a pluralist society. *Oxford Review of Education*, 1, 151–158.

Harré, R. (1977). Friendship as an accomplishment. In Duck (1977a), pp.339–354.

Harré, R. & Secord, P.F. (1972). *The explanation of social behaviour*. Oxford: Oxford University Press.

Harris, M.J., Milich, R., Corbitt, E.M., Hoover, D.W., & Brady, M. (1993). Self-fulfilling effects of stigmatizing information on children's social interactions. *JPSP*, 63, 41–50.

Hartup, W.W. (1995). The three faces of friendship. *JSPR*, 12, 569–574.

Harvey, J.H., Agostinelli, G., & Weber, A.L. (1989). Account-making and the formation of expectations about close relationships. In Hendrick (1989) pp.39–62.

Harvey, J.H., Barnes, M.K., Carlson, H.R., & Haig, J. (1995). Held captive by their memories: managing grief in relationships. In Duck & Wood (1995), pp.211–233.

Harvey, J.H., Hendrick, S.S., & Tucker, K. (1988). Self-report methods in studying personal relationships. In Duck (1988), pp.99–119.

Harvey, J.H., Weber, A.L, & Orbuch, T.L. (1990). *Interpersonal accounts*. Oxford: Blackwell.

Harvey, J.H., Weber, A.L., Yarkin, K.L., & Stewart, B.E. (1982). An attributional approach to relationship breakdown and dissolution. In Duck (1982a), pp.107–126.

Harvey, J.H., Wells, G.L., & Alvarez, M.D. (1978) Attribution in the context of conflict and separation in close relationships. In J.H. Harvey, W.J. Ickes & R.F. Kidd (Eds.), *New directions in attribution research*, 2, pp.235–259. Hillsdale, NJ: Lawrence Erlbaum Associates Inc.

Haslam, N. (1995). Factor structure of social relationships: an examination of relational models & resource exchange theories. *JSPR*, 12, 217–227.

Hassebrouck, M. (1987). The influence of

misattributions on reactions to inequity: towards a further understanding of inequity. *European Journal of Social Psychology*, *17*, 295–304.

Hatfield, E., Brinton, C., & Cornelius, J. (1989). Passionate love and anxiety in young adolescents. *Motivation and Emotion*, *13*, 271–289.

Hatfield, E., Schmitz, E., Cornelius, J., & Rapson, R.L. (1988). Passionate love: how early does it begin? *Journal of Psychology and Human Sexuality*, *1*, 35–51.

Hatfield, E., Traupmann, J., Sprecher, S., Utne, M., & Hay, J. (1985). Equity and intimate relations: recent research. In Ickes (1985), pp.91–117.

Hatfield, E. & Walster, G. (1978). *A new look at love*. San Francisco: Freeman.

Hatkoff, S. & Lasswell, T.E. (1979). Male–female similarities and differences in conceptualising love. In Cook & Wilson, (1979), pp.221–227.

Hays, R.B. (1984). The development and maintenance of friendship. *JSPR*, *1*, 75–98.

Hays, R.B. (1985). A longitudinal study of friendship development. *JPSP*, *48*, 909–924.

Hays, R.B. (1988). Friendships. In Duck (1988), pp.391–408.

Hays, R.B. (1989). The day-to-day functioning of close versus casual friendships. *JSPR*, *6*, 21–37.

Hazan, C. & Shaver, P. (1987). Romantic love conceptualised as an attachment process. *JPSP*, *52*, 511–524.

Hazan, C. & Shaver, P. (1994). Attachment as an organizational framework for research on close relationships. *Psychological Inquiry*, *5*, 1–22.

Heal, J. (1991). *Altruism*. In Hinde & Groebel (1991), pp.159–172.

Heaton, T.B. (1991). Time-related determinants of marital dissolution. *JMarFam*, *53*, 285–296.

Heaton, T.B. & Albrecht, S.L. (1991). Stable unhappy marriages. *JMarFam*, *53*, 747–758.

Heaton, T.B. & Pratt, E.L. (1990). The effects of religious homogamy on marital satisfaction and stability. *Journal of Family Issues*, *11*, 191–207.

Heavey, C.L., Layne, C., & Christensen, A. (1993). Gender and conflict structure in marital interaction: a replication and extension. *JCCP*, *61*, 16–27.

Hebb, D.O. (1949). *The organization of behavior*. New York: Wiley.

Hecht, M.L., Marston, P.J., & Larkey, L.K.

(1994). Love ways and relationship quality in heterosexual relationships. *JSPR*, *11*, 25–43.

Heider, F. (1958). *The psychology of interpersonal relations*. New York: Wiley.

Helgeson, V., Shaver, P., & Dyer, M. (1987). Prototypes of intimacy and distance in same-sex and opposite sex relationships. *JSPR*, *4*, 195–223.

Henderson, S. (1974). Care-eliciting behavior in man. *Journal of Nervous and Mental Diseases*, *159*, 172–181.

Henderson-King, D.H. & Veroff, J. (1994). Sexual satisfaction and marital well-being in the first years of marriage. *JSPR*, *11*, 509–534.

Hendrick, C. (Ed.) (1989). *Close relationships*. Newbury Park, CA: Sage.

Hendrick, C. & Brown, S. (1971). Introversion, extroversion and interpersonal attraction. *JPSP*, *20*, 31–36.

Hendrick, C. & Hendrick, S.S. (1986). A theory and method of love. *JPSP*, *50*, 392–402.

Hendrick, C. & Hendrick, S.S. (1989). Research on love: does it measure up? *JPSP*, *56*, 784–794.

Hendrick, C. & Hendrick, S.S. (1990). A relationship-specific version of the Love Attitudes scale. *Journal of Social Behaviour and Personality*, *5*, 239–254.

Hendrick, C., Hendrick S.S., & Adler, N.L. (1988). Romantic relationships: love, satisfaction and staying together. *JPSP*, *54*, 980–988.

Hendrick, C., Hendrick, S., Foote, F.H., & Slapion-Foote, M.J. (1984). Do men and women love differently?, *JSPR*, *1*, 177–195.

Hendrick, S.S. (1981). Self-disclosure and marital satisfaction. *JPSP*, *40*, 1150–1159.

Hendrick, S.S. & Hendrick, C. (1993). Lovers as friends. *JSPR*, *10*, 459–469.

Henley, N.M. (1977). *Body politics: power, sex, and non-verbal communication*. Englewood Cliffs, NJ: Prentice-Hall.

Hetherington, E.M. (1988). Parents, children, and siblings: six years after divorce. In Hinde & Stevenson-Hinde (1988), pp.311–331.

Hetherington, E.M., Cox, M., & Cox, R. (1982). Effects of divorce on parents and children. In M.E. Lamb (Ed.), *Non-traditional families: parenting and child development*, pp.233–288. Hillsdale, NJ: Lawrence Erlbaum Associates Inc.

Hewstone, M. & Antaki, C. (1988). Attribution theory and social explanations. In M. Hewstone et al. (Eds.), *Introduction to social psychology*, pp.111–141. Oxford: Blackwell.

Hicks, M.W. & Platt, M. (1970). Marital happiness and stability: a review of research in the sixties. *JMarFam*, *32*, 553–574.

Higgins, E.T., Loeb, I. & Moretti, M. (1995). Self-discrepancies and developmental shifts in vulnerability: life transitions in the regulatory significance of others. In Cicchetti & Toth (1995), pp.191–230.

Hilkevitch, R. (1960). Social interactional processes. *Psychological Reports*, *7*, 195–201.

Hill, C.A. (1991). Seeking emotional support: the influence of affiliative need and partner warmth. *JPSP*, *60*, 112–121.

Hill, C.T., Rubin, Z., & Peplau, L.A. (1976). Break-ups before marriage: the end of 103 affairs. *Journal of Social Issues*, *32*, 147–167.

Hill, M.S. (1988). Marital stability and spouses' shared time. *Journal of Family Issues*, *9*, 427–451.

Hill, T., Lewicki, P., Csyzewska, M., & Boss, A. (1989). Self-perpetuating development of encoding biases in person perception. *JPSP*, *57*, 373–387.

Hinchliffe, M.K., Vaughan, P.W., Hooper, D., & Roberts, F.J. (1977). The melancholy marriage: an enquiry into the interaction of depression. II Expressiveness. *British Journal of Medical Psychology*, *50*, 125–142.

Hinde, R.A. (Ed.) (1972). *Non-verbal communication*. Cambridge: Cambridge University Press.

Hinde, R.A. (1975). Interactions, relationships and social structure in non-human primates. *Symposium of the 5th Congress of the International Primatological Society*, pp.13–24. Japan Science Press.

Hinde, R.A. (1978a). Dominance and role—two concepts with dual meanings. *Journal of Social and Biological Structures*, *1*, 27–38.

Hinde, R.A. (1978b). Interpersonal relationships—in quest of a science. *Psychological Medicine*, *8*, 373–386.

Hinde, R.A. (1978c). Field Workers Questionnaire. *Laboratory Primates Newsletter and Supplement to Primate Eye No. 11.*

Hinde, R.A. (1979). *Towards understanding relationships*. London: Academic Press.

Hinde, R.A. (1985). Was "The Expression of the Emotions" a misleading phrase? *Animal Behavior*, *33*, 985–992.

Hinde, R.A. (1987). *Individuals, relationships and culture*. Cambridge: Cambridge University Press.

Hinde, R.A. (1989). Reconciling the family systems and the relationships approaches to child development. In K. Kreppner & R.M. Lerner (Eds.), *Family systems and life-span development*, pp.149–163. Hillsdale, NJ: Lawrence Erlbaum Associates Inc.

Hinde, R.A. (1991). A biologist looks at anthropology. *Man*, *26*, 583–608.

Hinde, R.A. & Dennis, A. (1986). Categorizing individuals: an alternative to linear analysis. *International Journal of Behavioural Development*, *9*, 105–119.

Hinde, R.A. & Groebel, J. (Eds.) (1991). *Co-operation and prosocial behaviour*. Cambridge: Cambridge University Press.

Hinde, R.A. & Herrmann, J. (1975). Frequencies, durations, derived measures and their correlations in studying dyadic and triadic relationships. In H.R. Schaffer (Ed.), *Studies in mother–infant interaction*, pp.19–46. London: Academic Press.

Hinde, R.A. & McGinnis, L. (1977). Some factors influencing the effects of temporary mother–infant separation—some experiments with rhesus monkeys. *Psychological Medicine*, *7*, 197–222.

Hinde, R.A. & Stevenson-Hinde, J. (Eds.) (1973). *Constraints on learning: limitations and predispositions*. London: Academic Press.

Hinde, R.A. & Stevenson-Hinde, J. (1976). Towards understanding relationships. In Bateson & Hinde (1976).

Hinde, R.A. & Stevenson-Hinde, J. (1987). Interpersonal relationships and child development. *Developmental Review*, *7*, 1–21.

Hinde, R.A. & Stevenson-Hinde, J. (Eds.) (1988). *Relationships within families: mutual influences*. Oxford: Clarendon.

Hinde, R.A., Tamplin, A., & Barrett, J. (1993a). Home correlates of aggression in pre-school. *Aggressive Behaviour*, *19*, 85–105.

Hinde, R.A., Tamplin, A., & Barrett, J. (1993b). A comparative study of relationship structure. *British Journal of Social Psychology*, *32*, 191–207.

Hinde, R.A., Tamplin, A., & Barrett, J. (1995). Consistency within and between relationships. *Czlowiek i Spoleczenstwo*, *12*, 7–18.

Hinde, R.A. & Watson, H. (Eds.) (1995). *War: a cruel necessity?* London: I.B. Tauris.

Hinsz, V.B. (1989). Facial resemblance in engaged and married couples. *JSPR*, *6*, 223–229.

Hodgins, H.S., Koestner, R., & Duncan, N. (1996). On the compatibility of autonomy and relatedness. *Personality and Social Psychology Bulletin*, *22*, 227–237.

Hoffman, M.L. (1975). Developmental synthesis of affect and cognition and its implications for altruistic motivation. *Developmental Psychology, 11*, 607–622.

Hofstee, W.K.B., de Raad, B., & Goldberg, L.R. (1992). Integration of the big five and the circumplex approaches to trait structure. *JPSP, 63*, 146–163.

Holman, T.B. and Jacquart, M. (1988). Leisure-activity patterns and marital satisfaction: a further test. *JMarFam, 50*, 69–77.

Holmberg, D. & Veroff, J. (1996). Rewriting relationship memories: the effects of courtship and wedding scripts. In Fletcher & Fitness, 1996, pp.345–368.

Holmes, J.G. (1981). The exchange process in close relationships: microbehavior and macromotives. In M.J. Lerner & S.C. Lerner (Eds.), *The justice motive in social behavior*, pp.261–284. New York: Plenum.

Holmes, J.G. (1991). Trust and the appraisal process in close relationships. In W.H. Jones & D. Perlman (Eds.), *Advances in Personal Relationships, 2*, 57–104.

Holmes, J.G. & Miller, D.T. (1976). Interpersonal conflict. In J.W. Thibaut, J.T. Spence, & R.C. Carson (Eds.), *Contemporary topics in social psychology*. Morristown, NJ: General Learning Press.

Holmes, J.G. & Rempel, J.K. (1989). Trust in close relationships. In Hendrick (1989), pp.187–220.

Holtgraves, T. & Yang, J-N. (1990). Politeness as universal: cross-cultural perceptions of request strategies and influences based on their use. *JPSP, 59*, 719–729.

Holtgraves, T. & Yang, J-N. (1992). Interpersonal underpinnings of request strategies: general principles and differences due to culture and gender. *JPSP, 62*, 246–256.

Homans, G.C. (1961, 1974). *Social behaviour: its elementary forms*. London: Routledge & Kegan Paul/New York: Harcourt, Brace Jovanovich.

Homans, G.C. (1974). *Social behavior: its elementary forms* (Revised edn). New York: Harcourt, Brace Jovanovich.

Homans, G.C. (1976). Commentary. *AdvExpSP*, pp.231–244.

Honeycutt, J.M. (1993). Memory structures for the rise and fall of personal relationships. In Duck (1993b), pp.60–86.

Honeycutt, J.M., Cantrill, J.G., & Allen, T. (1992). Memory structures for relational decay. *HCR, 18*, 528–562.

Honeycutt, J.M., Cantrill, J.G., & Greene, R.W. (1989). Memory structures for relational escalation: a cognitive test of the sequencing of relational actions and stages. *HCR, 16*, 62–90.

Honeycutt, J.M., Woods, B.L., & Fontenot, K. (1993). The endorsement of communication conflict rules as a function of engagement, marriage and marital ideology. *JSPR, 10*, 285–304.

Hooley, J.M. & Richters, J.E. (1995) Expressed emotion: a developmental perspective. In Cicchetti & Toth (1995), pp.133–166.

Hooley, J.M. & Teasdale, J.D. (1989). Predictors of relapse in unipolar depressives. *Journal of Abnormal Psychology, 98*, 229–235.

Hopper, J. (1993). The rhetoric of motives in divorce. *JMarFam, 55*, 801–813.

Hopper, R., Knapp, M.L., & Scott, L. (1981). Couples' personal idioms: exploring intimate talk. *Journal of Communication, 31*, 23–33.

Hornstein, G.A. (1985). Intimacy in conversational style as a function of the degree of closeness between members of a dyad. *JPSP, 49*, 671–681.

Horowitz, L.M., Locke, K.D., Morse, M.B., Waikar, S.V., Dryer, D.C., Tarnow, E., & Ghannan, J. (1991). Self-derogations and the interpersonal theory. *JPSP, 61*, 68–79.

Howard, J.A., Blumstein, P., & Schwartz, P. (1986). Sex, power, and influence tactics in intimate relationships. *JPSP, 51*, 102–109.

Howe, G.W. (1987). Attributions of complex cause and perception of marital conflict. *JPSP, 53*, 1119–1128.

Hsee, C.K., Hatfield, E., & Carlson, J.G. (1990). The effect of power on susceptibility to emotional contagion. *Cognition and Emotion, 4*, 327–340.

Humphrey, N.K. (1976). *The social function of intellect*. In Bateson & Hinde (1976), pp.303–318.

Humphrey, N.K. (1992). *A history of the mind*. London: Chatto & Windus.

Huston, T.L. (1973). Ambiguity of acceptance, social desirability and dating choice. *JESP, 9*, 32–42.

Huston, T.L. (Ed.) (1974). *Foundations of interpersonal attraction*. New York: Academic Press.

Huston, T.L. & Chorost, A.F. (1994). Behavioral buffers on the effect of negativity on marital satisfaction: a longitudinal study. *PR, 1*, 223–239.

Huston, T.L. & Levinger, G. (1978). Interpersonal attraction and relationships. *Annual Review of Psychology, 29*, 115–156.

Huston, T.L. & Vangelisti, A.L. (1991). Socioemotional behavior and satisfaction in marital relationships: a longitudinal study. *JPSP, 61*, 721–733.

Hutter, M. (1974). Significant others and

married student role attitudes. *J MarFam*, *36*, 31–36.

Ichheiser, G. (1970). *Appearances and realities*. San Francisco: Jossey-Bass.

Ickes, W. (1985). Sex-role influences on compatibility in relationships. In W. Ickes (Ed.), *Compatible and incompatible relationships*, pp.187–208. New York: Springer-Verlag.

Ingraham, L.J. & Wright, T.L. (1987). A social relations model test of Sullivan's anxiety hypothesis. *JPSP, 52*, 1212–1218.

Insko, C.A., Songer, E., & McGarvey, W. (1974). Balance, positivity and agreement in the Jordan paradigm: a defense of balance theory. *JESP, 10*, 53–83.

Isabella, R.A. (1993). Origins of attachment: maternal interactive behavior across the first year. *Child Development, 64*, 605–621.

Izard, C.E. (1960). Personality similarity and friendship. *Journal of Abnormal and Social Psychology, 61*, 47–51.

Jacobs, J.E. & Eccles, J.S. (1992). The impact of mother's gender-role stereotypic beliefs on mothers' and children's ability perceptions. *JPSP, 63*, 932–944.

Jacobson, N.J., Folletti, W.C., & McDonald, D. (1982). Reactivity to positive and negative behavior in distressed and nondistressed married couples. *JCCP, 50*, 706–714.

Jacobson, N.S. (1989). The politics of intimacy. *Behaviour Therapist, 12*, 29–32.

Jahoda, G. (1954). A note on Ashanti names and their relationship to personality. *British Journal of Psychology, 45*, 192–195.

Jamieson, D.W., Lydon, J.E., & Zanna, M.P. (1987). Attitude and activity preference similarity: differential bases of interpersonal attraction for low and high self-monitors. *JPSP, 53*, 1052–1060.

Jankowiak, W.R. & Fischer, E.F. (1992). A cross-cultural perspective on romantic love. *Ethnology, 31*, 149–155.

Jeffries, V. (1993). Virtue and attraction: validation of a measure of love. *JSPR, 10*, 99–117.

Jensen, A.R. (1978). Genetic and behavioral effects of non-random mating. In C.E. Noble, R.T. Osborne, & N. Weyle (Eds.), *Human variation*, pp.51–105. San Diego, CA: Academic Press.

Jensen-Campbell, L.A., Graziano, W.G., & West, S.G. (1995). Dominance, pro-social orientation and female preferences. *JPSP, 68*, 427–40.

John, O.P. (1990). The 'Big Five' factor taxonomy: dimensions of personality in the natural language and in questionnaires. In L.A. Pervin, (Ed.), *Handbook of personality*, pp.66–100. New York: Guilford.

Johnson, D.J. & Rusbult, C.E. (1989). Resisting temptation: devaluation of alternative partners as a means of maintaining commitment in close relationships. *JPSP, 57*, 967–980.

Johnson, D.R., White, L.K., Edwards, J.N., & Booth, A. (1986). Dimensions of marital quality. *Journal of Family Issues, 7*, 31–49.

Johnson, D.W. & Johnson, S. (1972). The effects of attitude similarity, expectation of goal facilitation and actual goal facilitation on interpersonal attraction. *JESP, 8*, 197–206.

Johnson, M.P. (1982). Social and cognitive features of the dissolution of commitment to relationships. In Duck (1982a), pp.51–74.

Johnson, M.P. (1991). Commitment in personal relationships. In W.H. Jones & D.W. Perlman (Eds.), *Advances in personal relationships, 3*, 117–143. London: Jessica Kingsley.

Johnson, M.P., Huston, T.L., Gaines, S.O. & Levinger, G. (1992). Patterns of married life among young couples. *JSPR, 9*, 343–364.

Johnson-George, C. & Swap, W. (1982). Measurement of specific interpersonal trust: construction and validation of a scale to assess trust in a specific order. *JPSP, 43*, 1306–1317.

Jones, D.C. (1991). Friendship satisfaction and gender: an examination of sex differences in contributors to friendship satisfaction. *JSPR, 8*, 167–186.

Jones, D.C., Bloys, N., & Wood, M. (1990). Sex roles and friendship patterns. *Sex Roles, 23*, 133–145.

Jones, E.E. & Archer, R.L. (1976). Are there special effects of personalistic self disclosure? *JESP, 12*, 180–193.

Jones, W.H. (1991). Personality and relationships. In V.J. Derlega, B.A. Winstead, & W.H. Jones (Eds.), *Personality: contemporary theory and research*, pp.510–535. Chicago: Nelson Hall.

Jones, W.H., Cavert, C.W., Snider, R.C., & Bruce, T. (1985). Relational stress: an analysis of situations and events associated with loneliness. In Duck & Perlman (1985), pp.221–242.

Jourard, S.M. (1971). *Self-disclosure*. New York: Wiley.

Jourard, S.M. & Friedman, R. (1970). Experimenter–subject "distance" and self-disclosure. *JPSP, 15*, 278–282.

Jussim, L. (1986). Self-fulfilling prophecies: a theoretical and integrative review. *PsychRev, 93*, 429–45.

Jussim, L. (1989). Teacher expectations: self-fulfilling prophecies, perceptual biases and accuracy. *JPSP*, *57*, 469–480.

Kagan, J. (1994). *Galen's prophecy: temperament in human nature*. New York: Basic Books.

Kahn, J., Coyne, J.C., & Margolin, G. (1985). Depression and marital disagreement: the social construction of despair. *JSPR*, *2*, 447–461.

Kahn, M. (1970). Nonverbal communication and marital satisfaction. *Family Process*, *9*, 449–456.

Kalick, S.M. & Hamilton, T.E. (1986). The matching hypothesis re-examined. *JPSP*, *51*, 673–682.

Kamo, Y. (1993). Determinants of marital satisfaction: a comparison of the United States and Japan. *JSPR*, *10*, 551–568.

Kandel, D.B. (1978). Similarity in real-life adolescent friendship pairs. *JPSP*, *36*, 306–312.

Karney, B.R. & Bradbury, T.N. (1995a). Assessing longitudinal change in marriage: an introduction to the analysis of growth curves. *JMarFam*, *57*, 1091–1108.

Karney, B.R. & Bradbury, T.N. (1995b). The longitudinal course of marital quality and stability: a review of theory, method and research. *PsychBull*, *118*, 3–34.

Karney, B.R., Bradbury, T.N., Fincham, F.D., & Sullivan, K.T. (1994). The role of negative affectivity in the association between attributions and marital satisfaction. *JPSP*, *66*, 413–424.

Katz, L.F. & Gottman, J.M. (1995). Marital interaction and child outcomes: a longitudinal study of mediating and moderating processes. In Cicchetti & Toth (1995), pp.501–542.

Keeley, M.P. & Hart, A.J. (1994) Nonverbal behavior in dyadic interactions. In Duck (1994a), pp.135–162.

Kellermann, K. (1991). The conversation MOP II. Progression through scenes in discourse. *HCR*, *17*, 385–414.

Kellermann, K., Broetzmann, S., Lim, T-S., & Kitao, K. (1989). The conversation MOP: scenes in the stream of discourse. *Discourse Processes*, *12*, 27–61.

Kelley, D.L. & Burgoon, J.K. (1991). Understanding marital satisfaction and couple type as functions of relational expectations. *HCR*, *18*, 40–69.

Kelley, H.H. (1971). *Attribution in social interaction*. Morristown, NJ: General Learning Press.

Kelley, H.H. (1972). Causal schemata in the attribution process. In E.E. Jones et al. (Eds.), *Attribution:perceiving the causes of behavior*. Morristown, NJ: General Learning Press.

Kelley, H.H. (1979). *Personal relationships*. Hillsdale, NJ: Lawrence Erlbaum Associates Inc.

Kelley, H.H. (1983). The concepts of love and commitment. In Kelley et al. (1983), pp.266–270.

Kelley, H.H., Berscheid, E., Christensen, A., Harvey, J.H., Huston, T.L., Levinger, G., McClintock, E., Peplau, L.A., & Peterson, D.R. (Eds.) (1983), *Close relationships*. New York: Freeman.

Kelley, H.H. & Stahelski, A.J. (1970a). Social interaction: basis of cooperators' and competitors' beliefs about others. *JPSP*, *16*, 66–91.

Kelley, H.H. & Stahelski, A.J. (1970b). Errors in perception of intentions in a mixed motive game. *JESP*, *6*, 379–400.

Kelley, H.H. & Stahelski, A.J. (1970c). The inference of intentions from moves in the Prisoner's Dilemma game. *JESP*, *6*, 401–419.

Kelley, H.H. & Thibaut, J.W. (1978). *Interpersonal relations*. New York: Wiley.

Kelley, K. & Rolker-Dolinsky, B. (1987). The psychosexology of female initiation and dominance. In Perlman & Duck (1987), pp.63–87.

Kelly, C., Huston, T.L., & Cate, R.M. (1985). Premarital relationship correlates of the erosion of satisfaction in marriage. *JSPR*, *2*, 167–178.

Kelly, E.L. (1955). Consistency of the adult personality. *American Psychologist*, *10*, 659–681.

Kelly, E.L. & Conley, J.J. (1987). Personality and compatibility: a prospective analysis of marital stability and marital satisfaction. *JPSP*, *52*, 27–40.

Kelly, G.A. (1955). *The psychology of personal constructs*. New York: Norton.

Kelvin, P. (1970). *The bases of social behaviour: an approach in terms of order and value*. London: Holt Rinehart & Winston.

Kelvin, P. (1977). Predictability, power and vulnerability in interpersonal attraction. In Duck (1977a), pp.355–378.

Kendon, A. (1967). Some functions of gaze direction in social interaction. *Acta Psychologica*, *26*, 22–63.

Kendon, A. & Ferber, A. (1973). A description of some human greetings. In R. Michael & J.H. Crook (Eds.), *Comparative ecology and behaviour in primates*. London: Academic Press.

Kenny, D.A., Horner, C., Kashy, D.A., & Chu, L-C. (1992). Consensus at zero acquaintance: replication, behavioral cues and stability. *JPSP*, *62*, 88–97.

Kenny, D.A. & Kashy, D.A. (1994). Enhanced co-orientation in the perception of friends: a social relations analysis. *JPSP*, *67*, 1024–1033.

Kenny, D.A. & La Voie, L. (1984). The social relations model. (Ed.), *AdvExpSP*, *18*, 142–183.

Kenrick, D.T., Groth, G.E., Trost, M.R., & Sadalla, E.K. (1993). Integrating evolutionary and social exchange perspectives on relationships: effects of gender, self-appraisal and involvement level on mate selection criteria. *JPSP*, *64*, 951–969.

Kerckhoff, A.C. (1974). The social context of interpersonal attraction. In Huston (1974), pp.61–78.

Kerckhoff, A.C. & Davis, K.E. (1962). Value consensus and need complementarity in mate selection. *American Sociological Review*, *27*, 295–303.

Kiesler, D.J. (1983). The 1982 interpersonal circle: a taxonomy for complementarity in human transactions. *PsychRev*, *90*, 187–214.

Kiesler, S.B. & Baral, R.L. (1970). The search for a romantic partner: the effects of self esteem and physical attractiveness on romantic behavior. In K. Gergen & D. Marlow (Eds.), *Personality and social behavior*. Reading, MA: Addison-Wesley.

Kihlstrom, J.F., Cantor, N., Albright, J.S., Chew, B.R., Klein, S.B., & Niedenthal, P.M. (1988). Information processing and the study of the self. In L. Berkowitz (Ed.), *AdvExpSP*, *21*, 145–180. San Diego, CA: Academic Press.

Kim, H.J. & Stiff, J.B. (1991). Social networks and the development of close relationships. *HCR*, *18*, 70–91.

King, L.A. (1993). Emotional expression, ambivalence over expression and marital satisfaction. *JSPR*, *10*, 601–617.

Kinget, G.M. (1979). The "Many-splendoured thing" in transition or "The Agony and the Ecstacy" revisited. In Cook & Wilson (1979), pp.251–255.

Kirchler, E. (1988). Marital happiness and interaction in everyday surroundings: a time-sample diary approach for couples. *JSPR*, *5*, 375–378.

Kirkpatrick, L.A. & Davis, K.E. (1994). Attachment style, gender, and relationship stability: a longitudinal analysis. *JPSP*, *66*, 502–512.

Kirkpatrick, L.A. & Hazan, C. (1994). Attachment styles and close relationships: a four year prospective study. *PR*, *1*, 123–142.

Kitson, G.C., Babri, K.B., & Roach, M.J. (1985). Who divorces and why. *Journal of Family Issues*, *6*, 255–293.

Klein, R. & Milardo, R.M. (1993). Third party influence on the management of personal relationships. In Duck (1993c), pp.55–77.

Klein, S.B., Loftus, J., Trafton, J.G., & Fuhrman, R.W. (1992). Use of examples and abstractions in trait judgements: a model of trait knowledge about the self and others. *JPSP*, *63*, 739–753.

Kleinke, C.L. & Kahn, M.L. (1980). Perceptions of self-disclosers: effects of sex and physical attractiveness. *JP*, *48*, 190–205.

Kling, J.W., & Schrier, A.M. (1971). Positive reinforcement. In J.W. Kling & L.A. Riggs (Eds.), *Experimental psychology*. New York: Holt, Rinehart & Winston.

Kobak, R.R. & Hazan, C. (1991). Attachment in marriage: effects of security and accuracy of working models. *JPSP*, *60*, 861–869.

Kobak, R.R. & Sceery, A. (1988). The transition to college. *Child Development*, *88*, 135–146.

Kolvin, I., Ounsted, C., Richardson, L.M., & Garside, R.F. (1971). The family and social background in childhood psychoses. *British Journal of Psychiatry*, *118*, 396–402.

Komarovsky, M. (1946). Cultural contradictions and sex roles. *American Journal of Sociology*, *52*, 186–188.

Krahe, B. (1990). *Situation, cognition and coherence in personality*. Cambridge: Cambridge University Press.

Kramer, L. & Baron, L.A. (1995). Intergenerational linkages: how experiences with siblings relate to the parenting of siblings. *JSPR*, *12*, 67–87.

Kreitman, N., Collins, J., Nelson, B., & Troop, J. (1970/1971). Neurosis and marital interaction. *British Journal of Psychiatry*, *117*, 33–46 & *119*, 243–252.

Krokoff, L.J. (1987). The correlates of negative affect in marriage. *Journal of Family Issues*, *8*, 111–135.

Krokoff, L.J. (1991). Job distress no laughing matter in marriage, or is it? *JSPR*, *8*, 5–25.

Krokoff, L.J., Gottman, J.M., & Roy, A.K. (1988). Blue-collar and white-collar marital interaction and communication orientation. *JSPR*, *5*, 201–221.

Kurdek, L.A. (1989). Relationship quality in gay and lesbian cohabiting couples: a 1-year follow-up study. *JSPR*, *6*, 39–59.

Kurdek, L.A. (1990). Spouse attributes and spousal interactions as dimensions of relationship quality in first-marriage and remarried newlywed men and women. *Journal of Family Issues, 11,* 91–100.

Kurdek, L.A. (1991a). Correlates of relationship satisfaction in cohabiting gay and lesbian couples: integration of contextual, investment, and problem-solving models. *JPSP, 61,* 910–922.

Kurdek, L.A. (1991b). Marital stability and changes in marital quality in newlywed couples: a test of the contextual model. *JSPR, 8,* 27–48.

Kurdek, L.A. (1992). Relationship stability and relationship satisfaction in cohabiting gay and lesbian couples: a prospective longitudinal test of the contextual and interdependence models. *JSPR, 9,* 125–142.

Kurdek, L.A. (1993). Predicting marital dissolution: a 5 year prospective longitudinal study of newlywed couples. *JPSP, 64,* 221–242.

Kurdek, L.A. (1994). Areas of conflict for gay, lesbian and heterosexual couples: what couples argue about influences relationship satisfaction. *JMarFam, 56,* 923–934.

Kurdek, L.A. (1995). Predicting change in marital satisfaction from husbands' and wives' conflict resolution styles. *JMarFam, 57,* 153–164.

Kurdek, L.A. & Schmitt, J.P. (1986a). Interaction of sex role self-concept with relationship quality and relationship beliefs in married, heterosexual cohabiting, gay and lesbian couples. *JPSP, 51,* 365–370.

Kurdek, L.A. & Schmitt, J.P. (1986b). Relationship quality of partners in heterosexual married, heterosexual cohabiting, and gay and lesbian relationships. *JPSP, 51,* 711–720.

Ladd, G.W. & Emerson, E.S. (1984). Shared knowledge in children's friendships. *Developmental Psychology, 20,* 932–940.

La Follette, H. & Graham, G. (1986). Honesty and intimacy. *JSPR, 3,* 3–18.

La Gaipa, J.J. (1977). Interpersonal attraction and social exchange. In Duck (1977a), pp.249–270.

La Gaipa, J.J. (1982). Rules and rituals in disengaging from relationships. In Duck (1982), pp.189–210.

Laing, R.D. (1969). *The divided self.* New York: Pantheon Books.

Laing, R.D., Phillipson, H., & Lee, A.R. (1966). *Interpersonal perception.* London: Tavistock.

Lamb, M.E. (Ed.) (1976). *Role of the father in child development.* New York: Wiley.

Lamke, L. (1989). Marital adjustment among rural couples: the role of expressiveness. *Sex Roles, 21,* 579–590.

Lamke, L.K., Solli, D.L., Durbin, R.G., & Fitzpatrick, J.A. (1994). Masculinity, femininity and relationship satisfaction: the mediating role of interpersonal competence. *JSPR, 11,* 535–554.

Landau, R. & Gewirtz, J.L. (1967). Differential satiation for a social reinforcing stimulus as a determinant of its efficacy in conditioning. *Journal of Experimental Child Psychology, 5,* 391–405.

Laner, M.R. (1989). Competitive vs. noncompetitive styles: which is most valued in courtship. *Sex Roles, 20,* 165–172.

Lang-Takac, E. & Osterweil, Z. (1992). Separateness and connectedness: differences between the genders. *Sex Roles, 27,* 277–289.

LaRossa, R. (1995). Stories and relationships, *JSPR, 12,* 553–558.

Larsen, K.S. (1971). An investigation of sexual behavior among Norwegian college students: a motivational study. *JMarFam, 33,* 219–227.

Larzelere, R.E. & Huston, T.L. (1980). The dyadic trust scale: toward understanding interpersonal trust in close relationships. *JMarFam, 42,* 595–604.

Latty-Mann, H. & Davis, K.E. (1996). Attachment theory and partner choice: preference and actuality. *JSPR, 13,* 5–23.

Lauer, R.H. & Lauer, J.C., (1986). Factors in long term marriages. *Journal of Family Issues, 7,* 382–390.

Lavin, T.J. (1987). Divergence and convergence in the causal attributions of married couples. *JMarFam, 49,* 71–80.

LaVine, L.O. & Lombardo, J.P. (1984). Self-disclosure: intimate and non-intimate disclosures to parents and best friends as a function of Bem sex-role category. *Sex Roles, 11,* 735–744.

Lawrence, K. & Byers, E.S. (1995). Sexual satisfaction in long-term heterosexual relationships: the interpersonal exchange model of sexual satisfaction. *PR, 2,* 267–285.

Layton, B.D. & Insko, C.A. (1974). Anticipated interaction and the similarity attraction effect. *Sociometry, 37,* 149–162.

Lea, M. (1989). Factors underlying friendship, an analysis of responses on the acquaintance description form in relation to Wright's friendship model. *JSPR, 6,* 275–292.

Leaper C. & Holliday, H. (1995). Gossip in same-gender and cross-gender friendships. *PR, 2,* 237–246.

Leary, M.R., Rogers, P.A., Canfield, R.W., &

Coe, C. (1986). Boredom in interpersonal encounters. *JPSP*, *51*, 968–975.

Leary, T. (1957). *Interpersonal diagnosis of personality*. New York: Ronald.

Lee, G.R. (1988). Marital satisfaction in later life: the effects of non-marital roles. *JMarFam*, *50*, 775–783.

Lee, J.A. (1973). *The colors of love: an explanation of the ways of loving*. Don Mills, Ontario: New Press.

Lefcourt, H.M., Martin, R.A., Fick, C.M., & Saleh, W.H. (1985). Locus of control for affiliation and behavior in social interactions. *JPSP*, *48*, 755–759.

Lefcourt, H.M., Martin, R.A., & Saleh, W.E. (1984). Locus of control and social support. *JPSP*, *47*, 378–389.

Lehman, D.R. & Hemphill, K.J. (1990). Recipients' perceptions of support attempts and attributions for support attempts that fail. *JSPR*, *7*, 563–574.

Lepore, S.J. (1992). Social conflict, social support and psychological distress: evidence of cross-domain buffering effects. *JPSP*. *63*, 857–867.

Lerner, M. (1974). Social psychology of justice and interpersonal attraction. In Huston (1974), pp.331–355.

Lerner, M.J. (1981). The justice motive in human relations. In M.B. Lerner & S.C. Lerner (Eds.), *The justice motive in social behaviour*. New York: Plenum.

Lerner, M.J., Miller, D.R., & Holmes, J.G. (1976). Deserving and the emergence of forms of justice. *AdvExpSP*, *9*, 133–162.

Leslie, L.A. (1989). Stress in the dual-income couple: do social relationships help or hinder? *JSPR*, *6*, 451–461.

Leslie, L.A., Huston, T.L., & Johnson, M.P. (1986). Parental reactions to dating relationships: do they make a difference? *JMarFam*, *48*, 57–66.

Levenson, R.W., Carstensen, L.L., & Gottman, J.M. (1994). The influence of age and gender on affect, physiology and their interrelations: a study of long-term marriages. *JPSP*, *67*, 56–68.

Levenson, R.W. & Gottman, J.M. (1978). Toward the assessment of social competence. *JCCP*, *46*, 453–462.

Levenson, R.W. & Gottman, J.M. (1983). Marital interaction: physiological linkage and affective exchange. *JPSP*, *45*, 587–597.

Levenson, R.W. & Gottman, J.M. (1985). Six physiological and affective predictors of change in relationship satisfaction. *JPSP*, *49*, 85–94.

Leventhal, G.S. & Lane, D. (1970). Sex, age and equity behavior. *JPSP*, *15*, 312–316.

Levine, T.R. & McCornack, S.A. (1992). Linking love and lies: a formal test of the McCornack and Parks model of deception detection. *JSPR*, *9*, 143–154.

Levinger, G. (1964). Note on need complementarity in marriage. *PsychBull*, *61*, 153–157.

Levinger, G. (1966). Systematic distortion in spouses' reports of preferred and actual social behavior. *Sociometry*, *29*, 291–299.

Levinger, G. & Breedlove, J. (1966). Interpersonal attraction and agreement: a study of marriage partners. *JPSP*, *3*, 367–372.

Levinger, G. & Snoek, J.D. (1972). *Attraction in relationships*. Morristown, NJ: General Learning Press.

Levitz-Jones, E.M. & Orlofsky, J. (1985). Separation-individuation and intimacy capacity in college women. *JPSP*, *49*, 156–169.

Levy, M.B. & Davis, K.E. (1988). Love styles and attachment styles compared. *JSPR*, *5*, 439–471.

Lewis, M. & Brooks-Gunn, J. (1979). Toward a theory of social cognition: the development of the self. In I. Uzziris (Ed.), *New directions in child development*, pp.183–221. San Francisco: Jossey-Bass.

Lewis, R.A. (1975). Social influences on marital choice. In S.E. Dragastin & G.H. Elder (Eds.), *Adolescence and the life cycle*. New York: Wiley.

Lewis, R.A. (1978). Emotional intimacy among men. *Journal of Social Issues*, *34*, 108–121.

Lewis, R. & Spanier G. (1979). Theorizing about the quality & stability of marriage. In W. Burr et al. (Eds.), *Contemporary theories about the family I*. New York: Free Press.

Li, J.T. & Caldwell, R.A. (1987). Magnitude and directional effects of marital sex-role incongruence on marital adjustment. *Journal of Family Issues*, *8*, 97–110.

Liddell, C. & Lycett, J. (in press). Simon or Sipho: South African children's given names and their academic achievement in grade one. *Applied Psychology*.

Lin, Y-H.W. & Rusbult, C.E. (1995). Commitment to dating relationships and cross-sex friendships in America and China. *JSPR*, *12*, 7–26.

Linton, R. (1936). *The study of man: an introduction*. New York: Appleton-Century-Crofts.

Lloyd, S.A. & Cate, R.M. (1985a). The developmental course of conflict in dissolution of premarital relationships. *JSPR*, *2*, 179–194.

Lloyd, S.A. & Cate, R.M. (1985b). Attributions associated with significant turning points in premarital relationship development and dissolution. *JSPR, 2,* 419–436.

Lloyd, S.A., Cate, R.M., & Henton, J. (1982). Equity and rewards as predictors of satisfaction in casual and intimate relationships. *Journal of Psychology, 110,* 43–48.

Lloyd, S.A., Cate, R.M., & Henton, J.M. (1984). Predicting premarital relationship stability. *JMarFam, 46,* 71–76.

Lobel, T.A. (1994). Sex-typing and the social perception of gender stereotypic and nonstereotypic behavior: the uniqueness of feminine males. *JPSP, 66,* 379–385.

Lock, A. (1976). Acts instead of sentences. In W. von Rafflet-Engel & Y. Lebrum (Eds.), *Neurolinguistics, 5: baby talk and infant speech.* Amsterdam: Swets & Zeitlinger.

Locke, H.J. & Wallace, K.M. (1959). Short marital-adjustment and prediction tests. *Marriage and Family Living, 21,* 251–255.

Locke, K.D. & Horowitz, L.M. (1990). Satisfaction in interpersonal interactions as a function of similarity in levels of dysphoria. *JPSP, 58,* 823–831.

Loehlin, J.C., Willerman, L., & Horn, J.M. (1988). Human behavior genetics. *Annual Review of Psychology, 39,* 101–133.

Long, E.C.J. & Andrews, D.W. (1990). Perspective taking as a predictor of marital adjustment. *JPSP, 59,* 126–131.

Lorr, M. & McNair, D.M. (1963). An interpersonal behavior circle. *Journal of Abnormal and Social Psychology, 67,* 68–75.

Lott, A.J. & Lott, B.E. (1974). The role of reward in the formation of positive interpersonal attitudes. In Huston (1974), pp.171–192.

Lund, M. (1985). The development of investment and commitment scales for predicting continuity of personal relationships. *JSPR, 2,* 3–23.

Lydon, J.E. & Zanna, M.P. (1990). Commitment in the face of adversity: a value affirmation approach. *JPSP, 58,* 1040–1047.

Lyons, J. (1972). Human language. In Hinde (1972), pp.49–85.

Maccoby, E. (1990). Gender and relationships: a developmental account. *American Psychologist, 45,* 513–520.

MacCorquodale, K. & Meehl, P.E. (1954). Edward C. Tolman. In W.K. Estes et al. (Eds.), *Modern learning theory.* New York: Modern Learning Theory.

MacDermid, S., Huston, T.L., & McHale, S. (1990). Changes in marriage associated with the transition to parenthood: individual differences as a function of sex role attitudes and changes in the division of labor. *JMarFam, 52,* 475–486.

MacEwen, K. & Barling, J. (1993). Type A behavior and marital satisfaction: differential effects of achievement striving and impatience/irritability. *JMarFam, 55,* 1001–1010.

Magnusson, D. & Endler, N.S. (Eds.), (1977). *Personality at the crossroads: current issues in interactional psychology.* Hillsdale, NJ: Lawrence Erlbaum Associates Inc.

Magnusson, D. & Olah, A. (1981). *Situation–outcome contingencies.* Reports from the Department of Psychology, University of Stockholm, Sweden.

Main, M. & Cassidy, J. (1988). Categories of responses to reunion with the parent at age six. *Developmental Psychology, 24,* 415–426.

Main, M. & Solomon, J. (1990). Procedures for identifying infants as disorganised/disoriented during the Ainsworth Strange Situation. In M. Greenberg, D. Cicchetti, & E.M. Cummings (Eds.), *Attachment in the preschool years,* pp.121–160. Chicago: Chicago University Press.

Main, M. & Weston, D. (1982). Avoidance of the attachment figure in infancy: descriptions and interpretations. In C.M. Parkes & J. Stevenson-Hinde (Eds.), *The place of attachment in human behaviour,* pp.31–59. New York: Basic Books.

Major, B., Bylsma, W.H., & Cozzarelli, C. (1989). Gender differences in distributive justice preferences. *Sex Roles, 21,* 487–497.

Major, B., McFarlin, D.B., & Gagnon, D. (1984). Overworked and underpaid: on the nature of gender differences in personal entitlement. *JPSP, 47,* 1399–1412.

Malloy, T.E. & Albright, L. (1990). Interpersonal perception in a social context. *JPSP, 58,* 419–428.

Manusov, V. (1990). An application of attribution principles to non-verbal behavior in romantic dyads. *Communication Monographs, 57,* 104–118.

Margolin, G. & Wampold, B.E. (1981). Sequential analysis of conflict and accord in distressed and non-distressed marital partners. *JCCP, 49,* 554–567.

Margolin, L. (1989). Gender and the prerogatives of dating and marriage: an experimental assessment of a sample of college students. *Sex Roles, 20,* 91–102.

Margolin, L. & White, L. (1987). The continuing role of physical attractiveness in marriage. *JMarFam, 49,* 21–27.

Markman, H.J. (1981). Predicting marital

distress: a 5-year follow-up. *JCCP*, *49*, 760–762.

Markman, H.J., Renick, M.J., Floyd, E., Stanley S.M., & Clements, M. (1992). Preventing marital distress through communication and conflict management training. *JCCP*, *61*, 70–77.

Markus, H. & Nurius, P. (1986). Possible selves. *American Psychologist*, *41*. 951–964.

Markus, H., Smith, J., & Moreland, R.L. (1985). Role of the self-concept in the perception of others. *JPSP*, *49*, 1494–1512.

Markus, H.M. & Kitayama, S. (1991). Culture and the self: implications for cognition, emotion and motivation. *PsychRev*, *98*, 224–253.

Martin, L.M. & Seta, J.J. (1983). Perceptions of unity and distinctiveness as determinants of attraction. *JPSP*, *44*, 755–764.

Marwell, G. & Hage, J. (1969). Personality and social interaction. In G. Lindzey & E. Aronson (Eds.), *Handbook of social psychology*. Vol. 4. Reading, MA: Addison-Wesley.

Masciuch, S. & Kienapple, K. (1993). The emergence of jealousy in children 4 months to 7 years of age. *JSPR*, *10*, 421–435.

Masheter, C. (1991). Post divorce relationships between ex spouses: the roles of attachment and interpersonal conflict. *JMarFam*, *55*, 103–110.

Masheter, C. & Harris, L. (1986). From divorce to friendship: a study of dialectic relationship development. *JSPR*, *3*, 177–190.

Mason, A. & Blankenship, V. (1987). Power and affiliation motivation, stress, and abuse in intimate relationships. *JPSP*, *52*, 203–210.

Matarazzo, J.D., Wiens, A.N., Saslow, G., Dunham, R.M., & Voas, R.B. (1964). Speech duration of astronaut and ground communicator, *Science*, *143*, 148–150.

Mathes, E.W., Adams, H.E., & Davies, R.M. (1985). Jealousy: loss of relationship rewards, loss of self-esteem, depression, anxiety and anger. *JPSP*, *48*, 1552–1561.

Maugham, W. S. (1976). *Sanatorium*, pp.541–556. London: Heinemann (Octopus).

Maxwell, G.M. (1985). Behaviour of lovers: measuring the closeness of relationships. *JSPR*, *2*, 215–238.

Maynard, A.E., Greenfield, P.M., & Childs, C.P. (1996). *Culture, history and body: how Zinacantecan Maya learn to weave*. Fyssen Foundation Conference, 1996, Paris.

McAdams, D.P. (1985). Motivation and friendship. In Duck & Perlman (1985a), pp.85–105.

McAdams, D.P. (1988). Personal needs and personal relationships. In Duck (1988), pp.7–22.

McAdams, D.P. & Losoff, M. (1984). Friendship motivation in fourth and sixth graders: a thematic analysis. *JSPR*, *1*, 11–27.

McCall, G.J. (1970). The social organization of relationships. In G.J. McCall et al. (Eds.), *Social relationships*. Chicago: Aldine.

McCall, G.J. (1974). A symbolic interactionist approach to attraction. In Huston (1974).

McCall, G.J. (1982). Becoming unrelated: the management of bond dissolution. In Duck (1982a), pp.211–232.

McCall, G.J. & Simmons, J.L. (1966). *Identities and interactions*. New York: Free Press.

McCall, M. (1970). Boundary rules in relationships and encounters. In G.J. McCall et al. (Eds.), *Social relationships*. Chicago: Aldine.

McCarthy, B. & Duck, S.W. (1976). Friendship duration and responses to attitudinal agreement–disagreement. *British Journal of Social and Clinical Psychology*, *15*, 377–386.

McClelland, D.C., Koestner, R., & Weinberger, J. (1989). How do self-attributed and implicit motives differ? *PsychRev*, *96*, 690–702.

McCornack, S.A. & Parks, M.R. (1986). Deception detection and relationship development: the other side of trust. In M.L. McLaughlin (Ed.), *Communication yearbook, 9*. Newbury Park, CA: Sage.

McCornack, S.A. & Parks, M.R. (1990). What women know that men don't: sex differences in determining the truth behind deceptive messages. *JSPR*, *7*, 107–118.

McDermott, J. (1992). Friendship and its friends in the late Ming. In Institute of Modern History, Academia Sinica, and University of California Press (Eds.), *Family process and political process in modern Chinese history*, pp.67–96. Nankang, Taipei: Institute of Modern History, Academia Sinica.

McFarland, C. & Miller, D.T. (1990). Judgements of self-other similarity: just like other people only more so. *Personality and Social Psychology Bulletin*, *16*, 475–484.

McGonagle, K.A., Kessler, R.C., & Gotlib, I.H. (1993). The effects of marital disagreement style, frequency and outcome on marital disruption. *JSPR*, *10*, 385–404.

McGonagle, K.A., Kessler, R.C., & Schilling, A.E. (1992). The frequency and determinants of marital disagreements in a community sample. *JSPR*, *9*, 507–524.

McGuire, W.J. & McGuire, C.V. (1988). Content and process in the experience of self. In L. Berkowitz (Ed.), *AdvExpSP*, *21*, 97–144. San Diego, CA: Academic Press.

McNulty, S.C. & Swann, W.B. (1994). Identity negotiation in room-mate relationships: the self as architect and consequence of social reality. *JPSP*, *67*, 1012–1023.

Mead, G.H. (1934). *Mind, self and society*. Chicago: University of Chicago Press.

Mearns, P. (1991). Coping with a breakup: negative mood regulation expectancies and depression following the end of a romantic relationship. *JPSP*, *60*, 327–334.

Messé, L.A. & Watts, B.L. (1983). Complex nature of the sense of fairness: internal standards and social comparison as bases of reward expectations. *JPSP*, *45*, 84–93.

Mettee, D.R. & Aronson, E. (1974). Affective reactions to appraisal from others. In Huston (1974), pp.236–284.

Metts, S. (1989). An exploratory investigation of deception in close relationships. *JSPR*, *6*, 159–179.

Metts, S., Cupach, W.R., & Bejlovec, R.A. (1989). "I love you too much to ever start liking you": redefining romantic relationships. *JSPR*, *6*, 259–274.

Meyer, H-J. (1988). Marital and mother–child relationships. In Hinde & Stevenson-Hinde (1988), pp.119–142.

Meyer, J.P. & Pepper, S. (1977). Need compatability and marital adjustment in young married couples. *JPSP*, *35*, 331–342.

Michaels, J.W., Acock, A.C., & Edwards, J.N. (1986). Social exchange and equity determinants of relationship commitment. *JSPR*, *3*, 161–175.

Midwinter, D.Y. (1992). Rule prescriptions for initial male–female interaction. *Sex Roles*, *26*, 161–173.

Miell, D. & Duck, S. (1986). Strategies in developing friendships. In V.J. Derlega & V.A. Winstead (Eds.), *Friendship and social interaction*, pp.129–143. New York: Springer-Verlag.

Miell, D.E., Duck, S.W., & La Gaipa, J.J. (1979). Some interactive effects of sex and timing in self disclosure. *British Journal of Social and Clinical Psychology*, *18*, 355–362.

Milardo, R.M. (1987). Changes in social networks of women and men following divorce. *Journal of Family Issues*, *8*, 78–96.

Milardo, R.M. (1992). Comparative methods for delineating social networks. *JSPR*, *9*, 447–461.

Milardo, R.M., Johnson, M.P., & Huston,

T.L. (1984). Developing close relationships: changing patterns of interaction between pair members and social networks. *JPSP*, *44*, 964–976.

Miller, G.A., Galanter, E., & Pribram, K. (1960). *Plans and the structure of behavior*. New York: Holt, Rinehart & Winston.

Miller, G.R. & Boster, F. (1988). Persuasion in personal relationships. In Duck (1988), pp.275–288.

Miller, G.R. & Parks, M.R. (1982). Communication in dissolving relationships. In Duck (1982a) pp.127–154.

Miller, J.G. (1984). Culture and the development of everyday social explanation. *JPSP*, *46*, 961–978.

Miller, J.G. & Bersoff, D.M. (1995). Development in the context of everyday family relationships: culture, interpersonal morality and adaptation. In M. Killen & D. Hart (Eds.), *Morality in everyday life*. pp.259–282. Cambridge: Cambridge University Press.

Miller, J.G., Bersoff, D.M., & Harwood, R.L. (1990). Perceptions of social responsibilities in India and in the United States: moral imperatives or personal decisions? *JPSP*, *58*, 33–47.

Miller, L.C. (1990). Intimacy and liking: mutual influence and the role of unique relationships. *JPSP*, *59*, 50–60.

Miller, L.C. & Kenny, D.A. (1986). Reciprocity of self disclosure at the individual and dyadic levels: a social relations analysis. *JPSP*, *50*, 713–719.

Miller, L.C. & Read, S.J. (1991). Interpersonalism: understanding persons in relationships. *Advances in Personal Relationships*, *2*, 233–268.

Miller, N.E. (1959), Liberalization of basic S–R concepts. In S. Koch (Ed.) *Psychology, a study of a science. Study 1 Vol. 2*, pp.196–292. New York: McGraw Hill.

Miller, P.C., Lefcourt, H.M., Holmes, J.G., Ware, E.E., & Saleh, W.E. (1986). Marital locus of control and marital problem solving. *JPSP*, *51*, 161–169.

Miller, R.S. & Lefcourt, H.M. (1982). Social intimacy. *American Journal of Community Psychology*, *11*, 127–139.

Millett, P. (1991). *Lending and borrowing in ancient Athens*. Cambridge: Cambridge University Press.

Mills, J. & Clark, M.S. (1982). Communal and exchange relationships. In L. Wheeler (Ed.), *Review of Personality and Social Psychology*, *3*, 121–144. Beverly Hills: Sage.

Minuchin, P. (1985). Families and individual development. *Child Development*, *56*, 289–301.

Minuchin, S. & Fishman, H.C. (1981). *Family therapy techniques.* Cambridge, MA: Harvard University Press.

Mischel, W. (1968). *Personality and assessment.* New York: Wiley.

Monsour, M. (1992). Meanings of intimacy in cross- and same-sex friendships. *JSPR, 9,* 277–295.

Monsour, M. (1994). Similarities and dissimilarities in personal relationships: constructing meaning and building intimacy through communication. In Duck (1994a), pp.112–134.

Monsour, M., Betty, S., & Kurzweil, N. (1993). Levels of perspectives and the perceptions of intimacy in cross-sex friendships: a balance theory explanation of shared perceptual reality. *JSPR, 10,* 529–550.

Montemayor, R. (1983). Parents and adolescents in conflict: all families some of the time and some families most of the time. *Journal of Early Adolescence, 3,* 83–103.

Montepare, J.M. & Zebrowitz-McArthur, L. (1989). Impressions of people created by age-related qualities of their gaits. *JPSP, 55,* 547–556.

Montgomery, B. (1988a). Communication—overview. In Duck (1988), pp.233–238.

Montgomery, B. (1988b). Quality communication in personal relationships. In Duck (1988) pp.343–59.

Montgomery, B. (1993). Relationship maintenance vs. relationship change: a dialectical dilemma. *JSPR, 10,* 205–224.

Moreland, R.L. & Zajonc, R.B. (1982). Exposure effects in person perception: familiarity, similarity and attraction. *JPSP, 22,* 8–12.

Mori, De A., Chaiken, S., & Pliner, P. (1987). "Eating lightly" and the self-presentation of femininity. *JPSP, 53,* 693–702.

Morris, M.W. & Kaiping Peng (1994). Culture and cause: American and Chinese attributions for social and physical events. *JPSP, 67,* 949–971.

Morrow, G.D., Clark, E.M., & Brock, K.F. (1995). Individual and partner love styles: implications for the quality of romantic involvements. *JSPR, 12,* 363–387.

Morton, T.L. (1978). Intimacy and reciprocity of exchange: a comparison of spouses and strangers. *JPSP, 36,* 72–81.

Moskowitz, G.B. (1993). Individual differences in social categorization: the influence of personal need for structure on spontaneous trait inferences. *JPSP, 65,* 132–142.

Mueser, K.T., Grau, B.W., Sussman, M.S., & Rosen, A.J. (1984). You're only as pretty as you feel: facial expression as a determinant of physical attractiveness. *JPSP, 46,* 469–478.

Mulac, A., Wiemann, J.M., Wildenmann, S.J., & Gibson, T.W. (1988). Male/female language differences and effects in same-sex and mixed-sex dyads. *Communication Monographs, 55,* 314–335.

Murphy-Berman, V., Berman, J.J., Singh, P., Pachauri, A., & Kumar, P. (1984). Factors affecting allocation to needy and meritorious recipients: cross-cultural comparison. *JPSP, 46,* 1267–1272.

Murray, S.L. & Holmes, J.G. (1993). Seeing virtues in faults: negativity and the transformation of interpersonal narratives in close relationships. *JPSP, 65,* 707–722.

Murray S.L. & Holmes, J.G. (1996). The construction of relationship realities. In Fletcher & Fitness (1996) pp.91–120.

Murstein, B.I. (1961). The complementary need hypothesis in newlyweds & middle-aged married couples. *Journal of Abnormal & Social Psychology, 63,* 194–197.

Murstein, B.I. (1967a). Empirical tests of role, complementary needs, and homogamy theories of marital choice. *JMarFam, 29,* 689–696.

Murstein, B.I. (1967b). The relationship of mental health to marital choice and courtship progress. *JMarFam, 29,* 447–451.

Murstein, B.I. (1971a). Self–ideal-self discrepancy and the choice of marital partner. *JCCP, 37,* 47–52.

Murstein, B.I. (1971b). Critique of models of dyadic attraction. In B.I. Murstein (Ed.), *Theories of attraction and love.* New York: Springer.

Murstein, B.I. (1971c). A theory of marital choice and its applicability to marriage adjustment. In B.I. Murstein (Ed.), *Theories of attraction and love,* pp.1–30. New York: Springer.

Murstein, B.I. (1972). Person perception and courtship progress among premarital couples. *JMarFam, 34,* 621–626.

Murstein, B.I. (1977). The stimulus-value-role (SVR) theory of dyadic relationships. In Duck (1977a), pp.105–128.

Murstein, B.I. (1987). A clarification and extension of the SVR theory of dyadic pairing. *JMarFam, 49,* 929–947.

Murstein, B.I. & Adler, E.R. (1995). Gender differences in power and self-disclosure in dating and married couples. *PR, 2,* 199–210.

Nadler, A. & Dotan, I. (1992). Commitment and rival attractiveness: their effects on male and female reactions to jealousy-arousing situations. *Sex Roles, 26*, 293–310.

Nardi, P.M. & Sherrod, D. (1994). Friendship in the lives of gay men and lesbians. *JSPR, 11*, 185–199.

Navran, L. (1967) Communication and adjustment in marriage. *Family Process, 6*, 173–184.

Neimeyer, G.J. & Hudson, J.E. (1985). Couple's constructs: personal systems in marital satisfaction. In D. Bannister (Ed.), *Issues and approaches in personal construct theory*. London: Wiley.

Neimeyer, G.J. & Neimeyer, R.A. (1985). Relational trajectories: a personal construct contribution. *JSPR, 2*, 325–349.

Neisser, U. (1976). *Cognition and reality*. San Francisco: Freeman.

Nelson, B., Collins, J., Kreitman, N., & Troop, J. (1970). Neurosis and marital interaction. II. Time sharing and social activity. *British Journal of Psychiatry, 117*, 47–58.

Neuberg, S.L. & Newsom, J.T. (1993). Personal need for structure: individual differences in the desire for simple structure. *JPSP, 65*, 113–131.

Newcomb, M.D. (1990). Social support by many other names: towards a unified conceptualization. *JSPR, 7*, 479–494.

Newcomb, M.D. & Bentler, P.M. (1981). Marital breakdown. In Duck & Gilmour (1981b), pp.57–96.

Newcomb, T.M. (1952). *Social psychology*. London: Tavistock.

Newcomb, T.M. (1956). The prediction of interpersonal attraction. *American Psychologist, 11*, 575–586.

Newcomb, T.M. (1961). *The acquaintance process*. New York: Holt, Rinehart & Winston.

Newcomb, T.M., Koenig, K.E., Flacks, R., & Warwick, D.P. (1967). *Persistence and change: Bennington College and its students after 25 years*. New York: Wiley.

Nezlek, J.B. (1995). Social construction, gender/sex, similarity and social interaction in close personal relationships. *JSPR, 12*, 503–520.

Nezlek, J.B. & Pilkington, C.J. (1994). Perceptions of risk in intimacy and social participation. *PR, 1*, 45–62.

Noller, P. (1980). Misunderstandings in marital communication: a study of couples' non-verbal communication. *JPSP, 39*, 1135–1148.

Noller, P. (1984). *Non-verbal communication and marital interaction*. Oxford: Pergamon.

Noller, P. (1985). Negative communications in marriage. *JSPR, 2*, 289–302.

Noller, P. (1987). Non-verbal communication in marriage. In Perlman & Duck (1987), pp.149–175.

Noller, P. (1996). What is this thing called love? Defining the love that supports marriage and the family. *PR, 3*, 97–115.

Noller, P., Feeney, J.A., Bonnell, D., & Callan, V.J. (1994). A longitudinal study of conflict in early marriage. *JSPR, 11*, 233–252.

Noller, P. & Guthrie, D. (1992). Studying communication in marriage: an integration and critical valuation. In W.H. Jones & D. Perlman (Eds.), *Advances in Personal Relationships, 3*, 37–24. London: Jessica Kingsley.

Noller, P. & Hiscock, H. (1989). Fitzpatrick's typology: an Australian replication. *JSPR, 6*, 87–91.

Noller, P. & Venardos, C. (1986). Communication awareness in married couples. *JSPR, 3*, 31–42.

Norton, R.W. (1988). Communication style theory in marital interaction: persistent challenges. In Duck (1988), pp.307–324.

Notarius, C.I. & Herrick, L.R. (1988). Listener responses to a distressed other. *JSPR, 5*, 97–108.

Nye, F.I. (1974). Emerging and declining family roles. *JMarFam, 36*, 238–245.

O'Connell, L. (1984). An explanation of exchange in three social relationships: kinship, friendship and the marketplace. *JSPR, 1*, 333–345.

O'Connor, P. & Brown, G.W. (1984). Supportive relationships: fact or fancy? *JSPR, 1*, 159–175.

O'Meara, J.D. (1994). Cross-sex friendship's opportunity challenge: uncharted terrain for exploration. *Personal Relationship Issues, 2*, 4–7.

Oggins, J., Veroff, L. & Leber, D. (1993). Perceptions of marital interaction among black and white newlyweds. *JPSP, 65*, 494–511.

Oppong, C. (1979). Changing family structure and conjugal love: the case of the Akan of Ghana. In Cook & Wilson (1979), pp.237–245.

Orbuch, T.L., Veroff, J., & Holmberg, D. (1993). Becoming a married couple: the emergence of meaning in the first years of marriage. *JMarFam, 55*, 815–826.

Ortega, S.T., Whitt, H.P. & Williams, J.A. (1988). Religious homogamy and marital happiness. *Journal of Family Issues, 9*, 224–239.

Orvis, B.R., Kelley, H.H., & Butler, D. (1976). Attributional conflict in young couples. In J.H. Harvey, W. Ickes, & R.E. Kidd (Eds.), *New directions in attribution research*.

Hillsdale, NJ: Lawrence Erlbaum Associates Inc.

Paikoff, R. & Brooks-Gunn, J. (1991). Do parent–child relationships change during puberty? *PsychBull, 110*, 47–66.

Papini, D., Datan, N., & McCluskey-Fawcett, K. (1988). An observational study of affective and assertive family interactions during adolescence. *Journal of Youth and Adolescence, 17*, 477–492.

Park, B., DeKay, M.L., & Kraus, S. (1994). Aggregating social behavior into person models: perceiver-induced consistency. *JPSP, 66*, 437–459.

Park, B. & Flink, C. (1989). A social relations analysis of agreement in liking judgements. *JPSP, 56*, 506–518.

Park, B. & Judd, C.M. (1989). Agreement on initial impressions: differences due to perceivers, trait dimensions, and target behaviors. *JPSP, 56*, 493–505.

Parke, R.D., Power, T.G., & Gottman, J. (1979). Conceptualizing and quantifying influence patterns in the family triad. In M.E. Lamb, S.J. Suomi, & G.R. Stephenson (Eds.), *The study of social interaction: methodological issues*. Madison: University of Wisconsin Press.

Parker, S.A. & de Vries, B. (1993). Patterns of friendship for women and men in same and cross-sex relationships. *JSPR, 10*, 617–626.

Parks, M.M., Stan, C.M., & Eggert, L.L. (1983). Romantic involvement and social network involvement. *Social Psychology Quarterly, 46*, 116–131.

Parks, M.R. & Eggert, L.L. (1991). The role of social context in the dynamics of personal relationships. *Advances in Personal Relationships, 2*, 1–24.

Parks, M.R. & Floyd, K. (1996). Meanings for closeness and intimacy in friendship. *JSPR, 13*, 85–107.

Parrott, W.G. & Smith, R.H. (1993). Distinguishing the experiences of envy and jealousy. *JPSP, 64*, 906–920.

Parsons, T. & Bales, R.F. (1955). *Family, socialization and interaction process*. New York: Free Press.

Pataki, S.P., Shapiro, C., & Clark, M.S. (1994). Children's acquisitions of appropriate norms for friendships and acquaintances. *JSPR, 11*, 427–442.

Patterson, G.R. (1982). *Coercive family process*. Eugene, OR: Castalia.

Patterson, G.R. & Dishion, T.J. (1988). Multilevel family process models. In Hinde & Stevenson-Hinde (1988), pp.283–310.

Patterson, M.L. (1976). An arousal model of interpersonal intimacy. *PsychRev, 83*, 235–245.

Patterson, M.L. (1988). Functions of nonverbal behavior in close relationships. In Duck (1988), pp.41–56.

Paulhus, D.L. & Bruce, M.N. (1992). The effect of acquaintanceship on the validity of personality impressions: a longitudinal study. *JPSP, 63*, 816–824.

Paulhus, D.L. & Martin, C.L. (1988). Functional flexibility: a new conception of interpersonal flexibility. *JPSP, 55*, 88–101.

Paunonen, S.V. (1991). On the accuracy of ratings of personality by strangers. *JPSP, 61*, 471–477.

Pawlik, K. & Buse, L. (1990). Felduntersuchungen zur Interaktionismuskontroverse. In D. Frey, (Ed.), *Bericht uber den 37. Kongress der Deutschen Gesellschaft fur Psychologie in Kiel, 1990*. (Bd.1, pp.321–322). Gottingen: Hogrefe.

Paykel, E.S. (1983). Methodological aspects of life events research. *Journal of Psychosomatic Research, 27*, 341–352.

Paykel, E.S., Myers, J.K., Dienelt, M.N., Klerman, G.L., Lindenthal, J.J., & Pepper, M.P. (1969). Life events and depression: a controlled study. *Archives of General Psychiatry, 21*, 753–760.

Pearlin, L.I. (1975). Status inequality and stress in marriage. *American Sociological Review, 40*, 344–357.

Pearson, J.C. (1981). The effects of setting and gender on self-disclosure. *Group and Organization Studies, 6*, 334–340.

Peplau, L.A. (1976). Impact of fear of success and sex-role attitudes on women's competitive achievement. *JPSP, 34*, 561–568.

Peplau, L.A. (1978). Loving women: attachment and autonomy in lesbian relationships. *Journal of Social Issues, 34*, 7–27.

Peplau, L.A. (1983). Roles and gender. In H.H. Kelley, et al. (1983), pp.220–264.

Peplau, L.A. & Cochran, S.D. (1990). A relational perspective on homosexuality. In D.P. McWhirter, S.A. Sanders, & J.M. Reinisch (Eds.).*Homosexuality/heterosexuality*, pp.321–49. New York: Oxford University Press.

Peplau, L.A. & Gordon, S.L. (1983). The intimate relationships of lesbians and gay men. In E.R. Allgeier & N.B. McCormick (Eds.), *The changing boundaries: gender roles and sexual behavior*. Palo Alto, CA: Mayfield.

Peplau, L.A. & Gordon, S.L. (1985). Women and men in love: gender differences in close heterosexual relationships. In V.E. O'Leary, R.K. Unger, & B.S. Wallston (Eds.), *Women, gender and social psychol-*

ogy, Hillsdale, NJ: Lawrence Erlbaum Associates Inc.

Peplau, L.A. & Perlman, D. (1982). *Loneliness*. New York: Wiley.

Perlman, D. & Duck, S.W. (Eds.) (1987). *Intimate relationships*. Beverley Hills, CA: Sage.

Perlman, D. & Fehr, B. (1987). The development of intimate relationships. In Perlman & Duck (1987), pp.13–42.

Perlman, S.D. & Abramson, P.R. (1982). Sexual satisfaction among married and cohabiting individuals. *JCCP, 50*, 458–460.

Pervin, L.A. (1993). *Personality: theory and research*. New York: Wiley.

Peterson, D.R. (1983). Conflict. In H.H. Kelley et al. (Eds.), *Close relationships*, pp.360–396. New York: Freeman.

Peterson, D.R. (1994). Fewer bricks, better buildings. *Psychological Inquiry, 5*, 56–58.

Pfeiffer, S.M. & Wong, P.T.P. (1989). Multidimensional jealousy. *JSPR, 6*, 181–196.

Pietromonaco, P.R., Rook, K.S. and Lewis, M.A. (1992). Accuracy in perceptions of interpersonal interactions. *JPSP, 63*, 247–259.

Pilkington, C.J., Tesser, A., & Stephens, D. (1991). Complementarity in romantic relationships: a self-evaluation maintenance perspective. *JSPR, 8*, 481–504.

Pistole, M.C. (1989). Attachment in adult romantic relationships: style of conflict resolution and relationship satisfaction. *JSPR, 6*, 505–510.

Planalp, S. (1985). Relational schemata. *HCR, 12*, 3–29.

Planalp, S. & Garvin-Doxas, K. (1994). Using mutual knowledge in conversation: friends as experts on each other. In Duck (1994), pp.1–26.

Planalp, S. & Rivers, M. (1996). Changes in knowledge of personal relationships. In Fletcher & Fitness (1996), 299–324.

Plomin, R. (1990). *Nature and nurture*. Pacific Grove, CA: Brooks-Cole.

Prager, K.J. (1991). Intimacy status and couple conflict resolution. *JSPR, 8*, 505–526.

Prins, K.S., Buunk, B.P., & Van Yperen, N.W. (1993). Equity, normative disapproval and extra marital relationships. *JSPR, 10*, 39–53.

Prusank, D.T., Duran, R.L., & DeLillo, D.A. (1993). Interpersonal relationships in women's magazines: dating and relating in the 1970s and 1980s. *JSPR, 10*, 307–320.

Radecki-Bush, C., Bush, J.P., & Jennings, J. (1988). Effects of jealousy threats on relationship perceptions and emotions. *JSPR, 5*, 285–303.

Radecki-Bush, C., Farrell, A.D., & Bush, J.P. (1993). Predicting jealous responses: the influence of adult attachment and depression on threat appraisal. *JSPR, 10*, 569–588.

Radke-Yarrow, M., Richters, J., & Wilson, W.E. (1988). Child development in a network of relationships. In Hinde & Stevenson-Hinde (1988), pp.48–67.

Rands, M., Levinger, G., & Mellinger, G.D. (1981). Patterns of conflict resolution and marital satisfaction. *Journal of Family Issues, 2*, 297–321.

Rausch, H.L., Barry, W.A., Hertel, R.K., & Swain, M.A. (1974). *Communication, conflict and marriage*. San Francisco: Jossey-Bass.

Raush, H.L., Dittman, A.T., & Taylor, T.J. (1959). Person, setting and change in social interaction. *Human Relations, 12*, 361–378.

Rawlins, W.K. (1994). Reflecting on (cross-sex) friendship: de-scripting the drama. *Personal Relationship Issues, 2*, 1–3.

Raz, J. (1994). *Ethics in the public domain*. Oxford: Clarendon.

Reedy, M.N., Birren, B.E., & Schaie, K.W. (1981). Age and sex differences in satisfying love relationships across the adult lifespan. *Human Development, 24*, 52–66.

Regan, P.C. & Berscheid, E. (1995). Gender differences in beliefs about the causes of male and female desire. *PR, 2*, 345–358.

Register, L.M. & Henley, T.B. (1992). The phenomenology of intimacy. *JSPR, 9*, 467–481.

Reis, H.T. (1995). Why I study the stream of ongoing experience. *International Society for the Study of Personal Relationships Bulletin, 11*, 6–8.

Reis, H.T. & Knee, C.R. (1996). What we know, what we don't know, and what we need to know about relationship knowledge structures. In Fletcher & Fitness (1996), pp.169–191.

Reis, H.T., Senchak, M., & Solomon, B. (1985). Sex differences in the intimacy of social interaction: further examination of potential explanation. *JPSP, 48*, 1204–1217.

Reis, H.T. & Shaver, P. (1988). Intimacy as interpersonal process. In Duck (1988) pp.367–389.

Reis, H.T. & Wheeler, L. (1991). Studying social interactions with the Rochester Interaction Record. *AdvExpSP, 24*, 269–318. San Diego, CA: Academic Press.

Reis, H.T., Wheeler, L., Spiegel, N., Kernis, M., Nezlek, J., & Peri, M. (1982). Physical attractiveness in social interaction: II. Why does appearance affect social experience? *JPSP, 43*, 979–996.

Reisman, J.M. (1990). Intimacy in same-sex friendships. *Sex Roles, 23*, 65–82.

Reisman, P. (1981). Adult friendships. In Duck & Gilmour (1981a) pp.205–230.

Reissman, C., Aron, A., & Bergen, M.R. (1993). Shared activities and marital satisfaction: causal direction and self-expansion versus boredom. *JSPR, 10*, 243–254.

Rempel, J.K., Holmes, J.G., & Zanna, M.P. (1985). Trust in close relationships. *JPSP, 49*, 95–112.

Reno, R.R., Cialdini, R.B., & Kallgren, C.A. (1993). The transituational influence of social norms. *JPSP, 64*, 104–112.

Retzinger, S.M. (1995). Shame and anger in personal relationships. In Duck & Wood (1995a), pp.22–42.

Rhodes, J.E., Ebert., L., & Meyers, A.B. (1994). Social support, relationship problems and the psychological functioning of young African-American mothers. *JSPR, 11*, 587–599.

Rholes, W.S., Simpson, J.A., & Blakely, B.S. (1995). Adult attachment styles and mothers' relationships with their young children. *PR, 2*, 35–54.

Richman, N. (1974). The effects of housing on pre-school children and their mothers. *Developmental Medicine and Child Neurology, 16*, 53–58.

Richman, N. (1977). Behaviour problems in pre-school children: family and social factors. *British Journal of Psychiatry, 131*, 523–527.

Riesmann, R. & Angleitner, A. (1993). Inferring interpersonal traits from behavior: act prototypicality versus conceptual similarity of trait concepts. *JPSP, 64*, 356–364.

Roberts, L.J. & Krokoff, L.J. (1990). A time-series analysis of withdrawal, hostility and displeasure in satisfied and dissatisfied marriages. *JMarFam, 52*, 95–105.

Rodin, M. (1982). Non-engagement, failure to engage, and disengagement. In Duck (1982), pp.31–50.

Rogers, C.R. (1959). A theory of therapy, personality and interpersonal relationships, as developed in the client-centred framework. In S. Koch (Ed.), *Psychology: a study of a science, 3*, pp.184–256. New York: McGraw Hill.

Rogers, L.E. & Farace, R.V. (1975). Analysis of relational communication in dyads: new measurement procedures. *HCR, 1*, 222–239.

Rogers, L.E. & Millar, F.E. (1988). Relational communication. In Duck (1988), pp.289–306.

Rogler, L.H. & Procidano, M.E. (1989). Marital heterogamy and marital quality in Puerto Rican families. *JMarFam, 51*, 363–372.

Rogoff, B., Baker-Sennett, J., Lacasa, P., & Goldsmith, D. (1995). Development through participation in sociocultural activity. In J.I. Goodnow, P.J. Miller, & F. Kessal (Eds.), *Cultural practices as contexts for development*, pp.45–65. San Francisco: Jossey-Bass.

Rollins, B.C. & Bahr, S.J. (1976). A theory of power relationships in marriage. *JMarFam, 38*, 619–627.

Roloff, M.E., Janiszewski, C.A., McGrath, M.A., Burns, C.S., & Manrai, L.A. (1988). Acquiring resources from intimates. *HCR, 14*, 364–396.

Rook, K.S. (1988) The negative side of social interaction: impact on psychological well-being. *JPSP, 46*, 1097–1108.

Roper, R. & Hinde, R.A. (1978). Social behavior in a play group: consistency and complexity. *Child Development, 49*, 570–579.

Rose, S.M. (1984). How friendships end: patterns among young adults. *JSPR, 1*, 267–278.

Rose, S.M. & Serafica, F.C. (1986). Keeping and ending close and best friendships. *JSPR, 3*, 275–288.

Rosenbaum, M. (1986). The repulsion hypothesis: on the non-development of relationships. *JPSP, 51*, 1156–1166.

Rosenberg, S. (1988). Self and others: studies in social personality and autobiography. In L. Berkowitz (Ed.), *AdvExpSP, 21*, 57–96. San Diego: Academic Press.

Rosenblatt, A. & Greenberg, J. (1991). Examining the world of the depressed: do depressed people prefer others who are depressed? *JPSP, 60*, 620–629.

Rosenblatt, P.C. (1974). Cross-cultural perspective on attraction. In Huston (1974), pp.79–99.

Rosenblatt, P.C. (1977). Needed research on commitment in marriage. In G. Levinger & H.L. Rausch (Eds.), *Close relationships: perspectives on the meaning of intimacy*. Amhurst, MA: University of Massachusetts Press.

Rosenbluth, S.C. & Steil, J.M. (1995). Predictors of intimacy for women in heterosexual and homosexual couples. *JSPR, 12*, 163–175.

Ross, H.S., Cheyne, J.A., & Lollis, S.P. (1988). Defining and studying reciprocity in young children. In Duck (1988), pp.143–160.

Ross, M.A. (1989). The relation of implicit

theories to the construction of personal histories. *PsychRev*, 96, 341–357.

Rubin, J. & Rubin, Z. (1993). Dynamics of conflict escalation in families. *Advances in Personal Relationships*, 4, 165–194.

Rubin, K.H., Bukowski, W., & Parker J.G. (in press). Peer interactions, relationships and groups. *Handbook of Child Psychology*.

Rubin, R. (1975). Maternal tasks in pregnancy. *Maternal Child Nursing Journal*, 4, 143–153.

Rubin, Z. (1974). *From liking to loving: patterns of attraction in dating relationships*. New York: Holt, Rinehart & Winston.

Ruble, D.N., Fleming, A.S., Hackel, L.S., & Strangor, C. (1988). Changes in the marital relationship during the transition to first time motherhood: effects of violated expectations concerning division of household labor. *JPSP*, 55, 77–87.

Ruble, D.N., Fleming, A.S., Stangor, C., Brooks-Gunn, J., Fitzmaurice, G., & Deutsch, F. (1990). Transition to motherhood and the self. *JPSP*, 58, 450–463.

Ruesch, J. & Bateson, G. (1951). *Communication: the social matrix of psychiatry*. New York: Norton.

Rusbult, C.E. (1980). Commitment and satisfaction in romantic associations: a test of the investment model. *JESP*, 16, 172–186.

Rusbult, C.E. (1983). A longitudinal test of the investment model: the development (and deterioration) of satisfaction and commitment in heterosexual involvements. *JPSP*, 45, 101–117.

Rusbult, C.E. (1987). Responses to dissatisfaction in close relationships: the exit–voice–loyalty–neglect model. In Perlman & Duck (1987), pp.209–237.

Rusbult, C.E. & Buunk, B.P. (1993). Commitment processes in close relationships: an interdependence analysis. *JSPR*, 10, 175–204.

Rusbult, C.E., Johnson, D.J., & Morrow, G.D. (1986a). Impact of couple patterns of problem solving on distress and non-distress in dating relationships. *JPSP*, 50, 744–753.

Rusbult, C.E., Johnson, D.L., & Morrow, G.D. (1986b). Predicting satisfaction and commitment in adult romantic involvements: an assessment of the generalization of the investment model. *Social Psychology Quarterly*, 49, 81–89.

Rusbult, C.E., Verette, J., Whitney, G.A., Slovik, L.P., & Lipkus, I. (1991). Accommodation processes in close relationships: theory and preliminary empirical evidence. *JPSP*, 60, 53–78.

Rusbult, C.E., Yovetich, N.A., & Verette, J. (1996). An interdependence analysis of accommodation processes. In Fletcher & Fitness (1996), pp.63–90.

Rusbult, C.E. & Zembrodt, I.M. (1983). Responses to dissatisfaction in romantic involvements: a multidimensional scaling analysis. *JESP*, 19, 274–293.

Rusbult, C.E., Zembrodt, I.M., & Gunn, L.K. (1982). Exit, voice, loyalty and neglect: responses to dissatisfaction in romantic relationships. *JPSP*, 43, 1230–1242.

Ruscher, J.B. & Hammer, E.D. (1994). Revising disrupted impressions through conversation. *JPSP*, 66, 530–541.

Rushton, J.P. (1989). Genetic similarity, human altruism and group selection. *Brain and Behavioral Sciences*, 12, 503–559.

Rutter, M. & Brown, G.W. (1966). The reliability and validity of measures of family life and relationships in families containing a psychiatric patient. *Social Psychiatry*, 1, 38–53.

Rychlak, J.F. (1965). The similarity, compatibility, or incompatibility of needs in interpersonal selection. *JPSP*, 2, 334–340.

Ryle, A. (1966). A marital patterns test for use in psychiatric research. *British Journal of Psychiatry*, 112, 285–293.

Ryle, A. & Breen, D. (1972). A comparison of adjusted and maladjusted couples using the double dyad grid. *British Journal of Medical Psychology*, 45, 375–382.

Ryle, A. & Lipshitz, S. (1975). Recording change in marital therapy with the reconstruction grid. *British Journal of Medical Psychology*, 48, 39–48.

Ryle, A. & Lipshitz, S. (1976). Repertory grid elucidation of a difficult conjoint therapy. *British Journal of Medical Psychology*, 49, 281–285.

Ryle, A. & Lunghi, M. (1970). The dyad grid: a modification of repertory grid technique. *British Journal of Psychiatry*, 117, 323–327.

Sabatelli, R.M. (1988). Measurement issues in marital research: a review and critique of contemporary survey instruments. *JMarFam*, 50, 891–915.

Sabatelli, R.M. & Cecil-Pigo, E.F. (1985). Relational interdependence and commitment in marriage. *JMarFam*, 47, 931–937.

Sabatelli, R. & Rubin, M. (1986). Non verbal expressiveness and physical attractiveness as mediators of interpersonal perceptions. *Journal of Nonverbal Behaviour*, 10, 120–133.

Sadalla, E.K., Kenrick, D.T., & Vershure, B. (1987). Dominance and heterosexual attraction. *JPSP*, 52, 730–738.

Safilios-Rothschild, C. (1970). The study of family power structure: a review 1960–1969. *JMarFam, 32,* 539–553.

Salmela-Aro, K. & Nurmi, J.E. (1996). Uncertainty and confidence in interpersonal projects: consequences for social relationships and well-being. *JSPR, 13,* 109–122.

Salovey, P. & Rodin, J. (1986). The differentiation of social-comparison jealousy and romantic jealousy. *JPSP, 50,* 1100–1112.

Salovey, P. & Rodin, J. (1989). Envy and jealousy in close relationships. In Hendrick (1989), pp.221–246.

Sameroff, A.J. & Chandler, M.J. (1975). Reproductive risk and the continuum of caretaking casualty. In F.D. Horowitz, M. Hetherington, S. Scarr-Salapatck, & G. Sregel (Eds.), *Review of child development research, Vol. 4.* Chicago: University of Chicago Press.

Sampson, E. & Insko, C. (1964). Cognitive consistency and performance in the autokinetic situation. *Journal of Abnormal and Social Psychology, 68,* 184–192.

Sander, L.W. (1977). The regulation of exchange in the infant–caretaker system and some aspects of the context–content relationship. In M. Lewis & L.A. Rosenblum (Eds.), *Interaction, conversation, and the development of language.* New York: Wiley.

Sander, L.W., Stechler, G., Burns, P., & Julia, H. (1970). Early mother–infant interaction and 24 hour patterns of activity and sleep. *Journal of Child Psychiatry, 9,* 103–123.

Sapadin, L.A. (1988). Friendship and gender: perspectives of professional men and women. *JSPR, 5,* 387–403.

Sarason, I.G., Pierce, G.R., & Sarason, B.R. (1990). Social support and interactional processes: a triadic hypothesis. *JSPR, 7,* 495–506.

Sarason, I.G., Sarason, B.R., & Pierce, G.R. (1995). Introduction: how should we study relationships? *JSPR, 12,* 521–522.

Saucier, G. (1992). Benchmarks: integrating affective and interpersonal circles with the big five personality factors. *JPSP, 53,* 1159–1177.

Schaap, C., Buunk, B., & Kerkstra, A. (1988). Marital conflict resolution. In P. Noller & M.A. Fitzpatrick (Eds.), *Perspectives on marital interaction,* pp.203–244. Clevedon, OH: Multilingual Matters.

Schachter, S. & Singer, J.E. (1962). Cognitive, social and physiological determinants of emotional state. *PsychRev, 69,* 379–399.

Schaefer, E.S. & Burnett, C.K. (1987). Stability and predictability of quality of women's marital relationships and demoralization. *JPSP, 53,* 1129–1136.

Schank, R.C. (1982) *Dynamic memory.* Cambridge: Cambridge University Press.

Scharfe, E. & Bartholomew, K. (1995). Accommodation and attachment representations in young couples. *JSPR, 12,* 389–401.

Schazer, S. de (1975). Brief therapy: two's company. *Family Process, 14,* 79–93.

Scheier, M.F. & Carver, C.S. (1988). A model of behavioural self-regulation. In L. Berkowitz (Ed.), *AdvExpSP, 21,* 303–346.

Scherer, K. & Ekman, P. (Eds.) (1982). *Handbook of methods in non-verbal behavior research.* New York: Cambridge University Press.

Scherer, K.R. & Wallbott, H.G. (1994). Evidence for universality and cultural variation of differential emotion response patterning. *JPSP, 66,* 310–328.

Schneider, B.H., Wiener, J., & Murphy, K. (1994). Children's friendships: the giant step beyond peer acceptance. *JSPR, 11,* 323–340.

Schriber, J.B., Larwood, L., & Peterson, J.L. (1985). Bias in the attribution of marital conflict. *JMarFam, 47,* 717–721.

Schumm, W.R. & Bugaighis, M.A. (1986). Marital quality over the marital career: alternative explanations. *JMarFam, 48,* 165–168.

Schutz, W.C. (1960). *FIRO: A three-dimensional theory of interpersonal behavior.* New York: Holt, Rinehart & Winston.

Schwab, J.J., Holzer, C.E., Warheit, G.J., & Schwab, R.J. (1976). Human ecology and depressive symptomatology. In J.H. Masserman (Ed.), *The range of normal in human behavior.* New York: Grune & Stratton.

Schwartz, B. (1968). The social psychology of privacy. *American Journal of Sociology, 73,* 741–752.

Schwartz, S.H. (1977). Normative influences on altruism. *AdvExpSP, 10,* 221–279.

Schweder, R.A. (1982). Fact and artifact in trait perception: the systematic distortion hypothesis. In B.A. Maher (Ed.), *Progress in Experimental Personality Research, 11,* 65–100. San Diego, CA: Academic Press.

Schweder, R.A. (1991). *Thinking through cultures.* Cambridge, MA: Harvard University Press.

Sears, D.O. (1986). College sophomores in the laboratory: influences of a narrow database on social psychology's view of human nature. *JPSP, 51,* 515–530.

Secord, P.F. & Backman, C.W. (1974). *Social psychology.* Tokyo: McGraw-Hill Kogakusta.

Sedikides, C., Oliver, M.B., & Campbell, W.K.

(1994). Perceived benefits and costs of romantic relationships for men and women: implications for exchange theory. *PR, 1,* 5–21.

Seeman, M.V. (1976). The psychopathology of everyday names. *British Journal of Medical Psychology, 49,* 89–95.

Seligman, M.E.P. (1975). *Helplessness: on depression, development and death.* San Francisco: Freeman.

Seligman, M.E.P. & Hager, J.L. (1972). *Biological boundaries of learning.* New York: Appleton-Century-Crofts.

Senchak, M. & Leonard, K.E. (1992). Attachment styles and marital adjustment among newlywed couples. *JSPR, 9,* 51–64.

Setterlund, M.O. & Niedenthal, P.M. (1993). Who am I? Why am I here?: Self-esteem, self-clarity and prototype matching. *JPSP, 65,* 769–780.

Seyfarth, R.M. (1977). A model of social grooming among adult female monkeys. *Journal of Theoretical Biology, 65,* 671–698.

Seyfarth, R.M., Cheney, D.L., & Hinde, R.A. (1978). Some principles relating social interactions and social structure among primates. In D.J. Chivers & J. Herbert (Eds.), *Recent advances in primatology.* London: Academic Press.

Seyfried, B.A. (1977). Complementarity in interpersonal attraction. In Duck (1977a), pp.165–185.

Shachar, R. (1991). His and her marital satisfaction: the double standard. *Sex Roles, 25,* 451–467.

Shaffer, D.R. & Ogden, J.K. (1986). On sex differences in self-disclosure during the acquaintance process: the role of anticipated future interaction. *JPSP, 51,* 92–101.

Shaffer, D.R., Ogden, K., & Wu, C. (1987). Effects of self-monitoring and prospect of future interaction on self-disclosure reciprocity during the acquaintance process. *JPSP, 55,* 75–96.

Shaffer, D.R., Pegalis, L., & Cornell, D.P. (1991). Interactive effects of social context and sex role identity on female self-disclosure during the acquaintance process. *Sex Roles, 24,* 1–19.

Shantz, C.U. & Hartup, W.W. (Eds.) (1992). *Conflict in child and adolescent development.* Cambridge: Cambridge University Press.

Sharabany, R. (1994). Intimate friendship scale: conceptual underpinnings, psychometric properties and construct validity. *JSPR, 11,* 449–469.

Sharpsteen, D.J. (1993). Romantic jealousy as an emotion concept: a prototype analysis. *JSPR, 10,* 69–82.

Sharpsteen, D.J. (1995). The effects of relationships and self-esteem threats on the liklihood of romantic jealousy. *JSPR, 12,* 89–101.

Shaver, P.R., Collins, N & Clark, C.L. (1996a). Attachment styles and internal working models of self and attachment partners. In Fletcher & Fitness (1996), pp.25–61.

Shaver, P., Furman, W., & Buhrmester, D. (1985). Transition to college: network changes, social skills and loneliness. In Duck and Perlman, (1985), pp.193–219.

Shaver, P.R. & Hazan, C. (1988). A biased overview of the study of love. *JSPR, 5,* 473–501.

Shaver, P.R. & Hazan, C. (1993). Adult romantic attachment: theory and evidence. In D. Perlman & W. Jones (Eds.), *Advances in Personal Relationships, 4,* 29–70. Greenwich, CT: JAI.

Shaver, P.R., Morgan, H.J., & Wu, S (1996b). Is love a "basic" emotion? *PR, 3,* 81–96.

Shaver, P.R., Schwartz, J., Kitson, D., & O'Connor, C. (1987) Emotion knowledge: further explorations of a prototype approach. *JPSP, 52,* 1061–1086.

Shea, L., Thompson, L., & Blieszner, R. (1988). Resources in older adults' old and new friendships. *JSPR, 5,* 83–96.

Shehan, C.L., Bock, E.W., & Lee, G.R. (1990). Religious heterogamy, religiosity and marital happiness: the case of Catholics. *JMarFam, 52,* 73–79.

Sheldon, A. (1992). Conflict talk: sociolinguistic challenges to self-assertion and how young girls meet them. *Merrill-Palmer Quarterly, 38,* 95–117.

Sherrod, D. (1989). The influence of gender on same-sex friendships. In C. Hendrick (Ed.), *Close relationships,* pp.164–186. Newbury Park, CA: Sage.

Shoda, Y., Mischel, W., & Wright, J.C. (1993). The role of situational demands and cognitive competencies in behavior organization and personality coherence. *JPSP, 65,* 1023–1035.

Shotland, R.L. (1989). A model of the causes of date rape in developing and close relationships. In Hendrick (1989), pp.247–270.

Shulman, S., Elicker, J., & Sroufe, L.A. (1994). Stages of friendship growth in preadolescence as related to attachment history. *JSPR, 11,* 341–361.

Siavalis, R.L. & Lamke, L.K. (1992). Instrumentalness and expressiveness: predictors of heterosexual relationship satisfaction. *Sex Roles, 26,* 149–159.

Sigall, H. & Aronson, E. (1967). Opinion change and the gain–loss model of interpersonal attraction. *JESP, 3,* 128–188.

Sillars, A.L., Folwell, A.L., Hill, K.C., Maki, B.K., Hurst, A.P., & Casano, R.A. (1994). Marital communication and the persistence of misunderstanding. *JSPR, 11,* 611–617.

Sillars, A.L. & Scott, M.D. (1983). Interpersonal perception between intimates: an integrative review. *HCR, 10,* 153–176.

Simpson, J.A. (1987). The dissolution of romantic relationships: factors involved in relationship stability and emotional distress. *JPSP, 53,* 683–692.

Simpson, J.A. (1990). Influence of attachment styles on romantic relationships. *JPSP, 59,* 971–980.

Simpson, J.A., Gangestad, S.W., & Lerma, M. (1990). Perception of physical attractiveness: mechanisms involved in the maintenance of romantic relationships. *JPSP, 59,* 1192–1201.

Simpson, J.A., Gangestad, S.W., & Nations, C. (1996). Sociosexuality and relationship initiation. In Fletcher & Fitness (1996), pp.121–147.

Singh, D. (1993). Adaptive significance of female physical attractiveness: role of waist-to-hip ratio. *JPSP, 65,* 293–307.

Smeaton, G., Byrne, D., & Murnen, S.K. (1989). The repulsion hypothesis revisited: similarity irrelevance or dissimilarity bias? *JPSP, 56,* 54–59.

Smith, E.R. (1978). Specification and estimation of causal models in social psychology: comment on Tesser and Paulhus. *JPSP, 36,* 34–38.

Smith, T.W., Sanders, J.D., & Alexander, J.F. (1990). What does the Cook & Medley Hostility Scale measure?: *JPSP, 58,* 698–708.

Smith, W.J. (1977). *The behavior of communicating.* Cambridge, MA: Harvard University Press.

Snodgrass, S.E. (1992). Further effects of role versus gender on interpersonal sensitivity. *JPSP, 62,* 154–158.

Snyder, D.K. (1979). Multi-dimensional assessment of marital satisfaction. *JMarFam, 44,* 739–741.

Snyder, D.K. & Smith, G.T. (1986). Classification of marital relationships: an empirical approach. *JMarFam, 48,* 137–146.

Snyder, M. (1984). When belief creates reality. In L. Berkowitz (Ed.), *AdvExpSP, 18,* 248–305. New York: Academic Press.

Snyder, M., Berscheid, E., & Glick, P. (1985). Focusing on the exterior and the interior: two investigations of the initiation of personal relationships. *JPSP, 48,* 1427–39.

Snyder, M., Gangestad, S., & Simpson, J.A. (1983). Choosing friends as activity partners: the role of self-monitoring. *JPSP, 45,* 1061–1071.

Snyder, M. & Simpson, J.A. (1987). Orientations towards romantic relationships. In Perlman & Duck (1987), pp.45–62.

Snyder, M., Simpson, J.A., & Gangestad, S. (1986). Personality and sexual relations. *JPSP, 51,* 181–190.

Snyder, M., Tanke, E., & Berscheid, E. (1977). Social perception and interpersonal behavior: on the self-fulfilling nature of social stereotypes. *JPSP, 35,* 656–666.

Sommer, R. (1965). Further studies of small group ecology. *Sociometry, 28,* 337–348.

Spanier, G.B. (1976). Measuring dyadic adjustment: new scales for assessing the quality of marriage and similar dyads. *JMarFam, 38,* 15–28.

Spence, J., Helmreich, R., & Stapp, J. (1975). Ratings of self and peers on sex role attributes and their relation to self-esteem and conceptions of masculinity and femininity. *JPSP, 32,* 29–39.

Spence, J.T. & Helmreich, R.L. (1978). *Masculinity and femininity.* Austin, TX: University of Texas Press.

Spencer, T. (1994). Transforming relationships through ordinary talk. In Duck (1994), pp.58–85.

Sperber, D. (1994). The modularity of thought and the epidemiology of representations. In L. Hirschfeld & S. Gelman (Eds.), *Mapping the mind,* pp. 39–67. Cambridge: Cambridge University Press.

Sperling, M.B. & Berman, W.H. (1994). *Attachment in adults.* New York: Guilford Press.

Spitzberg, B.H. (1993). The dialectics of (in)competence. *JSPR, 10,* 137–158.

Sprecher, S. (1986). The relations between inequity and emotions in close relationships. *Social Psychology Quarterly, 49,* 309–321.

Sprecher, S. (1994). Two sides to the break-up of dating relationships. *PR, 1,* 199–222.

Sprecher, S., Aron, A., Hatfield, E., Cortese, A., Potopova, E., & Levitskaya, A. (1994a). Love: American style, Russian style, and Japanese style. *PR, 1,* 349–370.

Sprecher, S. & Felmlee, D. (1992). The influence of parents and friends on the quality and stability of romantic relationships: a three-wave longitudinal investigation. *JMarFam, 54,* 888–900.

Sprecher, S. & McKinney, K. (1993). *Sexuality.* Newbury Park, CA: Sage.

Sprecher, S. & Metts, S. (1989). Development of the "romantic beliefs scale" and examination of the effects of gender and gender-role orientation. *JSPR, 6*, 387–411.

Sprecher, S., Sullivan, Q., & Hatfield, E. (1994b). Mate selection preferences: gender differences examined in a large national sample. *JPSP, 66*, 1074–1080.

Sprey, J. (1972). Family power structure: a critical comment. *JMarFam, 34*, 235–238.

Sroufe, L.A. (1983). Infant–caregiver attachment and patterns of adaptation in pre-school. In M. Perlmutter (Ed.), *Minnesota Symposia on Child Psychology, 16*, pp.41–83. Hillsdale, NJ: Lawrence Erlbaum Associates Inc.

Stafford, L. & Canary, D.J. (1991). Maintenance strategies and romantic relationship type, gender and relational characteristics. *JSPR, 8*, 217–242.

Stafford, R., Backman, E., & Dibona, P. (1977). The division of labor among co-habiting and married couples. *JMarFam, 39*, 43–57.

Stagner, R. (1971). Personality dynamics and social conflict. In C.G. Smith (Ed.), *Conflict resolution*. Notre Dame, IN: University of Notre Dame Press.

Stanley, S.M. & Markman, H.J. (1992). Assessing commitment in personal relationships. *JMarFam, 54*, 595–608.

Staub, E. (1974). Helping a distressed person: social, personality, and stimulus determinants. *AdvExpSP, 7*, 293–341.

Staub, E. & Sherk, L. (1970). Need for approval, children's sharing behavior, and reciprocity in sharing. *Child Development, 41*, 243–252.

Stebbins, R.A. (1969). On linking Barth and Homans: a theoretical note. *Man, 4*, 432–437.

Steck, L., Levitan, D., McClane, D., & Kelley, H.H. (1982). Care, need, and conceptions of love. *JPSP, 43*, 481–491.

Steele, C.M. (1988). The psychology of self-affirmation: sustaining the integrity of the self. In L. Berkowitz (Ed.) *AdvExpSP, 21*, 261–302.

Steele, H., Steele, M., & Fonagy, P. (1996). Associations among attachment classifications of mothers, fathers, and their infants. *Child Development, 67*, 541–555.

Steil, J.M. & Weltman, K. (1992). Influence strategies at home and at work: a study of sixty dual career couples. *JSPR, 9*, 65–88.

Stein, C.H. (1993). Felt obligation in adult family relationships. In Duck (1993c), pp.78–99.

Stein, C.H., Bush, E.G., Ross, R.R., & Ward, M. (1992). Mine, yours and ours: a con-figural analysis of the networks of married couples in relation to marital satisfaction and individual well-being. *JSPR, 9*, 365–383.

Stemp, P.S., Turner, R.J., & Noh, S. (1986). Psychological distress in the postpartum period: the significance of social support. *JMarFam, 48*, 271–277.

Stern, D. (1977). *The first relationship: infant and mother*. London: Fontana/Open Books.

Stern, D.N. (1995). *The motherhood constellation*. New York: Basic Books.

Sternberg, R.B. (1986). A triangular theory of love. *PsychRev, 93*, 119–135.

Sternberg, R.J. (1995). Love as a story. *JSPR, 12*, 541–546.

Sternberg, R.J. (1996). Love stories. *PR, 3*, 59–80.

Sternberg, R.J. & Barnes, M.L. (1985). Real and ideal others in romantic relationships: is four a crowd? *JPSP, 49*, 1586–1608.

Sternberg, R.J. & Barnes, M. (Eds.) (1988), *The psychology of love*. New Haven, CT: Yale University Press.

Sternberg, R.J. & Dobson, D.M. (1987). Resolving interpersonal conflicts: an analysis of stylistic consistency. *JPSP, 52*, 794–812.

Sternberg, R.J. & Grajek, S. (1984). The nature of love. *JPSP, 47*, 312–329.

Stets, J.E. (1993). Control in dating relationships. *JMarFam, 55*, 673–685.

Stets, J.E. & Pirog-Good, M.A. (1990). Interpersonal control and courtship aggression. *JSPR, 7*, 371–394.

Stevenson-Hinde, J. (1990). Attachment within family systems: an overview. *Infant Mental Health Journal, 11*, 218–227.

Stevenson-Hinde, J. & Glover, A. (1996). Shy girls and boys: a new look. *Journal of Child Psychology and Psychiatry, 37*, 181–187.

Stevenson-Hinde, J. & Hinde, R.A. (1986). Changes in associations between characteristics and interactions. In R. Plomin & J. Dunn (Eds.), *The study of temperament: changes, continuities and challenges* (pp.115–129). Hillsdale, NJ & London: Lawrence Erlbaum Associates Inc.

Stevenson-Hinde, J. & Shouldice, A. (1995). Maternal interactions & self-reports related to attachment classifications at 4.5 years. *Child Development, 66*, 583–96.

Stewart, A.J. & Rubin, Z. (1976). The power motive in the dating couple. *JPSP, 34*, 305.

Stiles, W.B., Walz, N.C., Schroeder, M.A.B., Williams, L.L., & Ickes, W. (1996) Attractiveness and disclosure in initial encounters of mixed-sex dyads. *JSPR*, *13*, 303–313.

Straus, M. & Sweet, S. (1992). Verbal/symbolic aggression in couples: incidence rates and relationships to personal characteristics. *JMarFam*, *54*, 346–357.

Street, R.L. (1984). Speech convergence and speech evaluation in fact-finding interviews. *HCR*, *11*, 139–169.

Stroebe, W. (1977). Self esteem and interpersonal attraction. In Duck (1977a), pp.79–104.

Stroebe, W., Insko, C.A., Thompson, V.D., & Layton, B.D. (1971). Effects of physical attractiveness, attitude similarity and sex on various aspects of interpersonal attraction. *JPSP*, *18*, 79–81.

Strong, S.R., Hills, H.I., Kilmartin, C.T., DeVries, H., Lanier, K., Nelson, B.N., Strickland, D., & Meyer, C.W. (1988). The dynamic relations among interpersonal behaviors: a test of complementarity and anticomplementarity. *JPSP*, *54*, 798–810.

Suitor, J.J. (1991). Marital quality and satisfaction with the division of household labor across the family life cycle. *JMarFam*, *53*, 221–230.

Suitor, J.J. & Pillemer, K. (1992). Status transitions and marital satisfaction: the case of adult children caring for elderly parents suffering from dementia. *JSPR*, *9*, 549–562.

Sullivan, H.S. (1953). *Conceptions of modern psychiatry*. New York: Norton.

Surra, C.A. (1985). Courtship types: variations in interdependence between partners and social networks. *JPSP*, *49*, 357–375.

Surra, C.A. (1996). Knowledge structures in close relationships. In Fletcher & Fitness (1996), pp.397–414.

Surra, C.A., Arizzi, P., & Asmussen, L.A. (1988). The association between reasons for commitment and the development and outcome of marital relationships. *JSPR*, *5*, 47–63.

Surra, C.A. & Huston, T.L. (1987). Mate selection as a social transition. In Perlman & Duck (1987), pp.88–120.

Surra, C.A. & Longstreth, M. (1990). Similarity of outcomes, interdependence, and conflict in dating relationships. *JPSP*, *59*, 501–516.

Surra, C.A. & Milardo, R.M. (1991). The social psychological context of developing relationships: interactive and psychological networks. *Advances in Personal Relationships*, *3*, 1–36.

Swann, W.B. (1987). Identity negotiation: where two roads meet. *JPSP*, *53*, 1038–1051.

Swann, W.B., de la Ronde, C., & Hixon, J.G. (1994). Authenticity and positivity showings in marriage and courtship. *JPSP*, *66*, 857–869.

Swann, W.B. & Hill, C.A. (1982). When our identities are mistaken: reaffirming self-conceptions through social interaction. *JPSP*, *43*, 59–66.

Swann, W.B., Stein-Seroussi, A., & Giesler, R.B. (1992a). Why people self-verify. *JPSP*, *62*, 392–401.

Swann, W.B., Stein-Seroussi, A., & McNulty, S.E. (1992b). Outcasts in a white-lie society: the enigmatic worlds of people with negative self-conceptions. *JPSP*, *62*, 618–624.

Swap, W.C. (1991). Perceiving the causes of altruism. In Hinde & Groebel (1991), pp.147–158.

Tajfel, H. (1978). The psychological structure of intergroup relations. In H. Tajfel (Ed.), *Differentiation between social groups*. London: Academic Press.

Taraban, B. & Hendrick, C. (1995). Personality perceptions associated with six styles of love. *JSPR*, *12*, 453–461.

Taylor, D.A. (1968). Some aspects of the development of interpersonal relationships: social penetration processes. *Journal of Social Psychology*, *75*, 79–90.

Taylor, D.A., Altman, I., & Sorrentino, R. (1969). Interpersonal exchange as a function of rewards and costs and situational factors: expectancy confirmation-disconfirmation. *JESP*, *5*, 324–339.

Taylor, D.A. & Hinds, M. (1985). Disclosure reciprocity and liking as a function of gender and personalism. *Sex Roles*, *12*, 1137–1153.

Teachman, J.D. & Polonko, K.A. (1990). Cohabitation and marital stability in the United States. *Social Forces*, *69*, 207–220.

Teevan, J.J. (1972). Reference groups and premarital sexual behavior. *JMarFam*, *34*, 283–291.

Teichman, M., Glaubman, H., & Garner, M. (1993). From early adolescence to middle-age adulthood. In Foa et al. (1993a), pp.157–168.

Tennen, H. & Herzberger, S. (1987). Depression, self-esteem, and the absence of self-protective attributional biases. *JPSP*, *52*, 72–80.

Terhune, K.W. (1970). The effects of personality in cooperation and conflict. In P. Swingle (Ed.), *The structure of conflict*, pp.193–234. New York: Academic Press.

Tesch, S.A. (1985). The psychosocial intimacy questionnaire: validational studies and an investigation of sex roles. *JSPR*, *2*, 471–488.

Tesser, A. (1971). Evaluative and structural similarity of attitudes as determinants of interpersonal attraction. *JPSP*, *18*, 92–96.

Tesser, A. (1978). Self-generated attitude change. *AdvExpSP*, *11*, 290–338.

Tesser, A. (1980). Self-esteem maintenance in family dynamics. *JPSP*, *39*, 77–91.

Tesser, A. (1986). Some effects of self-evaluation maintenance on cognition and action. In R.M. Sorrentino & E.T. Higgins (Eds.), *Handbook of motivation and cognition*, pp.435–464. New York: Guilford Press.

Tesser, A. (1988). Toward a self-evaluation maintenance model of social behavior. *AdvExpSP*, *21*, 181–228.

Tesser, A. & Danheiser, P. (1978). Anticipated relationship, salience of partner and attitude change. *Personal & Social Psychology Bulletin*, *4*, 358.

Tesser, A., Millar, M., & Moore, J. (1988). Some affective consequences of social comparison and reflection processes: the pain and pleasure of being alone. *JPSP*, *54*, 49–61.

Tesser, A. & Paulhus, D.L. (1976). Toward a causal model of love. *JPSP*, *34*, 1095–1105.

Tetlock, P.E. (1991). An alternative model of judgement and choice: people as politicians. *Theory and Psychology*, *1*, 451–477.

Tetlock, P.E., Peterson, R.S., & Berry, J.M. (1993). Flattering and unflattering personality portraits of integratively simple and complex managers. *JPSP*, *64*, 500–511.

Thagard, P. (1989). Explanatory coherence. *Behavioural and Brain Sciences*, *12*, 435–467.

Tharp, R.G. (1963a). Psychological patterning in marriage. *PsychBull*, *60*, 97–117.

Tharp, R.G. (1963b). Dimensions of marriage roles. *Marriage and Family Living*, *25*, 389–404.

Thelen, M.H., Fishbein, M.D., & Tatten, H.A. (1985). Interpersonal similarity: a new approach to an old question. *JSPR*, *2*, 437–446.

Thibaut, J. (1968). The development of contractual norms in bargaining: replication and variation. *Journal of Conflict Resolution*, *12*, 102–112.

Thibaut, J.W. & Kelley, H.H. (1959). *The social psychology of groups*. New York: Wiley.

Thompson, J.M., Whiffen, V.E., & Blain, M.D. (1995). Depressive symptoms, sex & perceptions of intimate relationships. *JSPR*, *12*, 49–66.

Thompson, L. & Walker, A.J. (1989). Gender in families: women and men in marriage, work and parenthood. *JMarFam*, *51*, 845–871.

Thompson, W.R. & Nishimura, R. (1952). Some determinants of friendship. *JP*, *20*, 305–314.

Thorne, A. (1987). The press of personality: a study of conversations between introverts and extroverts. *JPSP*, *53*, 718–26.

Tice, D.M. (1992). Self-concept change and self-presentation: the looking glass self is also a magnifying glass. *JPSP*, *63*, 435–451.

Tinbergen, N. (1951). *The study of instinct*. Oxford: Clarendon.

Tizard, B. & Hodges, J. (1978). The effect of early institutional rearing on the development of 8 year-old children. *Journal of Child Psychology and Psychiatry*, *19*, 99–118.

Tolhuizen, P.H. (1989). Communication strategies for intensifying dating relationships: identification, use and structure. *JSPR*, *66*, 413–434.

Tolsdorf, C. (1976). Social networks, support and coping: an exploratory study. *Family Process*, *15*, 407–417.

Tolstedt, B.E. & Stokes, J.P. (1984). Self-disclosure, intimacy and the depenetration process. *JPSP*, *46*, 84–90.

Toman, W. (1971). The duplication theorem of social relationships as tested in the general population. *PsychRev*, *78*, 380–390.

Tornblom, K.Y. (1992). The social psychology of distributive justice. In K. Scherer (Ed.), *Justice: interdisciplinary perspectives*. Cambridge: Cambridge University Press.

Tornblom, K.Y. & Nilsson, B.O. (1993). The effect of matching resources to source on their perceived importance and sufficiency. In Foa et al. (1993a), pp.81–96.

Toth, O. (1991). *Conservative gender roles and women's work*. Paper presented at the 10th EGOs Conference on societal change between market and organization. Vienna.

Trevarthen, C. (1979). Instincts for human understanding and for cultural co-operation. In M. von Cranach, K. Foppa, W. Lepenies, & D. Ploog (Eds.), *Human ethology*, pp.530–537. Cambridge: Cambridge University Press.

Triandis, H.C. (1991). Cross-cultural differences in assertiveness/competition versus group loyalty/cooperation. In Hinde & Groebel (1991), pp.178–188.

Tripathi, R.C., Caplan, R.D., & Naida, R.K. (1986). Accepting advice: a modifier of social supports' effect on well-being. *JSPR*, *3*, 213–228.

Trope, Y. (1986). Identification and inferential processes in dispositional attribution. *PsychRev*, *93*, 239–257.

Trower, P. (1981). Social skill disorder. In Duck & Gilmour (1981b), pp.97–110.

Tschann, J.M. (1988). Self-disclosure in adult friendship: gender and marital status differences. *JSPR*, 5, 65–82.

Turk, J.L. (1974). Power as the achievement of ends: a problematic approach in family and small group research. *Family Process*, *13*, 39–52.

Turner, P.J. (1991). Relations between attachment, gender, and behavior with peers in pre-school. *Child Development*, *62*, 1475–1488.

Turner, P.J., Gervai, J., & Hinde, R.A. (1993). Gender-typing in young children: preferences, behaviour and cultural differences. *British Journal of Developmental Psychology*, *11*, 323–342.

Tweedie, J. (1979). *In the name of love*. London: Cape.

Tzeng, M. (1992). The effects of socio-heterogamy and changes on marital dissolution for first marriages. *JMarFam*, *54*, 609–619.

Uddenberg, N., Englesson, I., & Nettelbladt, P. (1979). Experience of father and later relations to men. A systematic study of women's relations to their father, their partner and their son. *Acta Psychiatrica Scandinavia*, *59*, 87–96.

Uehara, E.S. (1995). Reciprocity reconsidered: Gouldner's "moral norm of reciprocity" and social support. *JSPR*, *12*, 483–502.

Ulrich, R.E. & Symannek, B. (1969). Pain as a stimulus for aggression. In S. Garattini & E.B. Sigg (Eds.), *Aggressive behavior*. Amsterdam: Excerpta Medica.

Utne, M.K. & Kidd, R. (1980). Equity and attribution. In G. Mikula (Ed.), *Justice and social interaction*, pp.63–94. Bern: Huber.

Utne, M.K., Hatfield, E., Traupmann, J., & Greenberger, D. (1984). Equity, marital satisfaction and stability. *JSPR*, *1*, 323–332.

Vaillant, C.O. & Vaillant, G.E. (1993). Is the U-curve of marital satisfaction an illusion? A 40-year study of marriage. *JMarFam*, *55*, 230–239.

Vandenberg, S.G. (1972). Assortative mating, or who marries whom. *Behavior Genetics*, *2*, 127–157.

Van der Geest, S. (1976). Role relationships between husband and wife in rural Ghana. *JMarFam*, *38*, 572–578.

Vangelisti, A.L. (1994). Family secrets: forms, functions and correlates. *JSPR*, *11*, 113–135.

Van IJzendoorn, M.H. (1995). Adult attachment representations, parental responsiveness and infant attachment. *PsychBull*, *117*, 387–403.

VanLear, C.A. (1987). The formation of social relationships. *HCR*, *13*, 299–322.

VanLear, C.A. (1990). Testing a cyclical model of communicative openness in relationship development: two longitudinal studies. *Communication Monographs*, *58*, 337–361.

VanLear, C.A. (1992). Marital communication across the generations: learning and rebellion, continuity and change. *JSPR*, *9*, 103–123.

VanLear, C.A. & Zietlow, P.H. (1990). Toward a contingency approach to marital interaction: an empirical integration of three approaches. *Communication Monographs*, *57*, 202–218.

Van Yperen, N.W. & Buunk, B.P. (1990). A longitudinal study of equity and satisfaction in intimate relationships. *European Journal of Social Psychology*, *20*, 287–309.

Vaughn, C.E. & Leff, J.P. (1976). The influence of family and social factors on the course of psychiatric illness. A comparison of schizophrenic and depressed neurotic patients. *British Journal of Psychiatry*, *129*, 125–137.

Vera, A., Berardo, D.H., & Berardo, F.M. (1985). Age heterogamy in marriage. *JMarFam*, *47*, 553–566.

Veroff, J., Sutherland, L., Chadiha, L., & Ortega, R.M. (1993a). Newlyweds tell their stories: a narrative method of assessing marital experience. *JSPR*, *10*, 437–457.

Veroff, J., Sutherland, L., Chadiha, L.A., & Ortega, R.M. (1993b). Predicting marital quality with narrative assessments of marital experience. *JMarFam*, *55*, 326–337.

Verplanck, W.S. (1955). The control of the content of conversation: reinforcement of statements of opinion. *Journal of Abnormal and Social Psychology*, *51*, 668–676.

Voelz, C.J. (1985). Effects of gender role disparity on couples' decision-making process. *JPSP*, *49*, 1532–1540.

Vonk, R. & van Nobelen, D. (1993). Masculinity and femininity in the self with an intimate partner: men are not always men in the company of women. *JSPR*, *10*, 627–630.

Vorauer, J.D. & Ross, M. (1996). The pursuit of knowledge in close relationships. In

Fletcher & Fitness, (1996), pp.369–396.

Wagner, R.V. (1975). Complementary needs, role expectations, interpersonal attraction and the stability of working relationships. *JPSP, 32*, 116–124.

Walster, E., Aronson, V., Abrahams, D., & Rottmann, L. (1966). Importance of physical attractiveness in dating behavior. *JPSP, 4*, 508–516.

Walster, E., Berscheid, E., & Walster, G.W. (1976). New directions in equity research. *AdvExpSP. 9*, 1–42.

Walster, E. & Walster, G.W. (1963). Effect of expecting to be liked on choice of associates. *Journal of Abnormal and Social Psychology, 67*, 402–404.

Walster, E., Walster, G.W., & Berscheid, E. (1978a). *Equity theory and research.* Boston, MA: Allyn & Bacon.

Walster, E., Walster, G.W., & Traupmann, J. (1978b). Equity and premarital sex. *JPSP, 36*, 82–92.

Walters, R.G. & Parke, R.D. (1964). Social motivation, dependency and susceptibility to social influence. *AdvExpSP, 1*, 232–279.

Waring, E., Tilliman, M., Frelick, L., Russell, L., & Weisz, G. (1980). Concepts of intimacy in the general population. *Journal of Nervous and Mental Disorders, 168*, 471–474.

Watson, D. (1989). Strangers' ratings of the 5 robust personality factors: evidence of a surprising convergence with self-report. *JPSP, 57*, 120–128.

Watzlawick, P., Beavin, J.H., & Jackson, D.D. (1967). *Pragmatics of human communication.* New York: Norton.

Weber, D.J. & Vangelisti, A.L. (1991). "Because I love you..." The tactical use of attributional expressions in conversation. *HCR, 17*, 606–624.

Wedell, D.H. (1994). Contextual contrast in evaluative judgements: a test of pre- versus post-integration models of contrast. *JPSP, 66*, 1007–1019.

Wegner, D.M., Lane, J.D., & Dimitri, S. (1994). The allure of secret relationships. *JPSP, 66*, 287–300.

Weigel, D.J. & Weigel, R.R. (1993). Intergenerational family communication: generational differences in rural families. *JSPR, 10*, 467–473.

Weiner, B., Amirkhan, J., Folkes, V.S., & Verette, J.A. (1987). An attributional analysis of excuse giving: studies of a naive theory of emotion. *JPSP, 52*, 316–324.

Weiss, R.L., & Perry, B.A. (1979). *Assessment and treatment of marital dysfunction.* University of Oregon Marital Studies Program, Eugene, Oregon.

Weiss, R.S. (1974). The provisions of social relationships. In Z. Rubin (Ed.), *Doing unto others.* New Jersey: Prentice-Hall.

Weiss, R.S. (1975). *Marital separation.* New York: Basic Books.

Weller, L. & Rofe, Y. (1988). Marital happiness among mixed and homogeneous marriages in Israel. *J MarFam, 50*, 245–254.

Wellman, B. & Wellman, B. (1992). Domestic affairs and network relations. *JSPR, 9*, 385–409.

Wener, A.E. & Rehm, A.P. (1975). Depressive affect: a test of behavioral hypotheses. *Journal of Abnormal Psychology, 84*, 221–227.

Werking, K.J. (1994). Hidden assumptions: a critique of existing cross-sex friendship research. *Personal Relationship Issues, 2*, 8–11.

Werner, C. & Parmelee, P. (1979). Similarity of activity preferences among friends: those who play together stay together. *Social Psychology Quarterly, 42*, 62–66.

Werner, C.M., Altman, I., Brown, B.B., & Ginat, J. (1993). Celebrations in personal relationships. In Duck (1993c), pp.109–138.

Wertheim, E.S. (1975a). Person–environment interaction: the epigenesis of autonomy and competence. II Review of developmental literature (normal development). *British Journal of Medical Psychology, 48*, 95–111.

Wertheim, E.S. (1975b). Person–environment interaction: the epigenesis of autonomy and competence. III Autonomy and para/pre-linguistic and linguistic action systems: review of developmental literature (normal development). *British Journal of Medical Psychology, 48*, 237–256.

Wertheim, E.S. (1975c). The science and typology of family systems II. Further theoretical and practical considerations. *Family Process, 14*, 285–309.

Wetsel, C.G. & Insko, C.A. (1982). The similarity–attraction relationship: is there an ideal one? *JESP, 18*, 153–276.

Whaley, K.L. & Rubinstein, T.S. (1994). How toddlers "do" friendship. *JSPR, 11*, 383–400.

Wheeler, L. (1974). *Social comparison and selective affiliation.* In Huston (1974), pp.309–330.

Wheeler, L. & Miyake, K. (1992). Social comparison in everyday life. *JPSP, 62*, 760–773.

Whisman, M.A. & Allan, L.E. (1996). Attachment and social cognition theories of romantic relationships: convergent or complementary perspectives? *JSPR*, *13*, 263–278.

White, G.L. (1980). Inducing jealousy: a power perspective. *Personality and Social Psychology Bulletin*, *6*, 222–227.

White, G.L. (1981). Jealousy and partner's perceived motives for attraction to a rival. *Social Psychology Quarterly*, *44*, 24–30.

White, G. (1984). Comparison of four jealousy scales. *Journal of Research in Personality*, *18*, 115–130.

White, G.L., Fishbein, S., & Rutstein, J. (1981). Passionate love and misattribution of arousal. *JPSP*, *41*, 56–62.

White, G. & Mullen, P. (1989). *Jealousy: theory, research and clinical strategies*. New York: Guilford Press.

White, J.M. (1985). Perceived similarity and understanding in married couples. *JSPR*, *2*, 45–57.

White, K.M., Speisman, J.C., Jackson, D., Bartis, S., & Costos, D. (1986). Intimacy maturity and its correlates in young married couples. *JPSP*, *50*, 152–162.

White, L.K. (1983). Determinants of spousal interaction: marital structure or marital happiness. *JMarFam*, *45*, 511–519.

White, L.K. (1990). Determinants of divorce: a review of research in the eighties. *JMarFam*, *52*, 904–912.

White, L.K. & Booth, A. (1991). Divorce over the life course. *Journal of Family Issues*, *12*, 5–21.

White, L.K., Booth, A., & Edwards, J.N. (1986). Children and marital happiness: why the negative correlation? *Journal of Family Issues*, *7*, 131–148.

Whitley, B.E. (1993). Reliability and aspects of the construct validity of Sternberg's triangular love scale. *JSPR*, *10*, 475–480.

Wiggins, J.S. (1982). Circumplex models of interpersonal behavior in clinical psychology. In P.C. Kendall & J.N. Butcher (Eds.), *Handbook of research methods in clinical psychology*, pp.183–221. New York: Wiley.

Williams, D.G., (1985). Gender, masculinity–femininity, and emotional intimacy in same-sex friendship. *Sex Roles*, *12*, 587–600.

Williams, J.A., White, L.K., & Ekaidem, B.J. (1979). Romantic love as a basis for marriage. In Cook & Wilson (1979), pp.245–251.

Williamson, G.M. & Clark, M.S. (1989). Providing help and desired relationship type as determinants of changes in moods and self-evaluations. *JPSP*, *56*, 722–734.

Williamson, R.N. & Fitzpatrick, M.A. (1985). Two approaches to marital interaction: relational control patterns in marital types. *Communication Monographs*, *52*, 236–252.

Winch, R.F. (1958). *Mate-selection: a study of complementary needs*. New York: Harper & Row.

Winch, R.F. (1967). Another look at the theory of complementary needs in mate selection. *JMarFam*, *29*, 756–762.

Wink, P. & Helson, R. (1993). Personality change in women and their partners. *JPSP*, *65*, 597–605.

Winstead, B.A., Derlega, V.J., Montgomery, M.J., & Pilkington, C. (1995). The quality of friendships at work and job satisfaction. *JSPR*, *12*, 199–215.

Wiseman, J.P. (1986). Friendship, bonds and binds in a voluntary relationship. *JSPR*, *3*, 191–212.

Wiseman, J.P. & Duck, S. (1995). Having and managing enemies. In Duck & Wood, pp.43–72.

Witteman, H. & Fitzpatrick, M.A. (1986). Compliance-gaining in marital interaction: power bases, processes and outcomes. *Communication Monographs*, *53*, 130–143.

Wood, J.T. (1993). Engendered relations: interaction, caring, power, and responsibility in intimacy. In Duck (1993c), pp.26–54.

Wood, J.T. (1995). The part is not the whole: weaving diversity into the study of relationships. *JSPR*, *12*, 563–567.

Worthy, M., Gary, A.L., & Kahn, G.M. (1969). Self disclosure as an exchange process. *JPSP*, *13*, 59–63.

Wright, P.H. (1982). Men's friendships, women's friendships and the alleged inferiority of the latter. *Sex Roles*, *8*, 1–20.

Wright, P.H. (1984). Self-referent motivation and the intrinsic quality of friendship. *JSPR*, *1*, 115–130.

Wright, P.H. (1985). The acquaintance description form. In Duck & Perlman (1985), pp.39–62.

Wright, P.H. (1988). Interpreting research on gender differences in friendship: a case for moderation and a plea for caution. *JSPR*, *5*, 367–373.

Wright, P.H. & Keple, T.W. (1981). Friends and parents of a sample of high school juniors: an explanatory study of relationship intensity and interpersonal rewards. *JMarFam*, *43*, 559–570.

Wright, P.H. & Wright, K.D.(1995). Co-dependency: personality or relationship distress. In Duck & Wood (1995), pp.109–128.

Wright, R.A, & Contrada, R.J. (1986). Dating selectivity and interpersonal attraction. *JSPR*, *3*, 131–148.

Wright, T.L. & Ingraham, L.J. (1986a). A

social relations model test of the interpersonal circle. *JPSP, 50,* 1285–1290.

Wright, T.L. & Ingraham, L.J. (1986b). Partners and relationships influence self-perceptions of self-disclosures in naturalistic interactions. *JPSP, 50,* 631–635.

Wyer, R.S., Budesheim, T.L., Lambert, A.J., & Swan, S. (1994). Person memory and judgement: pragmatic influences on impressions formed in a social context. *JPSP, 66,* 254–267.

Xiaohe Xu & Whyte, M.K. (1990). Love matches and arranged marriages: a Chinese replication. *J Mar Fam, 52,* 709–722.

Yingling, J. (1994). Constituting friendship in talk and meta talk. *JSPR, 11,* 411–426.

Yinon, Y., Bizman, A., & Yagil, D. (1989). Self-evaluation maintenance and the motivation to interact. *JSPR, 6,* 475–486.

Yogev, S. & Brett, J. (1985). Perceptions of the division of housework and child care and marital satisfaction. *J Mar Fam, 47,* 609–618.

Zigler, E. (1964). The effect of social reinforcement on normal and socially deprived children. *Journal of Genetic Psychology, 104,* 235–242.

Zimmer, T.A. (1986). Premarital anxieties. *JSPR, 3,* 149–159.

Zivin, G. (1982). Watching the sands shift: conceptualizing development of non verbal mastery with the assistance of instabilities and discontinuities. In R.S. Feldman (Ed.), *The development of nonverbal communication in children.* New York: Springer.

Zuckerman, M., Miyake, K., & Hodgins, H.S. (1991). Cross-channel effects of vocal and physical attractiveness and their implications for interpersonal attraction. *JPSP, 60,* 545–554.

Zuckerman, M., De Paulo, B.M., & Rosenthal, R. (1981). Verbal and nonverbal communication of deception. *AdvExpSP, 14,* 2–60.

Zuo, J. (1992). The reciprocal relationship between marital interaction and marital happiness: a three-wave study. *J Mar Fam, 54,* 870–878.

Zuroff, D.C. & de Lorimer, S. (1989). Ideal and actual romantic partners of women varying in dependency and self-criticism. *JP, 57,* 825–846.

Zvonkovic, A.M., Pennington, D.C., & Schmiege, C.J. (1994). Work and courtship: how college workload and perceptions of work environment relate to romantic relationships among men and women. *JSPR, 11,* 63–76.

Author Index

Schank, R.C. 33
Scharfe, E. 178
Schazer, S. de 294
Scheier, M.F. 30
Scherer, K.R. 88, 302
Schilling, A.E. 153, 160, 161, 163
Schilling, E.A. 285
Schmiege, C.J. 474
Schmitt, J.P. 139, 250
Schmitz, E. 441
Schneider, B.H. 410, 418, 420
Schriber, J.B. 327
Schrier, A.M. 334
Schumm, W.R. 247
Schutz, W.C. 141
Schwab, J.J. 292
Schwab, R.J. 292
Schwagler, J. 298
Schwartz, B. 208
Schwartz, J. 212, 452
Schwartz, P. 199
Schwartz, S.H. 366
Schweder, R.A. 228, 303
Scott, L. 469
Scott, M.D. 95
Sears, D.O. 19
Sears, R.R. 193
Secord, P.F. 28, 37, 283, 307
Sedikides, C. 442
Seeman, M.V. 314
Seligman, M.E.P. 157, 260, 371
Senchak, M. 116, 212, 253, 414, 416, 435
Serafica, F.C. 419, 422
Servis, L.J. 72
Seta, J.J. 230
Setterlund, M.O. 130
Seyfarth, R.M. 125
Seyfried, B.A. 138, 139, 147
Shabilske, L.J. 230
Shachar, R. 263
Shaffer, D.R. 212, 216
Shantz, C.U. 154
Shapiro, C. 354
Sharabany, R. 216, 412, 420
Sharpsteen, D.J. 163, 165, 166
Shaver, P. 35, 58, 59, 87, 211, 216, 253, 288, 388, 389, 391, 415, 430, 431, 434, 435, 438, 452, 466
Shea, L. 420
Shehan, C.L. 263
Sheldon, A. 84
Sherk, L. 402
Sherrod, D. 212, 414, 415
Shoda, Y. 288
Shotland, R.L. 188
Shouldice, A. 21, 286, 387
Shulman, S. 388
Siavalis, R.L. 252
Sigall, H. 106
Sillars, A.L. 95, 183, 213

Silver, R.C. 506
Simmons, J.L. 455
Simon, E.P. 484
Simpson, J.A. 88, 228, 276, 286, 339, 390, 391, 392, 394, 419, 473, 480, 499, 500, 506
Singer, J.E. 302
Singh, D. 448
Singh, P. 358
Skokan, L.A. 145
Slapion-Foote, M.J. 436
Slovik, L.P. 176, 177, 186
Smeaton, G. 118, 450
Smith, E.R. 224, 406
Smith, J. 228
Smith, P.M. 91
Smith, R.H. 163
Smith, T.W. 182, 189
Smith, W.J. 86
Smithson, M. 213
Smollan, D. 30, 58, 59
Smyer, M.A. 494, 501
Sneed, C.D. 224
Snider, R.C. 458
Snodgrass, S.E. 231
Snoek, J.D. 58, 205, 363, 447
Snyder, D.K. 344
Snyder, M. 29, 57, 226, 227, 233, 276, 284, 286, 419, 449, 454, 481
Solli, D.L. 138, 252, 266, 513
Sollie, D.L. 85
Solomon, B. 212, 414, 416, 435
Solomon, J. 386, 387, 394
Solomon, L. 322, 402
Sommer, R. 291
Songer, E. 323
Sorrentino, R. 205
Spangler, G. 387
Spanier, G. 234
Spanier, G.B. 156, 244
Sparks, G.G. 423
Speicher, H. 457
Speisman, J.C. 59
Spence, J. 138
Spence, J.T. 250
Spencer, T. 80, 204, 463
Sperber, D. 515
Sperling, M.B. 390
Spiegel, N. 286, 449
Spitzberg, B.H. 91, 92
Sprecher, S. 264, 347, 358, 437, 439, 440, 442, 448, 470, 491, 499
Sprey, J. 199
Sroufe, L.A. 387
Stafford, L. 482, 483
Stafford, R. 71
Stagner, R. 161
Stahelski, A.J. 156
Stan, C.M. 452
Stangor, C. 83

Stanley, S.M. 272, 503
Stapp, J. 139
Staub, E. 363, 402
Stebbins, R.A. 316, 336
Stechler, G. 91
Steck, L. 427
Stecker, H.L. 188
Steele, C.M. 28, 30
Steele, H. 388, 389
Steele, M. 388, 389
Steil, J.M. 182, 196, 198, 252
Stein, C.H. 297, 299
Stein-Seroussi, A. 85, 130, 451
Stemp, P.S. 265
Stephens, D. 141
Stephenson, G. 295
Stern, D. 70, 90
Stern, D.N. 32
Sternberg, R.J. 58, 59, 159, 178, 237, 245, 270, 429, 430, 431, 433, 439, 467
Stets, J.E. 182, 188, 196
Stevenson-Hinde, J. 21, 40, 41, 54, 124, 125, 228, 286, 293, 294, 297, 371, 387, 479
Stewart, A.J. 138
Stewart, B.E. 328, 492, 494
Stiff, J.B. 471
Stillwell, A. 329
Stillwell, A.M. 501
Stinson, L. 457
Stith, S.M. 179, 188
Stokes, J.P. 217
Stone, J.I. 93
Strangor, C. 73
Straus, M. 153
Street, R.L. 91
Strejc, H. 94, 467, 483
Strickland, D. 113, 114
Stroebe, W. 126, 323, 371, 402
Strong, S.R. 113, 114
Suess, G. 387
Suitor, J.J. 248, 265
Sullivan, H.S. 207, 217, 319, 410
Sullivan, K.T. 258
Sullivan, Q. 442, 448
Suomi, S. 295
Surra, C.A. 74, 260, 271, 299, 362, 363, 462, 467, 470, 471, 473, 475, 492, 505
Sussman, M.S. 448
Sutherland, L. 462, 467
Swain, M.A. 169, 179
Swan, S. 229
Swann, W.B. 30, 85, 130, 214, 225, 226, 227, 233, 284, 451
Swap, W. 275
Swap, W.C. 364
Sweet, S. 153

Subject Index